EARLY SETT

OF LOUISIANA
AS TAKEN FROM
LAND CLAIMS
IN THE
EASTERN DISTRICT OF THE
ORLEANS TERRITORY

By
Walter Lowrie
Editor, *American State Papers*, Vol. 2

Southern Historical Press, Inc.
Greenville, South Carolina

Please direct all correspondence and orders to:

www.southernhistoricalpress.com
or
SOUTHERN HISTORICAL PRESS, Inc.
PO BOX 1267
Greenville, SC   29601
southernhistoricalpress@gmail.com

ISBN #0-89308-582-0

Printed in the United States of America

AMERICAN STATE PAPERS.

PUBLIC LANDS.

VOLUME I.

DOCUMENTS,

LEGISLATIVE AND EXECUTIVE,

OF THE

Congress of the United States,

IN RELATION TO

THE PUBLIC LANDS,

FROM THE FIRST SESSION OF THE FIRST CONGRESS TO THE FIRST SESSION OF THE
TWENTY-THIRD CONGRESS :

MARCH 4, 1789, TO JUNE 15, 1834.

SELECTED AND EDITED,

UNDER THE AUTHORITY OF THE SENATE OF THE UNITED STATES;

BY WALTER LOWRIE,

SECRETARY OF THE SENATE.

VOLUME I.

FROM MARCH 4th, 1789, TO FEBRUARY 27th, 1809.

WASHINGTON:
PRINTED BY DUFF GREEN.

1834.

PUBLISHER'S PREFACE

When the *American State Papers* were first issued between 1834 and 1860, two different editions were published, one by the Duff Green Company Publishers and the other, and the most widely used, was that done by Gales & Seaton Publishers. Both series contained essentially the same information; the Duff Green series appeared in six volumes, and the Gales & Seaton edition appeared in eight volumes. As well as your publisher has been able to determine, the Gales & Seaton edition was limited to 750 sets, which heightens the problem of their obscurity and their importance to the general public.

Southern Historical Press has taken Volumes I and II of the Duff Green edition and has lifted out for publication those continuous sections that deal with the Land Grants and Claims for the present states of Louisiana, Mississippi and Missouri. It should be noted by the reader that the other volumes of both series of these land papers contain additional information pertaining to land grants and claims in these three states.

Southern Historical Press plans to reprint, with full-name indexes, the entire eight volumes of the Gales & Seaton edition of the *American State Papers – Land Grants and Claims, 1789-1837.*

Concerning Pagination

Please note that the pagination of these three books is the original pagination from Volumes I and II of the Duff Green series. We did not attempt to renumber the pages starting with page one and continuing to the last page of each book, and the full-name index at the back of each volume reflects these *original* page numbers.

AMERICAN STATE PAPERS, PUBLIC LANDS:
An Overview of the Series

By Elizabeth Shown Mills, C.G., F.A.S.G.

The story of America's *land* is the story of the American people. The hunger for *land* populated American shores and drove the settlers westward. *Land* was the American dream: a piece for every man, every family — *land* each could fertilize with his or her own sweat and pass to their own sons.

It was the abundance of land — for farming, for hunting, for mining — that brought the British and the German to the Atlantic Seaboards; the French and the Spanish to the Gulf; Canadians, British, French, and Poles to the Mississippi Valley and the Great Lakes. For land, they challenged the Native American wherever they found him. To keep their land, the Indian nations fought back, then bargained, before finally conceding defeat.

American State Papers, Public Lands Series documents the melding of these peoples on the first great frontiers of the new United States: the Old Southwest and the Old Northwest. *ASP-PL* is, beyond a doubt, the most neglected source — the most *important* neglected source — of data on ethnic settlement and migration within trans-Appalachian America. It also serves as a vital finding aid to rich stores of public land claim files within the National Archives. In overall importance, *ASP-PL* stands second to none but the Draper Papers.

Between 1832 and 1861, the United States Congress selected and published a series of 38 volumes, some 35,000 pages, of congressional documents, chosen for their importance to "the legislative and documentary history of the United States." (*ASP-Foreign Relations,* vol. V, p. vii.) Those records chosen for inclusion in *American State Papers: Documents Legislative and Executive of the Congress of the United States* were grouped into ten classes (*Foreign Relations, Indian Affairs, Finance, Commerce & Navigation, Military Affairs, Naval Affairs, Post Office, Public Lands, Claims,* and *Miscellaneous*), with one to eight volumes per group.

ASP-PL represents the largest class of this now rare series, offering 1,570 documents spanning some 7,728 pages, within 8 volumes. The number of Americans discussed is mind-boggling — 80,000-100,000 would be a conservative estimate of the men and women included in this rich fund of biographical data. The scope of the material which *ASP-PL* makes available to professional and family historians is of both wide range and momentous import. As a sampling:

- Settlements of the United Brethren in Ohio, 1826
- Colonial French, British, and Spanish land grants in the Gulf States throughout the 1700s and early 1800s
- Settlement of exiled supporters of Napoleon in Alabama's Vine and Olive Colony, 1825 (where records subsequent were destroyed by local officials —

on the premise that "no one could read those things anyway, since they're all written in a foreign language"!)

- Lead mining in Missouri, Illinois, and Michigan, ca. 1810-30
- Petitions for bounty land by Revolutionary soldiers of Virginia, and patriot refugees from Canada and Nova Scotia
- Early plats (designating land and lot owners) of such cities as Detroit, Green Bay, Peoria, Cahokia, and Kaskaskia (whose "old town" now lies under the Mississippi River)
- Requests of Polish exiles, deported by the emperor of Austria, to settle in Illinois or Michigan
- Choctaw Land Claimants (full and mixed-blood, as well as white countrymen) under the Treaty of Dancing Rabbit Creek, 1830
- Creek and Cherokee Reservees after the settlement of the War of 1812
- North Carolina payments to Indian reservees, in exchange for their abandonment of their lands
- Similar documents for the Potowatomie, Quapaw, Catawba, Wyandots and other tribes

Thirteen states are directly, and abundantly, treated in *ASP-PL*

Alabama	Indiana	Mississippi
Arkansas	Iowa	Missouri
Florida	Louisiana	Ohio
Illinois	Michigan	Wisconsin
	Minnesota	

At least nine others are less directly treated to an extent worth noting:

Georgia	Pennsylvania	Tennessee
New York	Rhode Island	Vermont
North Carolina	South Carolina	Virginia

Historical studies of the Old Southwest suffer immensely from the underuse of grassroots level resources — caused, in part, by haphazard recordkeeping, by courthouse fires, and by too-little awareness of the value of such materials. The eight volumes of *American State Papers, Public Lands* offers viable substitutes for destroyed or nonexisting records and an extremely convenient source of biographical data and local-oriented documents, all available to the scholar without travel.

Introduction to the Three Volumes on Louisiana, Mississippi and Missouri

These Land Grants are the public record of transactions presented to Congress relating uniquely to settlement of Public Domain between 1789–1837. Types of claims to land on Public Domain are primarily: preemption rights; homestead settlements; military bounty lands and militia claims.

Those persons who presented their claims before Congress receive extensive treatment only in the *State Papers*. Nearly 80,000 diverse claims to land in early America which are treated in this 8-volume series give such valuable genealogical/historical data as: ages of claimants; previous places of habitation; names of children, wives, and other relatives; exact location of claims; and the time period of "cultivation and habitation."

LOUISIANA AND MISSOURI

Louisiana is a major focal point for land grants and claims in the *State Papers*. When the Louisiana Purchase took place in 1803, only two territories were immediately formed—the Louisiana and Orleans territories. An act of Congress in 1812 provided that the territory heretofore called Louisiana should hereafter be called Missouri. The southern portion of the territory of Missouri became the Territory of Arkansas in 1819, and the northern portion became the state of Missouri in 1821. The Territory of Orleans became the state of Louisiana in 1812.

In these records the original proprietor is named, by whom the land is presently being claimed, reason for change of title (purchase or inheritance), nature and extent of claim, and, if the claim was disallowed, the reasons for disallowance.

MISSISSIPPI

Mississippi was formed from land ceded to the United States by South Carolina and Georgia. Part of the British Province of West Florida and part of the land ceded by the French made up the rest of the Territory of Mississippi in 1798. The Territory of Alabama was formed from the Territory of Mississippi in 1812. In 1817 statehood was granted to Mississippi.

The genealogical worth of the foregoing paragraph is evident. The present claimant and original claimant are given in addition to their location; from where the patent was derived; if claim was rejected an explanation was given, plus the exact period of known settlement. Also included are those settling under preemption rights without authority to settle from any governments. The location and nature of claim are listed, both the period of cultivation and habitation, plus the date of first settlement and the parish where these people are located.

EARLY SETTLERS
OF LOUISIANA
AS TAKEN FROM
LAND CLAIMS
IN THE
EASTERN DISTRICT OF THE
ORLEANS TERRITORY

LAND CLAIMS IN THE EASTERN DISTRICT OF THE ORLEANS TERRITORY.

COMMUNICATED TO THE HOUSE OF REPRESENTATIVES JANUARY 9, 1812.

TREASURY DEPARTMENT, *January* 8, 1812.
SIR:
I have the honor, in conformity with the act respecting claims to land in the Territories of Orleans and Louisiana, to transmit a copy of the report made by the Commissioners for the Eastern District of the Territory of Orleans, on the claims to land within the said district which they have not confirmed.* On inquiring why the claims in the said report were not arranged into three general classes, as directed by the act aforesaid, I was verbally informed by the commissioner who delivered the report, that all the claims thus rejected were considered by the Board as belonging to the third class: that is to say, as claims not entitled to confirmation, either under the acts of Congress, or in conformity with the laws, usages, and customs of the Spanish Government.
A letter subsequently received from another commissioner is also transmitted.
I have the honor to be, with great respect, sir,
Your most obedient servant,
ALBERT GALLATIN.
The Hon. the SPEAKER *of the House of Representatives.*

Decisions of the Board of Commissioners for the Eastern District of the Territory of Orleans, of Land Claims registered in the books of Michael Cautrelle, Deputy Register.

No. 1.—BELONY LANDRY claims a tract of land, situate on the east side of the river Mississippi, in the county of Acadia, containing three arpents in front, and forty

*The reports now published embrace the claims *confirmed,* as well as those *rejected.*

arpents in depth, and bounded on one side by land of Michel Judice, and on the other by land of Raphael Landry.

There was an order of survey in the year 1783, for fifty arpents front, and forty arpents depth, obtained by Louis Judice from Governor Miro. The three arpents of land now claimed are part of the said tract, and purchased by the wife of the claimant in the year 1799; the land having been inhabited and cultivated for more than ten years prior to the 20th December, 1803. Confirmed.

No. 2.—JOSEPH CALLIOT claims a tract of land, situate on the east side of the river Mississippi, in the county of Acadia, containing four arpents and twelve toises in front, and forty arpents in depth, and bounded on the lower side by land of Pablo David.

It appears that the claimant did actually inhabit and cultivate the land now claimed on the 20th December, 1803; and that the same was continually inhabited and cultivated for more than ten consecutive years next preceding. Confirmed.

No. 3.—OLIVIER TERRIO claims a tract of land, situate on the east side of the river Mississippi, in the county of Acadia, containing five arpents and seventeen toises in front, and forty arpents in depth, and bounded on the upper side by land of Estevan Landry, and on the lower by land of Pedro Leblanc.

This land was surveyed by Don Louis Andry, in the year 1773, in favor of Armand Babin, who obtained a complete grant to the same in the year 1775 from Don Louis de Unzaga, then Governor; the present claimant holds by different deeds of sale under the aforesaid grant. Confirmed.

No. 4.—BERGITE FOREST, widow of Pierre Braux, claims a tract of land, situate on the river Mississippi, in the county of Acadia, containing four arpents front, and forty in depth, and bounded on the upper side by land of Pedro Duplessy, and on the lower by land of Anselmo Landry.

This land is part of fifty arpents front on the usual depth of forty, for which Louis Judice obtained an order of survey, in the year 1783, from Governor Miro. Pierre Braux, the husband of the claimant, purchased of said Judice in the year 1787; the land having been inhabited and cultivated for more than ten years prior to the 20th December, 1803. Confirmed.

No. 5.—SILVAIN LEBLANC claims a tract of land, situate on the east side of the river Mississippi, in the county of Acadia, containing three arpents and twenty-four toises in front, and forty arpents in depth, and bounded on the upper side by the land of Mr. Judice, and on the lower by land of Joseph Hughes.

It appears that the land now claimed was inhabited and cultivated on the 20th December, 1803, and that Anselmo Landry obtained an order of survey for the same in the year 1785, under whose title the claimant holds; the land having been inhabited and cultivated for more than ten years prior to the 20th December, 1803. Confirmed.

No. 6.—SILVAIN LEBLANC claims a tract of land, situate on the east side of the river Mississippi, in the county of Acadia, containing five arpents and sixteen toises in front, and forty arpents in depth, and bounded on the upper side by land of Armand Babin, and on the lower by land of Simon Landry.

This land was surveyed by Don Louis Andry in the year 1773, in favor of Pedro Leblanc, who obtained a complete grant for the same in 1775 from Governor Unzaga; the present claimant holds as the representative of Pedro Leblanc, deceased, his father. Confirmed.

No. 7.—PIERRE HOUVRE claims a tract of land, situate on the east side of the river Mississippi, in the county of Acadia, containing two arpents and eighteen toises in front, and forty arpents in depth, and bounded on one side by land of Joseph Malbouroux.

It appears that the claimant did actually inhabit and cultivate the land now claimed on the 20th December, 1803, and that the same was continually inhabited and cultivated by him, or those under whom he claims, for more than ten consecutive years next preceding. Confirmed.

No. 8.—EDWARD GODWIN claims a tract of land, situate on the east side of the river Mississippi, in the county of Acadia, containing one arpent in front, and forty arpents in depth, and bounded on the upper side by land of Augustine Burleau, and on the lower by land of Pedro Braux.

The land is a part of five arpents front and forty depth, mentioned in No. 1; the present claimant holds by purchase, under the title mentioned in No. 1. Confirmed.

No. 9.—RAPHAEL LANDRY claims a tract of land, situate on the east side of the river Mississippi, in the county of Acadia, containing seven arpents front, and forty in depth, and bounded on the upper side by land of Bellony Landry, and on the lower by land of Augustine Burleau.

This land is part of a tract of fifty arpents front and forty in depth, mentioned in No. 1; the claimant holds by purchase, under Louis Judice, in the year 1793. Confirmed.

No. 10.—PIERRE CARMOUCHE claims a tract of land, situate on the west side of the river Mississippi, in the county of Acadia, containing five arpents and five feet in front, and forty arpents in depth, and bounded on the upper side by land of Maxin Prejeau, and on the lower by land of Juan Janesome.

This land was surveyed by Don Louis Andry in the year 1774, in favor of Amand Prejeau, who obtained a complete grant for the same, in the same year, from Governor Unzaga; under which grant the present claimant holds by regular deed of sale. Confirmed.

No. 11.—PIERRE CARMOUCHE claims a tract of land, situate on the west side of the river Mississippi, in the county of Acadia, containing four arpents twenty-four toises and two feet in front, and forty arpents in depth, and bounded on the upper side by land of Joseph Prejeau, and on the lower by land of Amand Prejeau.

The land was surveyed by Don Louis Andry, in the year 1774, in favor of Maxin Prejeau, who obtained a complete grant for the same, in the same year, from Governor Unzaga; under which grant the present claimant holds by regular deeds of sale. Confirmed.

No. 12.—PIERRE CARMOUCHE claims a tract of land, situate on the west side of the river Mississippi, in the county of Acadia, containing five arpents one toise and five feet in front, and forty arpents in depth, and bounded on the upper side by land of Carlos Prejeau, and on the lower by land of Maxin Prejeau.

This land was surveyed by Don Louis Andry in the year 1774, in favor of Joseph Prejeau. who obtained a complete grant for the same in the year 1775, from Governor Unzaga; under which grant the claimant holds by regular deed of sale. Confirmed.

No. 13.—ARMAND BABIN claims a tract of land, situate on the west side of the river Mississippi, in the county of Acadia, containing five arpents one toise and four feet in front, and forty arpents in depth; and bounded on the upper side by land of Joseph Richard, and on the lower by land of Joseph Prejeau.

This land was surveyed by Don Louis Andry in the year 1774, in favor of Carlos Prejeau, who obtained a complete grant for the same, in the same year, from Governor Unzaga; under which grant the present claimant holds. Confirmed.

No. 14.—PIERRE AVRIEUX claims a tract of land, situate on the west side of the river Mississippi, in the county of Acadia, containing six arpents and four toises in front, and forty arpents in depth, and bounded on the upper side by land of Carlos Dugast, and on the lower by land of Amable Robichaud.

This land was surveyed by Don Louis Andry in the year 1774, in favor of Francisco Dugast, who obtained for the same a complete grant in 1775, from Governor Unzaga; under which grant the present claimant holds by regular deeds of sale. Confirmed.

No. 15.—JEAN ORRY claims a tract of land, situate on the east side of the river Mississippi, in the county of Acadia, containing six arpents and one toise in front, and forty arpents in depth, and bounded on the upper side by land of Dominique Badeau, and on the lower by land of Pierre Chenet.

It appears that the claimant did actually inhabit and cultivate the land now claimed on the 20th December, 1803; and that the same was continually inhabited and cultivated for more than ten consecutive years next preceding. Confirmed.

No. 17.—JEAN REYNAUD and PETARIN claim a tract of land, situate on the west side of the river Mississippi, in the county of Acadia, containing three arpents and twenty-seven toises in front, and forty arpents in depth, and bounded on the upper side by land of Noel Dugast, and on the lower by land of Pablo Forest.

This is part of a tract of land of five arpents and four toises in front, on the usual depth, surveyed in the year 1774 by Don Louis Andry, in favor of Anselmo Forest, who obtained a complete grant to the same in 1775, from Governor Unzaga; the claimant holds three arpents and twenty-seven toises of said land by virtue of the successive sales. Confirmed.

No. 18.—JEAN ROM claims a tract of land, situate on the west side of the river Mississippi, in the county of Acadia, containing three arpents and twenty-four toises in front, and forty arpents in depth, and bounded on the upper side by land of Gabriel Rodrigue, and on the lower by land of Baptiste Luquel.

It appears that the claimant did actually inhabit and cultivate the land now claimed on the 20th December, 1803, and that the same was continually inhabited and cultivated for more than ten consecutive years next preceding. Confirmed.

No. 19.—ETIENNE BREAUX claims a tract of land, situate on the east side of the river Mississippi, in the county of Acadia, containing four arpents in front, and forty in depth, and bounded on the upper side by land of Anselmo Landry, and on the lower by land of Carlos Landry.

This is part of a tract of land of fifty arpents front, on the ordinary depth, mentioned in No. 1. The claimant holds by purchase under the title there mentioned; and it appearing that the land has been inhabited and cultivated for more than ten consecutive years prior to the 20th December, 1803. Confirmed.

29

No. 20.—JOSEPH and PIERRE LANDRY claim a tract of land, situate on the east side of the river Mississippi, in the county of Acadia, containing four arpents in front, and forty arpents in depth, and bounded on the upper side by land of Raphael Landry, and on the lower by land of Pedro Duplessy.

This is part of fifty arpents front on the usual depth, mentioned in No 1. The claimant holds by purchase under the title there mentioned; and the land having been inhabited and cultivated for more than ten consecutive years prior to the 20th December, 1803. Confirmed.

No. 21.—JEAN MARIE ARMANT claims a tract of land, situate on the west side of the river Mississippi, in the county of Acadia, containing eight arpents and ten toises in front, and eigh y arpents in depth, and bounded above by land of Saturn'n Bruno, and below by land of Francisco Lebœuf.

The first depth of forty arpents of the land now claimed was surveyed in the year 1771, in favor of Joseph Forest, who obtained a complete grant for the same, in 1773, from Governor Unzaga. Pierre Dupain obtained an order of survey, in 1795, for a second depth to the aforesaid land, from the Baron de Carondelet, then Governor. The present claimant holds under the above titles. Confirmed.

No. 22.—JEAN MARIE ARMANT claims a tract of land, situate on the west side of the river Mississippi, in the county of Acadia, containing seven arpents and twelve toises front, and forty arpents in depth, and bounded above by land of Mr. Godin, and below by land of Francisco Dominique Lebœuf.

There is a regular grant for six arpents and twelve toises front of this land in the year 1773, from Governor Unzaga, in favor of Saturnin Bruno, who purchased the remaining arpents in 1781, which has been inhabited and cultivated for more than ten years prior to the 20th December, 1803. The present claimant holds under the title of said Bruno. Confirmed.

No. 23.—LOUIS PARENT claims a tract of land, situate on the east side of the river Mississippi, in the county of Iberville, containing five and a half arpents in front, and forty in depth, and bounded on the upper side by land of Pedro Cloatre, and on the lower by land of Francisco Babin.

There is an order of survey in the year 1786, in favor of the claimant, by Don Estevan Miro, then Governor, the land having been inhabited and cultivated for more than ten consecutive years next preceding the 20th December, 1803. Confirmed.

No. 24.—RAIMOND BRAND claims a tract of land, situate on the west side of the river Mississippi, in the county of Acadia, containing five arpents and eight toises in front, and forty arpents in depth, and bounded on the upper side by land of Joseph Landry, and on the lower by land of Atanagio Dugast.

This land was surveyed by Don Louis Andry, in the year 1774, in favor of Maturin Landry, who obtained a complete grant for the same, in the year 1775, from Governor Unzaga; under which grant the present claimant holds. Confirmed.

No. 25.—PAUL MELANSON claims a tract of land, situate on the east side of the river Mississippi, in the county of Acadia, containing six arpents and ten toises in front, and forty arpents in depth, and bounded on the upper side by land of Maxin Landry, and on the lower by land of Joseph Dupuis.

It appears that the claimant did actually inhabit and cultivate the land now claimed on the 20th December, 1803, and that the same was continually inhabited and cultivated by him, or those under whom he claims, for more than ten consecutive years next preceding. Confirmed.

No. 26.—SILVAIN LEBLANC claims a tract of land, situate on the east side of the river Mississippi, in the county of Acadia, containing six arpents and twelve toises in front, and forty arpents in depth, and bounded on the upper side by land of Estevan Benois, and on the lower by land of Pedro Laurone.

This land was regularly surveyed, in the year 1782, for Joseph Dupuis, under whose title the claimant holds; and it having been continually inhabited and cultivated for more than ten consecutive years, prior to the 20th December, 1803. Confirmed.

No. 27.—MARIE LANDRY, widow of Joseph Conaes, claims a tract of land, situate on the west side of the river Mississippi, in the county of Acadia, containing five arpents twenty-five toises and three feet in front, and eighty arpents in depth, and bounded on the upper side by land of Desiderato Leblanc, and on the lower by land of Juan Chauvin.

The first depth of forty arpents of this land was regularly granted to Geromino Leblanc, in the year 1775, by Governor Unzaga: for the second depth of forty arpents Juan Baptiste Pechoux obtained a complete grant in the year 1790, from the Baron de Carondelet, then Governor. The present claimant holds by regular deeds under the aforesaid grant. Confirmed.

No. 28.—MARIE LANDRY, widow of Joseph Conaes, claims to a tract of land, situate on the west side of the river Mississippi, in the county of Acadia, containing four arpents and three feet in front, and forty arpents in depth, and bounded on the upper side by land of the claimant, and on the lower by land of Leno Picou.

It appears that the claimant did actually inhabit and cultivate the land now claimed on the 20th December, 1803, and that the same was continually inhabited and cultivated by her, or those under whom she claims, for more than ten consecutive years next preceding. Confirmed.

No. 29.—HENRY BERTHELOT claims a tract of land, situate on the east side of the river Mississippi, in the county of Acadia, containing four arpents twenty-seven toises, and four feet in front, and forty arpents in depth, and bounded on the upper side by land of Marguerite René Bourgeois, and on the lower by land of François Pochet.

It appears that the claimant did actually inhabit and cultivate the land now claimed on the 20th December, 1803, and that the same was continually inhabited and cultivated by him, or those under whom he claims, for more than ten consecutive years next preceding. Confirmed.

No. 30.—MARGUERITE RENE BOURGEOIS claims a tract of land, situate on the east side of the river Mississippi, in the county of Acadia, containing five arpents in front, and forty in depth, and bounded on the upper side by land of Étienne Renne, and on the lower by land of Henry Berthelot.

This is part of a tract of land of twelve arpents in front, for which there appears to have been a grant from the Spanish Government, and the land having been inhabited and cultivated for more than ten consecutive years prior to the 20th December, 1803. Confirmed.

No. 31.—ANTONIO BERRY claims a tract of land, situate on the east side of the river Mississippi, in the county of Acadia, containing five arpents twenty-three toises and three feet in front, and forty arpents in depth, and bounded on the upper side by land of Carlos Soroy, and on the lower by land of Antoine Labove.

It appears that the land now claimed was inhabited and cultivated on the 20th of December, 1803; and that the same was continually inhabited and cultivated, by those under whom the present claimant holds, for more than ten consecutive years next preceding. Confirmed.

No. 32.—ISIDORE BLANCHARD claims a tract of land, situate on the east side of the river Mississippi, in the county of Acadia, containing four arpents in front, and forty in depth, and bounded on the upper side by land of Anne Blanchard, and on the lower by land of Charles Melanson.

This is part of a tract of land of six arpents and one toise in front, on the ordinary depth, surveyed by Don Louis Andry, in the year 1774, in favor of Pablo Melanson, who obtained a complete grant for the same, in the year 1775, from Governor Unzaga; under which grant the claimant holds, by virtue of regular deeds of sale. Confirmed.

No. 33.—ANNE MARTHE BLANCHARD claims a tract of land, situate on the east side of the river Mississippi, in the county of Acadia, containing eight arpents in front, and forty in depth, and bounded on the upper side by land of Juan Brousard, and on the lower by land of Isidore Blanchard.

Two arpents one toise and four feet of this land is part of a grant to Pablo Melanson, mentioned in No. 32. The balance of the eight arpents now claimed was surveyed in the year 1774, by Don Louis Andry, in favor of Isaac Leblanc, who obtained a complete grant for the same, in 1775, from Governor Unzanga; under which titles the claimant holds, by regular deeds of sale. Confirmed.

No. 34.—SIMON RICHARD claims a tract of land, situate on the east side of the river Mississippi, in the county of Acadia, containing five arpents six toises and five feet in front, and forty arpents in depth, and bounded on the upper side by land of German Bergeron, and on the lower by land of André Bernard.

It appears that the land now claimed was inhabited and cultivated on the 20th December, 1803; and that the same was continually inhabited and cultivated by those under whom the claimant holds for more than ten consecutive years next preceding. Confirmed.

No. 35.—JOSEPH LAURENT FABRE claims two tracts of land, situate on the west side of the river Mississippi, in the county of Acadia: one of said tracts containing two arpents and ten toises in front, and sixty arpents in depth, and bounded on the upper side by land of Mr. Remy, and on the lower by land of Madame Croizet; and the other tract containing eight arpents in front, and sixty in depth, and bounded on the upper side by land of Madame Croizet, and on the lower by land of François Croizet.

The tracts now claimed are part of a tract of land, of thirty arpents front, on the ordinary depth of forty arpents, regularly granted to Louis Judice, in the year 1765. François Croizet obtained a grant for an addition of twenty arpents in depth to the aforesaid tract, in the year 1774, from Governor Unzaga; under which grant the claimant holds the lands now claimed, by regular deeds of sale. Confirmed.

No. 36.—JOSEPH LAURENT FABRE claims a tract of land, situate on the east side of the river Mississippi, in the county of Acadia, containing twenty-five arpents and twenty-six toises in front, and eighty arpents depth, and bounded on the upper side by land of Pedro Dupuis.

This tract of land is composed of three other tracts, for all of which complete grants have been obtained to the extent of fifty arpents in depth, either by their original proprietors or by the present claimant. Confirmed.

No. 37.—ELIGIUS FROMENTIN claims a tract of land, situate on the east side of the river Mississippi, in the county of Acadia, containing six arpents front, and forty arpents in depth, and bounded on the upper side by land of Basil Le Clerc.

This land was surveyed by Don Louis Andry, in the year 1776, in favor of Francisco Antailla, who obtained a complete grant for the same, in 1777, from Don Bernardo de Galvez, then Governor; under which title the claimant holds, by regular conveyance. Confirmed.

No. 38.—JEAN BAPTISTE TETE claims a tract of land, situate on the east side of the river Mississippi, in the county of Acadia, containing six arpents and one toise in front, and forty arpents in depth, and bounded on the upper side by land of Mathais y Guillermo, and on the lower by land of Simon Mir.

This land was regularly surveyed by Don Carlos Trudeau, in the year 1781, in favor of Bellony Mir, and it appearing to have been inhabited and cultivated until on and after the 20th December, 1803. Confirmed.

No. 39.—BAPTISTE LUGUET claims a tract of land, situate on the west side of the river Mississippi, in the county of Acadia, containing two and a half arpents in front, and forty arpents in depth, and bounded on the upper side by land of Jean Rhom, and the lower by land of Evariste Hautin.

It appears that the land now claimed was inhabited and cultivated on the 20th December, 1803; and that the same was continually inhabited and cultivated by the claimant, or those under whom he claims, for more than ten consecutive years next preceding. Confirmed.

No. 40.—FRANCISCO LANDRY claims a tract of land, situate on the east side of the river Mississippi, in the county of Acadia, containing two and a half arpents in front, and forty arpents in depth, and bounded on the upper side by land of Carlos Landry, and on the lower by land of Allin Babin.

This land was regularly surveyed by Don Carlos Trudeau, in the year 1795, in favor of Eusebe Landry, at whose decease it was purchased by his widow, the wife of the present claimant; the land having been inhabited and cultivated since that date until on and after the 20th December, 1803. Confirmed.

No. 41.—JEAN DUMAINE claims a tract of land, situate on the east side of the river Mississippi, in the county of Acadia, containing six arpents in front, and forty in depth, and bounded on the upper side by land of Bellony Mir, and on the lower by land of Michel Porrier.

This land was regularly surveyed by Don Carlos Trudeau, in the year 1782, in favor of Simon Mir, under whom the present claimant holds, by successive transfers; the land having been continually inhabited and cultivated since that period until on and after the 20th December, 1803. Confirmed.

No. 42.—VICTOR BLANCHARD claims a tract of land, situate on the east side of the river Mississippi, in the county of Iberville, containing six arpents and four feet in front, and forty arpents in depth, and bounded on the upper side by land of Anselme Blanchard, and on the lower by land of Firman Landry.

This land was surveyed by Don Louis Andry, in the year 1772, in favor of Joseph Blanchard, who obtained a complete grant for the same, in 1774, from Governor Unzaga; under which grant the present claimant holds, by regular deeds of sale. Confirmed.

No. 43.—FRANÇOIS POCHER claims a tract of land, situate on the east side of the river Mississippi, in the county of Acadia, containing three arpents and twenty-seven toises in front, and eighty arpents in depth, and bounded on the upper side by land of Henry Berthelot, and on the lower by land of Alexandre Briguoc.

It appears that the first depth of forty arpents of this land was inhabited and cultivated on the 20th December, 1803, and that for more than ten consecutive years prior. Pierre Bossie obtained a regular order of survey for the second depth of forty arpents, in the year 1783, from Governor Miro. The present claimant holds by virtue of regular transfer. Confirmed.

No. 44.—JOSEPH SIMON LANDRY claims a tract of land, situate on the east side of the river Mississippi, in the county of Acadia, containing five arpents and five toises in front, and forty arpents in depth, and bounded on one side by land of Madam Judice.

This land was surveyed by Don Louis Andry, in the year 1773, in favor of Simon Landry, who obtained a complete grant, in the year 1775, from Governor Unzaga, for twelve arpents and five toises front, of which this claim is part. The claimant holds under the said grant by purchase. Confirmed.

No. 45.—MARIE RASICOT, widow of Louis Judice, claims a tract of land, situate on the east side of the river Mississippi, in the county of Acadia, containing seven arpents in front, and forty in depth, and bounded on one side by land of Joseph Simon Landry.

This is part of a tract of land of twelve arpents and five toises in front, on the ordinary depth, surveyed by Don Louis Andry, in the year 1773, in favor of Simon Landry, who obtained a complete grant for the same, in 1775, from Governor Unzaga; under which grant the claimant holds the seven arpents, claimed by regular deeds. Confirmed.

No. 46.—JACQUES CANTRELLE claims a tract of land, situated on the west side of the river Mississippi, in the county of Acadia, containing five arpents and eleven toises in front, and forty arpents in depth, and bounded on the upper side by land of Anna Bergeron, and on the lower by land of Bentura Godin.

This land was surveyed by Don Carlos Trudeau, in the year 1780, for Philip Lachaussee, under whose title the present claimant holds by successive purchases; the land having been inhabited and cultivated since that period until on and after the 20th December, 1803. Confirmed.

No. 47.—JEAN BOUDIN claims a tract of land, situated on the west side of the river Mississippi, in the county of Acadia, containing four arpents in front, and sixty in depth, and bounded on one side by land of Jacques Chestaildre.

This is part of a tract of land of six arpents twenty six toises in front, and sixty arpents in depth; the first forty arpents in depth of which was surveyed by order of the Governor, in the year 1781, in favor of Juan Marcot, who obtained an order of survey for an addition of twenty arpents in depth, in the year 1783, from Governor Miro. The claimant holds under the above title, and the land having been inhabited and cultivated since that period to the present time. Confirmed.

No. 48.—PIERRE LOUP claims a tract of land, situate on the west side of the river Mississippi, in the county of Acadia, containing two arpents in front, and sixty in depth, and bounded on the upper side by land of George Himel, on the lower by land of Mr. Andry.

This is a part of a tract of land of six arpents and twenty-six toises, mentioned in No. 47, and having been inhabited and cultivated since 1781, until on and after the 20th December, 1803. Confirmed.

No. 49.—JOSEPH LANDRY claims a tract of land, situate on the west side of the river Mississippi, in the county of Acadia, containing six arpents fifteen toises and two feet in front, and forty arpents in depth, and bounded on the upper side by land of Estevan Landry, and on the lower by land of Silvain Leblanc.

This land was surveyed by Don Louis Andry, in the year 1774, in favor of the claimant, who obtained a complete grant for the same, in 1775, from Governor Unzaga. Confirmed.

No. 50.—JOSEPH LANDRY claims a tract of land situate on the west side of the river Mississippi in the county of Acadia, containing five arpents sixteen toises and five feet in front, and forty arpents in depth, and bounded on the upper side by land of Joseph Babin, and on the lower by land of the claimant.

This land was surveyed by Don Louis Andry, in the year 1774, in favor of Estevan Landry, who obtained a complete grant for the same, in 1775, from Governor Unzaga. The present claimant holds by purchase, under the title of the grantee. Confirmed.

No. 51.—JOSEPH LANDRY claims a tract of land being the second depth of forty arpents, situate immediately behind the two preceding tracts mentioned in Nos. 49 and 50; claimed by him, and bounded on the upper and lower sides by vacant lands.

This second depth of forty arpents was surveyed by Don Carlos Trudeau, in the year 1791, in favor of the claimant, who obtained a complete grant for the same in the same year from Don Estevan Miro, then Governor. Confirmed.

No. 52.—JOSEPH LANDRY claims a tract of land, situate on the east side of the river Mississippi, in the county of Acadia, containing five arpents fifteen toises and two feet in front, and forty arpents in depth, and bounded on the upper side by land of Juan Landry, and on the lower by land of Pedro Landry.

This land was surveyed by Don Louis Andry, in the year 1773, in favor of Joseph Granger, who obtained a complete grant for the same in 1775, from Governor Unzaga; under which grant the present claimant holds by virtue of regular deeds of sale. Confirmed.

No. 53.—JOSEPH LANDRY claims a tract of land, situate on the west side of the river Mississippi, in the county of Iberville, containing five arpents and two toises in front, and forty arpents in depth, and bounded on the upper side by land of Joseph Orillion, and on the lower by land of Madame Dupuis.

This land was surveyed by Don Louis Andry, in the year 1772, in favor of Blas Lejeune, who obtained a complete grant for the same, in 1774, from Governor Unzaga; under which grant the present claimant holds, by virtue of regular deeds of sale. Confirmed.

No. 54.—JOSEPH and JEAN ALEXIS LEBLANC claim a tract of land, situate on the east side of the river Mississippi, in the county of Iberville, containing ten arpents in front, and forty in depth, and bounded on the upper side by land of Mathurin Richard, and on the lower by land of Joseph Como, Jun.

This land was surveyed by Don Louis Andry, in the year 1772, in favor of Pedro Brasseux, who obtained a complete grant for the same in the year 1775, from Governor Unzaga; under which grant the claimant holds, by virtue of regular deeds of sale. Confirmed.

No. 55.—JEAN BAPTISTE LEBLANC claims a tract of land, situate on the east side of the river Mississippi, in the county of Iberville, containing five arpents five toises and three feet in front, and forty arpents in depth, and bounded on the upper side by land of Simon Babin, and on the lower by land of Joseph Leblanc.

This land was surveyed by Don Louis Andry, in the year 1772, in favor of Mathurin Richard, who obtained a complete grant for the same, in 1775, from Governor Unzaga; under which grant the claimant holds, by virtue of successive sales. Confirmed.

No. 56.—ALEXIS CESAR BONAMY claims a tract of land, situate on the east side of the river Mississippi, in the county of Acadia, containing six arpents front, and forty in depth, and bounded on the upper side by land of Jago Melanson, and on the lower by land of Simon Boudro.

This land was surveyed by an order of Governor Galvez, in the year 1782, by Don Carlos Trudeau, for Joseph Soiner; under which title the present claimant holds, by virtue of successive sales; the land having been inhabited and cultivated ever since that period, until on and after the 20th December, 1803. Confirmed.

No. 57.—ALEXIS CESAR BONAMY claims a tract of land situate on the east side of the river Mississippi, in the county of Acadia, containing six arpents and ten toises in front, and forty arpents in depth, and bounded on the upper side by land of Joseph Soiner, and on the lower by land of Francisco Antaya.

This land was surveyed by Don Carlos Trudeau, by an order of Governor Galvez, in the year 1782, in favor of Simon Boudro, under whose title the claimant holds, by successive sale; the land having been inhabited and cultivated ever since that period, until on and after the 20th December, 1803. Confirmed.

No. 58.—ALEXIS CESAR BONAMY claims a tract of land, situate on the east side of the river Mississippi, in the county of Acadia, containing six arpents and four toises in front, and forty arpents in depth, and bounded on the upper side by land of Simon Boudro, and on the lower by land of Alexandre Melanson.

This land was surveyed by Don Carlos Trudeau, by an order of Governor Galvez, in the year 1782, in favor of Francisco Antaya; under whose title the claimant holds, by virtue of successive sale; the land having been inhabited and cultivated ever since that period, until on and after the 20th December, 1803. Confirmed.

No. 59.—ALEXIS CESAR BONAMY claims a tract of land, situate on the east side of the river Mississippi, in the county of Acadia, containing four arpents in front, and forty in depth, and bounded on the upper side by land of the claimants, and on the lower by land of Pierre Dupuis.

This is part of a tract of land of six arpents in front, surveyed by Don Carlos Trudeau, by an order of Governor Galvez, in the year 1782, in favor of the widow of Alexandre Melanson; under whose title the claimant holds, by virtue of successive sales. The land having been inhabited and cultivated ever since that period, until on and after the 20th December, 1803. Confirmed.

No. 60.—DAVID ROM claims a tract of land, situate on the west side of the river Mississippi, in the county of Acadia, containing six arpents and five toises in front, and forty arpents in depth, and bounded on the upper side by land of Joseph Blanchard, and on the lower by land of Juan Leboeuf.

This land was surveyed in the year 1771, in favor of Pedro Lambert, who obtained a complete grant for the same in the year 1775, from Governor Unzaga: under which grant the present claimant holds, by virtue of a regular deed of sale. Confirmed.

No. 61.—JOSEPH LEBLANC claims a tract of land, situate on the east side of the river Mississippi, in the county of Iberville, containing five arpents and seventeen toises in front, and forty arpents in depth, and bounded on the upper side by land of Bernard Capedeville, and on the lower by land of Bonaventura Forest.

This land was surveyed by Don Louis Andry, in the year 1772, in favor of the claimant, who obtained a complete grant for the same in the year 1774, from Governor Unzaga. Confirmed.

No. 62.—LOUIS LANDRY, JUN. claims a tract of land, situate on the west side of the river Mississippi, in the county of Acadia, containing eight arpents seven toises and three feet in front, and forty arpents in depth, and bounded on the upper side by land of Aman Babin, and on the lower by land of Edward Godin.

It appears that the claimant did actually inhabit and cultivate the land now claimed on the 20th of December, 1803; and that the same was continually inhabited and cultivated for more than ten consecutive years next preceding. Confirmed.

No. 63.—MICHEL JUDICE claims a tract of land situate on the east side of the river Mississippi, in the county of Acadia, containing five arpents and two toises in front, and forty arpents in depth.

It appears that the land now claimed was inhabited and cultivated on the 20th December, 1803; and that the same was continually inhabited and cultivated by those under whom the claimant holds, for more than ten consecutive years next preceding. Confirmed.

No. 64.—ADAM CHISNAILDRE claims a tract of land, situate on the east side of the river Mississippi, in the county of Acadia, containing three arpents twenty-six toises and three feet in front, and forty arpents in depth, and bounded on the upper side by land of Juan Baptiste Curo, and on the lower by land of Mr. Mather.

This land was surveyed by Don Carlos Trudeau, by order of Governor Galvez, in the year 1781, in favor of George Treigle, under whose title the claimant holds, by virtue of successive sales; the land having been inhabited and cultivated ever since that period, until on and after the 20th December, 1803. Confirmed.

No. 65.—MARIE JEANNE TASSIN, widow of Jean Baptiste Curo, claims a tract of land, situate on the east side of the river Mississippi, in the county of Acadia, containing three arpents in front, and forty in depth, and bounded on the upper side by land of Baptiste Michel, and on the lower by land of Jean Baptiste Curo.

This land was surveyed by Don Carlos Trudeau, by an order of Governor Galvez, in the year 1781, in favor of Pedro Pierre Lejoye, under whose title the claimant holds by virtue of successive sales; the land having been inhabited and cultivated ever since that period, until on and after the 20th December, 1803. Confirmed.

No. 66.—SIMON BABIN claims a tract of land, situate on the west side of the river Mississippi, in the county of Acadia, containing five arpents nineteen toises and two feet in front, and forty arpents in depth, and bounded on the upper side by land of Pedro Landry, and on the lower by land of Joseph Athanas Landry.

This land was surveyed by Don Carlos Trudeau, in the year 1794, for Eusebo Landry, under whose title the claimant holds by virtue of successive sales; the land having been inhabited and cultivated ever since, until on and after the 20th December, 1803. Confirmed.

No. 67.—JOSEPH LEBLANC, Jun. claims a tract of land, situate on the West side of the river Mississippi, in the county of Acadia, containing five arpents one toise five feet and seven inches in front, and forty arpents in depth, and bounded on the upper side by land of Simon Gotreau, and on the lower by land of Gille Leblanc.

This land was surveyed by Don Carlos Trudeau, in the year 1780, for the claimant, who has continued to inhabit and cultivate the same ever since that period, until on and after the 20th December, 1803. Confirmed.

No. 68.—JOSEPH SAUNIER claims a tract of land, situate on the east side of the river Mississippi, in the county of Acadia, containing seven arpents in front, and forty in depth, and bounded on the upper side by land of Mauricio Cairoe, and on the lower by land of Francisco Autailla.

This land was surveyed by Don Louis Andry, in the year 1776, in favor of Miguel Chiasson, who obtained a complete grant for the same, in 1777, from Don Bernardo de Galvez, then Governor; under which grant the present claimant holds by virtue of regular deeds of sale. Confirmed.

No. 69.—JOSEPH ORILLION claims a tract of land, situate on the west side of the river Mississippi, in the county of Iberville, containing seven arpents twenty-two toises and some feet in front, and eighty arpents in depth, and bounded on the upper side by land of Pedro Segur, and on the lower by land of Joseph Mobre.

It appears that the first depth of forty arpents of this land has been inhabited and cultivated for more than ten consecutive years prior to the 20th December, 1803; the claimant obtained a complete grant for the second depth in the year 1796, from the Baron de Carondelet, then Governor. Confirmed.

No. 70.—MARIE CLOATRE, widow of Jean Dupuy, claims a tract of land, situate on the west side of the river Mississippi, in the county of Iberville, containing six arpents in front, and forty in depth, and bounded on the upper side by land of Blas Lejeune and on the lower side by land of Barthelemi Monpierre.

There appears to have been a grant for this land; and the same having been continually inhabited and cultivated for more than ten consecutive years prior to the 20th December, 1803. Confirmed.

No. 71.—JOSEPH ATHANAS LANDRY claims a tract of land, situate on the west side of the river Mississippi, in the county of Acadia, containing eight arpents two perches and three feet in front, and forty arpents in depth, and bounded on the upper side by land of Eusebo Landry, and on the lower by land of Aman Babin.

This land was surveyed by Don Carlos Trudeau, in the year 1796, in favor of the claimant, who obtained a complete grant for the same in the same year from the Baron de Carondelet, then Governor. Confirmed.

No. 72.—JOSEPH ATHANAS LANDRY claims a tract of land, situate on the east side of the river Mississippi, in the county of Acadia, containing six arpents and two toises in front, and forty arpents in depth, and bounded on the upper side by land of Efrem Babin, and on the lower by land of Estevan Landry.

This land was surveyed by Don Louis Andry, in the year 1773, in favor of Carlos Babin, who obtained a complete grant for the same, in the year 1775, from Governor Unzaga; under which grant the present claimant holds, by virtue of regular sales. Confirmed.

No. 73.—WILLIAM DONALDSON claims a tract of land, situate on the right bank of the bayou Lafourche, in the county of Acadia, containing four superficial arpents, and bounded on the north by the river Mississippi, on the east by the bayou Lafourche, and on the south and west by land of Mr. Hemby.

This land was granted to Louis Judice, in the year 1775, by Governor Unzaga; under which title the present claimant holds, by virtue of regular transfers. Confirmed.

No. 74.—JOSEPH TURULET claims a tract of land, situate on the west side of the river Mississippi, in the county of Acadia, containing three arpents in front, and forty in depth, and bounded on the upper side by land of Charles Fredric, and on the lower by land of Joseph Cloatre.

This is part of a tract of land of five arpents twenty-one toises two feet and six inches in front, on the ordinary depth, surveyed by Don Carlos Trudeau, in the year 1780, for Carlos Gaudet; under whose title the present claimant holds by virtue of successive transfers; this land having been inhabited and cultivated ever since 1780, until on and after the 20th December, 1803. Confirmed.

No. 75.—JOSEPH TURULET claims a tract of land, situate on the east side of the river Mississippi, in the county of Acadia, containing four arpents thirteen toises and three feet in front, and forty arpents in depth, and bounded on the upper side by land of Ambrose Terrio, and on the lower by land of Juan Baptiste Melanson.

This land was surveyed by Don Carlos Trudeau, by order of the Governor, in the year 1782, for Estevan Melanson; under whose title the claimant holds by successive sales; the land having been inhabited and cultivated ever since that period, until on and after the 20th December, 1803. Confirmed.

No. 76.—FRANÇOISE BLANCHARD, widow of Anselme Landry, claims a tract of land, situate on the east side of the river Mississippi, in the county of Acadia, containing six arpents six toises and two feet in front, and forty arpents in depth, and bounded on the upper side by land of Carlos Babin, and on the lower by land of Aman Babin.

This land was surveyed by Don Louis Andry, in the year 1773, in favor of Estevan Landry, who obtained a complete grant for the same in 1775, from Governor Unzaga; the claimant holds under said grant, by virtue of regular transfers. Confirmed.

No. 77.—JOSEPH BOURG claims a tract of land, situate on the west side of the river Mississippi, in the county of Acadia, containing four arpents in front, and forty in depth, and bounded on the upper side by land of Pedro Bourgeois, and on the lower by land of Juan Arcenaux.

This land was surveyed by Don Carlos Trudeau, in the year 1780, for Juan Carlos Arcenaux; under whose title the present claimant holds, in virtue of successive sales; the land having been inhabited and cultivated ever since that period, until on and after the 20th December, 1803. Confirmed.

No. 78.—JUSTIN TERREL claims a tract of land, situate on the east side of the river Mississippi, in the county of Acadia, containing two arpents in front, and forty in depth, and bounded on the upper side by land of Pierre Bruno, and on the lower by land of Joseph Blanchard.

It appears that the land now claimed was inhabited and cultivated on the 20th December, 1803, and that the same was continually inhabited and cultivated by those under whom the claimant holds for more than ten consecutive years next preceding. Confirmed.

No. 79.—JOSEPH POIRIE claims a tract of land, situate on the east side of the river Mississippi, in the county of Acadia, containing three arpents and twenty-six toises in front, and forty arpents in depth, and bounded on one side by land of Louis Part.

This is part of a tract of land of six arpents and twenty-six toises in front, on the ordinary depth, surveyed by Don Carlos Trudeau, in the year 1781, for the claimant, who sold the balance to Louis Part; the land having been inhabited and cultivated ever since that period, until on and after the 20th December, 1803. Confirmed.

No. 80.—PIERRE PLE claims a tract of land, situate on the west side of the river Mississippi, in the county of Iberville, containing three arpents five toises one foot and six inches in front, and forty arpents in depth, and bounded on the upper side by land of Pablo Hebert, and on the lower side by land of Madame Baudraux.

This is part of a tract of land of four arpents five toises one foot and six inches in front, on the usual depth, surveyed by Vincente Pintado, in the year 1796, in favor of Ambrosio Longue-Epée, who obtained a complete grant for the same in the same year, from the Baron de Carondelet, then Governor. The present claimant holds by purchase from the grantee. Confirmed.

No. 81.—PATRICE URIELL claims a tract of land, situate on the west side of the river Mississippi, in the county of Acadia, containing seven arpents in front, and sixty in depth, and bounded on one side by land of Hubert Remy.

This is part of a tract of land of thirty arpents in front, on the depth of forty, regularly granted to Louis Judice, in the year 1765. François Croizet obtained a complete grant for an addition of twenty arpents in depth, in the year 1774, from Governor Unzaga; under which titles the present claimant holds the part he claims by virtue of regular sales. Confirmed.

No. 82.—JOSEPH MENDEZ claims a tract of land, situate on the west side of the river Mississippi, in the county of Acadia, containing two arpents twenty-five toises and three feet in front, and forty arpents in depth, and bounded on the upper side by land of Juan Alleman, and on the lower by land of Bartholomew Hidalgo.

This land was surveyed by Don Carlos Trudeau, in the year 1791, for the claimant, and has been inhabited and cultivated ever since that period, until on and after the 20th December, 1803. Confirmed.

No. 83.—MARIE BONVILIAU, widow of Jacques Guedry, claims a tract of land situate on the east side of the river Mississippi, in the county of Acadia, containing three arpents in front, and forty in depth, and bounded on the upper side by land of Joseph Guedry, and on the lower by land of Jacques Bonviliau.

It appears that the present claimant did actually inhabit and cultivate the land now claimed on the 20th December, 1803; that the same was continually inhabited and cultivated for more than ten consecutive years next preceding. Confirmed.

No. 84.—JOSEPH MAZA LEBLANC claims a tract of land, situate on the west side of the river Mississippi, in the county of Acadia, containing two arpents, sixteen toises, and three feet in front, and forty arpents in depth, and bounded on one side by lands of Paul Breau.

This is part of a tract of four arpents sixteen toises and three feet in front, on the ordinary depth, surveyed by Don Carlos Trudeau, in the year 1798, for the claimant, who sold the balance to Paul Breau; the land having been inhabited and cultivated ever since that period, until on and after the 20th December, 1803. Confirmed.

No. 85.—SIMON PIERRE BABIN claims a tract of land, situate on the east side of the river Mississippi, in the county of Iberville, containing five arpents twenty-six toises and one foot in front, and forty arpents in depth, and bounded on the upper side by land of Timoleon Lesassier, and on the lower by land of Baptiste Leblanc.

It appears that the claimant did actually inhabit and cultivate the land now claimed on the 20th December, 1803, and that the same was continually inhabited and cultivated for more than ten consecutive years next preceding. Confirmed.

No. 86.—JEAN BAPTISTE LAISSARD claims a tract of land, situate on the west side of the river Mississippi, in the county of Acadia, containing one arpent one toise and two thirds of a toise in front, and forty arpents in depth, and bounded on the upper side by land of William Donaldson, and on the lower by land of William Conway.

It appears that the claimant did actually inhabit and cultivate the land now claimed on the 20th December, 1803, and that the same was continually inhabited and cultivated by him, or those under whom he claims, for more than ten consecutive years next preceding. Confirmed.

No. 87.—PIERRE FREDERIC claims a tract of land, situate on the west side of the river Mississippi, in the county of Arcadia, containing three arpents four feet and seven inches in front, and forty arpents in depth, and bounded on the upper side by land of the heirs of Mathias Frederic, deceased, and on the lower by land of Christophe Troxler.

This is a part of a tract of land of nine arpents and twenty-four toises in front, on the usual depth, for which there appears to have been an order of survey in the year 1756, from the French Government; the land having been inhabited and cultivated ever since that period, until on and after the 20th December, 1803. Confirmed.

No. 88.—PIERRE FREDERIC, for the heirs of Mathias Frederic, claims a tract of land, situate on the west side of the river Mississippi, in the county of Acadia, containing three arpents thirteen feet and nine inches in front, and forty arpents in depth, and bounded on the upper side by land of Pierre Frederic, and on the lower by land of Francis Frederic.

This is a part of the land for which there was an order of survey in the year 1756, mentioned in No. 87; and it having been inhabited and cultivated ever since that period, until on and after the 20th December, 1803. Confirmed.

No. 89.—JOSEPH FONTELET claims a tract of land, situate on the left bank of the bayou Lafourche, in the county of Acadia, containing three arpents twenty-six toises and one foot in front, and forty arpents in depth, and bounded on the upper side by land of Edward Landry, and on the lower by land of Nicholas Daublin.

This is part of a tract of land of eleven arpents eighteen toises and four feet in front, on the ordinary depth, for which, it appears, there was a grant; and the land having been inhabited and cultivated for more than ten consecutive years prior to the 20th December, 1803. Confirmed.

No. 90.—SIMON BOUDREAUX claims a tract of land, situate on the west side of the river Mississippi, in the county of Acadia, containing six arpents in front and eighty in depth, and bounded on the upper side by land of Madame Babin, and on the lower by land of Joseph Babin.

There was an order of survey in the year 1788, for the first depth of forty arpents, in favor of the claimant, by Governor Miro; and in the same year there was a complete grant for the second depth of forty arpents, obtained by the claimant from that Governor. Confirmed.

No. 91.—SIMON LEBLANC claims a tract of land, situate on the west side of the river Mississippi, in the county of Acadia, containing six arpents and twenty-one toises in front, and forty in depth, and bounded on the upper side by land of Carlos Forest, and on the lower by land of Estevan Leblanc.

This land was surveyed by Don Louis Andry, in the year 1774, in favor of the claimant, who obtained a complete grant for the same, in 1775, from Governor Unzaga. Confirmed.

No. 92.—MARIE LEBLANC, widow of Joseph Melanson, claims a tract of land, situate on the west side of the river Mississippi, in the county of Acadia, containing five arpents in front, and forty in depth, and bounded on one side by land of Eusebe Melanson.

This is part of a tract of land of six arpents in front, on a depth of forty, surveyed by Don Carlos Trudeau, in the year 1780, for Joseph Melanson, the husband of the claimant, and which has been inhabited and cultivated ever since. The claimant's husband obtained a complete grant for the second depth of forty arpents in 1791, from Governor Miro. The claimant sold one arpent of the six here mentioned to Eusebe Melanson. Confirmed.

No. 93.—HUBERT REMY claims a tract of land, situate on the west side of the river Mississippi, in the county of Acadia, containing ten arpents in front, and one hundred arpents in depth, and bounded on the upper side by land of Joseph L. Fabre, and on the lower by land of Mr. Uriell.

This land, to the extent of sixty arpents in depth, is part of a tract of thirty arpents front, and sixty in depth, granted to Louis Judice and François Croizet, mentioned in No. 35; and which the claimant holds, by virtue of regular sale. So much of this claim the Board confirm, but reject the balance of forty arpents in depth.

No. 94.—GILES LEBLANC claims a tract of land, situate on the west side of the river Mississippi, in the county of Acadia, containing eight arpents ten toises and six feet in front, and forty arpents in depth, and bounded on the upper side by land of Charles Gaudet, and on the lower by land of Honoré Breaux.

It appears that this land was inhabited and cultivated on the 20th December, 1803; and that the same was continually inhabited and cultivated, by those under whom the claimant holds, for more than ten consecutive years next preceding. Confirmed.

No. 95.—JEAN VESRIE claims a tract of land, situate on the west side of the river Mississippi, in the county of Acadia, containing six arpents and two feet in front, and forty arpents in depth, and bounded on the upper side by land belonging to the parish of Ascension, and on the lower by land of Gregoire Blanc.

This land was surveyed in the year 1774 for Abraham Landry, under whose title the present claimant holds, by virtue of successive sales; the land having been inhabited and cultivated ever since that period, until on and after the 20th December, 1803. Confirmed.

No. 96.—ARMAND BRAUX claims a tract of land, situate on the east side of the river Mississippi, in the county of Acadia, containing five arpents twenty-seven toises and four feet in front, and forty arpents in depth, and bounded on the upper side by land of Philip Lachaussée, and on the lower by land of Joseph Gravois.

This land was surveyed by Don Carlos Trudeau, in the year 1780, for Alexandria Godin, under whose title the claimant holds, in virtue of successive sales; the land having been inhabited and cultivated ever since that period, until on and after the 20th December, 1803. Confirmed.

No. 97.—JOSEPH LANDRY, JUN. claims a tract of land, situate on the east side of the river Mississippi, in the county of Acadia, containing four arpents in front, and forty in depth, and bounded on the upper side by land of Mr. Gillard, and on the lower by land of Madame Labonne.

It appears that the claimant did actually inhabit and cultivate the land now claimed on the 20th December, 1803; and that the same was continually inhabited and cultivated by him, or those under whom he claims, for more than ten consecutive years next preceding. Confirmed.

No. 98.—JEAN PIERRE RICHARD claims a tract of land, situate on the west side of the river Mississippi, in the county of Acadia, containing three arpents in front, and forty in depth, and bounded on the upper side by land of Michel Poirier, and on the lower by land of Madame Richard.

This is a part of a tract of land of thirteen arpents twenty-four toises and two feet in front, on the ordinary depth, surveyed in the year 1780, for Louis Andry. under whose title the claimant holds, by successive sales; the land having been inhabited and cultivated since 1780, until on and after the 20th December, 1803. Confirmed.

No. 99.—JEAN KLINGS claims a tract of land, situate on the east side of the river Mississippi, in the county of Acadia, containing four arpents in front, and forty arpents in depth, and bounded on the upper side by land of Firmin Guedry, and on the lower side by land of Laurenzo Fabre.

It appears that the claimant did actually inhabit and cultivate the land now claimed on the 20th December, 1803, and that the same was continually inhabited and cultivated by him, or those under whom he claims, for more than ten consecutive years next preceding. Confirmed.

No. 100.—FIRMIN DUPUY claims a tract of land, situate on the east side of the river Mississippi, in the county of Acadia, containing nine arpents in front, and forty in depth, and bounded on the upper side by land of Antoine Blanchard, and on the lower by land of Maria Dupuy.

This land was surveyed by Don Carlos Trudeau, in the year 1795, for the claimant; and having been inhabited and cultivated ever since that period, until on and after the 20th December, 1803. Confirmed.

No. 101.—BENJAMIN BABIN claims a tract of land, situate on the west side of the river Mississippi, in the county of Acadia, containing three arpents in front, and eighty arpents in depth, and bounded on the upper side by land of Pierre Richard, and on the lower by land of Madame Richard.

The first depth of forty arpents of this land is part of a tract of thirteen arpents twenty-four toises and two feet in front, on the ordinary depth, surveyed, in the year 1780, for Louis Andry, under which title the present claimant holds, by virtue of successive sales; and on the first depth of the land now claimed, having been inhabited and cultivated ever since 1780, until on and after the 20th December, 1803; the Board confirm the claim to that extent, but reject the claim to the second depth.

No. 102.—JOSEPH MELANSON, Jun. claims a tract of land, situate on the west side of the river Mississippi, in the county of Acadia, containing six arpents in front, and forty in depth, and bounded on the upper side by land of Ephraim Babin, and on the lower by land of Marguerita Landry.

It appears that the claimant did actually inhabit and cultivate the land now claimed, on the 20th December, 1803; and that the same was continually inhabited and cultivated by him, or those under whom he claims, for more than ten consecutive years next preceding. Confirmed.

No. 103.—ROSE BOURGEOIS, widow of —— Richard, claims a tract of land, situate on the west side of the river Mississippi, in the county of Acadia, containing twenty-seven toises and one foot in front, and forty arpents in depth, and bounded on the upper side by land of Jean Pierre Richard, and on the lower by land of Benjamin Babin.

This is part of a tract of land of thirteen arpents twenty four toises and two feet, surveyed for Louis Andry in the year 1780, under which title the claimant holds by virtue of successive sales; this land having been inhabited and cultivated ever since the above period, until on and after the 20th December, 1803. Confirmed.

No. 104.—PIERRE RICHARD claims a tract of land, situate on the west side of the river Mississippi, in the county of Acadia, containing five arpents in front, and forty in depth, and bounded on the upper side by land of Benjamin Babin, and on the lower by land of François Croizet.

This is part of a tract of land of ten arpents two toises and three feet in front, on the ordinary depth, surveyed in the year 1780, for Pierre Arcenaux, under whose title the claimant holds, by virtue of successive sales; the land having been inhabited and cultivated ever since that period, until on and after the 20th December, 1803. Confirmed.

No. 105.—ANTOINE FREDERIC claims a tract of land, situate on the west side of the river Mississippi, in the county of Acadia, containing four arpents eighteen feet and four inches in front, and eighty arpents in depth, and bounded on the upper side by land of Louis Mouton, and on the lower by land of Charlotte Frederic.

This part of a tract of land of fourteen arpents ten toises and four feet in front, said to have been granted to Mathias Frederic, Sen. under whose title the claimant holds, as one of the heirs of his father. The first depth of forty arpents having been inhabited and cultivated for more than ten consecutive years, prior to the 20th December, 1803, the Board confirm; but reject the balance of forty arpents, the second depth. But see No. 308, page 285, respecting second depth.

No. 106.—NOEL GISDAR claims a tract of land, situate on the west side of the river Mississippi, in the county of Acadia, containing two arpents nine feet and two inches in front, and eighty arpents in depth, and bounded on the upper side by land of Antoine Frederic, and on the lower by land of Francis Frederic.

This is part of a tract of land mentioned in the last No. 105, the claimant holds by right of his wife, one of the heirs of Mathias Frederic, deceased. The first depth of forty arpents having been inhabited and cultivated for more than ten years, prior to the 20th December, 1803, the Board confirm; but reject the balance. See No. 308, page 285, with respect to the second depth here claimed.

No. 107.—FRANCOIS FREDERIC claims a tract of land, situate on the west side of the river Mississippi, in the county of Acadia, containing four arpents eighteen feet and four inches in front, and eighty arpents in depth, and bounded on the upper side by land of Charlotte Frederic, and on the lower by land of the heirs of Mathias Frederic, deceased.

This is part of a tract of land mentioned in No. 105, the claimant holds as one of the heirs to his deceased father. The first depth of forty arpents having been inhabited and cultivated for more than ten consecutive years prior to the 20th December, 1803, the Board confirm; but reject the second depth of forty arpents.

No. 108.—EPHRAIM BABIN claims a tract of land, situate on the east side of the river Mississippi, in the county of Acadia, containing six arpents eight toises and one foot in front, and forty arpents in depth, and bounded on the upper side by land of Carlos Landry, and on the lower by land of Carlos Babin.

This land was surveyed by Don Louis Andry, in the year 1773, in favor of the claimant, who obtained a complete grant for the same, in the year 1775, from Governor Unzaga. Confirmed.

No. 109.—PIERRE BOURGEOIS claims a tract of land, situate on the west side of the river Mississippi, in the county of Acadia, containing six arpents in front, and forty in depth, and bounded on the upper side by land of Anna Arcenaux, and on the lower by land of Juan Carlos Arcenaux.

This land was surveyed by Don Carlos Trudeau, in the year 1780, for the claimant, and the land having been inhabited and cultivated ever since that period, until on and after the 20th December, 1803. Confirmed.

No. 110.—JOSEPH MELANSON claims a tract of land, situate on the west side of the river Mississippi, in the county of Acadia, containing two arpents twenty-nine toises and one foot in front, and forty arpents in depth, and bounded on the upper side by land of Jerome Melanson, and on the lower by land of Vincente Landry.

This is part of a tract of land of five arpents twenty-nine toises and one foot, surveyed by Don Louis Andry, in the year 1774, in favor of Aman Gautrot, who obtained a complete grant for the same, in the year 1775, from Governor Unzaga. The present claimant holds by purchase from said Aman Gautrot. Confirmed.

No. 111.—JOSEPH MELANSON claims a tract of land, situate on the west side of the river Mississippi, in the county of Acadia, containing five arpents twenty-two toises and two feet in front, and forty arpents in depth, and bounded on the upper side by land of Aman Landry and on the lower by land of Aman Gautrot.

This land was surveyed by Don Louis Andry, in the year 1774, in favor of Pedro Landry, who obtained a complete grant for the same, in the year 1775, from Governor Unzaga; under which grant the claimant holds by virtue of regular sales. Confirmed.

No. 112.—JEROME MELANSON claims a tract of land, situate on the west side of the river Mississippi, in the county of Acadia, containing three arpents in front and forty in depth, and bounded on the upper side by land of Madame Benjamin Leblanc, and on the lower by land of Joseph Melanson.

This is part of a tract of land of five arpents twenty-nine toises and one foot in front, on the ordinary depth, surveyed by Don Louis Andry, in the year 1774, in favor of Aman Gautrot, who obtained a complete title for the same, in 1775, from Governor Unzaga; the father of the claimant purchased from said Gautrot, and the claimant holds under his father by donation. Confirmed.

No. 113.—FRANCOIS ARCENAUX claims a tract of land, situate on the east side of the river Mississippi, in the county of Acadia, containing four arpents and twenty toises in front, and forty arpents in depth, and bounded on the upper side by land of Estevan Melanson, and on the lower by land of Pedro Braux.

This land was surveyed by Don Carlos Trudeau, in the year 1782, for Juan Baptiste Melanson, under whose title the claimant holds by purchase; and having been inhabited and cultivated ever since that period, until on and after the 20th December, 1803. Confirmed.

No. 114.—FRANCOIS ARCENAUX claims a tract of land, situate on the east side of the river Mississippi, in the county of Acadia, containing four arpents in front, and forty in depth, and bounded on the upper side by land of Juan Baptiste Melanson, and on the lower by land of Juan Carlos Arcenaux.

This land was surveyed by Don Carlos Trudeau, in the year 1782, for Pedro Braux, under whose title the present claimant holds, by virtue of successive sales; the land having been inhabited and cultivated ever since that period, until on and after the 20th December, 1803. Confirmed.

No. 115.—CATHARINE FREDERIC, widow of Nicholas Trosclair, claims a tract of land, situate on the west side of the river Mississippi, in the county of Acadia, containing two arpents in front, and forty in depth, and bounded on one side by land of Augustin Trosclair.

This land was surveyed by Don Carlos Trudeau, in the year 1781, for Nicholas Trosclair, the deceased husband of the claimant; the land having been inhabited and cultivated ever since that period, until on and after the 20th December, 1803. Confirmed.

No. 116.—MARTIN DUBOURG claims a tract of land, situate on the east side of the river Mississippi, in the county of Acadia, containing one arpent and forty-six feet in front, and forty arpents in depth, and bounded on the upper side by land of Jean Vebre, and on the lower by land of Christophe Mayer.

It appears that this land was inhabited and cultivated on the 20th December, 1803, and that the same was continually inhabited and cultivated by those under whom the claimant holds for more than ten consecutive years next preceding. Confirmed.

No. 117.—GEORGE AUTIN claims a tract of land, situate on the west side of the river Mississippi, in the county of Acadia, containing two arpents in front, and forty in depth, and bounded on the upper side by land of George Lequel, and on the lower by land of Etienne Toupe.

It appears that this land was inhabited and cultivated on the 20th December, 1803, and that the same was continually inhabited and cultivated by those under whom the claimant holds for more than ten consecutive years next preceding. Confirmed.

No. 118.—PIERRE MICHEL claims a tract of land, situate on the east side of the river Mississippi, in the county of Acadia, containing two arpents in front, and forty in depth, and bounded on the upper side by land of J. Godberry, and on the lower side by land of the claimant.

This is a part of six arpents in front on the ordinary depth, surveyed for François Savoy, under whose title the present claimant holds by virtue of successive sales; the land having been inhabited and cultivated for more than ten consecutive years prior to the 20th December, 1803. Confirmed.

No. 119.—SILVAIN LEBLANC claims a tract of land, situate on the west side of the river Mississippi, in the county of Acadia, containing five arpents and twenty toises in front, and forty arpens in depth, and bounded on the upper side by land of Joseph Landry, and on the lower by land of Pedro Bujeau.

This land was surveyed by Don Louis Andry, in the year 1774, in favor of the claimant, who obtained a complete grant for the same, in the year 1775, from Governor Unzaga. Confirmed.

No. 120.—SILVAIN LEBLANC claims a tract of land, being a second depth, situate immediately behind a tract of land in claim No. 119, and bounded on the upper and lower sides by vacant lands.

This land was surveyed by Don Carlos Trudeau, in the year 1796, in favor of the claimant, who obtained a complete grant for the same in the year 1796 from the Baron de Carondelet, then Governor. Confirmed.

No. 121.—CHARLES BABIN claims a tract of land, situate on the west side of the river Mississippi, in the county of Acadia, containing five arpents eight toises and one foot and a half in front, and forty arpents in depth, and bounded on the upper side by land of Louis Landry, and on the lower by land of Simon Leblanc.

This land was surveyed by Don Carlos Trudeau, in the year 1794, for Edward Godin, from whom the claimant purchased; the land having been inhabited and cultivated ever since that period, until on and after the 20th December, 1803. Confirmed.

No. 122.—SIMON BABIN claims a tract of land, situate on the west side of the river Mississippi, in the county of Acadia, containing four arpents sixteen toises and three feet in front, and forty arpents in depth, and bounded on the upper side by land of Edward Godin, and on the lower by land of Joseph Leblanc.

This land was surveyed by Don Carlos Trudeau, in the year 1794, for the claimant; and having been inhabited and cultivated ever since that period, until on and after the 20th December, 1803. Confirmed.

No. 123.—ATHANAS DUGAST claims a tract of land, situate on the west side of the river Mississippi, in the county of Acadia, containing four arpents in front, and forty arpents in depth, and bounded on the upper side by land of Joseph Leblanc, and on the lower by land of Ephraim Babin.

This land was surveyed by Don Carlos Trudeau, in the year 1793, in favor of Joseph Bretomiere, who obtained a complete grant for the same in the same year, from Don Manuel Gayoso de Lemos, then Governor. The claimant holds by purchase from said Bretomiere. Confirmed.

No. 124.—JOSEPH LEVERT claims a tract of land, situate on the east side of the river Mississippi, in the county of Acadia, containing four arpents twenty-nine toises and two feet in front, and forty arpents in depth, and bounded on the upper side by land of Joseph Gaudet, and on the lower by land of Mr. Bariouier.

This land was surveyed by Don Carlos Trudeau, in the year 1782, for André Bernard, deceased, under whose title the claimant holds, in right of his wife, widow of said Bernard; the land having been inhabited and cultivated ever since that period, until on and after the 20th December, 1803. Confirmed.

No. 125.—PIERRE PART claims a tract of land, situate on the east side of the river Mississippi, in the county of Acadia, containing four arpents in front, and forty in depth, and bounded on the upper side by land of Joseph Richard, and on the lower by land of Guiot Mathias, and William Caruthers.

This land was surveyed by Don Carlos Trudeau, in 1782, for the claimant; and it having been inhabited and cultivated ever since that period, until on and after the 20th December, 1803. Confirmed.

No. 126.—PIERRE PART claims a tract of land, situate on the east side of the river Mississippi, in the county of Acadia, containing three arpents and twenty toises in front, and forty arpents in depth, and bounded on the upper side by land of the claimant, and on the lower by land of Bellony Myr.

This land was surveyed by Don Carlos Trudeau, in the year 1782, for Guiot Mathias, and William Caruthers, from whom the claimant purchased; the land having been inhabited and cultivated ever since that period, until on and after the 20th December, 1803. Confirmed.

No. 127.—SIMON PIERRE BABIN claims a tract of land, situate on the west side of the river Mississippi, in the county of Acadia, containing five arpents and twenty-one toises in front, and forty arpents in depth, and bounded on the upper side by land of Joseph Athanas Landry, and on the lower by land of Silvain Leblanc.

This land was surveyed by Don Carlos Trudeau, in the year 1798, for Armand Babin, from whom the claimant purchased; the land having been inhabited and cultivated ever since that period, until on and after the 20th December, 1803. Confirmed.

No. 128.—PIERRE SIANNEAUX claims a tract of land, situate on the west side of the river Mississippi, in the county of Acadia, containing six arpents and two toises in front, and forty arpents in depth, and bounded on the upper side by land of Joseph Bourg, and on the lower by and of Joussett de Laloire.

This land was surveyed by Don Carlos Trudeau in the year 1782, for Juan Lebœuf, under whose title the claimant holds by virtue of successive sales; this land having been inhabited and cultivated ever since that period, until on and after the 20th December, 1803. Confirmed.

No. 129.—MARIE DUPUY, widow of —— Hebert, claims a tract of land, situate on the east side of the river Mississippi, in the county of Acadia, containing three arpents twenty-four toises and four feet in front, and forty arpents in depth, and bounded on one side by land of Jacques Hebert.

This is part of a tract of land of six arpents twenty-four toises and four feet in front, and forty arpents in depth, surveyed by Don Carlos Trudeau, in the year 1795, for the claimant, who sold three arpents of said land to her son, Jacques Hebert; the land having been inhabited and cultivated since 1795, until on and after the 20th December, 1803. Confirmed.

No. 130.—MARCELLY CORNU, Jun. claims a tract of land, situate on the west side of the river Mississippi, in the county of Acadia, containing four arpents and four toises in front, and forty arpents in depth, and bounded on the upper side by land of Jacques Cautrelle, and on the lower by land of Jean Marie Mallard.

This is part of a tract of land of twelve arpents in front, on the ordinary depth, surveyed by Don Carlos Trudeau, in the year 1780, for Bonaventura Bergeron, under whose title the claimant holds, by successive sales; the land having been inhabited and cultivated ever since that period, until on and after the 20th December, 1803. Confirmed.

No. 131.—JEAN MARIE MALLARD claims a tract of land, situate on the west side of the river Mississippi, in the county of Acadia, containing two arpents and six toises in front, and forty arpents in depth, and bounded on the upper side by land of Marcelly Cornu, and on the lower by land of Auguste Gravois.

This is part of a tract of land of twelve arpents in front, and forty in depth, mentioned in the last claim, No. 130. The claimant holds by virtue of successive sales; and the land having been inhabited and cultivated ever since the year 1780, until on and after the 20th December, 1803. Confirmed.

No. 132.—PIERRE CHENET claims a tract of land, situate on the east side of the river Mississippi, in the county of Acadia, containing five arpents in front, and forty in depth, and bounded on the upper side by land of Jean Orry, and on the lower by land of Etienne René.

It appears that the claimant did actually inhabit and cultivate the land now claimed on the 20th December, 1803, and that the same was continually inhabited and cultivated by him, or those under whom he claims, for more than ten consecutive years next preceding. Confirmed.

No. 133.—JACQUES HEBERT claims a tract of land, situate on the east side of the river Mississippi, in the county of Acadia, containing three arpents in front, and forty in depth, and bounded on one side by land of Etienne Hebert.

This is part of a tract of land of five and a half arpents in front, on the usual depth, surveyed for Antonio Blanchard, in the year 1795, under whose title the claimant holds by virtue of successive sales; the land having been inhabited and cultivated ever since the above period, until on and after the 20th December, 1803. Confirmed.

No. 134.—CHARLES GAUTROT claims a tract of land, situate on the east side of the river Mississippi, in the county of Acadia, containing three arpents nine perches and one toise in front, and forty arpents in depth, and bounded on the upper side by land of Baptiste Goutro, and on the lower by land of Simon Loutro.

This land was surveyed by Don Carlos Trudeau, in the year 1796, for the claimant; and having been inhabited and cultivated ever since that period, until on and after the 20th December, 1803. Confirmed.

No. 135.—AMANT GOUTRO claims a tract of land, situate on the west side of the river Mississippi, in the county of Acadia, containing four arpents in front, and forty in depth, and bounded on the upper side by land of Madame Bourg, and on the lower by land of Carlos Goutro.

This land was surveyed by Don Carlos Trudeau, in the year 1795, for Baptiste Goutro, under whose title the claimant holds by successive sales; the land having been inhabited and cultivated ever since that period, until and after the 20th December, 1803. Confirmed.

No. 136.—BALTIZAR PLAISANCE claims a tract of land, situate on the left bank of the bayou Lafourche, in the county of Acadia, containing three arpents in front, and forty in depth, and bounded on the upper side by land of Dominique Suares, and on the lower by land of Manuel Bermudez.

This land was surveyed by Don Carlos Trudeau, in the year 1780, for Sebastian Suares, under whose title the claimant holds by successive sales; the land having been inhabited and cultivated ever since that period, until on and after the 20th December, 1803. Confirmed.

No. 137.—FRANÇOIS MICHEL claims a tract of land, situate on the east side of the river Mississippi, in the county of Acadia, containing four arpents and four feet in front, and forty arpents in depth, and bounded on the upper side by land of Charles Gaudet, and on the lower by land of Joseph Bourgeois.

It appears that the claimant did actually inhabit and cultivate the land now claimed on the 20th December, 1803, and that the same was continually inhabited and cultivated for more than ten consecutive years next preceding. Confirmed.

No. 138.—FIRMIN and PIERRE N. LANDRY claim a tract of land, situate on the west side of the river Mississippi, in the county of Acadia, containing six arpents in front, and forty in depth, and bounded on the upper side by land of Silvain Leblanc, Sen., and on the lower by land of Armand Babin.

This land was surveyed by Don Carlos Trudeau, in the year 1780, for Silvain Leblanc, Sen., from whom the claimants purchased; the land having been inhabited and cultivated ever since that period, until on and after the 20th December, 1803. Confirmed.

No. 139.—JEAN CHARLES ARCENAUX claims a tract of land, situate on the east side of the river Mississippi, in the county of Acadia, containing three arpents three toises and five feet in front, and forty arpents in depth, and bounded on the upper side by land of——, and on the lower by land of——.

This is part of a tract of land of eight arpents three toises and five feet in front, and forty arpents in depth, surveyed by Don Carlos Trudeau, in the year 1782, for the claimant, who sold the remaining five arpents; the land having been inhabited and cultivated ever since that period, until on and after the 20th December, 1803. Confirmed.

No. 140.—GUILLAUME ARCENAUX claims a tract of land, situate on the west side of the river Mississippi, in the county of Acadia, containing four arpents twelve toises and one foot in front, and forty arpents in depth, to two of the front arpents; but a depth of eighty arpents to the remaining two arpents twelve toises and one foot; and bounded on the upper side by land of Juan Carlos Arcenaux, and on the lower side by land of Juan Roger.

This land, to the extent of forty arpents in depth, was surveyed for Juan Arcenaux, in the year 1780, by Don Carlos Trudeau. The claimant holds by donation from his father. The land, to the extent of the first depth, having been inhabited and cultivated ever since the above period, until on and after the 20th December, 1803, the Board confirm; but reject the second depth claimed.

No. 141.—LOUIS HYMEL claims a tract of land, situate on the west side of the river Mississippi, in the county of Acadia, containing three arpents twenty-three toises and five feet in front, and sixty arpents in depth, and bounded on one side by land of André Hymel.

This is part of a tract of land of four arpents twenty-three toises and five feet in front, on the depth of forty arpents, surveyed by Don Carlos Trudeau, in the year 1781, for Bastien Hymel. Jacques Trosclair obtained an order of survey for an additional depth of twenty arpents, in the year 1783, from Governor Miro. The claimant holds under the aforesaid titles, by virtue of successive sales. Confirmed.

No. 142.—RICHARD LEBLANC claims a tract of land, situate on the west side of the river Mississippi, in the county of Acadia, containing one arpent and two-thirds of an arpent fifty feet and nine inches in front, and forty arpents in depth, and bounded on the upper side by land of Madame Hyacinthe Landry, and on the lower by land of Madame Etienne Leblanc.

It appears that the land now claimed was inhabited and cultivated on the 20th December, 1803; and that the same was continually inhabited and cultivated by those under whom the claimant holds for more than ten consecutive years next preceding. Confirmed.

No. 143.—BAPTISTE BOURGEOIS claims a tract of land, situate on the east side of the river Mississippi, in the county of Acadia, containing five arpents twenty-six toises and three feet in front, and eighty arpents in depth, and bounded on the upper side by land of Paul Bourgeois, and on the lower by land of Miguel Bourgeois.

This is part of a tract of land of eleven arpents twenty-six toises and three feet in front, on the usual depth of forty arpents, surveyed by Don Carlos Trudeau, in the year 1781, for the claimant, who obtained an order of survey for a second depth of forty arpents, in 1791, from Governor Miro. The claimant sold the remaining six arpents of this land to his sons, Paul and Aman Bourgeois. Confirmed.

No. 144.—Madame BOURGEOIS, widow of Aman Bourgeois, claims a tract of land, situate on the east side of the river Mississippi, in the county of Acadia, containing three arpents in front, and eighty in depth, and bounded on the upper side by land of Joseph Poiré, and on the lower by land of Paul Bourgeois.

This is part of a tract of land mentioned in the last claim, No. 143. The deceased husband of the claimant purchased from his father Baptiste Bourgeois. Confirmed.

No. 145.—PAUL BOURGEOIS claims a tract of land, situate on the east side of the river Mississippi, in the county of Acadia, containing three arpents in front, and eighty in depth, and bounded on the upper side by land of Madame Aman Bourgeois, and on the lower by land of Baptiste Bourgeois.

This is part of the tract of land mentioned in No. 143. The claimant purchased of his father, Baptiste Bourgeois. Confirmed.

No. 146.—HONORE BRAUX claims a tract of land, situate on the west side of the river Mississippi, in the county of Acadia, containing six arpents four toises and one foot in front, and forty arpents in depth, and bounded on the upper side by land of Carlos Braux, and on the lower by land of Carlos Gaudet.

This land was surveyed by Don Carlos Trudeau, in the year 1780, for the claimant; and having been inhabited and cultivated ever since that period, until on and after the 20th December, 1803. Confirmed.

No. 147.—JOSEPH MICHEL claims a tract of land, situate on the east side of the river Mississippi, in the county of Acadia, containing six arpents in front, and forty in depth, and bounded on the upper side by land of Paul Bourgeois, and on the lower by land of François Duon.

It appears that the claimant did actually inhabit and cultivate the land now claimed on the 20th December, 1803; and that the same was continually inhabited and cultivated by him, or those under whom he claims, for more than ten consecutive years next preceding. Confirmed.

No. 148.—AUGUSTIN TROSLER claims a tract of land, situate on the west side of the river Mississippi, in the county of Acadia, containing three arpents in front, and forty in depth, and bounded on the upper side by land of André Hymel, and on the lower by land of Madame Nicholas Trosler.

This is part of a tract of land of five arpents in front, on the usual depth, surveyed by Don Carlos Trudeau, in the year 1781, for Nicholas Trosler, deceased, the father of the claimant; the land having been inhabited and cultivated ever since that period, until on and after the 20th December, 1803. Confirmed.

No. 149.—OLIVIER LANDRY claims a tract of land, situate on the west side of the river Mississippi, in the county of Acadia, containing four arpents seven toises and four feet in front, and forty arpents in depth, and bound on the upper side by land of Madame Pierre Landry, and on the lower by land of Joseph Landry.

This is part of a tract of land surveyed, in the year 1775, for Louis Leco upte, under whose title the claimant holds, in virtue of successive sales; the land having been inhabited and cultivated ever since that period, until on and after the 20th December, 1803. Confirmed.

No. 150.—FRANÇOIS DUHON claims a tract of land, situate on the east side of the river Mississippi, in the county of Acadia, containing three arpents and eleven feet in front, and forty arpents in depth, and bounded on the upper side by land of Joseph Michel, and on the lower by land of Joseph Leblanc.

It appears that the claimant did actually inhabit and cultivate the land now claimed on the 20th December, 1803; and that the same was continually inhabited and cultivated by him, or those under whom he claims, for more than ten consecutive years next preceding. Confirmed.

No. 151.—SIMON SAVOYE claims a tract of land, situate on the east side of the river Mississippi, in the county of Acadia, containing five arpents in front, and forty arpents in depth, and bounded on the upper side by land of Simon Gautrot, and on the lower by land of Madame Maxaut.

This land was surveyed by Don Carlos Trudeau, in the year 1796, for Francisco Duhon, under whose title the claimant holds by virtue of successive sales; the land having been inhabited and cultivated since that period, until on and after the 20th December, 1803. Confirmed.

No. 152.—JOSEPH THERIOT claims a tract of land, situate on the east side of the river Mississippi, in the county of Acadia, containing two arpents and six toises in front, and forty arpents in depth, and bounded on the upper side by land of Mr. Ouvre, and on the lower by land of André Bernard.

This is part of a tract of land of four arpents and twelve toises in front, on the ordinary depth of forty arpents, surveyed by Don Carlos Trudeau, in the year 1782, for Maurice Fontenau, under whose title the claimant holds by virtue of a judicial sale of the State, to said Fontenau; the land having been inhabited and cultivated ever since 1782, until on and after the 20th December, 1803. Confirmed.

No. 153.—ANDRE BERNARD claims a tract of land, situate on the east side of the river Mississippi, in the county of Acadia, containing two arpents and six toises in front, and forty arpents in depth, and bounded on the upper side by land of Joseph Theriot, and on the lower by land of Mr. Godberry.

This land is part of four arpents and twelve toises in front, on the ordinary depth, mentioned in No. 152. The claimant holds by virtue of a sale from Jean Theriot, who purchased at a judicial sale of the estate of Maurice Fontenau, deceased; the land having been inhabited and cultivated ever since the year 1782, until on and after the 20th December, 1803. Confirmed.

No. 154.—JOSEPH RICHARD, Junior, claims a tract of land, situate on the east side of the river Mississippi, in the county of Iberville, containing six arpents in front, and forty in depth, and bounded on the upper side by land of Pierre Allain, and on the lower by land of Simon Richard, Junior.

This land was surveyed by Don Louis Andry, in the year 1772, in favor of Pedro Casidau Hebert, who obtained a complete grant for the same, in 1775 from Governor Unzaga: under which grant the claimant holds by virtue of successive sales. Confirmed.

No. 155.—CHARLES and OLIVER THIBODEAU claim a tract of land, situate on the east side of the river Mississippi, in the county of Acadia, containing five and a half arpents in front, and forty arpents in depth, and bounded on the upper side by land of Pierre Blanchard, and on the lower by land of Mr. Fossié.

It appears that this land was actually inhabited and cultivated by the claimants on the 20th December, 1803, and that the same was continually inhabited and cultivated for more than ten consecutive years next preceding. Confirmed.

No. 156.—BAPTISTE BERNARD claims a tract of land, situate on the east side of the river Mississippi, in the county of Acadia, containing five arpents and twenty-nine toises in front, and forty arpents in depth, and bounded on the upper side by land of Pablo Bourgeois.

This land was surveyed by Don Carlos Trudeau, in the year 1782, for the claimant, who continued to inhabit and cultivate the same ever since that period, until on and after the 20th December, 1803. Confirmed.

No. 157.—CHARLES DUGAST claims a tract of land, situate on the west side of the river Mississippi, in the county of Acadia, containing five arpents eleven toises and five feet in front, and forty arpents in depth, and bounded on the upper side by land of Athanas Dugast, and on the lower by land of Francis Dugast.

This land was surveyed by Don Louis Andry, in the year 1774, in favor of the claimant, who obtained a complete grant for the same, in the year 1775, from Governor Unzaga. Confirmed.

No. 158.—JOSEPH LEBLANC, Junior, claims a tract of land, situate on the west side of the river Mississippi, in the county of Acadia, containing five arpents and twenty-one toises in front, and forty arpents in depth, and bounded on the upper side by land of Mr. Reynaud, and on the lower by land of Francis Blanchard.

It appears that the claimant did actually inhabit and cultivate the land now claimed on the 20th December, 1803, and that the same was continually inhabited and cultivated by him, or those under whom he claims, for more than ten consecutive years next preceding. Confirmed.

No. 159.—MICHEL POIRE claims a tract of land, situate on the west side of the river Mississippi, in the county of Acadia, containing four arpents and fifteen toises in front, and eighty arpents in depth, and bounded on the upper side by land of Guillaume Arcenaux, and on the lower by land of Jean Pierre Richard.

It appears that the claimant did actually inhabit and cultivate the first depth of forty arpents of the land now claimed, on the 20th December, 1803; and that the same was inhabited and cultivated for more than ten years prior thereto: so much the Board confirm, but reject the claim to the second depth. Confirmed.

No. 160.—GREGOIRE DUGAST claims a tract of land, situate on the west side of the river Mississippi, in the county of Acadia, containing four arpents and eleven toises in front, and forty arpents in depth, and bounded on the upper side by land of Raimond Braux, and on the lower by land of Paul Dugast.

It appears that the claimant did actually inhabit and cultivate the land on the 20th December, 1803, and that the same was continually inhabited and cultivated by him, or those under whom he claims, for more than ten consecutive years next preceding. Confirmed.

No. 161.—DANIEL BLOUIN claims a tract of land, situate on the east side of the river Mississippi, in the county of Acadia, containing five arpents and nineteen toises in front, and forty arpents in depth, and bounded on the upper side by land of Pablo Bourgeois, and on the lower by land of Miguel Bourgeois.

This land was surveyed by Don Carlos Trudeau, in the year 1782, for Joseph Bourgeois, under whose title the claimant holds by virtue of successive sales; the land having been inhabited and cultivated ever since that period, until on and after the 20th December, 1803. Confirmed.

No. 162.—JEAN BAPTISTE BOUCRY claims a tract of land, situate on the east side of the river Mississippi, in the county of Acadia, containing two arpents twenty-seven toises and one foot in front, and forty arpents in depth, and bounded on the upper side by land of Jean Baptiste Drorully, and on the lower by land of Joseph Normand.

It appears that this land was inhabited and cultivated on the 20th December, 1803; and that the same was continually inhabited and cultivated by those under whom the claimant holds, for more than ten consecutive years next preceding. Confirmed.

No. 163.—PIERRE MYR claims a tract of land, situate on the east side of the river Mississippi, in the county of Acadia, containing five arpents and fifteen toises in front, and forty arpents in depth, and bounded on the upper side by land of Joseph Bourgeois, and on the lower by land of Pedro Blanchard.

This land was surveyed by Don Carlos Trudeau in the year 1782, for Miguel Bourgeois, under whose title the claimant holds by virtue of successive sales; the land having been inhabited and cultivated ever since that period, until on and after the 20th December, 1803. Confirmed.

No. 164.—BONAVENTURE GOUDIN claims a tract of land, situate on the east side of the river Mississippi, in the county of Acadia, containing three arpents and fifteen toises in front, and forty arpents in depth, and bounded on the upper side by land of Marie Landry, and on the lower by land of Laurent Arcenaux.

This is part of a tract of land of six arpents and a half in front, and forty arpents in depth; surveyed in the year 1782 for Juan Arcenaux, under whose title the claimant holds by virtue of successive sales; the land having been inhabited and cultivated ever since that period, until on and after the 20th December, 1803. Confirmed.

No. 165.—GEORGE SAINT CYR claims a tract of land, situate on the east side of the river Mississippi, in the county of Acadia, containing one arpent in front, and forty arpents in depth, and bounded on the upper side by land of Honoré Durio, and on the lower by land of Paul Sechenedre.

It appears that the claimant did actually inhabit and cultivate the land now claimed on the 20th December, 1803; and that the same was continually inhabited and cultivated by him, or those under whom he holds, for more than ten consecutive years next preceding. Confirmed.

No. 166.—CHARLES FREDERIC claims a tract of land, situate on the west side of the river Mississippi, in the county of Acadia, containing one arpent in front, and forty arpents in depth, and bounded on the upper side by land of Polite Breux, and on the lower by land of Joseph Torulet.

This is part of a tract of land of five arpents twenty-one toises two feet and six inches in front, on the ordinary depth; surveyed by Don Carlos Trudeau, in the year 1780, for Carlos Gaudet, under whose title the claimant holds in virtue of successive sales; the land having been inhabited and cultivated ever since that period, until on and after the 20th December, 1803. Confirmed.

No. 167.—JOSEPH LEBLANC claims a tract of land, situate on the west side of the river Mississippi. in the county of Iberville, containing three arpents, twenty-four toises and four feet in front, and forty arpents in depth, and bounded on the upper side by land of Ambrose Longue-Epée, and on the lower by land of Juan Carlos Comeau.

This land was surveyed in the year 1796, in favor of the claimant, who obtained a complete grant for the same in the same year, from the Baron de Carondelet, then Governor. Confirmed.

No. 168.—JOSEPH BABIN claims a tract of land, situate on the west side of the river Mississippi, in the county of Acadia, containing five arpents eighteen toises and two feet in front, and forty arpents in depth, and bounded on the upper side by land of Vicente Landry, and on the lower by land of Estevan Landry.

This land was surveyed by Don Louis Andry, in the year 1774, in favor of the claimant, who obtained a complete grant for the same, in 1775, from Governor Unzaga. Confirmed.

No. 169.—JOSEPH BABIN claims a tract of land situate on the west side of the river Mississippi, in the county of Acadia, containing three arpents in front, and forty in depth, and bounded on the upper side by land of Amant Goutro, and on the lower by land of the claimant.

This land was surveyed by Don Louis Andry, in the year 1774, in favor of Vincente Landry, who obtained a complete grant for the same, in the year 1775, from Governor Unzaga; the claimant purchased at a judicial sale of the estate of the deceased grantee. Confirmed.

No. 170.—JOSEPH BABIN claims a tract of land, situate on the west side of the river Mississippi, in the county of Acadia, containing eight arpents and eleven toises in front, and forty arpents in depth, and bounded on the upper side by land of Louis Lecompte, and on the lower by vacant land.

This land was granted by Governor Miro, in the year 1789, to Pedro Lecompte, in consideration of his supporting the road and levée; but he being unable to comply with the conditions, made a donation of the land, before the commandant of the district, to the claimant, who engaged to perform the conditions annexed to the grant. Confirmed.

No. 171.—JOSEPH BABIN claims a tract of land, situate in the west side of the river Mississippi, in the county of Acadia, containing eight arpents and ten toises in front, and forty arpents in depth, and bounded on the upper side by vacant land, and on the lower by land of Pedro Lecompte.

This land was granted by Governor Miro, in the year 1789, to Louis Lecompte in consideration of his supporting the road and levée. The land, by the decease of the grantee, descended to his brother Pedro Lecompte, who made the same donation of it to the present claimant as that mentioned in the last, No: 170. Confirmed.

No. 172.—PIERRE THERIOT claims a tract of land, situate on the east side of the river Mississippi, in the county of Acadia, containing five arpents seven toises and three feet in front, and forty arpents in depth, and bounded on the upper side by land of Madame Palanquin, and on the lower by land of Jean Chapentier.

It appears that the land now claimed was inhabited and cultivated on the 20th of December, 1803, and that the same was continually inhabited and cultivated by the claimant, or those under whom he holds, for more than ten consecutive years next preceding. Confirmed.

No. 173.—CHRISTOPHER TROSLER claims a tract of land, situate on the west side of the river Mississippi, in the county of Acadia, containing two arpents in front, and forty in depth, and bounded on the upper side by land of Pierre Mathias, and on the lower by land of Gabriel Rodrigues.

It appears that the land now claimed was inhabited and cultivated on the 20th of December, 1803, and that the same was continually inhabited and cultivated by those under whom the claimant holds for more than ten consecutive years next preceding. Confirmed.

No. 174.—MICHEL and SIMON LANOUE claim a tract of land, situate on the east side of the river Mississippi, in the county of Acadia, containing three arpents and twenty toises in front, and forty arpents in depth, and bounded on one side by land of Pierre Lanoue.

This is part of a tract of land of fifteen arpents and twenty toises in front, on the ordinary depth. surveyed by Don Carlos Trudeau, in the year 1782, for Pierre Lanoue, the father of the claimants, from whom they purchased; the land having been inhabited and cultivated ever since the above period, until on and after the 20th of December, 1803. Confirmed.

No. 175.—DOUAT LANDRY claims a tract of land, situate on the east side of the river Mississippi, in the county of Acadia, containing two arpents in front, and forty in depth, and bounded on the upper side by land of Paul Melanson, and on the lower by land of Pierre Lanoue.

This is part of the land surveyed for Pierre Lanoue, mentioned in the last, No. 174 ; the claimant purchased of said Lanoue ; the land having been inhabited and cultivated ever since the year 1782, until on and after the 20th of December, 1803. Confirmed.

No. 176.—PAUL MYR claims a tract of land, situate on the east side of the river Mississippi, in the county of Acadia, containing two arpents in front, and forty in depth, and bounded on the upper side by land of Pierre Lanoue, and on the lower by land of Jacques Leblanc.

This is part of the land surveyed for Pierre Lanoue, mentioned in No. 174; the present claimant purchased of said Lanoue; and the land having been inhabited and cultivated ever since the year 1782, until on and after the 20th of December, 1803. Confirmed.

No. 177.—MARCU LANDRY claims a tract of land, situate on the east side of the river Mississippi, in the county of Acadia, containing four arpents in front and forty in depth, and bounded on the upper side by land of David Melanson, and on the lower by land of Paul Melanson.

It appears that the claimant did actually inhabit and cultivate the land now claimed on the 20th of December, 1803, and that the same was continually inhabited and cultivated for more than ten consecutive years next preceding. Confirmed.

No. 178.—DAVID MELANSON claims a tract of land, situate on the east side of the river Mississippi, in the county of Acadia, containing two arpents in front, and forty in depth, and bounded on the upper side by land of Eligius Fromentin, and on the lower by land of Marcu Landry.

It appears that the claimant did actually inhabit and cultivate the land now claimed on the 20th of December, 1803, and that the same was continually inhabited and cultivated by him, or those under whom he claims, for more than ten consecutive years next preceding. Confirmed.

No. 179.—MICHEL RICHARD claims a tract of land, situate on the west side of the river Mississippi, in the county of Acadia, containing three arpents thirteen toises and five feet in front, and forty arpents in depth, and bounded on the upper side by land of Simon Boudreau, Junior, and on the lower by land of Simon Boudreau, Senior.
It appears that the land now claimed was inhabited and cultivated on the 20th of December, 1803, and that the same was continually inhabited and cultivated by those under whom the claimant holds for more than ten consecutive years next preceding. Confirmed.

No. 180.—SIMON BOUDREAU, Junior, claims a tract of land, situate on the west side of the river Mississippi, in the county of Acadia, containing three arpents thirteen toises and five feet in front, and forty arpents in depth, and bounded on the upper side by land of Jacques Babin, and on the lower by land of Michel Richard.
It appears that the claimant did actually inhabit and cultivate the land now claimed on the 20th of December, 1803, and that the same was continually inhabited and cultivated by him, or those under whom he claims, for more than ten consecutive years next preceding. Confirmed.

No. 181.—MICHEL ARCENAUX claims a tract of land, situate on the west side of the river Mississippi, in the county of Acadia, containing two arpents three toises and two feet in front, and forty arpents in depth, and bounded on the upper side by land of Jacques Roman, and on the lower by land of Louis Arcenaux.
It appears that the claimant did actually inhabit and cultivate the land now claimed on the 20th of December, 1803, and that the same was continually inhabited and cultivated for more than ten consecutive years next preceding. Confirmed.

No. 182.—LOUIS ARCENAUX claims a tract of land, situate on the west side of the river Mississippi, in the county of Acadia, containing two arpents three toises and two feet in front, and forty arpents in depth, and bounded on the upper side by land of Michel Arcenaux, and on the lower by land of François Arcenaux.
It appears that the claimant did actually inhabit and cultivate the land now claimed on the 20th of December, 1803, and that the same was continually inhabited and cultivated for more than ten consecutive years next preceding. Confirmed.

No. 183.—FRANÇOIS ARCENAUX claims a tract of land, situate on the west side of the river Mississippi, in the county of Acadia, containing two arpents three toises and two feet in front, and forty arpents in depth, and bounded on the upper side by land of Louis Arcenaux, and on the lower by land of David Rom.
It appears that the claimant did actually inhabit and cultivate the land now claimed on the 20th of December, 1803, and that the same was continually inhabited and cultivated for more than ten consecutive years next preceding. Confirmed.

No. 184.—PIERRE BOURGEOIS claims a tract of land, situate on the east side of the river Mississippi, in the county of Acadia, containing two arpents in front, and forty arpents in depth, and bounded on the upper side by land of Madame Robert Longue, and on the lower by land of Juan Baptiste Vicher.
This is part of a tract of land of six arpents front, on the usual depth, surveyed by Don Carlos Trudeau, in the year 1791, for George Violon, under whose title the claimant holds in virtue of successive sales. The land having been inhabited and cultivated ever since that period, until on and after the 20th December, 1803. Confirmed.

No. 185.—SUSANNE LE ROS, widow of Robert Laringue, claims a tract of land, situate on the east side of the river Mississippi, in the county of Acadia, containing two arpents in front, and forty in depth, and bounded on the upper side by land of Madame Joseph Bourgeois, and on the lower by land of Pierre Bourgeois.
This is part of a tract of land of six arpents in front, on the usual depth, surveyed by Don Carlos Trudeau,

in the year 1781, for George Violon, under whose title the claimant holds by virtue of successive sales. The land having been inhabited and cultivated ever since that period, until on and after the 20th December, 1803. Confirmed.

No. 186.—JEAN BAPTISTE VICUER claims a tract of land, situate on the east side of the river Mississippi, in the county of Acadia, containing two arpents in front, and forty in depth, and bounded on the upper side by land of Pierre Bourgeois, and on the lower by land of Jacques Poché.
This is part of a tract of land of six arpents in front, on the ordinary depth, surveyed by Don Carlos Trudeau, in the year 1781, for George Violon, under whose title the claimant holds by virtue of successive sales. The land having been inhabited and cultivated ever since that period, until on and after the 20th December, 1803. Confirmed.

No. 187.—JACQUES BABIN claims a tract of land, situate on the west side of the river Mississippi, in the county of Acadia, containing five arpents fourteen toises and five feet in front, and forty arpents in depth, and bounded on the upper side by land of Joseph Bertouière, and on the lower by land of Bonaventure Babin.
The land was surveyed for the claimant in the year 1794, by Don Carlos Trudeau; and having been cultivated ever since, until on and after the 20th December, 1803. Confirmed.

No. 188.—NOEL LASSEIGNE claims a tract of land, situate on the east side of the river Mississippi, in the county of Acadia, containing one arpent in front, and forty arpents in depth, and bounded on the upper side by land of Mr. Millet, and on the lower by land of Martin Dubourg.
It appears that the land now claimed was inhabited and cultivated on the 20th December, 1803, and that the same was continually inhabited and cultivated by those under whom the claimant holds for more than ten consecutive years next preceding. Confirmed.

No. 189.—JEAN VEBRE claims a tract of land, situate on the east side of the river Mississippi, in the county of Acadia, containing one arpent in front, and forty in depth, and bounded on the upper side by land of Manuel Laisseigne, and on the lower by land of Martin.
It appears that this land was inhabited and cultivated by the claimant on the 20th December, 1803, and that the same was continually inhabited and cultivated by him, or those under whom he claims, for more than ten consecutive years next preceding. Confirmed.

No. 190.—JACQUES PLANCHE claims a tract of land, situate on the east side of the river Mississippi, in the county of Acadia, containing four arpents in front, and forty in depth, and bounded on the upper side by land of Jean Baptiste Vicher, and on the lower by land of Jean Decarreaux.
It appears that the claimant did actually inhabit and cultivate the land now claimed on the 20th December, 1803, and that the same was continually inhabited and cultivated by him, or those under whom he claims, for more than ten consecutive years next preceding. Confirmed.

No. 191.—JEAN DECARREAUX claims a tract of land, situate on the east side of the river Mississippi, in the county of Acadia, containing two arpents in front, and forty in depth, and bounded on the upper side by land of Jacques Planché and on the lower by land of Honoré Duris.
It appears that the claimant did actually inhabit and cultivate the land now claimed on the 20th December, 1803, and that the same was continually inhabited and cultivated by him, or those under whom he claims for more than ten consecutive years next preceding. Confirmed.

No. 192.—JOSEPH GUEDRY claims a tract of land situate on the east side of the river Mississippi, in the county of Acadia, containing four arpents and two toises in front, and forty arpents in depth, and bounded on the upper side by land of Donat Guedry, and on the lower by land of Madame Cadet.
It appears that the claimant did actually inhabit and cultivate the land now claimed on the 20th December, 1803, and that the same was continually inhabited and cultivated by him, or those under whom he claims, for more than ten consecutive years next preceding. Confirmed.

No. 193.—DONAT GUEDRY claims a tract of land, situate on the east side of the river Mississippi, in the county of Acadia, containing one arpent and two-thirds in front, and forty arpents in depth, and bounded on the upper side by land of Alexandre Guedry, and on the lower by land of Joseph Guedry.

It appears that the claimant did actually inhabit and cultivate the land now claimed on the 20th December, 1803, and that the same was continually inhabited and cultivated by him, or those under whom he claims, for more than ten consecutive years next preceding. Confirmed.

No. 194.—PIERRE GUEDRY claims a tract of land, situate on the east side of the river Mississippi, in the county of Acadia, containing one arpent and two-thirds in front, and forty arpents in depth, and bounded on the upper side by land of Jean Godet, and on the lower by land of Alexandre Guedry.

It appears that the land claimed was continually inhabited and cultivated on the 20th December, 1803, and that the same was continually inhabited and cultivated by those under whom the claimant holds for more than ten consecutive years next preceding. Confirmed.

No. 195.—ALEXANDRE GUEDRY claims a tract of land, situate on the east side of the river Mississippi, in the county of Acadia, containing one arpent and two-thirds in front, and forty arpents in depth, and bounded on the upper side by land of Pierre Guedry, and on the lower by land of Donat Guedry.

It appears that the land now claimed was inhabited and cultivated on the 20th December, 1803, and that the same was continually inhabited and cultivated by those under whom the claimant holds for more than ten consecutive years next preceding. Confirmed.

No. 196.—ETIENNE TOUR claims a tract of land, situate on the west side of the river Mississippi, in the county of Acadia, containing two arpents in front, and forty in depth, and bounded on the upper side by land of George Antin, and on the lower by land of Madame Trosler.

It appears that the claimant did actually inhabit and cultivate the land now claimed, on the 20th December, 1803, and that the same was continually inhabited and cultivated by him, or those under whom he claims, for more than ten consecutive years next preceding. Confirmed.

No. 197.—GABRIEL RODRIGUES claims a tract of land, situate on the west side of the river Mississippi, in the county of Acadia, containing two arpents in front, and forty in depth, and bounded on the upper side by land of Jean Rom, and on the lower by land of Christophe Trosler.

It appears that the claimant did actually inhabit and cultivate the land now claimed on the 20th December, 1803, and that the same was continually inhabited and cultivated by him, or those under whom he claims, for more than ten consecutive years next preceding. Confirmed.

No. 198.—JOSEPH PAUL EBER claims a tract of land, situate on the west side of the river Mississippi, in the county of Acadia, containing eight arpents fourteen toises and two feet in front, and forty arpents in depth, and bounded on the upper side by land of Joseph Dugast, and on the lower by land of Mr. Turreaud.

It appears that the claimant did actually inhabit and cultivate the land now claimed on the 20th December, 1803, and that the same was continually inhabited and cultivated by him, or those under whom he claims, for more than ten consecutive years next preceding. Confirmed.

No. 199.—JOSEPH DUGAST claims a tract of land, situate on the west side of the river Mississippi, in the county of Acadia, containing two arpents and one-third in front, and forty arpents in depth, and bounded on the upper side by land of Charles Thorué and Paul Babin, and on the lower by land of Joseph Eber.

It appears that the claimant did actually inhabit and cultivate the land now claimed on the 20th December, 1803, and that the same was continually inhabited and cultivated by him, or those under whom he claims, for more than ten consecutive years next preceding. Confirmed.

No. 200.—SIMON GOTEREAU claims a tract of land, situate on the west side of the river Mississippi, in the county of Acadia, containing one arpent twenty-four toises and two feet in front, and eighty arpents in depth, and bounded on the upper side by land of Raphael Gotereau; and on the lower by land of Joseph Gotereau.

The first depth of this land is part of a tract of five arpents and eighteen toises in front, on the ordinary depth, surveyed in the year 1771 for the claimant, who obtained a complete grant for the same in 1774, from Governor Unzaga. The Board confirm the title to the extent of the first depth, but reject the claim to the second depth.

No. 201.—RAPHAEL GOTEREAU claims a tract of land, situate on the west side of the river Mississippi, in the county of Acadia, containing one arpent twenty-four toises and two feet in front, and eighty arpents in depth, and bounded on the upper side by land of Olivier Leblanc, and on the lower by land of Simon Gotereau, Senior.

This is part of a tract of land mentioned in the last, No. 200, for which Simon Gotereau, Senior, obtained a complete grant to the extent of the first depth of forty arpents. The claimant holds by purchase from his father, said Simon Gotereau, Senior. The Board confirm the title to the extent of the first depth, but reject the claim to the second depth.

No. 202.—JOSEPH GOTEREAU claims a tract of land, situate on the west side of the river Mississippi, in the county of Acadia, containing one arpent twenty-four toises and two feet in front, and eighty arpents in depth, and bounded on the upper side by land of Simon Gotereau, Senior, and on the lower by land of Joseph Leblanc.

This is part of a tract of land mentioned in No. 200, for which Simon Gotereau, Senior, obtained a complete grant to the extent of the first depth of forty arpents. The claimant holds by purchase from his father, the said Simon Gotereau. The Board confirm the title to the extent of the first depth, but reject the claim to the second depth.

No. 203.—JOSEPH CLOATRE claims a tract of land, situate on the west side of the river Mississippi, in the county of Acadia, containing one arpent twenty-seven toises and one foot in front, and forty arpents in depth, and bounded on the upper side by land of Joseph Tornlet, and on the lower by land of Gisle Leblanc.

It appears that the claimant did actually inhabit and cultivate the land now claimed on the 20th December, 1803, and that the same was continually inhabited and cultivated by him, or those under whom he claims, for more than ten consecutive years next preceding. Confirmed.

No. 204.—LOUIS GAUTROT claims a tract of land, situate on the east side of the river Mississippi, in the county of Acadia, containing five arpents in front, and forty in depth, and bounded on the upper side by land of Madame Augustin, and on the lower by land of Madame Bourg.

It appears that the claimant did actually inhabit and cultivate the land now claimed on the 20th December, 1803, and that the same was continually inhabited and cultivated by him, or those under whom he claims, for more than ten consecutive years next preceding. Confirmed.

No. 205.—JACQUES LEBLANC claims a tract of land, situate on the east side of the river Mississippi, in the county of Acadia, containing three arpents in front, and forty in depth, and bounded on the upper side by land of Pierre Lanoue, and on the lower by land of Madame Augustin.

It appears that the claimant did actually inhabit and cultivate the land now claimed on the 20th December, 1803, and that the same was continually inhabited and cultivated for more than ten consecutive years next preceding. Confirmed.

No. 206.—ANTOINE LEDOUX claims a tract of land, situate on the east side of the river Mississippi, in the county of Acadia, containing one arpent in front, and forty in depth, and bounded on the upper side by land of Joseph Leblanc, and on the lower by land of Charles Gaudet.

It appears that the claimant did actually inhabit and cultivate the land now claimed on the 20th December, 1803, and that the same was continually inhabited and cultivated by him, or those under whom he claims, for more than ten consecutive years next preceding. Confirmed.

No. 207.—NICHOLAS KELLER claims a tract of land, situate on the east side of the river Mississippi, in the county of Acadia, containing three arpents and sixteen toises in front, and forty arpents in depth, and bounded on the upper side by land of François Duhon, and on the lower by land of Antoine Ledoux.

It appears that the land now claimed was inhabited and cultivated on the 20th December, 1803, and that the same was continually inhabited and cultivated by those under whom the claimant holds for more than ten consecutive years next preceding. Confirmed.

No. 208.—PAUL DUGAST claims a tract of land, situate on the west side of the river Mississippi, in the county of Acadia, containing three arpents and eleven toises in front, and forty arpents in depth, and bounded on the upper side by land of Charles Dugast, and on the lower by land of Gregoire Dugast.

It appears that the land now claimed was inhabited and cultivated on the 20th December, 1803, and that the same was continually inhabited and cultivated by those under whom the claimant holds for more than ten consecutive years next preceding. Confirmed.

No. 209.—HELENE LEBLANC, widow of Joseph Bourgeois, claims a tract of land, situate on the east side of the river Mississippi, in the county of Acadia, containing five arpents and four feet in front, and forty arpents in depth, and bounded on the upper side by land of François Michel, and on the lower by land of George Vellau.

It appears that the claimant did actually inhabit and cultivate the land now claimed on the 20th December, 1803, and that the same was continually inhabited and cultivated for more than ten consecutive years next preceding. Confirmed.

No. 210.—AUGUSTIN GRAVOIS claims a tract of land, situate on the west side of the river Mississippi, in the county of Acadia, containing two arpents in front, and forty in depth, and bounded on the upper side by land of Jean Mallard, and on the lower by land of Paulete Babin.

It appears that the claimant did actually inhabit and cultivate the land now claimed on the 20th December, 1803, and that the same was continually inhabited and cultivated by him, or those under whom he claims, for more than ten consecutive years next preceding. Confirmed.

No. 211.—ALEXIS MILLET claims a tract of land, situate on the west side of the river Mississippi, in the county of Acadia, containing three arpents in front, and forty in depth, and bounded on the upper side by land of Gabriel Arcenaux, and on the lower by land of Jacques Roman.

It appears that this land was inhabited and cultivated on the 20th December, 1803, and that the same was continually inhabited and cultivated by those under whom the claimant holds for more than ten consecutive years next preceding. Confirmed.

No. 212.—JEAN PAUL SECHENEDRE claims a tract of land, situate on the east side of the river Mississippi, in the county of Acadia, containing two arpents twenty-six toises and two feet in front, and forty arpents in depth, and bounded on the upper side by land of George St. Cyr, and on the lower by land of Adam Sechenedre.

It appears that the claimant did actually inhabit and cultivate the land now claimed, on the 20th December, 1803, and that the same was continually inhabited and cultivated by him, or those under whom he claims, for more than ten consecutive years next preceding. Confirmed.

No. 213.—JEAN LOUIS PART claims a tract of land, situate on the east side of the river Mississippi, in the county of Acadia, containing three arpents in front, and forty in depth, and bounded on the upper side by land of Joseph Poirié, and on the lower by land of Madame Bourgeois.

This is a part of a tract of land of six arpents and twenty-six toises in front, on the usual depth, surveyed by Don Carlos Trudeau, in the year 1781, for Joseph Poirié, from whom the claimant purchased; the land having been inhabited and cultivated ever since that period, until on and after the 20th December, 1803. Confirmed.

No. 214.—JACQUES BABIN claims a tract of land, situate on the west side of the river Mississippi, in the county of Acadia, containing two arpents in front, and forty in depth, and bounded on the upper side by land of Basil Prejeau, and on the lower by land of Simon Boudreau, Jun.

It appears that this land was inhabited and cultivated on the 20th December, 1803, and that the same was continually inhabited and cultivated by those under whom the claimant holds for more than ten consecutive years next preceding. Confirmed.

No. 215.—JOSEPH BABIN, Jun. claims a tract of land, situate on the east side of the river Mississippi, in the county of Acadia, containing four arpents in front, and forty in depth, and bounded on the upper side by land of Pierre Randal, and on the lower by land of Belony Landry.

It appears that the claimant did actually inhabit and cultivate the land now claimed on the 20th December, 1803, and that the same was continually inhabited and cultivated by him, or those under whom he claims, for more than ten consecutive years next preceding. Confirmed.

No. 216.—PIERRE BERTRAND claims a tract of land, situate on the west side of the river Mississippi, in the county of Acadia, containing three arpents and three toises in front, and eighty arpents in depth, and bounded on the upper side by land of Guillaume Dupart, and on the lower by land of Frederic Blanchard.

The first depth of this land is part of a tract of six arpents and three toises in front and forty arpents in depth, surveyed in the year 1771 for the claimant, who obtained a complete grant for the same, in 1773, from Governor Unzaga. The Board confirm to the extent of the first depth, but reject the claim to the second depth.

No. 217.—CHRISTOPHE MAYER claims a tract of land, situate on the east side of the river Mississippi, in the county of Acadia, containing two arpents in front, and forty in depth, and bounded on the upper side by land of Martin Dubourg, and on the lower by land of Antoine Frederic.

It appears that the claimant did actually inhabit and cultivate the land now claimed on the 20th December, 1803, and that the same was continually inhabited and cultivated by him, or those under whom he claims, for more than ten consecutive years next preceding. Confirmed.

No. 218.—JEROME GODED claims a tract of land, situate on the west side of the river Mississippi, in the county of Acadia, containing four arpents four toises and five feet in front, and forty arpents in depth, and bounded on the upper side by land of Augustin Goded, and on the lower by land of Joseph Arcenaux.

It appears that the claimant did actually inhabit and cultivate the land now claimed, on the 20th December, 1803; and that the same was continually inhabited and cultivated for more than ten consecutive years next preceding. Confirmed.

No. 219.—MICHEL GODET claims a tract of land, situate on the west side of the river Mississippi, in the county of Acadia, containing four arpents four toises and five feet in front, and forty arpents in depth, and bounded on the upper side by land of Honoré Brand, and on the lower by land of Augustine Godet.

It appears that the claimant did actually inhabit and cultivate the land now claimed on the 20th December, 1803, and that the same was continually inhabited and cultivated for more than ten consecutive years next preceding. Confirmed.

No. 220.—AUGUSTIN GODET claims a tract of land, situate on the west side of the river Mississippi, in the county of Acadia, containing four arpents four toises and five feet in front, and forty arpents in depth, and bounded on the upper side by land of Michel Godet, and on the lower by land of Jerome Godet.

It appears that the claimant did actually inhabit and cultivate the land now claimed on the 20th December, 1803; and that the same was continually inhabited and cultivated by him, or those under whom he claims, for more than ten consecutive years next preceding. Confirmed.

No. 221.—ANDRE HYMELLE claims a tract of land, situate on the west side of the river Mississippi, in the county of Acadia, containing two arpents in front, and sixty arpents in depth, and bounded on the upper side by land of Augustin Trosler, and on the lower by land of Louis Hymelle.

This is part of a tract of land surveyed by Don Carlos Trudeau, in the year 1781, for Bastian Hymelle. Jacques Trosler obtained an order of survey for an additional depth of twenty arpents, in the year 1783, from Governor Miro; under which titles the claimant holds by virtue of successive sales. Confirmed.

No. 222.—MARIE FOREST, widow of Jean Baptiste Bergeron, claims a tract of land, situate on the west side of the river Mississippi, in the county of Acadia, containing one arpent and four toises and a half in front, and eighty arpents in depth, and bounded on the upper side by land of Henry Landry, and on the lower by land of Michel Bergeron.

The first forty arpents in depth of this land is part of a tract of four arpents four toises and three feet, surveyed by Don Carlos Trudeau, in the year 1780, for the husband of the claimant. The land having been inhabited and cultivated ever since that period, until on and after the 20th December, 1803, the Board confirm the claim to the extent of the first depth of forty arpents, but reject the second of forty arpents.

No. 223.—HENRY LANDRY claims a tract of land, situate on the west side of the river Mississippi, in the county of Acadia, containing two arpents in front, and eighty arpents in depth, and bounded on the upper side by land of Joseph Arcenaux, and on the lower by land of Madame Jean Bte. Bergeron.

The first depth of this land is part of the tract of land mentioned in the last, No. 222, surveyed for Jean Baptiste Bergeron, under whose title the claimant holds in virtue of successive sales. The land having been inhabited and cultivated ever since the year 1780, until on and after the 20th December, 1803, the Board confirm the claim to the extent of the first depth, but reject the second depth.

No. 224.—MICHEL BERGERON claims a tract of land, situate on the west side of the river Mississippi, in the county of Acadia, containing two arpents twenty-one toises in front, and eighty arpents in depth, and bounded on the upper side by land of Jean Baptiste Bergeron, and on the lower by land of Jean Cox.

It appears that the first-depth of this land was inhabited and cultivated on the 20th December, 1803, and for more than ten consecutive years prior. So far the Board confirm the claim, but reject the claim to the second depth of forty arpents.

No. 225.—JEAN BAPTISTE VICUER claims a tract of land, situate on the east side of the river Mississippi, in the county of Acadia, containing two arpents in front, and forty in depth, and bounded on the upper side by land of Mr. Lanois, and on the lower by land of Mr. Lanois.

It appears that the claimant did actually inhabit and cultivate the land now claimed on the 20th December, 1803, and that the same was continually inhabited and cultivated by him, or those under whom he claims, for more than ten consecutive years next preceding. Confirmed.

No. 226.—ANTOINE TREGNE claims a tract of land, situate on the east side of the river Mississippi, in the county of Acadia, containing four arpents in front, and forty in depth, bounded on the upper side by land of Christophe Mayer, and on the lower by land of Pierre Lanois.

It appears that the claimant did actually inhabit and cultivate the land now claimed on the 20th December, 1803, and that the same was continually inhabited and cultivated by him, or those under whom he claims, for more than ten consecutive years next preceding. Confirmed.

No. 227.—ANTOINE CLAIRO claims a tract of land, situate on the east side of the river Mississippi, in the county of Acadia, containing two arpents in front, and forty in depth, and bounded on the upper side by land of Joseph Bourg, and on the lower by land of Christophe Roussel.

It appears that the claimant did actually inhabit and cultivate the land now claimed on the 20th December, 1803, and that the same was continually inhabited and cultivated by him, or those under whom he claims, for more than ten consecutive years next preceding. Confirmed.

No. 228.—CHRISTOPHE ROUSSEL claims a tract of land, situate on the east side of the Mississippi, in the county of Acadia, containing five arpents in front, and forty arpents in depth, and bounded on the upper side by land of Mr. Cairo, and on the lower by land of Jean Louis Bourgeois.

It appears that the land now claimed was inhabited and cultivated on the 20th December, 1803, and that the same was continually inhabited and cultivated by the claimant, or those under whom he claims, for more than ten consecutive years next preceding. Confirmed.

No. 229.—JOSEPH BOURG claims a tract of land, situate on the east side of the river Mississippi, in the county of Acadia, containing three arpents in front, and forty in depth, and bounded on the upper side by land of Mr. Houvre, and on the lower by land of Antoine Clairo.

It appears that the land now claimed was inhabited and cultivated on the 20th December, 1803, and that the same was continually inhabited and cultivated by the claimant, or those under whom he claims, for more than ten consecutive years next preceding. Confirmed.

No. 230.—PAULITE HERBERT claims a tract of land, situate on the east side of the river Mississippi, in the county of Acadia, containing three arpents and twenty-seven toises in front, and forty arpents in depth, and bounded on the upper side by land of Jean Bte. Charpentier, and on the lower by land of Felix Vincent.

It appears that the claimant did actually inhabit and cultivate the land now claimed on the 10th December, 1803, and that the same was continually inhabited and cultivated by him, or those under whom he claims, for more than ten consecutive years next preceding. Confirmed.

No. 231.—JOSEPH MICHEL claims a tract of land, situate on the east side of the river Mississippi, in the county of Acadia, containing one arpent in front, and forty arpents in depth, and bounded on the upper side by land of Joseph Caillet, and on the lower by land of Louis Gregoire.

This is part of a tract of land of eight arpents and two toises in front, on the ordinary depth, surveyed by Don Carlos Trudeau, in the year 1782, under whose title the claimant holds by virtue of successive sales; this land having been inhabited and cultivated ever since the above period, until on and after the 20th December, 1803.

No. 232.—JOSEPH CAILLET claims a tract of land, situate on the east side of the river Mississippi, in the county of Acadia, containing three arpents in front, and forty in depth, and bounded on the upper side by land of Mr. Lebare, and on the lower side by land of Joseph Michel.

This is part of a tract of land of eight arpents and two toises in front, mentioned in the last, No. 231; surveyed for Jean Baptiste Picou, under whose title the claimant holds by virtue of successive sales; the land having been inhabited and cultivated ever since that period, until on and after the 20th December, 1803. Confirmed.

No. 233.—LOUIS GREGOIRE claims a tract of land situate on the east side of the river Mississippi, in the county of Acadia, containing four arpents fourteen toises and four feet in front, and forty arpents in depth, and bounded on the upper side by land of Joseph Michel, and on the lower by land of Pierre Houvre.

This is part of a tract of land mentioned in No. 231, surveyed for Jean Baptiste Picou, under whose title the claimant holds by virtue of successive sales; the land having been inhabited and cultivated ever since the year 1782, until on and after the 20th December, 1803. Confirmed.

No. 234.—AUGUSTIN BROUSSARD claims a tract of land, situate on the west side of the river Mississippi, in the county of Acadia, containing two arpents in front, and forty in depth, and bounded on the upper side by land of Olivier Landry, and on the lower by land of Joseph Landry.

It appears that the land now claimed was inhabited and cultivated on the 20th December, 1803, and that the same was continually inhabited and cultivated by those under whom the claimant holds for more than ten consecutive years next preceding. Confirmed.

No. 235.—LUDIVINE GRANGER, widow of Jean Bourgeois, claims a tract of land, situate on the east side of the river Mississippi, in the county of Acadia, containing one arpent and twenty-six toises in front, and forty arpents in depth, and bounded on the upper side by land of Jean Louis Bourgeois, and on the lower by land of Edward Bourgeois.

It appears that the claimant did actually inhabit and cultivate the land now claimed on the 20th December, 1803, and that the same was continually inhabited and cultivated by him, or those under whom he claims, for more than ten consecutive years next preceding. Confirmed.

No. 236.—JEAN LOUIS BOURGEOIS claims a tract of land, situate on the east side of the river Mississippi, in the county of Acadia, containing two arpents in front, and forty in depth, and bounded on the upper side by land of Christophe Roussel, and on the lower by land of Ludivine Granger.

It appears that the claimant did actually inhabit and cultivate the land now claimed on the 20th December, 1803, and that the same was continually inhabited and cultivated by him or those under whom he claims for more than ten consecutive years next preceding. Confirmed.

No. 237.—EDWARD BOURGEOIS claims a tract of land, situate on the east side of the river Mississippi, in the county of Acadia, containing two arpents in front, and forty in depth, and bounded on the upper side by land of Ludivine Granger, and on the lower by land of Joseph Poirier.

It appears that the land now claimed was inhabited and cultivated on the 20th December, 1803, and that the same was continually inhabited and cultivated by those under whom the claimant holds for more than ten consecutive years next preceding. Confirmed.

No. 238.—JOSEPH LANDRY, Senior, claims a tract of land, situate on the west side of the river Mississippi, in the county of Acadia, containing six arpents and three toises in front, and forty arpents in depth, and bounded on the upper side by land of Diego Cantrelle, and on the lower by land of Diego Verret.

This land was surveyed by Don Carlos Trudeau, in the year 1780, for Basile Leclair, under whose title the claimant holds by virtue of successive sales; the land having been inhabited and cultivated ever since the above period, until on and after the 20th December, 1803. Confirmed.

No. 239.—FREDERIC BLANCHARD claims a tract of land, situate on the west side of the river Mississippi, in the county of Acadia, containing two arpents in front, and forty in depth, and bounded on the upper side by land of Pierre Bertrand, and on the lower by land of Pierre Blanchard.

It appears that the land now claimed was inhabited and cultivated on the 20th December, 1803, and that the same was continually inhabited and cultivated by the claimant, or those under whom he claims, for more than ten consecutive years next preceding. Confirmed.

No. 240.—HENRY MELANSON claims a tract of land, situate on the east side of the river Mississippi, in the county of Acadia, containing three and a half arpents in front, and forty arpents in depth, and bounded on the upper side by land of Jacques Leblanc and on the lower by land of Louis Gautreau.

It appears that the land now claimed was inhabited and cultivated on the 20th December, 1803, and that the same was continually inhabited and cultivated by those under whom the claimant holds for more than ten consecutive years next preceding. Confirmed.

No. 241.—LOUIS FALGOUT claims a tract of land, situate on the west side of the river Mississippi, in the county of Acadia, containing two arpents and twenty-six toises in front, and forty arpents in depth, and bounded on the upper side by land of Jean Baptiste Chenier, and on the lower by land of Pierre Olivier.

It appears that the land now claimed was inhabited and cultivated on the 20th December, 1803, and that the same was continually inhabited and cultivated by those under whom the claimant holds, for more than ten consecutive years next preceding. Confirmed.

No. 242.—MANUEL BREAUX claims a tract of land, situate on the east side of the river Mississippi, in the county of Acadia, containing two arpents in front, and forty in depth, and bounded on the upper side by land of Pierre Blanchard, and on the lower by land of Pierre Michel, Jun.

It appears that the claimant did actually inhabit and cultivate the land now claimed on the 20th December, 1803, and that the same was continually inhabited and cultivated by him, or those under whom he claims, for more than ten consecutive years next preceding. Confirmed.

No. 243.—CHARLES THIBODEAUX, Jun. claims a tract of land, situate on the east side of the river Mississippi, in the county of Acadia, containing two arpents and twenty-three toises in front, and forty arpents in depth, and bounded on the upper side by land of Pierre Myr, and on the lower by land of Pierre Blanchard.

It appears that the claimant did actually inhabit and cultivate the land now claimed on the 20th December, 1803, and that the same was continually inhabited and cultivated for more than ten consecutive years next preceding. Confirmed.

No. 244.—PIERRE BLANCHARD claims a tract of land, situate on the east side of the river Mississippi, in the county of Acadia, containing two arpents and twenty-three toises in front, and forty arpents in depth, and bounded on the upper side by land of Chas. Thibodeaux, and on the lower by land of Manuel Breaux.

It appears that the land now claimed was inhabited and cultivated on the 20th December, 1803, and that the same was continually inhabited and cultivated by those under whom the claimant holds for more than ten consecutive years next preceding. Confirmed.

No. 245.—MARGUERITE BRASSEUX, widow of Paul Babin, claims a tract of land, situate on the east side of the river Mississippi, in the county of Iberville, containing six arpents five toises three feet and six inches in front, and forty arpents in depth, and bounded on the upper side by land of Guillaume Germain, and on the lower by land of Joseph Brasset.

This land was surveyed by Don Louis Andry, in the year, 1774, in favor of Francisco Landry, who obtained a complete grant of the same, in 1775, from Governor Unzaga. The claimant holds under said grant by virtue of regular sales. Confirmed.

No. 246.—FERDINAND CAPDEVIELLE claims a tract of land, situate on the west side of the river Mississippi, in the county of Iberville, containing two and a half arpents in front, and forty arpents in depth, and bounded on the upper side by land of Madame Capdevielle, and on the lower by land of François Gallaugher.

It appears that the claimant did actually inhabit and cultivate the land now claimed on the 20th December, 1803; and that the same was continually inhabited and cultivated by him, or those under whom he claims, for more than ten consecutive years next preceding. Confirmed.

No. 247.—SIMON JACOB CRONE claims a tract of land, situate on the east side of the river Mississippi, in the county of Acadia, containing three arpents and twenty-six toises in front, and forty arpents in depth, and bounded on the upper side by land of Paul Landry, and on the lower by land of David, a free negro.

It appears that the land now claimed was inhabited and cultivated on the 20th of December, 1803, and that the same was continually inhabited and cultivated by those under whom the claimant holds for more than ten consecutive years next preceding. Confirmed.

No. 248.—JOSEPH CLOATRE claims a tract of land, situate on the west side of the river Mississippi, in the county of Iberville, containing three arpents and twenty toises in front, and forty arpents in depth, and bounded on the one side by land of Anselmo Blanchard.

It appears that the claimant did actually inhabit and cultivate the land now claimed on 20th of December, 1803, and that the same was continually inhabited and cultivated for more than ten consecutive years next preceding. Confirmed.

No. 249.—POLITE BABIN claims a tract of land, situate on the west side of the river Mississippi, in the county of Acadia, containing two arpents in front, and forty arpents in depth, and bounded on the upper side by land of Augustin Gravois, and on the lower by land of Joseph Dugast.

It appears that the land now claimed was inhabited and cultivated on the 20th of December, 1803, and that the same was continually inhabited and cultivated by those under whom the claimant holds for more than ten consecutive years next preceding. Confirmed.

No. 250. JACQUES ROMAN claims a tract of land, situate on the west side of the river Mississippi, in the county of Acadia, containing sixteen arpents and seven toises in front, and of an unlimited depth, and bounded on the upper side by land of Alexis Perret, and on the lower by land of Alexis Perret.

It appears that the land now claimed, to the extent of forty arpents in depth, was inhabited and cultivated on the 20th of December, 1803, and for more than ten consecutive years prior thereto. The Board confirm the claim to the extent of the first forty arpents in depth only.

No. 251.—JACQUES ROMAN claims a tract of land, situate on the west side of the river Mississippi, in the county of Acadia, containing nine arpents eight toises and one foot in front, and of an unlimited depth, and bounded on the upper side by land of Madame Bourg, and on the lower by land of Alexis Perret.

It appears that the first depth of forty arpents of this land was inhabited and cultivated on the 20th of December, 1803, and for more than ten consecutive years prior. The Board confirm the claim to the extent only of forty arpents in depth.

No. 252.—JACQUES ROMAN claims a tract of land, situate on the west side of the river Mississippi, in the county of Acadia, containing four arpents and fourteen toises in front, and forty arpents in depth, and bounded on the upper side by land of George Mouton, and on the lower by land of Mathias Frederic.

This land was surveyed in year 1771, in favor of Juan Saunier, who obtained a complete grant for the same in the year 1773, from Governor Unzaga; the present claimant holds under said grant by virtue of successive sales. Confirmed.

No. 253.—JACQUES ROMAN claims a tract of land, situate on the west side of the river Mississippi, in the county of Acadia, containing nine arpents and ten feet in front, and forty arpents in depth, and bounded on the upper side by land of Gabriel Arcenaux, and on the lower by land of Michel Arcenaux.

It appears that the land now claimed was inhabited and cultivated on the 20th of December, 1803, and that the same was continually inhabited and cultivated by those under whom the claimant holds for more than ten consecutive years next preceding. Confirmed.

No. 254.—JACQUES ROMAN claims a tract of land, situate on the west side of the river Mississippi, in the county of Acadia, containing two arpents in front, and forty in depth, and bounded on the upper side by land of Frederic Blanchard, and on the lower by land of Louis Mouton.

It appears that the land now claimed was inhabited and cultivated on the 20th of December, 1803, and that the same was continually inhabited and cultivated by those under whom the claimant holds for more than ten consecutive years next preceding. Confirmed.

No. 255.—JACQUES ROMAN claims a tract of land, situate on the west side of the river Mississippi, in the county of Acadia, containing fourteen arpents in front, and of a depth unlimited, and bounded on the upper side by land of Juan Baptiste Cautrelle, and on the lower by land of Michel Cautrelle.

It appears that the first depth of forty arpents of the land now claimed was inhabited and cultivated on the 20th December, 1803, and for more than ten consecutive years prior; the Board confirm the claim to the extent only of forty arpents in depth.

No. 256.—WILLIAM HUTCHERSON claims a tract of land, situate on the west side of the river Mississippi, in the county of Acadia, containing five arpents in front, and forty in depth, and bounded on one side by land of David Hanly, and on the other by land of John Walker.

It appears that the land now claimed was inhabited and cultivated on the 20th December, 1803, and that the same was continually inhabited and cultivated by those under whom the claimant holds for more than ten consecutive years next preceding. Confirmed.

No. 257.—JOSEPH CAPDEVIELLE claims a tract of land, situate on the west side of the river Mississippi, in the county of Iberville, containing two and a half arpents in front, and forty arpents in depth, and bounded on the upper side by land of Alexander Hebre, and on the lower by land of Frederic Capdevielle.

It appears that the land now claimed was inhabited and cultivated on the 20th December, 1803, and that the same was continually inhabited and cultivated by those under whom the claimant holds for more than ten consecutive years next preceding. Confirmed.

No. 258.—FIRMIN BROUSSARARD claims a tract of land, situate on the east side of the river Mississippi, in the county of Iberville, containing two arpents in front, and forty in depth, and bounded on the upper side by land of Michel Hebert, and on the lower by land of Louis Parent.

It appears that the land now claimed was inhabited and cultivated on the 20th December, 1803, and that the same was continually inhabited and cultivated by those under whom the claimant holds for more than ten consecutive years next preceding. Confirmed.

No. 259.—ANTOINE GARCIE claims a tract of land, situate on the west side of the river Mississippi, in the county of Acadia, containing fifteen toises in front, and two arpents in depth, and bounded on each side by land of Jean Baptiste Pœfarre.

It appears that the land now claimed was inhabited and cultivated on the 20th December, 1803, and that the same was continually inhabited and cultivated by those under whom the claimant holds for more than ten consecutive years next preceding. Confirmed.

No. 260.—DIEGO GOMEZ claims a tract of land, situate on the right side of the bayou La Fourche in the county of Acadia, containing two arpents in front, and forty arpents in depth, and bounded on the upper side by land of Antoine Monterino, and on the lower by land of Joseph Corbo.

It appears that the land now claimed was inhabited and cultivated on the 20th December, 1803, and that the same was continually inhabited and cultivated by those under whom the claimant holds for more than ten consecutive years next preceding. Confirmed.

No. 261.—ALEXANDRE HEBERT claims a tract of land, situate on the west side of the river Mississippi, in the county of Iberville, containing three arpents in front, and forty in depth, and bounded on the upper side by land of Edward Capdevielle, and on the lower by land of Madame Capdevielle.

It appears that the claimant did actually inhabit and cultivate the land now claimed on the 20th December, 1803, and that the same was continually inhabited and cultivated by him, or those under whom he claims, for more than ten consecutive years next preceding. Confirmed.

No. 262.—JOSEPH ORILLON claims a tract of land, situate on the west side of the river Mississippi, in the county of Iberville, containing six arpents in front, and eighty in depth, and bounded on the upper side by land of Atanasia Dardenne, and on the lower by land of Blas Lejeune.

The first depth of this land was surveyed by Don Louis Andry, in the year 1772, in favor of Louis Dardenne, who obtained a complete grant for the same, in the year 1774, from Governor Unzaga; under which grant the claimant holds by virtue of regular sales. The Board confirm the claim to the first depth, but reject the second depth of forty arpents.

No. 263.—JOSEPH ORILLON claims a tract of land, situate on the west side of the river Mississippi, in the county of Iberville, containing three arpents and twelve toises in front, and forty arpents in depth, and bounded on the upper side by land of Cadet Dupuis, and on the lower by land of Paul Babin.

It appears that the land now claimed was inhabited and cultivated on the 20th December, 1803, and that the same was continually inhabited and cultivated by those under whom the claimant holds for more than ten consecutive years next preceding. Confirmed.

No. 264.—ANTONIO MONTASINO claims a tract of land, situate on the right bank of the bayou La Fourche, in the county of Acadia, containing one arpent in front, and forty arpents in depth, and bounded on the upper side by land of Martin Kijoure, and on the lower by land of Diego Gomez.

It appears that the land now claimed was inhabited and cultivated on the 20th December, 1803, and that the same was continually inhabited and cultivated by those under whom the claimant holds for more than ten consecutive years next preceding. Confirmed.

No. 265.—Joseph Albarez claims a tract of land, situate on the right bank of the bayou La Fourche, in the county of Acadia, containing one arpent and twenty-eight toises and four feet in front, and a depth extending to the lands fronting on the river Mississippi, and bounded on the upper side by land of Jean Paredes, and on the lower by land of Joseph Gonzales.

This land is part of a tract surveyed by Don Carlos Trudeau, in the year 1791, for Jean Aleman, under whose title the claimant holds by virtue of successive sales; the land having been inhabited and cultivated ever since that period, until on and after the 20th December, 1803. Confirmed.

No. 266.—Jean Paredes claims a tract of land, situate on the right bank of the bayou La Fourche, in the county of Acadia, containing two arpents in front, and a depth extending to the land fronting on the river Mississippi, and bounded on the upper side by land of Joseph Hidalgo, and on the lower by land of Joseph Albarez.

This land is part of a tract of three arpents twenty-eight toises and four feet in front, on the ordinary depth, surveyed in the year 1791, for Jean Alman, under whose title the claimant holds by virtue of successive sale; the land having been inhabited and cultivated ever since that period, until on and after the 20th December, 1803. Confirmed.

No. 267.—Antonio Gomez claims a tract of land, situate on the right bank of the bayou La Fourche, in the county of Acadia, containing three arpents twenty-five toises and five feet in front, and of a depth extending to the lands fronting on the river Mississippi, and bounded on the upper side by land of Mr. Baptiste, and on the lower by land of François Hidalgo.

It appears that the land now claimed was inhabited and cultivated on the 20th December, 1803; and that the same was continually inhabited and cultivated by those under whom the claimant holds for more than ten consecutive years next preceding. Confirmed.

No. 268.—Lorenzo Hernandez claims a tract of land, situate on the right bank of the bayou La Fourche, in the county of Acadia, containing three arpents in front, and a depth extending to the lands fronting on the river Mississippi, and bounded on the upper side by land of Joseph Hidalgo, and on the lower by land of Gregorie Hidalgo.

It appears that the claimant did actually inhabit and cultivate the land now claimed on the 20th December, 1803; and that the same was continually inhabited and cultivated by him, or those under whom he claims, for more than ten consecutive years next preceding. Confirmed.

No. 269.—Thomas Albaredo claims a tract of land, situate on the right bank of the bayou La Fourche, in the county of Acadia, containing three arpents in front, and forty in depth, and bounded on the upper side by land of Watkins River.

It appears that the claimant did actually inhabit and cultivate the land now claimed on the 20th December, 1803; and that the same was continually inhabited and cultivated by him, or those under whom he claims, for more than ten consecutive years next preceding. Confirmed.

No. 270.—Manuel Romanos claims a tract of land, situate on the left bank of the bayou La Fourche, in the county of Acadia, containing three arpents four toises and five feet in front, and forty arpents in depth, and bounded on the upper side by land of Dominique Suares, and on the lower by land of Diego Gonzales.

It appears that the land now claimed was inhabited and cultivated on the 20th December, 1803, and that the same was continually inhabited and cultivated by those under whom the claimant holds for more than ten consecutive years next preceding. Confirmed.

No. 271.—Louis Dannequin claims a tract of land, situate on the west side of the river Mississippi, in the county of Acadia, containing three arpents in front, and forty in depth, and bounded on the upper side by land of Joseph Nicholas Landry, and on the lower by land of Jean Gravois.

It appears that the land now claimed was inhabited and cultivated on the 20th December, 1803; and that the same was continually inhabited and cultivated by those under whom the claimant holds for more than ten consecutive years next preceding. Confirmed.

No. 272.—Louis Mollere claims a tract of land, situate on the west side of the river Mississippi, in the county of Acadia, containing eighteen arpents one toise and four feet in front, and forty arpents in depth, and bounded on the upper side by land of Pierre Arrieux, and on the lower by land of Joseph Nicholas Landry.

It appears that the claimant did actually inhabit and cultivate the land now claimed on the 20th December, 1803; and that the same was continually inhabited and cultivated by him, or those under whom he claims, for more than ten consecutive years next preceding. Confirmed.

No. 273.—Augustin Dominique Tureaud claims a tract of land, situate on the west side of the river Mississippi, in the county of Acadia, containing four arpents in front, and forty in depth, and bounded on the upper side by land of Joseph Hebert, and on the lower by land of Benjamin Leblanc.

It appears that the land now claimed was inhabited and cultivated on the 20th December, 1803; and that the same was continually inhabited and cultivated by those under whom the claimant holds for more than ten consecutive years next preceding. Confirmed.

No. 274.—Augustin Dominique Tureaud claims a tract of land, situate on the west side of the river Mississippi, in the county of Acadia, containing three arpents and one-third and five feet in front, and forty arpents in depth, and bounded on the upper side by land of Ch. Gotereau, and on the lower by land of Basile Prejeau.

It appears that the land now claimed was inhabited and cultivated on the 20th December, 1803; and that the same was continually inhabited and cultivated by those under whom the claimant holds for more than ten consecutive years next preceding. Confirmed.

No. 275.—Joseph Boudreaux claims a tract of land, situate on the west side of the river Mississippi, in the county of Acadia, containing five arpents and twenty-three toises in front, and forty arpents in depth, and bounded on the upper side by land of Jean Baptiste Brand, and on the lower by land of Pedro Landry.

This land was surveyed by Don Louis Andry, in the year 1774, in favor of Aman Landry, who obtained a complete grant for the same, in the year 1775, from Governor Unzaga; under which grant the claimant holds, in right of his wife, by virtue of regular sales. Confirmed.

No. 276.—Joseph Godet claims a tract of land, situate on the east side of the river Mississippi, in the county of Iberville, containing three arpents and twelve toises in front, and forty arpents in depth, and bounded on the upper side by land of Mr. Gime, and on the lower by land of Jean Godet.

It appears that the land claimed was actually inhabited and cultivated on the 20th December, 1803, and that the same was continually inhabited and cultivated by those under whom the claimant holds for more than ten consecutive years next preceding. Confirmed.

No 277.—Jean Godet claims a tract of land, situate on the east side of the river Mississippi, in the county of Acadia, containing one arpent and twenty-three toises in front, and forty arpents in depth, and bounded on the upper side by land of Joseph Godet, and on the lower by land of P. Guedry.

It appears that the land now claimed was inhabited and cultivated on the 20th December, 1803, and that the same was continually inhabited and cultivated by those under whom the claimant holds for more than ten consecutive years next preceding. Confirmed.

No. 278.—Pierre Michel claims a tract of land, situate on the east side of the river Mississippi, in the county of Acadia, containing three arpents and six toises in front, and forty arpents in depth, and bounded on the upper side by land of Paul Materne, and on the lower by land of Mort Materne.

It appears that the land now claimed was inhabited and cultivated on the 20th December, 1803, and that the same was continually inhabited and cultivated by those under whom the claimant holds for more than ten consecutive years next preceding. Confirmed.

No. 279.—Alexis Rom claims a tract of land, situate on the east side of the river Mississippi, in the county of Acadia, containing two arpents in front, and forty in depth, and bounded on the upper side by land of Charles Vincent, and on the lower by land of George Mouton.

It appears that the land now claimed was inhabited and cultivated on the 20th December, 1803, and that the same was continually inhabited and cultivated by those under whom the claimant holds for more than ten consecutive years next preceding. Confirmed.

No. 280.—WILLIAM BELO claims a tract of land, situate on the west side of the river Mississippi, in the county of Acadia, containing one arpent in front, and forty arpents in depth, and bounded on the upper side by land of Pierre Olivier, and on the lower by land of André Joseph.

It appears that the land claimed was actually inhabited and cultivated on the 20th December, 1803, and that the same was continually inhabited and cultivated by those under whom the claimant holds for more than ten consecutive years next preceding. Confirmed.

No. 281.—JAMES GODBERRY claims a tract of land, situate on the east side of the river Mississsippi, in the county of Acadia, containing three arpents eighteen toises and three feet in front, and forty arpents in depth, and bounded on the upper side by land of André Bernard, and on the lower by land of Pierre Michel.

It appears that the land claimed was inhabited and cultivated on the 20th December, 1803, and that the same was continually inhabited and cultivated by those under whom the claimant holds for more than ten consecutive years next preceding. Confirmed.

No. 282.—CHARLES THOME claims a tract of land, situate on the west side of the river Mississippi, in the county of Acadia, containing fifteen toises in front, and two arpents in depth, and bounded on the upper side by land of Paulite Babin, and on the lower by land of Joseph Dugast.

It appears that the claimant did actually inhabit and cultivate the land now claimed on the 20th December, 1803, and that the same was continually inhabited and cultivated by him, or those under whom he claims for more than ten consecutive years next preceding. Confirmed.

No. 283.—ISABELLE BAUGARD, a free negro, claims a tract of land, situate on the left bank of the bayou La Fourche, in the county of Acadia, containing three arpents in front, and forty in depth, and bounded on the upper side by land of Francisco Diez, and on the lower by land of Antoine Melene.

It appears that the claimant did actually inhabit and cultivate the land now claimed on the 20th December, 1803, and that the same was continually inhabited and cultivated by her, or those under whom she claims, for more than ten consecutive years next preceding. Confirmed.

No. 284.—DOMINIQUE SUARES claims a tract of land, situate on the left bank of the bayou la Fourche, in the county of Acadia, containing three arpents four toises and five feet in front, and forty arpents in depth, and bounded on the upper side by land of Antonio Peres, and on the lower by land of Manuel Romanos.

It appears that the claimant did actually inhabit and cultivate the land now claimed on the 20th December, 1803, and that the same was continually inhabited and cultivated by him, or those under whom he claims, for more than ten consecutive years next preceding. Confirmed.

No. 285.—JOSEPH HERES claims a tract of land, situate on the right bank of the bayou la Fourche, in the county of Acadia, containing two arpents in front, and a depth extending to the bank fronting on the Mississippi, and bounded on the upper side by land of Louis Judice, and on the lower side by land of Mr. Baptiste.

It appears that the land now claimed was inhabited and cultivated on the 20th December, 1803, and that the same was continually inhabited and cultivated by those under whom the claimant holds for more than ten consecutive years next preceding. Confirmed.

No. 286.—JEAN CHARLES COUMO claims a tract of land, situate on the west side of the river Mississippi, in the county of Iberville, containing six arpents in front, and forty in depth, and bounded on one side by land of John Hull.

It appears that the claimant did actually inhabit and cultivate the land now claimed on the 20th December, 1803, and that the same was continually inhabited and cultivated for more than ten consecutive years next preceding. Confirmed.

No. 287.—ANTOINE BAYOU claims a tract of land, situate on the left bank of the bayou La Fourche, in the county of Acadia, containing six arpents in front, and forty in depth, and bounded on the upper side by land of Mr. Bartole, and on the lower by land of Mr. Balthazard.

It appears that the land now claimed was inhabited and cultivated on the 20th December, 1803, and that the same was continually inhabited and cultivated by those under whom the claimant holds for more than ten consecutive years next preceding. Confirmed.

No. 288.—OLIVIER BLANCHARD claims a tract of land, situate on the east side of the river Mississippi, in the county of Iberville, containing three arpents ten toises and four feet in front, and eighty arpents in depth, and bounded on one side by land of Jean Longue-Epée.

The first depth of forty arpents of this land was granted, in the year 1774, to Bernard Capdevielle; and Michel Gareuil having afterwards become the owner of it, by purchase, obtained a grant to a second depth of forty arpents in the year 1793; under which titles the present claimant holds by virtue of regular sales. Confirmed.

No. 289.—PAUL RICHARD claims a tract of land, situate on the east side of the river Mississippi, in the county of Iberville, containing five arpents and a half in front, and forty arpents in depth, and bounded on the upper side by land of Simon Richard, and on the lower by land of Pierre Richard.

It appears that the land now claimed was inhabited and cultivated on the 20th December, 1803, and that the same was continually inhabited and cultivated by those under whom the claimant holds for more than ten consecutive years next preceding. Confirmed.

No. 290.—JOHN HULL claims a tract of land, situate on the west side of the river Mississippi, in the county of Iberville, containing three arpents in front, and forty in depth, and bounded on the upper side by land of Jean Charles Comon, and on the lower by land of Edmond Capdevielle.

It appears that the claimant did actually inhabit and cultivate the land now claimed on the 20th December, 1803, and that the same was continually inhabited and cultivated by him, or those under whom he claims, for more than ten consecutive years next preceding. Confirmed.

No. 291.—JOSEPH MOLLERE claims a tract of land, situate on the west side of the river Mississippi, in the county of Iberville, containing five arpents in front, and forty in depth, and bounded on the upper side by land of Joseph and Pierre Lacroix, and on the lower by land of Philip Roth.

It appears that the land now claimed was inhabited and cultivated on the 20th December, 1803, and that the same was continually inhabited and cultivated by those under whom the claimant holds for more than ten consecutive years next preceding. Confirmed.

No. 293.—EDMOND CAPDEVIELLE claims a tract of land, situate on the east side of the river Mississippi, in the county of Iberville, containing six arpents and twenty toises in front, and forty arpents in depth, and bounded on the upper side by land of Alexis Leblanc, and on the lower by land of Jean Baptiste Allain.

This is part of a tract of land of seven arpents and twenty toises in front, on the ordinary depth, surveyed by Don Louis Andry, in the year 1772, in favor of Joseph Comon, who obtained a complete grant for the same in 1775 from Governor Unzaga; under which grant the claimant holds by virtue of regular sales. Confirmed.

No. 294.—SIMON BROUSSARD claims a tract of land, situate on the east side of the river Mississippi, in the county of Iberville, containing six arpents seven toises and four feet in front, and forty arpents in depth, and bounded on the upper side by land of André Bourg, and on the lower by land of Pierre Allain.

This land was surveyed by Don Louis Andry, in the year 1772, in favor of Maturin Benoit, who obtained a complete grant for the same in 1775, from Governor Unzaga; under which grant the claimant holds by virtue of successive sales. Confirmed.

No. 295.—SIMON BROUSSARD claims a tract of land, situate on the east side of the river Mississippi, in the county of Iberville, containing four arpents in front, and forty in depth, and bounded on the upper side by land of Firmin Pengrasse Landry, and on the lower by land of Madame Ch. Brand.

It appears that the claimant did actually inhabit and cultivate the land now claimed on the 20th December, 1803, and that the same was continually inhabited and cultivated for more than ten consecutive years next preceding. Confirmed.

No. 296.—ETIENNE COUMO claims a tract of land, situate on the east side of the river Mississippi, in the county of Iberville, containing seven arpents twenty-eight toises and three feet in front, and forty arpents in depth, and bounded on the upper side by land of Joseph Leblanc, and on the lower by land of Pedro Forest.

This land was surveyed by Don Louis Andry, in the year 1772, in favor of Bonaventura Forest, who obtained a complete grant for the same in 1774, from Governor Unzaga; under which grant the claimant holds by virtue of regular sales. Confirmed.

No. 297.—ETIENNE COUMO claims a tract of land, situate on the road leading to Galveztown, in the county of Iberville, containing eight hundred superficial arpents, and bounded on one side by land of Louis Lecompte, and on the lower side by vacant lands.

This land was surveyed by Don Carlos Trudeau, in the year 1789, in favor of Baptiste Allain, who obtained a complete grant for the same, in the same year, from Don Estevan Miro, then Governor; under which grant the claimant holds by virtue of regular sales. Confirmed.

No. 299.—SIMON RICHARD, Jun. claims a tract of land, situate on the east side of the river Mississippi, in the county of Iberville, containing five arpents and twenty-nine toises in front, and forty arpents in depth, and bounded on the upper side by land of Joseph Richard, and on the lower by land of Simon Richard, Sen.

This tract of land was surveyed in favor of Cerilo Rivet, in the year 1772, who was at the same time put in possession of it by Don Louis Andry, the authorized surveyor, and who, in the year 1775, obtained a complete title to the same from Governor Unzaga; under which title the claimant holds in virtue of successive sales. Confirmed.

No. 300.—SIMON RICHARD claims a tract of land, situate on the east side of the river Mississippi, in the county of Iberville, containing four arpents and five toises in front, and forty arpents in depth, and bounded on the upper side by land of Paul Richard, and on the lower by land of Daniel Richard.

This is part of a tract of land of six arpents and five toises in front, on the usual depth, surveyed in the year 1772 for the claimant, who obtained a complete grant for the same in 1776, from Governor Unzaga, of which he now claims four arpents and five toises, having sold two arpents to his son, Paul Richard. Confirmed.

No. 301.—SIMON RICHARD claims a tract of land, situate on the east side of the river Mississippi, in the county of Iberville, containing five arpents and twenty-seven toises in front, and forty arpents in depth, and bounded on the upper side by land of Marin Landry, and on the lower by land of the claimant.

This land was surveyed by Don Louis Andry, in the year 1772, in favor of Paul Richard, who obtained a complete grant for the same in 1776 from Governor Unzaga. The claimant holds by purchase of the grantee. Confirmed.

No. 302.—ALEXIS BREAUX claims a tract of land, situate on the west side of the river Mississippi, in the county of Acadia, containing five arpents seventeen toises one foot and six inches in front, and forty arpents in depth, and bounded on the upper side by land of Jean Baptiste Bergeron, and on the lower by land of Anne Bergeron.

This land was surveyed in the year 1771 in favor of Francisco Moreau, who obtained a complete title to the same in the year 1774 from Governor Unzaga; under which title the present claimant holds, by virtue of regular sales. Confirmed.

No. 303.—BAPTISTE LORREE claims a tract of land, situate on the west side of the river Mississippi, in the county of Iberville, containing four arpents in front, and forty in depth, and bounded on the upper side by land of Jean Charles Goumo, and on the lower by land of Joseph and Pierre Lacroix.

This is part of six arpents front, on the usual depth, surveyed in the year 1772 in favor of Louis Jousson, who obtained a complete grant for the same in 1774 from Go-

vernor Unzaga; under which grant the claimant holds by virtue of successive sales. Confirmed.

No. 304.—FIRMIN PENGRASSE LANDRY claims a tract of land, situate on the east side of the river Mississippi, in the county of Iberville, containing four arpents in front, and forty in depth, and bounded on the upper side by land of Joseph Docite Babin, and on the lower by land of Simon Broussard.

This is part of a tract of land of eight arpents in front, on the ordinary depth, surveyed in the year 1772 in favor of Joseph Brand, who obtained a complete grant for the same in 1776 from Governor Unzaga; under which grant the claimant holds by virtue of successive sales. Confirmed.

No. 305.—SIMON LEBLANC claims a tract of land, situate on the east side of the river Mississippi, in the county of Iberville, containing five arpents in front, and forty in depth, and bounded on the upper side by land of Jean Baptiste Allain, and on the lower by land of Marchel Dupuis.

This is part of a tract of land of twelve arpents in front, and forty in depth, surveyed in the year 1772 in favor of Carlos Coumo, who obtained a complete grant for the same in 1775 from Governor Unzaga; under which grant the claimant holds by virtue of successive sales. Confirmed.

No. 306.—MARCEL DUPUIS claims a tract of land, situate on the east side of the river Mississippi, in the county of Iberville, containing six arpents in front, and forty in depth, and bounded on the upper side by land of Simon Leblanc, and on the lower by land of Nathan Michel.

This is part of the tract of land mentioned in the last, No. 305, granted to Carlos Coumo; under which grant the present claimant holds by virtue of successive sales. Confirmed.

No. 307.—HYPOLITE LANDRY claims a tract of land, situate on the east side of the river Mississippi, in the county of Iberville, containing six arpents and five toises in front, and forty arpents in depth, and bounded on the upper side by land of Victor Blanchard, and on the lower by land of Guillaume Germain.

This is part of a tract of land of eight arpents and five toises in front, on the ordinary depth, surveyed in the year 1772 in favor of Firmin Landry, who obtained a complete grant for the same in 1775 from Governor Unzaga; under which grant the claimant holds by virtue of successive sales. Confirmed.

No. 308.—PIERRE FREDERIC, for himself, and for the infant heirs of Mathias Frederic, deceased, and also for François Frederic, Antoine Frederic, and Noel Guisclar, as husband of Charlotte Frederic, claims a tract of land, situate on the west side of the river Mississippi, in the county of Acadia, containing fourteen arpents and thirteen toises in front, to eight of which front arpents there is the ordinary depth of forty arpents, and to the remaining six arpents and thirteen toises front the depth of eighty arpents, and which said tract is bounded on the upper side by land of Louis Mouton, and on the lower by land of Estevan Tupo.

In the year 1775 a tract of land of twenty arpents front, on the usual depth of forty, was granted by Louis de Kerberrec, at that time Governor, to André Neau, which was afterwards transferred to one Delery, who being unable to support the road levée, twelve arpents of it were re-annexed by his consent, in writing, to the domain. The remaining eight arpents front, with the depth of forty, (part of the present claim,) passed, by virtue of successive sales, under the aforesaid grant, to Mathias Frederic; six arpents and thirteen toises in front, with the depth of forty, the balance of the tract here claimed, was granted to Juan Mouton by Don Louis de Unzaga, in the year 1773; and, in 1783, Mathias Frederic, who had become proprietor of said land, obtained a regular order of survey from Governor Miro, directing him to be put in possession of the second depth of the aforesaid six arpents and thirteen toises front. The tract now claimed is held under these several grants by the claimants, as heirs of Mathias Frederic, deceased. Confirmed.

N. B.—This tract of land was divided among the aforesaid claimants, whose several respective claims have been registered and acted upon by the Board; but, in consequence of the title to the second depth of the six arpents and thirteen toises mentioned above not having been recorded by Antoine Frederic, in claim No. 105, and by Noel Guisclar, in claim No. 106, whose shares include the said six arpents and thirteen toises, the second depth was rejected. The titles being here recorded, the second depth to said land is now confirmed.

No. 309.—Joseph Babin claims a tract of land, situate on the west side of the river Mississippi, in the county of Iberville, containing three arpents twenty-nine toises and two feet in front, and eighty arpents in depth, and bounded on the upper side by land of Hypolite Landry, and on the lower by land of Donat Landry.

Joseph Athanas Landry being proprietor of twelve arpents front, with the depth of forty, was, by a regular order of survey from the Baron de Carondelet, in the year 1794, put in possession of the second depth of forty arpents; of which land the present claimant now holds, by purchase, three arpents twenty-nine toises and two feet front, with the whole depth of eighty arpents. It appears, also, that said land was inhabited and cultivated on the 20th of December, 1803, and for more than ten consecutive years next preceding. Confirmed.

No. 310.—Donat Landry claims a tract of land, situate on the west side of the river Mississippi, in the county of Iberville, containing three arpents twenty-nine toises and two feet in front, and eighty arpents in depth, and bounded on the upper side by land of Joseph Babin, and on the lower by land of Paul Babin.

This is part of the tract of land of twelve arpents in front, and eighty in depth, mentioned in the last, No. 309; the claimant purchased from his father, Joseph Athanas Landry; the land having been inhabited and cultivated for more than ten consecutive years prior to the 20th of December, 1803.

No. 311.—Hypolite Landry claims a tract of land, situate on the west side of the river Mississippi, in the county of Iberville, containing three arpents twenty-nine toises and two feet in front, and eighty arpents in depth, and bounded on the upper side by land of Laurent Cigut, and on the lower by land of Joseph Babin.

This is part of a tract of land of twelve arpents front, and eighty in depth, mentioned in No. 309; the claimant purchased from his father, Joseph Athanas Landry; and the land having been inhabited and cultivated for more than ten consecutive years next preceding the 20th December, 1803. Confirmed.

No. 312.—Joseph Callouet claims a tract of land, situate on the east side of the river Mississippi, in the county of Acadia, containing three and a half arpents in front, and forty in depth, and bounded on the upper side by land of Pierre Houvre, and on the lower by land of the claimant.

It appears that the claimant did actually inhabit and cultivate the land now claimed on the 20th December, 1803, and that the same was continually inhabited and cultivated for more than ten consecutive years next preceding. Confirmed.

No. 313.—Eusebe Melanson claims a tract of land, situate on the west side of the river Mississippi, in the county of Acadia, containing five arpents in front, and eighty arpents in depth, and bounded on the upper side by land of Joseph Melanson, and on the lower by land of Donat Leblanc.

This tract of land is composed of a portion of two grants made in the year 1774 by Governor Unzaga; the one in favor of Santiago Leblanc, and the other in favor of Marcel Leblanc; to which tracts a grant of the second was made by Governor Miro, in the year 1791; under which titles the claimant holds. Confirmed.

No. 314.—Donat Leblanc claims a tract of land, situate on the west side of the river Mississippi, in the county of Acadia, containing two arpents in front, and eighty in depth, and bounded on the upper side by land of Eusebe Melanson, and on the lower by land of Joseph Melanson.

This tract of land is composed of a portion of the two grants mentioned in the last, No. 313, made in favor of Santiago Leblanc and Marcel Leblanc, to which grants there was a grant of a second depth, from Governor Miro, in the year 1791; under which title the claimant holds by virtue of successive sales. Confirmed.

No. 315.—Joseph Melanson claims a tract of land, situate on the west side of river Mississippi, in the county of Acadia, containing three arpents in front, and eighty arpents in depth, and bounded on the upper side by land of Donat Leblanc, and on the lower by land of Olivier Leblanc.

This land is part of the tracts granted to Santiago Leblanc and Marcel Leblanc, mentioned in No. 113, to which tracts a second depth was granted in the year 1791; the claimant holds under said grants by virtue of successive sales. Confirmed.

No. 316.—Olivier Leblanc claims a tract of land, situate on the west side of the river Mississippi, in the county of Acadia, containing three arpents eighteen toises and five feet in front, and eighty arpents in depth, and bounded on the upper side by land of Joseph Melanson, and on the lower by land of Raphael Gotereau.

This is part of the tracts of land granted to Santiago Leblanc and Marcel Leblanc, mentioned in No. 313 ; to said tracts a second depth was granted in the year 1791; under which titles the claimant holds by virtue of regular sales. Confirmed.

No. 317.—Pierre Labat claims a tract of land, situate on the left bank of the bayou La Fourche, in the county of Acadia, containing thirty-two toises and three feet in front, and the depth extending to land of Barthole Hernandez, and bounded on the upper side by land of Barthole Hernandez, and on the lower by land of Mr. Marmonde.

It appears that the land now claimed was inhabited and cultivated on the 20th December, 1803, and that the same was continually inhabited and cultivated by those under whom the claimant holds for more than ten consecutive years next preceding. Confirmed.

No. 318.—Jean Dugas claims a tract of land, situate on the west side of the river Mississippi, in the county of Acadia, containing two arpents in front, and forty in depth, and bounded on the upper side by land of Joseph Leblanc, and on the lower by land of Silvain Leblanc.

It appears that the land now claimed was inhabited and cultivated on the 20th December, 1803, and that the same was continually inhabited and cultivated by those under whom the claimant holds for more than ten consecutive years next preceding. Confirmed.

No. 319.—Mathurin Bergeron claims a tract of land, situate on the west side of the river Mississippi, in the county of Acadia, containing three arpents in front, and forty in depth, and bounded on one side by land of Joseph Bergeron.

This is part of a tract of land of five arpents nineteen toises and three feet in front, and forty arpents in depth, surveyed in the year 1780 in favor of Juan Baptiste Bergeron, from whom the claimant purchased; the land having been inhabited and cultivated ever since that period, until on and after the 20th December, 1803. Confirmed.

No. 320.—Etienne Reine claims a tract of land, situate on the east side of the river Mississippi, in the county of Acadia, containing four arpents in front, and forty in depth, and bounded on the upper side by land of Pierre Chenette, and on the lower by land of Madame Le Bourgeois.

It appears that the claimant did actually inhabit and cultivate the land now claimed on the 20th December, 1803, and that the same was continually inhabited and cultivated for more than ten consecutive years next preceding. Confirmed.

No. 321.—Jean Baptiste Leblanc claims a tract of land, situate on the west side of the river Mississippi, in the county of Acadia, containing three arpents in front, and forty in depth, and bounded on the upper side by land of Simon Boudro, and on the lower by land of Joseph Lalande.

This is part of a tract of land of five arpents in front, and forty in depth, granted to Joseph Babin by Don Louis de Unzaga in the year 1774; under which title the claimant holds by virtue of successive sales. Confirmed.

No. 322.—Joseph Edward Lalande claims a tract of land, situate on the west side of the river Mississippi, in the county of Acadia, containing two arpents in front, and forty in depth, and bounded on the upper side by land of Jean Baptiste Leblanc, and on the lower by land of Madame Melanson.

This is part of a tract of land mentioned in the last, No. 321, granted to Joseph Babin by Don Louis de Unzaga, in the year 1774; under which title the claimant holds by virtue of successive sales. Confirmed.

No. 323.—Pierre Richard claims a tract of land, situate on the east side of the river Mississippi, in the county of Acadia, containing one arpent and a half in front, and forty arpents in depth, and bounded on one side by land of James Mather.

This is part of a tract of land of three arpents front, on the ordinary depth of forty, surveyed in the year 1790. in favor of Sauveur Roy, under whose title the claimant holds by virtue of success.ve sales; the land having been inhabited and cultivated ever since that period, until on and after the 20th December, 1803. Confirmed.

No. 324.—PIERRE MICHEL, Jun. claims a tract of land, situate on the east side of the river Mississippi, in the county of Acadia, containing two arpents in front, and forty in depth, and bounded on the upper side by land of Manuel Breau, and on the lower by land of Charles Thibodeau.
It appears that this land was inhabited and cultivated on the 20th December, 1803, and that the same was continually inhabited and cultivated by those under whom the claimant holds for more than ten consecutive years next preceding. Confirmed.

No. 325.—ETELDER PICOU claims a tract of land, situate on the east side of the river Mississippi, in the county of Acadia, containing two and a half arpents in front, and forty arpents in depth, and bounded on the upper side by land of Joseph Dugas, Sen. and on the lower by land of Joseph Dugas, Jun.
It appears that this land was inhabited and cultivated on the 20th December, 1803, and that the same was continually inhabited and cultivated by those under whom the claimant holds for more than ten consecutive years next preceding. Confirmed.

No. 326.—ANTOINE MAXAUT claims a tract of land, situate on the left bank of the bayou La Fourche, in the county of Acadia, containing three arpents in front, and forty in depth, and bounded on the upper side by land of Lazaro Hernandez, and on the lower by land of Mr. Verzegue.
It appears that the land now claimed was inhabited and cultivated on the 20th December, 1803, and that the same was continually inhabited and cultivated by those under whom the claimant holds for more than ten consecutive years next preceding. Confirmed.

No. 327.—LAZARO HERNANDEZ claims a tract of land, situate on the left bank of the bayou La Fourche, in the county of Acadia, containing four arpents in front, and forty in depth, and bounded on the upper side by land of Dominique Bourgeois, and on the lower by land of Antoine Maxaut.
It appears that this land was inhabited and cultivated on the 20th December, 1803, and that the same was continually inhabited and cultivated for more than ten consecutive years next preceding. Confirmed.

No. 328.—DOMINIQUE BOURGEOIS claims a tract of land, situate on the left bank of the bayou La Fourche, in the county of Acadia, containing four arpents two toises and two feet in front, and forty arpents in depth, and bounded on the upper side by land of Francisco Mathieu. and on the lower by land of Lazaro Hernandez.
It appears that this land was inhabited and cultivated on the 20th December, 1803, and that the same was continually inhabited and cultivated by those under whom the claimant holds for more than ten consecutive years next preceding. Confirmed.

No. 329.—SIMON GOTROT, Jun. claims a tract of land, situate on the east side of the river Mississippi, in the county of Acadia, containing four arpents in front, and forty in depth, and bounded on the upper side by land of Charles Gotrot, and on the lower by land of Simon Savoye.
This is part of a tract of land of six arpents front, with the depth of forty, granted by Don Louis de Unzaga to Firmin Landry, in the year 1775; under which grant the claimant holds by virtue of successive sales. Confirmed.

No. 330.—CHARLES GOTROT claims a tract of land, situate on the west side of the river Mississippi, in the county of Acadia, containing two arpents thirteen toises and five feet in front, and forty arpents in depth, and bounded on the upper side by land of Augustin Dominique Turreau, and on the lower by land of Aman Prejeau.
This is part of a tract of four arpents twenty-seven toises and four feet in front, with the depth of forty arpents, granted by DonLouis de Unzaga to Juan Jansone in the year 1774; under which grant the claimant holds by virtue of successive sales. Confirmed.

No. 331.—MARTIN HOUSSOUS claims a tract of land, situate on the right bank of the bayou La Fourche, in the county of Acadia, containing three arpents in front, and such depth as extends to the lands fronting on the river Mississippi, and bounded on the upper side by land of Mr. Morice, and on the lower by lands of Antoine Montesano.
It appears that the land now claimed was inhabited and cultivated on the 20th December, 1803, and that the same was continually inhabited and cultivated by the claimant, or those under whom he holds, for more than ten consecutive years next preceding. Confirmed.

No. 332.—THEODORE BERGERON and BAPTISTE GAUDIN claim a tract of land, situate on the east side of the river Mississippi, in the county of Acadia, containing six arpents and two toises in front, and forty arpents in depth, and bounded on the upper side by land of Pedro Cheasson, and on the lower by land of Juan Arcenaux.
In the year 1782, by the order of Governor Galvez, this land was surveyed in favor of the widow Forest, who gave it to her two daughters (the wives of the claimants) as a marriage portion. The land has been inhabited and cultivated ever since the making of the survey. Confirmed.

No. 333.—ISAAC LEBLANC claims a tract of land, situate on the east side of the river Mississippi, in the county of Acadia, containing three arpents twenty-six toises and three feet in front, and eighty arpents in depth, and bounded on the upper side by land of Baptiste Bourgeois, and on the lower by land of Paul Bourgeois.
This is part of a tract of land of eleven arpents twenty-six toises and three feet in front, with a double concession, granted to Baptiste Bourgeois, in the year 1791, by Governor Miro; under which grant the claimant holds by virtue of successive sales. Confirmed.

No. 334.—ABRAHAM ROM claims a tract of land, situate on the west side of the river Mississippi, in the county of Acadia, containing four arpents in front, and eighty-four arpents in depth, and bounded on the upper side by land of Alexis Perret, and on the lower by land of Dominique le Bœuf.
It appears that the first depth of forty arpents of this land was inhabited and cultivated by the claimant, on the 20th December, 1803, and for more than ten consecutive years next preceding. So far the Board confirm the claim, but reject the second depth of forty-four arpents.

No. 335.—ALEXIS PERRET claims a tract of land, situate on the west side of the river Mississippi, in the county of Acadia, containing three arpents in front, and eighty-four arpents in depth, and bounded on the upper side by land of Jacques Roman, and on the lower by land of Abraham Rom.
It appears that the first depth of forty arpents of this land was inhabited and cultivated on the 20th December, 1803, and for more than ten consecutive years prior. So far the Board confirm the claim, but reject the second depth of forty-four arpents.

No. 336.—ALEXIS PERRET claims a tract of land, situate on the west side of the river Mississippi, in the county of Acadia, containing two arpents and three-fourths of an arpent in front, and eighty-four arpents in depth, and bounded on the upper side by land of Jacques Roman, and on the lower by land of Jacques Roman.
It appears that the first depth of forty arpents of this land was inhabited and cultivated on the 20th December, 1803, and for more than ten consecutive years next preceding. So far the Board confirm the claim, but reject the second depth of forty-four arpents.

No. 337.—DOMINIQUE LE BOEUF claims a tract of land, situate on the west side of the river Mississippi, in the county of Acadia, containing nine arpents in front, and eighty-four arpents in depth, and bounded on the upper side by land of Abraham Rom, and on the lower by land of Mr. Armant.
It appears that the first depth of forty arpents of this land was inhabited and cultivated on the 20th December, 1803, and that the same was continually inhabited and cultivated for more than ten years prior. So much of the claim the Board confirm, but reject the second depth of forty-four arpents.

No. 338.—ANASTASIA CORMICO, widow of Pierre Bourg, claims a tract of land, situate on the west side of the river Mississippi, in the county of Acadia, containing one arpent and two-thirds in front, and eighty-four arpents in depth, and bounded on the upper side by land of Mr. Armant, and on the lower by land of Jacques Roman.

It appears that the first depth of forty arpents of this land was inhabited and cultivated on the 20th December, 1803, and for more than ten consecutive years prior. So far the Board confirm the claim, but reject the second depth of forty-four arpents.

No. 339.—WILLIAM PRIESTLEY claims a tract of land, situate on the west side of the river Mississippi, in the county of Acadia, containing three arpents and one-third in front, and eighty-four arpents in depth, and bounded on the upper side by land of Paul David, and on the lower by land of Madame Bourg.

It appears that the first depth of forty arpents of the land now claimed was inhabited and cultivated on the 20th December, 1803, and that the same was continually inhabited and cultivated for more than ten consecutive years prior. So much of the claim the Board confirm, but reject the second depth of forty-four arpents.

No. 340.—PAUL DAVID claims a tract of land, situate on the west side of the river Mississippi, in the county of Acadia, containing two arpents in front, and eighty-four arpents in depth, and bounded on the upper side by land of Pierre Sionnaux, and on the lower by land of Mr. Armant.

It appears that the first forty arpents in depth of the land now claimed was inhabited and cultivated on the 20th December, 1803, and for more than ten consecutive years prior. So far the Board confirm the claim, but reject the second depth of forty-four arpents.

No. 341.—PAUL PERTUIT claims a tract of land, situate on the east side of the river Mississippi, in the county of Acadia, containing two arpents in front, and forty in depth, and bounded on the upper side by land of Jacques Graber, and on the lower by land of Joseph Caillet.

It appears that the claimant did actually inhabit and cultivate this land on the 20th December, 1803, and that the same was continually inhabited and cultivated by him, or those under whom he claims, for more than ten consecutive years next preceding. Confirmed.

No. 342.—JACQUES GRABER claims a tract of land, situate on the east side of the river Mississippi, in the county of Acadia, containing two arpents in front, and forty in depth, and bounded on the upper side by land of Charles Bertaut, and on the lower by land of Paul Pertuit.

It appears that the claimant did actually inhabit and cultivate this land on the 20th December, 1803, and that the same was continually inhabited and cultivated by him, or those under whom he claims, for more than ten consecutive years next preceding. Confirmed.

No. 343.—JOSEPH LANDRY claims a tract of land, situate on the west side of the river Mississippi, in the county of Acadia, containing six arpents and three feet in front, and forty arpents in depth, and bounded on the upper side by land of Zeno Pierre, and on the lower by land of Mr. Jones.

This is part of a tract of land of eleven arpents twenty-seven toises and two feet in front, with the depth of forty arpents, granted by Don Louis de Unzaga to Juan Chauvin, in the year 1775; under which grant the claimant holds, by virtue of successive sales. Confirmed.

No. 344.—JOSEPH MOLLERE claims a tract of land, situate on the west side of the river Mississippi, in the county of Iberville, containing thirteen arpents and nine toises in front, to nine and a half of which front arpents there is a depth of eighty arpents, and to the remaining three arpents and twenty-four toises front the ordinary depth of forty arpents; said tract being bounded on the upper side by land of Nicholas Orillon, and on the lower by land of Antoine Blanchard.

The claimant being in possession, and proprietor of nine arpents and a half front, and forty arpents in depth, at his request, was, by a written order of the Baron de Carondelet, in the year 1790, put in possession of the second depth of forty arpents. The balance of the tract of thirteen arpents and nine toises in front now claimed, being three arpents and twenty-four toises in front, on the ordinary depth of forty arpents, is a part of six arpents and twenty-four toises

front, on the ordinary depth, granted by Governor Unzaga, in the year 1774, to Pedro Priamo, which the claimant holds by purchase. Confirmed.

No. 347.—PIERRE OLIVIER claims a tract of land, situate on the west side of the river Mississippi, in the county of Acadia, containing five arpents in front, and forty in depth, and bounded on the upper side by land of William Billon, and on the lower by land of Louis Talgout.

It appears that the land now claimed was inhabited and cultivated on the 20th December, 1803, and that the same was continually inhabited and cultivated by the claimant, or those under whom he claims, for more than ten consecutive years next preceding. Confirmed.

No. 348.—THOMAS and DAVID URQUART claim a tract of land, situate on the east side of the river Mississippi, in the county of Acadia, containing nine arpents and twenty-seven toises in front, and forty arpents in depth, and bounded on the upper side by land of Pierre Proster, and on the lower by land of Oliver Breau.

It appears that the land now claimed was inhabited and cultivated on the 20th December, 1803, and that the same was continually inhabited and cultivated by those under whom the claimant holds for more than ten consecutive years next preceding. Confirmed.

No. 349.—ANTOINE MILIEU claims a tract of land, situate on the left bank of the bayou La Fourche, in the county of Acadia, containing seven arpents and twenty-three toises in front, and forty arpents in depth, and bounded on the upper side by land of Isabelle Bengard, on the lower by land of Mr. Seague.

It appears that the claimant did actually inhabit and cultivate the land now claimed on the 20th December, 1803, and that the same was continually inhabited and cultivated by him, or those under whom he claims, for more than ten consecutive years next preceding. Confirmed.

No. 350.—JEAN GRAVOIS claims a tract of land, situate on the west side of the river Mississippi, in the county of Acadia, containing four arpents and twenty-four toises in front, and forty arpents in depth, and bounded on the upper side by land of Francisco Andro, and on the lower by land of Nicholas Doblin.

This tract of land was regularly granted, in the year 1775, by Don Louis de Unzaga to Joseph Moran; and now held by the claimant under said grant, by virtue of successive sales. Confirmed.

No. 351.—JOSEPH DUHON claims a tract of land, situate on the west side of the river Mississippi, in the county of Acadia, containing three arpents in front, and forty in depth, and bounded on the upper side by land of Victor Blanchard, and on the lower by land of Messrs. Reynaud and Peytavin.

This is part of a tract of land of six arpents and six toises in front, on the ordinary depth, granted to Carlos Forest by Governor Unzaga, in the year 1775; under which grant the claimant holds, by virtue of successive sales. Confirmed.

No. 352.—PAUL LEBLANC claims a tract of land, situate on the west side of the river Mississippi, in the county of Acadia, containing two arpents in front, and forty in depth, and bounded on the upper side by land of Paul Forest, and on the lower by land of Joseph Duhon.

This is part of the tract mentioned in the last, No. 351, granted to Carlos Forest by Governor Unzaga, in the year 1775; under which grant the claimant holds the quantity here claimed, by virtue of successive sales. Confirmed.

No. 353.—FRANCISCO MATHIEU claims a tract of land, situate on the left bank of the bayou La Fourche, in the county of Acadia, containing four arpents six toises and three feet in front, and forty arpents in depth, and bounded on the upper side by land of Diego Gonzalez, and on the lower by land of Dominique Bourgeois.

It appears that the claimant did actually inhabit and cultivate the land now claimed on the 20th December, 1803, and that the same was continually inhabited and cultivated for more than ten consecutive years next preceding. Confirmed.

No. 354.—ANDRE VEGA claims a tract of land, situate on the left bank of the bayou La Fourche, in the county of Acadia, containing three arpents in front, and forty in depth, and bounded on the upper side by land of Antoine Misau, and on the lower by land of Barthole Hernandez.

It appears that the claimant did actually inhabit and cultivate the land now claimed on the 20th December, 1803, and that the same was continually inhabited and cultivated for more than ten consecutive years next preceding. Confirmed.

No. 355.—BARTHOLE HERNANDEZ claims a tract of land, situate on the left bank of the bayou La Fourche, containing three arpents in front, and forty in depth, and bounded on the upper side by land of André Vega, and on the lower by land of Antoine Bayau.

It appears that the land now claimed was inhabited and cultivated on the 20th December, 1803, and that the same was continually inhabited and cultivated by the claimant, or those under whom he claims, for more than ten consecutive years next preceding. Confirmed.

No. 356.—MICHEL HEBERT claims a tract of land, situate on the east side of the river Mississippi, in the county of Iberville, containing three arpents and eighteen toises in front, and forty arpents in depth, and bounded on the upper side by land of Juan Brand, and on the lower by land of Firmin Broussard.

This is part of a tract of land of five arpents and eighteen toises in front, on the ordinary depth, granted to Pedro Cloatre by Don Louis de Unzaga, in the year 1776 ; under which grant the claimant holds, by virtue of successive sales. Confirmed.

No. 357.—CHRISTOVAL FALCON claims a tract of land, situate on the right bank of the bayou La Fourche, in the county of Acadia, containing six arpents in front, and forty in depth, and bounded on the upper side by land of Thomas Dalbarado, and on the lower by land of Gaspar Falcon.

It appears that the land now claimed was inhabited and cultivated on the 20th December, 1803, and that the same was continually inhabited and cultivated by the claimant, or those under whom he claims, for more than ten consecutive years next preceding. Confirmed.

No. 358.—DOMINIQUE DESCAGUE claims a tract of land, situate on the left bank of the bayou La Fourche, in the county of Acadia, containing three arpents in front, and forty in depth, and bounded on the upper side by land of Antoine Miller, and on the lower side by land of Antoine Pevera.

It appears that the claimant did actually inhabit and cultivate the land now claimed on the 20th December, 1803, and that the same was continually inhabited and cultivated for more than ten consecutive years next preceding. Confirmed.

No. 359.—VICENTE RODRIGUES MORA claims a tract of land, situate on the right bank of the bayou La Fourche, in the county of Acadia, containing four arpents in front, and forty in depth, and bounded on the upper side by land of Dominique Cavalier, and on the lower by land of Dominique Serat.

It appears that the land now claimed was inhabited and cultivated on the 20th December, 1803, and that the same was continually inhabited and cultivated by the claimant, or those under whom he claims, for more than ten consecutive years next preceding. Confirmed.

No. 360.—ANTONIO PEVERA claims a tract of land, situate on the left bank of the bayou La Fourche, in the county of Acadia, containing three arpents in front, and forty in depth, and bounded on the upper side by land of Dominique Descague, and on the lower by land of Dominique Suares.

It appears that the land now claimed was inhabited and cultivated on the 20th December, 1803, and that the same was continually inhabited and cultivated by the claimant, or those under whom he claims, for more than ten consecutive years next preceding. Confirmed.

No. 361.—DOMINIQUE CAVALIER claims a tract of land, situate on the right bank of the bayou La Fourche, in the county of Acadia, containing two arpents in front, and forty in depth, and bounded on the upper side by land of Joseph Gonzalez, and on the lower by land of Vincente Rodrigues Mora.

It appears that the land now claimed was inhabited and cultivated on the 20th December, 1803, and that the same was continually inhabited and cultivated by the claimant, or those under whom he claims, for more than ten consecutive years next preceding. Confirmed.

No. 362.—JOSEPH GONZALEZ claims a tract of land, situate on the right bank of the bayou La Fourche, in the county of Acadia, containing three arpents in front, and forty in depth, and bounded on the upper side by land of Gaspar Falcon, and on the lower by land of the claimant.

It appears that the claimant did actually inhabit and cultivate the land now claimed on the 20th December, 1803, and that the same was continually inhabited and cultivated by him, or those under whom he claims, for more than ten consecutive years next preceding. Confirmed.

No. 363.—JOSEPH GONZALEZ claims a tract of land, situate on the right bank of the bayou La Fourche, in the county of Acadia, containing one arpent in front, and forty arpents in depth, and bounded on the upper side by land of the claimant, and on the lower by land of Dominique Cavalier.

It appears that the claimant did actually inhabit and cultivate the land now claimed on the 20th December, 1803, and that the same was continually inhabited and cultivated by him, or those under whom he claims, for more than ten consecutive years next preceding. Confirmed.

No. 364.—HYPOLITE BREAU claims a tract of land, situate on the west side of the river Mississippi, in the county of Acadia, containing four arpents eight toises four feet and four inches in front, and forty arpents in depth, and bounded on the upper side by land of Jean Baptiste Myr, and on the lower by land of Charles Frederick.

It appears that the claimant did actually inhabit and cultivate the land now claimed on the 20th December, 1803, and that the same was continually inhabited and cultivated by him, or those under whom he claims, for more than ten consecutive years next preceding. Confirmed.

No. 365.—CONSTANÇA BREAU, widow of Simonet Breau, claims a tract of land, situate on the west side of the river Mississippi, in the county of Acadia, containing four arpents eight toises four feet and four inches in front, and forty arpents in depth, and bounded on the upper side by land of Silvain Leblanc, and on the lower by land of Baptiste Myr.

It appears that the claimant did actually inhabit and cultivate the land now claimed on the 20th December, 1803, and that the same was continually inhabited and cultivated by her, or those under whom she claims, for more than ten consecutive years next preceding. Confirmed.

No. 366.—PAUL BOURGEOIS claims a tract of land, situate on the east side of the river Mississippi, in the county of Acadia, containing two arpents twenty-nine toises three feet and four inches in front, and forty arpents in depth, and bounded on the upper side by land of Baptiste Bourgeois, and on the lower by land of Joseph Michel.

It appears that the claimant did actually inhabit and cultivate the land now claimed on the 20th December, 1803, and that the same was continually inhabited and cultivated by him, or those under whom he claims, for more than ten consecutive years next preceding. Confirmed.

No. 367.—FRANÇOIS GALLAGHER claims a tract of land, situate on the west side of the river Mississippi, in the county of Iberville, containing three arpents in front, and forty in depth, and bounded on the upper side by land of Ferdinand Capdevielle, and on the lower by land of Alexandre McDougald.

It appears that the claimant did actually inhabit and cultivate the land now claimed on the 20th December, 1803, and that the same was continually inhabited and cultivated by him, or those under whom he claims, for more than ten consecutive years next preceding. Confirmed.

No. 368.—ALEXANDRE McDOUGALD claims a tract of land, situate on the west side of the river Mississippi, in the county of Iberville, containing three arpents in front, and forty in depth, and bounded on the upper side by land of François Gallaugher, and on the lower by land of Jean Baptiste Lorrié.

It appears that the land now claimed was inhabited and cultivated on the 20th December, 1803, and that the same was continually inhabited and cultivated by those under whom the claimant holds for more than ten consecutive years next preceding. Confirmed.

No. 369.—MICHEL DUGAS claims a tract of land, situate on the west side of the river Mississippi, in the county of Acadia, containing three arpents and twenty-seven toises in front, and such depth as extends to the line of division between the lands of the different sides of the point, and bounded on the upper side by land of Simon Leblanc, and on the lower by land of Mr. Raynaud.

It appears that this land was inhabited and cultivated on the 20th of December, 1803, and that the same was continually inhabited and cultivated by the claimant, or those under whom he claims, for more than ten consecutive years next preceding. Confirmed.

No. 370.—SIMONET LEBLANC claims a tract of land, situate on the west side of the river Mississippi, in the county of Acadia, containing two arpents thirteen toises and five feet in front, and such depth as extends to the line of division between the lands of the different sides of the point, and bounded on the upper side by land of Jean Gravois, and on the lower by land of Michel Dugas.

It appears that the land now claimed was inhabited and cultivated on the 20th of December, 1803, and that the same was continually inhabited and cultivated by the claimant, or those under whom he claims, for more than ten consecutive years next preceding. Confirmed.

No. 371.—JOHN COXE claims a tract of land, situate on the west side of the river Mississippi, in the county of Acadia, containing two arpents in front, and eighty arpents in depth, and bounded on the upper side by land of Michel Bergeron, and on the lower by land of Mathurin Bergeron.

It appears that the first forty arpents in depth of this land was inhabited and cultivated on the 20th of December, 1803, and for more than ten consecutive years next preceding. So far the Board confirm the claim, but reject the second depth of forty arpents.

No. 372.—JOSEPH LACROIX claims a tract of land, situate on the west side of the river Mississippi, in the county of Iberville, containing two arpents thirteen toises in front, and forty arpents in depth, and bounded on the upper side by land of Mr. Laurier, and on the lower by land of Pierre Lacroix.

It appears that the land now claimed was inhabited and cultivated on the 20th of December, 1803, and that the same was continually inhabited and cultivated by those under whom the claimant holds for more than ten consecutive years next preceding. Confirmed.

No. 373.—PIERRE LACROIX claims a tract of land, situate on the west side of the river Mississippi, in the county of Iberville, containing two arpents and thirteen toises in front, and forty arpents in depth, and bounded on the upper side by land of Joseph Lacroix, and on the lower by land of Joseph Mollere.

It appears that the land now claimed was inhabited and cultivated on the 20th of December, 1803, and that the same was continually inhabited and cultivated by those under whom the claimant holds for more than ten consecutive years next preceding. Confirmed.

No. 374.—PIERRE DUPUIS claims a tract of land, situate on the east side of the river Mississippi, in the county of Acadia, containing two arpents in front, and forty in depth, and bounded on the upper side by land of Marius Briugier, and on the lower by land of Thomas Terrio.

It appears that the claimant did actually inhabit and cultivate the land now claimed on the 20th of December, 1803, and that the same was continually inhabited and cultivated by him, or those under whom he claims, for more than ten consecutive years next preceding. Confirmed.

No. 375.—CHARLES and ETIENNE TERRIO claim a tract of land, situate on the east side of the river Mississippi, in the county of Acadia, containing five arpents in front, and forty in depth, and bounded on the upper side by land of Pierre Dupuy, and on the lower by land of the claimant.

This land was granted to Thomas Terrio by Don Louis de Unzaga, in the year 1774; the claimants now hold it by inheritance from their deceased father. Confirmed.

No. 376.—CHARLES and ETIENNE TERRIO claim a tract of land, situate on the east side of the river Mississippi, in the county of Acadia, containing four arpents in front, and forty in depth, and bounded on the upper

side by land of the claimants, and on the lower by land of Ambrose Terrio.

This land was granted to Francisco Terrio by Don Louis de Unzaga, in the year 1775; the present claimants hold by inheritance from their deceased father, Thomas Terrio, who held under the aforesaid grant by virtue of successive sales. Confirmed.

No. 377.—BAPTISTE MONTEL and JEAN LIGNAC claim a tract of land, situate on the east side of the river Mississippi, in the county of Acadia, containing six arpents and twenty toises in front, and forty arpents in depth, and bounded on the upper side by land of Joseph Martin, and on the lower by land of Mr. Gisme.

It appears that the claimant did actually inhabit and cultivate the land now claimed on the 20th of December, 1803, and that the same was continually inhabited and cultivated by them, or those under whom they claim, for more than ten consecutive years next preceding. Confirmed.

No. 378.—JEAN BAPTISTE LOUVIER claims a tract of land, situate on the east side of the river Mississippi, in the county of Acadia, containing two arpents in front, and forty in depth, and bounded on the upper side by land of Maclet Boura, and on the lower by land of Jacques Melanson.

It appears that the land now claimed was inhabited and cultivated on the 20th of December, 1803, and that the same was continually inhabited and cultivated by those under whom the claimant holds for more than ten consecutive years next preceding. Confirmed.

No. 379.—JOSEPH CORBO claims a tract of land, situate on the right bank of the bayou La Fourche, in the county of Acadia, containing three arpents in front, and forty in depth, and bounded on the upper side by land of Jean Lacoste, and on the lower by land of Maria Rodrigues.

It appears that the land now claimed was inhabited and cultivated on the 20th of December, 1803, and that the same was continually inhabited and cultivated for more than ten consecutive years next preceding. Confirmed.

No. 380.—JOSEPH CORBO claims a tract of land, situate on the right bank of the bayou La Fourche, in the county of Acadia, containing three arpents in front, and forty in depth, and bounded on the upper side by land of Diego Gomez, and on the lower by land of Jean Lacoste.

It appears that the land now claimed was inhabited and cultivated on the 20th of December, 1803, and that the same was continually inhabited and cultivated by the claimant, or those under whom he claims, for more than ten consecutive years next preceding. Confirmed.

No. 381.—JEAN LACOSTE claims a tract of land, situate on the right bank of the bayou La Fourche, in the county of Acadia, containing three arpents and eight toises in front, and forty arpents in depth, and bounded on the upper side by land of Joseph Corbo, and on the lower by land of Joseph Corbo.

It appears that the claimant did actually inhabit and cultivate the land now claimed on the 20th December, 1803, and that the same was continually inhabited and cultivated by him, or those under whom he claims, for more than ten consecutive years next preceding. Confirmed.

No. 382.—Madame MARIA RODRIGUES claims a tract of land, situate on the right bank of the bayou La Fourche, in the county of Acadia, containing two arpents and twenty-six toises in front, and forty arpents in depth, and bounded on the upper side by land of Joseph Corbo, and on the lower by land of Thomas Dalborado.

It appears that the claimant did actually inhabit and cultivate the land now claimed on the 20th December, 1803, and that the same was continually inhabited and cultivated by her, or those under whom she claims, for more than ten consecutive years next preceding. Confirmed.

No. 383.—FRANCISQUE DIEZ claims a tract of land, situate on the left bank of the bayou La Fourche, in the county of Acadia, containing one arpent in front, and forty in depth, and bounded on the upper side by land of Mr. Briugier, and on the lower by land of Isabelle Bengard.

It appears that the claimant did actually inhabit and cultivate the land now claimed on the 20th December,

1803, and that the same was continually inhabited and cultivated by him, or those under whom he claims, for more than ten consecutive years next preceding. Confirmed.

No. 384.—SIMON LANOUE claims a tract of land, situate on the east side of the river Mississippi, in the county of Acadia, containing four arpents in front, and forty in depth, and bounded on the upper side by land of Guillaume Canout, and on the lower by land of Baptiste Bourgeois.

It appears that the claimant did actually inhabit and cultivate the land now claimed on the 20th December, 1803, and that the same was continually inhabited and cultivated by him, or those under whom he claims, for more than ten consecutive years next preceding. Confirmed.

No. 385.—BAPTISTE BOURGEOIS claims a tract of land, situate on the east side of the river Mississippi, in the county of Acadia, containing four arpents in front, and forty in depth, and bounded on the upper side by land of Simon Lanoue, and on the lower by land of Edward Saunier.

It appears that the claimant did actually inhabit and cultivate the land now claimed on the 20th December, 1803, and that the same was continually inhabited and cultivated by him, or those under whom he claims, for more than ten consecutive years next preceding. Confirmed.

No. 386.—JOSEPH DAROZA claims a tract of land, situate on the east side of the river Mississippi, in the county of Acadia, containing one arpent in front, and forty arpents in depth, and bounded on the upper side by land of Mr. Blanchard, and on the lower by land of Mr. David.

It appears that the land now claimed was inhabited and cultivated on the 20th December, 1803, and that the same was continually inhabited and cultivated by those under whom the claimant holds for more than ten consecutive years next preceding. Confirmed.

No. 387.—AUGUSTIN MALLET, a free man of color, claims a tract of land, situate on the east side of the river Mississippi, in the county of Acadia, containing nine arpents in front, and forty in depth, and bounded on the upper side by land of Jean Baptiste Fata, and on the lower by land of Michel Verret.

This tract of land was granted in the year 1798 to Henrique Cline, by Don Manuel Gayoso, then Governor; under which grant the present claimant holds by regular deed of sale. Confirmed.

No. 388.—MARIE THERESE AUGUSTINE MALLET, a free woman of color, claims a tract of land, situate on the east side of the river Mississippi, in the county of Acadia, containing six arpents in front, and forty in depth, and bounded on the upper side by land of Mr. Fabre, and on the lower by land of Augustin Mallet.

It appears that the land now claimed was inhabited and cultivated on the 20th December, 1803, and that the same was continually inhabited and cultivated by those under whom the claimant holds for more than ten consecutive years next preceding. Confirmed.

No. 389.—JOSEPH DUGAS, Sen. claims a tract of land, situate on the east side of the river Mississippi, in the county of Acadia, containing five arpents and twenty-seven toises in front, and forty arpents in depth, and bounded on the upper side by land of Baptiste Melanson, and on the lower by land of Etelder Picou.

It appears that the claimant did actually inhabit and cultivate the land now claimed on the 20th December, 1803, and that the same was continually inhabited and cultivated for more than ten consecutive years next preceding. Confirmed.

No. 390.—JOSEPH DUGAS, Jun. claims a tract of land, situate on the east side of the river Mississippi, in the county of Acadia, containing two arpents and a half in front, and forty arpents in depth, and bounded on the upper side by land of Etelder Picou, and on the lower by land of Joseph Poirier.

It appears that the land now claimed was inhabited and cultivated on the 20th December, 1803, and that the same was continually inhabited and cultivated by those under whom the claimant holds, for more than ten consecutive years next preceding. Confirmed.

No. 393.—NOEL MATERNE claims a tract of land, situate on the east side of the river Mississippi, in the

county of Acadia, containing two arpents and twenty-six toises in front, and forty arpents in depth, and bounded on the upper side by land of Pierre Michel, and on the lower by land of Mr. Clay.

It appears that the claimant did actually inhabit and cultivate the land now claimed on the 20th December, 1803, and that the same was continually inhabited and cultivated by him, or those under whom he claims, for more than ten consecutive years next preceding. Confirmed.

No. 394.—SILVAIN LEBLANC claims a tract of land, situate on the west side of the river Mississippi. in the county of Acadia, containing three arpents fifteen toises one foot and nine inches in front, and forty arpents in depth, and bounded on the upper side by land of Jean Dugas, and on the lower by land of Simon Breau.

It appears that the land now claimed was inhabited and cultivated on the 20th December, 1803, and that the same was continually inhabited and cultivated by those under whom the claimant holds for more than ten consecutive years next preceding. Confirmed.

No. 395.—CHARLES BERTRAND claims a tract of land, situate on the east side of the river Mississippi, in the county of Acadia, containing four arpents and eighteen toises in front, and forty arpents in depth, and bounded on the upper side by land of Joseph Landry, and on the lower by land of Paul Pertuit.

It appears that the land now claimed was inhabited and cultivated on the 20th December, 1803, and that the same was inhabited and cultivated by the claimant, or those under whom he claims, for more than ten consecutive years next preceding. Confirmed.

No. 396.—MICHEL BREAUX claims a tract of land, situate on the east side of the river Mississippi, in the county of Acadia, containing twelve arpents in front, and forty in depth, and bounded on the upper side by land of Mr. Roussin, and on the lower by land of Mr. Judice.

It appears that the claimant did actually inhabit and cultivate the land now claimed on the 20th December, 1803, and that the same was continually inhabited and cultivated by him, or those under whom he claims, for more than ten consecutive years next preceding. Confirmed.

No. 397.—MARIANNE LEBLANC, widow of Firmin Landry, claims a tract of land, situate on the west side of the river Mississippi, in the county of Acadia, containing four arpents in front, and forty in depth, and bounded on the upper side by land of Augustin Broussard, and on the lower by land of Joseph Boudreau.

It appears that the land now claimed was inhabited and cultivated on the 20th December, 1803, and that the same was continually inhabited and cultivated by those under whom the claimant holds for more than ten consecutive years next preceding. Confirmed.

No. 398.—FREDERICK BLANCHARD claims a tract of land, situate on the east side of the river Mississippi, in the county of Acadia, containing three and a half arpents in front, and forty in depth, and bounded on one side by land of Philip Coussat.

This tract of land is a part of six arpents front, on the usual depth, surveyed by Don Carlos Trudeau, Surveyor general, in the year 1790, in favor of Joseph Paul, under whose title the claimant holds by successive sales; it appearing that the said land has continued to be inhabited and cultivated since the time of making the survey. Confirmed.

No. 399.—BENJAMIN MYR and JOSEPH PART claim a tract of land, situate on the east side of the river Mississippi, in the county of Acadia, containing five arpents in front, and forty in depth, and bounded on the upper side by land of Pedro Bernard, and on the lower by land of Francisco Par.

This land was surveyed by Don Carlos Trudeau, in the year 1782, in favor of Joseph Arcenaux, under whose title the claimants hold by virtue of successive sales; the land having been inhabited and cultivated ever since the time of making the survey. Confirmed.

No. 400.—JEAN ARCENAUX and LOUIS GAUDIN claim a tract of land, situate on the east side of the river Mississippi, in the county of Acadia, containing five arpents in front, and forty in depth, and bounded on the upper side by land of Olivier Par, and on the lower by land of Pedro Par.

This land was surveyed by Don Carlos Trudeau, in the year 1782, in favor of Joseph Richard, under whose title the claimants hold by virtue of successive sales; the land having been inhabited and cultivated ever since the time of making the survey. Confirmed.

No. 401.—JEAN BAPTISTE DOUCET claims a tract of land, situate on the west side of the river Mississippi, in the county of Iberville, containing seven superficial arpents, and eighty-three hundredths of an arpent, and bounded on the upper side by land of Olivier Arnandez, and on the lower by land of James Goodby.
The claimant was put in possession of this tract of land in conformity with an order of the Baron de Carondelet, dated in the year 1792, and has, since that period, continued to inhabit and cultivate the same. Confirmed.

No. 402.—JEAN BAPTISTE DOUCET claims a tract of land, situate on the west side of the river Mississippi, in the county of Iberville, containing six arpents in front, and forty in depth, and bounded on the upper side by land of Hubarto Jany, and on the lower by land of Vincente Depino.
This tract of land was surveyed in the year 1772, in favor of Blas Brasseux, who obtained a complete grant for the same in 1774, from Governor Unzaga; under which grants the claimant holds by deed from the grantee. Confirmed.

No. 403.—FELIX and CHARLES VINCENT claim a tract of land, situate on the east side of the river Mississippi, n the county of Acadia, containing four arpents in front and forty in depth, and bounded on the lower side by land of Alexis Rom, and on the upper by land of Augustin Foutuo.
This is part of seven arpents and twenty-five toises in front, on the ordinary depth, surveyed in the year 1782, in favor of the widow Vincent, under which title the claimants hold by inheritance; the land having been inhabited and cultivated ever since the making of the survey. Confirmed.

No. 404.—GEORGE MOUTON claims a tract of land, situate on the east side of the river Mississippi, in the county of Acadia, containing two arpents eleven toises and four feet in front, and forty arpents in depth, and bounded on the upper side by land of Alexis Rom, and on the lower by land of Joseph Theriot.
This is part of the land surveyed for the widow Vincent, mentioned in the last, No. 403, under which title the claimant holds by purchase; the land having been inhabited and cultivated ever since the year 1782. Confirmed.

No. 405.—JOSEPH NICHOLAS LANDRY claims a tract of land, situate on the west side of the river Mississippi, in the county of Acadia, containing one arpent in front, and forty arpents in depth, and bounded on the upper side by land of Louis Mollere, and on the lower by land of Louis Dannequin.
It appears that the claimant did actually inhabit and cultivate the land now claimed on the 20th December, 1803, and that the same was continually inhabited and cultivated by him, or those under whom he claims, for more than ten consecutive years next preceding. Confirmed.

No. 406.—JOSEPH HEBERT claims a tract of land, situate on the west side of the river Mississippi, in the county of Iberville, containing six arpents in front, and forty in depth, and bounded on the upper side by land of Blas Brasseux, and on the lower by land of Antoine Bernard Danterve.
This land was surveyed in the year 1772, in favor of Vincente Delpino, who obtained a complete grant for the same in the year 1774, from Don Louis de Unzaga; under which grant the claimant holds by purchase. Confirmed.

No. 407.—JOSEPH HEBERT claims a tract of land, situate on the west side of the river Mississippi, in the county of Iberville, containing eight arpents in front, and forty in depth, and bounded on the upper side by land of Joseph and Jacques Arnandez, and on the lower by land of James Goodby.
It appears that the claimant did actually inhabit and cultivate the land now claimed on the 20th December, 1803, and that the same was continually inhabited and cultivated by him, or those under whom he claims, for more than ten consecutive years next preceding. Confirmed.

No. 408.—JOSEPH PARVIE claims a tract of land, situate on the east side of the river Mississippi, in the county of Acadia, containing one arpent and a half in front, and forty arpents in depth, and bounded on the upper side by land of Antoine Robo, and on the lower by land of Jean Klings.
It appears that the claimant did actually inhabit and cultivate the land now claimed on the 20th December, 1803, and that the same was continually inhabited and cultivated by him, or those under whom he claims, for more than ten consecutive years next preceding. Confirmed.

No. 409.—ANTOINE ROBO claims a tract of land situate on the east side of the river Mississippi, in the county of Acadia, containing one arpent and a half in front, and forty arpents in depth, and bounded on the upper side by land of Douat Hebert, and on the lower by land of Joseph Parvie.
It appears that the land now claimed was inhabited and cultivated on the 20th December, 1803, and that the same was continually inhabited and cultivated by those under whom the claimant holds for more than ten consecutive years next preceding. Confirmed.

No. 410.—AUGUSTIN LANDRY claims a tract of land, situate on the east side of the river Mississippi, in the county of Acadia, containing three arpents in front, and forty in depth, and bounded on the upper side by land of Simon Dupuis, and on the lower by land of Michel Judice.
It appears that the claimant did actually inhabit and cultivate the land now claimed on the 20th December, 1803, and that the same was continually inhabited and cultivated by him, or those under whom he claims, for more than ten consecutive years next preceding. Confirmed.

No. 411.—SILVESTRE JUDICE claims a tract of land, situate on the east side of the river Mississippi, in the county of Acadia, containing two arpents in front and forty in depth, and bounded on the upper side by land of Michel Judice, and on the lower by land of Jean Cline.
It appears that the claimant did actually inhabit and cultivate the land now claimed on the 20th December, 1803, and that the same was continually inhabited and cultivated by him, or those under whom he claims, for more than ten consecutive years next preceding. Confirmed.

No. 412.—JACQUES HEBERT claims a tract of land, situate on the east side of the river Mississippi in the county of Acadia. containing two arpents in front, and forty in depth, and bounded on the upper side by land of Madame Olivier, and on the lower by land of Michel Brand.
It appears that the claimant did actually inhabit and cultivate the land on the 20th December, 1803, and that the same was continually inhabited and cultivated by him, or those under whom he claims. for more than ten consecutive years next preceding. Confirmed.

No. 413.—SIMON DUPUY claims a tract of land, situate on the east side of the river Mississippi, in the county of Acadia, containing three arpents three toises and two feet in front, and forty arpents in depth, and bounded on the upper side by land of Jacques Hebert, and on the lower by land of Augustin Landry.
It appears that the claimant did actually inhabit and cultivate the land now claimed on the 20th December, 1803, and that the same was continually inhabited and cultivated by him, or those under whom he claims, for more than ten consecutive years next preceding. Confirmed.

No. 414.—HENRY HOUVRE claims a tract of land, situate on the east side of the river Mississippi, in the county of Acadia, containing four arpents in front, and forty in depth, and bounded on the upper side by land of Jean David, and on the lower by land of Joseph Bourg.
It appears that the claimant did actually inhabit and cultivate the land now claimed on the 20th December, 1803, and that the same was continually inhabited and cultivated for more than ten consecutive years next preceding. Confirmed.

No. 415.—GABRIEL ARCENAUX claims a tract of land situate on the west side of the river Mississippi, in the county of Acadia, containing four arpents in front, and forty in depth, and bounded on the upper side by land of Aaron Heins, and on the lower by land of Jean Poirié.

This is part of a tract of seven arpents fourteen toises and six inches front, on the ordinary depth, surveyed in the year 1782, in favor of Carlos Thibodeau, from whom the claimant purchased, the land having been inhabited and cultivated ever since the above period. Confirmed.

No. 416.—AUGUSTIN BROUSSARD claims a tract of land, situate on the west side of the river Mississippi, in the county of Acadia, containing four arpents in front, and forty in depth, and bounded on the upper side by land of Joseph Landry, and on the lower by land of Marie Leblanc.

It appears that the land now claimed was inhabited and cultivated on the 20th December, 1803, and that the same was continually inhabited and cultivated by those under whom the claimant holds for more than ten consecutive years next preceding. Confirmed.

No. 417.—Madame HYACINTE LANDRY claims a tract of land, situate on the west side of the river Mississippi, in the county of Acadia, containing five arpents and one-third in front, and forty arpents in depth, and bounded on the upper side by land of Jerome Melanson, and on the lower by land of Richard Leblanc.

It appears that the claimant did actually inhabit and cultivate the land now claimed on the 20th December, 1803, and that the same was continually inhabited and cultivated by her, or those under whom she claims for more than ten consecutive years next preceding. Confirmed.

No. 418.—NATHAN MITCHELL for his daughter Priscilla Mitchell, a minor, claims a tract of land, situate on the west side of the river Mississippi, in the county of Iberville, containing five arpents in front, and forty in depth, and bounded on the upper side by land of Hypolite and Joseph Landry, and on the lower by land of James Goodby.

It appears that the land now claimed was inhabited and cultivated on the 20th December, 1803, and that the same was continually inhabited and cultivated by those under whom the claimant holds for more than ten consecutive years next preceding. Confirmed.

No. 419.—JEAN BAPTISTE ALLAIN claims a tract of land, situated on the east side of the river Mississippi, in the county of Iberville, containing four arpents and fourteen toises in front, and forty arpents in depth, and bounded on the upper side by land of Edmond Capdevielle, and on the lower by land of Simon Leblanc.

It appears that the claimant did actually inhabit and cultivate the land now claimed on the 20th December, 1803, and that the same was continually inhabited and cultivated by him, or those under whom he claims, for more than ten consecutive years next preceding. Confirmed.

No. 420.—JEAN BAPTISTE MYR claims a tract of land, situate on the west side of the river Mississippi, in the county of Acadia, containing four arpents eight toises four feet and four inches in front, and forty arpents in depth, and bounded on the upper side by land of Simonet Breau, and on the lower by land of Polite Breau.

It appears that the claimant did actually inhabit and cultivate the land now claimed on the 20th December, 1803, and that the same was continually inhabited and cultivated by him, or those under whom he claims, for more than ten consecutive years next preceding. Confirmed.

No. 421.—PIERRE and ALPHONSO PERRKT claim a tract of land, situate on the west side of the river Mississippi, in the county of Acadia, containing nine arpents and twenty-five toises in front, and of a depth extending to a particular lake, and bounded on the upper side by land of Basile Leclair, and on the lower by land of the claimants.

It appears that this tract of land was inhabited and cultivated on the 20th December, 1803, and for more than ten consecutive years next preceding. The Board confirm the claim to the extent of forty arpents in depth. The claimants pretend that this tract is part of a larger tract granted by the French Government to one Nicholas Verret, to run back from the river as far as land could be found, and that the records have been consumed by fire, and the title-papers destroyed; but the

Board having no evidence of the grant under which they claim, they reject so much of the claim as exceeds the usual depth of forty arpents.

No. 422.—PIERRE and ALPHONSO PERRET claim a tract of land, situate on the west side of the river Mississippi, in the county of Acadia, containing four arpents and twenty-four toises in front, and of a depth extending back to a particular lake, and bounded on the upper side by land of the claimants, and on the lower by land of Evariste Villiavasse.

It appears that this tract of land was inhabited and cultivated on the 20th December, 1803, and for more than ten consecutive years next preceding. The Board confirm the claim to the extent of forty arpents in depth, but reject so much as exceeds the depth of forty arpents, as in the preceding number; it being part of the grant then mentioned.

No. 423.—EVARISTE VILLIAVASE claims a tract of land, situate on the west side of the river Mississippi, in the county of Acadia, containing five arpents in front, and of a depth extending back to a particular lake, and bounded on the upper side by land of Pierre and Alphonso Perret.

It appears that this tract of land was inhabited and cultivated on the 20th December, 1803, and for more than ten consecutive years next preceding. The Board confirm the claim to the extent of forty arpents in depth, but reject so much as exceeds that depth; the land being part of the grant to Nicholas Verret, mentioned in No. 421.

No. 424.—VALENTIN LANDRY claims a tract of land, situate on the west side of the river Mississippi, in the county of Acadia, containing two arpents eight toises and one foot in front, and eighty arpents in depth, and bounded on the upper side, by land of Simon Bourgeois, and on the lower by land of Joseph Landry.

It appears that the first depth of this land was inhabited and cultivated on the 20th December, 1803, and for more than ten consecutive years prior thereto. So much the Board confirm, but reject the claim to the second depth of forty arpents.

No. 425.—SIMON BOURGEOIS claims a tract of land, situate on the west side of the river Mississippi, in the county of Acadia, containing two arpents in front, and eighty in depth, and bounded on the upper side by land of Baptiste Drouilly, and on the lower by land of Valentin Landry.

It appears that the first depth of this land was inhabited and cultivated on the 20th December, 1803, and for more than ten consecutive years next preceding. So much the Board confirm, but reject the claim to the second depth of forty arpents.

No. 426.—JOSEPH ARCENAUX, Sen. claims a tract of land, situate on the west side of the river Mississippi, in the county of Acadia, containing three arpents two toises and three feet in front, and eighty arpents in depth, and bounded on the upper side by land of Jerome Godet, and on the lower by land of Joseph Arcenaux, Jun.

It appears that the first depth of this land was inhabited and cultivated on the 20th December, 1803, and for more than ten consecutive years next preceding. The Board confirm the claim to the extent of forty arpents in depth, but reject the second depth of forty arpents.

No. 427.—JOSEPH ARCENAUX, Jun. claims a tract of land, situate on the west side of the river Mississippi, in the county of Acadia, containing four arpents three toises and one foot in front, and eighty arpents in depth, and bounded on the upper side by land of Joseph Arcenaux, Sen., and on the lower by land of Henry Landry.

It appears that the first depth of this land was inhabited and cultivated on the 20th December, 1803, and for more than ten consecutive years next preceding. So much the Board confirm, but reject the claim to the second depth of forty arpents.

No. 428.—BENJAMIN LEBLANC claims a tract of land, situate on the west side of the river Mississippi, in the county of Acadia, containing two arpents and twenty-five toises in front, and forty arpents in depth, and bounded on the lower side by land of Pedro Blanchard.

This is part of a tract of land of eight arpents and twenty-five toises in front, on the ordinary depth, and veyed in the year 1771 in favor of Simon Leblanc, who obtained a complete grant for the same in 1774 from Don Louis de Unzaga; under which grant the claimant holds by regular deeds. Confirmed.

No. 429.—ALEXANDRE Mc. DOUGALD claims a tract of land, situate on the east side of the river Mississippi, in the county of Iberville, containing thirty-six superficial arpents and sixty-hundredths, and bounded on the upper side by land of Desily Babin, and on the lower by land of Pierre Bassett.

It appears that the land now claimed was inhabited and cultivated on the 20th December, 1803, and that the same was continually inhabited and cultivated by those under whom the claimant holds for more than ten consecutive years next preceding. Confirmed.

No. 430.—LUC GAUDIN, BONAVENTURE GAUDIN, Jun., and BAPTISTE MELANSON, claim a tract of land, situate on the east side of the river Mississippi, in the county of Acadia, containing five arpents and fourteen toises in front, and forty arpents in depth, and bounded on the upper side by land of Juan Arcenaux, and on the lower by land of Iago Dugast.

This land was surveyed by Don Carlos Trudeau, in the year 1782, in favor of Batista Bonaventura, under whose title the claimants hold by virtue of successive sales; the land having been inhabited and cultivated ever since the time of making the survey. Confirmed.

No. 431.—JOSEPH BOURGEOIS claims a tract of land, situate on the east side of the river Mississippi, in the county of Acadia, containing one arpent and twenty-five toises in front, and forty arpents in depth, and bounded on the upper side by land of Baptiste Bernard, and on the lower by land of Louis Breau.

It appears that the claimant did actually inhabit and cultivate the land now claimed on the 20th December, 1803, and that the same was continually inhabited and cultivated by him, or those under whom he claims, for more than ten consecutive years next preceding. Confirmed.

No. 432.—JEAN KLINGS claims a tract of land, situate on the east side of the river Mississippi, in the county of Acadia, containing one arpent in front, and forty in depth, and bounded on the upper side by land of Joseph Pavie, and on the lower by land of Firmin Dupuy.

It appears that the land now claimed was inhabited and cultivated on the 20th December, 1803, and that the same was continually inhabited and cultivated by the claimant, or those under whom he holds, for more than ten consecutive years next preceding. Confirmed.

No. 433.—JEAN BAPTISTE CHIASSON claims a tract of land, situate on the east side of the river Mississippi, in the county of Acadia, containing six arpents six toises and three feet in front, and forty arpents in depth, and bounded on the upper side by land of Abraham Arcenaux, and on the lower by land of Jean Baptiste Gaudin.

It appears that the land now claimed was inhabited and cultivated on the 20th December, 1803, and that the same was continually inhabited and cultivated by the claimant, or those under whom he holds, for more than ten consecutive years next preceding. Confirmed.

No. 434.—AUGUSTIN MALLET, Jun., a free man of color, claims a tract of land, situate on the east side of the river Mississippi, in the county of Acadia, containing four arpents in front, and forty in depth, and bounded on the upper side by land of Augustin Mallet, Sen., and on the lower by land of Mr. Dejean.

It appears that the land now claimed was inhabited and cultivated on the 20th December, 1803, and that the same was continually inhabited and cultivated by the claimant, or those under whom he claims, for more than ten consecutive years next preceding. Confirmed.

No. 435.—CHEVALIER MELARCHER claims the following tracts of land, viz: the first, situate on the east side of the river Mississippi, in the county of Acadia, containing five arpents and one toise in front, and forty arpents in depth, and bounded on the upper side by land of Madame Michel Migot, and on the lower by land of Louis Gaudin; and the second tract, situate on the east side of the river Mississippi, in the county of Acadia, containing two arpents twenty-four toises and four feet in front, and forty arpents in depth, and bounded on the upper side by land of Benjamin Myr, and on the lower by land of Madame Michel Migot.

It appears that the land now claimed was inhabited and cultivated on the 20th December, 1803, and that the same was continually inhabited and cultivated for more than ten consecutive years prior, by those under whom the claimant holds. Confirmed.

No. 436.—MICHEL DORADOU BRIUGIER claims a tract of land, situate on the east side of the river Mississippi, in the county of Acadia, containing twenty arpents in front, and forty in depth, and bounded on the lower side by land of Firmin Broussard.

This land was regularly granted to Gregorio French, in the year 1775, by Don Louis de Unzaga, then Governor; under which grant the claimant holds by virtue of successive sales. Confirmed.

No. 437.—Mr. MERCIER claims a tract of land, situate on the east side of the river Mississippi, in the county of Acadia, containing thirteen arpents and three-fourths in front, and forty arpents in depth, and bounded on the upper side by land of Joseph Leblanc, and on the lower by land of John Wederstrand.

Gil Leblanc, having improved the tract of land now claimed, petitioned and obtained from Governor Gayoso, in the year 1798, a regular warrant of survey, under which title the present claimant holds by regular deeds. It also appears that said land was inhabited and cultivated on the 20th December, 1803, and for more than ten consecutive years next preceding. Confirmed.

No. 438.—PIERRE LANOIX claims a tract of land, situate on the east side of the river Mississippi, in the county of Acadia, containing two arpents five toises and five feet in front, and eighty arpents in depth, and bounded on the upper side by land of François Pochet, and on the lower by land of Mathieu Brignac.

It appears that the first depth of forty arpents of this land was inhabited and cultivated on the 20th December, 1803, and for more than ten consecutive years prior. So far the Board confirm, but reject the claim to the second depth of forty arpents.

No. 439.—MAGDELAINE BABIN, widow of Anselme Leblanc, claims a tract of land, situate on the west side of the river Mississippi, in the county of Acadia, containing eight arpents and eight toises in front, and forty arpents in depth, and bounded on the upper side by land of Madame Etienne Leblanc, and on the lower by land of Madame Pierre Landry.

It appears that the claimant did actually inhabit and cultivate the land now claimed on the 20th December, 1803, and that the same was continually inhabited and cultivated by her, or those under whom she claims, for more than ten consecutive years next preceding. Confirmed.

No. 440.—OZITTE LEBLANC, widow of Etienne Leblanc, claims a tract of land, situate on the west side of the river Mississippi, in the county of Acadia, containing four arpents in front, and forty in depth, and bounded on the upper side by land of Madame Hyacinte Landry, and on the lower by land of Madame Anselme Leblanc.

It appears that the claimant did actually inhabit and cultivate the land now claimed on the 20th December, 1803, and that the same was continually inhabited and cultivated by her, or those under whom she claims, for more than ten consecutive years next preceding. Confirmed.

No. 442.—RICHARD FOWLER claims a tract of land, situate on the west side of the river Mississippi, in the county of Acadia, containing twenty-one arpents and twenty-four toises in front, of which three arpents and fourteen toises have the ordinary depth of forty arpents, and the remaining eighteen arpents and ten toises have a depth of eighty arpents; and said tract of land being bounded on the upper side by land of Mr. Cantrelle, and on the lower by land of Gabriel Arcenaux.

It appears that the first depth of forty arpents of the land now claimed was inhabited and cultivated on the 20th December, 1803, and for more than ten consecutive years prior. So far the Board confirm, but reject the claim to the second depth.

No. 443.—MARGUERITE POIRIER, widow of Charles Hebert, claims a tract of land, situate on the east side of the river Mississippi, in the county of Acadia, containing five arpents in front, and forty in depth, and bounded on the upper side by land of Francisco Terrio, and on the lower by land of Estevan Melanson.

This tract of land was surveyed in the year 1782, in favor of Ambrosio Terrio, by Carlos Trudeau, Surveyor General, who put him at the same time in possession; to which title the present claimant has succeeded by regular deeds. It also appears that said land has been inhabited and cultivated ever since the making of the survey. Confirmed.

No. 444.—L. H. Gurlain, as agent for the "Eastern Shore of Maryland Louisiana Company," claims a tract of land, situate on the east side of the river Mississippi, in the county of Acadia, containing ten arpents and seven toises in front, and a depth extending back to the lake Maurepas, and bounded on the one side by land of J. Macdonough and Sheperd Brown, and on the other by land of Antoine Trigle.

It appearing to the satisfaction of the Board that this tract of land was inhabited and cultivated on the 20th December, 1803, and for more than ten consecutive years next preceding, the Board confirm the title to the extent of forty arpents in depth, and reject the claim to the balance.

No. 16.—Genezi Roussin claims a tract of land, situate on the east side of the river Mississippi, in the county of Acadia, containing six and a half arpents in front, and forty arpents in depth, and bounded on the upper side by land of Mr. Renio, and on the lower by land of Michel Braux.

It appears that the claimant did actually inhabit and cultivate the land now claimed on the 20th December, 1803, and that the same was continually inhabited and cultivated by him, or those under whom he claims, for more than ten consecutive years next preceding. Confirmed.

No. 292.—Edmond Capdevielle claims a tract of land, situate on the west side of the river Mississippi, in the county of Iberville, and containing two arpents twenty-seven toises and two feet in front, and forty arpents in depth, and bounded on the upper side by land of Jean Holl, and on the lower by land of Alexandre Hebert.

It appears that the claimant did actually inhabit and cultivate the land now claimed on the 20th December, 1803, and that the same was continually inhabited and cultivated by him, or those under whom he claims, for more than ten consecutive years next preceding.

No. 391.—Isidore Blanchard claims, for the parish church of the parish of Ascension, a tract of land, situate on the west side of the river Mississippi, in the county of Acadia, containing four arpents one toise and four feet in front, and forty arpents in depth, and bounded on the upper side by land of William Conway, and on the lower by land of Jean Vessier.

There is no written evidence of title to the land claimed: the church is built upon it, and it has been used as a glebe for a great number of years, and is claimed by the people of the parish, as belonging to them, for the use of the church. The Board are of opinion it ought to be confirmed.

No. 392.—Augustin Dominique Tureaud claims, for the church of the parish of St. Jacques, a tract of land, situate on the west side of the river Mississippi, in the county of Acadia, containing four arpents and four toises in front, and forty arpents in depth, and bounded on the upper side by land of Patrice Urielle, and on the lower by land of Mr. Poëyfarré.

There is no written evidence of the title to the land claimed; the church is built upon it, and it has been used as a glebe for a great number of years, and is claimed by the people of the parish, as belonging to them, for the use of the church. The Board are of opinion it ought to be confirmed.

P. GRYMEZ, R. E. D. Orl. Ter.
JOSHUA LEWIS.
THOS. B. ROBERTSON.

Rejected claims from the books of Michel Cantrelle, Deputy Register of the county of Acadia and part of the county of Iberville.

No. 93.—Hubert Remy claims a second concession of forty arpents in depth, lying immediately back of a front or first concession, which we have already confirmed to him in page 266, No. 93, among the confirmed claims.

This claim to a second depth is founded solely upon a petition (*requête*) to Governor Salcedo, in the year

1803, with the commandant's certificate that the land was vacant, and might be granted without prejudice, &c. Had the Governor even a right at that period to grant the land, he has never acted upon the petition, nor does it appear that it has ever been presented to him. We are of opinion that this claim to a second concession ought not to be confirmed under any law, custom, or usage of the Spanish Government, and do therefore reject it.

No. 101.—Benjamin Babin claims a second depth of forty arpents, lying immediately back of a front or first depth, which we have already confirmed to him in No. 101. page 267, among the confirmed claims.

The claimant has no other foundation for his title to this second depth than having occupied the front and first depth, and having occasionally supplied himself with timber from this second depth. According to the laws, customs, and usages of the Spanish Government, no front proprietor, by any act of his own, could acquire a right to lands further back than the ordinary depth of forty arpents; and although the Spanish Government has invariably refused to grant the second depth to any other than the front proprietor, yet nothing short of a grant or warrant of survey from the Governor could confer a title or right to the land; we therefore reject the claim.

No. 140.—Guillaume Arcenaux claims a second depth of forty arpents, lying immediately back of a first depth of two arpents twelve toises and one foot front, being part of a larger front, which we have already confirmed to him in page 271, No. 140, among the confirmed claims.

The claimant produces no manner of evidence whatever in support of his claim to this second depth. He merely states, in his notice, that his title to the part of this land, to which this additional depth is claimed, is founded upon a grant for the same in favor of Louis Andry, from whom, by different intermediate conveyances, it passed to the claimant's father, who made a donation of it to the claimant. No grant or title from the Government in favor of said Andry is exhibited, nor any evidence that such grant or title did ever exist. We are therefore of opinion that his claim to this second depth ought to be rejected.

No. 159.—Michel Poirie claims a second depth of forty arpents, lying immediately back of a first depth, which we have confirmed to him in page 272, No. 159, among the confirmed claims.

This claim to a second depth is of a similar nature to the preceding: there appears in support of it only the bare statement of the claimant, in his notice, that it is part of a tract for which there was a grant of the first and second depth, in favor of Louis Andry, from whom his title is derived. No grant or title from the Government is exhibited, nor is there any evidence whatever to substantiate the claimant's statement. We are therefore of opinion that his claim to this second depth ought to be rejected.

No. 200.—Simon Gotereau claims a second concession, lying immediately back of a front or first concession, which we have already confirmed to him in page 276, No. 200, among the confirmed claims.

This claim to a second depth is founded solely upon a petition (*requête*) to the Governor of the province, in the year 1798, with the commandant's certificate that the land was vacant, and might be granted without prejudice, &c. It does not appear that the petition was ever acted upon by the Governor, or that it was ever presented to him. We are of opinion that this claim to a second concession ought not to be confirmed under any law, usage, or custom of the Spanish Government, and do therefore reject it.

No. 201.—Raphael Gotereau claims a second concession, lying immediately back of a front or first concession, which we have already confirmed to him in page 276, No. 201, among the confirmed claims.

This second depth, together with the first depth of forty arpents, was conveyed, in the year 1804, to the claimant by Simon Gotereau, his father, and composes part of the land petitioned for in the year 1798 by him, as stated in the preceding claim; and for the reasons there assigned, we are of opinion that this claim ought to be rejected.

No. 202.—Joseph Gotereau claims a second concession, lying immediately back of a front or first concession, which we have already confirmed to him in page 276, No. 202, among the confirmed claims.

This second depth, together with the first depth of forty arpents, was conveyed in the year 1805 to the claimant by Simon Gotereau, his father, and composes part of the land petitioned for in the year 1798, by him, as stated in claim No. 200; and for the reasons there assigned, we are of opinion that this claim ought to be rejected.

No. 216.—PIERRE BERTRAND claims a second concession of forty arpents, lying immediately back of a front or first concession, which we have already confirmed to him in page 277, No. 216, among the confirmed claims.

This claim to a second depth is founded solely upon a petition (requête) to the Governor of the province, in the year 1791, with the commandant's certificate that the land was vacant, and might be granted without prejudice, &c. It does not appear that the petition was ever acted upon by the Governor, or that it was ever presented to him. We are of opinion that this claim ought not to be confirmed under any law, custom or usage of the Spanish Government, and do therefore reject it.

No. 222.—MARIE FOREST, widow of Jean Baptiste Bergeron, claims a second depth of forty arpents, lying immediately behind a first depth, which we have already confirmed to her in page 278, No. 222, among the confirmed claims.

The claimant has no other foundation for her title to this second depth than having occupied the front and first depth, and having occasionally supplied herself with timber from this second depth. According to the laws, customs, and usages of the Spanish Government, no front proprietor, by any act of his own, could acquire a right to lands further back than the ordinary depth of forty arpents; and although the Spanish Government has invariably refused to grant the second depth to any other than the front proprietor, yet nothing short of a grant or warrant of survey from the Governor could confer a title or right to the land. We do therefore reject the claim.

No. 223.—HENRY LANDRY claims a second depth of forty arpents, lying immediately back of a first depth, which we have already confirmed to him in page 278, No. 223, among the confirmed claims.

This claim to a second depth is in every respect similarly situated to that in the preceding number, being founded solely upon the claimant's having occupied the front depth, and occasionally supplying himself with timber from this back depth; and for the reasons already assigned, we are of opinion that the claim ought to be rejected.

No. 224.—MICHEL BERGERON claims a second depth of forty arpents, lying immediately back of a first depth, which we have already confirmed to him in page 278, No. 224, among the confirmed claims.

This claim to a second depth is in every respect similarly situated to those in the two preceding numbers, being founded solely upon the claimant's having occupied the first depth, and having occasionally supplied himself with timber from the second depth; and for reasons already assigned, we are of opinion that this claim ought to be rejected.

No. 334.—ABRAHAM ROM claims a second depth of forty-four arpents, lying immediately back of a first depth, already confirmed to him in page 288, No. 334, of the confirmed claims.

The claimant states this second depth is part of a larger tract, having a depth of eighty-four arpents, which was by Governor O'Reilly granted to one Petit Antoine, for the purpose of establishing a vacherie, and that the title-papers have by some means or other been destroyed; but there being no evidence whatever produced in support of this statement, we are of opinion that his claim to this second depth ought to be rejected.

No. 335.—ALEXIS PERRET claims a second depth of forty-four arpents, lying immediately back of a first depth, which we have already confirmed to him in page 288, No. 335, among the confirmed claims.

This claim to a second depth is founded upon the same pretensions as that of the preceding, viz: that it is a part of a tract having a depth of eighty-four arpents, which was formerly granted by O'Reilly, the first Spanish Governor of the province, to a certain Petit Antoine, and that the written evidence of title has by some

means been destroyed; but this being a bare statement, unsubstantiated by any evidence of its truth, we are of opinion that this claim ought to be rejected.

No. 336.—ALEXIS PERRET claims a second depth of forty-four arpents, lying immediately back of a first depth, which we have already confirmed to him in page 288, No. 336, among the confirmed claims.

This claim to a second depth is situated in all respects similarly to the preceding, being claimed by the same persons, and being part of the tract there said to have been granted by Governor O'Reilly. There being no manner of evidence whatever exhibited to prove that the title-papers, which are stated to have been either lost or destroyed, were ever in reality obtained from the Spanish Government, we are of opinion that this claim ought to be rejected.

No. 337.—DOMINIQUE LE BŒUF claims a second depth of forty-four arpents, lying immediately back of a first depth, which we have already confirmed to him in page 288, No. 337, among the confirmed claims.

This second depth is claimed as forming part of a larger tract, which is represented by the claimant, in No. 334 and No. 335 preceding, as having been granted formerly by Governor O'Reilly; and the claimant producing no evidence in support of his claim, we are of opinion that it ought to be rejected.

No. 338.—ANASTASIA CORMICO, widow of Pierre Bourg, claims a second depth of forty-four arpents, lying immediately back of a first depth, which we have already confirmed in page 228, No. 338, among the confirmed claims.

This claim to a second depth is founded upon the same pretensions as the preceding, being part of a tract which is represented in Nos. 334 and 335 to have been formerly granted by Governor O'Reilly. We are therefore of opinion, for reasons before assigned, that this claim ought to be rejected.

No. 339.—WILLIAM PRIESTLY claims a second depth of forty-four arpents, lying immediately back of a first depth, already confirmed to him in page 288, and No. 339, among the confirmed claims.

This second depth is claimed as being part of a larger tract, which is represented by the claimants, in Nos. 334 and 335, to have been granted formerly to one Petit Antoine by Governor O'Reilly; of which we have no manner of evidence, and are therefore of opinion that this claim ought to be rejected.

No. 340.—PAUL DAVID claims a second depth of forty-four arpents, lying immediately back of a first depth, which we have already confirmed to him in page 288, No. 340, among the confirmed claims.

This claim to a second depth is represented by the claimant as being part of a larger tract, which in the six preceding claims is stated to have been formerly granted by Governor O'Reilly to a certain Petit Antoine; in support of which statement no evidence has been produced to us, and we are therefore of opinion that this claim ought to be rejected.

No. 346.—JOSEPH LEBLANC claims a second depth or concession of forty arpents, lying immediately back of a front or first concession, which we have already confirmed to him in page 264, No. 61, among the confirmed claims.

This claim to a second depth is founded solely upon a petition (requête) to the Intendant General of the province, in the year 1801, with the commandant's certificate that the land was vacant, and might be granted without prejudice, &c. Had the Intendant even a right at that period to grant the land, he has never acted upon the petition, nor does it appear that it has ever been presented to him. We are of opinion that this claim to a second concession ought not to be confirmed under any law, custom, or usage of the Spanish Government, and do therefore reject it.

No. 371.—JOHN COXE claims a second depth of forty arpents, lying immediately back of a first depth, which we have already confirmed to him in page 291, No. 371, among the confirmed claims.

The claimant has no other foundation for his title to this second, than having occupied the front and first depth, and having occasionally supplied himself with timber from this second depth. According to the laws, customs, and usages of the Spanish Government, no front proprietor, by any act of his own, could acquire a right to lands further back than the ordinary depth of forty arpents; and although the Government has invariably refused to grant the second depth to any other than the front proprietor, yet nothing short of a grant or warrant of survey from the Government could confer a title or right to the land. We do therefore reject the claim.

No. 421.—PIERRE and ALPHONSE PERRET claim a second depth, and extending back to a particular lake, and lying immediately behind a first depth of forty arpents, which we have already confirmed to the claimants in page 295, No. 421, among the confirmed claims.

The claimants pretend that the tract of land to which they claim this additional depth is part of a larger tract granted by the French Government to one Nicholas Verret, to run back from the river Mississippi as far as the first lake, and that the records have been consumed by fire, and the title-papers destroyed. But they having presented no evidence of the grant under which they hold to the Board, we are of opinion that their claim to this additional depth ought to be rejected.

No. 422.—PIERRE and ALPHONSE PERRET claim a second depth, and extending back to a particular lake, and lying immediately behind the first depth of forty arpents, which we have already confirmed to them in page 295, and No. 422, among the confirmed claims.

This claim to a second or additional depth is in every point similarly situated to the preceding claim. The claimants state this is part of the tract formerly granted to Nicholas Verret by the French Government; the written evidence of which grant has been destroyed. But there being no evidence before the Board that such grant did ever exist, we are of opinion that their claim to this additional depth ought to be rejected.

No. 423.—EVARISTE VILLIAVASSE claims a second depth, extending back to a particular lake, and lying immediately behind a first depth of forty arpents, which we have already confirmed to him in page 295, No. 423, among the confirmed claims.

The claimant pretends that the tract of land to which he claims this second or additional depth is part of a larger tract, which was granted by the French Government to a certain Nicholas Verret, to run back from the river Mississippi to a particular lake; and that the records have been consumed by fire, and the title-papers destroyed. But he having produced no evidence to the Board in support of his statement that such grant ever existed, we are of opinion that this claim ought to be rejected.

No. 424.—VALENTIN LANDRY claims a second depth of forty arpents, lying immediately back of a first depth, which we have already confirmed to him in page 295, No. 424, among the confirmed claims.

The claimant states, as a foundation to his title to this second depth, that it is part of a larger tract of land, having a depth of eighty arpents, which was granted to M. Cantrelle by Governor Galvez, in the year 1780, and that the written evidence of the grant has either been lost, or was, whilst in the possession of Mr Trudeau, the then Surveyor General of the province, consumed in the general conflagration of the city of New Orleans, in 1788. But he having exhibited no manner of evidence to prove the existence of such a grant, we are of opinion that his claim to this second depth ought to be rejected.

No. 425.—SIMON BOURGEOIS claims a second depth of forty arpents, lying immediately back of a first depth, which we have already confirmed to him in page 295, No. 425, among the confirmed claims.

The claimant states that this second depth is part of the tract mentioned in the preceding number, and represented by the claimant to have been granted in the year 1780, by Governor Galvez, to M. Cantrelle, and that the title-papers have been lost, or consumed at New Orleans, in 1788, whilst in the possession of Mr Trudeau, Surveyor General. But there being no evidence exhibited to the Board to prove that such title-papers did ever exist, we are therefore of opinion that this claim ought to be rejected.

No. 426.—JOSEPH ARCENAUX, Sen. claims a second depth of forty arpents, lying immediately back of a first depth, which we have already confirmed to him in page 295, No. 426, among the confirmed claims.

The claimant shows no other foundation for his title to this second depth than having occupied the first depth, and having occasionally supplied himself with timber from this second depth. According to the laws, customs, and usages of the Spanish Government, no front proprietor could, by any act of his own, acquire a right to lands further back than the ordinary depth of forty arpents; we do therefore reject the claim.

No. 438.—PIERRE LANOIX claims a second depth of forty arpents, lying immediately back of a first depth, which we have already confirmed to him in page 296, No. 438, among the confirmed claims.

The claimant in support of his title to this second depth, produces the certificate of some old inhabitants, his neighbors, certifying that the second depth has, by the persons under whom the present claimant holds, been cultivated ever since the year 1772, until 1807, when it was purchased, together with the front and first depth, by the claimant. But according to the laws, usages, and customs of the Spanish Government, no front proprietor, by any act of his own, could acquire a right to lands further back than the ordinary depth of forty arpents; and although the Government has invariably refused to grant the second depth to any other than the front proprietor, yet nothing short of a grant or warrant of survey from the Governor could confer a title or right to the land; we therefore reject the claim.

No. 442.—RICHARD FOWLER claims a second depth, lying immediately back of a first depth, of eighteen arpents and ten toises in front, being part of a larger front, which we have confirmed to him in page 297, No. 442, among the confirmed claims.

The claimant states that his claim to this second depth is founded upon a grant from the Spanish Government, in favor of Manuel Andry, for a larger tract, of which this is part. But he has not produced the grant, or any evidence whatever, to prove that there ever was one, or any other sufficient title made by that Government; we are therefore of opinion that his claim to this second depth ought to be rejected.

No. 444.—L. H. GUERLAIN, as agent for the Eastern Shore of Maryland Louisiana Company, claims a second depth, extending back quite to the lake Maurepas, and lying immediately behind a front or first depth, which we have already confirmed to him in page 297, No. 444, among the confirmed claims.

The claimant states that this land is part of a tract sold by the Colapissas nation of Indians, in the year 1739, to one Delille Dupard, from whom the aforesaid company claims by successive transfers; and pretends that the land, whilst the property of said nation of Indians, had a depth extending back to lake Maurepas; but of this fact, there is no other evidence than the deposition of the late Surveyor General of the province, stating that he heard his father, who served as interpreter at the sale made by the Indians, say that the land sold was to extend back to the lake Maurepas. The sale is stated to have been a verbal one, but there is no certain evidence that a sale has been made as stated by the claimant, nor is there any act of Government respecting it, nor are there any defined limits given to the land by the pretended sale: we are therefore of opinion that the claim ought to be rejected.

P. GRYMES, R. E. D. Orl. Territory.
JOSHUA LEWIS,
THOMAS B. ROBERTSON.

SECOND SPECIES OF THE FIRST CLASS OF DECISIONS.

No. 3.—JOSEPH DECUIR claims a tract of land, situate in the county of Pointe Coupée, and fronting on the False river, containing six hundred and fifty-nine superficial arpents, bounded on the upper side by land of Henry Lagrange, and on the lower two sides by vacant land.

It appearing to the Board, from a patent exhibited, that said land was granted by the Spanish Government to the present claimant on the 2d day of April, 1790, they are of opinion that his claim ought, and the same hereby is confirmed.

No. 6.—PIERRE MICHEL claims a tract of land, situate in the county of Acadia, and on the left bank of the Mississippi, containing five arpents twelve toises in front, by the common depth of forty arpents, bounded on the upper side by land of Basile de Rocher, and on the lower by land of Paul Martin.

It appears to the Board, from a patent exhibited, that said land was granted by the Spanish Government to the present claimant on the 10th day of July, 1777; they are therefore of opinion that said claim ought, and it is hereby confirmed.

No. 7.—Pierre Michel claims another tract of two hundred and sixteen superficial arpents of land, situate in the county of Acadia, being what is called a second depth, and adjoining other land belonging to him.

It appearing to the Board, from an order of survey exhibited, that said land was granted by the Spanish Government to the present claimant on the 8th day of January, 1782; and from the certificate of Laveau Trudeau, late Surveyor General under the said Government for the province of Louisiana, that the survey was made on the 6th day of February following; and it further appearing to the Board that the requisitions under the first section of the law of Congress organizing this Board have been complied with, they are of opinion that the said claim ought, and the same hereby is confirmed.

No. 8.—Leonard Pomet claims a tract of land, situated in the county of Orleans, twenty-seven miles below the city, and on the right bank of the Mississippi, containing five arpents in front, by forty in depth, bounded on the upper side by land of John Donat, and by land of Charles Calphat on the lower.

It appears to the Board, from the documents exhibited, that said land is a part of twenty arpents of front by forty in depth, which was granted by the French Government to the late Simon Calphat, by a patent dated the 2d day of October, 1767; that, at his death, it descended to his son, Lewis Simons, from whom it was purchased, and is held by the present claimant. The Board is therefore of opinion that the said claim ought, and the same hereby is confirmed.

No. 9.—Mary Darden claims a tract of land, situated in the county of Iberville, containing six hundred and eighty superficial arpents, being what is called a second depth, and adjoining land that was granted by the Spanish Government to Anthony Rodriguez, her former husband, fronting on the Mississippi.

It appears to the Board, from an order of survey exhibited, that said land was granted by the Spanish Government to the present claimant on the 8th March, 1791; and, from the certificate of Laveau Trudeau, late Surveyor General under the Government aforesaid for the province of Louisiana, that the order of survey was duly executed on the 22d of November, 1799; and it also appearing to the satisfaction of the Board that the requisitions under the first section of the act of Congress organizing this Board have been complied with, they are of opinion that said claim ought, and the same hereby is confirmed.

No. 10.—Joseph McNeil claims a corner lot of ground, in the city of New Orleans, consisting of sixty feet fronting on Royal street, and one hundred and eighteen and a half on Custom-house street.

It appearing to the Board, from a patent exhibited, that said land was granted by the Spanish Government to Manuel Toledano on the 16th day of June, 1792, and, by purchase, the same has become the property of the present claimant, the Board is of opinion that said claim ought, and it is hereby confirmed.

No. 11.—Said McNeil claims another lot of ground, in the said city of New Orleans, containing seventy feet fronting on Royal street, by one hundred and twenty in depth.

It appears to the Board, from two patents exhibited, that said land was granted by the Spanish Government to Ambrose de Leibana in two separate parcels: one on the 24th September, 1793; the other on the 26th of the same month and year; and that, by divers sales since made, the whole has become the property of the present claimant; the Board is therefore of opinion that his claim ought, and the same hereby is confirmed.

No. 12.—Said McNeil claims another lot of ground, in the city of New Orleans, containing thirty feet in front on Chartres street, by one hundred and twenty in depth.

It appears to the Board, from a patent exhibited, that said lot was granted by the Spanish Government to Anthony Ceulino on the 2d day of September, 1793, and that, by sales of the same since that time, it has become the property of the present claimant; they are therefore of opinion that his claim ought, and the same hereby is confirmed.

No. 15.—Pierre Belly claims a tract of land, situated in the county of Iberville, consisting of twenty arpents, fronting on the Mississippi, and being upon its right bank, and varying in depth, bounded on the upper side by land of Philip Roth, and on the lower by land of Godfrey Roth.

It appearing to the Board, from patents exhibited, that said land was originally granted by the Spanish Government. in different parcels, to different individuals, and at different times, all prior to the 1st October, 1800, and, by divers sales since. the whole has become the property of the present claimant; the Board is therefore of opinion that his claim ought, and it hereby is confirmed.

No. 16.—Joseph McNeil claims a piece of ground, in the city of New Orleans, consisting of three lots, viz.: one forty feet in front, by one hundred and nine and a half in depth, on Royal street; another adjoining the former lot, and forming one of the corners of Royal and Custom-house streets, running ninety feet on the former, and fifty-six feet on the latter: the last lot having fifty-three and a half feet fronting on Royal street, by ninety feet in depth, and adjoining the other two lots.

It appears to the satisfaction of the Board, from a patent produced, that said land was granted by the Spanish Government to Elisha Winter on the 23d day of May, 1794, and by divers sales since made, the same has become the property of the present claimant; the Board is therefore of opinion that his claim ought, and it hereby is confirmed.

No. 17.—Alexander Milne claims a tract of land, situated on the bayou St. John, and on the left side thereof, about two miles below the bridge, containing seventeen arpents twenty-nine toises in front, by forty arpents in depth, bounded on the upper side by land of the widow Durrocher, and on the lower by land of Peter Palao.

It appears to the Board, from patents exhibited, that fifteen arpents twenty-nine toises in front, by the depth aforesaid, of said land, which had been, on the 12th day of June, 1766, conceded by the French Government to Bartholomew Roberts, was afterwards, viz., on the 27th day of August, 1771, confirmed to him by the Spanish Government by patent; that the remaining two arpents of front, with the depth aforesaid. was granted by the Spanish Government to John B. Blaize, under a patent bearing date the 20th April, 1771; and it appearing that said land has, by legal conveyances, become the property of the present claimant, the Board is of opinion that his claim ought, and it hereby is confirmed.

No. 18.—Philip Roth claims a tract of land, situated in the county of Iberville, and on the right bank of the Mississippi, containing five and a quarter arpents of front, by eighty arpents in depth, bounded on the upper side by land of Antoine Maxent, and on the lower by land of Pierre Belly.

It appearing to the Board, from a patent exhibited, that said land was granted by the Spanish Government on the 18th day of July, 1796, to the present claimant, the Board is of opinion that his claim ought, and the same hereby is confirmed.

No. 20.—Pierre Belly claims a tract of land, situated in the county of Iberville, and on the right bank of the Mississippi, bounded on the upper side by land of Godfrey Roth, and on the lower by land of John Serret, and containing three arpents forty-eight feet and seven inches in front, by forty arpents in depth.

It appears to the Board, from a patent exhibited, that said land was granted by the Spanish Government to Pierre Truhan, on the 7th July, 1774; and it appearing, from divers instruments of conveyance, also exhibited, that said land has become the property of the present claimant, the Board is of opinion that his claim ought, and it hereby is confirmed.

No. 21.—François Rivas claims a tract of land, situated in the county of Iberville, and on the left bank of the Mississippi, containing twelve arpents five toises and one foot in front, by forty arpents in depth, bounded on the upper side by land of Thomas Estevan, and on the lower by land of Thimoleon Lesassier.

It appearing to the Board, from a patent exhibited, that eight arpents four toises of front, by forty arpents in depth, of said land, was granted to Anselme Landry on the 5th day of February, 1775; and it appearing to the Board, from a certain decree in writing signed Louis Dotisné, commandant and judge of the district of Iberville, dated the 10th day of July, 1780, that four arpents one toise and one foot front, by the depth aforesaid, (remainder) of said land, having belonged to Jacob Landry, who had neglected to keep the levée in order, although twice required by him, the said commandant, &c. so to do; and that, in consequence of the necessary repairs having been made by Nicholas Triste, said land last aforesaid was by the commandant aforesaid adjudged to him; and it also appearing to the Board, from divers instruments of conveyance, also exhibited, that the whole of the said land has become the property of the present claimant, the Board is of opinion that his claim ought, and the same hereby is confirmed.

No. 22.—THIMOLFON LESASSIER claims a tract of land situated in the county of Iberville, and on the left bank of the Mississippi, containing six arpents two toises and a half of front, by forty arpents in depth, bounded on the upper side by land of François Rivas, and on the lower by land of Simon P. Babin.

It appearing to the Board, from a patent exhibited, that said land was granted by the Spanish Government to Joseph Landry on the 5th day of February, 1775, and from divers instruments of conveyance, also exhibited, that it has become the property of the present claimant; the Board is of opinion that this claim ought, and the same hereby is confirmed.

No. 23.—JOSEPH McNEIL claims a lot of ground, in the suburb of St. Mary, in the county of Orleans, consisting of sixty feet on the side of the levée, by three hundred and thirteen feet in depth, bounded on the upper side by land of John Rhea and Cohgran, on the lower by land of Samuel Corp, and in the rear by Magazine street.

It appearing to the Board, from a decree in writing signed by Manuel Gayoso de Lemos, Governor General of the province of Louisiana, dated the 8th day of August, 1797, that said land was adjudged to John Gravier, in consideration of its having belonged to his brother, Bertrand Gravier, who died intestate; and it likewise appearing to this Board, from divers instruments of conveyance, also exhibited, that said land has been transferred to, and is now held by the present claimant, the Board is therefore of opinion that his claim ought, and the same is hereby confirmed.

No. 24.—JOHN RHEA and COHGRAN claim a lot of ground, in the suburb of St. Mary, in the county of Orleans, consisting of sixty feet fronting on Levée street, sixty-one feet in the rear, three hundred and three feet on one side, and three hundred and thirteen on the other, bounded on the northeast by a lot of ground of Joseph McNeil, and on the northwest by Magazine street, and on the southwest by Gravier street.

It appearing to the Board, by the bill of sale produced that Bertram Gravier, having inherited said land from Mary Derlond, his deceased wife, did, on the 15th day of March, 1794, convey the same to Joseph Hervier; and it also appearing, from an instrument of conveyance, dated in 1803, that said Hervier sold it to the present claimants, the Board is therefore of opinion that their claim ought, and it is hereby confirmed.

No. 25.—THOMAS McCORMICK claims a lot of ground in the city of New Orleans, containing thirty feet fronting on Custom-house street, by one hundred and fifty in depth, bounded on the northeast side by land of William Garland, and on the northwest by land of Hardy de Boisblanc.

It appears to the Board, from an instrument of conveyance exhibited to the Board, that Charles Hardy Boisblanc, having inherited said land from his deceased mother, on the 3d day of April, 1797, sold it to Anne Brune; and it likewise appearing, from a like instrument of conveyance, also exhibited, that, on the 27th day of December, 1805, she sold it to the present claimant, the Board is of opinion that his claim ought, and the same is hereby confirmed.

No. 28.—CATHARINE LAJONCHERE claims a tract of land, situated at a place called the English Turn, about twelve miles below the city of New Orleans, and on the right bank of the Mississippi, containing two hundred and eighty superficial arpents, bounded on the upper side by land of Charles Lacheregue, and on the lower by land of Louis Ducreau.

It appears to the Board, from an order of survey exhibited, that the same was issued by the Spanish Government, on the 12th day of February, 1790, in favor of Charles Lajonchere Danois, late husband of the present claimant, for the land in question; and it moreover appearing to the satisfaction of the Board that the requisitions under the first section of the law of Congress establishing this Board have been complied with, the Board is of opinion that the claim aforesaid ought, and it hereby is established and confirmed.

No. 29.—BONAVENTURA LEBLANC claims a tract of land, situated in the county of Iberville, and on the left bank of the Mississippi, containing nine arpents and twelve toises in front, by forty arpents in depth, bounded on the upper side by land of Peter Alain, and on the lower by land of Joseph Richard.

It appearing to the Board, from a patent exhibited, that said land was granted by the Spanish Government to the claimant, on the 5th day of November, 1774, they are of opinion that his claim ought, and it is hereby confirmed.

No. 30.—JOSEPH LEBLANC claims a tract of land, situated in the county of Iberville, and on the left bank of the Mississippi, containing four arpents in front, by forty in depth, bounded on the upper side by land of Francis Hebert, and on the lower by land of John B. Babin.

It appears to the Board, from a patent exhibited, that said land was granted by the Spanish Government, on the 5th day of November, 1774, to the present claimant; they are therefore of opinion that his claim ought, and the same is hereby confirmed.

No. 31.—STEPHEN HEBERT claims a tract of land, situated in the county of Iberville, and on the left bank of the Mississippi, containing seven arpents and thirteen toises of front, by forty arpents in depth, bounded on the lower sides by land of Alexander Hebert, and on the other sides by vacant land.

It appearing to the Board, from a patent exhibited, that said land was granted by the Spanish Government to the present claimant, on the 5th day of November, 1774, they do confirm his said claim.

No. 32.—MARIA BERMUDEZ claims a lot of ground, in the county of Iberville, and in the town of Galvez, forming one of the corners of St. Mark and Claiborne streets, containing ninety feet on the former, and ninety on the latter, bounded on the southeast by land of Ferdinand Percy, and on the remaining sides by vacant land.

It appearing to the Board, upon the oaths of Joseph Sanchez, Francis Massias, and Joseph Capitan, inhabitants of the county of Iberville, that Joseph Bermudez, deceased, late husband of the claimant, was one of the settlers of the post of Galveztown, who came from the Canary Islands in the year 1779, at the expense of the King of Spain, and that to him was given by the Spanish Government a piece of ground of about one hundred superficial arpents, within the district of Galveztown aforesaid, and also a lot of ground in the town of Galvez, containing ninety feet square, the Board therefore confirm said claim.

No. 33.—Said MARIA BERMUDEZ also claims a tract of land, situated in the county of Iberville, and the post of Galveztown, containing five arpents fronting on the river Iberville, by twenty arpents in depth, bounded on the north by the river aforesaid, on the east by land of John Hernandez, on the west by land of Wykoff, and on the south by vacant land.

From the evidence offered in the preceding case of the present claimant, the Board do confirm her said claim.

Nos. 34 and 35.—MICHAEL MASSIAS claims a tract of land, situated in the county of Iberville, containing one hundred and twenty superficial arpents, bounded on the north by land of Thomas Collado, on the west by land of Diego Quintana, and on the other sides by vacant land.

He also claims a lot of ground in Galveztown, containing ninety feet square, and fronting on Iberville street, bounded on the northeast by land of Augustin Lombardo, and by land of John Hernandez on the southeast.

It appears to the Board, upon the oaths of Joseph Sanchez, Francis Massias, and Joseph Capitan, inhabitants of the county of Iberville, that the said Michael Massias, the claimant, is one of the first settlers of the post of Galveztown, who came from the Canary Islands in the year 1779, at the expense of the King of Spain, for the purpose of promoting agriculture in the province of Louisiana; on which account the Spanish Government assigned him a piece of land in the post of Galveztown aforesaid, of about one hundred superficial arpents, together with a lot in Galveztown, containing ninety feet square; and it further appearing to the Board, from the certificate of Charles Laveau Trudeau, Esq. late Surveyor General under the Spanish Government aforesaid for the province of Louisiana aforesaid, that the aforesaid one hundred and twenty arpents of land was, on the 15th of November, 1793, duly surveyed in favor of the present claimant, the Board do hereby confirm the whole of his claim.

Nos. 36 and 37.—JOSEPH MASSIAS claims a tract of land, in the county of Iberville and district of Galveztown, containing eighty superficial arpents, bounded on the north by land of Fabien Ramos, on the east by land of Joseph Pino, on the west by land of Joseph Capitan, and on the south by vacant land.

Also two lots of ground, situated in the town of Galvez, fronting each other, and forming two of the corners of Claiborne and Galvez streets, containing each ninety feet square.

It appearing to the Board, upon the oaths of Joseph Capitan, Joseph Sanchez, and Francis Massias, inhabitants of the county of Iberville, that said Joseph Massias, the present claimant, is one of the first settlers of the post of Galveztown, who came from the Canary Islands in the year 1779, at the expense of the King of Spain, for the purpose of improving agriculture in the province of Louisiana; on which account the Spanish Government assigned him a piece of land to establish himself upon, situated in the district aforesaid, consisting of about one hundred superficial arpents, together with a lot in Galveztown, containing ninety feet square; that the same quantity of land was in like manner aforesaid assigned, at the same epoch, to Joseph Massias, deceased, father of the claimant, which, at his death, was left to the claimant; and it further appearing to the Board, from the certificate of Charles Laveau Trudeau, late Surveyor General under the Spanish Government for the province of Louisiana, that the said eighty arpents of said land was duly surveyed in 1794 in favor of the claimant, the Board do hereby confirm the whole of his claim aforesaid.

Nos. 38 and 39.—JOSEPH CAPITAN claims a tract of land, situated in the county of Iberville, containing one hundred superficial arpents, bounded northerly by land of Maria Ramos, on the east by land of Joseph Massias, on the west by land of Francis Massias, and on the south by vacant land. He also claims a lot of ground, in the county aforesaid, and in the town of Galvez, forming the southwest corner of Claiborne, and Galvez streets, and containing ninety feet square.

It appearing to the Board, upon the oaths of Francis Massias and Joseph Sanchez, inhabitants of the county of Iberville aforesaid, that Joseph Capitan, the present claimant, is one of the first settlers of the post of Galveztown, who came from the Canary Islands in the year 1779, at the expense of the King of Spain, for the purpose of promoting agriculture in the province of Louisiana; on which account the Spanish Government assigned him a piece of land to establish himself upon, situated in the district of Galveztown aforesaid, containing about one hundred superficial arpents, together with a lot in the town of Galvez, containing ninety feet square, the Board do hereby confirm the claimant in the whole of his claim aforesaid.

Nos. 40 and 42.—FRANCIS MASSIAS claims a tract of land, situated in the county of Iberbille, and in the district of Galveztown, containing one hundred and twenty superficial arpents, bounded on the north and on the east by vacant land, on the west by land of Joseph Capitan, and on the south by land of John Medina. Also, a lot of ground in the district aforesaid, and in Galveztown, forming the southwest corner of St. Matthew and Humas streets.

It appearing to the Board, upon the oaths of Joseph Capitan and Joseph Sanchez, inhabitants of the district aforesaid, that the said Francis Massias, the present claimant, is one of the first settlers of the post of Galveztown aforesaid, who came from the Canary Islands in the year 1779, at the expense of the King of Spain, for the purpose of improving agriculture in the province of Louisiana; on which account the Spanish Government assigned him a piece of land to establish himself upon, situated in said district, and containing about one hundred superficial arpents, together with a lot of ground in Galveztown, in said district, containing ninety feet square, the Board do hereby confirm the present claimant in his claim aforesaid.

No. 41.—WILLIAM BLAKE claims a tract of land, situated in the county of Iberville, and on the left bank of the bayou Plaquemine, bounded on the east by land of Alexander Darden, and on the west by land of Pedro Egrimier, and on the south by vacant land, and containing four hundred superficial arpents.

An order of survey being exhibited to the Board, appearing to have been issued by the Spanish Government, on the 1st day of July, 1794, in favor of the present claimant, for the land in question; and it likewise appearing to the Board, from the certificate of Charles Laveau Trudeau, Esq., Surveyor General under the Spanish Government for the province of Louisiana, dated November 15, 1802, that the order of survey aforesaid was duly executed; and it also appearing to the satisfaction of the Board that the 'requisitions under the first section of the act of Congress establishing this Board have been complied with, they do hereby confirm the claim aforesaid.

No. 43.—JOSEPH PEREIRA claims a lot of ground in Galveztown, in the county of Iberville, forming one of the corners of St. Matthew and Galvez streets, and containing ninety feet square, and adjoining land of Maria Ramos.

It appearing to the Board, upon the oaths of Joseph Capitan, Joseph Sanchez, and Francis Massias, inhabitants of the district of Galveztown, that said Joseph Pereira, the present claimant, is one of the first settlers of the post of Galveztown, who came from the Canary Islands in the year 1779, at the expense of the King of Spain, for the purpose of improving agriculture in the province of Louisiana; on which account the Spanish Government assigned him a piece of land in the said district, together with a lot of ground in Galveztown, containing ninety feet square, the Board do hereby confirm the claim aforesaid.

No. 44.—JOHN HERNANDEZ claims a lot of ground in Galveztown, in the county of Iberville, containing ninety feet square, and forming the northeast corner of Jefferson and Acadian streets.

It appearing to the Board, that the oaths of Francis Massias, Joseph Sanchez, and Joseph Capitan, inhabitants of the county of Iberville, that John Hernandez aforesaid is one of the first settlers of the post of Galveztown, who came from the Canary Islands in the year 1779, at the expense of the King of Spain, for the purpose of promoting agriculture in the province of Louisiana; on which account the Spanish Government assigned him a piece of land in the district aforesaid, containing about one hundred superficial arpents, together with a lot of ground in Galveztown, ninety feet square, the Board do hereby confirm the claim last aforesaid.

No. 46.—THOMAS DURNFORD, as acting executor of John Harrison, deceased, claims a tract of land, situated in the county of Iberville, and on the left bank of the Mississippi, containing twenty arpents and seventeen toises of front, and converging towards the rear twenty-five degrees; bounded on the upper side by vacant lands, and on the lower by land of one Michel.

It appearing to the Board, from a letter exhibited, signed by Francis Rivas, and dated 30th of October, 1802, and addressed to Thomas Durnford, aforesaid, executor as aforesaid, that he, the said Durnford, was called upon, in virtue of his said executorship, to make or repair the levée and road upon the said tract of land, from which it is made to appear that the said John Harrison, deceased, was recognised by the authority aforesaid as having been, in his lifetime, the proprietor of said land; it further appearing to the Board, from a memorial dated the 23d day of November, 1802, and addressed by the said Thomas Durnford, in his capacity of executor as aforesaid, to the Intendant General of the province of Louisiana, that it was therein stated that the land aforesaid had been conceded by the Baron de Carondelet, whilst Governor of Louisiana, (which must have been prior to 1798,) to John Harrison, deceased; which fact appears to have been recognised by the patent which was upon said memorial, ordered by the Intendant General aforesaid to be issued; which order is dated on the 15th day of November, 1802, and is exhibited to the Board; and it further appearing to the Board, from the certificate of Charles Laveau Trudeau, Esq. late Surveyor General under the Spanish Government, dated the 27th of March, 1803, that a survey of said land was duly made in favor of the estate of the deceased John Harrison; under all these circumstances, the Board are of opinion that the claim of Thomas Durnford aforesaid, as executor of John Harrison, deceased, aforesaid, ought, and the same hereby is confirmed.

No. 48.—MARGUERITE ROBERT, widow of the late Bartholomew Durrocher, claims a tract of land, situated in the county of Orleans, and on the right bank of the bayou St. John, containing four hundred superficial arpents, bounded on the upper side by vacant land, and on the lower partly by land of Alexander Milne, and partly by vacant land.

It appearing to the Board, from a patent exhibited, that said land was granted by the French Government to Andrew Jung, the 22d day of June, 1766, and, from divers instruments of conveyances, that said property has been transferred to the present claimant, they do hereby confirm her in her said claim.

No. 49.—JOSEPH ENRY claims a tract of land, situated in the county of Iberville, and on the right bank of the Mississippi, containing three hundred and sixty-six superficial arpents forty-three toises and thirty feet, bounded on the upper side by land of Peter Landry, and on the lower by land of John B. Lambremont.

It appearing to the Board, from a patent exhibited, that said land was granted by the Spanish Government, on the 20th July, 1796, to the present claimant, they do hereby confirm his said claim.

No. 50.—JOHN B. LAMBREMONT claims a tract of land, situated in the county of Iberville, and on the right bank of the Mississippi, containing two hundred and forty-seven superficial arpents, bounded on the upper side by land of Joseph Henrique, and on the lower by land of Simon Leblanc.

It appearing to the Board, from a patent exhibited, that said land was granted by the Spanish Government to the claimant on the 20th day of July, 1796, they do hereby confirm his said claim.

No. 51.—MATURIN LANDRY claims a tract of land, situated in the county of Iberville, and on the right bank of the Mississippi, containing five arpents seventeen and a half toises in front, by the common depth of forty arpents, bounded on the upper side by land of Batiste Leblanc, and on the lower by land of Joseph Landry.

It appears to the Board from a patent exhibited, that said land was granted by the Spanish Government to Augustin Landry on the 7th July, 1774; and it appearing from an instrument of conveyance, also exhibited, that he afterwards transferred it to the present claimant, they do therefore confirm his said claim.

No. 52.—IGNATIUS LANDRY claims a tract of land, situated in the county of Iberville, and on the right bank of the Mississippi, containing five arpents seventeen and a half toises in front, by forty arpents in depth, bounded on the upper side by land of Maturin Landry, and on the lower by land of Amant Melanson.

It appearing to the Board, from a patent exhibited, that said land was granted by the Spanish Government to Augustin Landry on the 7th day of July, 1774; and it also appearing, from divers instruments of conveyance, likewise exhibited, that the land was transferred to the present claimant, the Board do hereby confirm his claim aforesaid.

No. 53.—AMANT HEBERT claims a tract of land, situated in the county of Iberville, and on the right bank of the Mississippi, containing five arpents in front, by forty in depth, bounded on the upper side by land of Peter Hebert, and on the lower by land of Joseph Depuis.

It appears to the Board, from a patent exhibited, that said land was granted by the Spanish Government to Augustin Morino on the 11th day of July, 1774; and it also appearing to the Board, from an instrument of conveyance likewise produced, that he afterwards conveyed it to the present claimant, they do hereby confirm his said claim.

No. 54.—Said AMANT HEBERT claims another tract of land, situated in the county of Iberville, and on the right bank of the Mississippi, containing five arpents six toises one foot and a half in front, by forty arpents in depth, bounded on the upper side by land of Batiste Hebert, and on the lower by other lands of the claimant.

It appearing to the Board, from a patent exhibited, that said land was granted by the Spanish Government to Peter Hebert on the 11th day of July, 1774; and it also appearing, from a deed of conveyance exhibited, that he afterwards conveyed it to the claimant, the Board do hereby confirm the claim aforesaid.

No. 55.—DIEGO HERNANDEZ claims a tract of land, situated in the county of Iberville, and on the right bank of the Mississippi, containing four arpents in front, by a depth of forty arpents, bounded on one side by land of Amant Hebert, and on the other by land of Augustin Landry.

It appearing to the Board, from a patent exhibited, that said land, together with two arpents of front more, was granted by the Spanish Government to Stephen Rivet on the 7th day of July, 1774; and it also appearing, from divers deeds of conveyance since made, that said land was last conveyed to the present claimant, the Board do hereby confirm his claim aforesaid.

No. 56.—Said DIEGO HERNANDEZ claims another tract of land, situated in the county of Iberville aforesaid, and on the right bank of the Mississippi, containing six arpents in front, by the depth of forty arpents, bounded on the upper side by land of John B. Dupuis, and on the lower by vacant lands.

It appearing to the Board, from a patent exhibited, that said land was granted by the Spanish Government to John Alenacio Landry, on the 11th day of July, 1774; and it appearing to the Board, from divers instruments of conveyance, also produced to the Board, that said land was last conveyed to the present claimant, they do hereby confirm his said claim.

No. 57.—Said DIEGO HERNANDEZ claims another tract of land, situated in the said county of Iberville, and on the right bank of the Mississippi, containing five arpents twenty-eight toises and five feet front, by forty in depth, bounded on one side by land of Amant Hebert, and on the other by land of Charles Hebert.

It appearing to the Board, from a patent exhibited, that said land was granted by the Spanish Government to Joseph Dupuis, on the 11th day of July, 1774, and it also appearing, from two different instruments of conveyance, likewise produced, that it was last conveyed to the present claimant, the Board hereby confirm his said claim.

No. 58.—SIMON MELANSON claims a tract of land, situated in the county of Iberville, and on the right bank of the Mississippi, containing four and a half arpents in front, by forty in depth, bounded on one side by land of Theodore Rivet, and on the other by land of Anne Babin.

It appears to the Board, from a patent exhibited, that said land, together with a larger quantity, was granted by the Spanish Government to Amant Melanson, on the 7th day of July, 1774; and it appearing, from divers deeds of conveyance also exhibited before the Board, that the land now claimed was last transferred to the present claimant, the Board do hereby confirm the said claim.

No. 59.—GREGOIRE MELANSON claims a tract of land, situated in the county of Iberville, and on the right bank of the Mississippi, containing five arpents in front by forty in depth, bounded on the upper side by land of Ignatius Landry, and on the lower by land of Joseph Hebert.

It appearing to the Board, from the patent exhibited, that said land, together with a larger quantity, was granted by the Spanish Government to Amant Melanson on the 7th day of July, 1774; and it appearing further to the Board, from divers conveyances also produced before the Board that the quantity of land now claimed was last transferred to the present claimant, they do hereby confirm his said claim.

No. 60.—PETER JOSEPH LANDRY claims a tract of land, situated in the county of Iberville, and on the right bank of the Mississippi, containing six arpents ten toises in front, by forty arpents in depth, bounded on the upper side by land of Charles Breaud, and on the lower by land of Joseph Henry.

It appearing to the Board, from the certificate of Pierre Belly, Judge of the county of Iberville, dated 11th February, 1806, that said Landry, the claimant, was put in possession of the land in question by Anselme Blanchard, agent of the Spanish Government, for the purpose of promoting agriculture in the said district of Iberville, and that he has continued to occupy and improve the same for more than twenty years, and that it was once surveyed in his favor by Laveau Trudeau, by direction of the same Anselme Blanchard, the Board do hereby confirm said claim.

No. 61.—AMANT HEBERT claims a tract of land, situated in the county of Iberville, and on the right bank of the Mississippi, containing ninety arpents in front, by forty in depth, bounded on the upper side by land of J. Villier, and on the lower by land of Oliver Lebrusseau. Two orders of survey being exhibited to the Board, appearing to have been issued by the Spanish Government, viz: one for eight arpents in front, by the depth aforesaid, in favor of John Alexander Darden, dated 1788; the other, in favor of the claimant, for the remaining eleven arpents in front, by the depth aforesaid, together with a larger quantity, dated 28th March, 1795; and it also appearing, from a conveyance, also exhibited to the Board, that the aforesaid eight arpents in front, by the depth aforesaid, have been legally conveyed to the claimant; and it further appearing to the satisfaction of the Board that all the requisitions under the first section of the act of Congress establishing this Board have, in relation to these two tracts of land, been complied with, the Board do hereby confirm the aforesaid claim.

No. 1.—ALEXANDER MILNE claims a tract of land, situated in the county of Orleans, on the south side of lake Pontchartrain, six arpents from the mouth of the Bayou St. John, and on the right side thereof, containing two thousand one hundred and sixty-seven superficial arpents, being ninety-four arpents in front, and limited in its depth by the lands of Chantilly.

It appearing to the Board, upon the certificate of Francis Durcy, Raymond Gaillard, Joseph Lestenet, Charles Laveau Trudeau, Esq., late Surveyor General of the province of Louisiana, and A. Argote, ancient inhabitants of said province, that Charles de Lachaise held uninterrupted and peaceable possession of the land in question for more than twenty years, and was during that time acknowledged to be the true and only proprietor thereof; and it appearing to the Board, from divers instruments of conveyance also exhibited before them, that said land was last conveyed in due form to the present claimant by those who derived their title from the aforesaid Lachaise, the Board do hereby confirm the said claimant in his claim aforesaid.

No. 2.—Said ALEXANDER MILNE claims another tract of land, situated in the county of Orleans, and on the north bank of the bayou or canal Carondelet, fronting its basin, containing one hundred and ninety-four feet upon said canal, ninety-five feet in depth at one end, and one hundred and eight feet on the other end of the aforesaid front.

It appearing to the Board, from the certificate of Henry Metzinguer, dated 10th January, 1805, that the land in question was, in the year 1796, settled with the permission of the Baron de Carondelet, then Governor of the province of Louisiana, by one Pierre, upon the condition that he would take care of the basin, keep a public house for the convenience of those who might pass that way, and pay annually the sum of ten dollars for the use of the city, all of which he did; and it appearing to the Board, from sundry instruments of conveyance likewise exhibited, that said land had passed out of the hands of the original grantee, and was last conveyed to the present claimant, they do hereby confirm his said claim.

No. 5.—ANTHONY DECUIR claims a tract of land, situated in the county of Pointe Coupée, and fronting on the False River, containing eight hundred superficial arpents, bounded on the upper side by land of Joseph Decuir, and on the lower by vacant land.

It appearing to the Board, from an order of survey exhibited, that the same was issued by the Spanish Government on the 12th day of July, 1788, in favor of the claimant, for the land in question; and it also appearing to the Board, from the certificate of Charles Laveau Trudeau, late Surveyor General of the province of Louisiana, that the aforesaid order of survey was duly executed on the 18th day of February, 1790; and it further appearing to the Board that all the requisitions under the first section of the act of Congress establishing this Board have been complied with, the Board do hereby confirm the claim of the present claimant.

No. 26.—PAUL CHIASSON claims a tract of land, situated in the county of Iberville, and district of Galveztown, containing four hundred superficial arpents bounded on the north by land of Benjamin Leblanc, and on the south by vacant land.

An order of survey being exhibited to the Board, purporting to have been issued by the Spanish Government, the 30th day of January, 1789, in favor of the claimant, for the land in question; and it appearing, from the certificate of Charles Laveau Trudeau, late Surveyor General of the province of Louisiana, that the aforesaid order of survey was duly executed on the 11th day of December, 1799; and it moreover appearing to the satisfaction of the Board that all the requisitions under the first section of the act of Congress establishing this Board have been complied with, the Board do hereby confirm the claim aforesaid.

No. 62.—FRANCIS XAVIER TERRIOT claims a tract of land, situated in the county of Iberville, on the right bank of the Mississippi, containing five arpents in front by forty in depth, bounded on the upper side by vacant land, and on the lower side by land of Ambrosio Terriot.

It appearing to the Board, from the patent exhibited, that said land was granted by the Spanish Government to Michael Mayer, on the 22d day of April, 1790; and it also appearing, from an instrument of conveyance exhibited, that said Mayer has since conveyed it to the claimant, the Board do confirm his claim aforesaid.

No. 63.—FABIAN GUILLOT claims a tract of land, situated in the county of La Fourche, on the left bank of the bayou of that name, and about fifteen miles from its confluence with the Mississippi, containing two hundred and fifty-three and one third superficial arpents, bounded on the upper side by land of Joseph Landry, and on the lower by land of John Charles Gautro.

An order of survey being exhibited to the Board, purporting to have been issued by the Spanish Government, on the 2d day of October, 1790, in favor of the claimant, for the land in question; and it also appearing, from the certificate of Charles Laveau Trudeau, Esq., late Surveyor General for the province of Louisiana, that the order of survey aforesaid was duly executed on the 4th day of March, 1792; and it also appearing to the satisfaction of the Board that all the requisitions under the first section of the law of Congress establishing this Board have been complied with, the Board do hereby confirm the claim aforesaid.

No. 64.—JOSEPH PINO claims a tract of land, situated in the county of Iberville, containing one hundred and forty superficial arpents, bounded on the north by land of Joseph Pereira, on the south by land of George Hulsell, on the east by land of Philip Ramirez, and on the west by land of Joseph Massias.

An order of survey being exhibited, purporting to have been issued by the Spanish Government, on the 6th day of February, 1794, in favor of the claimant, for the land aforesaid; and it appearing to the Board, from the certificate of Charles Laveau Trudeau, Esq., that the order of survey aforesaid was duly executed on the 14th of September, 1794; and it likewise appearing to the satisfaction of the Board that all the requisitions of the first section of the act of Congress establishing this Board have been complied with, the Board do hereby confirm the claimant in his claim aforesaid.

No. 65.—Said JOSEPH PINO claims two lots of ground in Galveztown, in the county of Iberville, each of ninety feet square, bounded by St. John street on the northeast, by land of Mr. Romiro and A. Lombardo on the northwest, by Miranda street on the west, and by Jefferson street on the south.

It appearing to the Board, from the depositions of Michael Massias and Joseph Pereira, ancient inhabitants of the district of Galveztown, taken before William Reed, Justice of the Peace of said place, dated 30th January, 1806, and exhibited before the Board, that said lots were granted to the claimant, in the year 1780, by Don Francis Collell, then commandant of Galveztown, who then settled thereon, and has had peaceable possession thereof ever since; and it also appearing, from the certificate of Bartholomew Lafon, that, in the year 1803, being employed by the Spanish commandant of Galveztown to survey the land occupied in said post, he then surveyed the said lots in favor of the claimant, the Board do hereby confirm him in his claim aforesaid.

No. 66.—GASPER TILLANO claims a lot of ground in Galveztown, in the county of Iberville, containing ninety feet square, and fronting on St. Matthew street, bounded on the west by lot of Augustin Lombardo, and on the southeast by a lot of Joseph Alamo.

It appearing to the Board, upon the oath of Don Manuel Dias, an ancient inhabitant of the county of Iberville, that the present claimant is one of the first settlers of the post of Galveztown, who came from the Canary Islands in the year 1779, at the expense of the King of Spain, for the purpose of promoting agriculture in the province of Louisiana; on which account, the Spanish Government granted to him a piece of land to establish himself upon, containing about one hundred superficial arpents, together with a lot in Galveztown, containing ninety feet square, being the one now claimed, which lot he has continued ever since to occupy and cultivate, the Board do hereby confirm the claimant in his claim aforesaid.

No. 67.—FRANCIS RAUSMAN claims a lot of ground in Galveztown, in the county of Iberville, forming the southwest corner of Jefferson and Humas streets.

It appearing to the Board, from the warrant of Baron de Carondelet, Governor of Louisiana, dated the 20th day of May, 1796, and addressed to the commandant of the post of Galveztown, that the said commandant was, in virtue thereof, authorized and directed to put the claimant in possession of the lot of ground aforesaid, the Board do hereby confirm the claimant in his claim aforesaid.

No. 68.—ANTHONY RAUSMAN claims a lot of ground in Galveztown, in the county of Iberville, and forming the southwest corner of Humas and Iberville streets.

It appearing to the Board, from an order in writing, signed by the Baron de Carondelet, Governor of Louisiana, dated the 20th May, 1796, and addressed to the commandant of the post of Galveztown, that said commandant was, in virtue thereof, authorized and directed to put the claimant in possession of the lot aforesaid, the Board do hereby confirm the claimant in his claim aforesaid.

No. 69.—ISIDORE LEBLANC, J. BLANCHARD, and J. LANDRY claim a tract of land, situated in the county of Iberville, containing eleven arpents ten toises and five feet in front, on the left bank of the Mississippi, by the common depth of forty arpents, bounded on the upper side by land belonging to the heirs of Paul Melanson, deceased, and on the lower by land of Joseph Melanson, deceased.

It appears to the Board, from the petition of Bonaventura Babin, who married the wife of Charles Melanson, dated the 7th September, 1796, and addressed to his excellency the Baron de Carondelet, Governor of the province of Louisiana, that the seven arpents eleven toises and three feet front, by forty arpents in depth, of the land aforesaid, which had been granted by the Spanish Government to the said Charles Melanson, deceased, by virtue of a patent dated the 5th November, 1775, was then formally abandoned; and it also appearing to the Board, from a certificate of Louis Judice, commandant of the county of Iberville, dated 19th August, 1797, that the present claimant was then put in possession of the land last aforesaid, together with three arpents twenty-nine toises and two feet of front, by the depth aforesaid, (which having been granted to Olivier Melanson, by a patent bearing date the 5th day of November, 1775, had been abandoned,) conformable to a decree of Don Manuel Gayoso de Lemos, then Governor of the province of Louisiana, the Board do hereby confirm the claimants aforesaid in their said claim.

No. 70.—MANUEL DIAS claims a tract of land, situated in the county of Iberville, and about three miles to the eastward of the fort at Galveztown, containing fifty-six superficial arpents, bounded on the north by land of Madame Nicholas, on the west by land of Joseph Pereira, on the south by land of Thomas Collado, and on the east by vacant land.

It appearing to the Board, upon the oath of Mary Dias, an ancient inhabitant of the county of Iberville aforesaid, that said land was granted by the Spanish Government to Bartholomew Dias, deceased, in the year 1781, who was one of the first settlers of the post of Galveztown, and who came from the Canary Islands in the year 1780; and that, at the death of Josepha Pabona, his widow, it descended to the present claimant; and it further appearing to the Board, from the certificate of Charles Laveau Trudeau, late Surveyor General of the province of Louisiana, that the land aforesaid was, in the year 1793, duly surveyed in favor of the said Josepha Pabona, the Board do hereby confirm the claimant in his claim aforesaid.

No. 71.—MATHIAS MARTIN claims a tract of land, situated in the county of Iberville, and about one mile to the north-northeast of the fort at Galveztown, containing one hundred and ten superficial arpents, bounded on the north by Galveztown lands, on the east by land of Juan Medina, on the west by land of John Milcher, and on the south by vacant land.

It appearing to the Board, upon the oath of Manuel Dias, of the county of Iberville, that Mathias Martin, the present claimant, is one of the first settlers of the post of Galveztown, who came from the Canary Islands in the year 1779, and that the Spanish Government granted him about one hundred superficial arpents of land in said district, together with a lot of ground in Galveztown, and that he has ever since continued to occupy and cultivate said tract of land first above mentioned; and it appearing, from the certificate of Charles Laveau Trudeau, late Surveyor General of the province of Louisiana, also exhibited, that the land claimed by the said Mathias Martin was, in the month of September, 1794, duly surveyed in favor of the claimant, by the verbal order of the Baron de Carondelet, then Governor of said province, the Board do hereby confirm the said Mr. Martin in his claim aforesaid.

No. 72.—Said MATHIAS MARTIN claims a lot of ground in Galveztown, in the county of Iberville aforesaid, fronting on St. Matthew street, adjoining a lot of Mr. Pino on the northeast, and a lot of Joseph Capitan on the southeast, and containing ninety feet square.

From the evidence of the aforesaid Manuel Dias, offered in support of the preceding claim of the said Matthias Martin, the Board do hereby confirm the claim of the present claimant.

No. 73.—JOHN DIAS claims a lot of ground in Galveztown, in the county of Iberville, containing ninety feet square, and forming the northwest corner of St. Matthew and Humas streets.

It appearing to the Board, upon the oath of Mary Dias, of the county of Iberville, that the claimant is one of the first settlers of the post of Galveztown, who came from the Canary Islands in the year 1780, and that the Spanish Government granted him about one hundred superficial arpents of land in said place, together with a lot of ground in Galveztown, which lot of land he has continued ever since to occupy and cultivate, the Board do hereby confirm said claimant in his claim aforesaid.

No. 74.—JOSEPH ALAMO claims a lot of ground in Galveztown, in the county of Iberville, fronting Claiborne street to the south, and adjoining a lot of Gaspar Tellano on the northwest, containing ninety feet square.

It appearing to the Board, upon the oath of Manuel Dias, of the county of Iberville, that Joseph Alamo, the present claimant, is one of the first settlers of the post of Galveztown, who came from the Canary Islands in the year 1779; on which account the Spanish Government granted him about one hundred superficial arpents of land in said district, together with a lot of ground in Galveztown, which lot he has ever since that period occupied and improved, the Board do hereby confirm said claimant in his claim aforesaid.

No. 75.—MARIE DEL PINO claims a lot of ground, in the county of Iberville, and forming the southwest corner of Humas and St. Matthew streets in Galveztown, containing ninety feet square.

It appearing to the Board, from the order, in writing, of the Baron de Carondelet, Governor of Louisiana, exhibited to the Board, dated the 18th day of March, 1794, directed to the commandant of Galveztown, that said commandant was thereby directed to put the claimant in possession of the lot aforesaid; and it further appearing to the Board, from the certificate of Marcos Derilliers, that, by virtue of the order aforesaid, he did, in the year aforesaid, put the claimant in possession of said lot, the Board do hereby confirm the claimant in her said claim.

No. 76.—AUGUSTIN LOMBARDO claims one superficial arpent of ground in Galveztown, in the county of Iberville, fronting on Humas street on the west, and on Iberville street on the southwest.

It appears to the Board, from the oath of Manuel Dias, of the county of Iberville, that, about the year 1795, Dr. Francis Rivas, being then commandant of Galveztown, granted to one Peter Junipero Sacristain, at that time of the parish of St. Bernard, a lot of ground in Galveztown aforesaid, containing a square arpent, which land was five years after given by the grantee aforesaid to Francis Bony, Senior; and it further appearing to the Board, upon the oaths of Joseph Pereira and Michael Massias, inhabitants of the county of Iberville, that said Francis Bony, Senior, at his death, left the said land to his son, Francis Bony, Jun., who, on the 27th day of September, 1803, conveyed it to the claimant; which last circumstance appears by the bill of sale from the former to the latter, dated the day and year last aforesaid, the Board do therefore confirm the present claimant in his claim.

No. 77.—DIEGO QUINTANA claims a tract of land, situated in the county of Iberville, containing forty-eight superficial arpents, bounded on the north by land of Philip Ramirez, on the east by land of Michael Massias, on the south by land of Frederic Kitten, and on the west by land of Joseph Pino.

It appearing to the Board, from the depositions of Joseph Pino, Joseph Massias, and Michael Massias, inhabitants of the county of Iberville, taken before William Reed, Esq. Justice of the Peace in said county, on the 28th January, 1806, and exhibited to the Board, that the above tract of land was granted to the claimant by the Spanish Government in the year 1794, and that he has ever since been, and still is, in peaceable possession thereof; and it further appearing, from the certificate of Charles Laveau Trudeau, Esq., late Surveyor General of the province of Louisiana, dated 5th October, 1794, and exhibited to the Board, that said tract of land was duly surveyed by him in favor of the present claimant, by order of the Baron de Carondelet, Governor of the province of Louisiana, the Board do hereby confirm the claimant in his claim aforesaid.

No. 78.—AUGUSTIN LOMBARDO claims a lot of ground in Galveztown, in the county of Iberville, forming the southeast corner of Miranda and Iberville streets, containing ninety feet square.

It appearing to the Board, upon the oath of Manuel Dias, of the county of Iberville, that Diego Quintana is one of the first settlers of the post of Galveztown, who came from the Canary Islands in the year 1779, and that the commandant of Galveztown made him a verbal concession of about one hundred superficial arpents of land in said post, together with a lot of ground in Galveztown, which he has always occupied and improved; and it appearing, from a deed of conveyance exhibited to the Board, executed by said Diego Quintana on the 7th day of October, 1805, that he then conveyed the said lot of ground to the present claimant, the Board do hereby confirm him in his claim aforesaid.

No. 79.—MARIA ROMEO claims a tract of land, situated in the county of Iberville, about one mile to the northeast of the fort of Galveztown, containing thirty-two superficial arpents, bounded on the north by land of Joseph Pereira, on the east by land of Michael Massias, on the south by land of Diego Quintana, and on the west by land of Joseph Pino.

It appearing to the Board, from the certificate of Charles Laveau Trudeau, Esq., late Surveyor General of the province of Louisiana, that said land was duly surveyed in favor of Philip Romero, (the late husband of the claimant,) on the 23d day of March, 1802, in conformity to a verbal order of the Baron de Carondelet, Governor of the province of Louisiana, given in the month of September, 1794, the Board do therefore confirm the said Maria Romero, widow of the late Philip Romero, in her claim aforesaid.

No. 80.—Said MARIA ROMERO claims a lot of ground, in Galveztown, in the county of Iberville, containing ninety feet square, and forming the southwest corner of St. John and Iberville streets.

It appearing to the Board, from the depositions of Michael Massias and Joseph Pereira, ancient inhabitants of the county of Iberville, taken before William Reed, Esq. Justice of the Peace for said county, dated 30th day of January, 1806, that said lot was granted to the claimant in 1780, by Don Francis Collell, former commandant of Galveztown, at the time of the claimant's settling on said lot, and that she has had peaceable and quiet possession thereof ever since, the Board do hereby confirm said claimant in her claim last aforesaid.

No. 81.—FRANCIS MORALES claims a tract of land, in the county of Iberville, about one mile to the northeast of the fort at Galveztown, containing eighty superficial arpents, bounded on the east by land of Matthias Martin, on the south by land of John Milcher, and on the north and west by vacant land.

It appearing to the Board, upon the certificate of Charles Laveau Trudeau, Esq., late Surveyor General of the province of Louisiana, that said land was duly surveyed in favor of the claimant in the month of September, 1794, in pursuance of an order of the Baron de Carondelet, Governor of the province of Louisiana, the Board do therefore confirm the claimant in his claim aforesaid.

No. 82.—Said FRANCIS MORALES claims a lot of ground in Galveztown, in the county of Iberville, containing ninety feet square, and forming the southwest corner of Humas and Claiborne streets.

It appearing to the Board, upon the oath of Manuel Dias, of the county of Iberville, that the claimant is one of the first settlers of the post of Galveztown, who came from the Canary Islands in the year 1779, and that the then commandant of Galveztown made him a verbal concession of about one hundred arpents of land in said district, together with a lot of ground in Galveztown, which he has always continued to occupy and cultivate, the Board do hereby confirm the claimant in his claim last aforesaid.

No. 83.—AUGUSTIN LOMBARDO claims a lot of ground in Galveztown, in the county of Iberville, containing one hundred and eighty feet square, and forming the southwest corner of Miranda and Iberville streets, and the northwest corner of Miranda and Jefferson streets.

It appearing to the Board, upon the oath of Manuel Dias, of the county of Iberville, that the commandant of Galveztown made a verbal concession of two lots of ground in Galveztown, each of ninety feet square, to Joseph Quintero and Anna his wife, when they came as settlers to the province of Louisiana, in the year 1799; that, at the death of them, the said Joseph and Anna, the property left by them descended to Alexander Lopez; and it appearing, from an instrument of conveyance executed by said Alexander Lopez the 25th February, 1804, that he then conveyed said lots of ground to the present claimant, the Board do hereby confirm the claimant in his claim aforesaid.

No. 84.—MARIA DIAS claims a tract of land, situate in the county of Iberville, about three miles above the fort at Galveztown, and on the right bank of the river Iberville, containing eight hundred superficial arpents, bounded on the west by land of Marcos Coullon Devilliers, and on the remaining sides by vacant land.

It appearing, from the certificate of Charles Laveau Trudeau, Esq., late Surveyor General of the province of Louisiana, that said land was granted to one Joseph Cabo, late husband of the claimant, by Don Manuel Gayoso de Lemos, whilst Governor of the province of Louisiana, and that afterwards, viz. on the 10th day of February, 1802, the Intendant General of said province ordered a survey of said land to be made in favor of the claimant, the Board do hereby confirm the claimant in her said claim.

No. 87.—FRANCIS BERMUDEZ claims a tract of land, situate in the county of Orleans, on the south side of the Canal de Carondelet, containing two arpents of front, by four and a half in depth, bounded on the remaining sides by vacant land.

A royal order of the Court of Spain being exhibited to the Board, dated at Aranjuez, 3d day of May, 1799, in favor of the claimant, for the land in question, the Board do hereby confirm the claim aforesaid.

No. 88.—JACOB STATENFELD claims a tract of land, situate in the county of Iberville, and on the right bank of the bayou Manchack, containing two hundred and forty superficial arpents, bounded on the east by land of William Spaun, and on the west by land of John Hernandez.

A warrant of survey being exhibited to the Board, purporting to have been issued by the Baron de Carondelet, Governor of the province of Louisiana, the 2d day of July, 1794, in favor of the claimant, for the land in question; and it appearing, from the certificate of Charles Laveau Trudeau, Esq., late Surveyor General of said province, that the order of survey was duly executed on the 17th day of September of the year last aforesaid; and it also appearing to the satisfaction of the Board that all the requisitions of the first section of the law of Congress establishing this Board, have been complied with, the Board do hereby confirm the claimant in his claim aforesaid.

No. 95.—FRANCIS M. GUERIN claims a tract of land, situate in the county of Orleans, on the left bank of the Mississippi, containing seven arpents of front, by eighty in depth, bounded on the upper side by land of Norbert Boudusquier, and on the lower by land of the widow Dupré.

It appearing to the Board, from a written concession of his excellency Stephen Miro, Governor of the province of Louisiana, dated the 8th day of August, 1787, and exhibited to the Board, that Anthony Decalogne, being at that time owner and possessor of that part of said land fronting on the river, obtained a grant for the second depth thereof; and it appearing to the Board, that, after several legal transfers of the land aforesaid, it has become the property of the present claimant, the Board do hereby confirm the said claim.

No. 96.—FRANCIS JOSEPH LEBRETON claims a tract of land, situate in the county of Orleans, at a place called Barataria, and on the lake Perrier, or Ouachas, fronting on the north side thereof, and about two miles from the bayou Pouba to the west.

An order of survey being exhibited, purporting to have been issued by the Spanish Government, on the 10th day of July, 1781, in favor of the claimant, for the land in question; and it appearing to the satisfaction of the Board that all the requisitions under the first section of the act of Congress establishing this Board have been fully complied with, the Board do hereby confirm the claimant in his claim aforesaid.

No. 97.—ANTHONY SILVIO claims a tract of land, situate in the county of Iberville, on the right bank of the bayou Manchack, containing one hundred superficial arpents, bounded on the upper side by land of John Harrison, and on the lower by land of Bartholomew Hernandez.

It appearing to the Board from the certificate of Charles Laveau Trudeau, Esq., late Surveyor General of the province of Louisiana, exhibited before the Board, that said land was conceded to the claimant in the year 1794, by the verbal order of the Baron de Carondelet, and surveyed in his favor, in the year 1802, by the directions of the then Intendant General of the province aforesaid, the Board do therefore confirm the claimant in his claim aforesaid.

No. 98.—JOSEPH DEBORA claims a tract of land, situate in the county of Iberville, and on the right bank of the Petit Bayou, containing one hundred superficial arpents, bounded on the upper side by land of John Hernandez, and on the lower by land of Bartholomew Hernandez.

It appearing to the Board, from a certificate of Charles Laveau Trudeau, late Surveyor General of the province of Louisiana, that said land was duly surveyed, in favor of the present claimant, in the year 1794, pursuant to the verbal orders of the Baron de Carondelet, and that his rights thereto were recognised by the decree of the late Intendant General of the province of Louisiana, bearing date the 11th January, 1802, the Board do hereby confirm the claimant in his claim aforesaid.

No. 99.—JOHN SILVERIO claims a tract of land, in the county of Iberville, and on the right bank of the bayou Manchack, containing one hundred superficial arpents, bounded on the upper side by land of William Spaun, by land that is vacant in the rear, and by Galveztown on the lower side.

It appearing to the Board, from the certificate of Charles Laveau Trudeau, Esq., late Surveyor General of the province of Louisiana, exhibited to the Board, that said land was duly surveyed in 1794, in favor of the claimant, by the verbal order of the Baron de Carondelet, Governor of the province aforesaid, as one of the settlers of the post of Galveztown, and that his claim or right was afterwards recognised by the decree of the late Intendant General of said province, the Board do hereby confirm the claimant in his claim aforesaid.

No. 100.—ALEXANDRE MILNE claims a tract of land, situate in the county of Orleans, and on the right bank of the bayou St. John, about three miles below the bridge, containing four hundred superficial arpents, bounded on the north by land of Madame Cartillon, and on the south by land belonging to the claimant.

It appearing to the Board, from the patent exhibited, that said land was granted by the French Government to John Tuon, 21st July, 1776, and from divers conveyances from him and others since that time, it has become the property of the present claimant, the Board therefore confirm the claim aforesaid.

No. 101.—THOMAS URQUHART, executor of the estate of the late John Alman, claims, in behalf of said estate, a tract of land, situate in the county of Iberville, about nine miles to the eastward of the fort of Manchack, containing eleven hundred and forty-six superficial arpents; bounded on the north by land of John B. Hebert, on the south by land of Stephen Hebert, and on the other sides by vacant land.

It appears to the Board, from a deed of conveyance produced before the Board, that said land was, with a greater quantity, sold, in the year 1788, by one James

Nicolson, to Isaac and Joseph Leblanc; and it further appearing, from an instrument of conveyance, duly executed by the said Isaac Leblanc, dated the 7th day of April, 1795, and passed before the other commandant of Galveztown, that he, the said Leblanc, conveyed said land to the aforesaid John Alman, the Board do hereby confirm the claimant in his claim aforesaid.

No. 102.—JOHN B. SAUSSIER claims a tract of land, situate at a place called "Le Quartier de la Concession," on the left bank of the Mississippi, about twenty miles below the city of New Orleans, containing one hundred and sixty superficial arpents, bounded on the upper side by land of Maxent Aimé, and on the lower by land of the claimant.

An order of survey being exhibited to the Board, purporting to have been issued by the Spanish Government, on the 6th day of December, 1788, in favor of the present claimant, for the land in question; and it appearing to the Board that all the requisitions of the first section of the act of Congress establishing this Board have been fully complied with, the Board do hereby confirm the claimant in his claim aforesaid.

No. 103.—ALEXANDRE MILNE claims a tract of land, situate in the county of Orleans, and on the right bank of the bayou St. John, half a league below the bridge, containing two hundred and seventy-three superficial arpents and ten toises, bounded on the north by land of Stephen Roquigny, and on the south by land of Madame Maxent, and on the back side by the lands of Jentilly.

It appears to the Board, upon the oath of Don Andreas Lopez de Armento, corroborated by the certificate of Charles Laveau Trudeau, Esq., late Surveyor General of the province of Louisiana, dated 25th August, 1802, by the certificate of Louis Leblanc, dated 5th June, 1804, and by the certificate of Joseph Duparc, dated 25th July, 1804, that said land was, in the latter end of the year 1799, conceded to one P. Palao by Don Manuel Gayoso de Lemos, Governor of the province of Louisiana; that said Palao took possession of and cultivated the same; and it appearing to the Board, from the certificate of Anthony Argote, Justice of the Peace under the temporary Government of Louisiana, that the said Peter Palao was authorized to make sale of the land aforesaid; and, lastly, it appearing to the Board, from a deed of conveyance executed by the said Peter Palao, the 13th day of February, 1805, that he conveyed the said land to the present claimant, the Board do therefore confirm his claim aforesaid.

No. 104.—DANIEL CLARK claims a piece of land, in the city of New Orleans, containing nineteen hundred and twenty toises square, bounded on the upper side by vacant lands, and on the lower by the city of New Orleans aforesaid.

It appearing to the Board, from a royal order of the court of Spain, dated Madrid, 23d May, 1791, that said land was thereby granted to Elisha Winter; and it appearing to the Board, from sundry deeds of conveyance, that said land has been transferred to the present claimant, the Board do therefore confirm him in his claim aforesaid.

No. 105.—JOSEPH McNEIL claims a lot of ground, in the city of New Orleans, containing thirty feet fronting on Conty street, by one hundred and seventy-seven in depth; bounded on the north by land of Thomas Urquhart, and on the south by land of ———— Harrang.

A deed of conveyance being exhibited to the Board by Peter D. Delaronde, executor of the late Mrs. Delaronde, his mother, and dated 13th day of November, 1805, whereby it appears that said P. D. Delaronde, as executor aforesaid, sold said land to the present claimant, the Board do therefore confirm him in his claim aforesaid.

No. 106.—DANIEL CLARK claims a tract of land, situate in the county of Orleans, and on the left bank of the Mississippi, containing eighteen acres in front, by forty in depth, bounded on the upper side by land of Edward Livingston, and on the lower by land of one Pierre Gautier.

It appearing to the Board, from a deed of conveyance exhibited, executed by Edward Livingston, and dated the 18th day of August, 1805, that he thereby conveyed the said land to the present claimant, the Board do hereby confirm the claim aforesaid.

No. 107.—Said DANIEL CLARK claims another tract of land, situate in the county of Orleans, and on the

34

left bank of the Mississippi, containing twenty acres of front, by forty in depth, bounded on the upper side by land of one Dupré, and on the lower by land of C. Robin.

It appearing to the Board, from a deed of conveyance exhibited, executed by Gilbert Andry, dated the 11th day of November, 1803, that the said Andry, having obtained said land from Nicolas Cayeux, by a regular transfer before Peter Pedersclaw, notary public, in the city of New Orleans, thereby sold it to Daniel Clark, the present claimant, the Board do therefore hereby confirm his claim aforesaid.

No. 108.—DANIEL McCONNELL claims a tract of land, situate in the county of Iberville, containing three hundred superficial arpents, bounded on the west by land of Baptiste Habair, and on the other sides by vacant land.

It appearing to the Board, from a patent exhibited, that said land was granted to the present claimant by the Spanish Government on the 10th day of February, 1795, the Board do hereby confirm the claimant in his claim aforesaid.

No. 109.—JAMES JONES claims a tract of land, situate in the county of Iberville, and on the right bank of the bayou Manchack, containing one hundred and twenty superficial arpents, bounded on the upper side by land of Joseph Bermudez, and on the other by land of Jacob Stanfield.

It appearing to the Board, from the certificate of Charles Laveau Trudeau, Esq., late Surveyor General of the province of Louisiana, that said land was granted by the Spanish Government, in the year 1780, to John Hernandez, as one of the first settlers of the post of Galveztown, and that it was duly surveyed in his favor, on the 25th day of January, 1794; and it appearing to the Board, upon the oaths of Francis Massias, Joseph Sanchez, and Joseph Capitan, ancient inhabitants of the county of Iberville aforesaid, that John Hernandez is one of the first settlers of the post of Galveztown, who came from the Canary Islands in the year 1779, at the expense of the King of Spain, for the purpose of promoting agriculture in the colony of Louisiana; on which account the Spanish Government made him a verbal concession of a tract of land, situated in said district, containing about one hundred superficial arpents, together with a lot of ground in Galveztown of ninety feet square; and it appearing to the Board, from a deed of conveyance from the said John Hernandez to the claimant, bearing date the 28th day of January, 1806, that he has conveyed the aforesaid one hundred and twenty arpents of land to the claimant, the Board do therefore confirm him in his claim aforesaid.

No. 110.—JAMES BAZILICO claims a tract of land, situate in the county of Iberville, and on the right bank of the river Amite, in the post of Galveztown, containing one hundred and forty superficial arpents, bounded on the upper side by lands of Mr. Nicolas, and on the lower by vacant land.

It appearing to the Board, upon the depositions of Joseph Pereira, Joseph Massias, Joseph Capitan, and Michael Massias, ancient inhabitants of the county aforesaid, taken before William Reed, Esq., Justice of the Peace in said county, and dated 27th January, 1806, that said land was granted to the claimant, in the year 1782, by Governor Galvez, as a settler, that he lived on and cultivated it for a number of years after, and has always been considered as the rightful owner thereof; and it further appearing to the Board, from a certificate of Charles L. Trudeau, Esq., late Surveyor General of the province of Louisiana, that said land was duly surveyed in favor of the claimant on the 17th day of January, 1794, the Board do hereby confirm the claim aforesaid.

No. 111.—WILLIAM SPAUN claims a tract of land, situate in the county of Iberville, and on the right bank of the bayou of that name, containing two hundred and forty superficial arpents, bounded on the upper side by land of Jacob Statenfeld, and on the lower by land of John Silverio.

It appears to the Board, from the depositions of Joseph Massias, Michael Massias, Joseph Capitan, and Joseph Sanchez, taken before William Reed, Esq., Justice of the Peace in said county, dated 23d January, 1806, that the claimant settled on the said land in the year 1794, with the permission of the then commandant of Galveztown, and has continued ever since to inhabit and cultivate it; and it appearing also, from the certificate of Charles L. Trudeau, Esq., late Surveyor General of the province of Louisiana, that the said land was surveyed in favor of the claimant in the year 1794, the Board do therefore confirm the claim aforesaid.

No. 112.—FREDERICK BROWN claims a tract of land, situate in the county of Iberville, and on the right bank of the bayou of that name, bounded on the east by land of William Wykoff, and on the west by land of William Pepe Cabo, and containing two hundred and forty superficial arpents.

It appearing to the Board, from the depositions of Joseph Pereira, John Hernandez, Joseph Pino, and Michael Massias, taken before Wm. Reed, Esq., Justice of the Peace in said county, and dated 23d day of January, 1806, that the claimant settled on said land in the year 1795, with the consent of the then commandant of Galveztown, and that he has ever since continued to occupy and cultivate it; and it further appearing to the Board, from the certificate of Bartholomew Lafon, deputy surveyor of the county of Orleans, that the land aforesaid was, in the year 1794, duly surveyed by order of the Spanish Government in favor of the claimant, the Board do therefore confirm him in his claim aforesaid.

No. 116.—JEAN BAPTISTE SAUSSIER claims a tract of land, situate in the county of Orleans, and on the left bank of the Mississippi, containing four arpents in front, by forty in depth, bounded on the upper side by other land of the claimant, and on the lower by land of Jean B. Saussier, Jun.

It appears to the Board, from the order in writing of Stephen Miro, Governor of the province of Louisiana, dated 23d day of June, 1787, exhibited to the Board, that Louis Cuillerez and Madame Garelle, then proprietors of said land, were ordered to make certain repairs upon the levée and roads appertaining thereto, and, in default thereof, they, the said proprietors, should forfeit said lands, and authorizing Jean B. Saussier, in that case, to make the necessary repairs, whereby the said land should belong to him; and it appearing further, from the certificate of Charles Delatour, Justice of the Peace in the county of Orleans, dated the 10th day of February, 1806, exhibited to the Board, that it is within his knowledge that the levée and roads appertaining to the land aforesaid, which had been abandoned, have been, for thirteen years last past, kept in repair by the present claimant, the Board do therefore confirm his said claim.

No. 118.—JOHN F. JACOB claims a tract of land, situate in the county of Orleans, and on the left bank of the Mississippi, containing six arpents and ten toises of front, by the depth to lake Borgue in the rear, bounded on the upper side by land of Mr. Prevost, and on the lower by land of Mr. Delery.

It appearing to the Board, from an attested copy of a patent exhibited, that six arpents ten toises of front, by the depth of one hundred arpents of said land, were granted with a larger quantity by the French Government, in 1754, to one Anthony Bienvenu; and it appearing to the Board, from a deed of conveyance executed by Anthony Bienvenu, (son and her of the grantee,) dated 11th day of August, 1803, that he conveyed six of them to the claimant; and it appearing to the Board, from another instrument of conveyance exhibited, executed by Francis Chauvin Delery Dezelet, and dated the 10th day of September, 1804, that, having that same day the remaining ten toises (of the land first above mentioned) of Anthony Bienvenu last aforesaid, he thereby conveyed it to the present claimant; the Board do hereby confirm him in his claim aforesaid.

No. 120.—DANIEL CLARK claims a tract of land, situate in the county of La Fourche, containing eleven arpents four toises and one foot in front, on the Mississippi, by fourteen arpents in depth, bounded on the upper side by land of John Vessier, and on the lower by land of Louis Judice.

It appearing to the Board, from the certificate of Bartholomew Lafon, present deputy surveyor of the county of Orleans, dated March 6, 1805, that said land was surveyed on the 5th October, 1791, by Charles Laveau Trudeau, Esq., then Surveyor General of the province of Louisiana, in favor of Paul Colet and Charles Liencourt; and it appearing to the Board, from the deed of conveyance exhibited, executed by Simon Ducourneau, dated the 17th day of November, 1803, that he thereby conveyed said land to the present claimant, the Board do hereby confirm the claim aforesaid.

No. 121.—DANIEL CLARK claims a tract of land, situate in the county of La Fourche, containing six acres in front, on the bayou of that name, by forty in depth, bounded on the upper side by land of Louis Hacher, and on the lower by the same.

It appears to the Board, from the certificate of Charles Laveau Trudeau, Esq., late Surveyor General of the Spanish Government, that said land was duly surveyed in favor of Pierre Hacher, conformably to an order for that purpose from the Spanish Government aforesaid, on the 25th April, 1799; and it appearing, from a deed of conveyance exhibited, executed by Lewis Stevens, dated 29th April, 1795, that he thereby conveyed said land to one James Favre, the Board do hereby confirm the claimant in his claim aforesaid.

No. 122.—Said DANIEL CLARK claims another tract of land, situate in the county of La Fourche, and on the bayou of that name, containing twenty arpents ten toises in front, by forty arpents in depth, bounded on the upper side by land of Mathurin Huzet, and on the lower by land of Joseph Arrari.

It appearing to the Board, from the certificate of Charles Laveau Trudeau, Esq., late Surveyor General of the province of Louisiana, that said land was granted by the Spanish Government to Ignatius Mathews, 25th April, 1799, and that it was only surveyed in his favor on — day of March, 1800; and it further appearing to the Board, from a deed of conveyance executed by Joseph Sausa, Josepha Augustina Romano, and Antonio Dias, dated the 9th of March, 1804, that they conveyed the land aforesaid to the present claimant, the Board do hereby confirm his claim aforesaid.

No. 128.—JOHN C. WEDERSTRANDT claims a tract of land, situate in the county of Iberville, and on the left bank of the Mississippi, containing twelve arpents eleven toises and three feet of front, by the depth of forty arpents.

It appearing to the Board, from two original patents or complete titles exhibited, both dated the 5th day of November, 1775, that said land was granted by the Spanish Government, as follows, viz: eight arpents front, by forty in depth, to one Jermin Broussard, and the four arpents eleven toises and three feet remaining to John Martin; and it appearing to the Board, from a deed of conveyance exhibited, dated the 7th day of May, 1804, and executed by Marine Briugier, that he conveyed said land to the present claimant, the Board do confirm his claim aforesaid.

No. 129.—WILLIAM DONALDSON claims a tract of land, situate in the county of La Fourche Chatimachas, and on the right bank of the Mississippi, containing seven arpents and one toise in front, by twenty-four arpents in depth, with an opening of six degrees towards the rear; bounded on the upper side by the bayou La Fourche, and on the lower by land of John B. Leisard, alias Villeneuve.

It appearing to the Board, from a patent or complete title produced, bearing date the 5th day of November, 1775, that said land was granted by the Spanish Government to Peter Landry; and it also appearing to the Board, from a deed of conveyance also exhibited, bearing date the 10th day of February, 1806, that said Landry thereby conveyed said land to the present claimant, the Board do hereby confirm the claim aforesaid.

No. 130.—JOHN E. BORE claims a tract of land, situate in the county of Orleans, and on the left bank of the Mississippi, containing nine hundred and fifty-two superficial arpents, bounded on the upper side by land of James Fontenet and by vacant land, and on the lower by land of Mr. Ducros and some vacant land.

It appearing to the Board, from a proces-verbal made by C. Laveau Trudeau, Esq., late Surveyor General of the province of Louisiana, that eight hundred and seventy-five arpents of said land have beeen successively transferred by several proprietors thereof, since the year 1729, down to the present claimant; and it appearing further, from a patent or complete title exhibited, that the remaining seventy-seven arpents back were granted by the Spanish Government to the present claimant on the 7th day of April, 1791, the Board do therefore confirm him in his claim aforesaid.

No. 135.—CHARLES DEVILLIERS claims a tract of land, situate in the county of Orleans, and on the left bank of the Mississippi, containing nineteen arpents and twelve toises of front, by the depth back to the lake, bounded on the upper side by land of John B. Mercier, and on the lower by land of Joseph S. Dufossat.

It appearing to the Board, from a patent or complete title exhibited, that thirteen arpents twelve toises of front, by the depth aforesaid, were granted by the French Government to one Gerard Pery on the 5th day of November, 1764; and it also appearing, from a deed of conveyance executed by Française Aufure, widow of the grantee, dated 20th day of December, 1765, and from a deed of conveyance executed by Renato Kermon, dated 16th day of November, 1795, that the whole of said land first above mentioned, having become the property of the said Ronato Kirmon, was, on the day and year last aforesaid, conveyed to the present claimant, the Board do hereby confirm his claim aforesaid.

No. 117.—FRANCIS D. DIZILET claims a tract of land, situate in the county of Orleans, about three miles below the city, containing eight arpents in front, on the left bank of the Mississippi, by the depth of eighty arpents, bounded on the upper side by land of John Jacob, and on the lower by land of the estate of Mrs. Bienvenu.

The Board confirm the claimant in his claim to four arpents and two-thirds of front, by forty in depth, to which a second depth of sixty arpents was granted by the French Government on the 12th day of April, 1754, as appears from page 7, book No. 1, of grants received from the Spanish Government of the province of Louisiana, to Antoine Bienvenu, whose heirs sold five arpents of it to the claimant on the 10th day of September, 1804, who, on the same day, sold the third of an arpent to John Jacob; and the Board further confirm the claimant in his claim to three and one-third arpents of front, by forty in depth, part of his claim aforesaid, on the oath of Jacques Villeré, who declares that the widow Bienvenu has possessed the lands of the claimant for more than twenty years last past. But the Board reject the claim of the said Francis D. Dizilet to forty arpents more in depth, made by said Dizilet, because he has produced no evidence, although repeatedly required so to do, to support that part of his said claim.

No. 124.—WILLIAM CONWAY claims a tract of land, situate in the county of Acadia, and on the right bank of the Mississippi, containing two arpents in front, by forty in depth, bounded on the upper side by land of one Leisard, and on the lower by land of the parish.

It appearing to the Board, from the testimony of Joseph Landry, that said land has been in the possession of, and cultivated by, several persons, from whom it was successively conveyed during the space of about thirty-eight years, when it became the property of John Maguire, parson of the parish; and it appearing, from a deed of conveyance executed on the 17th day of June, 1801, that said Maguire transferred said land to the present claimant, the Board do confirm him in his claim aforesaid.

No. 126.—DANIEL CLARK claims a tract of land, situate near the city of New Orleans, containing twelve arpents in front, on the road leading to the bayou St. John, and varying in depth, bounded on the north by the road aforesaid, on the south by the canal Carondelet, on the east by land of Joseph Suares, and on the west by land of Louis Blanc, and on the bayou St. John aforesaid.

It appears to the Board, from a deed of conveyance dated 3d day of September, 1793, executed by Andreas Almonaster, that he conveyed part of the lands in question to Louis Antoine Blanc; and it appearing, from a patent or complete title exhibited, that another part of said land was granted by the Spanish Government to Nicholas Vidal, on the 18th day of April, 1800 ; and it appearing also, from deeds of conveyance exhibited to the Board, that they, the said Blanc and Vidal, have conveyed to the claimant the whole of the land now claimed by him, the Board do hereby confirm him in his said claim.

No. 131.—MICHAEL BELANGER claims a tract of land, situate in the county of Iberville, on the right bank of the Mississippi, twelve miles below the fort of Baton Rouge, containing one hundred and eighty-three and one-third superficial arpents, bounded on the north by land of Francis Arbour, and on the south by land of Peter Lavergne.

It appearing to the Board, from the certificate of S. Pintado, late deputy surveyor under the Spanish Government of the province of Louisiana, dated October 25, 1803, that he did, on the 6th day of August, 1800, survey said land for Anthony Barbera, who had then lived on and cultivated the same for some time ; and a warrant of survey being exhibited, purporting to have been issued by the Spanish Government on the 14th day of September, 1803, in favor of said Anthony Barbera, for said land ; and it also appearing to the Board, from a deed of conveyance exhibited, that said Anthony Barbera did, on the 21st April, 1801, convey said land to the present claimant, the Board do therefore confirm him in his claim aforesaid.

No. 132.—JOHN BAPTISTE DEJEAN claims a tract of land situate in the county of Iberville, on the left bank of the Mississippi, containing nine arpents and ten toises in front, by forty arpents in depth, with the opening of eleven degrees towards the rear, bounded on the upper side by land of Augustus Malet, and on the lower by land of one Voussin.

It appears to the Board, from an instrument of conveyance executed before Rafael Croquer, then commandant of La Fourche, on the 1st day of December, 1798, that Peter Bore then sold to Messrs. Debuys and Remy six arpents of front, or thereabouts, by forty in depth, of said land, alleging to have obtained the same by a concession of the Spanish Government, which assertion is corroborated by the registry of a warrant of survey issued by the Government aforesaid, on the 13th day of July, 1798, in favor of one Michael Verret, in which warrant said Bore is recognised as the proprietor of the said six arpents of front, by forty in depth ; and it also appearing to the Board, from the same registered warrant of survey aforesaid, in favor of the said Michael Verret, that four arpents in front, by forty in depth, (remainder of the land now claimed,) was, with a larger quantity, conceded by the Spanish Government to him, the said Verret, at the time above mentioned ; and it further appearing to the Board, from sundry deeds of conveyance exhibited, that the whole of the land claimed as aforesaid, has been transferred to the present claimant, the Board do hereby confirm this claim.

No. 136.—SAMUEL WINTER and THOMAS HARMAN claim a tract of land, situate in the county of Orleans, at the settlement of St. Bernard, on both sides of the Bayou aux Bœufs, about two miles below the church, containing two arpents and twenty-eight toises in front, on each side, by the common depth of forty arpents, bounded on the upper side by land of J. Sanchez, and on the lower by land of Juliana Broussard.

An order of survey being exhibited to the Board, purporting to have been issued by the Spanish Government on the 4th day of February, 1792, in favor of Honoratus Duhon, for the land in question ; and it appearing to the satisfaction of the Board that all the requisitions under the first section of the act of Congress establishing this Board have been complied with ; and it further appearing, from divers deeds of conveyance, likewise exhibited to the Board, that said land has become the property of the present claimants, the Board do hereby confirm them in their claim aforesaid.

No. 140.—MARIA JOSEPHE ROCHEJEAN claims a tract of land, situate in the county of Orleans, at a place called *Quartier des Familles*, on the right bank of the bay of the same name, six miles from the Mississippi, containing one thousand five hundred and nine superficial arpents, bounded on the north by land of Francis Dauphin, on the south by land of the widow Pablo, on the east by the Bayou des Familles, and on the west by vacant land.

It appears to the Board, from a patent or complete title exhibited, that part of said land was, with a greater quantity, granted by the Spanish Government to Jean Baptiste Flaurian on the 11th day of May, 1797 ; and it also appearing, from the certified plat of survey of Charles L. Trudeau, Esquire, late Surveyor General of the province of Louisiana, dated the 29th day of November, 1802, that the remaining part of the land claimed as aforesaid was bought by one Peter Lartique at the public sale made of the property of one Wart and Nicolas Daumé, who had been in the possession of and cultivated the same for twenty years, as appears by the testimony of Enould Dugay Livaudais taken before the Board ; and it further appearing, from sundry deeds of conveyance exhibited to the Board, that the two parcels of land above described and claimed by the present claimant have become transferred to him, the Board do hereby confirm his said claim.

No. 141.—BARTHOLOME DUVERGES claims a tract of land, situate in the county of Orleans, on the right bank of the Mississippi, and opposite to the city of New Orleans, forming a triangle, and containing ten arpents in front, and converging towards the rear twenty-three degrees ; the upper line, adjoining land of S. Amant

directed south forty degrees, twenty degrees east ; and the lower, adjoining land of Martial Le Bœuf, directed seventeen degrees, twenty degrees east ; which gives a superficies of one hundred and twenty-four arpents and one hundred and twenty toises.

It appears to the Board, from a deed of conveyance exhibited, that one Louis Borepo sold said land to one James Rixner, on the 9th September, 1777 ; and it appearing, from sundry deeds of conveyance, likewise exhibited to the Board, that said land has become transferred to the present claimant, the Board do therefore confirm him in his said claim ; saving and reserving that part which was occupied by the Spanish Government of the military guard of the powder magazine ; and which is considered as having been transferred by said Government to that of the United States among the items of public property.

No. 142.—MARGUERITE WILTZ claims a tract of land, situate in the county of Orleans, and on the left bank of the Mississippi, about one league above the city of New Orleans, containing four hundred and fifty superficial arpents, bounded on the upper side by land of James Livaudais, and on the lower by land claimed by the nuns of the city of New Orleans.

It appears to the Board, from a deed of conveyance executed 28th March, 1758, before Jean Baptiste Garric, notary public, that Augustus Chantaloux sold eight arpents of front, by a depth not defined, of said land, to Stephen Vaugaine, which he alleges to have acquired as follows, viz: six arpents at the public sale made of the estate of one Dilmo, in 1752; and the other two arpents of front, by the depth aforesaid, of one Pidet, who had purchased the same of one Lagotré: and it also appearing to the Board, from a deed of conveyance likewise exhibited, that on the —— day of ——, 1769, the two arpents of front, by the depth aforesaid, (remainder of the quantity now claimed,) was sold by the widow Laronde to James Livaudais; and it further appearing, from deeds of conveyance exhibited, that the several tracts of land above described have been transferred to the present claimant, the Board do hereby confirm her said claim.

No. 143.—SAMUEL WINTER and THOMAS HARMAN claim a lot of ground, situate in the suburb of St. Mary, containing sixty feet front on the Rue du Camp, by one hundred and sixty in depth, bounded on the north by land belonging to Mr. Decalogne, and on the south by other land of the claimants.

It appearing to the Board, from a deed of conveyance exhibited, dated 27th day of September, 1800, that John Gravier then sold said lot to René Theard; and it appearing also, from another deed of conveyance, likewise exhibited, that said René has since conveyed said lot to the claimants; and the Board being satisfied that said John Gravier had, when he conveyed, a good and sufficient title to said land, the Board hereby confirm the claimants in their claim aforesaid.

No. 144.—Said WINTER and HARMAN claim a tract of land, situate in the suburb of St. Mary, containing four lots, and part of another, consisting each of sixty feet front, by one hundred and sixty in depth; the part of a lot containing twenty-four feet in front, by the depth aforesaid, bounded on the north by land of René Theard and John Clay, on the south by land of Nicholas Delille and John Dawson, on the west by St. Charles street, and on the east by Rue du Camp.

It appearing to the Board, from a deed of conveyance exhibited, that the four lots aforesaid were sold by Jean Baptiste Sarpy to Jacinto Bernard, on the 30th day of January, 1798; and it also appearing to the Board, from another deed of conveyance exhibited, that the remaining part of a lot was bought of Mathurin Guerin on the 15th June, 1799, by the said Jacinto Bernard: and it also appearing, from a deed of conveyance exhibited, that said Bernard has since conveyed the whole of said land to the claimants, the Board do therefore confirm their claim aforesaid.

No. 145.—Said WINTER and HARMAN claim another lot of ground, in the suburb of St. Mary, containing sixty feet front on St. Charles street, by one hundred and sixty in depth, bounded on the north by land of one Roselle, a free mulatto woman, and on the south by land of John Clay.

It appearing to the Board, from a deed of conveyance exhibited to the Board, dated the 10th day of April, 1804, that said land was then sold by Magdaline, a free negress, to Messrs. Amory and Callender; and it appearing also, from a like instrument of conveyance, that said Amory and Callender have since conveyed to the present claimants; and the Board being satisfied that said Magdaline, free mulatto woman aforesaid, had, when she conveyed, a good and sufficient title to the said land, the Board do hereby confirm the claimants in their said claim.

No. 147.—PHILIP LANAUD claims a tract of land, situate in the county of Orleans, and on the left bank of the Mississippi, about four miles below the city of New Orleans, containing three arpents twenty-six toises and four feet in front, by eighty arpents in depth, bounded on the upper side by land of the estate of the late Madame Bienvenu, and on the lower by land of Laurent Sigur.

It appears to the Board, from a warrant of survey exhibited, that Espiritus Lioland and Augustus Faure, were in possession of the front of said land, together with a larger quantity obtained from the Spanish Government, on the 12th day of June, 1790, a concession of the second depth; and it appearing to the Board, from sundry deeds of conveyance exhibited, that said land has become transferred to the present claimant; and it moreover appearing to the satisfaction of the Board that all the requisitions under the first section of the act of Congress establishing this Board have been complied with, the Board do hereby confirm the claimant in his claim aforesaid.

No. 149.—THOMAS ESTEVAN claims a tract of land, situate in the county of Iberville, and on the left bank of the Mississippi, containing four arpents in front, by forty in depth, bounded on the upper side by land of John B. Dupuis, and on the lower by land of Francis Ribas.

It appearing to the Board, from a patent exhibited, that part of said land, viz: two arpents in front, by the depth aforesaid, was, with a greater quantity, granted by the Spanish Government to Paul Landry, on the 5th day of February, 1775; and it appearing to the Board, from a warrant of survey, likewise exhibited, dated 1st day of September, 1786, that the two remaining arpents of front, by the depth aforesaid, were, with a larger quantity, conceded by the Spanish Government to one Paul Chiasson, and it appearing to the satisfaction of the Board, in regard to this latter quantity, that all the provisions of the first section of the act of Congress establishing this Board have been fulfilled; and it moreover appearing, from instruments of conveyance exhibited, that the land thus claimed by the present claimant has been transferred to him, the Board do hereby confirm him in his claim aforesaid.

No. 150.—ANTHONY DERUCLET claims a tract of land, situate in the county of Iberville, and on the right bank of the Mississippi, containing six arpents eighteen toises and three feet in front, by the common depth of forty arpents, with an opening towards the rear of ten degrees, bounded at present on the upper side by land of Peter Belly, Esq., and on the lower by land of Peter Sigur.

It appearing to the Board, from a patent or complete title exhibited, that said land was granted by the Spanish Government to Honoré Trahan, on the 7th of July, 1774; and it appearing to the Board, from sundry deeds of conveyance, likewise exhibited, that said land has become conveyed to the present claimant, the Board do hereby confirm him in his claim aforesaid.

No. 153.—Messieurs JOHNSTON and BRADDISH claim a tract of land, situate in the county of Orleans, on the right bank of the Mississippi, about sixty miles below the city, containing twenty arpents in front, by forty in depth, bounded on the upper side by the land of Peter Burat, and on the lower and other sides by vacant land.

It appearing to the Board, from a warrant of survey exhibited, purporting to have been issued by the Spanish Government the 27th day of August, 1798, that said land was then conceded by the Spanish Government to one Peter Martin; and it appearing also, from a deed of conveyance from him to the claimant, that he has transferred said land to them, the 3d August, 1805; and it moreover appearing to the satisfaction of the Board, that all the provisions under the first section of the act of Congress establishing this Board have, in regard to said land, been complied with, the Board do hereby confirm the claimants in their claim aforesaid.

No. 27.—JAMES LIVAUDAIS claims a tract of land, situate about eighteen miles below the city of New Orleans, on the left bank of the Mississippi, containing twelve arpents in front, by forty in depth, bounded on the upper side by land of Jacques Bachemin, and on the lower by land of John B. Saucier.

It appears to the Board, from the oath of Gilbert Leonard, that he is knowing to Mr. Livaudais, the claimant, having obtained from the Baron de Carondelet, while Governor of the province of Louisiana, a concession for a tract of land, containing about twelve arpents in front, by forty in depth, situate on the left bank of the Mississippi, about six leagues from New Orleans, it being land that had been abandoned by the former owner; that, in the year 1800, said Livaudais put into the hands of this deponent, who was then Fiscal to His Catholic Majesty (the same being the office next below the Intendant) for the province of Louisiana, the petition and decree in relation to said land, which papers he lodged with Mr. Lopez, then Intendant of said province, and that he has reason to believe said papers are among the papers of Mr. Morales, the late Intendant of the province aforesaid; which testimony is confirmed by that of Don Andreas Lopez Almestre; and it further appearing to the Board, from the registry of a warrant of survey found in No. 6, page 19, of the public records, received from the Spanish Government of the province of Louisiana, that said land was granted to the claimant on the 25th day of January, 1793; and it appearing to the satisfaction of the Board that all the requisites of the first section of the act of Congress establishing this Board have, in relation to said land, been complied with, the Board do hereby confirm the claimant in his claim aforesaid.

No. 47.—JOSEPH McNEIL claims a tract of land, situated in the county of Orleans, at a place called Pointe St. Antoine, three miles below the city of New Orleans, and on the left bank of the Mississippi, containing two hundred feet front, by one thousand in depth, bounded on the upper side by land of Messrs. Davis and Harper, and on the lower by land of John Clay.

It appears to the Board, upon the oath of James Villeré, that said land was in the possession, and the property of Madame Bienvenue, for more than twenty years; and it appearing also, from divers deeds of conveyance exhibited, that it has been duly transferred to the present claimant, the Board do therefore confirm him in his claim aforesaid.

No. —. JOHN BAPTISTE BABIN claims a tract of land, situate in the county of Iberville, and on the left bank of the Mississippi, containing five arpents and twenty-five toises in front, by forty in depth, bounded on the upper side by land of Joseph Leblanc, and on the lower by land of John Baptiste Hebert.

It appearing to the Board, from a patent or complete title exhibited, that said land was granted by the Spanish Government to the claimant on the 5th day of November, 1774, the Board do therefore confirm him in his claim aforesaid.

No. —. PAUL CHIASSON claims a tract of land, situate in the county of Iberville, and on the left bank of the river Mississippi, containing five arpents three toises and three feet in front, by forty arpents in depth, bounded on the upper side by land of Peter Forest, and on the lower by land of Anselme Blanchard.

It appearing to the Board, from a patent or complete title exhibited, that said land was granted by the Spanish Government to the claimant on the 5th day of November, 1774, the Board do hereby confirm him in his claim aforesaid.

No. 151.—JUDAH TURO claims a tract of land, situate in the county of Orleans, about eighteen leagues below the city of New Orleans, on the left bank of the Mississippi, containing forty-five arpents in front, by the depth of forty, converging twenty degrees towards its rear, and bounded on all sides by vacant lands.

It appears to the satisfaction of the Board that said land was regularly surveyed by Charles Laveau Trudeau, Esq., late Surveyor General of the province of Louisiana, on the 19th day of September, in the year 1789; and that a patent was issued, on the 28th day of September in the same year, by the Spanish Government, in favor of James Pierrot, from whom, by subsequent conveyances, the claimant derives title. Confirmed.

No. 161.—GREGORY BERGEL claims a tract of land, situate in the county of Iberville, on the right bank of the river Amite, containing eight arpents in front, by twenty in depth, and bounded on the upper side by lands of Fabian Ramos, and on the lower by lands of widow Nicholas.

It appears that Joseph Pereira was put in possession of said land in the year 1794, by the Surveyor General, by order of the Governor, Baron de Carondelet, and from whom tne claimant derives his title; and that said land has since that period been inhabited and cultivated. Confirmed.

No. 162.—THOMAS COLLADO claims a tract of land, situate in the county of Iberville, containing sixty superficial arpents, bounded on the north by lands of Joseph Pabona, on the west by Joseph Prara, on the south by those of Michael Massias, and on the east by vacant lands.

It appears that the claimant was put in possession of said land in the year 1794, by the Surveyor of the province, and that he has continued to inhabit and cultivate the same since that period. Confirmed.

No. 163.—STEPHEN H. PLANCHE claims a tract of land, situate in the county of Orleans, on the right bank of the Mississippi, twenty-one miles below the city of New Orleans, containing fifteen arpents in front, by the common depth of forty, bounded on the upper side line by lands of Simon Ducoumeau, and on the lower by those of Peter Tassin.

It appears that said land was surveyed by the Surveyor General of the province, in the year 1774, in favor of ——— Troufleau, being then in possession of the same, under whom the present claimant derives his title. It also appears that said land was inhabited and cultivated on the 20th December, 1803, and for more than ten consecutive years next preceding. Confirmed.

No. 164.—ALEXANDRE MILNE claims a tract of land, situate in the county of Orleans, on the left bank of the bayou St. John, about two miles below the bridge thereof, containing seventeen arpents and twenty-nine toises in front, by forty in depth, bounded on the upper side by lands of James Proffit, and on the lower by the lands of claimant.

It appears that the claimant derives his title to the aforesaid land by virtue of a regular patent issued by the French Government, on the 16th day of June, 1766. Confirmed.

No. 165.—DOMINGO PREVOST claims a tract of land, situate in the county of Iberville, on the right bank of the river St. Bernard, about nine miles to the southeast of the fort of Galveztown, containing twenty arpents in front, by forty in depth, and bounded on all sides by vacant land.

It appears that the claimant obtained from the Spanish Government a regular patent for the aforesaid land, on the 23d day of June, 1788. Confirmed.

No. 166.—JEANNE DELATRE claims a tract of land, situate in the county of Pointe Coupée, on the northern bank of False river, containing seven hundred and fifty-four superficial arpents, bounded on the upper side by lands of Leblond and Francis Porche, and on the lower by those of William Goutrie.

It appears that the claimant obtained a regular warrant of survey from the Spanish Government, on the 19th day of April, 1784, and a patent from the same Government on the 19th day of June, 1802; the land having been inhabited and cultivated for more than ten consecutive years prior to the 20th of December, 1803. Confirmed.

No. 160.—THOMAS COLLADO claims a tract of land, situate in the county of Iberville, and settlement of Galveztown, on the right bank of bayou Manchack, containing five arpents in front, by forty in depth, bounded on the upper side line by the lands of Joseph Ramirez, and on the lower by those of Don Marcos Devilliers.

It appears that Juan Tilano was put in possession of said land, in the year 1794, by the Surveyor General of the province, by order of the Governor, Baron de Carondelet, and that the claimant derives his title from intermediate sales made thereof, and that said land has been inhabited and cultivated since the period above mentioned. Confirmed.

No. 156.—THOMAS and DAVID URQUHART claim a lot of ground, situate in the suburb of St. Mary, containing one hundred and ninety-eight feet in front, by fifty-nine feet and four inches in depth.

It appears to the satisfaction of the Board that said lot of ground was in the uninterrupted possession of the claimants, or of those under whom they claim, on the 20th December, 1803, and for more than ten consecutive years prior thereto. Confirmed.

No. 168.—AMANT HEBERT claims a tract of land, situate in the county of Iberville, on the right bank of the Mississippi, containing thirteen chains in front, by ninety-three chains in depth, bounded on the upper side line by lands of Jean Charles Hebert, and on the lower by those of Narcissus Hebert.

It appears that the claimant made the road and levee upon said land, and was put in possession of the same, conformably to an order of the Baron de Carondelet, dated the 10th August, 1792, and that he has inhabited and cultivated it from the period aforesaid. Confirmed.

No. 170.—PETER VOIRIN claims a tract of land, situate in the county of Iberville, on the left bank of the Mississippi, containing ten arpents in front; the upper side line, adjoining lands of Mr. Degruis, measures twenty-seven arpents two toises and three feet; and the lower, adjoining lands of Mr. Gagne, measures twenty-four arpents fifteen toises and three feet; producing a superfices of two hundred and fifty-seven arpents four perches and ten feet.

It appears that the claimant has been in possession of said land since the year 1792, and that he obtained a regular warrant of survey for the same in the year 1794, from the Governor, Baron de Carondelet, and that the same has been inhabited and cultivated since the period aforesaid. Confirmed.

No. 176.—EVAN JONES claims a tract of land, situate in the county of Acadia, on the right bank of the Mississippi, containing eight arpents eighteen toises and three feet in front, by eighty arpents in depth; the upper line adjoining lands of Joseph Bujeaux, and the lower those of Geromino Leblanc.

It appears that the claimant derives his title from regular grants of said land made by the Spanish Government in the years 1775 and 1787. Confirmed.

No. 177.—EVAN JONES claims a tract of land, situate in the county of Acadia, on the right bank of the river Mississippi, containing nine arpents eighteen toises and one foot in front; the upper line, adjoining lands of Mr. Biddel, running south, seven degrees thirty minutes west, measures twenty arpents in depth; and the lower, bounded by lands of Mr. Rody, running south, thirty degrees west, and measures sixteen arpents and fifteen toises.

It appears that the claimant derives his title to the aforesaid land from regular grants made of the same by the Spanish Government in the year 1775. Confirmed.

No. 184.—JEANNE LARABELLE, widow DUPRE, claims a tract of land, situate in the county of Iberville, on the left bank of the Mississippi, containing ten arpents in front; the upper line, adjoining lands of Mr. Clairmont, runs south, eight degrees thirty minutes one second and a quarter and measures twenty-seven arpents; and the lower, adjoining lands of Louis Dauterive, runs north, nine degrees east, and measures thirty-five arpents.

It appears that the claimant has possessed and occupied said land by virtue of a regular warrant of survey issued by the Baron de Carondelet on the first day of July, 1794, and that the same has been inhabited and cultivated ever since that period. Confirmed.

No. 185.—FRANCIS B. LANGUILLE claims a tract of land, situate in the county of Orleans, at the place called Pointe St. Antoine, about four miles below the city of New Orleans, on the left bank of the Mississippi, containing eight arpents and nine toises in front; the upper line, adjoining lands of Delery Desitet, running north, thirteen degrees thirty minutes east, and measures one hundred twenty-three arpents and twenty toises the lower line; adjoining lands of Philip Laneau, measures one hundred and thirty-two arpents, with five toises in depth; bounded on the rear by the plantation of Louis Druaux.

It appears that the front of said land was inhabited and cultivated by the claimant, or those under whom he claims, on the 20th December, 1803, and for more than ten consecutive years prior thereto. The Board confirm him in his claim as far as forty arpents in depth.

No. 186.—ISELENE MODESTE BARBIN claims a tract of land, situate in the county of Orleans, at the place known by the name of La Grande Chênaie containing about eight arpents in front on each side of the Bayou du Petit Lac, and sixty arpents depth on each side of said bayou, and bounded on all sides by vacant lands.

The husband of the claimant, Prosper Casimir Barbin, obtained for this land, in the year 1787, a regular warrant of survey from the Spanish Government; and it appears that the land was actually inhabited and cultivated on the 1st day of October, 1800. Confirmed.

No. 187.—LOUIS DAUTERIVE claims a tract of land, situate in the county of Iberville, on the left bank of the Mississippi, containing seventeen arpents in front, by forty in depth, bounded on the upper side line by lands of Laurent Dupuis, and on the lower by lands of Antoine Dauterive.

It appears that this claim is founded upon two regular warrants of survey issued by the Baron de Carondelet; the first, in favor of the claimant, dated 22d February, 1793, for eleven arpents front, by forty in depth; and the second, for six arpents, in favor of Joseph Babin, dated the 11th day of April, 1796; and that the said land has been continually inhabited and cultivated by virtue of said warrants of survey. Confirmed.

No. 188.—SAMUEL PACKWOOD claims a lot of land, situate in the county of Orleans, in the city of New Orleans, fronting on Levee street, containing fifty feet in front, by ninety-one and a half in depth.

It appears that said lot was in the individual possession of the claimant, or by those under whom he claims, on the 20th December, 1803, and for more than ten consecutive years prior thereto. Confirmed.

No. 189.—SAMUEL PACKWOOD claims a tract of land, situate in the county of Orleans, thirteen and a half miles below the city of New Orleans, on the left bank of the Mississippi, containing three arpents in front, by forty in depth, bounded on the upper side by land of Edward Livingston, and on the lower by land of John B. Lajonchere.

It appears that said land was inhabited and cultivated by the claimant, or by those under whom he claims, on the 20th December, 1803, and for more than ten consecutive years prior thereto. Confirmed.

No. 190.—JOSEPH DUCROS claims a tract of land, situate in the county of Orleans, on the left bank of the Mississippi, four and a half miles above the city of New Orleans, containing four hundred superficial acres, bounded on the upper side by land of Estevan Bore, and on the lower by land of Valentine R. Avar.

It appears that said land was inhabited and cultivated by the claimant, or by those under whom he claims, on the 20th December, 1803, and for more than ten consecutive years prior thereto; that the survey of said land was executed under the French Government in the year 1767. Confirmed.

No. 193.—CIRCIL FAZAND, SEBASTIAN FAZAND, and LOUIS C. LEBRETON claim a tract of land, situate in the county of Orleans. nine miles above the city of New Orleans, on the right bank of the Mississippi, containing nine arpents four toises and six feet in front, by eighty arpents in depth, the side lines converging two degrees towards the rear, the upper line adjoining to lands of Francis Lebreton Dorgenois, and the lower adjoining to those of Joseph Zeringue.

It appears that said land was inhabited and cultivated by the claimants, or by those under whom they claim, on the 20th December, 1803, and for more than ten consecutive years prior thereto. Confirmed.

No. 198.—PIERRE CLAIRMONT claims a tract of land, situate in the county of Iberville, on the left bank of the Mississippi, containing one hundred and sixty-seven superficial arpents and six hundredths, bounded on the upper side by lands of Urbain Gagné, and on the lower by vacant lands.

It appears that Jean Saussier did inhabit and cultivate said land by virtue of a warrant of survey obtained from the Spanish Government in the year 1795, and continued to possess and cultivate the same until the year 1806, when he transferred the same to the claimant. Confirmed.

No. 199.—HYPOLITE and JOSEPH LANDRY claim a tract of land, situate in the county of Iberville, on the right bank of the Mississippi, containing six arpents in front, by forty in depth, bounded on the upper side by the lands of James Goodby, and on the lower by the lands of John L. Bouche.

It appears that Joseph Duprée obtained a regular patent for the aforesaid land from Louis de Unzaga, in the year 1774, who was then Governor of the province, and that, by regular successive conveyances, the claimant has become the proprietor. Confirmed.

No. 200.—JOSEPH and HYPOLITE LANDRY claim a tract of land, situate in the county of Iberville, on the right bank of the Mississippi, containing thirty-five superficial acres and twenty-nine hundredths, and bounded on the upper side by lands of P. Mitchell, and on the lower by those of Joseph Hebert.

It appears that, conformably to an order from the Baron de Carondelet, the claimants made the road and levee in August, 1792. We consider them entitled to the lands claimed, as aforesaid, and do accordingly confirm their title to the same. Confirmed.

No. 202.—JOSEPH ENOUL DUGUES LIVAUDAIS claims a tract of land, situate in the county of Orleans, containing three leagues front, on Bayou des Allemands, by one arpent in depth, on the northern bank of said bayou, beginning at Petit Lac, and extending as far as the lands of Michael Zeringue.

It appears that the claimant petitioned Governor Miro for said land for the purpose of raising stock, and obtained, in the year 1789, a regular warrant of survey for the quantity of land claimed as aforesaid; and that the same has, ever since that period, continued to be occupied, by virtue of said warrant of survey, for the purposes mentioned in said petition; which, according to the laws, usages, and customs of the Spanish Government, we consider ought to be confirmed.

No. 203.—JOSEPH E. D. LIVAUDAIS claims a tract of land, situate in the county of La Fourche, on the left bank of the bayou of the same name, about seventy-five miles from the Mississippi, at the establishment called Valenzuela, containing one hundred and eighty arpents in front, by forty in depth, bounded on the upper side by lands of Jean Baptiste Demorville, and by vacant lands on the lower.

It appears that the claimant obtained a regular warrant of survey from his excellency Ramon Lopez de Angulo, at that time Intendant, on the 24 day of July, 1800, and that, since that period, he has continued to possess and occupy the same. Confirmed.

No. 205.—LAURENT DUPRES claims a tract of land, situate in the county of Iberville, on the left bank of the Mississippi, containing fourteen arpents in front, by forty in depth. with an opening of four degrees towards the rear, bounded on the upper side by lands of Mopes Lacroix and Flechier, and on the lower by lands of Baptiste Duprés.

It appears that ten arpents of said land were regularly granted by the Spanish Government, on the 11th day of February, 1799, to Bartholomew Duverges; and it further appears, from the testimony of Amant Hebert, that the remaining four arpents were purchased from Diego Nemandez, who purchased them from Narcisse O'Donnate Hebert, to whom they formerly belonged. Confirmed.

No. 206.—BARBRE CHLATRE claims a tract of land, situate in the county of Iberville, on the right bank of the Mississippi, containing ten arpents and six toises in front, by forty in depth, bounded on the upper side by lands of John A. B. Dauterive, and by vacant lands on the lower.

It appears that Antoine M. Dorville obtained a complete grant to said land from the Spanish Government on the 7th day of July, 1774, from whom the present claimant derives his title. Confirmed.

No. 208.—ANDRE GIROD claims a tract of land, situate in the county of Orleans, about thirty miles below the city of New Orleans, on the right bank of the Mississippi, at the place called Quartier du Portage, containing fourteen arpents in front, by the common depth of forty, bounded on the upper side by lands of Mr. Bernandy, and on the lower by those of Simon Girod.

It appears that said land was granted by the French Government to Laloire Jousset, from whom, by subsequent intermediate conveyances, the claimant derives his title. Confirmed.

No. 209.—SIMON GIROD claims a tract of land, situate in the county of Orleans, about thirty miles below the city of New Orleans, on the right bank of the Mississippi, at the place called Quartier du Portage, containing six arpents in front, by forty in depth, bounded on the upper side by lands of Andre Girod, and on the lower by those of John Girod.

It appears that said land was granted by the French Government to Laloire Jousset, from whom, by subsequent intermediate conveyances, the claimant derives his title. Confirmed.

No. 210.—JOHN GIROD claims a tract of land, situate in the county of Orleans, about thirty miles below the city of New Orleans, on the right bank of the Mississippi, at the place called Quartier du Portage, bounded on the upper side by lands of Simon Girod, and on the lower by those of James Hollier.

It appears that said land was granted by the French Government to Laloire Jousset, from whom, by subsequent intermediate conveyances, the claimant derives his title. Confirmed.

No. 212.—JOSEPH ZERINGUE claims a tract of land, situate in the county of Orleans, about eight miles above the city of New Orleans, on the right bank of the Mississippi, containing nine arpents twenty-three toises and three feet in front, by eighty arpents in depth, bounded on the upper side by lands of Godfroi Oliver, and on the lower by lands of Lebreton Dorgenois.

It appears that the front of said land, by forty arpents in depth, was inhabited and cultivated on the 20th December 1803, and for more than ten consecutive years prior thereto; and that, for the second depth of forty arpents, the claimant obtained a complete title from the Spanish Government, dated the 10th day of November, 1775. Confirmed.

No. 215.—ARCENE BRAUD claims a tract of land, situate in the county of Iberville, on the right bank of the Mississippi, containing three arpents two toises and two feet in front, by forty arpents in depth, bounded on the upper side by lands of Honoré Daigle, and on the lower by those of widow Josephe Henry.

It appears that the claimant did inhabit and cultivate said land, by permission of the proper Spanish officers, on the 20th December, 1803, and for more than ten consecutive years prior thereto. Confirmed.

No. 213.—CHARLES J. B. FLORIAN claims a tract of land, situate in the county of Orleans, containing a superficies of forty-five thousand nine hundred and eighty-six and a half arpents, bounded on the north by the Grand Lac des Allemands, on the east by Bayou des Allemands and Lac de Barataria, on the south by bayou Cataoulou, and on the west by Lac de la Fourche.

It appears that the aforesaid tract of land was regularly granted by the French Government, on the 1st day of June, 1763, in favor of Joseph Villars Dubreuils, from whom, by conveyances, the present claimant derives his title. Confirmed.

No. 216.—JOSEPH DOSITE BABIN claims a tract of land, situate in the county of Iberville, on the left bank of the Mississippi, containing seven arpents three toises and three feet in front, by forty in depth, bounded on the upper side by lands of Peter Richard, and on the lower by those of Fernin Pangrasse.

It appears that said land was granted by the Spanish Government, on the 3d day of January, 1776, in favor of Joseph Hebert, under whom the claimant derives his title. Confirmed.

No. 217.—HONORE DAIGLE claims a tract of land, situate in the county of Iberville, on the right bank of the Mississippi, containing three arpents two toises and four feet in front, by forty in depth, with an opening of three degrees and eighty-two minutes towards the rear.

It appears that said land was inhabited and cultivated by the claimant, or by those under whom he claims, on the 20th December, 1803, and for more than ten consecutive years prior thereto. Confirmed.

No. 218.—CHARLES BRAUD claims a tract of land, situate in the county of Iberville, on the right bank of the Mississippi, containing three arpents fifteen toises and six feet in front, by forty in depth, with an opening of three degrees towards the rear, bounded on the upper side by lands of Louis Braud, and on the lower by those of Peter J. Landry.

It appears that said land was inhabited and cultivated by the claimant on the 20th December, 1803, and for more than ten consecutive years preceding that day. Confirmed.

No. 219.—LOUIS BRAUD claims a tract of land, situate in the county of Iberville, on the right bank of the Mississippi, containing three arpents and six feet in front, by forty in depth, bounded on the upper side by lands of Joseph Hebert, and on the lower by those of Charles Braud.

It appears that said land was inhabited and cultivated by the claimant on the 20th December, 1803, and for more than ten consecutive years prior thereto. Confirmed.

No. 220.—ROSALIA COMEAU claims a tract of land, situate in the county of Iberville, on the right bank of the Mississippi, containing four arpents in front, by forty in depth, bounded on the upper side by lands of Arcené Braud, and on the lower by those of Peter Plet.

It appears that said land was inhabited and cultivated by the claimant, or by those under whom she claims, on the 20th December, 1803, and for more than ten consecutive years prior thereto. Confirmed.

No. 221.—MARGARITA BRAUD claims a tract of land, situate in the county of Iberville, on the right bank of the Mississippi, containing four arpents and twenty-nine toises in front, by forty arpents in depth, opening five and a half degrees towards the rear.

It appears that Simon Leblanc, under whom the present claimant derives his title, obtained from the Spanish Government, on the 20th July, 1796, a complete title to the aforesaid land. Confirmed.

No. 222.—MARIA JOSEPH HABERT claims a tract of land, situate in the county of Iberville, on the right bank of the Mississippi, containing six arpents in front, by forty in depth, bounded on the upper side by lands of Joseph Mollere, and on the lower by those of Joseph Orillon.

It appears that Athanasse Daiden, under whom the claimant derives her title, obtained from the Spanish Government a complete title to the aforesaid land, dated the 7th July, 1774. Confirmed.

No. 223.—JOSEPH BRAUD and MARIQUE GUEDRY claim a tract of land, situate in the county of Iberville, on the left bank of the Mississippi, containing eight arpents in front, by forty in depth, with an opening of seven degrees towards the rear.

It appears that Anthony Braud, under whom the claimants derive their title, obtained from the Spanish Government a complete title to the aforesaid land, dated the 3d January, 1776. Confirmed.

No. 224.—JOSEPH BRAUD and LOUIS LANDRY claim a tract of land, situate in the county of Iberville, on the left bank of the Mississippi, containing six arpents and seven toises in front, by forty arpents in depth, with an opening of twelve degrees towards the rear.

It appears that Oliver Babin, under whom the claimants derive their title, obtained from the Spanish Government a complete title to said land, dated on the 3d day of January, 1776. Confirmed.

No. 225.—LOUIS LANDRY claims a tract of land, situate in the county of Iberville, on the left bank of the Mississippi, containing two and a half arpents in front, by forty in depth, bounded on the upper side by lands of Joseph Braud, and on the lower by those of John W. Gurley.

It appears that Estevan Benoit, under whom the claimant derives his title, obtained from the Spanish Government on the 3d day of January, 1776, a complete title to the aforesaid land. Confirmed.

No. 226.—MARTIN DUPLESSIS claims a tract of land, situate in the county of Orleans, at the place called Quartier du Bois d'Amourette, thirteen leagues below the city of New Orleans, on the left bank of the Mississippi, containing twenty-eight arpents and fifteen toises in front, by forty arpents in depth, bounded on the upper side by the lands of widow Jacques Billaud, and on the lower by those of —— Martin.

It appears that the claimant was put in possession of twenty arpents of the aforesaid land by a regular warrant of survey from the Intendant, dated the 26th day of June, 1790, and purchased the other eight arpents and fifteen toises, which were inhabited and cultivated on the 20th December, 1803, and for more than ten consecutive years prior thereto. Confirmed.

No. 229.—JAMES GOODBY claims a tract of land, situate in the county of Iberville, on the right bank of the Mississippi, containing eight arpents in front, by forty in depth, converging eight degrees towards the rear, bounded on the upper side by the lands of Paul M. Landry, and on the lower by those of the claimant.

It appears that Joseph Hamilton, from whom the claimant derives his title, obtained from the Spanish

Government a patent concession for said land, dated the 16th day of July, 1796. Confirmed.

No. 231.—JAMES GOODBY claims a tract of land, situate in the county of Iberville, on the right bank of the Mississippi, containing thirty-seven superficial arpents and eighty-two hundredths, bounded on the upper side by the lands of Maniah Mitchel, and on the lower by those of Joseph Hernandez.

It appears from the testimony of Armand Hebert, that said land was inhabited and cultivated on the 20th of December, 1803, and for more than ten consecutive years prior thereto. Confirmed.

No. 233.—JEAN BAPTISTE BAGNERIS claims a tract of land, situate in the county of Orleans, on the left bank of the Mississippi, twelve leagues below the city of New Orleans, containing nine arpents in front, by forty in depth, bounded on the upper side by the lands of S. B. Davis, and on the lower by those of S. B. Davis.

It appears that the claimant did inhabit and cultivate said land on the 20th December, 1803, and for more than ten consecutive years prior to that period. Confirmed.

No. 234.—JEAN LOUIS BOUCHE claims a tract of land, situate in the county of Iberville, on the right bank of the Mississippi, containing six arpents in front, by forty in depth, bounded on the upper side by lands of widow Paul Landry, and on the lower by those of Baptiste Doucet.

It appears that Huberto Jany, from whom the claimant derives his title, obtained from the Spanish Government a patent for the aforesaid land, dated the 11th day of July, 1774. Confirmed.

No. 235.—CHARLOTTE ROUX claims a tract of land, situate in the county of Orleans, at the place called District de la Maitairie, about six miles from the city of New Orleans, containing three arpents in front, on both sides of the Bayou de la Maitairie, bounded on the west by lands of Auguste Savane, on the south by the rear of the plantations fronting the Mississippi, on the east by lands of Charles Ximenez, and on the north by lake Pontchartrain.

It appears that the claimant, or those under whom she claims, did inhabit and cultivate said land on the 20th December, 1803, and for more than ten consecutive years prior thereto. Confirmed.

No. 236.—FRANCIS DUVERNEY claims a tract of land, situate in the county of Orleans, twelve leagues below the city of New Orleans, on the left bank of the Mississippi, containing three hundred and fifty-two superficial arpents and six hundred toises, bounded on the upper side by lands of Charles B. Frederick, and on the lower by those of ———.

It appears that Charles Canel was put in possession of said land by virtue of a regular warrant of survey issued by the Baron de Carondelet, dated the 6th day of February, 1793, from whom the claimant derives his title by purchase, and that said land has been inhabited and cultivated since the period aforesaid. Confirmed.

No. 240.—LOUIS B. DECLOUET claims a tract of land, situate in the county of Orleans, four leagues below the city of New Orleans, on the left bank of the Mississippi, containing one hundred and eighty-six superficial arpents, bounded on the upper side by the lands of the widow Beauregard, and on the lower by those of the claimant.

It appears that the claimant obtained from the Spanish Government a complete title to the aforesaid land, dated the 17th December, 1799. Confirmed.

No. 241.—DOMINIQUE DOMINGUEZ claims a tract of land, situate in the county of Iberville, on the right bank of the Mississippi, containing two arpents one hundred feet and three inches in front, by forty arpents in depth, bounded on the upper side by lands of John Leblanc, and on the lower by those of Honoré Daigle.

It appears that this is part of a larger tract of land, of five arpents one toise two feet and six inches in front, which was surveyed in the year 1796, in favor of John Leblanc, who obtained a complete grant to the same on the 20th day of July, 1796, from the Spanish Government; under which grant the claimant derives his title. Confirmed.

No. 243.—PETER PHILIBERT claims a tract of land, situate in the county of Orleans, about twenty-two leagues below the city of New Orleans, on the left bank

of the Mississippi, containing eight arpents in front, by forty in depth, bounded on the upper side by vacant lands, and on the lower by those of the claimant.

It appears that said land was inhabited and cultivated by the claimant, or by those under whom he claims, on the 20th December, 1803, and for more than ten consecutive years prior thereto. Confirmed.

No. 244.—PETER PHILIBERT claims a tract of land, situate in the county of Orleans, below the city of New Orleans, about two and a half miles above Fort Placquemines, on the left bank of the Mississippi, containing twenty arpents in front, by the common depth of forty, bounded on the lower side by the lands of Pedro Roigas, and on the upper by vacant lands.

It appears that the claimant, or those under whom he claims, inhabited and cultivated said land on the 20th December, 1803, and for more than ten consecutive years prior thereto. Confirmed.

No. 245.—PETER HONORE VEILLON claims a tract of land, situate in the county of Orleans, at the settlement of St. Bernard, about four miles from the Mississippi, containing twelve toises and four feet in front on each side of the Bayou aux Bœufs, by forty arpents in depth, bounded on the upper side by lands of Joseph Ogeda, and on the lower by those of the present claimant.

It appears that Antonio Ogeda, under whom the claimant derives his title, was put in possession of said land by the Surveyor General of the province on the 3d day of April, 1792, and that said land was inhabited on the 20th December, 1803, and for more than ten consecutive years prior thereto. Confirmed.

No. 246.—JOSEPH HENDERSON claims a tract of land, situate in the county of Iberville, on the left bank of the Mississippi, containing five arpents and eleven toises in front, by forty in depth, bounded on the upper side by lands of James Teyset, and on the lower by those of Michel Hebert.

It appears that John Braud, from whom the claimant derives his title, obtained from the Spanish Government a patent concession for said land dated the 3d day of January, 1776. Confirmed.

No. 247.—JAMES GOODBY claims a tract of land, situate in the county of Iberville, on the right bank of the Mississippi, containing six arpents in front, by forty in depth, bounded on the upper side by lands of the claimant, and on the lower by those of Hypolite and Joseph Landry.

It appears that John Landry, under whom, by conveyances, the claimant derives his title, obtained from the Spanish Government a complete title to the aforesaid land, dated the 11th day of July, 1774. Confirmed.

No. 248.—NATHANIEL CROPPER claims a tract of land, situate in the county of Iberville, on the right bank of the Mississippi, containing three hundred and three acres and fifty-seven hundredths superficial; bounded on all sides by vacant land.

It appears that Denis Landry obtained from the Spanish Government a regular warrant of survey, dated the 20th January, 1799, and that, by virtue of which, said land has been inhabited and cultivated ever since that period. Confirmed.

No. 249.—PETER HONORATIO VEILLON claims a tract of land, situate in the county of Orleans, at the settlement of St. Bernard, about one mile from the church thereof, containing fifty-three and a half toises in front, on each side of the Bayou aux Bœufs, adjoining lands of Anthony Ogeda and Pedro R. de St. Germain.

It appears that Ramon Palacios was put in possession of said land by the Surveyor General of the province on the 3d February, 1792, under whom the claimant derives his title, and that said land has been inhabited and cultivated by virtue of this possession ever since that period, and for ten consecutive years prior to the 20th December, 1803. Confirmed.

No. 250.—SILVANO VEILLON claims a tract of land, situate in the county of Orleans, at the settlement of St. Bernard, three miles from the Mississippi, containing three arpents twenty-nine toises and three feet in front, by forty in depth, on the left bank of Bayou aux Bœufs; bounded on the upper side by lands of Joseph Querido and on the lower by those of John Estevans.

It appears that the claimant was put in possession of said land by the Surveyor General of the province on the 14th of April, 1792, and that said land was inhabited and cultivated on the 20th December, 1803, and for more than ten consecutive years prior thereto. Confirmed.

No. 251.—SILVANO VEILLON claims a tract of land, situate at the settlement of St. Bernard, about three miles from the Mississippi, containing one arpent in front, on the right bank of the Bayou aux Bœufs, by forty in depth, bounded on the upper side by lands of Joseph Querido, and on the lower by those of Isidro Rodriguez.

It appears that the Surveyor General of the province did, on the 14th March, 1792, put Joseph Querido in possession of two arpents sixteen toises and five feet front, on Bayou aux Bœufs, and also Isidro Rodriguez in possession of three arpents twenty-three toises and five feet adjoining; from each of whom the present claimant has purchased half an arpent. It appears, moreover, that said land was inhabited and cultivated on the 20th December, 1803, and for more than ten consecutive years prior thereto. Confirmed.

No. 252.—ASRICA SANCHEZ claims a tract of land, situate in the county of Orleans, at the settlement of St. Bernard, containing fifty-five toises and five feet in front, on each side of Bayou aux Bœufs, by forty in depth, bounded on the upper side by lands of Jasper Sanchez and on the lower by those of Anthony Lopez.

It appears that the claimant was put in possession of said land by the Surveyor General of the province on the 15th day of March, 1792, and that said land was inhabited and cultivated on the 20th December, 1803, and for more than ten consecutive years prior thereto. Confirmed.

No. 253.—FRANCIS COLONIA and SEBASTIANA RAMIREZ claim a tract of land, situate in the county of Orleans, at the settlement of St. Bernard, containing one hundred and twenty French feet front, by forty arpents in depth, on each side of Bayou aux Bœufs, bounded on the upper side by lands of Mr. Petit, and on the lower by those of Mr. Delille.

It appears that the claimants were put in possession of said land by the Surveyor General of the province on the 15th of March, 1792, and that said land was inhabited and cultivated on the 20th of December, 1803, and for ten consecutive years prior to that period. Confirmed.

No. 254.—MANUEL OGEDA claims a tract of land, situate in the county of Orleans, at the settlement of St. Bernard, containing four arpents two toises and four feet in front, on each side of the Bayou aux Bœufs, by forty arpents in depth, bounded on the upper side by lands of Vincent Delgado, and on the lower by those of Heloix Hachez.

It appears that the claimant was put in possession, by the Surveyor General of the province, of sixty-three toises front, on each side by the bayou, and that he purchased the remainder from Mariano Padron, who was put in possession of said land by the Surveyor General, on the 4th day of February, 1792; that said land has been inhabited for ten consecutive years next preceding the 20th December, 1803. Confirmed.

No. 255.—NICHOLAS GODFROY OLIVIER claims a tract of land, situate in the county of Orleans, at the settlement of St. Bernard, about four miles distant from the church thereof, containing eleven arpents eighteen toises and one foot in front, on each side of the Bayou aux Bœufs, by forty arpents in depth, bounded on the upper side by the lands of widow Padron, and on the lower by lands of widow Curé.

It appears that, in the year 1792, the Surveyor General of the province laid off said land into five several parcels, on each side of the bayou, viz.: to Madame widow Padron, one arpent and thirty-four toises; to Heloix Hachez, three arpents five toises and one foot; to Madame widow Benois two arpents and twenty-four toises; to Gille Robin, two arpents and fourteen toises; and to Bartholomew Cazal, one arpent twenty-nine toises and two feet, with the depth of forty arpents to each, on each side of the bayou; from whom the claimant derives his title by purchase. It also appears that said land was inhabited and cultivated on the 20th of December, 1803, and for more than ten consecutive years prior to that period. Confirmed.

No. 256.—NICHOLAS G. OLIVER claims a tract of land, situate in the county of Orleans, at the settlement of St. Bernard, two leagues from the church thereof, containing two arpents seventeen toises and three feet in front, on each side of the Bayou aux Bœufs; bounded on the upper side by the lands of Francisco Dominguez, and on the lower by those of Diego Belligo.

It appears that Bartholomew Benges, from whom the claimant derives his title, was put in possession of said land, by the Surveyor General of the province, on the 4th day of February, 1792; and, further, it appears that said land was inhabited and cultivated on the 20th of December, 1803, and for ten consecutive years prior to that period. Confirmed.

No. 258.—SAMUEL WINTER and THOMAS L. HARMAN claim a tract of land, situate in the county of Orleans, at the settlement of St. Bernard, about one mile beyond the parish church thereof, containing five arpents two toises and three feet in front, by forty in depth, on each side of the Bayou aux Bœufs, bounded on the upper side by lands of Joseph Williams, and on the lower by those of John Sanchez.

It appears that said land was parcelled out to different individuals by the Spanish Government, in the year 1792, from whom, by purchase, the claimants derive their title; and also that said land was inhabited and cultivated on the 20th of December, 1803, and for ten consecutive years prior to that period. Confirmed.

No. 259.—TOUSSAINT MASSEY claims a tract of land, situate in the county of Orleans, opposite the city of New Orleans, on the right bank of the Mississippi, containing four arpents in front; the upper side, adjoining lands of John Ray, measures twenty arpents and twelve toises; and the lower, adjoining lands of Bartholomew Duverges, measures twenty-two arpents and five toises, &c.

It appears that said land has been inhabited and cultivated by those under whom the claimant derives his title for more than forty years; that the same was inhabited and cultivated on the 20th of December, 1803. Confirmed.

No. 261.—LOUIS DE REGGIO claims a tract of land, situate in the county of Orleans, at the settlement of St. Bernard, about ten miles from the Mississippi, containing one league in front, by ten arpents in depth, on each side of the bayou Yeslocsy, bounded on the west by the lands of Juan Guzman, and on the other side by vacant lands.

It appears that Don Pedro Laronde, from whom the claimant derives his title, obtained a complete grant of said land from the Baron de Carondelet, dated the 4th of April, 1795. Confirmed.

No. 262.—LOUIS DE REGGIO claims a tract of land, situate in the county of Orleans, at the settlement of St. Bernard, about four miles from the church thereof, containing twenty-seven arpents and two toises in front, on each side of the Bayou aux Bœufs, by forty arpents in depth; bounded by the lands of Carlos Maclé on one side, and by the lands of Anthony de Armas on the other.

It appears that Juan Guzman, from whom the claimant derives his title, was put in possession of said land by the Surveyor General of the province, on the 17th day of March, 1792. It further appears that said land was inhabited and cultivated on the 20th of December, 1803, and for ten consecutive years prior thereto. Confirmed.

No. 263.—MICHEL ZERINGUE claims a tract of land, situate in the county of Orleans, on lake Ferrier, or Ouachas, district of Barataria, containing twelve arpents in front, by thirty in depth, bounded on the southwest by bayou Pouba, and on the other sides by vacant lands.

It appears that Alexander Harrang, from whom the claimant derives his title, obtained from the Spanish Government a complete title to the aforesaid land, dated the 12th day of March, 1794. Confirmed.

No. 264.—MICHEL ZERINGUE claims a tract of land, situated in the county of Orleans, containing twelve hundred superficial arpents, bounded on the west by Bayou des Allemands, on the north by vacant lands and the bay Bohia de los Cazadones.

It appears that Alexander Harrang, from whom the claimant derives his title, obtained a complete grant for one thousand arpents of the aforesaid land from the Spanish Government, dated the 12th day of March, 1794; which quantity, agreeably to the grant, the Board do hereby confirm.

No. 266.—CHARLES GARRELLE claims a tract of land, situate in the county of Orleans, about twelve leagues below the city of New Orleans, on the left bank of the

Mississippi, containing six hundred and forty-eight arpents and four hundred toises superficial, bounded on the upper side by lands of Daquine, and on the lower by those of Charles B. Frederick.

It appears that the claimant or those under whom he derives his title, were in possession of said land on the 20th December, 1803, and that the same has been inhabited and cultivated for more than ten consecutive years prior to that period. Confirmed.

No. 267.—CHARLES S. FREDERICK claims a tract of land, situate in the county of Orleans, twelve leagues, below the city of New Orleans, on the left bank of the Mississippi, containing one hundred and seventy-three superficial arpents and three hundred toises, bounded on the upper side by lands of Charles Garrelle, and on the lower by those of François Duvernay.

It appears that the claimant was in possession of said land on the 20th December, 1803, and that the same has been inhabited and cultivated for more than ten consecutive years prior thereto. Confirmed.

No. 268.—LOUIS DE REGGIO claims a tract of land, situate in the county of Orleans, at the settlement of St. Bernard, about four miles from the church thereof, containing three arpents one toise and four feet in front, on each side of the Bayou aux Bœufs, by forty arpents in depth, bounded on the upper side by lands of John Lorenzo Morales, and on the lower by those of Juan Guzman.

It appears that Carlos Maelé, from whom the claimant derives his title, was put in possession of said land on the 15th day of May, 1792, by the Surveyor General of the province, and that said land was inhabited and cultivated on the 20th December, 1803, and for ten consecutive years prior thereto. Confirmed.

No. 269.—LOUIS DE REGGIO claims a tract of land, situate in the county of Orleans, at the settlement of St. Bernard, about four miles below the church thereof, containing two arpents seventeen toises and two feet in front, on each side of the Bayou aux Bœufs, by forty in depth, bounded on the upper side by lands of M. Olivier, and on the lower by lands of Joseph Gutines.

It appears that Madame widow Curé, from whom the claimant derives his title, was put in possession of said land by the Surveyor General of the province, on the 28th day of March, 1792, and that said land was inhabited and cultivated on the 20th December, 1803, and for more than ten consecutive years prior to that period. Confirmed.

No. 270.—LOUIS DE REGGIO claims a tract of land, situate in the county of Orleans, at the settlement of St. Bernard, about six and a half miles below the church thereof, containing three arpents and six toises in front, on each side of the Bayou aux Bœufs, bounded on the upper side by lands of Joseph Hernandez, and on the lower by those of Antonio Perez.

It appears that Joseph Augustin, from whom the claimant derives his title, obtained regular possession of said land from the Surveyor General of the province, on the 28th day of March, 1792, and that the same was inhabited and cultivated on the 20th December, 1803, and for ten consecutive years prior thereto. Confirmed.

No. 295.—JAMES BROWN claims a tract of land, situate in the county of German Coast, nine leagues above the city of New Orleans, and on the same side of the Mississippi, containing sixteen acres in front, by forty in depth, bounded on the upper side by lands of Pierre Paine, and on the lower by those of Pierre Rillieau.

It appears that the claimant, or those under whom he claims, was in possession of said land on the 20th December, 1803, and that the same was inhabited and cultivated for more than ten consecutive years prior to that period. Confirmed.

No. 373.—LUCIEN DRAUSIER and JOHN BAPTISTE LABRANCHE, brothers, claim a tract of land, situate in the county of Orleans, about twelve miles above the city of New Orleans, on the right bank of the Mississippi, containing twenty-five arpents and five toises in front, by the common depth of forty, bounded on the upper side by lands of Dusseau, and on the lower by those of Charlotte Lacombe.

It appears that the claimants did inhabit and cultivate said land on the 20th December, 1803, and for more than ten consecutive years prior to that period. Confirmed.

No. 371.—ALEXANDER HARRANG claims a tract of land, situate in the county of Orleans, on lake Perrier, or Ouachas, containing twenty arpents in front, by three in depth, bounded on the north side by St. Catharine river, on the west by the lake aforesaid, and by low and swampy lands on the other.

It appears that John Joseph Dauphin, under whom the claimant derives his title, obtained from the French Government, in the year 1750, a grant for the aforesaid land; and the same was completed to his heirs, in the year 1783, by the Spanish Government. Confirmed.

No. 374.—JOHN B. SAUSSIER claims a tract of land, situate in the county of Orleans, about eighteen miles below the city of New Orleans, on the left bank of the Mississippi, containing ten arpents in front, by forty in depth, bounded on the upper side by lands of Decalogne, and on the lower by those of Henry Saussier.

It appears that the claimant was put in possession of said land by the Surveyor General of the province, in the year 1800, and that he has continued to inhabit and cultivate the same, by virtue of such possession, since that period to the present day. Confirmed.

No. 257.—MICHAEL DUGAT claims a tract of land, situate in the county of Acadia, on the left bank of the bayou La Fourche, containing four hundred and seventy-one superficial arpents and two hundred toises, bounded on the upper side by lands of Comvery, the new town, and B. Landry, and on the lower by those of Nicholas Doublin.

It appears that said land was inhabited and cultivated by the claimant, or by those under whom he claims, on the 20th December, 1803, and for ten consecutive years prior thereto. Confirmed.

No. 230.—HONORÉ and MICHEL DUPLESSIS claim a tract of land, situate in the county of Orleans, fourteen leagues below the city of New Orleans, on the right bank of the Mississippi, containing seventeen arpents in front, by forty in depth, bounded on the upper side by lands of Bartholomew Duverges, and on the lower by those of Baptiste Iris.

It appears that Francis Vignette, from whom the claimants derive their title, obtained from the French Government, on the 19th day of July, 1764, a complete title to thirty arpents front on the river, of which the present claim is a part. Confirmed.

No. 191.—WALTER BURK claims a tract of land, situate in the county of Iberville, on the left bank of the Mississippi, containing eighteen arpents and eighteen toises in front, by thirty-one arpents and twenty toises in depth; the upper side line, and that of the lower, adjoining Simon Broussard's, are thirty arpents in depth.

It appears that said land was inhabited and cultivated by the claimant, or by those under whom he claims, on the 20th December, 1803, and for more than ten consecutive years prior to that period. Confirmed.

No. 355.—JAMES JONES claims two tracts of land, situate in the county of Iberville, on the right bank of the bayou Manchack, the one containing six hundred superficial arpents, and the other three hundred and twenty superficial arpents; bounded on the upper side by vacant lands, and on the lower by those of the late John Harrison.

It appears that, in the year 1797, the Surveyor General of the province, by virtue of two regular warrants of survey from the Governor General, put Joseph Richard in possession of six hundred arpents of said land, and Santiago McCollock in possession of three hundred and twenty arpents of the aforesaid land, from whom the claimant derives his title; and that said land has been inhabited and cultivated, by virtue of such warrants of survey, ever since that period aforesaid. Confirmed.

No. 354.—SAMUEL YOUNG claims a tract of land, situate in the county of Pointe Coupée, containing twenty arpents in front, by forty in depth, bordering upon False river; the upper line adjoining lands of Benjamin Farrar, and that of the lower adjoining lands of Margarita Farrar.

It appears that Anna Francisca Farrar, who intermarried with the claimant, obtained from the Spanish Government a regular patent concession for said land, on the 17th day of July, 1790. Confirmed.

No. 356.—JULIA RAMOS claims a tract of land, situate in the county of Iberville, at the settlement of Galveztown, about one mile from the fort thereof, on the right bank of the river Amite, containing ten arpents in front, by twenty in depth, bounded on the upper side by the limits of the fort, and on the lower by lands of Joseph Pereira.

It appears that Fabian Ramos, late husband of the claimant, was put in possession of said land in the month of March, 1803, by the Surveyor General of the province, and was by said Ramos inhabited and cultivated on the 20th December, 1803, and has since that period continued to be possessed and occupied. Confirmed.

No. 271.—JOSEPH FOUQUE claims a tract of land, situate in the county of Orleans, at the settlement of St. Bernard, about fourteen acres front on each side of the Bayou aux Bœufs, by forty in depth, bounded on the upper side by the lands of Jean Fuertes, and on the lower by those of John Perez.

It appears that Antonio Gonzalez, from whom the claimant derives his title, was put in possession of said land on the 30th day of March, 1792, by the Surveyor General of the province, and that said land, by virtue of that possession, has been inhabited and cultivated since that period, and for ten consecutive years prior to the 20th December, 1803. Confirmed.

No. 352.—SAMUEL YOUNG, MARGARITA BUTLER, and BENJAMIN FARRAR claim a tract of land, situate in the county of Pointe Coupée, on False river, containing ten thousand five hundred arpents, of which there are two hundred and thirty-six fronting on False river.

It appears that Benjamin Farrar, from whom the claimants derive their title, obtained from the Spanish Government, on the 26th day of April, 1790, a complete title to the aforesaid land. Confirmed.

No. 272.—MARTIAL LE BŒUF claims a tract of land, situate in the county of Orleans, at the place called Quartier du Bois d'Amourette, thirteen leagues below the city of New Orleans, on the right bank of the Mississippi, containing ten arpents in front, by forty in depth, bounded on the upper side by lands of Nicholas Toulouse, and on the lower by those of Bartholomew Duverges.

It appears that John C. Tizoneau, from whom the claimant derives his title, obtained from the French Government, on the 9th day of July, 1766, a complete title to the aforesaid land. Confirmed.

No. 273.—JOSEPH GUTIERREZ claims a tract of land, situate in the county of Orleans, at the settlement of St. Bernard, containing two arpents and twenty-one toises in front, on each side of the Bayou aux Bœufs, by forty arpents in depth, bounded on the upper side by the lands of Madame widow Curé, and on the lower by those of John Quintana.

It appears that the claimant was put in possession of said land by the Surveyor General of the province, on the 18th day of March, 1792, and that said land has been inhabited and cultivated ever since that period. Confirmed.

No. 274.—SAMUEL YOUNG claims a tract of land, situate in the county of Pointe Coupée, containing twelve arpents, fronting the Mississippi, by forty in depth, bounded on the upper side by the lands of Madame widow Decour, and on the lower by those of Madame widow Decuir.

It appears that the said land was formerly the property of Colin Lacour; after whose death, it was sold, by a judicial sale under the Spanish Government, in the year 1797, to Jean Baptiste Saizan, from whom the claimant derives his title. Confirmed.

No. 275.—CHARLES J. B. FLEUREAU claims a tract of land, situate in the county of Orleans, at the place called Petit Desert, about six miles above the city of New Orleans, on the right bank of the Mississippi, containing six arpents twenty-six toises and two feet in front, by one hundred in depth, bounded on the upper side by lands of Alexander Harrang, and on the lower by those of Joseph E. Dugué Livaudais.

It appears to be a part of an ancient concession, which was consumed with the public records of this country; it further appears that said land has been inhabited and cultivated upwards of forty years. Confirmed.

No. 276.—JOSEPH GUTIERREZ claims a tract of land, situate in the county of Orleans, at the settlement of St. Bernard, two leagues distant from the church thereof, containing three arpents and thirteen toises in front, on each side of the Bayou aux Bœufs, adjoining lands of Mr. Lacroix; the line on one side, running north, fifty-three degrees west, measures six hundred and fifty toises, and south, fifty-three degrees east, measures one hundred and eighty-five toises; and that of the lower,

bounded by lands of Anthony Montag, running north, eighty-five degrees west, measures one thousand toises, and south, eighty-five degrees east, measures one hundred and sixty-five toises.

It appears that Santiago Molina was put in possession of said land on the 19th day of March, 1792, by the Surveyor General of the province, from whom the claimant derives his title; it further appears that said land was inhabited and cultivated on the 20th December, 1803, and for ten consecutive years prior to that period. Confirmed.

No. 277.—MICHAEL ZERINGUE claims a tract of land, situate in the county of Orleans, on the right bank of the Mississippi, containing thirty-four arpents in front, running in its depth as follows: the lower twelve arpents, adjoining lands of Charles J. B. Fleureau, measure one hundred arpents in depth; the eight next above measure eighty arpents, and the remaining fourteen forty arpents in depth.

It appears that the front, with forty arpents in depth of said land, has been inhabited and cultivated for more than forty years; and that, for the second depth, the claimant derives his title by regular warrants of survey. Confirmed.

No. 278.—ANTONIA SUARES, widow MORALES, claims a tract of land, situate in the county of Orleans, at the settlement of St. Bernard, containing two arpents thirteen toises and three feet in front, on each side of the Bayou aux Bœufs; the upper line adjoining lands of John Quintana, and the lower adjoining lands of Carlos Morales.

It appears that Juan Alonzo Morales, from whom the claimant derives her title, was put in possession of said land on the 17th March, 1792, by the Surveyor General of the province; it further appears that said land was inhabited and cultivated on the 20th December, 1803, and for ten consecutive years prior to that date. Confirmed.

No. 279.—RICHARD BUTLER claims a tract of land, situate in the county of German Coast, on the left bank of the Mississippi, containing eighteen arpents in front, by the ordinary depth of forty, bounded by the lands of ——— on the upper side, and by those of ——— on the lower side.

It appears that said land was inhabited and cultivated on the 20th December, 1803, and for more than ten consecutive years prior to that period. Confirmed.

No. 280.—PETER CRAIG claims a tract of land, situate in the county of Iberville, at the settlement of Galveztown, on the right bank of the bayou Manchack, containing three hundred superficial arpents, bounded on the upper side by the lands of Anthony Gonzalez, and on the other by vacant lands.

It appears that James Kelly, from whom the claimant derives his title, was put in possession of said land by the Surveyor General of the province, in the year 1794, and that said land has been inhabited and cultivated ever since that period. Confirmed.

No. 282.—PETER DELARONDE claims a tract of land, situate in the county of Orleans, at the settlement of St. Bernard, about five miles above the Mississippi, containing one hundred and sixty-eight arpents in front, on the left or northern bank of the Bayou aux Bœufs, by five arpents in depth; bounded on the west by lands of Mr. Fisher.

It appears that the claimant obtained from the Baron de Carondelet a complete grant for the aforesaid land, dated the 4th day of April, 1795. Confirmed.

No. 285.—JOACHIN ASCARGA claims a tract of land, situate in the county of Orleans, at the place called Quartier du Portage, about ten leagues below the city of New Orleans, on the right bank of the Mississippi, containing five arpents in front, by the depth of forty, bounded on the upper side by lands of Desdune Leclerc, and on the lower by those of J. B. Gautier.

It appears that said land has been inhabited and cultivated by the claimant, or by those under whom he claims, for more than ten consecutive years prior to the 20th December, 1803. Confirmed.

No. 289.—PETER SIGUR claims a tract of land, situate in the county of Iberville, above the place called l'Isle aux Marais, containing seven arpents twenty-one toises and four feet in front, by eighty arpents in depth, bounded on the upper side by lands of Peter Belly, the lower side line diverging ten degrees towards the rear.

It appears to the Board that said land, with the front forty arpents in depth, was granted by the Spanish Government to Anthony Belas, on the 7th day of July, 1774; and that the second depth of forty arpents was granted by the same Government to Laurent Sigur, on the 7th day of July, 1779; from each of whom the present claimant derives his title. Confirmed.

No. 288.—GEORGE BRADDISH and WILLIAM H. JOHNSON claim a tract of land, situate in the county of Orleans, at the place called Quartier de la Pointe à la Hache, about fourteen leagues below the city of New Orleans, on the right bank of the Mississippi, containing twenty eight arpents in front, by forty in depth.

It appears that said land is a part of a larger tract, which was granted by the French Government to Philip Floté on the 29th day of January, 1764, from whom the claimants derive their title to the land aforesaid. Confirmed.

No. 286.—JOSEPH BURAT claims a tract of land, situate in the county of Orleans, at the place called Quartier du Portage, eleven leagues below the city of New Orleans, on the right bank of the Mississippi, containing ten arpents in front, by forty in depth; bounded on the upper side line by the lands of Jacques Frederick, and on the lower by those of Desdune Leclerc.

It appears that said land was inhabited and cultivated by the claimant, or by those under whom he claims, on the 20th December, 1803, and for more than ten consecutive years prior to that date. Confirmed.

No. 290.—BARTHOLOMEW BAPTISTE claims a tract of land, situate in the county of Orleans, at the place called Quartier de la Pointe à la Hache, below the city of New Orleans, on the right bank of the Mississippi, containing six arpents in front, by forty in depth, bounded on the upper side by lands of John Lafrance, and on the lower by those of Francis Romset.

It appears that two arpents of the aforesaid land, by forty in depth, were inhabited and cultivated on the 20th December, 1803, and for more than ten consecutive years prior to that period; and that, upon the remaining four, the claimant made and kept in repair the road and levée, in the year 1801, in pursuance of an order from the commanding officer of that place. The land being of little value, we are of opinion that the claim ought to be confirmed.

No. 291.—JOHN LAFRANCE claims a tract of land, situate in the county of Orleans, at the place called Pointe à la Hache, on the right bank of the Mississippi, containing three and a half arpents in front, by forty in depth, bounded on the upper side by lands of Messrs. Braddish and Johnson, and on the lower by those of Bartholomew Baptiste.

It appears that said land was inhabited and cultivated on the 20th December, 1803, by the claimant, or by those under whom he claims, and for more than ten consecutive years prior to that period. Confirmed.

No. 297.—JEANNE LARRABLE claims a tract of land, situate in the county of Orleans, about three miles below the city of New Orleans, on the left bank of the Mississippi, containing six arpents and two toises in front, by the depth of eighty arpents, bounded on the upper side by lands of Mr. Guerin, and on the lower by those of Solomon Prevost.

It appears that the claimant, or those under whom he claims, inhabited and cultivated the first forty arpents in depth of said land on the 20th December, 1803, and for more than ten consecutive years prior to that period, and that the claimant obtained from the Spanish Government a regular warrant of survey for the second depth of forty arpents, dated the 9th July, 1790. Confirmed.

No. 298.—URBAIN GAGNE claims a tract of land, situate in the county of Iberville, on the right bank of the Mississippi, containing eight arpents in front, by forty in depth, bounded on the upper side by vacant lands, and on the lower by those of Peter Voisin.

It appears that Pierre Clairmont, from whom the claimant derives his title, obtained from the Spanish Government a patent concession of said land, dated the 15th day of May, 1795. Confirmed.

No. 301.—CHARLOTTE DREUX claims a tract of land, situate in the county of Orleans, at the place called Quartier de la Concession, six leagues below the city of New Orleans, on the right bank of the Mississippi, con-

taining thirty-four arpents in front, with an extension of depth to lake Barataria; bounded by lands of Gabriel Fazand.

It appears to be a part of a tract of land which, in the year 1780, belonged to Charles Favre Daunois; after whose death it was sold, by order of Government, and the husband of the claimant, in his lifetime, became the purchaser; it also appears that said land has been inhabited and cultivated more than ten consecutive years prior to the 20th December, 1803; but the claim to the extent of forty arpents in depth only is hereby confirmed. Confirmed.

No. 302.—GABRIEL TIXERANT claims a tract of land, situate in the county of Orleans, about twelve leagues below the city of New Orleans, on the right bank of the Mississippi, containing ten arpents in front, by forty in depth, adjoining on the upper side to lands of T. P. Gautrie, and on the lower to those of Mr. Duplessis.

It appears that said land was inhabited and cultivated on the 20th December, 1803, by the claimant, or those under whom he claims, and for ten consecutive years prior to that period. Confirmed.

No. 303.—FRANCIS ROUSSET claims a tract of land, situate in the county of Orleans, about fifteen leagues below the city of New Orleans, on the right bank of the Mississippi, containing seven arpents in front, by forty in depth, bounded on the upper side by lands of Bartholomew Batiste, and on the lower by those of Jeremie Treaudnique.

It appears that Joseph Hernandez, from whom the claimant derives his title, made an actual settlement on said land, prior to the 20th December, 1803, by virtue of a written permission from the proper Spanish officer; it appears further, that said land has been inhabited and cultivated since the time of the written permission as aforesaid. Confirmed.

No. 304.—MARGARITA BARON claims a tract of land, situate in the county of Orleans, opposite the city of New Orleans, containing four arpents in front, by seven hundred and seven toises in depth, bounded on the upper side by lands of Bartholomew Duverges, and on the lower by lands of the widow Bienveau.

It appears that said land was inhabited and cultivated by the claimant, or by those under whom she claims, on the 20th December, 1803, and for more than ten consecutive years prior to that period. Confirmed.

No. 305.—JEREMIAH TRENDWING claims a tract of land, situate in the county of Orleans, at the place called Pointe à la Hache, below the city of New Orleans, on the right bank of the Mississippi, containing seventeen arpents in front, by forty in depth, bounded on the upper side by lands of Francis Rousset, and on the lower by lands of Bartholomew Baptiste.

It appears that John Lafrance was in possession of ten acres of said land in the year 1789, by virtue of a regular warrant of survey, and that, upon the remaining seven, settlement was made by Francis Toupart, anterior to that period, from each of whom the claimant derives his title; it appears, also, that said land was inhabited and cultivated on the 20th December, 1803, and for more than ten consecutive years prior to that period. Confirmed.

No. 309.—JOSEPH BUJAU claims a tract of land, situate in the county of Acadia, at the place called Quartier de l'Ascension, on the right bank of the Mississippi, containing five arpents and fourteen toises in front; the upper side line, adjoining lands of Etienne Bujau, running south, eighty-seven degrees thirty-five minutes west, measures sixty-six arpents, the lower side line, adjoining lands of Evan Jones, running south, sixty-six degrees thirty-five minutes west, measures sixty-five arpents.

It appears that the claimant obtained from the Spanish Government a complete title to five arpents fourteen toises and three feet in front, by forty arpents in depth, dated the 5th day of November, 1775. Confirmed; but so much as exceeds the quantity specified in the patent is rejected.

No. 310.—JOHN ETIENNE BUJAU claims a tract of land, situate in the county of Acadia, at the place called Quartier de l'Ascension, on the right bank of the Mississippi, containing five arpents and fifteen toises in front, by the depth of eighty arpents, bounded on the upper side by lands of widow Pierre Bujau, and on the lower by those of Joseph Bujau.

It appears that Etienne Bujau, father of the claimant, and from whom he derives his title, obtained from the Spanish Government, on the 5th day of November, 1775, a patent concession for the aforesaid land, with the depth only of forty arpents, which, agreeably to the patent, is hereby confirmed.

No. 311.—MADELAINE BUJAU claims a tract of land, situate in the county of Acadia, at the place called Quartier de l'Ascension, on the right bank of the Mississippi, containing five arpents twenty-four toises and two feet in front, by the depth of eighty arpents, bounded on the upper side by lands of Silvain Leblanc, and on the lower by those of Etienne Bujau.

It appears that Peter Bujau, from whom the claimant derives her title, obtained from the Spanish Government a patent concession for the front of the aforesaid land, with the depth only of forty arpents, dated the 5th day of November, 1775; which quantity, agreeably to the patent, is hereby confirmed.

No. 316.—BARTHOLOMEW LAFON claims a tract or point of land, situate in the county of Orleans, bounded by lake Pontchartrain on the north side, and on the east by bayou Chef Menteur.

It appears that Maxent, from whom the claimant derives his title, obtained from the French Government a patent concession for the aforesaid land, dated 10th March, 1763. Confirmed.

No. 318.—FRANCIS VERSAILLE claims two tracts of land, situate in the county of Orleans, settlement of St. Bernard; the first containing three arpents and twelve toises in front, on the right bank of the Bayou aux Bœufs, by forty arpents in depth: and the other, containing four arpents and twenty-five toises in front, by the common depth as aforesaid, on the left side of the same bayou, lying about forty-eight acres distant from the Mississippi; bounded on the upper side by the lands of the late widow De Mandeville, and on the lower by those of Maria Morales.

It appears that said land was inhabited and cultivated by the claimant, or by those under whom he claims, on the 20th December, 1803, and for ten consecutive years prior to that period. Confirmed.

No. 319.—PETER R. ST. GERMAIN claims a tract of land, situate in the county of Orleans, at the settlement of St. Bernard, about a mile above the parish church, containing four arpents and nine toises in front, on the left bank of Bayou aux Bœufs, by forty arpents in depth; and upon the right bank of the same bayou, opposite the first, four arpents and five toises in front, by forty arpents in depth; bounded on the upper side by lands of Raymond Palacio, and on the other by those of John Fouquet.

It appears that said land was inhabited and cultivated by the claimant, or by those under whom he claims, on the 20th December, 1803, and for more than ten consecutive years prior to that period. Confirmed.

No. 321.—FRANCIS and LEUFROY DREUX claim a tract of land, situate in the county of Orleans, at the place called Gentilly, about five miles from the city of New Orleans, containing thirty-three arpents in front, on each bank of the bayou Gentilly, by twenty arpents in depth, bounded on the upper side by lands of Guid Dreux, and on the lower by those of M. de Morant.

It appears that Mathurin Dreux, from whom the claimants derive their title, obtained from the French Government a patent concession for the aforesaid land, dated on the 8th day of March, 1763. Confirmed.

No. 322.—FRANCIS and LEUFROY DREUX claim a second tract of land, situate in the county of Orleans, at the place called Chantilly, about ten miles from the city of New Orleans, containing seventy-five arpents in front, on each side of the bayou Chantilly, by twenty arpents in depth, bounded by lands of Guid Dreux on the upper side, and on the lower by lands of Louis Dectouet.

It appears that the aforesaid tract of land is a part of a patent concession for one hundred and seventy-three and a half acres, granted by the French Government to Mathurin Dreux, on the 8th day of March, 1763. Confirmed.

No. 330.—THE ABBESS AND COMMUNITY OF THE URSULINE CONVENT AT THE CITY OF NEW ORLEANS claim a tract of land, situate in the county of Orleans, on the right bank of the Mississippi, consisting of a second

depth, and containing a total superficies of seven hundred and sixty-five arpents sixteen perches and twelve toises in the rear of their plantation.

It appears that the first forty arpents in depth were inhabited and cultivated on the 20th December, 1803, and for more than ten consecutive years prior thereto; and that a regular patent was issued by the Spanish Government for the land claimed as aforesaid, on the 2d day of December, 1789. Confirmed.

No. 331.—LOUIS DE REGGIO claims a tract of land, situate in the county of Orleans, at the settlement of St. Bernard, about five miles from the church thereof, containing one arpent and a half in front, on each side of the Bayou aux Bœufs, with the depth of forty arpents on the northeast side of the bayou, and twenty arpents in depth on the southwest, bounded on the upper side line by lands of Joseph Gutierrez, and on the lower by those of John Alonzo Morales.

It appears that Juan Quintana, from whom the claimant derives his title, was put in possession of said land by the Surveyor General of the province on the 18th day of March, 1792; it appears also that said land was inhabited and cultivated on the 20th December, 1803, and for ten consecutive years prior thereto. Confirmed.

No. 334.—JOHN MARI CORNER claims a tract of land, situate in the county of Orleans, at the place called Quartier du Portage, twelve and a half leagues below the city of New Orleans, on the left bank of the Mississippi, containing fifteen arpents and twelve toises in front, by forty arpents in depth, bounded on the upper side by lands of John Lauthois, and on the lower by those of Augustin Bineau.

It appears that Louis Buison obtained from the French Government a patent concession for thirteen arpents front of said land, on the 24th day of July, 1766, and that for the remaining two arpents and twelve toises a regular warrant of survey was issued by the Spanish Government, in favor of James Billaud, on the 22d of July, 1791; from each of whom the claimant derives his title. Confirmed.

No. 336.—ALEXANDER HARRANG claims two tracts of land, situate in the county of Orleans, at the place called Quartier des Chapitoulas, on the right bank of the Mississippi, three leagues below the city of New Orleans; the first containing two arpents in front of the Mississippi, by forty in depth; the second, being at the distance of one arpent eastward of the rear of the former, having two acres in front, by forty in depth; the first being bounded on the upper side by lands of Nicholas Bacchus.

It appears that the first tract of two arpents, by forty in depth, was inhabited and cultivated on the 20th December, 1803, and for more than ten consecutive years prior to that period; and that for the second depth Nicholas Bacchus obtained from the Spanish Government a regular warrant of survey in the year 1790, from whom the claimant derives his title by purchase. Confirmed.

No. 339.—LOUIS TRUDEAU claims a tract of land, situate in the county of Orleans, six leagues above the city of New Orleans, on the left bank of the Mississippi, containing twenty arpents in front, with an extension of depth to lake Pontchartrain, adjoining the plantation of Mr. Foreman on the lower side, and that of Mr. Meuillons on the upper side.

It appears that the front and first depth of forty arpents of this land was actually inhabited and cultivated on the 20th of December, 1803, and for more than ten consecutive years next preceding. So much of the claim the Board confirm, but reject it as to the second extension of depth.

No. 340.—WILLIAM G. GARLAND claims a tract of land, situate in the county of Orleans, at the settlement of St. Bernard, about nine miles from the parish church thereof, containing six arpents nine toises and seven feet in front, on each side of the Bayou aux Bœufs, by forty in depth, bounded on the upper side by lands of Domingo Martel, and on the lower by those of Luc Gonzalez.

It appears that said land was inhabited and cultivated on the 20th December, 1803, by the claimant, or by those under whom he claims, and for more than ten consecutive years prior to that period. Confirmed.

No. 345.—ARNAUD BEAUVAIS claims a tract of land, situate in the county of Pointe Coupée, on the right bank of the Mississippi, containing four hundred and fifteen acres, bounded on the upper side by lands of widow Decour, and on the lower by lands of Pierre Laurent.

It appears that the said land was inhabited and cultivated on the 20th December, 1803, and for more than ten consecutive years prior thereto. Confirmed.

No. 348.—JOSEPH M. WHITE claims a tract of land, situate in the county of Iberville, on the right bank of the Mississippi, containing five arpents twenty-two toises and two feet in front, by eighty arpents in depth, bounded on the upper side by lands of ————, and on the lower by those of ————.

It appears to the satisfaction of the Board, that the first depth of forty arpents was inhabited and cultivated on the 20th December 1803, and for more than ten consecutive years prior to that period, which quantity is hereby confirmed; but the second depth having never been inhabited or cultivated, nor any sufficient written evidence of title exhibited, it is hereby rejected.

No. 351.—BERNARD MARIGNY claims a tract of land, situate in the county of Orleans, about twelve miles above the city of New Orleans, on the left bank of the Mississippi, containing thirty-eight arpents in front; the upper line, adjoining to lands of Forcel, measures thirty-two arpents and twenty toises, running north, fifty-six degrees east; the lower side line, adjoining lands of widow Arnout, running north, fifteen degrees ten minutes west, measures thirty-five arpents and four toises.

It appears that the said land was inhabited and cultivated on the 20th December, 1803, by the claimant, or by those under whom he claims, and for more than ten consecutive years prior to that period. Confirmed.

No. 350.—BERNARD MARIGNY claims a tract of land, situate in the county of Orleans, on the right bank of the Mississippi, five leagues above the city of New Orleans, containing five arpents and five inches in front, with an extension of depth as far as lake Ouachas; the lower line adjoining lands of Jean Louis Zeringue, and that of the upper those of Mrs. Duval and Fortier.

It appears that Charles de St. Pierre, from whom the claimant derives his title, obtained from the French Government a regular patent concession for twenty arpents front, by the depth aforesaid, dated the 13th day of January, 1722. Confirmed.

No. 358.—JAMES and SILVESTER VINET claim a tract of land, situate in the county of Orleans, nine leagues below the city of New Orleans, on the left bank of the Mississippi, containing ten arpents in front, by eighty arpents in depth, bounded on the upper side by lands of widow Francis Vinet, and on the lower by those of Mr. Gentilly.

It appears that John Denesse, from whom the claimants derive their title, obtained from the Spanish Government a regular warrant of survey for the second depth of forty arpents, dated 1783; and also that the first depth of land was inhabited and cultivated on the 20th December, 1803, and for more than ten consecutive years prior thereto. Confirmed.

No. 361.—JOHN VINET and brothers claim a tract of land, situate in the county of Orleans, about ten leagues below the city of New Orleans, on the left bank of the Mississippi, containing twenty-one arpents in front, by forty arpents in depth, bounded on the upper side by lands of Louis Dreux Gentilly, and on the lower by those of Silvester Vinet.

It appears that said land was inhabited and cultivated by the claimants, or by those under whom they claim, on the 20th December, 1803, and for more than ten consecutive years prior to that period. Confirmed.

No. 362.—JAMES SMITH and HARRIS HOVE claim a tract of land, situate in the county of Orleans, on the right bank of the Mississippi, containing six thousand six hundred and twenty-four superficial arpents and five hundred and eighty-four toises, bounded on the upper side by the bayou Liard, and on the lower by the bayou Caranas.

It appears that an order of survey for said land was duly issued by the Baron de Carondelet in favor of Anthony de St. Maxent, from whom the claimants derive their title, dated the 14th day of January, 1795, which the Board do hereby confirm, agreeably to the terms and conditions specified in the petition, reserving to the United States the ground within two hundred toises of Fort Bourbon.

No. 366.—The ABBESS AND COMMUNITY OF THE URSULINE CONVENT IN NEW ORLEANS claim a tract of land, situate about three miles above the city, on the left bank of the Mississippi, containing five arpents in front, by sixty-six in depth, bounded on the upper side by the lands of widow Panis, and on the lower by those of Mr. Livaudais, Junior.

It appears that said land was inhabited and cultivated by the claimants on the 20th December, 1803, and for more than ten consecutive years prior to that period. Confirmed.

No. 378.—GABRIEL FAZAND claims a tract of land, situate in the county of Orleans, on the right bank of the Mississippi, eighteen miles from the city of New Orleans, containing ten arpents in front, by eighty in depth, bounded on the upper side by lands of widow Lajonchere, and on the lower by those of widow Fazand.

It appears that Joseph Dugruis, from whom the claimant derives his title, being in possession of the first depth of forty acres of said land, petitioned for and obtained from the Spanish Government a regular warrant of survey for the second depth of forty arpents, dated the 5th day of July, 1796. It also appears that said land has been inhabited and cultivated for more than ten consecutive years prior to the 20th December, 1803. Confirmed.

No. 389.—ALEXANDER HARRANG claims a tract of land, situate in the county of Orleans, three and a half leagues above the city of New Orleans, on the right bank of the Mississippi, at the place called Quartier des Chapitoulas, containing twenty one arpents and seven toises in front, by forty arpents in depth, bounded on the upper side by lands of Nicholas Bacchus, and on the lower by those of Francis J. Lebreton Dorgenois.

It appears that said land was inhabited and cultivated on the 20th December, 1803, by the claimant, or by those under whom he claims, and for more than ten consecutive years prior to that period. Confirmed.

No. 383.—MANON, EMELIE, and ROSALIE MALINES claim a tract of land, situate between lakes Maurepas and Pontchartrain, bounded on the west by the former lake, and on the east by the latter, on the north by the river Manchack, and on the south by lands of Lactete, containing ten thousand one hundred and twenty Paris arpents.

It appears that Marie Rillieux, deceased, mother of the claimants, obtained from the Spanish Government a patent concession of the aforesaid land, dated the 13th day of July, 1764. Confirmed.

No. 369.—HENRY MENTZINGER claims a lot of ground, situate in the city of New Orleans, fronting the Levée, containing fifty-three feet in front, the upper line, adjoining lands of Artutuise, measures fifty-six feet in depth; the lower line, adjoining lands of Arnaud Magnon, measures fifty-eight feet.

It appears that the claimant obtained from the Spanish Government a complete title to the aforesaid lot of ground, dated the 10th day of August, 1795. Confirmed.

No. 359.—JOSEPH PRARA claims a tract of land, situate on the right bank of the river Amite, in the county of Iberville, containing eight arpents in front, and twenty arpents in depth, and bounded on the upper side by lands of the representatives of Fabian Ramos, deceased, and on the lower by land of Madame Nicolas.

It appears to the satisfaction of the Board that this land was inhabited and cultivated on and before the 1st day of October, 1800, and that the same continued to be inhabited and cultivated until on and after the 20th December, 1803. Confirmed.

No. 94.—VICTOR LEBLANC claims a tract of land, situate on the left bank of the bayou Placquemines, in the county of Iberville, containing ten arpents in front, by forty arpents in depth, and bounded on the upper side by land of Nicolas Huller, and on the lower by land of Alexander Darden.

It appears to the satisfaction of the Board that this land was settled by permission of the proper Spanish officer, prior to the 20th December, 1803, and that the same was actually inhabited and cultivated on that day. Confirmed.

No. 158.—HONORATO LEONARD claims a tract of land, situate on the left bank of the bayou Placquemines, in the county of Iberville, containing eight arpents and six toises in front, and forty arpents in depth, with an opening of fifteen degrees towards the rear, and bounded on the upper side by land of F. A. Darden, and on the lower by land of Henry Rigé.

It appears to the satisfaction of the Board that this land was settled by permission of the proper Spanish officer, prior to the 1st December, 1803, and that the same was actually inhabited and cultivated on that day. Confirmed.

No. 138.—JOSEPH LANDRY claims a tract of land, situate on the west side of the river Mississippi, in the county of Iberville, containing twelve arpents in front, and forty arpents in depth, and bounded on the upper side by land of Jean Prosper, and on the lower by vacant lands.

It appears that the claimant did actually inhabit and cultivate the land now claimed on the 20th of December, 1803, and for more than ten consecutive years prior. Confirmed.

No. 370.—NATHAN MITCHELL claims a tract of land, situate on the east side of the river Mississippi, in the county of Iberville, containing forty-four and twenty-hundredths superficial arpents, and bounded on the upper side by land of Mercel Dupuis, and on the lower by land of S. Leblanc.

It appears to the satisfaction of the Board that this land was inhabited and cultivated on and before the 1st day of October, 1800, and that the same continued to be inhabited and cultivated until on and after the 20th December, 1803. Confirmed.

No. 365.—AMBROISE GARIDELLE claims a tract of land, situate on the right bank of the bayou La Fourche, in the county of la Fourche, containing six arpents and twenty-four toises in front, and forty arpents in depth, and bounded on the upper side by land formerly the property of the claimant, and on the lower by land of Peter Aucoin.

It appears to the satisfaction of the Board that there was an order of survey for this land, in favor of the claimant, from the Spanish Government, in the year 1790, and that the same has continued to be inhabited and cultivated ever since, until on and after the 20th December, 1803. Confirmed.

No. 351.—MARGARITE BOURGEAT claims a tract of land, situate on the river Mississippi, in the county of Pointe Coupée, containing one thousand two hundred and forty-one superficial arpents, being eighty arpents in depth.

It appears to the satisfaction of the Board that the first depth of forty arpents of this land was inhabited and cultivated on the 20th December, 1803, and for more than ten consecutive years prior, and that the husband of the claimant obtained a warrant of survey from the Spanish Government, in the year 1785, for the second depth of forty arpents. Confirmed.

No. 201.—SAMUEL YOUNG claims a tract of land, situate on the east side of the river Mississippi, in the county of Orleans, containing twenty arpents in front, and extending back as far as lake Borgne, and bounded on the upper side by land of Charles Devilliers Jumonville and on the lower by land of Madame de Lachaise.

Part of this land, viz: eight arpents front, and forty arpents depth, was granted by the French Government, in the year 1730, to Michel de Vauxparis; the remaining twelve arpents front, on the ordinary depth, have been actually inhabited and cultivated for a great number of years. Jean Baptiste Prevost, who had acquired a title to the whole front of twenty arpents, with the usual depth of forty, obtained from the French Government, in 1764, a complete grant for an extension of depth as far back as the lake Borgue. Under the above titles the present claimant holds by virtue of different intermediate conveyances. Confirmed.

No. 299.—GEORGE BRADISH and W. H. JOHNSON claim a tract of land, situate on the west side of the river Mississippi, in the county of Orleans, containing a superficies of nine hundred and seventy-three arpents and three hundred toises, and bounded on each side by the bayou Liard.

It appears to the satisfaction of the Board that this land was settled, with the permission of the proper Spanish officer, prior to the 20th December, 1803, and that the same was actually inhabited and cultivated on that day by those under whom the present claimants hold. Confirmed.

No. 337.—SEBASTIAN BURAT claims a tract of land, situate on the west side of the river Mississippi, in the county of Orleans, containing twenty arpents in front, and forty in depth, and bounded on the upper side by land of Pierre Colette, and on the lower by land of Bradish and Johnson.

It appears to the satisfaction of the Board that the land now claimed was actually settled prior to the 1st day of October, 1800, and that the same was continually inhabited and cultivated by those under whom the present claimant holds, until on and after the 20th day of December, 1803. Confirmed.

No. 338.—SEBASTIAN BURAT claims a tract of land, situate on the west side of the river Mississippi, in the county of Orleans, containing fourteen arpents in front, and forty in depth, and bounded on the upper side by land of Joseph Chevreuse.

It appears to the satisfaction of the Board that the land now claimed was actually settled prior to the 1st day of October, 1800, and that the same was continually inhabited and cultivated until on and after the 20th day of December, 1803. Confirmed.

No. 353.—JOHN LAVALDE claims a tract of land, situate on the west side of the river Mississippi, in the county of Orleans, containing twenty arpents in front, and forty in depth, and bounded on the upper side by land of Honore Duplessis, and on the lower by land of John Toulouse.

It appears that Martin Duplessis obtained from the Spanish Government, in the year 1785, an order of survey for this land, to be established as a vacherie, and that it has ever since been occupied for the purpose intended; the present claimant holds under the right of said Duplessis, by virtue of divers intermediate transfers. Confirmed.

No. 377.—SOLOMON PREVOST claims a tract of land, situate on the east side of the river Mississippi, in the county of Orleans, containing nineteen arpents and nine toises in front, and a depth extending as far as the rear of the plantations bordering on the bayou Chantilly, (being about one hundred arpents,) and bounded on the upper side by land of the widow Dupuis, and on the lower by land of Madame Piernas.

It appearing to the Board that the claimant did actually inhabit and cultivate the front and ordinary depth of the land now claimed on the 20th day of December, 1803, and for more than ten consecutive years prior, they hereby confirm his claim to the extent of forty arpents depth, but reject his claim to the balance.

No. 396.—JAMES LACOUTURE, alias TOURANGAIS claims a tract of land, situate on the west side of the river Mississippi, in the county of Orleans, containing seventeen arpents in front, and forty in depth, and bounded on the upper side by land of Charles Duplessis, and on the lower by land of Honore Duplessis.

It appears to the satisfaction of the Board that the claimant was put in possession of this land by the commandant of the district, in the year 1798, and that he continued to inhabit and cultivate it until on and after the 20th December, 1803. Confirmed.

No. 397.—HONORE DUPLESSIS claims a tract of land, situate on the west side of the river Mississippi, in the county of Orleans, containing ten arpents in front, and forty in depth, and bounded on the upper side by land of Jacques Lacouture.

It appears to the satisfaction of the Board that the claimant did actually settle this land, with the permission of the commandant of the district, prior to the 20th of December, 1803, and that he did actually inhabit and cultivate the same on that day. Confirmed.

No. 398.—MICHEL DUPLESSIS claims a tract of land, situate on the west side of the river Mississippi, in the county of Orleans, containing ten arpents in front, and forty in depth, and opening seventeen degrees thirty minutes towards the rear; and bounded on the upper side by land of Gabriel Tixerant, and on the lower by land of Jacques Lacouture.

It appears to the satisfaction of the Board that the claimant did actually settle this land, by the permission of the commandant of the district, prior to the 20th December, 1803, and that he did actually inhabit and cultivate the same on that day. Confirmed.

No. 400.—JOHN BAPTISTE GAUTIER claims a tract of land, situate on the west side of the river Mississippi, in the county of Orleans, containing twelve arpents in front, and forty in depth, and bounded on the upper side by land of Jacques Hollier, and on the lower by land of Tixerant.

It appears that Peter Boye obtained from the Spanish Government, in the year 1791, a regular warrant of survey for this land; and it also appears that the same has been since inhabited and cultivated. The present claimant holds under title of said Boye, by virtue of intermediate conveyances. Confirmed.

No. 402.—JOHN MARIE SILVE claims a tract of land, situate on the west side of the river Mississippi, in the county of Orleans, containing seven arpents in front, and forty in depth, and bounded on the upper side by land of T. Bister, and on the lower by land of Bradish and Johnson.

This is part of a tract of land which was granted in the year 1764, by the French Government, to Philip Floté, under whose title the present claimant holds the land now claimed, by virtue of divers intermediate conveyances. Confirmed.

No. 404.—HUBERT BURAT claims a tract of land, situate on the west side of the river Mississippi, in the county of Orleans, containing three arpents in front, and forty in depth, with an opening of six degrees towards the rear; and bounded on the lower side by land of Ramond Thomas.

It appears to the satisfaction of the Board that this land was settled prior to the 1st day of October, 1800, and that the same was actually inhabited and cultivated until on and after the 20th December, 1803. Confirmed.

No. 364.—THOMAS HEBERT claims a tract of land, situate on the west side of the river Mississippi, in the county of Iberville, containing four and a half arpents in front, and eighty arpents in depth, and bounded on the upper side by land of Olivier Hernandez, and on the lower by land of Pierre Rivet.

The front and ordinary depth of this land is part of a tract surveyed in the year 1772, in favor of Estevan Rivet, who obtained a complete grant for the same in 1774, from the Governor Don Louis de Unzaga; the present claimant holds the part now claimed under said title, which is confirmed; but the claim to a second depth of forty arpents is rejected.

No. 401.—ALEXANDER BABIN claims a tract of land, situate on the west side of the river Mississippi, in the county of Acadia, containing three arpents and twenty-six toises in front, and seventy-one arpents in depth, and bounded on the upper side by land of Firmin Landry, and on the lower by land of Simon Babin.

It appears that the front and first depth of this land was actually inhabited and cultivated on the 20th December, 1803, and for more than ten consecutive years prior thereto. The Board confirm the claim to so much, but reject it as to the balance of thirty-one arpents in depth.

No. 386.—WILLIAM BROWN claims a tract of land, situate on the east side of the river Mississippi, in the county of Orleans, containing sixteen arpents eleven toises and three feet in front, with a depth extending back as far as lake Borgue, and bounded on the upper side by land of J. M. Pintard, and on the lower by land of Chalmet Delino.

It appears that the front and first depth of forty arpents of this land was actually inhabited and cultivated on the 20th day of December, 1803, and for more than ten consecutive years prior thereto. So much the Board confirm, but reject the claim to the remaining extension of depth.

No. 395.—HELENE BETET, widow BIENVENU, claims a tract of land, situate on the west side of the river Mississippi, in the county of Orleans, containing sixteen arpents in front, and extending back in depth as far as the bayou Ouachas, or Villars, and bounded on the upper side by land of the widow Gonsolin, and on the lower by land of Chevalier Macarty.

This is part of a larger tract of land, of forty-six and one-sixth arpents in front, and one hundred and sixty arpents in depth, surveyed in the year 1737, by Chevalier François Brutin, (Surveyor General at that time under the French Government,) in favor of Chevalier Bienville. The present claimant holds this part under said title; the land having been inhabited and cultivated ever since the above period. Confirmed.

No. 320.—URBAIN GAGNE claims two tracts of land, situate on the east side of the river Mississippi, in the county of Iberville; the first containing four hundred

and twenty-four superficial arpents and eleven toises, and bounded on the upper side by land of Pierre Roisin and Pierre Clairmont, and on the lower by land of Laurent Duprés; the second containing seven hundred and seventy-six superficial arpents, and bounded on the upper side by the Pointe de Manchack, and on the lower by the first tract of the claimant.

One of the tracts now claimed, viz.: that of four hundred and twenty-four arpents and eleven toises, was regularly granted to Pierre Clairmont, by the Spanish Government, in the year 1794, together with a larger quantity. The present claimant purchased this part of said Clairmont, which is hereby confirmed to him; but the Board reject his claim to the second tract of seven hundred and seventy-six arpents.

No. 137.—OLIVIER BROSSET claims a tract of land, situate on the west side of the river Mississippi, in the county of Iberville, containing three hundred and twenty superficial arpents, and bounded on the upper side by land of Amant Hebert, and on the lower by land of Pierre Floré.

It appears that this land was actually inhabited and cultivated on the 20th December, 1803, and that the same was continually inhabited and cultivated by those under whom the claimant holds for more than ten consecutive years next preceding. Confirmed.

No. 140.—MARIE J. P. ROCHEJEAN claims a tract of land, situate in the county of Orleans, at the place called Quartier des Familles, on the right bank of the bayou of the same name, six miles from the Mississippi, containing one thousand one hundred and nine superficial arpents, and bounded on the north by lands belonging to Francis Dauphin, and on the south by those of the widow Pablo, on the east by the Bayou des Familles, and on the west by vacant lands.

Part of this land was regularly granted, in the year 1797, to Jean Bte. Florian by the Baron de Carondelet; the remaining part has actually been inhabited and cultivated for more than ten consecutive years prior to the 20th day of December, 1803. The present claimant holds under these titles, in virtue of successive intermediate conveyances. Confirmed.

No. 140.—MARIE DE MOLEON claims a tract of land, situate on the east side of the river Mississippi, in the county of Orleans, containing three hundred and ninety-three superficial arpents, and bounded on the upper side by land of Mr. Mercier, and on the lower by land of Francis Mericutt.

It appears that this land was actually inhabited and cultivated on the 20th December, 1803, and that the same was continually inhabited and cultivated by the claimant, or those under whom she claims, for more than ten consecutive years next preceding. Confirmed.

No. 152.—ANTHONY BIENVENU claims a tract of land, situate on the east side of the river Mississippi, in the county of Orleans, containing eighteen arpents in front, and a depth extending back as far as lake Borgue, and bounded on the upper side by land of Charles de Reggio, and on the lower by land of Joseph Connaud.

François Reggio being proprietor of part of the front of this land, viz.: fourteen arpents, on the usual depth of forty, obtained from the Spanish Government, in the year 1775, a complete grant for an extension of depth, to the aforesaid front, as far as lake Borgue; the widow of said Reggio conveyed to the present claimant in 1794. The remaining four front arpents now claimed, it appears, have been inhabited and cultivated for more than ten consecutive years prior to the 20th December, 1803; and the present claimant holds under the original proprietor, by virtue of successive intermediate transfers. The Board confirm the whole claim except as to the second extension of depth to the four arpents front last above mentioned, which they reject.

No. 157.—THOMAS and DAVID URQUHART claim a lot of ground, situate in the suburb St. Mary, of the city of New Orleans, containing ninety-eight feet in front, and one hundred and sixty feet in depth, and bounded on the south by Girod street, on the east by Magazine street, on the north by the lot of Barbay, and on the west by that of Michel Fortier.

It appears that they under whom the claimants hold have been in possession and occupation of said lot for more than ten consecutive years prior to the 20th December, 1803. Confirmed.

No. 159.—PETER GRENIER claims a tract of land, situate on the left bank of the bayou Placquemines, in the county of Iberville, containing ten arpents in front, and forty in depth, and bounded on the upper side by and of William Blake, and on the lower by land claimed by the Indians.

The claimant obtained a regular order of survey for this land from the Baron de Carondelet, in the year 1797, and the land was by him inhabited and cultivated on the 1st day of October, 1800. Confirmed.

No. 196.—BARTHOLOMEW DUVERGES claims a tract of land, situate on the west side of the river Mississippi, in the county of Orleans, containing twenty-two arpents in front, and forty in depth, and bounded on the upper side by land of Martial Le Bœuf, and on the lower by land of Honoré and Michel Duplessis; he also claims a piece of land called *le Chemin du Bayou qui conduit a Barataria*, with an extension of depth of six arpents on each side of said bayou. On the 8th day of July, 1766, the French Government granted to Jacques Larche twenty arpents front, and forty depth, of the first tract above mentioned, together with the second tract now claimed. Said Larche, on the 1st of July, 1805, conveyed to the present claimant. The Board confirm the title according to grant, but reject the surplus of two arpents front now claimed.

No. 201.—JOHN LANTHOIS claims a tract of land, situate on the east side of the river Mississippi, in the county of Orleans, containing thirteen arpents and eight toises in front, and forty arpents in depth, (the lines closing one degree towards the rear,) and bounded on the upper side by land of Daniel Clark, and on the lower by land of John Maurice Corner.

It appears that the land now claimed was actually inhabited and cultivated on the 20th day of December, 1803, and that the same was continually inhabited and cultivated by those under whom the present claimant holds for more than ten consecutive years next preceding. Confirmed.

No. 204.—Jos. E. D. LIVAUDAIS claims a tract of land, situate on the west side of the river Mississippi, in the county of Orleans, containing three arpents in front, and forty in depth, and bounded on the upper side by land of Charles Flaurian, and on the lower by land of Jean Baptiste Sarpy.

It appears that the land now claimed was inhabited and cultivated on the 20th December, 1803, and that the same was continually inhabited and cultivated by the claimant, or those under whom he claims, for more than ten consecutive years next preceding. Confirmed.

No. 228.—FRANCIS WOOD claims a tract of land, situate on the east side of the river Mississippi, in the county of Orleans, containing two hundred and sixty-five superficial arpents, and bounded on the upper side by land of Cadet Leonard and B. Duverges, and on the lower by land of Barbin de Bellevue.

It appears that the land now claimed was actually inhabited and cultivated on the 20th day of December, 1803, and for more than ten consecutive years prior thereto. Confirmed.

No. 86.—JOHN TULEY claims a tract of land, situate on the river Amite, at the place called and known by the name of Third Bluff, in the county of Iberville, containing six hundred and forty superficial acres.

It appears to the satisfaction of the Board that the land now claimed was actually settled, with the permission of the proper Spanish officer, prior to the 20th December, 1803, and that the same was actually inhabited and cultivated on that day by those under whom the present claimant holds. Confirmed.

No. 242.—PETER PHILIBERT claims a tract of land, situate at the place called *Quartier de Placquemines*, on the east side of the river Mississippi, in the county of Orleans, containing thirty-one arpents in front; the upper line, running north, eight degrees east, and measuring sixty-seven arpents; and the lower, running north, ten degrees west, and measuring forty arpents; the line meeting towards the rear, so as to form a superficies of four hundred and forty-seven arpents and six hundred and fifteen toises; and adjoining on the lower side to the land of the fort of Placquemines.

It appears to the satisfaction of the Board that the claimant made an actual settlement on the land prior to the 1st day of October, 1800, and that he did actually inhabit and cultivate the same on the 20th December, 1803. Confirmed.

No. 265.—PHILIP E. DUGUE LIVAUDAIS claims a tract of land, situate in the county of Orleans, on the east side of lake Perrier, or Barataria, containing seventeen arpents in length, and, by reason of its narrowness, a superficies of thirteen arpents and five toises.

It appears to the satisfaction of the Board that the land now claimed was actually inhabited and cultivated on the 20th December, 1803, and that the same was continually inhabited and cultivated by those under whom the present claimant holds for more than ten consecutive years next preceding.

No. 281.—MARTIN DUPLESSIS claims a tract of land, situate in the county of Orleans, at the place called *Quartier de Babbancha*, on the east side of the river Mississippi, containing twenty-two arpents and ten toises in front, and thirty-four arpents in depth, and bounded on the upper side by land of Pierre Charretier, and on the lower by land of James Magnon.

It appears to the satisfaction of the Board that this land was settled prior to the 1st day of October, 1800, and that the same was inhabited and cultivated on the 20th December, 1803. Confirmed.

No. 284.—PETER DELARONDE claims a tract of land, situate on the east side of the river Mississippi, in the county of Orleans, containing twelve arpents in front, and extending in depth back as far as lake Borgue, and bounded on the upper side by land of Francisco Maria de Reggio, and on the lower by land of Chauvin Delery.

It appears that one Balthazar Mazange was, in the year 1762, in possession of part of this land, to wit: eight arpents in front, with a depth extending back to the prairie; and, that for the purpose of enlarging his tract, he petitioned, in that year, Governor Kellerick to grant him eight arpents more in width, to begin at the end of the land granted to the Ursuline convent, which adjoined his tract, and to run back to the prairie. A grant accordingly issued in his name in the same year, conformably to the terms of the petition; which land the present claimant holds by purchase. The balance of this claim (four arpents front, and forty depth) the claimant holds by purchase under the grant made to the nuns of the Ursuline convent; all of which land having continually been inhabited and cultivated since the year 1762, the Board confirm the whole as far as the prairie, but reject the balance of extension to lake Borgue.

No. 300.—DANIEL CLARK and FRANCIS D. DE LA CROIX claim a tract of land, situate in the county of Orleans and parish of St. Bernard, measuring about seventy arpents in front, on the right side of the bayou of Terre aux Bœufs, from the limits of the land of Alonzo Diego to the entrance of the bayou leading to lake Lery, and on the left side of the bayou of Terre aux Bœufs, three hundred or more arpents in front, with the usual depth of forty, from the lands of Lorenzo downwards.

It appearing to the Board that seventy arpents front, on the right side of bayou Terre aux Bœufs, and three hundred arpents front on the left side of the bayou of the tract of land now claimed, were sold by the commandant, by order of the Governor, in 1795, as the property of Michael Fisher; they do hereby confirm the claim to that extent, but reject the surplus as embraced in the survey and claimed by the present claimants.

No. 314.—BARTHELEMY LAFON claims a lot of ground, situate in the city of New Orleans, opposite to the place called the Orange Grove, and between that and the river, containing eighty feet in front, by forty-two in depth.

Bernard Tremolet obtained a complete grant for the aforesaid lot of ground from the Baron de Carondelet, dated the 9th day of August, 1796, and conveyed the same, on the 26th of August of the same year, to the present claimant. Confirmed.

No. 315.—MARIE DAUBERVILLE, widow BOULIGNY, claims a tract of land, situate in the county of Orleans, in the district of Barataria, containing seven arpents and eight toises in front, by forty arpents in depth, on each side of the creek which empties itself into the bayou leading to lake Barataria; the upper line adjoining lands of one Daumé, and running north seventy-two degrees thirty minutes west, and south, seventy-two degrees thirty minutes east.

It appears that Marie Olivarez, testatrix of the claimant, did actually inhabit and cultivate this land on the 20th day of December, 1803, and for more than ten consecutive years prior thereto. Confirmed.

No. 357.—CHARLES GRIFFIN claims a tract of land, situate in the county of Orleans, on the south side of the Bayou St. John road, at the distance of about ten arpents from the city of New Orleans, containing two arpents in front, and extending in depth as far as the lands of John Gravier, and bounded on the northwest by land of J. B. Castillon, and on the southeast by those of Claude Trémé, and by lands claimed by the city as commons.

It appears that this land was actually inhabited and cultivated on the 20th day of December, 1803, and that the same was continually inhabited and cultivated by the claimant, or those under whom he claims, for more than ten consecutive years next preceding. Confirmed.

No. 363.—RAMON THOMAS & CO. claim a tract of land, situate in the county of Orleans, on the west side of the river Mississippi, about three miles above the fort of Placquemines, containing eight arpents in front, and forty in depth, and opening ten degrees towards the rear, and bounded on the upper side by land of Hubert Burat, and on the lower by land of Peter Silve.

It appears to the satisfaction of the Board that this land was actually settled prior to the 1st day of October, 1800, and that the same was continually inhabited and cultivated by the claimants, or those under whom they claim, until on and after the 20th December, 1803. Confirmed.

No. 368.—JOHN MCDONOUGH, Jun., and SHEPHERD BROWN claim a tract of land, situate on the east side of the river Mississippi, in the county of Acadia, containing eighteen arpents three toises and three feet in front, and eighty arpents in depth, opening twenty degrees seventy-one minutes towards the rear, and bounded on the upper side by lands of Marianne Lanoix, and on the lower by lands of Ambroise Garidelle.

In the year 1791, Peter Le Bourgeois, who was proprietor of part of this land, to wit, sixteen arpents eight toises and three feet in front on the ordinary depth, obtained from the Spanish Government a complete grant to the second depth of forty arpents to the aforesaid front; the complement to the front of the tract now claimed, viz., one arpent and twenty-five toises, with forty arpents in depth, was regularly granted by the same Government, in the same year, to said Le Bourgeois. The Board do hereby confirm the title to the whole claim, except the second depth claimed to the one arpent and twenty-five toises as aforementioned, which they reject.

No. 375.—SOLOMON PREVOST, for himself, and in behalf of those claiming under him, claims a tract of land, situate in the county of Orleans, on the west side of the river Mississippi, at the place called *Quartier du Detour des Anglais*, containing forty-six arpents and ten toises in front, and forty arpents in depth, and bounded on the upper side by land of Augustin Mallet, and on the lower by land of James Chaperon.

It appears that this land was actually inhabited and cultivated on the 20th December, 1803, and for more than ten consecutive years next prior thereto. Confirmed.

No. 379.—GABRIEL FAZENDE claims a tract of land, situate on the west side of the river Mississippi, in the county of Orleans, containing nine and a half arpents in front, and extending in depth back as far as the bayou of Barataria, (about seventy-five arpents from the river,) and bounded on the upper side by land formerly belonging to the widow of Gabriel Fazende, senior, and on the lower by land of Nicholas Daunois.

It appears that the front and first depth of this land was actually inhabited and cultivated on the 20th December, 1803, and for more than ten consecutive years prior thereto. The Board confirm to that extent, but reject the second depth as claimed.

No. 384.—MANICHE LACHAISE claims a tract of land, situate on the west side of the river Mississippi, in the county of Orleans, containing three arpents in front, and forty in depth, and bounded on the upper side by land of Baptiste Lafrance, and on the lower by land of Edward Livingston.

It appears that the land now claimed was actually settled prior to the first day of October, 1800, and that the same was continually inhabited and cultivated by the claimant until on and after the 20th day of December, 1803. Confirmed.

No. 394.—DOMINIC and URSINO BOULIGNY claim a tract of land, situate in the county of Pointe Coupée,

on the river Mississippi, containing eighty arpents in front, and forty in depth, and bounded on the lower side by land claimed by Montchosie.

It appears that each of the claimants, in the year 1796, obtained from the Spanish Government separate orders of survey, for the quantity of forty arpents front, and forty arpents depth; the orders of survey were located adjoining each other. It further appears that one of the tracts were actually inhabited and cultivated on the 1st day of October, 1800. The Board hereby confirm the claim to the tract of forty arpents front, including the settlement; but the other tract having never been settled, they reject the claim to it.

No. 376.—FRANCIS J. LEBRETON DORGENOIS claims a tract of land, situate in the county of Orleans, on the left side of the Bayou St. John road, containing two arpents in front, and extending back as far as within sixty feet of the canal Carondelet, and bounded by the lands of Domingo Fleitas and Daniel Clark.

It appears that the land now claimed was actually inhabited and cultivated on the 20th December, 1803, and that the same was continually inhabited and cultivated by those under whom the present claimant holds for more than ten consecutive years next preceding. Confirmed.

No. 381.—FRANCIS J. DEBRETON DORGENOIS claims a tract of land, situate in the county of Orleans, on the left side of the Bayou St. John road, containing sixty toises in front, and extending back as far as the land of John Gravier, bounded on one side by land of Michel, a free negro, and on the other by land of John Bte. Castillon.

It appears that this land was actually inhabited and cultivated on the 20th December, 1803, and that the same was continually inhabited and cultivated by those under whom the claimant holds for more than ten consecutive years next preceding. Confirmed.

No. 391.—FRANCIS J. LEBRETON DURGENOIS claims a tract of land, situate in the county of Orleans, at the place called Chapitoulas, on the west side of the river Mississippi, containing six arpents in front, and eighty in depth, and bounded on the upper side by land of Alexander Harrang, and on the lower by land of Lebreton des Chapelles.

It appears that the front and first depth of this land was actually inhabited and cultivated on the 20th December, 1803, and for more than ten consecutive years prior thereto; and it further appears that there was a survey of the second depth of forty arpents executed by the Surveyor General of the province in the year 1786. Confirmed.

No. 119.—JAMES VILLERY claims a tract of land, situate on the east side of the river Mississippi, in the county of Orleans, containing five arpents two toises and four feet front, and extending in depth as far as lake Pontchartrain, and bounded on the upper side by land of Norbert Boudusquier, and on the lower by land of Soignac Dufossat.

It appears that the front and first depth of this land was actually inhabited and cultivated on the 20th day of December, 1803, and for more than ten consecutive years prior thereto; so much the Board confirm. For the second extension of depth, as far back as lake Pontchartrain, the claimant produces consecutive sales for a great number of years back; but as it appears to this Board that, by continuing the lines in the direction of those of the first depth, they would not fall on lake Pontchartrain, but on lake Borgue, the claim cannot be confirmed for more than the front and ordinary depth; but the Board are of opinion that the claimant ought, in justice, to receive a concession for a second depth of forty arpents.

No. 392.—NORBERT BOUDUSQUIER claims a tract of land, situate in the county of Orleans, on the east side of the river Mississippi, containing five arpents twenty-eight toises and four feet in front, and extending back as far as lake Pontchartrain, and bounded on the upper side by land of Mr. Doriocour, and on the lower by land of James Villery.

It appears that the front and first depth of this land was actually inhabited and cultivated on the 20th of December, 1803, and for more than ten consecutive years prior thereto; so much the Board confirm. For the second extension of depth, as far back as lake Pontchartrain, the claimant produces consecutive sales for a great number of years back; but as it appears to the

Board that, by continuing the lines in the direction of those of the first depth, they would not fall on lake Pontchartrain, but on lake Borgue, the claim cannot be confirmed for more than the front and ordinary depth, but the Board are of opinion that the claimant ought, in justice, to receive a concession for a second depth of forty arpents.

No. 148.—WILLIAM DONALDSON claims a tract of land, situate in the county of Orleans, on the east side of the river Mississippi, at the place called the English Turn, containing seven arpents in front, and forty in depth, and bounded on the upper side by land of Louis Brognier Declouet, and on the lower by land of Edward Livingston.

It appears that part of this land, viz., three arpents front, with the depth of forty, was actually inhabited and cultivated on the 20th December, 1803, and for more than ten consecutive years next preceding; so much the Board confirm. The balance of the claim, viz. four arpents front, and forty deep, is founded on an order of survey issued by the Intendant General, on the 4th January, 1802; which claim the Board are not authorized to confirm.

No. 151.—DOMINGO FLEITAS claims a tract of land, situate in the county of Orleans, on the bayou St. John road, at the distance of a mile from the city of New Orleans, containing fifty-three toises and one foot in front, on said road, and extending back as far as the land of Gravier, but varying in its width towards the rear, and bounded on the land of Madame Bertran and vacant lands, and on the west by land of Joseph Suarez and vacant lands.

It appears that part of this land, viz. the front, and depth as far back as the letters A, B, on the plat executed by Charles Trudeau, late Surveyor General, dated May 9, 1801, was actually inhabited and cultivated on the 20th of December, 1803, and for more than ten consecutive years prior thereto; so much the Board confirm. The balance of the land now claimed was regularly granted on the 20th day of May, 1801, by the Intendant General, in favor of Charles Guardiola, under whom the claimant holds; but the Board, agreeably to the act of Congress, are not authorized to confirm the title to said part.

No. 135.—CHARLES DEVILLIERS claims a tract of land, situate in the county of Orleans, on the east side of the river Mississippi, containing nineteen arpents and twelve toises in front, and a depth extending back as far as the lake, and bounded on the upper side by land of Jean Baptiste Mercier, and on the lower by Joseph Soignat Dufossat.

Part of this land, viz. thirteen arpents and twelve toises in front, on the depth to the lake, was regularly granted by the French Government, in the year 1764, in favor of Grand Pevy, under whose title the present claimant holds.

It appears that the front and first depth of forty arpents of the remaining six arpents now claimed was actually inhabited and cultivated on the 20th December, 1803, and for more than ten consecutive years prior thereto. The Board confirm the whole claim, except as to the second extension of depth claimed to the six arpents front, not included in the grant, which they reject.

No. 238.—LOUIS B. DECLOUET claims a tract of land, situate in the county of Orleans, fronting partly on the east side of the river Mississippi, containing four thousand two hundred and twenty superficial arpents, and bounded on the north by land of the claimant, on the east by the settlement of St. Bernard, and on the south and west by land formerly abandoned by the widow of Henry Desprest.

It appears that this land was surveyed in favor of Peter de Marigny, under the Spanish Government by the Surveyor General of the province, and that it was actually inhabited and cultivated on the 20th December, 1803, and for more than ten consecutive years prior thereto, either by the present claimant, who purchased from said Marigny, or by those under whom he claims. Confirmed.

No. 294.—JOHN FOLEY claims a tract of land, situate in the county of Orleans, on the west side of the river Mississippi, containing forty-six arpents in front and forty in depth, and bounded on the upper side by land of John Denesse, and on the lower by land of James Frederick.

It appears that this land is part of an old concession, and that it was actually inhabited and cultivated on the 20th December, 1803, and for more than ten consecutive pears prior thereto. Confirmed.

No. 323.—GENEVIEVE MILLET, widow of John Adam Frederick, claims a tract of land, situate in the county of Orleans, on the west side of the river Mississippi, containing forty arpents in front, and forty in depth; the lines running in such manner as to include a superficies of seventeen hundred and eighty-eight arpents.

The husband of the claimant obtained from the Spanish Government a regular warrant of survey for this land in the year 1790; and the land having been inhabited and cultivated on the 1st of October, 1800. Confirmed.

No. 324.—JOHN BAPTISTE FREDERICK claims a tract of land, situate in the county of Orleans, on the west side of the river Mississippi, containing twenty-five arpents in front, and forty in depth, and bounded on the upper side by land of John James Frederick, and on the lower by vacant lands.

The claimant obtained from the Spanish Government a regular warrant of survey for this land in the year 1790; and it having been inhabited and cultivated on the 1st of October, 1800. Confirmed.

No. 325.—GENEVIEVE MILLET, widow of John Adam Frederick, claims a tract of land, situate in the county of Orleans, on the west side of the river Mississippi, containing twenty-eight arpents in front, and forty in depth, and bounded on the upper side by land of Jairus Wilcox, and on the lower by land of Homére Frederick.

Charles Adam Frederick, deceased, son of the claimant, obtained from the Spanish Government a regular warrant of survey for this land in the year 1790; and the same having been inhabited and cultivated on the 1st of October, 1800. Confirmed.

No. 326.—JOHN JAMES FREDERICK claims a tract of land, situate on the west side of the river Mississippi, in the county of Orleans, containing twenty-five arpents in front, and forty in depth, and bounded on the upper side by vacant lands, and on the lower by land of Peter Joseph Burat.

The claimant obtained from the Spanish Government a regular warrant of survey for the land, in the year 1790; and the land having been inhabited and cultivated on the 1st day of October, 1800. Confirmed.

No. 327.—GENEVIEVE MILLET, widow of John Adam Millet, claims a tract of land, situate on the west side of the river Mississippi, in the county of Orleans, containing twenty-five arpents in front, and forty in depth, and bounded on the upper side by land of Charles Adam Frederick, and on the lower by vacant lands.

Homère Frederick, deceased, son of the claimant, obtained from the Spanish Government a regular warrant of survey for this land in the year 1790; and the land having been inhabited and cultivated on the 1st of October, 1800. Confirmed.

No. 328.—GENEVIEVE MILLET, widow of John Adam Frederick, claims a tract of land, situate on the west side of the river Mississippi, in the county of Orleans, containing twenty-five arpents in front, and forty in depth, and bounded on the upper side by land of Peter Joseph Burat, and on the lower by vacant lands.

Claude Frederick, deceased, son of the claimant, obtained from the Spanish Government a regular warrant of survey for this land in the year 1790; and the land having been inhabited and cultivated on the 1st of October, 1800. Confirmed.

No. 387.—PETER MARTIN claims a tract of land, situate in the county of Orleans, on the east side of the river Mississippi, at the place called La Pointe à la Hache, containing twenty-five arpents in front, and forty in depth, and bounded on the upper side by land of Joseph Martin, and on the lower by vacant lands.

The claimant obtained from the Spanish Government a regular warrant of survey for this land in the year 1791; and the land having been inhabited and cultivated on the 1st of October, 1800. Confirmed.

No. 403.—CHARLES BASTIEN FREDERICK claims a tract of land, situate in the county of Orleans, on the east side of the river Mississippi, containing forty arpents in front, and seventeen in depth, and bounded on the upper side by land of Bastien Frederick, and on the lower by land of Ronquillo.

It appearing to the satisfaction of the Board that the land now claimed was actually settled prior to the 1st of October, 1800, and that the same was continually inhabited and cultivated by the claimant until on and after the 20th December, 1803. Confirmed.

No. 123.—DANIEL CLARK claims a tract of land, situate in the county of Orleans, on the Bayou aux Bœufs, containing seventy arpents in front, on said bayou.

This is part of the land confirmed to Daniel Clark and Francis D. de la Croix, in No. 300, page 331.

No. 312.—ARNAUD MAGNON claims a lot of ground, situate in the city of New Orleans, on the front side of the same, containing one arpent and nineteen toises in superficies, and bounded on the east side by the river Mississippi, on the south by the property of Henry Metzinger, on the west by the main road, and on the north by vacant land.

The Board confirmed so much of this claim as is embraced by the red lines on the plat of survey; it appearing that the Baron de Carondelet did, in the year 1797, according to the claimant's petition, decree to him part of the ground described in the red lines, and that the claimant, in the year 1799, presented a petition to the Intendant to grant him the remainder, which was referred to the officer of the Fiscal Department for his opinion, and was by him approved; and the country having been ceded to France before this opinion was communicated to the Intendant, no complete title issued; we are of opinion that, according to the usages and customs of the Spanish Government, a complete title would have issued, had an application afterwards been made to the Intendant.

N. B. The lot of ground embraced by the red lines marked in the plat referred to has a front of one hundred and fifteen French feet; and one part of that front, viz. sixty-six feet, has a depth of the upper line sixty-two feet, and the lower sixty-six feet; the remaining part of the front, viz. eighty-nine feet, has a depth of thirty-three feet; the whole containing a superficies of seven thousand seven hundred and sixty-five French feet.

It appears that the claimant occupied and possessed the balance of the ground claimed for more than twelve consecutive years prior to the 20th December, 1803, viz. a small slip, enclosed as a yard, in the rear of his dwelling, and the remainder as a ship-yard; and, at the time of taking possession, he enclosed a considerable part of the ship-yard, and erected work-houses on it, which yet exist, and which he still occupies. This was done with the knowledge and permission of the Spanish Government. We know of no law or usage of that Government respecting claims similarly situated, but think it highly probable that, had the claimant applied, he would have obtained a grant for it, as a grant was made to a lot of ground adjoining him under no higher pretensions. Nor does this appear to come within any of the provisions of the laws of the United States: although there have been ten consecutive years' possession, the land has not been inhabited and cultivated. This part of the claim we do not feel ourselves authorized to decide on, but are of opinion that, in justice, the claim ought to be confirmed.

No. 211.—SAMUEL PERRY claims a tract of land, situate in the county of Pointe Coupée, below the place known by the name of the Pointe Racourci, on the west side of the river Mississippi, containing sixty-one chains and fifty links in front, and one hundred and four chains in depth, forming a superficies of six hundred and forty acres, and bounded on the upper side by land claimed by John McClanahan, and on the lower by land claimed by Charles Morgan.

It appears that the claimant inhabited and cultivated this land in the year 1802, by the permission of the proper Spanish officer, and that it was continued to be inhabited and cultivated, for his benefit, until on and after the 20th December, 1803; we therefore confirm him in his title to the depth of twenty chains. The reason why we limit him to that depth is, that the land is situated at the neck of a large bend of the river, and, by giving him the ordinary depth of forty arpents, his land would stretch across to the river, on the opposite neck; and in this we pursue the custom of the Spanish Government, which was, not to permit the same survey to have two fronts on the river, but limited each front proprietor by a line drawn through the middle. And this rule was never departed from when the facts were known at the time of granting the land; and we therefore reject the balance of the claim.

No. 367.—BARTHELEMY LAFON claims a lot of ground, situate in the city of New Orleans, between the city and the suburb St. Mary, and containing a superficies of eight arpents and one hundred and fourteen toises, as is more fully described in the plat of survey, executed by Carlos Trudeau, Surveyor General of the province, dated March 16, 1798.

It appears that the claimant, on the 1st of March, 1798, petitioned Governor Gayoso for the land in question, and also for certain privileges relative to the establishment of a foundry; that the Governor, without hesitation, accorded to him that part of his petition which related to the land, and directed the Surveyor General to lay it off for him in the customary manner, and referred the claimant to the King as to the objects asked for relative to the foundry; that, in obedience to the Governor's order, the Surveyor General, on the 16th of the same month, surveyed, in favor of the claimant, the land now claimed; that, shortly after the survey was executed, the claimant took possession of the land, and enclosed with piquets a portion of it, and erected on it sheds to shelter his materials, &c., and commenced a foundry on a small scale, by way of experiment, and continued in the undisturbed possession of it until about a year thereafter, when, by a report of the engineer, he was forbidden, by a military order, to erect any buildings thereon which might interfere with the fire of the fort St. Louis, the fortifications of which were about that time enlarged and improved, in consequence of an apprehended invasion of the province. By reason of this order, the claimant was constrained to cease his operations on the land in question, and transported his materials to another place. Since the change of Government, and the demolition of the fortifications, he has attempted to resume possession, but has been prevented by the interference of the city corporation, who claim it as commons belonging to the city. We have no doubt that this land appertained to the domain, and not to the city, and was so considered by the King of Spain and the Governors of this province, and that they had a right to grant it; for sundry grants have been made to lots situate between this land and the city, and, among others, two grants to Elisha Winter: one by virtue of a royal order, and the other by the Governor himself. This land having been surveyed for the claimant, by the authority of the Governor, and he having been in quiet possession and enjoyment of it until interrupted by a military order, we are of opinion that the claim ought to be confirmed, and do accordingly confirm it.

To the above confirmation of the claim of Barthelemy Lafon, as aforesaid, by a majority of the Board of Commissioners, viz.: Messrs. Lewis and Robertson, Philip Grymes, one of the commissioners, dissented as follows:

I, Philip Grymes, one of the members of the Board of Commissioners of Land Claims for the eastern district of the Territory of Orleans, do disagree to the statement of facts on which is predicated the confirmation of the foregoing claim to a lot of land, situate between the faubourg St. Mary and the city of New Orleans, because I am of opinion that the facts assumed in that statement are not established by the testimony in the case; and I dissent from the decision of the majority of the commissioners on that claim: 1st, Because I am convinced the claimant never did receive from any legitimate authority, either French or Spanish, such a grant or permission to settle upon, inhabit, and cultivate the lot of ground in question, as is contemplated by any of the several acts of Congress giving the right of confirmation of claims to land in this Territory. 2dly, Because it is evident that the lot of ground makes a part of what is called the commons of the city; which commons attached to the corporation in such manner as that the sovereignty of neither France nor Spain could alienate or appropriate them, without the consent of the corporation, to any other than some object of common advantage and utility. No consent appears to have been given by the corporation, nor does the claimant pretend to rest his title to the property on the common utility of its appropriation; and 3dly, Because I do not believe that the claimant ever had such occupancy or possession of the premises as gives an equitable right to the confirmation of his claim.

No. 232.—BERNARD MARIGNY claims a tract of land, situate in the county of Orleans, on the east side of the river Mississippi, containing thirteen hundred and seventy-two superficial arpents, and bounded on the upper side by a line running parallel to the city of New Orleans, at the distance of two arpents and twelve toises from the barracks, and on the lower by Nicholas Daunoy.

It appears that this land was actually inhabited and cultivated on the 20th December, 1803, and that the same was continually inhabited and cultivated by the claimant, or those under whom he claims, for more than ten consecutive years next preceding. Confirmed.

No. 283.—GEORGE BRADISH and WM. H. JOHNSON claim a tract of land, situate in the county of Orleans, at the Balise, containing fifty-five superficial arpents and three hundred and sixty toises, and bounded by the bayou Johnson on one side, and by the ground on which is erected the light-house on the other.

It appears that John Ronquillo, a Spanish piloto, settled himself on this land in the year 1789, and with much labor, he cleared and rendered it habitable; that he continued to reside on it until some time in the year 1804, when it was sold by him to the present claimants. The Board confirm this claim in such manner, that the line dividing this land from the land of the public shall run perpendicular to the bayou, at the distance of three hundred and thirty-two feet from the block house.

No. 313.—DOMINIQUE BOULIGNY claims a tract of land, situate in the county of Orleans, on the west side of the river Mississippi, containing seven thousand six hundred and seventeen superficial arpents, and bounded on the upper side by land of Peter Aurin, and on the lower by land of Francis Delery.

It appears that Joseph Ducros, being proprietor of part of this land, viz.: twelve arpents front, with the ordinary depth of forty arpents, obtained from Governor Galvez, in the year 1777, a complete grant for the whole of the back land, to lake Barataria, continuing the direction of the lines of his front tract; it appears, also, that another part of the tract claimed, viz.: twelve arpents front, with the depth of forty, situate on the bayou leading to lake Barataria, was granted in the year 1794, by the Baron Carondelet, to Nicholas Domé; and also another tract, adjoining this last, having fifteen arpents front, and the depth of forty, on each side of the same bayou, was granted in the same year to Antonio Wort; there was also granted, in the year 1797, to Carlos Juan Baptiste Florian, a tract of land of forty arpents front, with forty depth, on each side of the aforesaid bayou. The whole of the land claimed having been regularly granted, and now held by the claimant, by purchase under those grants, the Board confirm the claim.

No. 134.—THOMAS POWER claims a tract of land, situate in the county of Iberville, on the right bank of the river Amite, at the place commonly called Crow Bluff, containing two thousand five hundred arpents.

It appearing to the satisfaction of the Board that this land was settled with the permission of the proper Spanish officer prior to the 20th December, 1803, and that the same was actually inhabited and cultivated on that day, the Board confirm the claim to the extent of six hundred and forty superficial acres, to be laid off so as to include the improvement; the centre, with a front of sixteen acres on the river Amite, and a depth of forty acres, the balance of the claim, the Board reject.

No. 197.—THOMAS POWER claims a tract of land, situate in the county of Orleans, on the west and northwest bank of the bayou of Barataria, commencing at a small bayou known by the name of bayou Chalan, and extending about four leagues to the Bayou aux Oies, and being forty arpents in depth.

It appears that an inventory was made of the estate of Claude Joseph Villars, in the year 1760, of which the tract of land now claimed formed a part; that at a judicial sale of said land, in the same year, Joseph Villars, the son, became the purchaser; after whose death, an inventory was made of his estate, and this land sold again by a judicial sale to the highest bidder, and was purchased by Louis Trudeau, who has since sold it to the present claimant. The Board confirm the claim.

No. 14.—ELISHA WINTER claims a lot of ground, situate between the city of New Orleans and the suburb St. Mary, containing one hundred feet in front, by six hundred feet in depth.

It appears that, in the year 1791, the claimant obtained a regular order from the King of Spain for this land, for the purpose of erecting a rope-walk, and, in the same year, obtained a grant from Governor Miro, pursuant to royal order; that, in or about the year 1793, by order of the Baron de Carondelet, part of this land was retrenched; the whole length of the side next to the fortifications, containing about eight hundred and forty-two superficial toises, to be used as a curtain to the same, and the claimant was ordered and compelled to demolish his buildings which were erected thereon. The claimant remonstrated against the injustice of this order, and the Go-

vernor ultimately granted him, as an indemnity, an additional quantity of ground in the rear of his rope-walk, making, in quantity, somewhat more than the ground retrenched, but not equal in point of value, nor was its value at the time equal to the value of the buildings demolished. The only difficulty appears to be, whether the grant of the additional quantity of ground adjoining the rope-walk was given and accepted, not only as an indemnity for the buildings demolished, and the consequent losses and inconveniences, but also as an extinguishment of all right and title in the claimant to the land retrenched from him. It seems to have been the practice of the Spanish Government in this country, when private property has been invaded by the law of public necessity, to indemnify the individual to the extent of his sacrifice. In this case, the indemnity given was not at the time equivalent to the buildings demolished, nor to the ground retrenched. This right of the Spanish Government is founded upon public necessity, and the principles which apply to it we consider are precisely analogous with those that apply to the laying out of public highways, &c; in which case the individual is indemnified for the privation and resulting inconveniences only, and the land reverts to him when it ceases to be a public highway. The Spanish Government, at the time, seemed to consider the indemnity as extending not even to the privation of the ground, but merely to the demolition of the buildings; for the Surveyor General, who, by the order of the Governor, surveyed for the claimant the ground which was given as an indemnity, states, in his proces-verbal of survey, (upon which the patent issued) "land surveyed for the claimant as an indemnity for demolishing his buildings." The fortifications having since been rased, we are of opinion that the land reverts to the claimant, and do accordingly confirm him in histitle.

No. 308.—JEAN BAPTISTE CASTILLON claims the following tracts of land, situate in the county of Orleans, viz: 1st. A tract of land, situate about half a league below the city of New Orleans, on the Mississippi river, containing six arpents in front, and extending back to the lands of Gentilly, and bounded on the upper side by land of Laveau Trudeau, and on the lower by land of the claimant. 2d. A tract adjoining the aforegoing tract, containing three arpents front, and eighty arpents depth. 3d. A tract situate on the bayou Terre aux Bœufs, containing three arpents front on each side of said bayou, and forty arpents depth, and bounded on the upper side by land of José Ruse, and on the lower by land of Carlos Tardy. 4th. A tract situate on the bayou of Terre aux Bœufs, containing two arpents front on each side of said bayou, and forty arpents depth, and bounded on one side by land of Manuel de la Caridad, and on the other by land of St. Yago Molina. 5th. A tract on the bayou of Terre aux Bœufs, containing five arpents and nineteen toises on both sides of said bayou, and forty arpents in depth, and bounded on the upper side by land of Bartholomew Molar, and on the lower by land of Diego Bertrand. 6th. A tract situate on the river Mississippi, about two and a half leagues above the city of New Orleans, containing nineteen arpents and eighteen toises in front, and extending back to lake Pontchartrain, and bounded on the upper side by land of Chevalier Hazeur, and on the lower by land of the claimants. 7th. A tract of land adjoining the last tract, and containing twenty arpents in front, and the upper line running back forty arpents, and the lower sixty arpents. 8th. A tract situate on the left side of the Bayou St. John road, in going from the city, containing six arpents in front, and extending back to the lands of Jean Gravier, and bounded on one side by land of Mr. Griffon, and on the other by land of Mr. Castanedo. 9th. A tract of land situate on the bayou St. John, containing seven hundred and eighty-eight superficial arpents, and bounded on one side by land of Mr. Deveniseaux, and on the other by lands of Metairie.

It appearing that the front and first depth of the first tract of land claimed was actually inhabited and cultivated on the 20th of December, 1803, and for more than ten consecutive years prior thereto, the Board confirm the claim to that extent, but reject it as to the second extension of the depth to the lands of Gentilly. It appears that the front and first depth of the second tract of land was actually inhabited and cultivated on the 20th December, 1803, and for more than ten consecutive years prior thereto, and the second depth was granted by the French Government to Mr. Decalogne, in the year 1764; the Board do therefore confirm the claim. It appears that the third tract of land claimed was actually inhabited and cultivated on the 20th of December, 1803, and for more than ten consecutive years prior thereto, by those under whom the claimant holds; the Board therefore confirm the claim. It appearing that the fourth tract of land now claimed was actually inhabited and cultivated on the 20th December, 1803, and for more than ten consecutive years prior thereto, by those under whom the present claimant holds, the Board therefore confirm the claim. It appearing that the fifth tract of land claimed was actually inhabited and cultivated on the 20th December, 1803, and for more than ten consecutive years prior thereto, the Board confirm the claim. It appears that the sixth tract of land claimed was granted by the India Company to Mr. Dubreuil, in the year 1708, and subsequently transferred to the present claimant; the Board therefore confirm the claim. It appearing that the front and first depth of the seventh tract of land claimed was inhabited and cultivated on the 20th December, 1803, and for more than ten consecutive years prior thereto, the Board confirm the claim to that extent, but reject the balance claimed. It appearing that the eighth tract claimed was actually inhabited and cultivated on the 20th December, 1803, and for more than ten consecutive years prior thereto, the Board confirm the claim. The ninth tract of land now claimed it appears was granted by the French Government in 1758, to Mr. Monleon, under whose title the present claimant holds. The Board confirm the claim.

No. 125.—WILLIAM CONWAY claims a tract of land, situate in the county of Acadia, at the place called the Houmas, on the left bank of the Mississippi, containing twenty-two and a half arpents in front, with an opening towards the rear of sixty degrees forty-five minutes; the upper line running north, nine degrees fifteen minutes east, three hundred and fifty-one arpents; and on the lower line directed north, seventy degrees east, and measuring four hundred and fifty-five arpents; bounded on the upper side by Daniel Clark's land, and on the lower by land of Simon Laveau.

It appearing to the Board, from a patent or complete title exhibited, that seventeen arpents of front were, together with a greater quantity, granted by the Spanish Government to Maurice Conway, 21st June, 1777; and it appearing that the five and a half arpents of front remaining of the land aforesaid were purchased by Pierre Part, at the public sale of the estate of the late Joachin Mire, alias Belony, on the 7th day of December, 1788; and it further appearing to the Board, from the several instruments of conveyance offered in testimony, that the two tracts of land aforesaid have been conveyed to the present claimant, the Board do hereby confirm his claim aforesaid.

No. 127.—DANIEL CLARK claims a tract of land, situate in the county of Acadia, at a place called the Houmas, containing ten acres in front, on the left bank of the Mississippi, and running back to the river Amite, bounded on the upper side by lands of Donaldson and Scott, and on the lower by those of W. Conway.

It appears to the Board, from a patent or complete title exhibited, that said land, together with a greater quantity, was granted by the Spanish Government to one Maurice Conway, on the 21st of June, 1777; and it appearing, from divers deeds of conveyance also exhibited, that the land now claimed by the present claimant has been legally conveyed to him, the Board do therefore confirm him in his said claim.

No. 133.—WILLIAM DONALDSON and JOHN W. SCOTT claim a tract of land, situate in the county of Acadia, on the left bank of the Mississippi, about twenty-two leagues above the city of New Orleans, containing twenty-nine acres in front, with the depth to the river Amite, bounded on the upper side by land of one Simonet, and on the lower by land of Daniel Clark.

It appearing to the Board, from an instrument of writing exhibited, that said land was sold at public auction on the 12th day of August, 1798, before Evan Jones, at that time commandant of La Fourche, to Louis Faure; and it appearing, from sundry deeds of conveyance, likewise exhibited, that said land has become the property of the present claimant, the Board do hereby confirm his said claim.

NOTE.—The three foregoing decisions were made before I became a member of the Board; as far as I am authorized to do so, I dissent from the same.
THOMAS B. ROBERTSON.

No. 306.—CLAUDE TREME, for himself, and in behalf of those who claim under him, claims a tract of land, situate on the northwest side of the city of New Orleans, and bounded on the north by lands of Bernard Marigny, on the west by those of C. Griffon, on the south by the canal Carondelet, and on the east by the city aforesaid.

Ten arpents front, and seven arpents depth, of this land, situate upon the ancient road leading from the city to the bayou St. John is claimed by virtue of a deed of sale made by the India Company, in the year 1731, and has been inhabited and occupied ever since that period; under which title the claimant holds that part of this land lying on the west side of said road; the other part of this land, to wit, ten arpents front, situate on the northeast side of said road, running in depth to the land of Dubreuil, he claims by a grant of the French Government, in the year 1756; all which land has become the property of the claimant by successive deeds of sale. The Board confirm him in his title.
JOSHUA LEWIS,
THOMAS B. ROBERTSON.

Rejected claims from those enregistered in the office of the Register of the Eastern District.

No. 4.—JOSEPH DECUIR claims a tract of land, being a second depth, and lying immediately behind a front depth of the claimant, situate in the county of Pointe Coupée, on the south side of False river, containing forty-two and one-third arpents in front, and forty in depth, with such an opening as to give a superficies of sixteen hundred and ninety arpents, and bounded on the two sides and in the rear by vacant lands.

It appears to the Board, from an order of survey exhibited, that said land was granted by the Spanish Government to the claimant on the 6th of September, 1802, for which land said Decuir was to pay said Government at the rate of five dollars for each front arpent, agreeably to a valuation made by Carlos Trudeau, Surveyor General of the province of Louisiana, dated November 20, 1802; but it appearing to the Board that, in consequence of a suspension of the proceedings relative to the land office having taken place before the valuation money could be paid, there is no power vested in the Board to receive, on the part of the United States, said valuation money, they feel themselves compelled to reject the claim.

No. 89.—BENJAMIN M. STOKES claims a tract of land, situate in the county of Pointe Coupée, on the river Mississippi, below the Pointe Racourci, containing six hundred and forty superficial acres, and bounded on each side by vacant lands.

The claimant claims this land in virtue of a permission from the commandant of the district given to Aaron Cadwell, senior, (under whose right he claims,) and an actual settlement and cultivation prior to and on the 20th December, 1803. In support of this, he produces the testimony of one witness, a son of the aforesaid Aaron Cadwell. It appears to the Board that the said Cadwell did settle on this land some time in the year 1802, and they have reason to believe with the verbal permission of the proper Spanish officer; but it further appears that he had not remained long on the land before he died, and that neither his family, nor any one for them, did inhabit or cultivate the same on the 20th December, 1803; and consequently, the claim does not fall under the provisions of the act of Congress relative to donations, and they accordingly reject the claim.

No. 90.—SUSANNA HONEYMAN claims a tract of land, situate in the county of Pointe Coupée, on the river Mississippi, below the place known by the name of Pointe Racourci, containing six hundred and forty superficial acres, and bounded on one side by land claimed by John McClanahan.

The claimant pretends title to this tract of land by virtue of a settlement made previous to the 20th December, 1803. There is no evidence that the land has ever been settled, either by her, or any other person for her. She resides in West Florida, and we have no doubt that the land is not yet settled. We have rejected the claim of Charles Morgan to a tract of land in the same neighborhood, sold to him by the present claimant, in the year 1806, and founded on a similar title. (See No. 93, next page.) By the act of Congress, the claimant could not hold two tracts under a settlement right, had there been an actual settlement. We consider this to be a feigned claim, and reject it.

No. 91.—ANDRY ROBINSON claims a tract of land, situate in the county of Pointe Coupée, on the river Mississippi, just at the mouth of the bayou Atchafalaya, (a small part being above said bayou, but the greater part lying below it,) containing six hundred and forty superficial acres.

This land is claimed in virtue of a settlement made prior to the 20th of December, 1803, and cultivation on that day. In support of which, the claimant produces two certificates, not sworn to, stating that the claimant was on the land in 1802, and one of them that he remained on it until on and after the 20th December, 1803. He pretends not that he settled with the permission of the proper Spanish officer; and it appears to the Board, from satisfactory testimony, that he did not actually settle the land until some time subsequent to the 20th December, 1803. The claim does not come within the provisions of the acts of Congress relative to donations, and the Board reject it, except as to the small part falling without the limits of their district.

No. 92.—JOHN McCLANAHAN claims a tract of land, situate in the county of Pointe Coupée, on the river Mississippi, below the place called and known by the name of Pointe Racourci, containing six hundred and forty superficial arpents, and bounded on the upper side by land claimed by Benjamin M. Stokes, and on the lower by land claimed by Susanna Honeyman.

This land is claimed in virtue of a settlement made with the permission of the proper Spanish officer prior to the 20th December, 1803, and cultivation on that day by Aaron Cadwell, Jun., under whose right the present claimant holds. In support of which, the claimant presents the testimony of one witness, a brother of the aforesaid Aaron Cadwell, Jun., stating that he had obtained permission from the commandant to settle vacant land, and did actually inhabit and cultivate this land on the 20th December, 1803. It appears satisfactorily to the Board that this land was settled neither by said Cadwell, nor any person for him, until long after the 20th December, 1803; we are therefore of opinion that the claim ought to be rejected.

No. 93.—CHARLES MORGAN claims a tract of land, situate in the county of Pointe Coupée, on the river Mississippi, below the place known by the name of Pointe Racourci, containing six hundred and forty superficial arpents.

The claimant purchased this tract of land of Susanna Honeyman, a resident of West Florida, in the year 1806, and founds his title upon a settlement made prior to the 20th of December, 1803; of this fact he has not, and we have no doubt cannot, produce any evidence. He has been called upon for proof. From the best information we have been able to obtain, this land has not been settled to this day. We have already rejected the claim of Susanna Honeyman to another tract of land claimed by her as a settlement right. (See No. 90, page 287.) We consider this claim a feigned one, and do therefore reject it.

No. 117.—FRANCIS D. DEZILET claims a tract of land, being a second depth of forty arpents, and lying immediately back of a first depth of forty arpents, situate in the county of Orleans, and containing eight arpents in front, which we have already confirmed to him in No. 117 among the confirmed claims.

The claimant shows no other foundation for his title to this second depth than having occupied the front and first depth, and having occasionally supplied himself with timber from the second depth. According to the laws, usages, and customs of the Spanish Government, no front proprietor, by any act of his own, could acquire a right to lands further back than the ordinary depth of forty arpents; and although the Spanish Government has invariably refused to grant the second depth to any other than the front proprietor, yet nothing short of a grant or warrant of survey from the Governor could confer a title or right to the land. We therefore reject the claim.

No. 119.—JAMES VILLERY claims a second depth of land, extending back to lake Pontchartrain, and lying immediately behind a tract of five arpents two toises and four feet front, on the ordinary depth of forty arpents, situate in the county of Orleans, on the east side of the river Mississippi, and which has already been confirmed to him in No. 119 among the confirmed claims.

In support of his claim to this second extension of depth to lake Pontchartrain, the claimant produces consecutive sales for a great number of years back; but it appears to the Board that, by continuing the lines in the direction of those of the first depth, they would fall, not on lake Pontchartrain, but on on lake Borgue: the claim cannot be confirmed for more than the front and ordinary depth, but the Board are of opinion that the claimant ought, in justice, to receive a concession for a second depth of forty arpents.

No. 152.—ANTHONY BIENVENU claims a second depth of land, extending to lake Borgue, and lying immediately back of a front of four arpents, by forty in depth, being part of a large front of eighteen arpents, situate in the county of Orleans, on the east side of the river Mississippi, and which has already been confirmed to him in No. 152 among the confirmed claims.

The claimant shows, for this second extension of depth to the four arpents aforesaid, no other title than that of having purchased it, together with a greater quantity of land. It does not appear that those from whom he purchased ever acquired a title to this part of the land. According to the laws, usages, and customs of the Spanish Government, no front proprietor could, by any act of his own, acquire a right to lands further back than the ordinary depth of forty arpents, and although that Government invariably refused to grant the land to any other than the front proprietor, yet nothing short of a grant or warrant of survey from the Governor could confer a title or right to the land. We do therefore reject the claim.

No. 155.—EBENEZER COOLEY claims a tract of land, situate in the county of Pointe Coupée, on the west side of the river Mississippi, containing twenty arpents in front, viz.: ten arpents on each side of the bayou Atanache, with the depth of forty arpents, and bounded on each side by vacant lands.

It appears that one Joseph Bourgeat made a settlement on this tract of land upwards of forty years ago, and resided on it some years; one witness, a kinsman of the claimant, says ten or twelve consecutive years. This part of the river was settled by a number of families about the same time, (Bourgeat's was one,) and a few years afterwards they abandoned it, by reason of a great inundation from the river, and settled elsewhere. Neither Bourgeat nor any of his family have ever resumed possession of the land, or exercised any act of ownership over it. The claimant purchased this land from Bourgeat's widow, in the year 1806. We consider that Bourgeat forfeited all claim to this land after having left it and established himself elsewhere, having no other title than a naked possession; and it is probable that neither Bourgeat, nor his heirs, nor any person claiming under him, would have pretended any claim to this land, had not its value been so much enhanced by the change of Government. We have no doubt that, according to the usages of the Spanish Government, the Governor would not have hesitated to grant this land to any other individual applying, with a full knowledge of Bourgeat's claim, after he had left it and settled elsewhere. We are of opinion that the claim is not warranted by any law, usage, or custom of the Spanish Government, or any law of the United States; and do accordingly reject it.

No. 172.—JOSEPH FREDERICK claims a tract of land, situate in the county of Pointe Coupée, on the river Mississippi, containing four hundred and forty-four and twenty-six hundredths superficial acres, being eighty arpents in depth, and bounded on the upper side by the Apeloussas road, and on the lower by land claimed by William Welborne.

It appears that this land has been abandoned for upwards of twenty-five years, and that possession has never been resumed, nor any acts of ownership exercised, either by those who were originally in possession and occupation of the land, or any one claiming under them, until long since the change of Government, in 1803, and probably never would have been to this day, had not the value of the land been so much enhanced thereby. We entertain not the least doubt that, if application had been made by any other individual for this land, the Governor, with a full knowledge of the pretensions of those under whom the present claimant holds, would not have made the least difficulty on that account in granting the land. We are of opinion that the claim is not sanctioned by any law, custom, or usage of the Spanish Government, nor by any law of the United States; and do accordingly reject it.

No. 173.—JOHN TOWLES claims a tract of land, situate in the county of Pointe Coupée, on the bayou Gros Tête, or Grand Bayou, containing nine hundred and sixty-nine and seventy-four hundredths superficial acres, and bounded on the upper side by other land of the claimant, on the lower by vacant land, and on the rear by land of Narcisse Carmouche.

George Olivo, under whose title the claimant holds by virtue of a conveyance from his widow, in the year 1806, obtained a regular warrant of survey for this land, in the year 1787, from Don Estevan Miro, the Governor: but it appears that the land was never occupied to this day. We are therefore of opinion that, according to the laws, usages, and customs of the Spanish Government, and consistently with the provisions of the acts of Congress, the claim ought to be rejected.

No. 174.—JOHN TOWLES claims a tract of land, situate in the county of Pointe Coupée, on the bayou Gros Tête, or Grand Bayou, containing nine hundred and sixty-nine and seventy-four hundredths superficial acres, and bounded on the lower side by other lands of the claimant.

Simon Porche, from whom the present claimant purchased in 1806, obtained a regular warrant of survey for this land, in the year 1787, from Don Estevan Miro; but it appears that the land was never occupied to this day either by said Porche or any other person for him. We are therefore of opinion that, according to the laws, usages, and customs of the Spanish Government, as also to the laws of the United States, the claim ought to be rejected.

No. 178.—CHARLES MORGAN claims a tract of land, situate on the river Mississippi, below the place called Pointe Racourci, in the county of Pointe Coupée, containing six hundred and forty superficial acres, and bounded on the upper side by land claimed by Benjamin M. Stokes, and on the lower by vacant lands.

The claimant purchased this land of John McClanahan, in the year 1806, who had purchased the said tract of land in the same year of John Barclay and wife. He produces two certificates from Barclay's family, not sworn to, stating that Barclay settled this land, by permission of Grand Pré, previous to the year 1800. We have the most satisfactory evidence that the land was not inhabited or cultivated in any part of the year 1803, or since; and therefore reject the claim.

No. 180.—BELONY CHATELIN claims a tract of land, situate in the county of Pointe Coupée, on the river Mississippi, above the Pointe Racourci, containing four hundred and six and twenty-one hundredths superficial acres, and bounded on the upper side by land claimed by Baptiste Lamour, and on the lower by vacant land.

It appears that this land was abandoned upwards of twenty-five years, and that possession had not been resumed, either by the present claimant, or those under whom he claims, until long since the 20th December, 1803. We have not a doubt but that the Governor would have granted the land to any person applying, with a full knowledge of the claim, after those under whom the present claimant holds had left it and settled elsewhere. We are of opinion that the claim is not warranted by any law, usage, or custom of the Spanish Government, or any law of the United States; and do therefore reject it.

No. 181.—WILLIAM WELBORNE claims a tract of land, situate in the county of Pointe Coupée, on the west side of the river Mississippi, containing six arpents in front, and forty in depth, and bounded on the upper side by land claimed by Joseph Frederick, and on the lower by land claimed by Charles Morgan.

It appears that this land was settled upwards of twenty-five years ago, when those who were in possession of it were forced, by reason of an inundation from the river, to leave it and settle elsewhere; since which time it has always remained abandoned, and possession has never been resumed by the original occupants, or any person for them, until long since the change of Government in 1803. From no acts of ownership having been exercised over the land under the Spanish Government for upwards of twenty-five years, the presumption is strong that it would never have been claimed again, had not its value been so much enhanced by the change of Government. We have no doubt the Governor would not have hesitated to grant the land, with a perfect knowledge of the pretensions of the original occupant. We are therefore of opinion that the claim is not sanctioned by any custom of the Spanish Government, or

any law of the United States; and do accordingly reject it.

No. 182.—JOSEPH RABALES claims a tract of land, situate in the county of Pointe Coupée, on the west side of the river Mississippi, containing six hundred and seventy-seven superficial acres, and bounded on the upper side by vacant lands, and on the lower by land claimed by Julian Poydras.

It appears that this land has been abandoned for upwards of twenty-five years, and that possession has never been resumed, either by the original occupant, or any one for him, until long since the year 1803. We have not the least doubt that the land would never have been again claimed, had not its value been so much increased by the change of Government; and we hesitate not to believe that the Governor would have granted it to any other individual applying, after the first settler had left it and settled on other lands. We are of opinion that the claim is unwarranted by any law, either of the Spanish Government or of the United States; and do therefore reject it.

No. 183.—JOSEPH DECUIR, Jun. claims a tract of land, situate in the county of Pointe Coupée, on the west side of the river Mississippi, containing two hundred and eighty-nine and thirty-one hundredths superficial acres, and bounded on the upper side by land claimed by J. B. Tunoir, and on the lower by land claimed by Charles Dufour, Jun.

It appears that this land was settled upwards of twenty-five years ago, and that, by reason of an inundation of the river, the original occupant was forced to leave it and settle elsewhere, and that it has remained abandoned for more than twenty-five years, and possession never resumed, nor any acts of ownership exercised, by the first occupant, or any one for him, until long since the 20th of December, 1803. We have every reason to believe that it never would have been again claimed, had not its value been so considerably increased by the change of Government. We are of opinion that the claim is not sanctioned by any law or custom of the Spanish Government, or any act of Congress; and do accordingly reject it.

No. 192.—CHARLES MORGAN claims a tract of land, situate in the county of Pointe Coupée, on the west side of the river Mississippi, containing twelve hundred and twenty-four and ninety-nine hundredths superficial arpents, and bounded on the upper side by land claimed by William Welborne, and on the lower by land claimed by Mr. Barry.

It appears that one John Decuir resided on this land about forty years ago, and continued there some years, when he was compelled to abandon it, by reason of the inundation of the river. He then settled on other lands, and has never since resumed possession of the land so abandoned, nor has any one for him, until within three or four years past; nor does it appear that he ever had any other title to the land than his old possession. We consider that John Decuir, by abandoning this land and settling elsewhere, has forfeited all the right which his settlement gave him, and that the Spanish Government would not have hesitated to have granted it to any other person applying for the same. It is not believed that either John Decuir or his heirs would ever have claimed this land, had not the change of Government made it valuable. As an evidence of the low value set upon this land, it was sold to the present claimant for the sum of four hundred dollars in the year 1806, and he now rates it at ten thousand dollars. We are of opinion that this claim cannot be maintained by any law, usage, or custom of the Spanish Government, or any law of the United States; and do therefore reject it.

No. 196.—BERTHELEMY DUVERGES claims a tract of land, situate in the county of Orleans, on the west side of the river Mississippi, containing two arpents in front, and forty in depth, it being part of a larger tract, of twenty-two arpents front, on the aforesaid depth; twenty arpents front of which we have already confirmed to him, in No. 196 among the confirmed claims.

The claimant pretends title to the land now claimed as having been granted by the French Government, in the year 1766, to Jacques Larche, under whom he holds. Twenty arpents front, on the ordinary depth, actually were granted, at that time, to said Larche; but as he can produce no title for the remaining two arpents front, on the ordinary depth, the Board reject the claim thereto.

No. 211.—SAMUEL PERRY claims a tract of land, situate in the county of Pointe Coupée, below the place known by the name of Pointe Racourci, on the west side of the river Mississippi, containing sixty-one chains and fifty links in front, and a depth of one hundred and four chains, forming a superficies of six hundred and forty acres, and bounded on the upper side by land claimed by John McClanahan, and on the lower by land claimed by Charles Morgan.

For the decision on the *part* of this claim that the Board reject, viz. twenty arpents of its width and depth towards the rear, see the claim No. 211 among the confirmed claims.

No. 227.—EDWARD CADWELL claims a tract of land, situate in the county of Pointe Coupée, below the place called Pointe Racourci, on the west side of the river Mississippi, containing six hundred and forty superficial acres, and bounded on the upper side by land claimed by Mrs. Trantham, and on the lower by land claimed by Edward Cadwell.

This land is claimed, as is pretended, by virtue of a settlement made in 1802, and cultivation on the 20th of December, 1803, by one Mason, from whom the present claimant purchased in 1806. The claimant produces the testimony of one witness in support of this. We have the best reasons for believing that the evidence is false, and have the most undoubted testimony that, if *ever* said Mason was on the land, he did not remain there but a very short time, and was not there on the 20th December, 1803, or for some time previous, or since. We consider the claim entirely a feigned one, and do therefore reject it.

No. 237.—FRANCIS MAYRONNE and J. B. DEGRUIS claim two tracts of land, adjoining each other, and situate in the county of Iberville, on the east side of the river Mississippi, about three miles below the Bayou of Manchack, at the place called Pointe de Manchack, containing each eighteen arpents in front, and forty in depth, and bounded on the upper side by land of Mr. Villars, and on the lower by land of Peter Voisin.

The claimants purchased this land of Francis Bouligny, about twenty years ago, but they produce no written evidence of title in said Bouligny; and the land never having been inhabited or cultivated to this day, we are of opinion the claim ought to be rejected.

No. 171.—ANTHONY DECUIR claims a tract of land, situate in the county of Pointe Coupée, on the Chenelle, containing sixteen hundred and twenty-six and thirty-one hundredths superficial acres, and bounded on the upper side by land of Joseph Decuir, and on the lower by land of —— Savoye.

The claimant states that he had an order of survey from the Spanish Government, but he produces no evidence of the fact, nor can it be found on the Spanish records relative to lands. It appears that the land was not settled until a short time after the year 1803; and, had it been previously settled, the claimant would have been excluded from a *donation*, as having actually received other lands from the Spanish Government. We are therefore of opinion that his claim ought to be rejected.

No. 214.—GEORGE POLLOCK, JOHN PALFREY, and CONSTANT FREEMAN, claim a tract of land, situate in the county of Orleans, on the southern border of lake Pontchartrain, about four miles eastward of the mouth of bayou St. John, containing three thousand nine hundred and twenty-six superficial arpents, and bounded on the north by lake Pontchartrain, on the east by bayou Cochon, on the south by the lands of Gentilly, and on the west by land of Alexander Milne.

The claimants hold this land, by successive conveyances, under Charles de Lachaise, whose title was founded upon possession and cultivation for upwards of ten consecutive years prior to the 20th of December, 1803. Lachaise claimed considerably more land than he conveyed to those from whom the present claimants hold; and the quantity of two thousand acres has already been confirmed to Alexander Milne, (No. 1,) who held by a precedent conveyance to that of the present claimants. The extent of land that the act of Congress allows under the principle of ten consecutive years having been already confirmed, the Board reject this claim.

No. 239.—XAVIER ROBICHAUX claims a tract of land, situate in the county of Iberville, on the right bank of the bayou of Placquemines, opposite to the land formerly belonging to Alexander Dardenne, containing

three hundred and thirty-seven and fifty-six hundredths superficial acres.

It appears that the claimant obtained an order of survey for this land, in the year 1794, from the Baron de Carondelet; but it also appearing that the land was never inhabited or cultivated until after the 20th December, 1803, we do therefore reject the claim.

No. 260.—HONORE PRINCE claims a tract of land, situate in the county of Orleans, at the place called *Quartier de Placquemines*, on the west side of the river Mississippi, containing four hundred and forty-two superficial arpents, and bounded on the upper side by land of Ramond Thomas, and on the lower by the bayou Liard.

The claimant founds his title to this land on a settlement prior to the 20th December, 1803, and habitation and cultivation on that day; but it appearing to the satisfaction of the Board that the land was not inhabited or cultivated until after the 20th December, 1803, they therefore reject the claim.

No. 284.—PETER DE LA RONDE claims a tract of land, lying back of a front which has already been confirmed to him, together with a depth extending to the prairie, and situate on the east side of the river Mississippi, in the county of Orleans. See No. 284 among the confirmed claims.

For the part of this claim which has been confirmed, viz: the front, and a depth back to the prairie, see the aforesaid number. The balance, viz: from the prairie to lake Borgne, the Board reject; the claimant having shown no manner of title to it.

No. 292.—JAIRUS WILCOX claims a tract of land, situate in the county of Orleans, on the west side of the river Mississippi, containing sixty-eight arpents in front, and forty in depth.

The claimant sets up title to this land under the will of John Gates, deceased, who, he alleges, purchased it in his lifetime of John and Charles Adam Frederick. He exhibits no evidence of title in said Gates, as stated in his notice. This land is also claimed by the Fredericks, and confirmed to them in different numbers among the confirmed claims.

No. 293.—CLAUDE TREME claims a tract of land, situate in the county of Pointe Coupée, on the west side of the river Mississippi, containing two hundred and thirty-six and ninety-two hundredths superficial acres, and bounded on the lower side by land claimed by Joseph Frederick.

The claimant pretends title to this land in the right of Mutin Moreau, who is said to have been in possession for more than twenty years. The land was settled upwards of twenty-five years ago, but, by reason of the inundation of the river, the first settler was forced to abandon it and settle on other lands. It has remained abandoned for upwards of twenty-five years, and possession has never been resumed, either by the first settler, or any one for him, until since the 20th of December, 1803. We are of opinion, for reasons assigned in claims founded on similar pretensions, that it ought to be rejected.

No. 296.—CLAUDE TREME claims a tract of land, situate in the county of Pointe Coupée, on the west side of the river Mississippi, containing forty arpents in front, viz: twenty on each side of the bayou Moreau, and forty arpents in depth, and bounded on each side by vacant land.

This land was settled about forty years ago by Paul Moreau, the father-in-law of the claimant, but has been abandoned for upwards of five-and-twenty years, and possession never since resumed, until long since the change of Government in 1803, either by said Moreau, or any one for him; nor do we suppose it would ever have been again claimed, had not its value been so much enhanced by the change of Government. We do not hesitate to believe that the Spanish Government would have granted the land to any body else applying, after the first occupant had left it and settled elsewhere. We are therefore of opinion that the claim is not sanctioned by any law or custom of that Government, or any law of the United States; and do accordingly reject it.

No. 300.—DANIEL CLARK and FRANCIS D. DELACROIX claim a tract of land, situate in the county of Orleans, on the bayou of Terre aux Bœufs, containing thirty-four thousand one hundred and two superficial arpents, part of which has been confirmed. See No. 300 among the confirmed claims.

The claimants showing no evidence of title whatever to the part not confirmed, (the extent of which see in number as above,) the Board do hereby reject the claim.

No. 301.—CHARLOTTE DREUX, widow FAZENDE, claims a second depth to a tract of land of thirty-four arpents front, situate in the county of Orleans, on the west side of the river Mississippi, which, together with the ordinary depth of forty arpents, has already been confirmed to her in No. 301 among the confirmed claims. The depth now claimed extends back to the bayou Barataria.

The claimant shows no evidence of title to the second depth, which we therefore reject.

No. 309.—JOSEPH BUJAU claims a second depth of land, the upper line being twenty-six, and the lower twenty-five arpents in depth, and lying immediately back of a front of five arpents fourteen toises and three feet, on the ordinary depth of forty arpents, situate in the county of Acadia, on the west side of the river Mississippi, and which we have confirmed to him in No. 309 among the confirmed claims.

The claimant shows no written evidence of title to this second depth, which is therefore rejected.

No. 310.—JEAN ETIENNE BUJAU claims a second depth of land, lying immediately back of a front and first depth of forty arpents, the front containing five arpents and fifteen toises, and situate in the county of Acadia, on the west side of the river Mississippi, and which we have confirmed to him in No. 310 among the confirmed claims.

The claimant shows no other foundation for his title to this second depth than having occupied the first depth, and occasionally supplied himself with timber from the second depth. According to the laws, customs, and usages of the Spanish Government, no front proprietor, by any act of his own, could acquire a right to lands further back than the ordinary depth of forty arpents ; and although that Government has invariably refused to grant the second depth to any other than the front proprietor, yet nothing short of a grant or warrant of survey from the Governor could confer a title or right to the land. We therefore reject the claim.

No. 311.—MAGDELAINE BUJAU claims a second depth of forty arpents, lying immediately back of a front of five arpents twenty-four toises and two feet, on the ordinary depth of forty arpents, situate in the county of Acadia, on the west side of the river Mississippi, and which we have confirmed to her in No. 311 among the confirmed claims.

The claimant's pretensions to this second depth of land are in every respect similar to those in the preceding claim, No. 310; and we therefore reject her claim.

No. 317.—FRANCIS DUBOIS claims a tract of land, situate in the county of Pointe Coupée, on the west side of the river Mississippi, containing twenty arpents in front, and forty in depth, and bounded on the upper side by the bayou Moreau, and on the lower by vacant lands.

It appears that the claimant obtained a warrant of survey for this land from the Spanish Government in the year 1793 ; but it appears that it was not inhabited and cultivated on the 1st of October, 1800, nor does it appear, from every information that we can obtain, that it ever was ; at all events, if it ever was, it has been abandoned for a great many years past. We are therefore of opinion that the claim ought to be rejected.

No. 320.—URBAINE GAGNE claims a tract of land, situate in the county of Iberville, on the east side of the river Mississippi, containing seven hundred and seventy-six superficial arpents, and bounded on the upper side by the Pointe de Manchack, and on the lower by other land of the claimant.

The claimant obtained a warrant of survey for this land from the Spanish Government in the year 1797, but it appears that the land never was inhabited or cultivated. The Board therefore reject the claim.

No. 332.—LANDRY BABIN claims a second depth of land, lying immediately back of a front and first depth of land belonging to Louis Landry, situate in the county of Acadia, on the west side of the river Mississippi. The second depth now claimed contains two hundred and ten superficial arpents, and bounded on the north by lands of Louis Landry, on the west by land of Simon Babin, on the south by land of Joseph Melanson, and on the east by vacant lands.

The claimant founds his pretensions to this land on possession and cultivation prior to the 1st October, 1800, and ever since that date. It was a custom with the Spanish Government, which we believe was invariably adhered to, never to grant the back depth to any other than the front proprietor. As far as they have fallen under our observation, wherever there were petitions to the Spanish Government, by any others than the front proprietors, for the back lands, that Government has always refused to grant these lands. We are therefore of opinion that this claim ought to be rejected.

No. 333.—SIMON BABIN claims a second depth of land of two hundred and eighteen superficial arpents five toises and six feet, lying immediately back of land claimed in part by the present claimant, and the remainder by Landry Babin, and situate in the county of Acadia, on the west side of the river Mississippi.

The claimant founds his pretensions to this second depth of land on possession and cultivation prior to the 1st of October, 1800, and ever since. We reject the claim to the part behind the land of Landry Babin for the reasons assigned in the preceding claim, No. 332, which was similarly situated to the present ; and the balance, as the claimant has no evidence of, nor does he pretend to, a title from the Spanish Government; and nothing short of a grant or warrant of survey from the Governor could confer a title or right to the second depth of lands.

No. 312.—MADAME (widow) DECUIR claims a tract of land, situate in the county of Pointe Coupée, on the west side of the river Mississippi, containing three hundred and twenty-three and thirteen hundredths superficial acres, and bounded on the upper side by land claimed by Pierre Decuir, and on the lower by land claimed by Joseph Ispion.

It appears that this land was settled upwards of twenty-five years ago, and, by reason of the inundation of the river, the first settler was compelled to abandon it, and settle on other lands ; the land has remained so abandoned for more than twenty-five years, and possession not resumed, either by the first settler, or any one for him, until after the 20th December, 1803. For reasons which we have assigned in preceding claims, similarly situated, we are of opinion that this claim ought to be rejected.

No. 344.—LOUIS ROUGE claims a tract of land, situate in the county of Pointe Coupée, above the bayou Racourci, on the west side of the river Mississippi, containing six hundred and forty superficial acres, and bounded on the upper side by vacant lands, and on the lower by land of Marie L. Courtesy.

It appears that this land was settled upwards of five-and-twenty years ago, and that, by reason of the inundation of the river, the first settler was forced to abandon it, and settle on other lands ; it remained so abandoned for more than twenty-five years, and possession has never been resumed, either by the original occupant, or any one for him, until since the 20th of December, 1803. For reasons which we have assigned in claims similarly situated, we are of opinion that this claim ought to be rejected.

No. 346.—LOUIS HART claims a tract of land, situate in the county of Pointe Coupée, on the west side of the river Mississippi, above the Pointe Racourci, containing six hundred and forty superficial acres, and bounded on the upper side by land that is vacant, and on the lower by land claimed by Jean Pierre Darquilon.

This land, it appears, was settled considerably upwards of twenty-five years ago, and was, by reason of the inundation of the river, abandoned by the first settler, who settled on other lands ; and possession has never been resumed, either by said person, or any one for him, until after the 20th of December, 1803. We are of opinion that the claim ought to be rejected, for reasons which we have assigned in claims founded on similar pretensions.

No. 347.—MARIE LOUISE COURTESY claims a tract of land, situate in the county of Pointe Coupée, on the west side of the river Mississippi, above the bayou Racourci, containing six hundred and thirty-seven superficial acres, and bounded on the upper side by land of Louis Rouge, and on the lower by vacant lands.

This land it appears was settled upwards of thirty years ago, and, by reason of the inundation of the river, the first settler was compelled to leave it and settle elsewhere, and it has remained so abandoned for more than twenty-five years ; and possession has never been resumed, either by the original occupant, or any other person for her, until since the 20th of December, 1803. This claim being similarly situated to many others which we have rejected, for the reasons there given, we reject it.

No. 348.—JOSEPH M. WHITE claims a second depth of forty arpents, lying immediately back of a front of five arpents twenty-two toises and two feet, on the ordinary depth of forty arpents, situate on the west side of the river Mississippi, in the county of Iberville, and which we have confirmed to him in No. 348 among the confirmed claims.

The claimant produces no evidence of title to this second depth of land, and his only pretensions are those of having been proprietor of the front, and having occasionally supplied himself with timber from this second depth. According to the usages of the Spanish Government, no front proprietor, by any act of his own, could acquire a right to lands further back than the ordinary depth of forty arpents: and although that Government has invariably refused to grant the back depth to any other than the front proprietor, yet nothing short of a grant or warrant of survey from the Governor could confer a right or title to the land. We are therefore of opinion that the claim ought to be rejected.

No. 349.—ABNER GRAY claims a tract of land, situate in the county of Iberville, on the east side of the river Mississippi, a little below the bayou Manchack, containing six hundred and thirty and eighty hundredths superficial acres.

This land is claimed, as is pretended, in virtue of a settlement made, in the year 1802, by George Mars, and cultivation on the 20th of December, 1803. The present claimant purchased of said Mars. The claim includes other lands to which we have already confirmed the title, as being inhabited and cultivated prior to the 1st of October, 1800, with the permission of the proper Spanish officer, and having continued so to be inhabited and cultivated until on and after the 20th of December, 1803. The claimant pretends not that the land was settled by permission of the proper Spanish officer; and, from the most correct evidence we could procure, it was not settled in the right of him under whom the claimant holds until since the 20th of December, 1803. We therefore reject the claim.

No. 364.—THOMAS HEBERT claims a tract of land, being a second depth, and lying immediately back of a front of four and a half arpents, on the ordinary depth of forty arpents, situate in the county of Iberville, on the west side of the river Mississippi, which we have confirmed in No. 364 among the confirmed claims.

This claim to a second depth is founded solely upon a petition (requette) to the Intendant General, in the year 1802, with the commandant's certificate that the land was vacant, and might be granted without prejudice, &c. Had the Intendant ever a right at that period to grant the land, he has never acted upon the petition; nor does it appear that it has ever been presented to him. We are therefore of opinion that the claim ought to be rejected.

No. 368.—JOHN McDONOUGH and SHEPHERD BROWN claim a second depth of forty arpents, lying immediately back of a front of one arpent and twenty-five toises, on the ordinary depth of forty arpents, being part of a larger front, situate in the county of Acadia, on the east side of the river Mississippi, and which we have confirmed in No. 368 among the confirmed claims.

The claimants state in their notice that there was an order of survey or grant for this second depth obtained from the Spanish Government, but that it has by some means or other been lost. But of its existence we find no evidence on the original record relative to the concessions of land; and we therefore reject the claim.

No. 377.—SOLOMON PREVOST claims a second depth of about sixty arpents, lying immediately back of a front of nineteen arpents and nine toises, on the ordinary depth of forty arpents, situate in the county of Orleans, on the east side of the river Mississippi, and which we have confirmed to him in No. 377 among the confirmed claims.

The claimant shows no other foundation for his title to this second depth than having occupied the front, and having occasionally supplied himself with timber from this second depth. According to the laws, usages, and customs of the Spanish Government, no front proprietor, by any act of his own, could acquire a right to lands

further back than the ordinary depth of forty arpents; and although the Spanish Government invariably refused to grant the second depth to any other than the front proprietor, yet nothing short of a grant or warrant of survey from the Governor could confer a title or right to the land. We are therefore of opinion that the claim ought to be rejected.

No. 379.—GABRIEL FAZENDE claims a second extension of depth back to the bayou of Barataria, being about thirty-five arpents, and lying immediately back of a front of nine and a half arpents, on the ordinary depth of forty arpents, situate in the county of Orleans, on the west side of the river Mississippi, and which we have already confirmed to him in No. 379 among the confirmed claims.

The claimant's only pretensions to this second depth of land are, possession of the front and first depth, and having occasionally supplied himself with timber from this second depth. We reject this claim for the reasons assigned in the preceding claim, No. 377, and in many others similarly situated.

No. 382.—MARIE JEANNE HELENE claims a tract of land, situate in the county of Orleans, at the place called Quartier des Bois d'Amourettes, on the west side of the river Mississippi, containing thirteen arpents in front, and forty in depth, and bounded on the upper side by land of Honoré Duplessis, and on the lower by land of Bradish and Johnson.

The claimant produces the permission of the commandant, in the year 1798, to settle this land; but it does not appear that she ever actually settled it until after the 20th of December, 1803, or that she caused the road and levée to be made. We are of opinion that her claim ought to be rejected.

No. 385.—JEAN BAPTISTE SAUSSIER claims a tract of land, situate in the county of Orleans, at the place called Quartier de la Riviere aux Chiens, containing one hundred and eighty arpents in front on each side of the Rivière aux Chiens, by five arpents in depth on each side.

The claimant pretends title to this land, in virtue of possession and cultivation for more than ten consecutive years prior to the 20th of December, 1803; but it appearing to the Board that the land has never been inhabited or cultivated until since the 20th of December, 1803, and that that being the only title the claimant sets up to the land, they do therefore reject the claim.

No. 386.—WILLIAM BROWN claims a second depth of land, extending back to lake Borgue, and lying immediately back of a front of sixteen arpents eleven toises and three feet on the ordinary depth of forty arpents, situate in the county of Orleans, on the east side of the river Mississippi, and which we have confirmed in No. 386 among the confirmed claims.

The claimant produces no evidence of title to this second extension of depth; the Board therefore reject the claim, for reasons assigned in preceding claims founded on similar pretensions.

No. 392.—NORBERT BOUDUSQUIER claims a second depth, extending back to lake Pontchartrain, and lying immediately back of a front of five arpents twenty-eight toises and four feet, on the ordinary depth of forty arpents, situate in the county of Orleans, on the east side of the river Mississippi, and which we have confirmed to him in No. 392 among the confirmed claims.

In support of his claim, the claimant produces consecutive sales for many years back; but it appearing to the Board, that by continuing the lines in the direction of those of the first depth, they would fall not on lake Pontchartrain, but on lake Borgue, the claim cannot be confirmed for more than the ordinary depth of forty arpents; but the Board are of opinion that the claimant ought, in justice, to receive a concession for an additional depth of forty arpents.

No. 393.—CHARLES JUMONVILLE VILLIER claims a tract of land, situate in the county of La Fourche, between the bayou La Fourche and the Atchafalaya, containing eighty arpents in front on each side of the bayou, and eighty in depth, and bounded on the lower side by the place called l'Ancien Campement de Monsieur Darbonne, and on the upper by vacant lands.

The claimant founds his title to this land upon the permission of the commandant of the district to settle it, given in the year 1799; but it appearing to the Board that the land was never inhabited or cultivated from that time to this, they therefore reject the claim.

No. 394.—Dominic and Ursino Bouligny claim a couple of tracts of land, situate in the county of Pointe Coupée, on the west side of the river Mississippi, containing each forty arpents front, and forty deep, and adjoining each other; one of which said tracts has been confirmed in No. 394 among the confirmed claims.

The tract of land now rejected, viz: forty arpents front, and forty deep, is claimed in virtue of an order of survey from the Spanish Governor, dated the 10th of January, 1796. The claimants have satisfactorily proved that they had a tenant on one of said tracts on the 1st of October, 1800, the title to which tract we have confirmed; but as it appears that the other tract was never inhabited or cultivated, either by them or any one for them, we therefore reject the claim to that tract.

No. 399.—Louis Joli claims a tract of land situate in county of Acadia, about sixty arpents back from the eastern bank of the river Mississippi. The quantity claimed is not specified, having never been surveyed.

The land now claimed lies immediately back of the lands facing on the river. It was a custom we believe, never departed from by the Spanish Government, if they possessed a correct knowledge of the situation of the land, not to grant lands to others than the front proprietors, which lay behind the lands fronting on the river. In this instance, it appears that the land was not actually inhabited and cultivated until after the 20th December, 1803; and possession and cultivation being the only grounds on which the claimant founds his title, the Board accordingly reject the claim.

No. 401.—Alexander Babin claims a second depth of land of thirty-one arpents, lying immediately back of a front of three arpents and twenty-six toises, on the ordinary depth of forty arpents, situate in the county of Acadia, on the west side of the river Mississippi, and which has been confirmed to him in No. 401 among the confirmed claims.

The only foundation of title which the claimant shows for this second depth is, his being proprietor of the front and first depth, and having occasionally supplied himself with timber from the second depth. The claimant produces no written evidence of title whatever; and the Board therefore reject the claim.

No. 195.—Alexander Leblanc, as agent for the inhabitants of Pointe Coupée, claims for the said inhabitants the rights of cuttting and taking timber from the cypress swamps of the place called Pointe Racourci.

The aforesaid inhabitants claim this privilege as having been accorded to them by the French Government, previous to the cession of the province to Spain; the written evidence of which they state to have been lost or in some way destroyed. The claimants produce, in support of their claim, the depositions of three or four inhabitants of the Territory, that it is within their knowledge that the aforesaid privilege has been accorded to the inhabitants of Pointe Coupée; but not feeling satisfied as to the fact, nor authorized to confirm a claim of this nature, we do therefore reject it.

No. 343.—Ebenezer Cooley, as agent for the inhabitants of Pointe Coupée, claims the same right of timber as above claimed, in No. 195, by another agent of said inhabitants. (See our opinion as above.)

No. 194.—Jean Baptiste Macarty claims a tract of land, situate back of the city of New Orleans, and adjoining the canal Carondelet, containing about thirteen hundred acres.

The claimant pretends that this land was surveyed for him, by virtue of an order from the Baron de Carondelet, dated 1795, and that the papers relative to his title have since been destroyed by fire. In support of this, he exhibits the certificate of Pintado, who states that the survey was executed by him, by the order of Carondelet. Admitting it as a fact that the land was surveyed for him by the order of the Baron de Carondelet, it must have been upon the condition that the land was vacant; but it appears clearly that the whole of this land is covered by grants long antecedent to the period that the land is stated to have been surveyed for the claimant; we therefore reject the claim.

No. 390.—Joseph Villars claims a tract of land, situate in the county of Orleans, on the left bank of the grand bayou of Barataria, or river Ouachas, containing about five leagues in front on said bayou, and forty arpents in depth, and bounded on the upper side by the bayou Dupont, and on the lower by the bayou St. Denis.

The claimant alleges that this land was formerly granted by the French Government to his grandfather, and that it has descended to him as heir; that the title-papers have all been destroyed. He has not been able to satisfy us that his grandfather ever obtained a grant to this land. The land has never been inhabited or cultivated by the claimant, or by any person for him; we therefore reject the claim.

No. 134.—Thomas Power claims a tract of land, situate in the county of Iberville, on the right bank of the river Amite, at the place called Crow Bluff, containing two thousand five hundred superficial arpents.

This claim is founded upon settlement, by permission of the proper Spanish officer, prior to the 20th December, 1803, and cultivation on that day. We have already confirmed to the claimant the quantity of six hundred and forty arpents (see No. 134 among the confirmed claims,) which is as much as he is entitled to under the act of Congress; and we therefore reject the balance.

No. 19.—Elisha Winter claims a lot of ground, situate in the city of New Orleans, containing two hundred and fifty feet on its longest side, one hundred and twenty-six feet fronting on Royal street, and one hundred and forty feet on the line H S on the plat of survey.

It appearing to the Board that the said Winter has parted with all his title to this lot of ground, by a competent conveyance or conveyances made to particular individuals, they therefore reject his claim.

No. 185.—Francis B. Languille claims a second depth of land, the upper line measuring eighty-three arpents and twenty toises, and the lower ninety-two arpents and five toises, and lying immediately back of a front of eight arpents and nine toises, on the ordinary depth of forty arpents, situate on the east side of the river Mississippi, in the county of Orleans, and which we have confirmed to him in No. 185 among the confirmed claims.

The claimant states that Antoine Bienvenu, from whom he purchased, obtained a grant from the French Government, in 1754, for this back depth, together with a larger quantity; but he not having produced any evidence of such grant, and it not appearing on the records of the book of grants, we therefore reject the claim.

No. 339.—Louis Trudeau claims a second extension of depth, extending back to lake Pontchartrain, and lying immediately behind a front of twenty arpents, and depth of forty, situate on the east side of the river Mississippi, in the county of Orleans, and which we have confirmed to him in No. 339 among the confirmed claims.

This land is claimed as having been granted by the India Company. The former Surveyor General of the province, Carlos Trudeau, certifies that the title-papers were deposited in his office, and were, at the time of the general conflagration of the city of New Orleans, consumed, together with a great many other papers. We do not feel ourselves authorized to confirm the title to this second extension of depth, but think that it would not be unjust were the General Government to sanction it.

No. 308.—Jean Baptiste Castillon claims a second depth, extending back to the lands of Gentilly, and lying immediately back of a front and first depth of land, confirmed to him in No. 308 among the confirmed claims. He also claims a second depth to one of twenty arpents, lying immediately back of a front and first depth, confirmed to him in the aforesaid number.

The claimant produces no evidence of title whatever to either of these second depths; the Board therefore reject the claim to them.

No. 175.—The Mayor, Aldermen, and Inhabitants of the city of New Orleans claim a parcel of land as commons, designated in a plat, recorded in the register of claims, book 2, folio 70.

This claim is in part settled by the acts of Congress of 1807 and 1811, which confirm to the corporation six hundred yards from the fortifications. The acts are silent as to vacant lands within the fortifications and the city, but which are, nevertheless, embraced by the claim aforesaid. In vain have the commissioners searched in the documents Nos. 3 and 5, to which they are referred for proof, for even a shadow of title to this land. There is no evidence of its ever having been granted, or considered as belonging to the city, by either the French or Spanish Government. The Board therefore reject the claim of the corporation to all the land now or formerly occupied by the fortifications erected by the Baron de Carondelet, and to all the lots and vacant parcels of land between the said fortifications and the city, and within and in front of the city, between Leveé street and the river.

JOSHUA LEWIS,
THOMAS B. ROBERTSON.

No. 113.—THOMAS POREE claims a tract of land, situate in the county of Orleans, on the west side of the river Mississippi, containing ninety-seven superficial arpents, and bounded on one side by land of John B. C. Blanquet, and on the other by land of Francis Corbin.

This land is claimed in virtue of a survey made the 19th of November, 1803, and a patent obtained on the 28th of the same month and year from Ventura Morales, the Spanish Intendant. The claimant having no other evidence of title, and the grant under which he claims having been made by a Spanish officer subsequent to the 1st of October, 1800, according to the fifth section of the act of Congress passed on the 2d of March, 1805, the Board are not authorized to make any decision hereon.

No. 114.—FRANCIS MANHALL claims a tract of land, situate in the county of Orleans, on the west side of the river Mississippi, containing two hundred and forty-six superficial arpents, and bounded on the west side by land of Bartholomew Duverges, and on the east by vacant lands.

This land is claimed in virtue of a patent issued in favor of James P. Guinault, (from whom the claimant purchased,) on the 27th of March, 1803, by Juan Ventura Morales, Intendant General of the province. According to the fifth section of the act of Congress passed on the 2d of March, 1805, the Board are not authorized to decide on grants made subsequent to the 1st of October, 1800.

No. 115.—THOMAS VILLANUEVA claims a tract of land, situate in the county of La Fourche, on each side of the bayou Darbonne, at the settlement called Valenzuela, containing eight hundred superficial arpents, and bounded on the south by land of Joseph Mollere, on the north by the Acadian settlement, and on the east and west by vacant lands.

This claim is founded upon an order of survey issued in favor of the claimant by Juan Ventura Morales, Intendant General of the province, dated the 19th of September, 1802. In conformity to the fifth section of the act of Congress passed on the 2d of March, 1805, the Board make no decision on the above claim.

No. 139.—JOSEPH LERLANC claims a tract of land, situate in the county of Iberville, on the west side of the river Mississippi, containing four hundred superficial arpents, and bounded on the upper side by land of Paul Charpe, and on the lower by land of Charles Hebert.

This land is claimed in virtue of a petition to the Intendant in the year 1801, and approved by the Fiscal del Real Hacienda. In conformity to the fifth section of the act of Congress passed on the 2d of March, 1805, the Board make no decision on the above claim.

No. 148.—WILLIAM DONALDSON claims a tract of land, situate in the county of Orleans, on the east side of the river Mississippi, containing four arpents in front, and forty in depth, being part of the tract of seven arpents front, on the ordinary depth; three arpents front of which we have confirmed in No. 148 among the confirmed claims.

The present four arpents front, on the depth of forty, are claimed in virtue of an order of survey from the Intendant, dated the 4th of January, 1802, in favor of Jean Bertran Dejean, from whom the claimant holds by successive transfers. The warrant of survey having issued subsequent to the 1st day of October, 1800, the Board make no decision thereon.

No. 151.—DOMINGO FLEITAS claims a tract of land, situate in the county of Orleans, on the Bayou St. John road, at the distance of a mile from the city of New Orleans, containing fifty-three toises and one foot in front on said road, and extending back as far as the lands of Gravier, but varying in its width.

For the part of this land not confirmed by the Board, see No. 151 among the confirmed claims.

No. 335.—ALEXANDER HARRANG claims a tract of land, situate in the county of Orleans, on the west side of the river Mississippi, at the place called Quartier des Chapitoulas, containing five hundred and twenty-five superficial arpents, and bounded on the south and north by lands of the claimant, on the west by land of Norbert Fortier, and on the east by vacant lands.

The claimant obtained an order of survey for this land, on the 31st of August, 1802, from the Intendant General, which was executed by the Surveyor General on the 16th of April, 1803. The land was to be granted to the claimant upon the condition of his paying to the Government the amount of its valuation money, which the Surveyor General was appointed to ascertain, and estimated it at one hundred and fifty-seven dollars and four cents. The grant has never been issued, nor has the money, or any part been paid; nor has the land been inhabited or cultivated. This title having originated under the Spanish Government subsequent to the 1st of October, 1800, the Board make no decision thereon.

No. 167.—JEANNE DELATRE claims a tract of land, situate in the county of Pointe Coupée, on the southern bank of the False river, containing two thousand six hundred and sixty-nine superficial arpents, bounded on the upper side by land of Jean Baptiste Baras, and on the lower by land of Joseph Janis.

The claimant obtained a complete grant from the Intendant of the province for this land, on the 9th of August, 1802; the board therefore make no decision thereon.

No. 169.—FRANCIS LANDON claims a tract of land, situate in the county of Orleans, on the east side of the river Mississippi, containing seven arpents in front, by forty in depth, and opening ten degrees towards the rear, and bounded on the upper side by land of Louis Declouet, and on the lower by land of Daniel Clark.

This land is claimed in virtue of a warrant of survey issued by the Spanish Government, in favor of Jean Baptiste, on the 4th of January, 1802. The Board, consequently, make no decision on the claim aforesaid.

No. 179.—JEAN BAPTISTE BARAS claims a tract of land, situate in the county of Iberville, on the west side of the river Mississippi, containing twenty arpents in front, and forty in depth, and bounded on all sides by vacant lands.

This land is claimed in virtue of a complete grant issued by the Intendant General, on the 23d of February, 1802. The Board make no decision thereon.

No. 388.—ALEXANDER HARRANG claims a tract of land, situate in the county of Orleans, at the place called Banio de Chepitoulas, or Island Verret, about two miles to the southward of the Mississippi, and containing two hundred superficial acres.

This land is claimed in virtue of a complete grant issued by the Intendant General, in favor of the claimant, on the 11th day of August, 1802. The Board therefore make no decision thereon.

JOSHUA LEWIS,
THOS. B. ROBERTSON.

No. 312.—ARNAUD MAGNON claims a lot of ground, situate in the city of New Orleans, on the front side of the same, containing one arpent and nineteen toises in superficies, and bounded on the east side by the river Mississippi, on the south by the property of Henry Metzinger, on the west by the main road, and on the north by vacant land. For the part of this land which we have confirmed to the claimant, see No. 312 among the confirmed claims.

It appears that the claimant occupied and possessed the balance of the ground (viz.: all that not included in the red lines, which was confirmed to him per the above number) for more than twelve consecutive years prior to the 20th of December, 1803; part of it, being a small slip, he enclosed as a yard, in the rear of his dwelling, and the remainder as a ship-yard; and, at the time of taking possession, he enclosed a considerable part of the ship-yard, and erected work-houses on it, which yet exist, and which he still occupies. This was done with the knowledge and permission of the Spanish Government. We know of no law or usage of that Government respecting claims similarly situated, but think it highly probable that, had the claimant applied, he would have obtained a grant for it, as a grant was made to a lot of ground adjoining him under no higher pretensions. Nor does this appear to come within any of the provisions of the laws of the United States: although there have been ten consecutive years' possession, the land has not been inhabited and cultivated. This part of the claim we do not feel ourselves authorized to decide on, but are of opinion that, in justice, the claim ought to be confirmed.

No. 329.—CATHARINE GONZALES BERTRAND, widow, claims a lot of ground, situate in the city of New Orleans, fronting on the Levée, and containing a superficies of three thousand one hundred and seventy-six feet and four inches, in a square form, and bounded on the northeast by the property of Domingo Gonzales, on the northwest by the main road, on the southwest by vacant land, and on the southeast by the Levée aforesaid.

It appears that, on the 27th of March, 1788, a few days after the fire which consumed a considerable portion of this city, Thomas Bertrand, the late husband of the claimant, and who was a sufferer by the fire, petitioned Governor Miro for leave to build himself a house on the lot of ground now claimed; which was accorded to him by the Governor. It appears, also, that in the year 1794, he presented another petition to the Baron de Carondelet, requesting permission to reconstruct his house, as the materials of which it was built were much decayed; which request was also accorded, upon condition that the house should be reconstructed according to its former dimensions. This lot of ground has been inhabited by the late husband of the claimant from the year 1788 until his death, and by the claimant since that period to this day. As we do not feel authorized to make any decision on this claim, we think it would be more an act of justice than of generosity if the Government should confirm it.

No. 380.—PETER URTUBUISE claims a lot of ground, situate in the city of New Orleans, fronting on the Levée, containing a superficies of two thousand one hundred and seventy-five feet, and bounded on one side by the property of Henry Metzinger, on another by St. Philip street, and in the rear by the main road.

The claimant states, that one Peter Breaux, of whom he purchased, in the year 1790, obtained a written permission from the Governor to build and settle himself on the lot of ground now claimed, which written permission was destroyed by fire in the year 1794. Of this we have no evidence. It appears that the claimant has his dwelling-house and blacksmith's shop on the lot, and has had the quiet possession of it for ten years prior to the 20th of December, 1803, and still has. We know of no law or usage of the Spanish Government respecting claims similarly situated, and it does not appear to come within any of the provisions of the laws of Congress, it being a small lot which has never been cultivated, nor intended for cultivation. The lot of ground was considered of little value at the time it was taken possession of, and we have no doubt but the Governor would have granted it to the claimant had he have asked it, as grants were made of lots near to this, under similar circumstances, to other individuals. We do not feel ourselves authorized to make any decision on this claim, but we think it would be more an act of justice than of generosity if the Government should confirm it.

No. 372.—JOHN J. CHESSE claims a lot of ground, situate in the city of New Orleans, between the Levée and the river, containing two thousand two hundred and ninety feet in superficies, and bounded on the northeast by the continuation of St. Philip street.

It appears that one Etienne Planché, the father-in-law of the claimant, petitioned the Cabildo, of which the Governor was president, in May, 1783, for, and obtained, permission to erect a shed on the lot of ground claimed, for the purpose of repairing vessels, and continued to occupy it until the year 1788, when he sold it to the present claimant, who has continued to possess and occupy it since that time to the present period, for the purposes aforesaid. We know of no law or usage of the Spanish Government respecting claims similarly situated, and it does not appear to come within any of the provisions of the laws of Congress, it being a small lot which has never been cultivated, nor intended for cultivation. But the claimant has his dwelling-house on it, and did actually inhabit it on the 20th of December, 1803, and for more than ten consecutive years next preceding. This lot of ground was considered of little value at the time it was taken possession of, and we have no doubt that the Governor would have granted it to the claimant had he have asked it, as grants were made of lots near to this, under similar circumstances, to other individuals. We do not feel authorized to make any decision on this claim, but we think it would be more an act of justice than of generosity if the Government should confirm it.

No. 360.—MARY L. DAUBERVILLE, widow of BOULIGNY, claims a lot of ground, situate in the city of New Orleans, at the corner of Dumaine and Condé streets, measuring twenty-three feet on the former, and sixty-five on the latter, containing a superficies of four thousand seven hundred and forty-five feet, and bounded on one side by the public magazine, and on the other by the public ball room.

It appears that this lot was granted to Don Guido Dufossat, upon condition that he should pay for it twelve dollars per month; that he not having taken possession of it, nor complied with the condition, it was, upon the representation of the Intendant to the King, annexed to the domain by a royal order, dated on the 5th of September, 1787. This lot is adjoining the public magazine, in which powder was occasionally deposited; and the King, in his order annexing it to the domain, forbids that it should be granted to any individual. The late husband of the claimant was commandant of the forts at this place under the Spanish Government, and cultivated this lot as a garden. The claimant sets up no other title than the possession of her husband. We are therefore of opinion that her claim ought to be rejected, and do accordingly reject it.

No. 307.—JOHN B. LABATUT, in behalf of the heirs of St. Maxent, claims a tract or parcel of land of two arpents and twelve toises in front, adjoining the lower limits of the city of New Orleans, at the distance of twenty toises from the barracks, and running parallel to said limits.

The facts in the case are as follows, viz: M. Dubreuil was the reputed owner of a plantation of seven arpents and eighteen toises front, bounded on the lower side by lands of ——— Amelot, and on the upper by the city. After his death, this plantation was sold at auction, in the year 1758, and described as containing seven arpents and eighteen toises in front; and it was also then publicly declared, that a parcel of land, within these limits, on which the principal buildings stood, belonged to the King, (see sale in 1758.) This declaration was repeated on the third day of setting up the plantation for sale, by Villars Dubreuil, one of the heirs, and tutor to the minors, who said that two arpents and twelve toises, on which had been erected the dwelling-house and other buildings of value, belonged to the King, who, out of favor, had permitted his father to occupy the same. This declaration was made with much solemnity before Mr. De Rochemore, Ordonnateur General, (see the declaration.) Under these circumstances, Mr. Lachaise became the purchaser; and, at his death, in the year 1771, it was sold to Madame de Moleon. The papers relative to this sale cannot be found, so that we are ignorant of the manner in which the plantation was, in that instance, described. In the year 1776, it was sold by Madame de Moleon to Colonel St. Maxent, and is spoken of as containing seven arpents and eighteen toises front, and at the same time is bounded as formerly on the lower line, but on the upper by the gate of France and the "fortificaciones antiguas 5 estacadas serviendo de muralla á esta ciudad." (see the act of sale.) Colonel St. Maxent sold this tract of land to Mr. Sigur, in the year 1789, limiting it on the upper side by the city, (see the sale;) the Baron de Carondelet, in the year 1794, erected fortifications around the town, and intrenched considerably on the land purchased by Sigur of Maxent. Sigur demanded of the Government an indemnity; but this was refused, on the ground that, in all French grants a reservation was made of all land necessary for fortifications. (see decree.) Sigur, after failing in this application, filed his petition for redress against the syndics of Maxent, and after very voluminous and tardy proceedings, obtained, from the Spanish tribunal of justice, a decree for twenty-five thousand five hundred and seventy-five dollars, (see the decree,) which was deducted from the sum he owed for the plantation. In the year 1797, a survey was made, for the purpose of ascertaining the lines of the former fortifications, and signed by all parties interested; this survey gives the position of the gate of France, and the ancient fortifications and stockades spoken of in the sale of Madame de Moleon. In 1798, Sigur sold the said plantation to Mr. P. Marigny, with a reservation of the lands taken by the Baron de Carondelet; and, in the same year, Governor Gayoso fixed the upper line of the plantation of Marigny at the distance of two arpents and twelve toises from the city. It is proper further to remark, that lots in Garrison street, running over the line established in 1760, and now contended for, were, in the year 1793, granted by the Baron de Carondelet to divers individuals. These are the most important facts which militate against the claim. On the other hand, in support of the pretensions of the syndic of Maxent, two plans are produced; one executed in the year 1760, and signed by De Rochemore and Governor Kerlerec, on which the line of separation between the plantation of Dubreuil (at that time belonging to Lachaise) and the city, runs at the distance from the latter of only twenty toises; the other, executed in 1769, when O'Reilly took possession of the country, on which the line aforesaid is laid down precisely in the same manner. It further appears that all the acts of sale speak of the plantation as containing seven arpents and eighteen toises front, (see the sale.) And it is in evidence that, in the year 1780, the fortifications being abandoned, Colonel St. Maxent was put in possession of the land on which they had been erected, by order of Governor Galvez; that he built several houses on, and continued in the full enjoyment of the same, until he sold the plantation, in the year 1789, to Laurence Sigur, limiting it by the city.

I have now, with all possible fairness, stated the material facts connected with this claim. Considering, then, the description of the plantation when purchased by Lachaise, in 1758; the declaration of Villars Debreuil; the limits mentioned in the sale of Madame Moleon to Colonel Maxent; the decree of Sigur's application to the Government for indemnity, and that for redress against the syndics of Maxent; the survey of 1797, showing the situation of the gate of France, and the old lines of the French fortifications; the grants of lots on Rue Quartier, by the Baron de Carondelet, in 1793; the line established by Gayoso, in 1798; and, finally, a fact omitted to be stated in its proper place, that when the Jesuits' plantation was granted, a space of ground of the same magnitude with that now claimed was left vacant between said plantation and the city, on the opposite side: I am of opinion that the claim of the syndic of Colonel Gilbert Antonio de St. Maxent ought not to be confirmed, and therefore do reject the same.

THOMAS B. ROBERTSON.

I concur in the foregoing statement of facts, but disagree as to the deduction made from them, and the evidence to which they refer. I am of opinion that the land in question forms part of the plantation formerly of Dubreuil, containing seven arpents eighteen toises in front, and bounded by the lands of Amelot below, and the limits of the city above, viz. twenty toises from the barracks; First, Because, many years antecedent to the time of constructing the French fortifications, Dubreuil cultivated the whole extent of this plantation between these limits and his dwelling-house, and sugar-houses and other permanent buildings were erected on the land now claimed. Secondly, Because all the deeds of sale give it the same extent of front. Thirdly, Because, by a plat of the city, made by the order of Rochemore, the Ordonnateur, and Kerlerec, the Governor, in the year 1760, signed and approved by them, a line at twenty toises from the barracks, and running parallel with the city, is recognised as the limits of the boundary of the city and the lands of Dubreuil. Fourthly, Because the same boundary is recognised by a plat made by the Count O'Reilly, in the year 1769, at the time the province came under the Spanish Government. Fifthly, Because the fortifications having fallen into disuse in the year 1780, St. Maxent, whose heirs claim under the title of Dubreuil, was put in possession of this land by the order of Governor Galvez.

I cannot perceive that the title to this part of the plantation has been extinguished by any surrender on the part of Dubreuil or his successors, or by any act of the French or Spanish Government. The first and only evidence that this land was reserved by the King is, the declaration of Villars Dubreuil, one of the heirs, and tutor to the minor children, in the year 1758, at the time the plantation was exposed to sale; stating that two arpents twelve toises of this plantation were reserved by the King, and that his father had possessed it by permission. Yet the plantation is described both by the advertisement and adjudication as having seven arpents eighteen toises front, which brings it up to the limits of the city. There is no vestige of the original grant (nor indeed of any grants of the same antiquity) by which the original limits can be ascertained; but it is scarcely to be presumed that Dubreuil, the father, would have made establishments of such magnitude on lands known to be reserved by the King, when, a few paces from it, he might have built on his own land, and on a site equally eligible. At the time this declaration was made the fortifications were erected, and there is invariably in all French grants to land in this country a special reserva-

tion, that the King shall take any part of the land granted, for the use of fortifications, when he may deem it necessary. This I consider the kind of reserve alluded to in the declaration, and rather admits it a part of the original grant; because, if the title was never out of the King, I cannot see how he could have reserved this land, as his reservations are only to be found in his grants. I do not consider that any act of the Spanish Government bars the right of Dubreuil's heirs, or those rightfully claiming under them, to this land. Laurence Sigur, one of the purchasers, being dispossessed, in 1794, by the Baron de Carondelet, made application to that Government for indemnity, which was refused, upon the principle that the Spanish Government succeeded to all the rights of the French Government, and that the latter never made indemnity in the like cases, this being one of the conditions of the grant; and upon this principle damages were awarded against the heirs of St. Maxent. Nor do I think the circumstance of the Baron de Carondelet's granting a small part of this land can impair the title of Dubreuil, or those who hold under him, if the land previously belonged to them, as his power to grant extended only to vacant land, and all the Spanish grants contain a proviso that the land be vacant. Upon the whole evidence of this case, I am of opinion that this land was a part of the estate of Dubreuil; that the French Government had a right, in virtue of the reservations in all their grants, to appropriate it to the use of the fortifications; but this was a right only to the use of soil, whilst the right of property remained in the individual; and as soon as the fortifications are demolished, and cease to be used, the land reverts to the individual, and he has a right to enter upon it.

J. LEWIS.

JOSHUA LEWIS,
THOMAS B. ROBERSTON.

Decisions of the Board of Commissioners for the eastern district of the Territory of Orleans, on land claims registered in the books of William Wikoff, Deputy Surveyor for the county of Pointe Coupée and part of the county of Iberville.

No. 1.—RICHARD MURPHY claims a tract of land, situate on the right bank of the bayou Manchack, in the county of Iberville and district of Baton Rouge, containing four hundred superficial arpents.

It appears that on the 23d of September, 1797, Don Carlos Trudeau, Surveyor General of the province, surveyed this tract of land in favor of William Black, and put him in possession thereof; and that, on the 7th of December in the same year, a complete grant was made in his favor to said land, by Manuel Gayoso de Lemos, then Governor; under which title the present claimant holds. Confirmed.

No. 2.—SAMUEL FULTON claims a tract of land, situate on the river Mississippi, in the county of Iberville and district of Manchack, containing six arpents in front, and forty in depth.

It appears that the land claimed was surveyed by Don Louis Andry, in the year 1772, in favor of Philip Englehart, and possession given at the same time; and that a complete grant was made in his favor, in the year 1772, by Don Louis de Unzaga, then Governor. Samuel Fulton now claims as one of the representatives of Hebert Powell, deceased, who held under the first grantee. Confirmed.

No. 3.—SAMUEL FULTON claims a tract of land, situate on the river Mississippi, in the county of Iberville and district of Manchack, containing six arpents in front, and forty in depth.

It appears that the land now claimed was surveyed by Don Louis Andry, in the year 1772, in favor of Adam Sastre, and possession given at the same time; and that a complete grant was made in his favor, in the year 1774, by Don Louis de Unzaga, then Governor. Samuel Fulton now claims it as one of the representatives of Hebert Powell, deceased, who held under the first grantee. Confirmed.

No. 4.—JOSEPH LELONG claims a tract of land, situate on the river Mississippi, in the county of Iberville and district of Manchack, containing six arpents in front, and forty in depth, and opening five degrees.

It appears that the land now claimed was surveyed by Don Louis Andry, in the year 1772, in favor of John Bullon, and possession given at the same time; and that a complete grant was made in his favor, in the year 1774, by Don Louis de Unzaga. Joseph Lelong claims it by purchase, under the title of the first grantee. Confirmed.

No. 7.—MICHEL MAHIER claims a tract of land, situate on the west side of the river Mississippi, in the county of Iberville and district of Baton Rouge, containing ten and a half arpents in front, on the ordinary depth of forty arpents; and bounded on one side by land of Madame Ayet, and on the other by land of Adam Boyd.

It appears that the present claimant did actually inhabit and cultivate the land now claimed on the 20th of December, 1803, and that the same was continually inhabited and cultivated by him, or those under whom he claims, for more than ten consecutive years next preceding. Confirmed.

No. 11.—PIERRE FARROT claims a tract of land, situate on the west side of the river Mississippi, in the county of Iberville and district of Baton Rouge, containing eighteen arpents in front, and depth uncertain, and bounded on one side by land of Jean Baptiste Bienville, and on the other by land of Joseph Mallet.

It appearing that the claimant did actually inhabit and cultivate the land now claimed on the 20th December, 1803, and that the same was continually inhabited and cultivated by him, or those under whom he claims, for more than ten consecutive years next preceding, the Board confirm the claim to the extent of the first forty arpents in depth.

No. 13.—JOSEPH DUPUY claims a tract of land, situate on the east side of the river Mississippi, in the county of Iberville and district of Manchack, containing seven and a half arpents front, and forty in depth, and bounded on the upper side by land of Armand Richard, and on the lower by land belonging to the church of St. Gabriel.

It appears that the claimant did actually inhabit and cultivate the land now claimed on the 20th December, 1803, and that the same was continually inhabited and cultivated by him, or those under whom he claims, for more than ten consecutive years next preceding. Confirmed.

No. 14.—JOSEPH DUPUY claims a tract of land, situate in the county of Iberville and district of Galveztown, containing six arpents front, on the ordinary depth of forty.

The tract now claimed is part of twelve arpents front, by forty in depth, surveyed by Don Carlos Trudeau, in the year 1789, in favor of Batista Hebert, who obtained a complete grant for the same in the same year, from Don Estevan Miro, then Governor; six arpents of which are claimed by the present claimant, by virtue of purchases made under the grant aforesaid. Confirmed.

No. 15.—JOSEPH LEBLANC, as executor of Joseph Landry, claims a tract of land, situate on the river Mississippi, in the county of Iberville and district of Manchack, containing three arpents in front, and forty in depth.

This tract is part of seven and a half arpents in front, with the ordinary depth of forty, surveyed in favor of Joseph Landry, in the year 1772, who obtained in the same year a complete grant for the same from Don Louis de Unzaga, then Governor; three arpents front of which are claimed by the present claimant, as executor of Joseph Landry; the deceased having sold the other part in his lifetime. Confirmed.

No. 16.—JOSEPH LEBLANC claims a tract of land, situate on the river Mississippi, in the county of Iberville and district of Manchack, containing five arpents and three toises front, on the ordinary depth of forty arpents.

This tract is a part of ten arpents and seven toises front, and forty arpents in depth, surveyed in favor of Pablo Hebert, in the year 1772, who obtained a complete grant for the same in the same year, from Don Louis de Unzaga, then Governor; five arpents three toises of which are claimed by the present claimant in virtue of regular deeds of sale. Confirmed.

No. 17.—DENY LANDRY claims a tract of land, situate on the river Mississippi, in the county of Iberville and district of Manchack, containing five arpents and three toises front, and forty arpents in depth.

This tract is part of the grant of Pablo Hebert, referred to in the claim No. 16. Confirmed.

No. 18.—PIERRE PALLIOT claims a tract of land, situate on the west side of the river Mississippi, in the county of Iberville and district of Baton Rouge, containing six arpents front, and forty deep, and bounded on one side by land of Francisco Arbour, and on the other by land of Juan Marie Traban.

It appears that the claimant did actually inhabit and cultivate the land now claimed on the 20th of December, 1803, and that the same was continually inhabited and cultivated by him, or those under whom he claims, for more than ten consecutive years next preceding. Confirmed.

No. 19.—JUAN PEDRO HEBERT and JUAN CARLOS HEBERT claim a tract of land, situate on the west side of the river Mississippi, in the county of Iberville and district of Manchack, containing five arpents and six toises front, and forty arpents in depth, and bounded on one side by land of Juan Batista Arnandez, and on the other by land of Armand Hebert.

It appears that the claimants did actually inhabit and cultivate the land now claimed on the 20th December, 1803, and that the same was continually inhabited and cultivated by them, or those under whom they claim, for more than ten consecutive years next preceding. Confirmed.

No. 20.—BARTHOLOMEW HAMILTON claims a tract of land, situate on the west side of the river Mississippi, in the county of Iberville and district of Manchack, containing three arpents three toises and three feet in front, and eighty arpents in depth, and bounded on one side by land of Jacques Leblanc, and on the other by land of N. Rousseau.

It appears that the claimant did actually inhabit and cultivate the first forty arpents depth of the land now claimed on the 20th December, 1803, and that the same was continually inhabited and cultivated by him, or those under whom he claims, for more than ten years prior to that period. So far the Board confirm his claim, but reject the balance.

No. 21.—WILLIAM WIKOFF, Jun. claims a tract of land, situate on the bayou of Iberville, in the county of Iberville and district of Galveztown, containing eight hundred superficial arpents.

This land was surveyed by Don Carlos Trudeau, in the year 1794, in favor of Marcos Coulon de Villiers, who obtained a complete title to the same, in the same year, from the Baron de Carondelet, at that time Governor. William Wikoff, Jun. now claims it under the original grant, through divers intermediate sales. Confirmed.

No. 22.—GEORGE T. Ross claims a tract of land, situate on the east side of the river Mississippi, in the county of Iberville and district of Manchack, containing six arpents front, and forty in depth.

This tract of land was surveyed in the year 1772, and a complete title issued in the year 1774, by Don Louis de Unzaga, at that time Governor, in favor of Juan Batista Aury, and is claimed by the present claimant, in virtue of different deeds of sale, under the original title. Confirmed.

No. 27.—JAMES MELANSON claims a tract of land, situate on the west side of the river Mississippi, in the county of Iberville and district of Baton Rouge, containing five arpents and three fourths in front, and forty arpents in depth, and bounded on one side by land of Peter Servants, and on the other by land of Louis d'Aigle.

It appears that the claimant did actually inhabit and cultivate the land now claimed on the 20th December, 1803, and that the same was continually inhabited and cultivated by him, or those under whom he claims, for more than ten consecutive years next preceding. Confirmed.

No. 28.—LOUIS D'AIGLE claims a tract of land, situate on the west side of the river Mississippi, in the county of Iberville and district of Baton Rouge, containing five arpents in front, and forty in depth, and bounded on one side by land of James Melanson, and on the other by land of Batista Hebert.

It appears that the claimant did actually inhabit and cultivate the land now claimed on the 20th December, 1803, and that the same was continually inhabited and cultivated by him, or those under whom he claims, for more than ten consecutive years next preceding. Confirmed.

No. 29.—FRANCIS MARIONNEAUX claims a tract of land, situate on the river Mississippi, in the county of Iberville and district of Manchack, containing four and a half arpents front, and forty in depth.

The tract of land now claimed is part of six arpents front, and forty in depth, surveyed, in the year 1772, in favor of Maximo River, and granted to him, in 1774, by Governor Unzaga. The present claimant derives title by regular deeds under the original grant. Confirmed.

No. 30.—FRANCIS MARIONNEAUX claims a tract of land, situate on the river Mississippi, in the county of Iberville and district of Manchack, containing two and a half arpents front, with the ordinary depth of forty.

This claim is part of a claim of six arpents fourteen toises front, surveyed in favor of Pedro Landry, in the year 1772, and by Governor Unzaga granted to him, in 1774. The present claimant holds under the original grant, by regular deeds. Confirmed.

No. 32.—BERNARD DUBROCA claims a tract of land, situate on the river Mississippi, in the county of Iberville and district of Baton Rouge, containing six arpents front, and forty in depth.

This tract is part of a claim of twelve arpents front, on the usual depth of forty, for which there was an order of survey, in the year 1773, and which was granted to Germain and Juan Marseille, in 1776, by Governor Unzaga. The present claimant holds under the original grant, by regular deeds. Confirmed.

No. 33.—WILLIAM WIKOFF, Jun. claims a tract of land, situate on the river Mississippi, in the county of Iberville and district of Baton Rouge, containing twelve arpents in front, with the depth of eighty arpents.

This tract of land was surveyed by Don Carlos Trudeau, in the year 1789, in favor of Armand Duplantier, as far as the first forty arpents in depth, and regularly granted to him, in the same year, by Governor Miro. In the year 1799, Carlos Trudeau surveyed for, and put him in possession of, the second depth of forty arpents. The claimant holds said land by purchase from Duplantier. Confirmed.

No. 39.—GREGOIRE LEJEUNE claims a tract of land, situate on the west side of the river Mississippi, in the county of Iberville and district of Baton Rouge, containing three hundred and sixty-seven and ninety-four hundredths superficial arpents, and bounded on one side by land of Valerian Allain, and on the other by land of John B. Lejeune.

It appearing that this tract of land was inhabited and cultivated by the claimant on the 20th December, 1803, and that the same was continually inhabited and cultivated by him, or those under whom he claims, for more than ten consecutive years next preceding, the Board confirm the claim to the extent of the first forty arpents depth.

No. 40.—BELONY HEBERT claims a tract of land, situate on the river Mississippi, in the county of Iberville and district of Baton Rouge, containing six arpents front, and forty deep.

This land was surveyed by Don Carlos Trudeau, in the year 1795, in favor of Yves Francisco Lejeuche, who obtained a complete grant for the same, in the same year, from the Baron de Carondelet; under which grant the present claimant holds. Confirmed.

No. 41.—SIMON BABIN claims a tract of land, situate on the west side of the river Mississippi, in the county of Iberville and district of Manchack, containing four arpents front, and forty deep, and bounded on one side by land of Mr. Robin, and on the other by land of Alexandre d'Aigle.

It appears that this tract of land was inhabited and cultivated by the claimant on the 20th December, 1803, and that the same was continually inhabited and cultivated by him, or those under whom he claims, for more than ten consecutive years next preceding. Confirmed.

No. 42.—JOSEPH BABIN claims a tract of land, situate on the west side of the river Mississippi, in the county of Iberville and district of Baton Rouge, containing four arpents and seven toises front, and forty arpents deep, and bounded on one side by land of William Cunningham, and on the other by land of James Hebert.

It appears that the present claimant did actually inhabit and cultivate the land now claimed on the 20th December, 1803, and that the same was continually inhabited and cultivated by him, or those under whom he claims, for more than ten consecutive years next preceding. Confirmed.

No. 43.—JEAN BAPTISTE LEJEUNE claims a tract of land, situate on the west side of the river Mississippi, in the county of Iberville and district of Baton Rouge, containing three hundred and fourteen and thirty-five hundredths superficial arpents, and bounded on one side by land of Gregoire Lejeune, and on the other by land of François Lejeune.

It appearing that the present claimant did actually inhabit and cultivate the land now claimed on the 20th December, 1803, and that the same was continually inhabited and cultivated by him, or those under whom he claims, for more than ten consecutive years next preceding, the Board confirm the claim to the extent of the first forty arpents depth.

No. 44.—FRANÇOIS LEJEUNE claims a tract of land, situate on the west side of the river Mississippi, in the county of Iberville and district of Baton Rouge, containing two hundred and seven and fifty seven hundredths superficial arpents, and bounded on one side by land of Jean B. Lejeune, and on the other by Peter Broussard.

It appearing that the present claimant did actually inhabit and cultivate the land now claimed on the 20th December, 1803, and that the same was continually inhabited and cultivated by him, or those under whom he claims, for more than ten consecutive years next preceding, the Board confirm the claim to the extent of the first forty arpents depth.

No. 45.—SIMON BABIN claims a tract of land, situate on the west side of the river Mississippi, in the county of Iberville and district of Baton Rouge, containing three hundred and fifteen and twenty-eight hundredths superficial arpents, and bounded on one side by land of Peter Broussard, and on the other by land of James Melanson.

It appearing that the claimant did actually inhabit and cultivate the land now claimed on the 29th December, 1803, and that the same was continually inhabited and cultivated by him, or those under whom he claims, for more than ten consecutive years next preceding, the Board confirm the claim to the extent of the first depth of forty arpents.

No. 47.—PAUL and JULIAN (free men of color) claim a tract of land, situate on the river Mississippi, in the county of Iberville, and district of Baton Rouge, containing twelve arpents front, and forty deep.

This land was regularly granted in the year 1774, by Governor Unzaga, to Pedro Pero; under whose title the claimants hold. Confirmed.

No. 49.—JEAN TEMPLET claims a tract of land, situate on the west side of the river Mississippi, in the county of Iberville and district of Baton Rouge, containing six hundred and twenty-five superficial arpents, and bounded on one side by land of Victor Hebert, and on the other by land of Andrew Martin.

It appearing that the claimant did actually inhabit and cultivate the land now claimed on the 20th December, 1803, and that the same was continually inhabited and cultivated by him, or those under whom he claims, for more than ten consecutive years next preceding, the Board confirm the claim to the extent of the first forty arpents depth.

No. 50.—DANIEL DENOIT claims a tract of land, situate on the west side of the river Mississippi, in the county of Iberville and district of Baton Rouge, containing two hundred and fifty-five and twenty hundredths superficial arpents, and bounded on one side by land of Peter Lebaure, and on the other by land of Belony Hebert.

It appearing that the claimant did actually inhabit and cultivate the land now claimed on the 20th December, 1803, and that the same was continually inhabited and cultivated by him, or those under whom he claims, for more than ten consecutive years next preceding, the Board confirm the claim to the extent of the first forty arpents depth.

No. 54.—JULIAN POYDRAS claims a tract of land, situate on Fausse river in the county of Pointe Coupée, containing eighty arpents and one-third in front, with the ordinary depth of forty arpents.

This claim is founded upon a complete grant made in favor of Benjamin Farrar, whose heirs have conveyed the land to the claimant. Confirmed.

No. 55.—JULIAN POYDRAS claims a tract of land, situate on the west side of the river Mississippi, in the county of Iberville and district of Baton Rouge, containing twenty arpents in front, and forty in depth, and bounded on one side by land of P. Allain, and on the other side by land of Valerian Allain.

It appears that this tract of land was inhabited and cultivated on the 20th December, 1803, and for more than ten consecutive years next preceding that period, by those under whom the claimant holds. Confirmed.

No. 56.—JULIAN POYDRAS claims a tract of land, situate on the river Mississippi, in the county of Pointe Coupée, containing twenty-six arpents and three perches in front, and forty arpents in depth, and lying about three-fourths of a league above the church of Pointe Coupée.

It appears that the present claimant did actually inhabit and cultivate the land now claimed on the 20th December, 1803, and that the same was continually inhabited and cultivated by him, or those under whom he claims, for more than ten consecutive years next preceding. Confirmed.

No. 57.—JOSEPH BOIDORE, by his agent Julian Poydras, claims a tract of land, situate on the Fausse river, in the county of Pointe Coupée, containing five hundred superficial arpents.

This land was surveyed by Carlos Trudeau, in the year 1789, in favor of Benjamin Farrar, who obtained, in the year 1790, a complete grant from Governor Miro; under whose title the claimant holds. Confirmed.

No. 59.—VALENTIN HEBERT claims a tract of land, situate on the west side of the river Mississippi, in the county of Iberville and district of Baton Rouge, containing six arpents and six toises front, and forty arpents deep, and bounded on one side by land of Xavier Robichaux, and on the other by land of Isidore Lebaure.

It appears that the present claimant did actually inhabit and cultivate the land now claimed on the 20th December, 1803, and that the same was continually inhabited and cultivated by him, or those under whom he claims, for more than ten consecutive years next preceding. Confirmed.

No. 60.—ALEXIS HEBERT claims a tract of land, situate on the west side of the river Mississippi, in the county of Iberville and district of Baton Rouge, containing four arpents and ten toises front, and forty arpents deep, and bounded on one side by land of Belony Hebert, and on the other by land of John B. Hebert.

It appears that the claimant did actually inhabit and cultivate the land now claimed on the 20th December, 1803, and that the same was continually inhabited and cultivated by him, or those under whom he claims, for more than ten consecutive years next preceding. Confirmed.

No. 61.—ANDREW MARTIN claims a tract of land, situate on the west side of the river Mississippi, in the county of Iberville and district of Baton Rouge, containing five arpents front, and forty deep, and bounded on one side by land of William Cunningham, and on the other by land of John Templet.

It appears that the present claimant did actually inhabit and cultivate the land now claimed on the 20th December, 1803, and that the same was continually inhabited and cultivated by him, or those under whom he claims, for more than ten consecutive years next preceding. Confirmed.

No. 62.—MATHURIN DOYRON claims a tract of land, situate on the west side of the river Mississippi, in the county of Iberville and district of Baton Rouge, containing four arpents front, and forty in depth, and bounded on the upper side by land of Charles Hebert, and on the other by land of John B. Doyron.

It appears that the present claimant did actually inhabit and cultivate the land now claimed on the 20th December, 1803, and that the same was continually inhabited and cultivated by him, or those under whom he claims, for more than ten consecutive years next preceding. Confirmed.

No. 64.—PIERRE DANIZE claims a tract of land, situate on the west side of the river Mississippi, in the county of Iberville and district of Baton Rouge, containing six and one-third arpents in front, and forty arpents in depth, and bounded on one side by land of James Hebert, and on the other by land of James Stawesbury.

It appears that the claimant was put in possession of the land claimed by the proper Spanish officer, in May, 1800, and continued to inhabit and cultivate the same until the 20th December, 1803, and afterwards. Confirmed.

No. 65.—PIERRE LE BERT claims a tract of land, situate on the west side of the river Mississippi, in the county of Iberville and district of Baton Rouge, containing five hundred and eight and thirty-two hundredths superficial arpents, and bounded on one side by land of Peter Landry, and on the other by land of Louis Hait.

It appearing that the claimant did actually inhabit and cultivate the land now claimed on the 20th December, 1803, and that the same was continually inhabited and cultivated by him, or those under whom he claims, for more than ten consecutive years next preceding, the Board confirm the claim to the extent of the first depth of forty arpents.

No. 67.—FRANCIS MARIONNEAUX, by his agent Thomas Crapper, claims a tract of land, situate on the west side of the river Mississippi, in the county of Iberville, containing eighty superficial arpents, and bounded on one side by land of the claimant, and on the other by land of Terece Riels.

It appears that the land now claimed was actually inhabited and cultivated on the 20th December, 1803, and that the same was continually inhabited and cultivated by those under whom the claimant holds for more than ten consecutive years next preceding. Confirmed.

No. 68.—GERTRUDE CLINEPETER, by her agent John Clinepeter, claims a tract of land, situate on the west side of the river Mississippi, in the county of Iberville and district of Baton Rouge, containing six arpents in front, and forty deep, and bounded on one side by land of Charles Hebert, and on the other by land of Joseph Sharp.

It appears that the claimant did actually inhabit and cultivate the land now claimed on the 20th December, 1803, and that the same was continually inhabited and cultivated by her, or those under whom she claims, for more than ten consecutive years next preceding. Confirmed.

No. 69.—LYOCADE HEBERT claims a tract of land, situate on the west side of the river Mississippi, in the county of Iberville and district of Baton Rouge, containing two and a half arpents in front, and forty in depth, and bounded on one side by land of John B. Hebert, and on the other by land of Mr. Forest.

It appears that the claimant did actually inhabit and cultivate the land now claimed on the 20th December, 1803, and that the same was continually inhabited and cultivated by her, or those under whom she claims, for more than ten consecutive years next preceding. Confirmed.

No. 70.—PAUL SHARP, by his agent Joseph Sharp, claims a tract of land, situate on the west side of the river Mississippi, in the county of Iberville and district of Baton Rouge, containing six arpents front, and forty deep, and bounded on one side by land of Pedro d'Acoste, and on the other by vacant land.

It appears that the claimant did actually inhabit and cultivate the land now claimed on the 20th December, 1803, and that the same was continually inhabited and cultivated by him, or those under whom he claims, for more than ten consecutive years next preceding. Confirmed.

No. 71.—JOSEPH SHARP, for Madam Henson, claims a tract of land, situate on the west side of the river Mississippi, in the county of Iberville and district of Manchack, containing six arpents front and forty deep, and bounded on one side by land of Gertrude Clinepeter, and on the other by vacant land.

It appears that Basticus Quidres, in the year 1774, petitioned Governor Unzaga for this tract of land, and, by a written order of the Governor, in the year 1775, he was put in possession of it by the commandant; it appears further, that the said land was conveyed to the husband of the claimant, since deceased, by the said Quidres, in the year 1780, and that she has continued to inhabit and cultivate the same since that time to the present day. Confirmed.

No. 72. PAUL SHARP, by his agent Joseph Sharp, claims a tract of land, situate on the river Mississippi, in the county of Iberville and district of Baton Rouge, containing eight arpents front, and forty deep.

The claimant was by a written order of Governor Unzaga, put in possession of this tract of land in the year 1773, and in the year following obtained from that Governor a complete grant to the same. Confirmed.

No. 73.—VALERY BERGERON claims a tract of land, situate on the west side of the river Mississippi, in the county of Iberville and district of Baton Rouge, containing three arpents and a fourth in front, and forty in depth, and bounded on one side by land of John Plaresbury.

It appears that the claimant was in possession of this tract of land in the year 1798, and that he continued to inhabit and cultivate the same until the 20th December, 1803, and afterwards. Confirmed.

No. 74.—JOSEPH BABIN claims a tract of land, situate on the east side of the river Mississippi, in the county of Iberville and district of Manchack, containing four and a half arpents front, and forty deep, and bounded on one side by land of Dienne Mecoleur, and on the other by land of Senateur Babin.

It appears that the present claimant did actually inhabit and cultivate the land now claimed on the 20th December, 1803, and that the same was continually inhabited and cultivated by him, or those under whom he claims, for more than ten consecutive years next preceding. Confirmed.

No. 75.—JOSEPH BURKE claims a tract of land, situate on the west side of the river Mississippi, in the county of Iberville and district of Baton Rouge, containing four arpents front, and forty deep, and bounded on one side by land of Louis Arbour, and on the other by land of Carlos Tibodeaux.

It appears that the claimant did actually inhabit and cultivate the land now claimed on the 20th December, 1803, and that the same was continually inhabited and cultivated by him, or those under whom he claims, for more than ten consecutive years next preceding. Confirmed.

No. 76.—CHARLES ROBERT claims a tract of land, situate on the west side of the river Mississippi, in the county of Iberville and district of Baton Rouge, containing three arpents, front, and forty deep, and bounded on one side by land of Jacques Blanchard, and on the other by land of Jean Pasqual.

It appears that the land now claimed was inhabited and cultivated on the 20th December, 1803, and that the same was continually inhabited and cultivated by those under whom the claimant holds for more than ten consecutive years next preceding. Confirmed.

No. 77.—JOSEPH CHLATRE claims a tract of land, situate on the river Mississippi, in the county of Iberville and district of Manchack, containing six arpents front, and forty deep.

This land was surveyed in favor of Martin Chlatre, in the year 1787, who obtained a complete title to the same in the same year, from Estevan Miro, then Governor; under whose title the claimant holds by purchase. Confirmed.

No. 78.—JAMES HEBERT claims a tract of land, situate on the west side of the river Mississippi, in the county of Iberville and district of Baton Rouge, containing six hundred and thirty-five and sixty-six hundredths superficial arpents, and bounded on one side by land of Joseph Babin, and on the other by land of Peter Franyer.

It appears that the claimant did actually inhabit and cultivate the land now claimed on the 20th December, 1803, and that the same was continually inhabited and cultivated by him, or those under whom he claims, for more than ten consecutive years next preceding. Confirmed.

No. 79.—THOMAS HAIT claims a tract of land, situate on the west side of the river Mississippi, in the county of Iberville and district of Baton Rouge, containing one hundred and eighty-five and twenty-eight hundredths superficial arpents, and bounded on one side by land of Juan Dugar, and on the other by land of Pedro Servantes.

It appearing that the claimant did actually inhabit and cultivate the land now claimed on the 20th December, 1803, and that the same was continually inhabited and cultivated by him, or those under whom he claims, for more than ten consecutive years next preceding, the Board confirm the claim to the extent of the first depth of forty arpents.

No. 80.—ANTONIO GROSS claims a tract of land, situate on the west side of the river Mississippi, in the county of Iberville and district of Baton Rouge, containing three arpents front, and forty deep, and bounded on one side by land of Noel O'Brian, and on the other side by land of Ricard de Rentard.

It appears that the present claimant did actually inhabit and cultivate the land now claimed on the 20th December, 1803, and that the same was continually inhabited and cultivated by him, or those under whom he claims, for more than ten consecutive years next preceding. Confirmed.

No. 81.—MARY TRAHANT claims a tract of land, situate on the west side of the river Mississippi, in the county of Iberville and district of Baton Rouge, containing eight arpents front, and forty in depth, and bounded on one side by land of Thomas Feriot, and on the other by land of Joel Brand.

It appears that the claimant did actually inhabit and cultivate the land now claimed on the 20th December, 1803, and that the same was continually inhabited and cultivated by her, or those under whom she claims, for more than ten consecutive years next preceding. Confirmed.

No. 82.—THOMAS HEBERT claims a tract of land, situate on the river Mississippi, in the county of Iberville and district of Manchack, containing eight arpents in front, with the ordinary depth of forty.

This tract of land was surveyed in favor of Arnaud Hebert, in the year 1787, who obtained a complete grant for the same in the same year; under whose title the claimant holds. Confirmed.

No. 83.—PETER C. TIBODEAUX claims a tract of land, situate on the west side of the river Mississippi, in the county of Iberville and district of Baton Rouge, containing three arpents front, and forty deep, and bounded on one side by land of Joseph Burke, and on the other by land of John B. Coms.

It appears that the claimant did actually inhabit and cultivate the land now claimed on the 20th December, 1803, and that the same was continually inhabited and cultivated by him, or those under whom he claims, for more than ten consecutive years next preceding. Confirmed.

No. 84.—FELIX BERNARD claims a tract of land, situate on the west side of the river Mississippi, in the county of Iberville and district of Baton Rouge, containing eight arpents and one hundred and twenty feet in front, and forty arpents in depth, and bounded on one side by land of Joseph Granger, and on the other by land of James Mathers.

It appears that the claimant did actually inhabit and cultivate the land now claimed on the 20th December, 1803, and that the same was continually inhabited and cultivated by him, or those under whom he claims, for more than ten consecutive years next preceding. Confirmed.

No. 85.—LOUIS DEBARDEAU claims a tract of land, situate on the west side of the river Mississippi, in the county of Iberville and district of Baton Rouge, containing two arpents in front, and forty in depth, and bounded on one side by land of Hipolito Mallet, and on the other by land of Marin J. Marion.

It appears that the present claimant did actually inhabit and cultivate the land now claimed on the 20th December, 1803, and that the same was continually inhabited and cultivated by him, or those under whom he claims, for more than ten consecutive years next preceding. Confirmed.

No. 86.—JAMES BLANCHARD claims a tract of land, situate on the west side of the river Mississippi, in the county of Iberville, in the district of Baton Rouge, containing five arpents front, and forty in depth, and bounded on one side by land of José Grange, and on the other by land of Francis G. Arbour.

It appears that the claimant did actually inhabit and cultivate the land now claimed, on the 20th December, 1803, and that the same was continually inhabited and cultivated by him, or those under whom he claims, for more than ten consecutive years next preceding. Confirmed.

No. 87.—JAMES MELANSON claims a tract of land, situate on the west side of the river Mississippi, in the county of Iberville and district of Baton Rouge, containing two arpents and three-fourths in front, and forty arpents depth, and bounded on one side by land of José Doyron, and on the other by land of Olivier Leblanc.

It appears that the claimant did actually inhabit and cultivate the land now claimed on the 20th December, 1803, and that the same was continually inhabited and cultivated by him, or those under whom he claims, for more than ten consecutive years next preceding. Confirmed.

No. 88.—MADELON LANDRY claims a tract of land, situate on the west side of the river Mississippi, in the county of Iberville, containing four arpents front, and twenty in depth, and bounded on one side by land of Alexandre Hebert, and on the other by land of Madame Melanson.

It appears that the claimant did actually inhabit and cultivate the land now claimed, on the 20th December, 1803, and that the same was continually inhabited and cultivated by her, or those under whom she claims, for more than ten consecutive years next preceding. Confirmed.

No. 89.—JOHN DOYRON claims a tract of land, situate on the west side of the river Mississippi, in the county of Iberville and district of Baton Rouge, containing four arpents in front, and forty in depth, and bounded on one side by land of Mathurin Landry, and on the other by land of Victor Hebert.

It appears that the claimant did actually inhabit and cultivate the land now claimed, on the 20th December, 1803, and that the same was continually inhabited and cultivated by him, or those under whom he claims, for more than ten consecutive years next preceding. Confirmed.

No. 90.—JOSEPH DOYRON claims a tract of land, situate on the west side of the river Mississippi, in the county of Iberville and district of Baton Rouge, containing two arpents and three-fourths in front, and forty arpents in depth, and bounded on one side by land of Mathurin Landry, and on the other by land of Santiago Melanson.

It appears that the claimant did actually inhabit and cultivate the land now claimed on the 20th December, 1803, and that the same was continually inhabited and cultivated by him, or those under whom he claims, for more than ten consecutive years next preceding. Confirmed.

No. 91.—ABRAHAM HEBERT claims a tract of land, situate on the west side of the river Mississippi, in the county of Iberville and district of Manchack, containing five arpents and seven toises front, and forty arpents in depth, and bounded on one side by land of Francisco Hebert, and on the other by land of José Leblanc.

It appears that the present claimant did actually inhabit and cultivate the land now claimed on the 20th December, 1803, and that the same was continually inhabited and cultivated by him, or those under whom he claims, for more than ten consecutive years next preceding. Confirmed.

No. 92.—SIMON ALLAIN claims a tract of land, situate on the river Mississippi, in the county of Iberville and district of Baton Rouge, containing seven arpents twenty-five toises and four feet front, and forty arpents in depth, and bounded on one side by land of Bonaventura Leblanc, and on the other side by Juan Hebert.

It appears that the claimant did actually inhabit and cultivate the land now claimed on the 20th December, 1803, and that the same was continually inhabited and cultivated by him, or those under whom he claims, for more than ten consecutive years next preceding. Confirmed.

No. 93.—JEAN PIERRE BABIN claims a tract of land, situate on the west side of the river Mississippi, in the county of Iberville and district of Baton Rouge, containing four arpents front, and forty in depth, and bounded on one side by land of Olivier Brassat, and on the other by land of Joseph Babin.

It appears that the claimant did actually inhabit and cultivate the land now claimed on the 20th December, 1803, and that the same was continually inhabited and cultivated by him, or those under whom he claims, for more than ten consecutive years next preceding. Confirmed.

No. 95.—PAUL BABIN claims a tract of land, situate on the river Mississippi, in the county of Iberville, and district of Baton Rouge, containing four arpents and twenty-three toises front, and forty arpents in depth, and bounded on one side by land of Jean B. Babin, and on the other by land of Simon Allain.

It appears that the claimant did actually inhabit and cultivate the land now claimed on the 20th December, 1803, and that the same was continually inhabited and cultivated by him, or those under whom he claims, for more than ten consecutive years next preceding. Confirmed.

No. 96.—JEAN PROSPERE claims a tract of land, situate on the west side of the river Mississippi, in the county of Iberville and district of Baton Rouge, containing five arpents front, and forty in depth, and bounded on one side by land of Pierre Lardois, and on the other by land of J. A. Landry.

It appears that the claimant did actually inhabit and cultivate the land now claimed on the 20th December, 1803, and that the same was continually inhabited and cultivated by him, or those under whom he claims, for more than ten consecutive years next preceding. Confirmed.

No. 97.—XAVIER LANDRY claims a tract of land, situate on the west side of the river Mississippi, in the county of Iberville and district of Baton Rouge, containing two hundred and ten and forty-four hundredths superficial arpents, and bounded on one side by land of Joseph Doyron, and on the other by land of Pierre Lebert.

It appearing that the land claimed was inhabited and cultivated on the 20th December, 1803, and that the same was continually inhabited and cultivated by those under whom the claimant holds for more than ten consecutive years next preceding, the Board confirm the claim to the extent of the first forty arpents depth.

No. 98.—SIMON and PAUL BABIN, by their agent Jean P. Babin, claim a tract of land, situate in the county of Iberville and district of Galveztown, containing six arpents front, and forty in depth.

The tract now claimed is part of twelve arpents front, by forty in depth, surveyed, in the year 1789, in favor of Batista Hebert, who obtained a complete grant for the same, in the same year, from Don Estevan Miro, then Governor. The present claimants hold by virtue of purchase made under the original grant. Confirmed.

No. 99.—LOUIS HAIT claims a tract of land, situate on the west side of the river Mississippi, in the county of Iberville and district of Baton Rouge, containing one arpent front, and forty arpents in depth, and bounded on one side by land of Pierre Lebaure, and on the other by Thomas Hait.

It appears that the land claimed was inhabited and cultivated on the 20th December, 1803, and that the same was continually inhabited and cultivated by those under whom the claimant holds for more than ten consecutive years next preceding. Confirmed.

No. 101.—THOMAS HEBERT claims a tract of land, situate on the west side of the river Mississippi, in the county of Iberville and district of Manchack, containing two arpents and one hundred and forty feet front, and forty arpents in depth, and bounded on one side by land of Deny Landry, and on the other by land of Joseph Arnandez.

The claimant was put in possession of this tract of land by Nicolas de Verbois, at that time commandant, conformably to an order (see below) of the Baron de Carondelet, in the year 1792; and having complied with the condition thereof, to wit, making the road and levée, has become entitled to the land under said order. Confirmed.

Translation of the order of the Baron de Carondelet to the commandant relative to the levées.

NEW ORLEANS, *August* 10, 1792.

I have examined and reflected upon the reasons which you expose to me in your letter No. 2, relative to the levées of the lands abandoned by Messrs. Riano, Loris, Peret, Guyot, Mueillon, Monsanto, F. Bouligny, William and Henry Thomas. It is absolutely necessary to eradicate the prevailing abuse of not putting into immediate execution the orders issued by Government thereupon; the last of which I render you responsible is, that within this year the levées shall be made: for which purpose you will give the ownership of the lands to those individuals who will undertake to make their levées without further order. You shall appoint your syndics, who, with yourself, may inspect and attend to the good condition of the levées, without having any other regard than to impartial justice.

THE BARON DE CARONDELET.

To Mr. NICOLAS DE VERBOIS.

No. 102.—ETIENNE THERIOT claims a tract of land, situate on the river Mississippi, in the county of Iberville and district of Baton Rouge, containing six arpents front, and the ordinary depth of forty.

This land was surveyed in the year 1790, by Don Carlos Trudeau, in favor of Don Joseph Basques Bahamond, who, in the same year, obtained a complete title to the same from Governor Miro; under which title the present claimant holds. Confirmed.

No. 103.—THOMAS HEBERT claims a tract of land, situate on the west side of the river Mississippi, in the county of Iberville and district of Baton Rouge, containing six arpents front, and forty in depth, and bounded on one side by land of Bernard Dautrière, and on the other by land of Pedro Flores.

It appears that the land now claimed was inhabited and cultivated on the 20th December, 1803, and that the same was continually inhabited and cultivated by those under whom the claimant holds for more than ten consecutive years next preceding. Confirmed.

No. 104.—JEAN BAPTISTE LEBLANC claims a tract of land, situate on the river Mississippi, in the county of Iberville, containing six and a half arpents front, on the usual depth of forty.

This tract of land was surveyed by Don Louis Andry, in the year 1772, in favor of Baulio Landry, who obtained a complete grant, in 1774, from Don Louis de Unzaga, then Governor. The claimant derives his title from the original grant by purchase. Confirmed.

No. 105.—PETER BROUSSARD claims a tract of land, situate on the west side of the river Mississippi, in the county of Iberville and district of Baton Rouge, containing three arpents in front, and forty in depth, and bounded on one side by land of Francis Lejeune, and on the other by land of Simon Babin.

It appears that the claimant did actually inhabit and cultivate the land now claimed on the 20th December, 1803, and that the same was continually inhabited and cultivated by him, or those under whom he claims, for more than ten consecutive years next preceding. Confirmed.

No. 106.—PAUL and MAGLOIRE DUPUIS claim a tract of land, situate on the river Mississippi, in the county of Iberville and district of Baton Rouge, containing four arpents front, and forty in depth.

This is part of a tract of land containing eight arpents and twenty-one toises front, with the depth of forty arpents, surveyed in the year 1772, and granted in 1774, by Governor Unzaga, in favor of Blas Rivet; under which grant the claimants derive title. Confirmed.

No. 107.—MOSES FOREST claims a tract of land, situate on the west side of the river Mississippi, in the county of Iberville and district of Baton Rouge, containing four arpents wanting five toises in front, and forty arpents in depth, and bounded on one side by land of Jean B. Hebert, and on the other by Pedro Lebaure.

It appears that the claimant did actually inhabit and cultivate the land now claimed on the 20th December, 1803, and that the same was continually inhabited and cultivated by him, or those under whom he claims, for more than ten consecutive years next preceding. Confirmed.

No. 110.—CHARLES HEBERT claims a tract of land, situate on the west side of the river Mississippi, in the county of Iberville, containing four and a half arpents in front, and forty in depth, and bounded on one side by land of Narcisse Hebert, and on the other by land of Charles Hebert.

The claimant was put in possession of this tract of land by Nicolas de Verbois, at that time commandant, conformably to an order (see page 301) of the Baron de Carondelet, in the year 1792; and, having complied with the conditions thereof, to wit, making the road and levée, has become entitled to the land under said order. Confirmed.

No. 111.—CHARLES HEBERT claims a tract of land, situate on the river Mississippi, in the county of Iberville, containing six arpents front, and forty in depth.

It appears that this land was surveyed in the year 1772, in favor of Ignatio Hebert, and granted to him by Governor Unzaga, in the year 1774; under which title the claimant holds. Confirmed.

No. 113.—ISIDORE LEBAURE claims a tract of land, situate on the west side of the river Mississippi, in the county of Iberville and district of Baton Rouge, containing five arpents front, and forty in depth, and bounded on one side by land of Xavier Theriot, and on the other by land of Madame Buther.

It appears that the land now claimed was inhabited and cultivated on the 20th December, 1803, and that the same was continually inhabited and cultivated by those under whom the claimant holds for more than ten consecutive years next preceding. Confirmed.

No. 114.—MICHEL LAMBREMONT claims a tract of land, situate on the river Mississippi, in the county of Iberville, containing six arpents eighteen toises and four feet front, and forty arpents in depth.

This land was surveyed in the year 1772, in favor of Alexander Landry, and to him granted by Governor Unzaga, in 1774; under which grant the present claimant holds. Confirmed.

No. 115.—CHARLES HEBERT, Sen. claims a tract of land, situate on the west side of the river Mississippi, in the county of Iberville, containing two arpents front, and forty in depth, and bounded on one side by land of Pierre Hebert, and on the other by Michel Guarud.

The claimant was put in possession of this tract of land by Nicolas de Verbois, at that time commandant, conformably to an order (see page 301) of the Baron de Carondelet, in the year 1792; and, having complied with the conditions thereof, to wit, making the road and levée, has become entitled to the land under said order. Confirmed.

No. 117.—JACQUES VIGNES claims a tract of land, situate on Fausse river, in the county of Pointe Coupée, containing twelve arpents and thirty feet front, and forty arpents in depth.

This is part of one thousand arpents of land, surveyed in favor of Benjamin Farrar, in the year 1789, and granted to him by Governor Miro, in 1790. The claimant holds by purchase under said grant. Confirmed.

No. 118.—MICHEL LEJEUNE, Jun., and JOSEPH LEJEUNE, Sen., by Nathan Meriam, their agent, claim a tract of land, situate on Fausse river, in the county of Pointe Coupée, containing twelve arpents front, and forty in depth.

This tract of land was surveyed in favor of Michel Lejeune, Sen., in the year 1795, in whose favor a complete grant issued, in the same year, by the Baron de Carondelet; under which grant the claimants derive title by purchase. Confirmed.

No. 119.—MICHEL LEJEUNE, Jun., by his agent Nathan Meriam, claims a tract of land, situate on Fausse river, in the county of Pointe Coupée, containing five arpents front, and forty in depth, and bounded on one side by land of Charles Lejeune, and on the other by land of Michel Lejeune.

It appears that the land claimed was inhabited and cultivated on the 20th December, 1803, and that the same was continually inhabited and cultivated by those under whom the claimant holds for more than ten consecutive years next preceding. Confirmed.

No. 121.—MADAME P. DESCUIR claims a tract of land, situate on the river Mississippi, in the county of Pointe Coupée, containing four arpents and three perches front, and forty arpents in depth, and bounded on one side by land of Samuel C. Young, and on the other by land of Baptiste Descuir.

It appears that the present claimant did actually inhabit and cultivate the land now claimed on the 20th December, 1803, and that the same was continually inhabited and cultivated by her, or those under whom she claims, for more than ten consecutive years next preceding. Confirmed.

No. 122.—JEAN BAPTISTE SAIZAN claims a tract of land, situate on Fausse river, in the county of Pointe Coupée, containing four arpents front, and forty in depth, and bounded on one side by land of George Bergeron, and on the other by land of Gausseraud.

It appears that the claimant did actually inhabit and cultivate the land now claimed on the 20th December, 1803, and that the same was continually inhabited and cultivated by him, or those under whom he claims, for more than ten consecutive years next preceding. Confirmed.

No. 126.—PIERRE BODILLARD claims a tract of land, situate on Fausse river, in the county of Pointe Coupée, containing two arpents front, and forty in depth, and bounded on one side by land of P. Bergeron, and on the other by land of Jacques Fabre.

It appears that the claimant did actually inhabit and cultivate the land now claimed on the 20th December, 1803, and that the same was continually inhabited and cultivated by him, or those under whom he claims, for more than ten consecutive years next preceding. Confirmed.

No. 127.—ANTOINE GAUSSERAND claims a tract of land, situate on Fausse river, in the county of Pointe Coupée, containing four and a half arpents in front, and forty in depth, and bounded on one side by land of Pierre Bergeron, and on the other by land of Jean B. Saizan.

It appears that the land claimed was actually inhabited and cultivated on the 20th December, 1803, and that the same was continually inhabited and cultivated by those under whom the claimant holds for more than ten consecutive years next preceding. Confirmed.

No. 128.—HUBERT PERRIOT claims a tract of land, situate on Fausse river, in the county of Pointe Coupée, containing two arpents front, and forty in depth, and bounded on one side by land of José Janes, and on the other by land of Francis Gross.

It appears that the land now claimed was inhabited and cultivated on the 20th December, 1803, and that the same was continually inhabited and cultivated by those under whom the claimant holds for more than ten consecutive years next preceding. Confirmed.

No. 129.—JOSEPH AGUILAR claims a tract of land, situate on Fausse river, in the county of Pointe Coupée, containing seven arpents front, and forty deep, and bounded on one side by land of Jacques Vignes, and on the other by land of Baptiste Saizan.

It appears that the claimant did actually inhabit and cultivate the land now claimed on the 20th of December, 1803, and that the same was continually inhabited and cultivated by him, or those under whom he claims, for more than ten consecutive years next preceding. Confirmed.

No. 130.—AUGUSTIN PORCHE claims a tract of land, situate on Fausse river, in the county of Pointe Coupée, containing eight arpents front, and forty in depth, and bounded on one side by land of Louis Flores, and on the other by land of Baptiste Porche.

It appears that the claimant did actually inhabit and cultivate the land now claimed on the 20th December, 1803, and that the same was continually inhabited and cultivated by him or those under whom he claims, for more than ten consecutive years next preceding. Confirmed.

No. 131.—LOUIS RICHE claims a tract of land, situate on the river Mississippi, in the county of Pointe Coupée, containing four and a half arpents front, and eighty in depth, and bounded on one side by land of Madame Bourgeat, and on the other by land of Martin Bourgeat.

The claimant, being in possession of the first depth of forty arpents, petitioned Governor Miro for a grant of the second depth, which was accordingly granted to him in the year 1791; since which time said land has been inhabited and cultivated. Confirmed.

No. 132.—LOUIS RICHE claims a tract of land, situate on the river Mississippi, in the county of Pointe Coupée, containing six arpents front, and eighty in depth, and bounded on one side by land of Joseph Tunoir, and on the other by land of F. Grenillon.

It appears that, in the year 1788, Joseph Carmonde was proprietor of the first forty arpents in depth of the land claimed, in which year he petitioned for a second concession; and Governor Miro granted him an order of survey, directing the Surveyor General to put him in possession. By means of several intermediate sales, this land has come to the possession of the present claimant; and has been inhabited and cultivated for more than ten consecutive years prior to the 20th December, 1803. Confirmed.

No. 133.—BAPTISTE SAIZAN claims a tract of land, situate on Fausse river, in the county of Pointe Coupée, containing three arpents front, and forty in depth, and bounded on one side by land of V. Tunoir, and on the other by land of J. Slynder.

It appears that the land claimed was inhabited and cultivated on the 20th December, 1803, and that the same was continually inhabited and cultivated by those under whom the claimant holds for more than ten consecutive years next preceding. Confirmed.

No. 134.—LOUIS LANGLOIS claims a tract of land, situate on Fausse river, in the county of Pointe Coupée, containing five arpents front, and forty in depth, and bounded on one side by land of Joseph Porche, and on the other by land of Augustin Porche.

It appears that the land claimed was inhabited and cultivated on the 20th December, 1803, and that the same was continually inhabited and cultivated by those under whom the claimant holds for more than ten consecutive years next preceding. Confirmed.

No. 135.—SIMON PORCHE claims a tract of land, situate on the river Mississippi, in the county of Pointe Coupée, containing fourteen arpents front, and forty in depth, and bounded on one side by land of Polite Porche, and on the other by land of V. P. Patin.

It appears that the claimant did actually inhabit and cultivate the land now claimed on the 20th December, 1803, and that the same was continually inhabited and cultivated by him, or those under whom he claims, for more than ten consecutive years next preceding. Confirmed.

No. 136.—PIERRE JOSEPH PORCHE claims a tract of land, situate on Fausse river, in the county of Pointe Coupée, containing three arpents front, and forty in depth, and bounded on one side by land of Louis David, and on the other by land of Madame Legras.

It appears that the claimant did actually inhabit and cultivate the land now claimed on the 20th December, 1803, and that the same was continually inhabited and cultivated by him, or those under whom he claims, for more than ten consecutive years next preceding. Confirmed.

No. 137.—PIERRE JOSEPH PORCHE claims a tract of land, situate on the Fausse river, in the county of Pointe Coupée, containing four arpents front, and forty in depth, and bounded on one side by land of Louis David, and on the other by land of B. C. Porche.

It appears that the claimant did actually inhabit and cultivate the land now claimed on the 20th December, 1803, and that the same was continually inhabited and cultivated by him, or those under whom he claims, for more than ten consecutive years next preceding. Confirmed.

No. 138.—GEORGE LEMENT claims a tract of land, situate on Fausse river, in the county of Pointe Coupée, containing six arpents in front, and forty in depth, and bounded on one side by land of Francis Lebreau, and on the other by land of George Bergeron, Sen.

It appears that the land claimed was inhabited and cultivated on the 20th December, 1803, and that the same was continually inhabited and cultivated by him, or those under whom he claims, for more than ten consecutive years next preceding. Confirmed.

No. 139.—SIMON DAVID claims a tract of land, situate on Fausse river, in the county of Pointe Coupée, containing two arpents front, and forty in depth, and bounded on one side by land of V. Tunoir, and on the other by land of Joseph Descuir.

It appears that the claimant did actually inhabit and cultivate the land now claimed on the 20th December, 1803, and that the same was continually inhabited and cultivated by him, or those under whom he claims, for more than ten consecutive years next preceding. Confirmed.

No. 140.—BAPTISTE PORCHE claims a tract of land, situate on Fausse river, in the county of Pointe Coupée, containing three arpents front, and forty in depth, and bounded on one side by land of Joseph Ennet, and on the other by land of Augustin Porche.

It appears that the land now claimed was inhabited and cultivated on the 20th December, 1803, and that the same was continually inhabited and cultivated by those under whom the claimant holds for more than ten consecutive years next preceding. Confirmed.

No. 141.—MARTIN BOURGEAT claims a tract of land, situate on the river Mississippi, in the county of Pointe Coupée, containing eight arpents front, and a double concession of eighty in depth, and bounded on one side by land of Louis Riché, and on the other by land of F. Gremillon.

It appears that the claimant did actually inhabit and cultivate the front and first depth of the land now claimed on the 20th December, 1803, and that the same was continually inhabited and cultivated by him, or those under whom he claims, for more than ten consecutive years next preceding; and that Francisco Riché, under whom the present claimant holds, obtained from the Spanish Government a regular warrant of survey for the second depth in the year 1788. Confirmed.

No. 143.—NICOLAS DE VILLIAN claims a tract, of land situate on Fausse river, in the county of Pointe Coupée, containing nine arpents five perches and three feet front, and forty arpents in depth, and bounded on one side by land of Baptiste Porche, and on the other by land of Hyacinthe Schick.

It appears that the claimant did actually inhabit and cultivate the land claimed on the 20th December, 1803, and that the same was continually inhabited and cultivated by him, or those under whom he claims, for more than ten consecutive years next preceding. Confirmed.

No. 144.—HYACINTE SCHICK claims a tract of land, situate on Fausse river, in the county of Pointe Coupée, containing four arpents in front, and forty in depth, and bounded on one side by land of Francis Demouchet, and on the other by land of Mr. Labigan.

It appears that the claimant did actually inhabit and cultivate the land now claimed on the 20th December, 1803, and that the same was continually inhabited and cultivated by him, or those under whom he claims, for more than ten consecutive years next preceding. Confirmed.

No. 145.—GUILLAUME GAUTIER claims a tract of land, situate on Fausse river, in the county of Pointe Coupée, containing six arpents front, and forty in depth, and bounded on one side by land of Jean L'Abbé, and on the other by land of Madame Le Cloud.

It appears that the land now claimed was inhabited and cultivated on the 20th December, 1803, and that the same was continually inhabited and cultivated by those under whom the claimant holds for more than ten consecutive years next preceding. Confirmed.

No. 146.—CHARLES LEJEUNE claims a tract of land, situate on Fausse river, in the county of Pointe Coupée, containing thirteen arpents front, and forty in depth, and bounded on one side by land of Joseph Ennet, and on the other by land of Michel Lejeune.

It appears that the land now claimed was inhabited and cultivated on the 20th of December, 1803, and that the same was continually inhabited and cultivated by those under whom the claimant holds for more than ten consecutive years next preceding. Confirmed.

No. 147.—FRANCIS LEBEAU claims a tract of land, situate on Fausse river, in the county of Pointe Coupée, containing five arpents front, and forty in depth, and bounded on one side by land of George Schack, and on the other by land of Pierre Joir.

It appears that the claimant did actually inhabit and cultivate the land now claimed on the 20th December, 1803, and that the same was continually inhabited and cultivated by him, or those under whom he claims, for more than ten consecutive years next preceding. Confirmed.

No. 148.—AUGUSTIN ALLAIN claims two tracts of land, situate on the river Mississippi, in the county of Pointe Coupée, one tract containing nine arpents front, and forty deep, and bounded on one side by land of Mr Leblanc, and on the other by land of Francis Barras; and the other tract, containing thirty-six arpents front, and forty in depth, and bounded on one side by Madame Jacques Jarreau, and on the other by land of ——.

It appears that the claimant did actually inhabit and cultivate the tracts of land now claimed on the 20th December, 1803, and that the same were continually inhabited and cultivated by him, or those under whom he claims, for more than ten consecutive years next preceding. Confirmed.

No. 149.—MARIANNE BACON, widow of Pierre Descoux, claims a tract of land, situate on the river Mississippi, in the county of Pointe Coupée, containing four arpents in front, and forty in depth, and bounded on one side by land of J. B. Beauvais, and on the other by land of Madame Beauvais.

It appears that the claimant did actually inhabit and cultivate the land now claimed on the 20th December, 1803, and that the same was continually inhabited and cultivated by her, or those under whom she claims, for more than ten consecutive years next preceding. Confirmed.

No. 150.—MARIANNE BACON, widow of Pierre Descoux, claims a tract of land, situate on the river Mississippi, in the county of Pointe Coupée, containing four arpents front, and forty in depth, and bounded on one side by land of Julian Poydras, and on the other by land of Santiago Vignes.

It appears that the claimant did actually inhabit and cultivate the land now claimed on the 20th December, 1803, and that the same was continually inhabited and cultivated by her, or those under whom she claims, for more than ten consecutive years next preceding. Confirmed.

No. 152.—ALEXANDER LABRY claims a tract of land, situate on Fausse river, in the county of Pointe Coupée, containing seventy-one and fifty-six hundredths superficial arpents, and bounded on one side by land of Louis Buther, and on the other by land of Gabriel Fusilier.

It appears that the land now claimed was inhabited and cultivated on the 20th December, 1803, and that the same was continually inhabited and cultivated by those under whom the claimant holds for more than ten consecutive years next preceding. Confirmed.

No. 153.—FRANCIS CHASSE claims a tract of land, situate on the river Mississippi, in the county of Pointe Coupée, containing four arpents front, and forty in depth, and bounded on one side by land of Mr. Belanger, and on the other by land of Julian Poydras.

It appears that the claimant did actually inhabit and cultivate the land now claimed on the 20th December, 1803, and that the same was continually inhabited and cultivated by him, or those under whom he claims, for more than ten consecutive years next preceding. Confirmed.

No. 155.—JOSEPH ENNET claims a tract of land, situate on Fausse river, in the county of Pointe Coupée, containing five arpents front, with the usual depth of forty, and bounded on one side by land of Charles Lejeune, and on the other by land of Baptiste Porche.

It appears that the claimant did actually inhabit and cultivate the land now claimed on the 20th December, 1803, and that the same was continually inhabited and cultivated by him, or those under whom he claims, for more than ten consecutive years next preceding. Confirmed.

No. 156.—JASON JAFFRION claims a tract of land, situate on the river Mississippi, in the county of Pointe Coupée, containing six arpents front, and forty in depth, and bounded on one side by land of P. Canon, and on the other by land surveyed for Madame Descuir.

It appears that the claimant did actually inhabit and cultivate the land now claimed on the 20th December, 1803, and that the same was continually inhabited and cultivated by him, or by those under whom he claims, for more than ten consecutive years next preceding. Confirmed.

No. 157. JASON JAFFRION claims a tract of land, situate on Fausse river, in the county of Pointe Coupée, and containing seven arpents and two-thirds in front, and forty arpents in depth, and bounded on one side by land of A. Major, and on the other by land of Decreat.

Five arpents and two-thirds front of this land is part of a complete grant of twenty arpents front on Fausse river, made to Margarita Farrar on the 17th ——, 1780; the balance, being two arpents front, has been inhabited and cultivated by those under whom the claimant holds for ten consecutive years prior to the 20th December, 1803. Confirmed.

No. 158.—ETIENNE MAJOR claims a tract of land, situate on Fausse river, in the county of Pointe Coupée, containing six hundred and forty superficial arpents, and bounded on one side by land of ——, and on the other by land of ——.

It appears that this land was inhabited and cultivated on the 20th December, 1803, and that the same was continually inhabited and cultivated by the claimant, or those under whom he holds, for more than ten consecutive years next preceding. Confirmed.

No. 159.—ETIENNE MAJOR claims a tract of land, situate on Fausse river, in the county of Pointe Coupée, containing five arpents front, and forty in depth, and bounded on one side by land of Joseph Jaffrion, and on the other by land of Eliza Picar.

It appears that the land claimed was inhabited and cultivated on the 20th December, 1803, and that the same was continually inhabited and cultivated by those under whom the claimant holds for more than ten consecutive years next preceding. Confirmed.

No. 160.—ETIENNE MAJOR claims a tract of land, situate on the Fausse river, in the county of Pointe Coupée, containing five arpents and two-thirds in front, and forty arpents in depth, and bounded on one side by land of Benjamin Farrar, and on the other by land of Margarita Farrar.

This tract has a parcel of twenty arpents front, granted to Anne Farrar, in the year 1790, and by her husband, Samuel Young, sold to the present claimant, on the 3d of August, 1797. Confirmed.

No. 162.—CHARLES GREMILLON claims a tract of land, situate on the Fausse river, in the county of Pointe Coupée, containing eight arpents in front, and forty in depth, and bounded on one side by land of Joseph Descuir, and on the other by land of Julian Poydras.

This land being a parcel of a tract of land granted to Benjamin Farrar, was by him sold to the claimant, in the year 1798. Confirmed.

No. 163.—JOSEPH DESCUIR claims a tract of land, situate on Fausse river, in the county of Pointe Coupée, containing twenty arpents front, and eighty in depth, and bounded on one side by land of Antoine Beauvais, and on the other by land of Pierre Olau.

This being a parcel of a tract of land granted to Benjamin Farrar, and sold to the claimant, by the heirs of the said Farrar, the Board confirm the title to the extent of forty arpents in depth, but reject the balance.

No. 164.—AUGUSTE PATIN, widow of J. PATIN, claims a tract of land, situate on the river Mississippi, in the county of Pointe Coupée, containing seven arpents and three perches in front, and forty arpents in depth, and bounded on one side by land of F. Porche.

It appears that the land claimed was inhabited and cultivated on the 20th December, 1803, and that the same was continually inhabited and cultivated by the claimant, or those under whom the claimant holds, for more than ten consecutive years next preceding. Confirmed.

No. 165.—FRANCIS BARRA claims a tract of land, situate on the river Mississippi, in the county of Pointe Coupée, containing three hundred and twenty-nine and ninety-nine hundredths superficial arpents, and bounded on one side by land of Madame V. Porche, and on the other by land of Augustin Allain.

It appears that the claimant did actually inhabit and cultivate the land now claimed on the 20th December, 1803, and that the same was continually inhabited and cultivated by him, or those under whom he claims, for more than ten consecutive years next preceding. Confirmed.

No. 166.—VINCENT PORCHE claims a tract of land, situate on the river Mississippi, in the county of Pointe Coupée, containing three hundred and sixty-three and and seventy-four hundredths superficial arpents, and bounded on one side by land of Polite Porche, and on the other by land of Francis Barra.

It appears that the land now claimed was inhabited and cultivated on the 20th December, 1803, and that the same was continually inhabited and cultivated by those under whom the claimant holds for more than ten consecutive years next preceding. Confirmed.

No. 667.—JOSEPH TUNOIR claims a tract of land, situate on the river Mississippi, in the county of Pointe Coupée, containing six arpents front, and forty in depth, and bounded on one side by land of Louis Riché, and on the other by land of Francis Chessé.

It appears that the land now claimed was inhabited and cultivated on the 20th December, 1803, and that the same was continually inhabited and cultivated by those under whom the claimant holds for more than ten consecutive years next preceding. Confirmed.

No. 168.—VINCENT TERNANT, Sen. claims a tract of land, situate on Fausse river, in the county of Pointe Coupée, containing twelve arpents and a half in front, and forty in depth, and bounded on one side by land of Saintville Ternant, and on the other by land of Simon Daird.

It appears that the claimant did actually inhabit and cultivate the land claimed on the 20th December, 1803, and that the same was continually inhabited and cultivated by him, or those under whom he claims, for more than ten consecutive years next preceding. Confirmed.

No. 169.—SAINTVILLE TERNANT claims a tract of land, situate on Fausse river, in the county of Pointe Coupée, containing eight arpents three perches and three feet front, and bounded on one side by land of Pierre Bahand, and on the other by land of Vincent Ternant, Sen.

It appears that the land claimed was inhabited and cultivated on the 20th December, 1803, and that the same was continually inhabited and cultivated by those under whom the claimant holds for more than ten consecutive years next preceding. Confirmed.

No. 170.—VINCENT TERNANT, Jun. claims a tract of land, situate on the Fausse river, in the county of Pointe Coupée, containing thirteen arpents front, and forty in depth, and bounded on one side by land of Madame Olivian, and on the other by land of Pierre Bahand.

It appears that the land now claimed was inhabited and cultivated on the 20th December, 1803, and that the same was continually inhabited and cultivated by those under whom the claimant holds for more than ten consecutive years next preceding. Confirmed.

No. 171.—PIERRE BAHAND claims a tract of land, situate on Fausse river, in the county of Pointe Coupée, containing nine arpents front, and forty in depth, and bounded on one side by land of Vincent Ternant, Sen., and on the other by land of Vincent Ternant.

It appears that the claimant did actually inhabit and cultivate the land now claimed on the 20th December, 1803, and that the same was continually inhabited and cultivated by him, or those under whom he claims, for more than ten consecutive years next preceding. Confirmed.

No. 172.—LOUIS BISETTE claims a tract of land, situate on Fausse river, in the county of Pointe Coupée, containing two arpents front, and forty in depth, and bounded on one side by land of Antoine Descuir, and on the other by land of Mr. Labore.

The claimant having inhabited and cultivated said land on and before the 1st day of October, 1800, and continued to inhabit and cultivate the same until the 20th December, 1803, and afterwards. Confirmed.

No. 173.—JEAN BAPTISTE PORCIEAU claims a tract of land, situate on Fausse river, in the county of Pointe Coupée, containing seven arpents front, and forty in depth, and bounded on one side by land of Pierre Porche, and on the other by land of N. Villian.

It appears that the claimant did actually inhabit and cultivate the land now claimed on the 20th December, 1803, and that the same was continually inhabited and cultivated by him, or those under whom he claims, for more than ten consecutive years next preceding. Confirmed.

No. 174.—JEAN BAPTISTE PORCIEAU claims a tract of land, situate on Fausse river, in the county of Pointe Coupée, containing thirteen arpents front, and forty in depth, and bounded on one side by land of N. Villian, and on the other by land of Grisent Large.

This tract of land is a parcel of a greater quantity granted to Benjamin Farrar, by him conveyed to Julian Poydras, and by the latter to the present claimant. Confirmed.

No. 176.—ANTOINE BEAUVAIS claims a tract of land, situate on Fausse river, in the county of Pointe Coupée, containing six arpents in front, and forty in depth, and bounded on one side by land of Joseph Descuir, and on the other by land of Joseph Guidreau.

It appears that the claimant did actually inhabit and cultivate the land now claimed on the 20th of December, 1803, and that the same was continually inhabited and cultivated by him, or those under whom he claims, for more than ten consecutive years next preceding. Confirmed.

No. 177.—FRANÇOISE RICARD, widow of Francis Allain, claims a tract of land, situate on the river Mississippi, in the county of Pointe Coupée, containing eight hundred and ten and forty-four hundredths superficial arpents, and bounded on one side by land of the

United States, and on the other by land of Madame Jarreau.

It appears that the claimant did actually inhabit and cultivate the land now claimed on the 20th December, 1803, and that the same was continually inhabited and cultivated by her, or those under whom she claims, for more than ten consecutive years next preceding. Confirmed.

No. 178.—JEAN F. PORCHE claims a tract of land, situate on the river Mississippi, in the county of Pointe Coupée, containing ten arpents front, and forty in depth, and bounded on one side by land of Augustine P. Patin; and on the other by land of ———.

It appears that the claimant did actually inhabit and cultivate the land now claimed on the 20th December, 1803, and that the same was continually inhabited and cultivated by him, or those under whom he claims, for more than ten consecutive years next preceding. Confirmed.

No. 179.—NATHAN MERIAM, as agent for the heirs of George Olivet, claims a tract of land, situate on Fausse river, in the county of Pointe Coupée, containing eighteen arpents front, and eighty in depth, and bounded on one side by land of Mr. Fabre, and on the other by land of Benjamin Farrar.

The father of the claimant having obtained a complete title to the first forty arpents in depth in the year 1791, and a regular order of survey for the second depth of forty arpents in 1793. Confirmed.

No. 180.—HYPOLITE PORCHE claims a tract of land, situate on the river Mississippi, in the county of Pointe Coupée, containing four arpents front, and forty in depth, and bounded on each side by lands of Vincent Porche.

It appears that the claimant did actually inhabit and cultivate the land now claimed on the 20th December, 1803, and that the same was continually inhabited and cultivated by him, or those under whom he claims, for more than ten consecutive years next preceding. Confirmed.

No. 181.—HYPOLITE BARON claims a tract of land, situate on the river Mississippi, in the county of Pointe Coupée, containing six arpents in front, and forty in depth, and bounded on one side by land of J. Jaffrion, and on the other by land of Madame Champinole.

It appears that the land claimed was inhabited and cultivated on the 20th December, 1803, and that the same was continually inhabited and cultivated by those under whom the claimant holds for more than ten consecutive years next preceding. Confirmed.

No. 182.—SALVADOR PAMIAS claims a tract of land, situate on the river Mississippi, in the county of Pointe Coupée, containing one hundred and sixty-one and a half superficial arpents, and bounded on one side by land of Santiago Vignes, and on the other by land of Jean B. Beauvais.

It appears that the land now claimed was inhabited and cultivated on the 20th December, 1803, and that the same was continually inhabited and cultivated by those under whom the claimant holds for more than ten consecutive years next preceding. Confirmed.

No. 183.—Madame J. B. LACOUR claims a tract of land, situate on the river Mississippi, in the county of Pointe Coupée, containing fifteen arpents in front, and eighty in depth, and bounded on one side by land of N. Lacour, and on the other by land of Samuel C. Young.

It appears that the claimant did actually inhabit and cultivate the first depth of forty arpents of the land she claims on the 20th December, 1803, and that the same was continually inhabited and cultivated by her, or those under whom she claims, for more than ten consecutive years next preceding. The Board confirm her claim to the extent of forty arpents, but reject the balance of the claim.

No. 184.—LOUIS DAVID claims a tract of land, situate on Fausse river, in the county of Pointe Coupée, containing four arpents front, and forty in depth, and bounded on each side by land of Pierre Porche.

It appears that the claimant did actually inhabit and cultivate the land now claimed on the 20th December, 1803, and that the same was continually inhabited and cultivated by him, or those under whom he claims, for more than ten consecutive years next preceding. Confirmed.

No. 185.—CHARLES DUFOUR, Sen. claims a tract of land, situate on the river Mississippi, in the county of Pointe Coupée, containing seven arpents in front, and forty in depth, and bounded on one side by land of Madame Bourgeat, and on the other by land of Madame Ledoux.

It appears that the claimant did actually inhabit and cultivate the land now claimed on the 20th December, 1803, and that the same was continually inhabited and cultivated by him, or those under whom he claims, for more than ten consecutive years next preceding. Confirmed.

No. 188.—JACQUES FABRE claims a tract of land, situate on Fausse river, in the county of Pointe Coupée, containing four arpents front, and forty in depth, and bounded on one side by land of Pierre Robillard, and on the other by land of George Olivet.

It appears that the land now claimed was inhabited and cultivated on the 20th December, 1803, and that the same was continually inhabited and cultivated by the claimant, or those under whom he holds, for more than ten consecutive years next preceding. Confirmed.

No. 189.—FRANÇOISE BOILEAU, by her agent Nathan Meriam, claims a tract of land, situate on Fausse river, in the county of Pointe Coupée, containing eleven and a half arpents front, and forty in depth, and bounded on one side by land of Julian Poydras, and on the other by land of Antoine Descuir.

It appears that the land claimed was inhabited and cultivated on the 20th December, 1803, and that the same was continually inhabited and cultivated by those under whom the claimant holds for more than ten consecutive years next preceding. Confirmed.

No. 190.—JOHN L'ABBE claims a tract of land, situate on Fausse river, in the county of Pointe Coupée, containing six arpents front, and forty in depth, and bounded on one side by land of Michel Lejeune, and on the other by land of G. Gautier.

It appears that the claimant did actually inhabit and cultivate the land now claimed on the 20th December, 1803, and that the same was continually inhabited and cultivated by him, or those under whom he claims, for more than ten consecutive years next preceding. Confirmed.

No. 191.—JEAN BATISTE DESCUIR claims a tract of land, situate on the river Mississippi, in the county of Pointe Coupée, containing three arpents and ——— perches front, and forty arpents in depth, and bounded on one side by land of Mr. Ladoux, and on the other by land of Madame Descuir.

It appears that the claimant did actually inhabit and cultivate the land now claimed on the 20th December, 1803, and that the same was continually inhabited and cultivated by him, or those under whom he claims, for more than ten consecutive years next preceding. Confirmed.

No. 192.—GABRIEL FUSILIER claims a tract of land, situate on Fausse river, in the county of Pointe Coupée, containing seven arpents two perches and fifteen and a half feet front, and forty arpents in depth, and bounded on one side by land of Jean B. Beauvais, and on the other by land of E. Labry.

It appears that the land now claimed was inhabited and cultivated on the 20th December, 1803, and that the same was continually inhabited and cultivated by the claimant, or those under whom he holds, for more than ten consecutive years next preceding. Confirmed.

No. 193.—GEORGE BERGERON claims a tract of land, situate on Fausse river, in the county of Pointe Coupée, containing six arpents front, and forty in depth, and bounded on one side by land of Mr. Schits, and on the other by land of Batista Saizan.

It appears that the claimant did actually inhabit and cultivate the land now claimed on the 20th December, 1803, and that the same was continually inhabited and cultivated by him, or those under whom he claims, for more than ten consecutive years next preceding. Confirmed.

No. 195.—PIERRE BERGERON, Jun. claims a tract of land, situate on Fausse river, in the county of Pointe Coupée, containing three arpents front, and forty in depth, and bounded on one side by land of Antoine Gausseraud, and on the other by land of Pierre Robillard.

It appears that the land now claimed was inhabited and cultivated on the 20th December, 1803, and that the same was continually inhabited and cultivated by the claimant, or those under whom he holds, for more than ten consecutive years next preceding. Confirmed.

No. 196.—ALEXIS PICARD claims a tract of land, situate on Fausse river, in the county of Pointe Coupée, containing five arpents and three-fourths in front, and forty in depth, and bounded on one side by land of A. Major, and on the other by land of Joseph John.

This tract being a parcel of lands granted to Benjamin Farrar by the Spanish Government, under which grant the claimant holds. Confirmed.

No. 197.—NICHOLAS LACOUR claims a tract of land, situate on the river Mississippi, in the county of Pointe Coupée, containing seven arpents in front, and forty in depth, and bounded on one side by land of Madame Lacour, and on the other by land of Simon Croiset.

It appears that the claimant did actually inhabit and cultivate the land now claimed on the 20th December, 1803, and that the same was continually inhabited and cultivated by him, or those under whom he claims, for more than ten consecutive years next preceding. Confirmed.

No. 198.—HUBERT DAVID claims a tract of land, situate on Fausse river, in the county of Pointe Coupée, containing ten arpents front, and forty in depth, and bounded on one side by land of Charles Quibaldo, and on the other by land of Joseph Chanvert.

It appears that the claimant did actually inhabit and cultivate the land now claimed on the 20th December, 1803, and that the same was continually inhabited and cultivated by him, or those under whom he claims, for more than ten consecutive years next preceding. Confirmed.

No. 199.—ALEXANDRE DESCUIR claims a tract of land, situate on Fausse river, in the county of Pointe Coupée, containing ten arpents front, and forty in depth, and bounded on one side by land of Julian Poydras, and on the other by land of Mr. Baudery.

It appears that the claimant did actually inhabit and cultivate the land now claimed on the 20th December, 1803, and that the same was continually inhabited and cultivated by him, or those under whom he claims, for more than ten consecutive years next preceding. Confirmed.

No. 200.—ANTOINE DESCUIR claims a tract of land, situate on Fausse river, in the county of Pointe Coupée, containing thirteen and a half arpents in front, and forty in depth, and bounded on one side by land of Benjamin Farrar, and on the other by land of Doctor Buch.

The claimant is entitled to this tract of land by a complete grant made in favor of Isaac Gaillard, from whom the claimant purchased. Confirmed.

No. 202.—JACQUES VITRAC claims a tract of land, situate on Fausse river, in the county of Pointe Coupée, containing five arpents and six-tenths front, and forty arpents in depth, and bounded on one side by land of G. Andrées, and on the other by land of Madame Lagrange.

It appears that the claimant inhabited and cultivated said land on and before the 1st day of October, 1800, and continued to inhabit and cultivate the same until on and after the 20th December, 1803; and it not appearing that he claims in his own right any other tract in the territory. Confirmed.

No. 204.—SIMON CROISET claims a tract of land, situate on the river Mississippi, in the county of Pointe Coupée, containing seven arpents and three-fourths front, and forty arpents in depth, and bounded on one side by land of the claimant, and on the other by land of Mr. Tunoir.

It appears that the claimant did actually inhabit and cultivate the land now claimed on the 20th December, 1803, and that the same was continually inhabited and cultivated by him, or those under whom he claims, for more than ten consecutive years next preceding. Confirmed.

No. 206.—JOSEPH FABRE claims a tract of land, situate on Fausse river, in the county of Pointe Coupée, containing two arpents front, and forty in depth, and bounded on one side by land of Joseph Bergeron, and on the other by land of Joseph St. Cyr, Jun.

This appears to be part of a tract of land sold by Benjamin Farrar to Julian Poydras, and to which said Farrar had obtained a complete title from the Spanish Government; under which title the claimant holds. Confirmed.

No. 207.—VINCENT TERNANT, Sen. claims a tract of land, situate on Fausse river, in the county of Pointe Coupée, containing four arpents front, and forty in depth, and bounded on one side by land of Dominique Saizan, and on the other by land of Gabriel Fusilier.

It appears that the land now claimed was inhabited and cultivated on the 20th December, 1803, and that the same was continually inhabited and cultivated by those under whom the claimant holds for more than ten consecutive years next preceding. Confirmed.

No. 208.—FRANCIS SAMPSON claims a tract of land, situate on Fausse river, in the county of Pointe Coupée, containing fifteen arpents front, and forty in depth, and bounded on one side by land of Berthelemy Olinde.

It appears that the claimant did actually inhabit and cultivate the land now claimed on the 20th December, 1803, and that the same was continually inhabited and cultivated by him, or those under whom he claims, for more than ten consecutive years next preceding. Confirmed.

No. 209.—MADAME JARREAU claims a tract of land, situate in the county of Pointe Coupée, containing four arpents front, and forty in depth, and bounded on one side by land of Madame Legros, and on the other by land of Joseph Le Bœuf.

It appears that the claimant did actually inhabit and cultivate the land now claimed on the 20th December, 1803, and that the same was continually inhabited and cultivated by her, or those under whom she claims, for more than ten consecutive years next preceding. Confirmed.

No. 213.—PIERRE GUICHO claims a tract of land, situate on Fausse river, in the county of Pointe Coupée, containing three arpents front, and forty in depth, and bounded on one side by land of Honoré Fabre, and on the other by land of Francis Lebeau.

It appears that the claimant did actually inhabit and cultivate the land now claimed on the 20th December, 1803, and that the same was continually inhabited and cultivated by him, or those under whom he claims, for more than ten consecutive years next preceding. Confirmed.

No. 214.—JEAN BAPTISTE GUIDROS claims a tract of land, situate on Fausse river, in the county of Pointe Coupée, containing three arpents front, and forty in depth, and bounded on one side by land of E. Lardoin, and on the other by land of Joseph Le Bœuf.

It appears that the land now claimed was inhabited and cultivated on the 20th December, 1803, and that the same was continually inhabited and cultivated by the claimant, or those under whom he holds, for more than ten consecutive years next preceding. Confirmed.

No. 215.—JOSEPH SAINT CYR claims a tract of land, situate on Fausse river, in the county of Pointe Coupée, containing four arpents front and forty in depth, and bounded on one side by land of Louis David, and on the other by land of Pierre Guicho.

It appears that the claimant did actually inhabit and cultivate the land now claimed on the 20th December, 1803, and that the same was continually inhabited and cultivated by him, or those under whom he claims, for more than ten consecutive years next preceding. Confirmed.

No. 216.—PIERRE BERGERON, Sen. claims a tract of land, situate on Fausse river, in the county of Pointe Coupée, containing four and a half arpents front, and forty in depth, and bounded on one side by land of Julian Poydras, and on the other by land of Samuel Young.

This being part of a tract of land to which Benjamin Farrar had obtained a complete title from the Spanish Government. Confirmed.

No. 217.—PIERRE BERGERON, Sen. claims a tract of land, situate on Fausse river, in the county of Pointe Coupée, containing eight and a half arpents in front, and forty in depth, and bounded on one side by land of —— and on the other by land of ——.

It appears that the claimant did actually inhabit and cultivate the land now claimed on the 20th December, 1803, and that the same was continually inhabited and cultivated by him, or those under whom he claims, for more than ten consecutive years next preceding. Confirmed.

No. 218.—MADAME P. LATOUR claims a tract of land, situate on the river Mississippi, in the county of Pointe Coupée, and containing three arpents front, forty in depth, and bounded on one side by land of Julian Poydras, and on the other by land of Madame St. Eloy.

It appears that the claimant did actually inhabit and cultivate the land now claimed on the 20th December, 1803, and that the same was continually inhabited and cultivated by him, or those under whom he claims, for more than ten consecutive years next preceding. Confirmed.

No. 220.—LOUIS BERGERON claims a tract of land, situate on Fausse river, in the county of Pointe Coupée, containing two arpents front, and forty in depth, and bounded one side by land of Baptiste Guidros, and on the other by land of Julian Poydras.

This is part of a tract of land to which Benjamin Farrar had obtained a complete title from the Spanish Government; under which title the claimant holds. Confirmed.

No. 221.—JOSEPH BERGERON claims a tract of land, situate on Fausse river, in the county of Pointe Coupée, containing two arpents front, and forty in depth, and bounded on one side by land of Hyacinthe Schits, and on the other by land of Julian Poydras.

This is part of a tract of land to which Benjamin Farrar had obtained a complete title from the Spanish Government; under which title the claimant holds. Confirmed.

No. 222.—JOSEPH BRESA claims a tract of land, situate on Fausse river, in the county of Pointe Coupée, containing four arpents front, and forty in depth, and bounded on one side by land of Joseph Janes, and on the other by land of Madame Bara.

This tract of land having been inhabited and cultivated on and before the 1st of October, 1800, and having continued to be inhabited and cultivated until on and after the 20th December, 1803. Confirmed.

No. 223.—PIERRE LAURENT claims a tract of land, situate on the river Mississippi, in the county of Pointe Coupée, containing six arpents front, and forty in depth, and bounded on one side by land of Madame Beauvais, and on the other by land of Simon Croiset.

It appears that the land now claimed was inhabited and cultivated on the 20th December, 1803, and that the same was continually inhabited and cultivated by those under whom the claimant holds for more than ten consecutive years next preceding. Confirmed.

No. 224.—GEORGE ANDRE claims a tract of land, situate on Fausse river, in the county of Pointe Coupée, containing six arpents front, and forty in depth, and bounded on one side by land of J. Chessé, and on the other by land of M. Vitrois.

This land having been inhabited and cultivated on and before the 1st of October, 1800, and having continued to be inhabited and cultivated until on and after the 20th December, 1803. Confirmed.

No. 228.—GEORGE POCK claims a tract of land, situate on Fausse river, in the county of Pointe Coupée, containing eight arpents front, and forty in depth, and bounded one side by land of Francis Sampson, and on the other by land of Pierre Carmouche.

It appears that the claimant did actually inhabit and cultivate the land now claimed on the 20th December, 1803, and that the same was continually inhabited and cultivated by him, or those under whom he claims, for more than ten consecutive years next preceding. Confirmed.

No. 229.—JOSEPH PIERRE GUIDROS claims a tract of land, situate on Fausse river, in the county of Pointe Coupée, containing two arpents front, and forty in depth, and bounded on one side by land of Pierre Bergeron, and on the other by land of Julian Poydras.

This is part of a tract of land to which Benjamin Farrar obtained a complete title from the Spanish Government; under which title the claimant holds. Confirmed.

No. 230.—NARCISSE CARMOUCHE claims a tract of land, situate on Fausse river, in the county of Pointe

Coupée, containing two arpents in front, and forty in depth, and bounded on one side by land of Augustin Pock, and on the other by land of the claimant.

This land having been inhabited and cultivated on and before the 1st of October, 1800, and having continued to be inhabited and cultivated until on and after the 20th December, 1803. Confirmed.

No. 231.—JOSEPH PORCHE claims a tract of land, situate on Fausse river, in the county of Pointe Coupée, containing two arpents front, and forty in depth, and bounded on one side by land of George Pock, and on the other by land of Louis Langlois.

This land having been inhabited and cultivated on and before the 1st of October, 1800, and having continued to be inhabited and cultivated on and after the 20th December, 1803. Confirmed.

No. 232.—FRANCIS LEGROS claims a tract of land, situate on Fausse river, in the county of Pointe Coupée, containing six arpents front, and forty in depth, and bounded on one side by land of Madame Janes, and on the other by land of Joseph Janes.

This land having been inhabited and cultivated on and before the 1st of October, 1800, and having continued to be inhabited and cultivated until on and after the 20th December, 1803. Confirmed.

No. 233.—FRANCIS MAYEUX claims a tract of land, situate in the county of Pointe Coupée, containing five arpents and eight perches front, and forty arpents in depth, and bounded on one side by land of Madame Descuir, and on the other by land of S. Lacour.

It appears that the claimant did actually inhabit and cultivate the land now claimed on the 20th December, 1803, and that the same was continually inhabited and cultivated by him, or those under whom he claims, for more than ten consecutive years next preceding. Confirmed.

No. 234.—MARGARITA BARON, widow of J. P. Ladoux, claims a tract of land, situate on the river Mississippi, in the county of Pointe Coupée, containing eight arpents front, and forty in depth, and bounded on one side by land of Jean Baptiste Descuir, and on the other by land of Charles Dufour.

It appears that the claimant did actually inhabit and cultivate the land now claimed on the 20th December, 1803, and that the same was continually inhabited and cultivated by her, or those under whom she claims, for more than ten consecutive years next preceding. Confirmed.

No. 235.—ETIENNE ARDOINE claims a tract of land, situate on the Fausse river, in the county of Pointe Coupée, containing three arpents front, and forty in depth, and bounded on each side by lands of Jean Baptiste Saizan.

This land having been inhabited and cultivated on and before the 1st of October, 1800, and the same having continued to be inhabited and cultivated until on and after the 20th December, 1803. Confirmed.

No. 236.—Madame J. ECOFFIE claims a tract of land, situate on Fausse river, in the county of Pointe Coupée, containing ten arpents front, and forty in depth, and bounded on one side by land of Demeiselle P. Merieau, and on the other by land of George André.

It appears that the claimant did actually inhabit and cultivate the land now claimed on the 20th December, 1803, and that the same was continually inhabited and cultivated by her, or those under whom she claims, for more than ten consecutive years next preceding. Confirmed.

No. 237.—JOSEPH JANES claims a tract of land, situate on the Fausse river, in the county of Pointe Coupée, containing three arpents front, and forty in depth, and bounded on one side by land of Francis Legros.

This land having been inhabited and cultivated on and before the 1st of October, 1800, and the same having continued to be inhabited and cultivated until on and after the 20th December, 1803. Confirmed.

No. 238.—CHARLES EDMOND claims a tract of land, situate on Fausse river, in the county of Pointe Coupée, containing four arpents front, and forty in depth, and bounded on one side by land of Joseph Bergeron, and on the other by land of Julian Poydras.

This land being part of a tract of land to which Benjamin Farrar had obtained a complete title from the

Spanish Government, under which title the claimant holds. Confirmed.

No. 239.—JEAN BAPTISTE BERGERON, Jun. claims a tract of land, situate on Fausse river, in the county of Pointe Coupée, containing four arpents front, and forty in depth, and bounded on one side by land of Jacques Jarreau, and on the other by land of Pierre Bergeron, Sen.

This is part of a tract of land to which Benjamin Farrar obtained a complete title from the Spanish Government; under which title the claimant holds. Confirmed.

No. 240.—FRANCIS GREMILLON claims a tract of land, situate on the river Mississippi, in the county of Pointe Coupée, containing seven arpents in front; to four of said arpents he claims a depth of eighty arpents, and the ordinary depth of forty arpents to the remaining three front arpents; the said land being bounded on one side by land of Mr. Bellager, and on the other by land of Mr. Carmouche.

It appears that the claimant did actually inhabit and cultivate the seven arpents front, and forty deep, of the land now claimed, on the 20th December, 1803, and for more than ten consecutive years prior to that date; and it appears, also, that he obtained an order of survey for a double concession to four of the front arpents claimed, from Governor Miro, in the year 1785. Confirmed.

No. 241.—FRANCIS GUICHO claims a tract of land, situate on Fausse river, in the county of Pointe Coupée, containing two arpents front, and forty in depth, and bounded on one side by land of J. B. Bergeron, and on the other by land of Sesain Olinde.

This land is part of a tract to which Benjamin Farrar obtained a complete title; under which title the claimant holds. Confirmed.

No. 242.—MICHEL LEJEUNE Sen. claims a tract of land, situate on Fausse river, in the county of Pointe Coupée, containing five arp:nts front, and forty in depth, and bounded on one side by land of Charles Lejeune, and on the other by land of John L'Abbé.

It appears that the claimant did actually inhabit and cultivate the land now claimed on the 20th December, 1803, and that the same was continually inhabited and cultivated by him, or those under whom he claims, for more than ten consecutive years next preceding. Confirmed.

No. 243.—MICHEL LEJEUNE, Sen. claims a tract of land, situate on Fausse river, in the county of Pointe Coupée, containing five arpents front, and forty in depth, and bounded on one side by land of Madame Lejeune, and on the other by land of Joseph Ennet.

It appears that the claimant did actually inhabit and cultivate the land now claimed on the 20th December, 1803, and that the same was continually inhabited and cultivated by him, or those under whom he claims, for more than ten consecutive years next preceding. Confirmed.

No. 244.—JOSEPH ANDRE claims a tract of land, situate on Fausse river, in the county of Pointe Coupée, containing six arpents front, and forty in depth, and bounded on one side by land of Martin Taudrique, and on the other by land of J. B. Legros.

It appears that the claimant did actually inhabit and cultivate the land now claimed on the 20th December, 1803, and that the same was continually inhabited and cultivated by him, or those under whom he claims, for more than ten consecutive years next preceding. Confirmed.

No. 245.—JOSEPH ANDRE claims a tract of land, situate on Fausse river, in the county of Pointe Coupée, containing three arpents front, and forty in depth, and bounded on one side by land of Hebert David, and on the other by land of Baptiste Guidros.

It appears that the land now claimed was inhabited and cultivated on the 20th December, 1803, and that the same was continually inhabited and cultivated by those under whom the claimant holds for more than ten consecutive years next preceding. Confirmed.

No. 246.—AUGUSTINA MARIONNEAUX, wife of Daniel Filoux, claims a tract of land, situate on Fausse river, in the county of Pointe Coupée containing one arpent and a half in front, and forty arpents in depth, and bounded on one side by land of Marie J. Marionneaux, and on the other by land of Madame Bellanger.

It appears that the land claimed was inhabited and cultivated on the 20th December, 1803, and that the same was continually inhabited and cultivated by those under whom the claimant holds for more than ten consecutive years next preceding. Confirmed.

No. 247.—JEAN PIERREBERGERON, Jun. claims a tract of land, situate on Fausse river, in the county of Pointe Coupée, containing four arpents in front, and forty in depth, and bounded on one side by land of Pierre Bergeron, Sen., and on the other by land of Jean Baptiste Bergeron.

This land is part of a tract of land to which Benjamin Farrar obtained a complete title; under which the claimant holds. Confirmed.

No. 248.—PIERRE OLINDE claims a tract of land, situate on Fausse river, in the county of Pointe Coupée, containing three arpents in front, and forty in depth, and bounded on one side by land of Joseph Descuir, and on the other by land of Jacques Jarreau.

This land is part of a tract of land to which Benjamin Farrar obtained a complete title; under which the claimant holds. Confirmed.

No. 249.—FRANCIS LEMAY claims a tract of land, situate on Fausse river, in the county of Pointe Coupée, containing two arpents front, and forty in depth, and bounded on one side by land of Pierre Olinde, and on the other by land of J. Jarreau.

This land is part of a tract of land to which Benjamin Farrar obtained a complete title; under which the claimant holds. Confirmed.

No. 250.—GEORGE SAIZAN claims a tract of land, situate on Fausse river, in the county of Pointe Coupée, containing three arpents in front, and forty in depth, and bounded on one side by land of Etienne Bergeron, and on the other by land of Francis Lemay.

This is a part of a tract of land to which Benjamin Farrar obtained a complete title; under which title the claimant holds. Confirmed.

No. 251.—GUILLAUME GUERIN claims a tract of land, situate on Fausse river, in the county of Pointe Coupée, containing three arpents front, and forty in depth, and bounded on one side by land of Alexis Lebeau, and on the other by land of Francis G. Saizan.

This land is part of a tract to which Benjamin Farrar obtained a complete title; under which the claimant holds. Confirmed.

No. 252.—ALEXIS LEBEAU claims a tract of land, situate on Fausse river, in the county of Pointe Coupée, containing three and a half arpents front, and forty arpents in depth, and bounded on one side by land of Etienne Bergeron, and on the other by land of J. Jarreau.

This land is part of a tract to which Benjamin Farrar obtained a complete title; under which title the claimant holds. Confirmed.

No. 253.—ETIENNE MAJOR, as guardian to the heirs of George Olivot, claims a tract of land, situate on Fausse river, in the county of Pointe Coupée, containing six arpents front, and forty in depth, and bounded on one side by land of Cesair Olinde, and on the other by land of Alexis Lebeau.

This land is part of a tract of land to which Benjamin Farrar obtained a complete title; under which title the claimant holds. Confirmed.

No. 254.—CESAIR OLINDE claims a tract of land, situate on Fausse river, in the county of Pointe Coupée, containing six arpents front, and forty in depth, and bounded on one side by land of George Olivot, and on the other by land of Antoine Nicolas.

This land is part of a tract to which Benjamin Farrar obtained a complete title; under which title the claimant holds. Confirmed.

No. 255.—ANTOINE NICOLAS claims a tract of land, situate on Fausse river, in the county of Pointe Coupée, containing two arpents front, and forty in depth, and bounded on one side by land of Cesair Olinde, and on the other by land of Baptiste Bergeron.

This land is part of a tract to which Benjamin Farrar obtained a complete title; under which title the claimant holds. Confirmed.

No. 256.—CATHARINE MOREAU, widow of Henry Legrange, claims a tract of land, situate on Fausse river, in the county of Pointe Coupée, containing four arpents in front, and forty in depth, and bounded on one side by land of Pierre St. Pierre, and on the other by land of Julian Poydras.

This land is part of a tract to which Benjamin Farrar obtained a complete title; under which title the claimant holds. Confirmed.

No. 258.—MARIE TUNOIR, widow of ——— Jarreau, claims a tract of land, situate in the county of Pointe Coupée, containing fifteen arpents front, and forty in depth, and bounded on one side by land of Augustin Allain, and on the other side by land of Madame Françoise Allain.

It appears that the land now claimed was inhabited and cultivated on the 20th December, 1803, and that the same was continually inhabited and cultivated by those under whom the claimant holds for more than ten consecutive years next preceding. Confirmed.

No. 259.—MARIE PARCIEAU, widow of Charles Robillard, claims a tract of land, situate on Fausse river, in the county of Pointe Coupée, containing five and a half arpents front, and forty arpents in depth, and bounded on one side by land of Etienne Major, and on the other by land of Mr. Goregés.

It appears that the claimant did actually inhabit and cultivate the land now claimed on the 20th December, 1803, and that the same was continually inhabited and cultivated by her, or those under whom she claims, for more than ten consecutive years next preceding. Confirmed.

No. 260.—BAPTISTE OLINDE claims a tract of land, situate on Fausse river, in the county of Point Coupée, containing two arpents front, and forty in depth, and bounded on one side by land of Pierre Bergeron, Sen., and on the other by land of Hyacinthe Schits.

It appears that the land now claimed was inhabited and cultivated on the 20th December, 1803, and that the same was continually inhabited and cultivated by those under whom the claimant holds for more than ten consecutive years next preceding. Confirmed.

No. 261.—MADAME BELLANGER claims a tract of land, situate on Fausse river, in the county of Pointe Coupée, containing three arpents front, and forty in depth, and bounded on one side by land of Mr. St. Eloy, and on the other by land of Julian Poydras.

It appears that the claimant did actually inhabit and cultivate the land now claimed on the 20th December, 1803, and that the same was continually inhabited and cultivated by her, or those under whom she claims, for more than ten consecutive years next preceding. Confirmed.

No. 262.—JOSEPH ST. CYR, Jun. claims a tract of land, situate on Fausse river, in the county of Pointe Coupée, containing two arpents front, and forty in depth, and bounded on one side by land of Hyacinthe Schits, and on the other by land of Joseph St. Cyr, Sen.

This land is part of a tract to which Benjamin Farrar obtained a complete title; under which title the claimant holds. Confirmed.

No. 263.—ALEXANDRE LEBLANC claims a tract of land, situate on the river Mississippi, in the county of Pointe Coupée, containing twenty-three and a half arpents front, and forty arpents in depth, and bounded on one side by land of Augustin Allain, and on the other by land of ———.

It appears that the claimant did actually inhabit and cultivate the land now claimed on the 20th December, 1803, and that the same was continually inhabited and cultivated by him, or those under whom he claims, for more than ten consecutive years next preceding. Confirmed.

No. 264.—GEORGE MATURIN claims a tract of land, situate on Fausse river, in the county of Pointe Coupée, containing four arpents in front, and forty in depth, and bounded on one side by land of ———, and on the other by land of ———.

It appears that the claimant did actually inhabit and cultivate the land now claimed on the 20th December, 1803, and that the same was continually inhabited and cultivated by him, or those under whom he claims, for more than ten consecutive years next preceding. Confirmed.

No. 265.—JOSEPH ST. CYR claims a tract of land, situate on Fausse river, in the county of Pointe Coupée,

containing two arpents front, and forty in depth, and bounded on one side by land of Louis Bergeron, and on the other by land of Julian Poydras.

This land is part of a tract of land to which Benjamin Farrar obtained a complete title; under which title the claimant holds. Confirmed.

No. 266.—PHILIP ROBILLARD claims a tract of land, situate on Fausse river, in the county of Pointe Coupée, containing four arpents and seventy-nine feet front, and forty arpents in depth, and bounded on one side by land of Pierre Olinde, and on the other by land of Cesair Gausseraud.

It appears that the land claimed was inhabited and cultivated on the 20th December, 1803, and that the same was continually inhabited and cultivated by the claimant, or those under whom he holds, for more than ten consecutive years next preceding. Confirmed.

No. 267.—CHARLES HEBERT claims a tract of land, situate on the west side of the river Mississippi, in the county of Iberville and district of Baton Rouge, containing four arpents in front, and forty in depth, and bounded on one side by land of Jean Baptiste Hebert, and on the other by land of Maturin Doyron.

It appears that the claimant did actually inhabit and cultivate the land now claimed on the 20th December, 1803, and that the same was continually inhabited and cultivated by him, or those under whom he claims, for more than ten consecutive years next preceding. Confirmed.

No. 268.—PETER LAVARU claims a tract of land, situate on the west side of the river Mississippi, in the county of Iberville and district of Baton Rouge, containing two arpents front, and forty in depth, and bounded on one side by land of Valery Bergeron, and on the other by land of Pierre Lardoin.

It appears that the land now claimed was inhabited and cultivated on the 20th December, 1803, and that the same was continually inhabited and cultivated by those under whom the claimant holds for more than ten consecutive years next preceding. Confirmed.

No. 270.—PAULAIN ALLAIN claims a tract of land, situate on the west side of the river Mississippi, in the county of Pointe Coupée, containing twenty-three and a half arpents front, and forty in depth, and bounded on one side by land of Mr. Patin, and on the other by land of Julian Poydras.

It appears that the claimant did actually inhabit and cultivate the land now claimed on the 20th December, 1803, and that the same was continually inhabited and cultivated by him, or those under whom he claims, for more than ten consecutive years next preceding. Confirmed.

No. 271.—MADAME PATIN, widow of Alexander Patin, claims a tract of land, situate on the river Mississippi, in the county of Iberville and district of Baton Rouge, containing fourteen arpents front, and forty in depth, and bounded on one side by land of Charles Templet, and on the other by land of Charles Broussard.

This tract of land was surveyed in the year 1794, in favor of Adam Boyd, who, in the same year, obtained a complete grant for the same from the Baron de Carondelet, then Governor; under which title the claimant holds. Confirmed.

No. 273.—PEDRO GAUDREAU claims a tract of land, situate on the river Mississippi, in the county of Iberville and district of Baton Rouge, containing three arpents front, and forty in depth, and bounded on one side by land of Peter Huiress, and on the other by land of Francis Broussard.

It appears that the claimant did actually inhabit and cultivate the land now claimed on the 20th December, 1803, and that the same was continually inhabited and cultivated by him, or those under whom he claims, for more than ten consecutive years next preceding. Confirmed.

No. 274.—THOMAS COURTIN claims a tract of land, situate on the west side of the river Mississippi, in the county of Iberville and district of Baton Rouge, containing three arpents front, and forty in depth, and bounded on one side by land of Felix Bernard, and on the other by land of Felix Bernard.

It appears that the claimant did actually inhabit and cultivate the land now claimed on the 20th December, 1803, and that the same was continually inhabited and

No. 275.—PETER SERVANT claims a tract of land, situate on the west side of the river Mississippi, in the county of Iberville and district of Baton Rouge, containing three arpents front, and forty in depth, and bounded on one side by land of Thomas Ayet, and on the other by land of Jacques Maison.
It appears that the land now claimed was inhabited and cultivated on the 20th December, 1803, and that the same was continually inhabited and cultivated by those under whom the claimant holds for more than ten consecutive years next preceding. Confirmed.

No. 276.—VALERIAN ALLAIN claims a tract of land, situate on the west side of the river Mississippi, in the county of Iberville and district of Baton Rouge, containing nine arpents front, and forty in depth, and bounded on one side by land of Julian Poydras, and on the other by land of Gregoire Lejeune.
It appears that the land now claimed was inhabited and cultivated on the 20th December, 1803, and that the same was continually inhabited and cultivated by those under whom the claimant holds for more than ten consecutive years next preceding. Confirmed.

No. 278.—ELI HEBERT claims a tract of land, situate on the river Mississippi, in the county of Iberville and district of Baton Rouge, containing three arpents front, and forty in depth, and bounded on one side by land of Pedro Hebert, and on the other by land of Santiago Arnandez.
It appears that the claimant did actually inhabit and cultivate the land now claimed on the 20th December, 1803, and that the same was continually inhabited and cultivated by him, or those under whom he claims, for more than ten consecutive years next preceding. Confirmed.

No. 279.—PAUL HUBEAU claims a tract of land, situate on the west side of the river Mississippi, in the county of Iberville and district of Baton Rouge, containing six arpents front, and forty in depth, and bounded on one side by land of —— Degrass, and on the other by land of Pierre Farrat.
It appears that the claimant did actually inhabit and cultivate the land now claimed on the 20th December, 1803, and that the same was continually inhabited and cultivated by him, or those under whom he claims, for more than ten consecutive years next preceding. Confirmed.

No. 280.—JOSEPH GRANGER claims a tract of land, situate on the west side of the river Mississippi, in the county of Iberville and district of Baton Rouge, containing three arpents front, and forty in depth, and bounded on one side by land of Germain Magloire, and on the other by land of Felix Doumontier.
It appears that the claimant did actually inhabit and cultivate the land now claimed on the 20th December, 1803, and that the same was continually inhabited and cultivated by him, or those under whom he claims, for more than ten consecutive years next preceding. Confirmed.

No. 281.—FRANCIS SEGUIN claims a tract of land, situate on the west side of the river Mississippi, in the county of Iberville, containing four arpents front, and forty in depth, and bounded on one side by land of Jean Marie Trahan, and on the other by land of Thomas Courtin.
It appears that the claimant did actually inhabit and cultivate the land now claimed on the 20th December, 1803, and that the same was continually inhabited and cultivated by him, or those under whom he claims, for more than ten consecutive years next preceding. Confirmed.

No. 282.—HENRY COLLAIN claims a tract of land, situate on the river Mississippi, in the county of Iberville, containing four and a half arpents front, and forty in depth, and bounded on one side by land of Baptiste Borsel, and on the other by land of Mr. Blanchard.
It appears that the claimant did actually inhabit and cultivate the land now claimed on the 20th December, 1803, and that the same was continually inhabited and cultivated by him, or those under whom he claims, for more than ten consecutive years next preceding. Confirmed.

No. 283.—JEAN BAPTISTE CORNEAU claims a tract of land, situate on the west side of the river Mississippi, in the county of Iberville, containing three arpents front, and forty in depth, and bounded on one side by land of Pierre Quisbedeaux, and on the other by land of Thomas Lilly.
It appears that the claimant did actually inhabit and cultivate the land now claimed on the 20th December, 1803, and that the same was continually inhabited and cultivated by him, or those under whom he claims, for more than ten consecutive years next preceding. Confirmed.

No. 284.—JEAN BAPTISTE BOISSEL claims a tract of land, situate on the river Mississippi, in the county of Iberville, containing six arpents front, and forty in depth, and bounded on one side by land of Joseph Baure, and on the other by land of Joseph Granger.
The claimant having obtained a permission from the proper Spanish officer, and a regular warrant of survey from the Governor of the province, in the year 1794, for the land now claimed, and having continued to inhabit and cultivate the same until on and after the 20th December, 1803. Confirmed.

No. 288.—CHRISTOPHE ARTACHE claims a tract of land, situate on the west side of the river Mississippi, in the county of Iberville and district of Baton Rouge, containing two arpents front, and forty in depth, and bounded on one side by land of Alexandre d'Aigle, and on the other by land of Isidore Lebaure.
It appears that the land now claimed was inhabited and cultivated on the 20th December, 1803, and that the same was continually inhabited and cultivated by those under whom the claimant holds for more than ten consecutive years next preceding. Confirmed.

No. 289.—BERNARD FERRARY claims a tract of land, situate on the west side of the river Mississippi, in the county of Iberville and district of Baton Rouge, containing two and a half arpents front, and forty in depth, and bounded on one side by land of Francis Broussard, and on the other by land of Louis Dubardeau.
It appears that the land now claimed was inhabited and cultivated on the 20th December, 1803, and that the same was continually inhabited and cultivated by those under whom the claimant holds for more than ten consecutive years next preceding. Confirmed.

No. 290.—MADAME CHLATRE, widow of Jacob Chlatre, claims a tract of land, situate on the river Mississippi, in the county of Iberville, containing six arpents front, and forty in depth, and bounded on one side by land of Jacob Chlatre, and on the other by the bayou Placquemines.
The husband of the claimant obtained a regular warrant of survey for the land now claimed, in the year 1795, from the Governor of the province; which was executed, in the year 1802, by the Surveyor General of the province, and a complete grant was issued in the same year, in her name, by the Intendant: she has continued to reside on the same since the time of obtaining the warrant of survey. It is the opinion of the Board that, according to the usages and customs of the Spanish Government, the claim ought to be confirmed.

No. 291.—GEORGE PERRIN claims a tract of land, situate on the west side of the river Mississippi, in the county of Iberville, containing seven arpents front, and forty in depth, and bounded on one side by land of Joseph Vahamonde, and on the other by land of Michel Mahier.
It appears that the land now claimed was inhabited and cultivated on the 20th December, 1803, and that the same was continually inhabited and cultivated by those under whom the claimant holds for more than ten consecutive years next preceding. Confirmed.

No. 292.—JEAN BAPTISTE LEBLANC claims a tract of land, situate on the river Mississippi, in the county of Iberville, containing four arpents one toise and one foot front, and forty arpents in depth, and bounded on one side by land of Eli Hebert, and on the other by land of Charles Hebert.
This is part of a tract of land to which Jean Baptiste Dupuy obtained a complete title, in the year 1774; from which the claimant derives his title. Confirmed.

No. 294.—ALEXANDRE D'AIGLE claims a tract of land, situate on the river Mississippi, in the county of Iberville and district of Baton Rouge, containing two arpents front, and forty in depth, and bounded on one side by land of Simon Babin, and on the other by land of Christophe Artache.

It appears that the land now claimed was inhabited and cultivated on the 20th December, 1803, and that the same was continually inhabited and cultivated by him, or those under whom the claimant holds, for more than ten consecutive years next preceding. Confirmed.

No. 295.—BERNARD DAUTERIVE claims a tract of land, situate on the west side of the river Mississippi, in the county of Iberville and district of Manchack, containing seven arpents and two toises front, and forty arpents in depth, and bounded on one side by land of Joseph M. Landry, and on the other by land of Blas Rivet.

It appears that the land now claimed was inhabited and cultivated on the 20th December, 1803, and that the same was continually inhabited and cultivated by the claimant, or those under whom he holds, for more than ten consecutive years next preceding. Confirmed.

No. 299.—PIERRE ALLAIN claims a tract of land, situate on the west side of the river Mississippi, in the county of Pointe Coupée, containing six arpents and two perches front, and forty arpents in depth, and bounded on one side by land of Marie Trahan, and on the other by land of Hypolite Mallet.

It appears that the land now claimed was inhabited and cultivated on the 20th December, 1803, and that the same was continually inhabited and cultivated by those under whom the claimant holds for more than ten consecutive years next preceding. Confirmed.

No. 304.—PIERRE HENRY claims a tract of land, situate on the west side of the river Mississippi, in the county of Iberville and district of Baton Rouge, containing three arpents front, and forty in depth, and bounded on one side by land of Thomas Courtin, and on the other by land of Peter Guideau.

It appears that the claimant did actually inhabit and cultivate the land now claimed on the 20th December, 1803, and that the same was continually inhabited and cultivated by him, or those under whom he claims, for more than ten consecutive years next preceding. Confirmed.

No. 305.—JAMES BLANCHARD, JOHN LONGUE-EPEE, and JOSEPH BRAND claim a tract of land, situate on the river Mississippi, in the county of Iberville and district of Baton Rouge, containing ten arpents front, and forty in depth, and bounded on one side by land of Anselmo Blanchard, and on the other by land of Francis d'Aigle.

This claim is founded upon a complete grant made by the Spanish Governor in favor of Ambrose Terriot, in the year 1787; under which title the claimants hold. Confirmed.

No. 306.—MICHEL GARDE claims a tract of land, situate on the river Mississippi, in the county of Iberville, containing two arpents front, and forty in depth, and bounded on one side by land of Charles Hebert, and on the other by land of Nicholas de Verbois.

It appears that the claimant did actually inhabit and cultivate the land now claimed on the 20th December, 1803, and that the same was continually inhabited and cultivated by him, or those under whom he claims, for more than ten consecutive years next preceding. Confirmed.

No. 307.—MICHEL GARRELL claims a tract of land, situate on the east side of the river Mississippi, in the county of Iberville, containing two arpents front, and forty in depth, and bounded on one side by land of Paul Hebert, and on the other by land of Narcisse Hebert.

It appears that the land now claimed was inhabited and cultivated by those under whom the claimant holds for more than ten consecutive years next preceding. Confirmed.

No. 310.—SIMON LANDRY claims a tract of land, situate on the east side of the river Mississippi, in the county of Iberville, containing four arpents and twenty-seven toises front, and forty arpents in depth, and bounded on one side by land of Pierre Rivet, and on the other by land of Paul Hebert.

It appears that the land now claimed was inhabited and cultivated on the 20th December, 1803, and that the same was continually inhabited and cultivated by those under whom the claimant holds for more than ten consecutive years next preceding. Confirmed.

No. 314.—ALEXANDRE LANDRY claims a tract of land, situate on the west side of the river Mississippi, in the county of Iberville, containing five arpents nine toises and three feet front, and eighty arpents in depth, and bounded on one side by land of Pierre Rivet, and on the other by land of Paul Hebert, Jun.

It appears that the claimant did actually inhabit and cultivate the first forty arpents in depth now claimed on the 20th December, 1803, and that the same was continually inhabited and cultivated for more than ten consecutive years prior to that period. The Board confirm the claim to the extent of forty arpents in depth, but reject the balance.

No. 316.—JEAN FRANCHBOIS claims a tract of land, situate on the river Mississippi, in the county of Iberville, containing eight arpents front, and eighty in depth, and bounded on one side by land of Pierre Brand, and on the other by land of A. Rodrigues.

It appears that the claimant continually inhabited and cultivated the first forty arpents in depth for more than ten consecutive years prior to the 20th December, 1803; and that he obtained an order of survey for the second depth of forty arpents, in the year 1784, from the Spanish Governor. Confirmed.

No. 317.—WILLIAM FLOOD claims a tract of land, situate on the river Mississippi, in the county of Iberville, containing twelve arpents front, and forty in depth, and bounded on one side by land of Julian Bienville, and on the other by land of William Wikoff.

This claim is founded upon a complete grant obtained by Nicholas Bellanger from the Spanish Governor, in the year 1776; under which grant the claimant holds. Confirmed.

No. 318.—JAMES MATHER, by his agent William Wikoff, claims a tract of land, situate on the river Mississippi, in the county of Iberville and district of Baton Rouge, containing eight arpents front, and eighty in depth, and bounded on one side by land of Felix Bernard, and on the other by land of Joisine Escalin.

It appears that forty arpents in depth of the land now claimed were inhabited and cultivated on the 20th December, 1803, and for more than ten consecutive years prior to that period, by those under whom the claimant holds. The Board confirm the claim to the extent of forty arpents depth, but reject the balance.

No. 322.—ALEXANDRE DARDEN claims a tract of land, situate in the county of Iberville, and on the bayou Placquemines, containing four hundred and forty superficial arpents, and bounded by vacant lands.

This tract of land was surveyed in favor of the claimant, in the year 1795, who obtained a complete grant to the same in 1796, from the Baron de Carondelet, then Governor. Confirmed.

No. 329.—PIERRE RIVET claims a tract of land, situate on the east side of the river Mississippi, in the county of Iberville, containing six arpents one toise and five feet front, and forty arpents in depth, and bounded on one side by land of Joseph Leblanc, and on the other by land of Simon Landry.

It appears that the claimant did actually inhabit and cultivate the land now claimed on the 20th December, 1803, and that the same was continually inhabited and cultivated by him, or those under whom he claims, for more than ten consecutive years next preceding. Confirmed.

No. 330.—NARCISSE HEBERT claims a tract of land, situate on the east side of the river Mississippi, in the county of Iberville, containing four arpents and twenty-seven toises front, and forty arpents in depth, and bounded on one side by land of Michel Garell, and on the other by land of Alexandre Hebert.

It appears that the land now claimed was inhabited and cultivated on the 20th December, 1803, and that the same was continually inhabited and cultivated by those under whom the claimant holds for more than ten consecutive years next preceding. Confirmed.

No. 331.—WILLIAM WIKOFF, in behalf of the parishioners of the parish church of Manchack, claims a tract of land belonging to the said church, and situate on the river Mississippi, in the county of Iberville, containing one hundred and one and seventy-three hundredths superficial arpents, and bounded on one side by land of Oliver Blanchard, and on the other by land of Joseph Dupuy.

This claim is founded upon a complete grant made in the year 1774, in favor of the parish church of Manchack, of ten arpents twenty toises and four feet front, on the depth of forty arpents. Confirmed.

No. 334.—THERESA HAMILTON claims a tract of land, situate on the river Mississippi, in the county of Iberville, containing three and a half arpents front, and eighty in depth, and bounded on one side by land of Santiago Leblanc, and on the other by land of Leonard Alos.

It appears that the present claimant did actually inhabit and cultivate the land now claimed on the 20th December, 1803, and that the same, to the full extent of eighty arpents in depth, was, by permission of the proper Spanish officer, continually inhabited and cultivated by those under whom the present claimant holds for more than ten consecutive years next preceding. Confirmed.

No. 335.—MADAME LEONARD, widow of Louis Leonard, claims a tract of land, situate on the river Mississippi, in the county of Iberville, containing six and a half arpents front, and eighty arpents in depth, and bounded on one side by land of Francis Marion, and on the other by land of Philip Roth.

The claimant having inhabited and cultivated the first depth of forty arpents of the land claimed on the 20th December, 1803, and for ten consecutive years prior to that period, the Board confirm the claim to that extent; and she having been put in possession of the second depth by the Surveyor General, in the year 1801, by order of the Intendant, it is the opinion of the Board that, according to the usages and customs of the Spanish Government, the claim to the second depth ought to be confirmed: provided it be considered by the Government of the United States that the Intendant General had a right to dispose of public lands subsequent to the 1st day of October, 1800.

No. 336.—PIERRE BRAND claims a tract of land, situate on the river Mississippi, in the county of Iberville, containing four arpents and four toises front, and forty arpents in depth, and bounded on one side by land of Louis Nero, and on the other by land of Paul and Magloire Dupuy.

This is part of a tract of land of seven arpents four toises and two feet front, and forty arpents in depth, for which Joseph Landry obtained a complete grant in the year 1772. Confirmed.

No. 340.—JOHN VARNARD claims a tract of land, situate on the river Mississippi, in the county of Iberville and district of Baton Rouge, containing two arpents front, and forty in depth, and bounded on one side by land of Louis Dubardeau, and on the other by land of Louis Marion.

It appears that the land now claimed was inhabited and cultivated on the 20th December, 1803, and that the same was continually inhabited and cultivated by those under whom the claimant holds for more than ten consecutive years next preceding. Confirmed.

No. 341.—JEAN BAPTISTE HEBERT claims a tract of land, situate on the river Mississippi, in the county of Iberville and district of Baton Rouge, containing twelve arpents front, and forty in depth, and bounded by vacant lands.

The claimant having obtained from the Governor of the province, in the year 1795, a regular warrant of survey for the land he now claims, and having actually resided on and cultivated the same on the 20th December 1803. Confirmed.

No. 344.—JOSEPH DEVILLIERS claims a tract of land, situate on the river Mississippi, in the county of Iberville, containing five arpents front, and forty in depth, and bounded on one side by the bayou Placquemines, and on the other by land of Antoine Rodrigues. This is a tract of land for which Joseph Macho obtained a complete grant from the Spanish Governor of the province, in the year 1774; under which grant the claimant holds. Confirmed.

No. 359.—JEAN LOUIS DARDENNES claims a tract of land, situate on the bayou Placquemines, in the county of Iberville, containing three hundred and twenty superficial arpents, and bounded on one side by land of Xavier Robichaux, and on the other by vacant land.

This is tract of land for which there was an order of survey in the year 1795, in favor of the claimant, who obtained a complete grant for the same from the Governor of the province in the year 1796. Confirmed.

No. 362.—PIERRE LAURENS claims a tract of land, situate on Fausse river, in the county of Pointe Coupée, containing twenty arpents front, and forty in depth, and bounded on one side by land of Julian Poydras, and on the other by land of Benjamin Farrar.

This is part of a tract of land to which Benjamin Farrar obtained a complete grant; under which the claimant holds. Confirmed.

No. 371.—ELLEN RUSS claims a tract of land, situate on Fausse river, in the county of Pointe Coupée, containing eighty superficial arpents, and bounded on one side by land of Jean Jones, and on the other by land of Joseph Baudgard.

It appears that the claimant did actually inhabit and cultivate the land now claimed on the 20th December, 1803, and that the same was continually inhabited and cultivated by her, or those under whom she claims, for more than ten consecutive years next preceding. Confirmed.

No. 374.—ANTHONY DAUTERIVE claims a tract of land, situate on the river Mississippi, in the county of Iberville, containing six arpents front, and forty in depth, and bounded on one side by land of Santiago Larche, and on the other by land of Joseph Miguel.

It appears that the claimant obtained a regular warrant of survey to said tract of land in the year 1796, from the Governor of this province, and that he did actually inhabit and cultivate the same on the 20th December, 1803, and for some time prior to that period. Confirmed.

No. 379.—PIERRE MOREAU claims a tract of land, situate on Fausse river, in the county of Pointe Coupée, containing one arpent front, and forty arpents in depth, and bounded on one side by land of Etienne Ardoin, and on the other by land of Madame Escofié.

It appears that the claimant did actually inhabit and cultivate the land now claimed on the 20th December, 1803, and that the same was continually inhabited and cultivated by him, or those under whom he claims, for more than ten consecutive years next preceding. Confirmed.

No. 382.—JEAN FRANCHBOIS claims a tract of land, situate on the river Mississippi, in the county of Iberville, containing two arpents front, and forty in depth, and bounded on one side by land of Augustin Richard, and on the other by land of the claimant.

It appears that the claimant did actually inhabit and cultivate the land now claimed on the 20th December, 1803, and that the same was continually inhabited and cultivated by him, or those under whom he claims, for more than ten consecutive years next preceding. Confirmed.

No. 5.—DOMINIC DE VERBOIS claims a tract of land, situate on the east side of the river Mississippi, in the county of Iberville, containing six hundred superficial arpents, and bounded on the upper side by the bayou Manchack.

This land having been inhabited and cultivated on and before the 1st of October, 1800, and having continued to be inhabited and cultivated until on and after the 20th December, 1803: Confirmed.

No. 24.—JOSEPH MOLLERE claims a tract of land, situate on the west side of the river Mississippi, in the county of Iberville, containing eight hundred superficial arpents, and bounded on the upper side by land of Helena Soileau, and on the lower by vacant land.

It appears that Antoine Blanchard, deceased, under whose title the claimant holds, obtained a regular order of survey from Governor Gayoso, in the year 1798, for this land, and that the same was continually inhabited and cultivated on the 1st day of October, 1800. Confirmed.

No. 26.—ANNE BRUNTEAU claims a tract of land, situate on the west side of the river Mississippi, in the county of Iberville, containing six arpents twenty-seven toises and two feet in front, and forty arpents in depth, and bounded on the upper side by land of Nicholas Rousseau, and on the lower by land of Michel Lambremont.

It appears that the claimant did actually inhabit and cultivate the land now claimed on the 20th December, 1803, and that the same was continually inhabited and cultivated by her, or those under whom she claims for more than ten consecutive years next preceding. Confirmed.

No. 38.—EMANUEL LANDRY claims a tract of land, situate on the west side of the river Mississippi, in the county of Iberville, containing four arpents in front, and forty in depth, and bounded on the upper side by land of Jean Prospère, and on the lower by land of William Cunningham.

This land having been inhabited and cultivated on and before the 1st day of October 1800, and having continued to be inhabited and cultivated until on and after the 20th December, 1803: Confirmed.

No. 203.—SIMON CROISET claims a tract of land, situate on the river Mississippi, in the county of Pointe Coupée, containing eight arpents in front, and forty in depth, and bounded on one side by land of Mr. Darquilon.

It appears that the land now claimed was inhabited and cultivated on the 20th December, 1803, and for more than ten consecutive years next preceding. Confirmed.

No. 205.—SIMON CROISET claims a tract of land, situate on the river Mississippi, in the county of Pointe Coupée, containing sixteen arpents in front, and forty in depth, and bounded on one side by land of Nicolas Lacour.

It appears that the land now claimed was inhabited and cultivated on the 20th December, 1803, and for more than ten consecutive years next preceding. Confirmed.

No. 210.—JEAN BAPTISTE BEAUVAIS claims a tract of land, situate on the river Mississippi, in the county of Pointe Coupée, containing nine arpents in front, and forty in depth, and bounded on the upper side by land of ——, and on the lower by land of ——.

It appears that the land now claimed was inhabited and cultivated on the 20th December, 1803, and that the same was continually inhabited and cultivated by the claimant, or those under whom he claims, for more than ten consecutive years next preceding. Confirmed.

No. 226.—Madame PIERRE DESCUIR claims a tract of land, situate on the river Mississippi, in the county of Pointe Coupée, containing five arpents in front, and forty in depth.

It appears that the land now claimed was inhabited and cultivated on the 20th December, 1803, and for more than ten consecutive years next preceding. Confirmed.

No. 269.—ANDREW ACHEMAN claims a tract of land, situate on the bayou Jacques, in the county of Iberville, containing one hundred and forty-four and fifty-three hundredths superficial acres, and bounded on one side by land of Antoine Langlos, and on the other by land of P. Langlos.

It appears that the land now claimed was inhabited and cultivated on and before the 1st day of October, 1800; and having continued to be inhabited and cultivated until on and after the 20th December, 1803: Confirmed.

No. 285.—WILLIAM CUNNINGHAM claims a tract of land, situate on the west side of the river Mississippi, in the county of Iberville containing eight arpents in front, and forty in depth, and bounded on one side by land of Joseph Landry.

It appears that the land now claimed was inhabited and cultivated on the 20th December, 1803, and that the same was continually inhabited and cultivated by those under whom the claimant holds for more than ten consecutive years next preceding. Confirmed.

No. 293.—THOMAS LILLY claims a tract of land, situate on the west side of the river Mississippi, in the county of Iberville, containing twenty arpents in front, and forty in depth, and bounded on one side by land of Jean Bte. Comeau, and on the other by land of Mr. Robin.

This land was surveyed for François Poinsett, in the year 1785, and, in the year 1786, he obtained a complete grant for the same from Governor Miro; the present claimant holds under said grant, by virtue of successive transfers. Confirmed.

No. 296.—MATHURIN LANDRY claims a tract of land, situate on the west side of the river Mississippi, in the county of Iberville, containing seven arpents in front, and eighty in depth, and bounded on one side by land of Pierre Lebert, and on the other by land of Xavier Landry.

It appearing that the land was inhabited and cultivated on the 20th December, 1803, and for more than ten con-

secutive years next preceding, the Board confirm the title to the extent of forty arpents in depth, and reject the claim to the balance.

No. 297.—OLIVIER LEBLANC claims a tract of land, situate on the river Mississippi, in the county of Iberville, containing five arpents in front, and forty in depth, and bounded on the upper side by land of Antonio Barbara, and on the lower by land of Joseph Bourge.

It appears that the claimant did actually inhabit and cultivate the land now claimed on the 20th December, 1803, and that the same was continually inhabited and cultivated by him, or those under whom he claims, for more than ten consecutive years next preceding. Confirmed.

No. 300.—JEAN BAPTISTE HEBERT claims a tract of land, situate on the west side of the river Mississippi, in the county of Iberville, containing five hundred and seventy-four and sixty-five hundredths superficial acres, and bounded on one side by land of Alexis Hebert, and on the other by land of Charles Hebert.

It appearing that the land now claimed was inhabited and cultivated on the 20th December, 1803, and for more than ten consecutive years prior, the Board confirm the title to the quantity of superficial acres contained in the ordinary depth of forty arpents, and reject the claim as to the balance.

No. 301.—WILLIAM CUNNINGHAM claims a tract of land, situate on the west side of the river Mississippi, in the county of Iberville, containing three hundred and sixteen and fifty-six hundredths superficial acres, and bounded on one side by land of Andrew Martin, and on the other by land of T. Babin.

It appears that the land now claimed was inhabited and cultivated on the 20th December, 1803, and that the same was continually inhabited and cultivated by the claimant, or those under whom he claims, for more than ten consecutive years next preceding. Confirmed.

No. 302.—FRANCIS DUPLESIS claims a tract of land, situate on the west side of the river Mississippi, in the county of Iberville, containing four arpents in front, and forty in depth, and bounded on one side by land of Peter Paillard, and on the other by land of Francis Seguin.

It appears that the land now claimed was inhabited and cultivated on the 20th December, 1803, and that the same was continually inhabited and cultivated by those under whom the claimant holds for more than ten consecutive years next preceding. Confirmed.

No. 303.—PIERRE LEBAURE claims a tract of land, situate on the west side of the river Mississippi, in the county of Iberville, containing five arpents in front, and forty in depth, and bounded on one side by land of Moses Forest, and on the other by land of Daniel Benoit.

It appears that the land now claimed was inhabited and cultivated on the 20th December, 1803, and that the same was continually inhabited and cultivated by the claimant, or those under whom he claims, for more than ten consecutive years next preceding. Confirmed.

No. 308.—ALEXANDRE LANCLOS claims a tract of land, situate on the bayou Jacques, in the county of Iberville, containing four arpents seven and a half toises in front, and forty arpents in depth, and bounded on one side by land of Amerant Lanclos, and on the other by land of Vital Rivet.

This land having been inhabited and cultivated on and before the 1st day of October, 1800, and having continued to be inhabited and cultivated until on and after the 20th day of December, 1803. Confirmed.

No. 309.—NARCISSE HEBERT claims a tract of land, situate on the river Mississippi, in the county of Iberville, containing four arpents in front, and forty arpents in depth, and bounded on the upper side by land of Armant Hebert, and on the lower by land of Pierre Hebert.

It appears that the land now claimed was inhabited and cultivated on the 20th December, 1803, and that the same was continually inhabited and cultivated by those under whom the claimant holds for more than ten consecutive years next preceding. Confirmed.

No. 315.—VICTOR HEBERT claims a tract of land, situate on the west side of the river Mississippi, in the county of Iberville, containing two hundred and ninety-two superficial acres, and bounded on the upper side by land of Jean Doyron, and on the lower by land of Jean Templette.

It appearing that this land was inhabited and cultivated on the 20th December, 1803, and for more than ten consecutive years prior, the Board confirm the title to the quantity of superficial acres contained in the ordinary depth of forty arpents, and reject the claim as to the balance.

No. 326.—Estevan Hebert claims a tract of land, situate in the county of Iberville, containing two hundred and twenty-three and eighty hundredths superficial acres, and bounded on one side by land of Joseph Dupuis, and on the other by land of John Almon.

This land having been inhabited and cultivated on and before the 1st day of October, 1800, and having continued to be inhabited and cultivated on and after the 20th of December, 1803. Confirmed.

No. 327.—Henry Vige claims a tract of land, situate on the bayou Placquemines, in the county of Iberville, containing seven arpents in front, and forty arpents in depth, and bounded on the upper side by land of André Langlois, and on the lower by land of Pierre Collaire.

It appearing to the satisfaction of the Board that this land was settled, by permission of the proper Spanish officer, prior to the 20th day of December, 1803, and that the same was actually inhabited and cultivated on that day. Confirmed.

No. 332.—Henry Vige claims a tract of land, situate on the bayou Placquemines, in the county of Iberville, containing four arpents and four feet in front, and forty arpents in depth, and bounded on one side by land of Honorato Leonard.

It appearing to the satisfaction of the Board that André Langlois, from whom the present claimant purchased, settled this land, by permission of the proper Spanish officer, prior to the 20th December, 1803, and that the same was actually inhabited and cultivated on that day. Confirmed.

No. 337.—Pierre Lebaure claims a tract of land, situate on the west side of the river Mississippi, in the county of Iberville, containing three hundred and thirty-seven and fifty-six hundredths superficial acres, and bounded on one side by land of Delaide Legendre.

It appears that the claimant did actually inhabit and cultivate the land now claimed on the 20th of December, 1803, and for more than ten consecutive years next preceding. Confirmed.

No. 338.—Joachim Escallain claims a tract of land, situate on the west side of the river Mississippi, in the county of Iberville, containing two arpents in front, and forty arpents in depth, and bounded on one side by land of James Mather, and on the other by land of Joseph Vahamonde.

It appearing that the land now claimed was inhabited and cultivated on the 20th December, 1803, and for more than ten consecutive years prior, the Board confirm the title to the extent of the first forty arpents in depth, and reject the claim to the second depth of forty arpents.

No. 339.—Francis Broussard claims a tract of land, situate on the west side of the river Mississippi, in the county of Iberville, containing three arpents in front, and forty arpents in depth, and bounded on one side by land of Peter Godeau, and on the other by land of Felicity Bernard.

It appears that the claimant did actually inhabit and cultivate the land now claimed on the 20th December, 1803, and for more than ten consecutive years next preceding. Confirmed.

No. 342.—William Wikoff, Jun. claims a tract of land, situate on the bayou of Manchack, in the county of Iberville, containing twelve arpents in front, and ten arpents in depth, and bounded on one side by land of William Spain.

It appears that the land now claimed was inhabited and cultivated on the 20th December, 1803, and that the same was continually inhabited and cultivated by the claimant, or by those under whom he claims, for more than ten consecutive years next preceding. Confirmed.

No. 343.—William Wikoff, Jun., as administrator to the estate of Richard Werge, deceased, claims a tract of land, situate on the bayou of Manchack, in the coun-

ty of Iberville, containing five arpents in front, and forty arpents in depth.

It appears that the land now claimed was inhabited and cultivated on the 20th December, 1803, and for more than ten consecutive years next preceding. Confirmed.

No. 346.—Jacques de Villiers claims a tract of land, situate on the west side of the river Mississippi, in the county of Iberville, containing four arpents in front, and forty arpents in depth, and bounded on the upper side by land of Diego Arnandez, and on the lower by land of Amant Hebert.

It appearing to the satisfacton of the Board that this land was settled by permission of the proper Spanish officer, prior to the 20th December, 1803, and that the same was actually inhabited and cultivated on that day: Confirmed.

No. 348.—Jean Baptiste Dupuis claims a tract of land, situate on the west side of the river Mississippi, in the county of Iberville, containing four arpents in front, and forty arpents in depth, and bounded on the upper side by land of ———, and on the lower by land of ———.

It appears that the land now claimed was inhabited and cultivated on the 20th December, 1803, and for more than ten consecutive years next preceding. Confirmed.

No. 351.—Athanas Darden claims a tract of land, situate on the bayou Placquemines, in the county of Iberville, containing ten arpents in front, and forty arpents in depth, and bounded on one side by land of Joseph Orillion, and on the other by vacant land.

This land having been inhabited and cultivated on and before the 1st day of October, 1800, and having continued to be inhabited and cultivated until on and after the 20th day of December, 1803: Confirmed.

No. 358.—Felicien Escalain claims a tract of land, situate on the west side of the river Mississippi, in the county of Iberville, containing four arpents in front, and forty arpents in depth, and bounded on one side by land of Mr. Vernard, and on the other by land of Archibald Brooks.

There is an order of survey for this land from Governor Miro, in the year 1789, in favor of Claude Delatre, under whose title the present claimant holds; and the land having been actually inhabited and cultivated on the 1st day of October, 1800: Confirmed.

No. 361.—Jacques Pasqual claims a tract of land, situate on the west side of the river Mississippi, in the county of Iberville, containing sixty-six and ninety hundredths superficial acres, and bounded on one side by land of Charles Robert, and on the other by land of Jean Bte. Moutchas.

It appears that the land now claimed was inhabited and cultivated by the claimant, or those under whom he claims, for more than ten consecutive years next preceding. Confirmed.

No. 347.—Archibald Brooks claims a tract of land, situate on the west side of the river Mississippi, in the county of Iberville, containing three hundred superficial arpents, and bounded on one side by land of Louis Marion, and on the other by land of Richard Reutard.

It appears that the land now claimed was inhabited and cultivated on the 20th December, 1803, and that the same was continually inhabited and cultivated by those under whom the claimant holds for more than ten consecutive years next preceding. Confirmed.

No. 352.—David C. Hatch claims the following lots of ground, situate in Galveztown, in the county of Iberville, viz: a lot of a quarter of an arpent, designated on a plan of said town by the letter O; also another lot of half an arpent, designated on said plan by the letters P and Q; also one other lot of a quarter of an arpent, designated by the letter R; also one other lot of a quarter of an arpent, designated by the letter S, and bounded on one side by the common; also one other lot of a quarter of an arpent, designated by the letter N.

It appearing that the aforesaid lots of ground were inhabited and cultivated on and before the 1st day of October, 1800, and that the same continued to be inhabited and cultivated until on and after the 20th day of December, 1803: Confirmed.

No. 354.—Frederick H. Summer claims the following lots of ground, situate in Galveztown, in the county of Iberville, viz: four lots, containing each a quarter of an arpent, and designated on a plan of said town by the letters A, B, C, and D; also two other lots of a quarter of an arpent each, and designated on said plan by the letters E and F; also one other lot of a quarter of an arpent, designated by the letter G; also one other lot of a quarter of an arpent, designated by the letter K ; also one other lot of a quarter of an arpent, designated by the letter I.

It appearing that the aforesaid lots of ground were inhabited and cultivated on and before the 1st day of October, 1800, and that the same continued to be inhabited and cultivated until on and after the 20th day of December, 1803: Confirmed.

No. 364.—JAMES SMITH YARBOROUGH claims a lot of ground, situate in Galveztown, in the county of Iberville, and being No. 4.

It appearing that the aforesaid lot of ground, was inhabited and cultivated on and before the 1st day of October, 1800, and that the same continued to be inhabited and cultivated until on and after the 20th day of December, 1803: Confirmed.

No. 365.—JAMES SMITH YARBOROUGH claims a tract of land, situate on the bayou of Manchack, in the county of Iberville, containing two hundred superficial arpents, and bounded on one side by land of John Tilano, and on the other by vacant land.

This land was surveyed in the year 1794, by Carlos Trudeau, Surveyor General, in favor of Joseph Ramirez, from whom the present claimant purchased; and the same having been inhabited and cultivated ever since the above period, until on and after the 20th December, 1803: Confirmed.

No. 366.—THOMAS COURTIN claims a tract of land, situate on the west side of the river Mississippi, in the county of Iberville, containing six arpents in front, and forty arpents in depth.

It appears that the claimant did actually inhabit and cultivate the land now claimed on the 20th December, 1803, and for more than ten consecutive years next preceding. Confirmed.

No. 373.—JAMES DE VILLIERS claims a tract of land, situate on the east side of the river Mississippi, in the county of Iberville, containing ten arpents in front, and forty arpents in depth, and bounded on the upper side by land of George T. Ross, and on the lower by land of Jean Bte. Degruis.

It appears that the claimant obtained from the Spanish Government a regular warrant of survey for this land in the year 1796; and the same having been inhabited and cultivated ever since that time, until on and after the 20th December, 1803: Confirmed.

No. 383.—WILLIAM WIKOFF, Jun. claims a lot of ground, situate in Galveztown, in the county of Iberville.

It appearing to the satisfaction of the Board that the claimant was put in possession of the aforesaid lot by the proper Spanish officer, prior to the 20th day of December, 1803, and that the same was continually inhabited and cultivated on that day: Confirmed.

No. 277.—LOUIS ALLAIZ claims a tract of land, situate on the west side of the river Mississippi, in the county of Iberville, containing four hundred superficial acres, and bounded on the upper side by land of Michel Mahier, and on the lower by land of ———— Bossell.

This land having been inhabited and cultivated on and before the 1st day of October, 1800, and having continued to be inhabited and cultivated until on and after the 20th day of December, 1803: Confirmed.

No. 353.—FREDERICK H. SUMMER claims three different tracts of land, situate in the county and parish of Iberville, as follows, to wit: a tract lying in the neighborhood of Galveztown, and containing one hundred and twenty superficial arpents, and bounded on the east by land of José Capitaine, on the west by land of Matthias Martin, and on the north and south by other lands; also, a tract lying in the neighborhood of Galveztown, containing eighty superficial arpents, and bounded northerly by land of Fabien Ramos, southerly by vacant lands, east by land of Joseph Delpino, and west by land of José Capitaine; also, a tract fronting on the river Amite, containing two hundred superficial arpents, and bounded on the upper side by Galveztown.

It appears to the satisfaction of the Board that the several persons, under whose titles the present claimant holds the aforesaid tracts of land now claimed, did actually inhabit and cultivate the said tracts on and before the 1st day of October, 1800, and that the same continued to be inhabited and cultivated until on and after the 20th day of December, 1803. Confirmed.

No. 355.—STEPHEN H. HOPKINS claims a tract of land, situate in the parish and county of Iberville, and containing two hundred and eighty superficial arpents.

This land having been inhabited and cultivated on and before the 1st of October, 1800, and having continued to be inhabited and cultivated until on and after the 20th day of December, 1803: Confirmed.

No. 356.—HYPOLITE LANDRY claims the following parcels of land, to wit: a lot of land, situate in the county and parish of Iberville, on the bayou St. Bernard, near Galveztown, containing sixteen superficial arpents, and bounded on one side by land of Joseph Parcird; also a lot of ground, situate in Galveztown, containing a superficies of half an arpent, fronting on the commons of said town, and designated on a plan of the same by the letters L and M; also a tract of land, situate in the county and parish aforesaid, in the neighborhood of Galveztown, and containing eighty superficial arpents.

It appearing that the above-mentioned lots and tract of land were inhabited and cultivated by the several persons under whose titles the present claimant holds on and before the 1st day of October, 1800, and that they continued to be inhabited and cultivated until on and after the 20th day of December, 1803: Confirmed.

No. 380.—JOSEPH VARGE VAHAMONDE claims a tract of land, situate on the west side of the river Mississippi, in the county of Iberville, containing fourteen arpents six perches and three feet in front, and eighty arpents in depth, and bounded on the upper side by land of ————, and on the lower by land of Madame Ayet.

The claimant having been put in possession of the first depth of forty arpents of this land, in the year 1798, by the Surveyor General of the province, and having continued to inhabit and cultivate the land ever since that period, the Board confirm the claim to that extent; and he having obtained a grant for the second depth of forty arpents from the Intendant General of the province, in the year 1802, the Board are of opinion that his claims ought to be confirmed, provided it be considered by the Government of the United States that the Intendant General had a right to dispose of public lands subsequent to the 1st October, 1800.

No. 324.—ANTOINE LANCLOS, Sen. claims a tract of land, situate on the bayou Jacques, in the county of Iberville, containing seven arpents in front, and forty arpents in depth, and bounded on one side by land of André Acheman, and on the other by land of Antoine Lanclos, Senior.

This is part of a tract of thirty-five arpents front, with forty in depth, purchased by the claimant of the Chitimachas Indians, in the year 1801, and a deed of sale regularly passed in the same year from said Indians, by their chiefs, to the claimant, before Rivas, the commandant of the district, under the written authority of the Intendant General of the province; which land the claimant has since sold to divers individuals, except the part now claimed by him; and it further appears that the part now claimed was inhabited and cultivated by the claimant on the 20th December, 1803; we are therefore of opinion that his claim ought to be confirmed, provided it be considered by the Government of the United States that the Intendant General had a right to dispose of public lands subsequent to the 1st day of October, 1800.

No. 313.—VITAL RIXET claims a tract of land, situate on the bayou Jacques, in the county of Iberville, containing four arpents and sixteen and a half toises in front, and forty arpents in depth, and bounded on the upper side by land of Antoine Lanclos, Jun., and on the lower by land of ————.

This is part of the tract of land purchased of the Indians, by Antoine Lanclos, Sen. as stated in his claim, No. 324, under which title the claimant holds; and it moreover appears that the land was inhabited and cultivated on the 20th December, 1803.

No. 319.—FRANCIS NERO claims a tract of land, situate on the bayou Jacques, in the county of Iberville, containing four arpents and seven and a half toises in front, and forty arpents in depth, and bounded on the upper side by vacant land, and on the lower by land of Antoine Lanclos, Sen.

This is part of the tract of land purchased of the Indians by Antoine Lanclos, Sen., as stated in his claim, No. 324, under which title the present claimant holds ; and it appears that the land was inhabited and cultivated on the 20th December, 1803.

No. 323.—ANTOINE LANCLOS, Jun. claims a tract of land, situate on the bayou Jacques, in the county of Iberville, containing four arpents and seven and a half toises in front, and forty arpents in depth, and bounded on one side by land of Antoine Lanclos, Sen., and on the other by land of Vital Rixet.

This is part of the tract of land purchased of the Indians by Antoine Lanclos, Sen., as stated in his claim, No. 324, under which title the claimant holds; and it appears that the land was inhabited and cultivated on the 20th December, 1803.

No. 328.—AMERANT LANCLOS claims a tract of land, situate on the bayou Jacques, in the county of Iberville, containing four arpents eleven toises one foot and a half in front, and forty arpents in depth, and bounded on one side by land of Alexandre Lanclos, and on the other by land of Lussin Lanclos.

This is part of the tract of land purchased of the Indians by Antonio Lanclos, Sen., as stated in his claim, No. 324, under which title the claimant holds; and it appears that the now claimed was inhabited and cultivated on the 20th December, 1803.

No. 333.—LUSSIN LANCLOS claims a tract of land, situate on the bayou Jacques, in the county of Iberville, containing four arpents eleven toises and one foot and a half in front, and forty arpents in depth, and bounded on the upper side by land of Amerant Lanclos and on the lower by land of Felix Brand.

This is part of the tract of land purchased of the Indians by Antoine Lanclos, Sen., as stated in his claim, No. 324, under which title the present claimant holds ; and it appears that the land was inhabited and cultivated on the 20th December, 1803.

No. 381.—JEAN BAPTISTE HEBERT claims a tract of land, situate on the west side of the river Mississippi, in the county of Iberville, containing nine arpents in front, and twenty-four in depth.

The claimant was put in possession of this land, conformably to an order (see page 301) of the Baron de Carondelet, in the year 1792; and having complied with the conditions thereof, to wit, making the road and levee, has become entitled to the land. Confirmed.

No. 349.—JOHN DRAUGHAN claims a tract of land, situate near Galveztown, in the county of Iberville, (the quantity not specified,) and adjoining on one side land of Adam Sides.

It appearing that the land now claimed was settled, with the permission of the proper Spanish officer, prior to the 20th December, 1803, and that the same was actually inhabited and cultivated by those under whom the present claimant holds on that day, the Board confirm the claim to the quantity of six hundred and forty acres, to be laid off with a front of sixteen acres, and a depth of forty.

P. GRYMES, R. E. D. Orl. Ter.
THOMAS B. ROBERTSON.

Decisions of the Board of Commissioners for the eastern district of the Territory of Orleans, on land claims registered in the books of Achille Trouard, Deputy Register for the county of German Coast.

No. 1.—LEONARD PERILLON claims a tract of land, situate in the county of German Coast, about thirteen leagues above the city of New Orleans, on the left bank of the Mississippi, containing five arpents six toises and four feet in front, by the depth of eighty arpents, bounded by lands of Baptiste Peritton on the one side, and by those of Francis Noel Dupont on the other.

It appears that the first forty arpents of said land were purchased at a judicial sale made of it in the year 1785, and that, for the second depth, the claimant obtained from Governor Estevan Miro a complete grant, dated the 8th June, 1787. Confirmed.

No. 2.—MICHEL LISCHE claims a tract of land, situate in the county of German Coast, on the left bank of the Mississippi, containing five arpents in front, by forty in depth, bounded on one side by land of Jago Leitche, and on the other by land of Pedro Anchepetre.

It appears that the said land was inhabited and cultivated on the 20th December, 1803, and that the same was continually inhabited and cultivated by those under whom the claimant derives his title for more than ten consecutive years prior thereto. Confirmed.

No. 3.—PIERRE MARIE CABARET D'ETREPY claims a tract of land, situate in the county of German Coast, containing fifteen arpents eleven toises and nine links, on the left bank of the river Mississippi, with an extension of depth to the lake.

It appears that the front, by forty arpents in depth, of said land, was inhabited and cultivated on the 20th December, 1803, and that the same was continually inhabited and cultivated by those under whom the claimant derives his title for more than ten consecutive years prior to that period; it appears, also, that the claimant obtained from Unxaga, then Governor of the province, on the 26th September, 1777, a concession of the second depth, claimed as aforesaid. Confirmed.

No. 4.—MADAME MAYER, widow of Philip Mayer, claims a tract of land, situate on the west side of the river Mississippi, in the county of German Coast, containing two arpents in front, and forty in depth, and bounded on the upper side by land of —— and on the lower by land of ——.

This is part of a tract of land of three arpents front, on the usual depth of forty, surveyed for Michel Arcenaux in the year 1776, and sold by him to the husband of the claimant in 1783; and it appears that the land has been inhabited and cultivated ever since the last-mentioned period, until on and after the 20th December, 1803. Confirmed.

No. 5.—ANTOINE TREIGNER claims a tract of land, situate on the west side of the river Mississippi, in the county of German Coast, containing five arpents in front, and forty in depth, and bounded on the upper side by land of Michael Arcenaux, and on the lower by land of David Rhom.

It appears that the claimant did actually inhabit and cultivate the land now claimed on the 20th December, 1803, and for more than ten consecutive next preceding. Confirmed.

No. 6.—MADAME MILLET claims a tract of land, situate on the west side of the river Mississippi, in the county of German Coast, containing five and a half arpents in front, and sixty-one arpents in depth, and bounded on the upper side by land of Pablo Obert, and on the lower by land of the heirs of —— Rhom, deceased.

It appears that the depth of forty arpents of the land now claimed was inhabited and cultivated on the 20th December, 1803, and that the same was continually inhabited and cultivated by the claimant, or those under whom she claims, for more than ten consecutive years next preceding. The Board confirm the claim to the extent of the first depth of forty arpents, but reject it as to the balance of twenty-one arpents depth.

No. 7.—ANTOINE MORIN claims a tract of land, situate on the west side of the river Mississippi, in the county of German Coast, containing four arpents twenty toises and two feet[in front, and forty arpents in depth, and bounded on the upper side by land of George Schneller, and on the lower by land of Jean Louis Balsoms.

It appears that the land claimed was inhabited and cultivated on the 20th December, 1803, and that the same was continually inhabited and cultivated by the claimant, or those under whom he claims, for more than ten consecutive years next preceding. Confirmed.

No. 8.—JOSEPH LAMORA claims a tract of land, situate on the west side of the river Mississippi, in the county of German Coast, containing six arpents and fifty-three feet in front, and forty arpents in depth, and bounded on the upper side by land of ——, and on the lower by land of ——.

It appears that the land now claimed was inhabited and cultivated on the 20th December, 1803, and that the same was continually inhabited and cultivated by the claimant, or those under whom he claims, for more than ten consecutive years next preceding. Confirmed.

No. 9.—JACQUES LEISCHE claims a tract of land, situate on the east side of the river Mississippi, in the county of German Coast, containing five arpents in front, and forty in depth, and bounded on the upper side by land o

Francisco Leische, and on the lower by land of Miguel Leische.

This land was surveyed by Don Carlos Trudeau, in the year 1785, for the claimant, who has continued to inhabit and cultivate the same ever since that period, until on and after the 20th December, 1803. Confirmed.

No. 10.—JACQUES LAGROVE claims a tract of land, situate on the west side of the river Mississippi, in the county of German Coast, containing four arpents in front, and forty in depth and bounded on the upper side by land of Jean Charles Rodrigues, and on the lower by land of Joseph Pichof.

This land was surveyed in the year 1776, in favor of Antoine Seiche, and has, ever since that period, been inhabited and cultivated; the present claimant now holds it under the title of said Antoine Seiche, by regular deeds. Confirmed.

No. 11.—PIERRE MARMILLON claims a tract of land, situate on the west side of the river Mississippi, in the county of German Coast containing twelve arpents in front, and forty in depth.

It appears that the claimant did actually inhabit and cultivate the land now claimed on the 20th December, 1803, and that the same was continually inhabited and cultivated by him, or those under whom he claims, for more than ten consecutive years next preceding. Confirmed.

No. 12.—GEORGE SEXNAITRE claims a tract of land, situate on the west side of the river Mississippi, in the county of German Coast, containing three arpents nine toises and four feet in front, and forty arpents in depth, and bounded on the upper side by land of Juan Robert, and on the lower by land of Juan de Lavilheuve.

It appears that the claimant did actually inhabit and cultivate the land now claimed on the 20th December, 1803, and for more than ten consecutive years next preceding. Confirmed.

No. 13.—JEAN ROBERT claims a tract of land, situate on the west side of the river Mississippi, in the county of German Coast, containing one arpent and a half and twelve feet in front, and forty arpents in depth, and bounded on the upper side by land of Pierre Faucheux, and on the lower by land of André Sexnaitre.

It appears that this land was inhabited and cultivated on the 20th December, 1803, and that the same was continually inhabited and cultivated by those under whom the claimant holds for more than ten consecutive years next preceding. Confirmed.

No. 14.—MICHEL CAMBER claims a tract of land, situate on the east side of the river Mississippi, in the county of German Coast, containing nineteen arpents in front, and eighty arpents in depth, and bounded on the upper side by land of Francisco Noel Dupont, and on the lower by land of Jacob Christian.

This land was surveyed in the year 1791, in favor of the claimant, who obtained a complete grant for the same in the same year from Don Estevan Miro, then Governor. Confirmed.

No. 15.—JEAN NOEL DESTREHAN claims a tract of land, situate on the east side of the river Mississippi, in the county of German Coast, containing twenty-eight arpents in front, of which six have a depth of one hundred and twenty arpents, and the remaining twenty-two arpents a depth extending to the lake.

The six arpents front, with the depth of one hundred and twenty arpents of this land, were granted in the year 1759 to Claude Renaudin; the balance, twenty-two arpents front, and extending in depth to the lake, was granted to Jean Baptiste Garie, in the year 1766. Under said grants the present claimant holds, in virtue of successive sales. Confirmed.

No. 16.—ANDRE HYMEL claims a tract of land, situate on the west side of the river Mississippi, in the county of German Coast, containing six arpents in front, and forty in depth, and bounded on the upper side by land of Madame Myettes, and on the lower by land of Madame Hautin.

It appears that the claimant did actually inhabit and cultivate the land now claimed on the 20th December, 1803, and that the same was continually inhabited and cultivated by him, or those under whom he claims, for more than ten consecutive years next preceding. Confirmed.

No. 17.—ANDRE HYMEL claims a tract of land, situate on the west side of the river Mississippi, in the county of German Coast, containing sixteen arpents in front, and forty arpents in depth.

It appears that the land now claimed was inhabited and cultivated on the 20th December, 1803, and that the same was continually inhabited and cultivated by the claimant, or those under whom he claims, for more than ten consecutive years next preceding. Confirmed.

No. 18.—JEAN BAPTISTE LABATUT claims a tract of land, situate on the west side of the river Mississippi, in the county of German Coast, containing ten arpents in front, and forty in depth, and bounded on the upper side by land of François Weber, and on the lower by land of Antoine Folse.

It appears that the land now claimed was inhabited and cultivated on the 20th December, 1803, and that the same was continually inhabited and cultivated by those under whom the claimant holds for more than ten consecutive years next preceding. Confirmed.

No. 19.—MADAME PAUL AUBERT claims a tract of land, situate on the west side of the river Mississippi, in the county of German Coast, containing three arpents and four toises in front, and forty arpents in depth, and bounded on the upper side by land of George Hymel, and on the other by land of Jean Mayer.

This land was surveyed in the year 1781 for Paul Aubert, the claimant's husband, and has been inhabited and cultivated ever since, until on and after the 20th December, 1803. Confirmed.

No. 20.—JEAN FOLSE claims a tract of land, situate on the east side of the river Mississippi, in the county of German Coast, containing seven arpents and seven toises in front, and forty arpents in depth, and bounded on the upper side by land of Pierre Becuelle, and on the lower by land of André Lasseigne.

It appears that the land now claimed was inhabited and cultivated on the 20th December, 1803, and that the same was continually inhabited and cultivated by those under whom the claimant holds for more than ten consecutive years next preceding. Confirmed.

No. 21.—JACQUES CLEMENT claims a tract of land, situate on the east side of the river Mississippi, in the county of German Coast, containing two arpents in front, and forty in depth, and bounded on the upper side by land of Daniel Materu, and on the lower by land of Adam Vicuer.

It appears that this land was actually inhabited and cultivated on the 20th December, 1803, and that the same was continually inhabited and cultivated by those under whom the claimant holds for more than ten consecutive years next preceding. Confirmed.

No. 22.—ALEXANDRE LABRANCHE claims a tract of land, situate on the east side of the river Mississippi, in the county of German Coast, containing thirty-five arpents and a half in front; twenty-five and a half of which have a depth of one hundred arpents, and the remaining ten front arpents a depth of forty arpents.

It appears that the ten arpents in front, on the ordinary depth here claimed, were inhabited and cultivated on the 20th December, 1803, and for more than ten consecutive years prior; and it also appears that the remaining twenty-five and a half front arpents, with the ordinary depth of forty arpents, were inhabited and cultivated on the 20th December, 1803, and for more than ten consecutive years prior; and that, in the year 1801, there was a concession for a second depth of sixty arpents to the aforesaid twenty-five and a half front arpents. Confirmed.

No. 23.—ALEXANDRE LABRANCHE claims a tract of land, situate on the east side of the river Mississippi, in the county of German Coast, containing fifteen arpents in front, and a depth extending back to the lake, and bounded on the upper side by land of ———, and on the lower by land of ———.

It appearing that the land now claimed was inhabited and cultivated on the 20th December, 1803, and for more than ten consecutive years prior, the Board confirm the claim to the extent of the first forty arpents in depth, and reject it as to the balance.

No. 24.—ANDRE TREIGLE claims a tract of land, situate on the east side of the river Mississippi, in the county of German Coast, containing four arpents ten toises and two feet in front, and eighty arpents in depth, and bounded on the upper side by land of Pedro San-souci, and on the lower by land of Theodore Treigle.

This is part of a tract of land of eight arpents twenty toises and four feet in front, and eighty arpents depth; the first depth of forty arpents of which has been inhabited and cultivated for more than ten consecutive years prior to the 20th December, 1803; and the second depth of forty arpents was granted to the father of the claimant, in the year 1780. Confirmed.

No. 25.—THEODORE TREIGLE claims a tract of land, situate on the east side of the river Mississippi, in the county of German Coast, containing four arpents ten toises and two feet in front, and eighty arpents in depth, and bounded on the upper side by land of André Treigle, and on the lower by land of Jean Treigle.

This is part of the tract of eight arpents twenty toises and four feet front, mentioned in the last, No. 24; the first depth of forty arpents of which has been inhabited and cultivated for more than ten consecutive years prior to the 20th December, 1803; and the second depth of forty arpents was granted to the father of the claimant, in the year 1780. Confirmed.

No. 26.—DANIEL MADERE claims a tract of land, situate on the east side of the river Mississippi, in the county of German Coast, containing six arpents nineteen toises and five feet in front, and forty arpents in depth, and bounded on the upper side by land of Charles Pontif, and on the lower by land of Jean Baptiste Vicuer.

The claimant having been put in possession of part of the land now claimed in the year 1785, and there having been a continued possession of the balance for more than ten years next preceding the 20th December, 1803. Confirmed.

No. 27.—JEAN PRECOEUR claims a tract of land, situate on the east side of the river Mississippi, in the county of German Coast, containing four arpents and eighteen toises in front, and forty arpents in depth, and bounded on the upper side by land of Joseph Bertrand, and on the lower by land of Madame Alexandre Chenet.

It appears that the land now claimed was inhabited and cultivated on the 20th December, 1803, and that the same was continually inhabited and cultivated by those under whom the claimant holds for more than ten consecutive years next preceding. Confirmed.

No. 28.—JEAN PRECOEUR claims a tract of land, situate on the east side of the river Mississippi, in the county of German Coast, containing two arpents and four toises in front, and forty arpents in depth, and bounded on the upper side by land of Louis Picou, and on the lower by land of Pierre Matherne.

It appears that the land now claimed was inhabited and cultivated on the 20th December, 1803, and that the same was continually inhabited and cultivated by those under whom the claimant holds for more than ten consecutive years next preceding. Confirmed.

No. 29.—MADAME QUARENTIN, widow of Joseph Quarentin, claims a tract of land, situate on the east side of the river Mississippi, in the county of German Coast, containing five arpents front, and eighty in depth, and bounded on the upper side by land of Adam Vicuer, and on the lower by land of Jean Albert.

It appears that the first depth of forty arpents of this land was inhabited and cultivated on the 20th December, 1803, and for more than ten years prior; and that the second depth of forty arpents was regularly granted to the claimant, in the year 1791, by Governor Miro. Confirmed.

No. 31.—MADAME STAIRE, widow of Jacques Staire, claims a tract of land, situate on the west side of the river Mississippi, in the county of German Coast, containing fourteen arpents in front, and forty in depth.

It appears that the land now claimed was inhabited and cultivated by the claimant on the 20th December, 1803, and that the same was continually inhabited and cultivated for more than ten consecutive years next preceding. Confirmed.

No. 32.—GEORGE HYMEL claims a tract of land, situate on the west side of the river Mississippi, in the county of German Coast, containing four arpents and four toises in front, and of which front arpents three and four toises have sixty arpents in depth, and the remaining arpent the ordinary depth of forty arpents; and which said tract is bounded on the upper side by land of Pierre Loup, and on the lower by land of Pablo Obert.

Three arpents and four toises front, on the ordinary depth, of this land, the claimant was put in possession of by the Surveyor General of this province in the year 1781 ; and, in 1783, he obtained an order of survey from Governor Miro for an additional depth of twenty arpents ; the remaining arpent front, with the usual depth of forty arpents, has been inhabited and cultivated for more than ten years next preceding the 20th December, 1803. Confirmed.

No. 33.—MICHEL VEBER claims a tract of land, situate on the west side of the river Mississippi, in the county of German Coast, containing six arpents in front, and forty arpents in depth, and bounded on the upper side by land of Jacques Estayre, and on the lower by land of Christophe Mayere.

It appears that the claimant did actually inhabit and cultivate the land now claimed on the 20th December, 1803, and that the same was continually inhabited and cultivated by him, or those under whom he claims, for more than ten consecutive years next preceding. Confirmed.

No. 34.—MADAME CHENET, widow of Alexandre Chenet, claims a tract of land, situate on the east side of the river Mississippi, in the county of German Coast, containing five arpents and sixteen toises in front, and forty arpents in depth, and bounded on the upper side by land of Pedro Chenet, and on the lower by land of Nicolas Vicuer.

The claimant was regularly put in possession of this land, in the year 1783, by the Surveyor General ; and it having continued to be inhabited and cultivated ever since that period, until on and after the 20th December, 1803. Confirmed.

No. 35.—ACHILLE TROUARD claims a tract of land, situate on the east side of the river Mississippi, in the county of German Coast, containing fifteen arpents twenty-six toises and four feet in front ; to twelve of which front arpents he claims a depth of eighty arpents, and to the remaining three arpents twenty-six toises and four feet front the ordinary depth of forty arpents ; and said tract is bounded on the upper side by land of George Wenprender, and on the lower by land of Jean Pinckley and Pierre Dunlap.

It appears that the first depth of forty arpents of this land was inhabited and cultivated on the 20th December, 1803, and for more than ten years prior. The Board confirm to the extent of the first forty arpents in depth, but reject the claim to the second depth of forty arpents, and to the twelve arpents front of this land.

No. 36.—PIERRE DRAGUE claims a tract of land, situate on the east side of the river Mississippi, in the county of German Coast, containing two arpents and a half in front, and forty arpents in depth, and bounded on the upper side by land of George T. Ross, and on the lower by land of Jean Held.

It appears that the land now claimed was inhabited and cultivated on the 20th December, 1803, and that the same was continually inhabited and cultivated by those under whom the claimant holds for more than ten consecutive years next preceding. Confirmed.

No. 36.—ANTOINE DORVIN claims a tract of land, situate on the west side of the river Mississippi, in the county of German Coast, containing six arpents and eight toises in front, and forty arpents in depth, and bounded on the upper side by land of Paul Chauvin, and on the lower by land of the widow Lorio.

It appears that the land now claimed was inhabited and cultivated on the 20th December, 1803, and that the same was continually inhabited and cultivated by the claimant, or those under whom he claims, for more than ten consecutive years next preceding. Confirmed.

No. 37.—ANTOINE DORVIN claims a tract of land, situate on the west side of the river Mississippi, in the county of German Coast, containing three arpents and twenty-two toises in front, and forty arpents in depth, and bounded on the upper side by land of Madame Chenier, and on the lower by land of Mr. Barran.

This land was surveyed in the year 1770, in favor of Alphonse Dorvin, who obtained a complete grant for the same in the year 1777; under which grant the present claimant holds. Confirmed.

No. 38.—ADAM JACOB claims a tract of land, situate on the east side of the river Mississippi, in the county of German Coast, containing seven arpents in front, and forty in depth, and bounded on the upper side by land of Vincent Marson, and on the lower by land of Jean Baptiste Miller.

The claimant having purchased part of the land claimed at a judicial sale made in the year 1793, and the balance at private sale in the year 1790, the whole of which has been inhabited and cultivated for more than ten consecutive years next preceding the 20th December, 1803: Confirmed.

No. 39.—PIERRE BECNEL claims a tract of land, situate on the east side of the river Mississippi, in the county of German Coast, containing five arpents and twenty feet in front, and forty arpents in depth, and bounded on the upper side by land of Adam Vicuer, and on the lower by land of Jean Folse.

This land was sold to F. Clement, in the year 1796, at a judicial sale, and, in 1804, to the present claimant, by a like sale. It having been continually inhabited and cultivated for more than ten consecutive years prior to the 20th December, 1803: Confirmed.

No. 40.—MADAME KERNER, widow of George Kerner, claims a tract of land, situate on the east side of the river Mississippi, in the county of German Coast, containing two arpents in front, and forty in depth, and bounded on the upper side by land of Christian Jacob, and on the lower by land of Jean Secheneder.

The husband of the claimant, in the year 1777, purchased this tract of land from Christian Jacob, and, after his death, it was purchased by his widow at a judicial sale. It appearing to have been continually inhabited and cultivated for more than ten consecutive years preceding the 20th December, 1803: Confirmed.

No. 41.—JEAN SECHENEDER claims a tract of land, situate on the east side of the river Mississippi, in the county of German Coast, containing two arpents in front, and forty in depth, and bounded on the upper side by land of Madame Kerner, and on the lower by land of Madame Saubel.

This is part of a tract of land surveyed for George Kerner, in the year 1776, and by his widow conveyed to the present claimant; and it appearing that the land has been continually inhabited and cultivated for more than ten consecutive years prior to the 20th December, 1803: Confirmed.

No. 42.—CHRISTOPHE OCTZIGUER claims a tract of land, situate on the east side of the river Mississippi, in the county of German Coast, containing four arpents seventeen toises and three feet in front, and forty arpents in depth, and bounded on the upper side by land of Madame Sivil Pichof, and on the lower by land of Noel Perret.

It appears that the claimant did actually inhabit and cultivate the land now claimed on the 20th December, 1803, and for more than ten consecutive years next preceding. Confirmed.

No. 43.—JEAN BTE. and LOUIS LAUBEL claim a tract of land, situate on the east side of the river Mississippi, in the county of German Coast, containing six arpents front, and forty in depth, and bounded on the upper side by land of George Kerner, and on the lower by land of Alphonse Faussier.

It appears that the claimants did actually inhabit and cultivate the land now claimed on the 20th December, 1803, and for more than ten consecutive years next preceding. Confirmed.

No. 44.—JEAN JACQUES HAYDEL claims a tract of land, situate on the west side of the river Mississippi, in the county of German Coast, containing seventeen arpents in front, and forty in depth, and bounded on the upper side by land of Matthias Roussel, and on the lower by land of Nicholas and Jacques Haydel.

It appears that the claimant did actually inhabit and cultivate the land now claimed on the 20th December, 1803, and that the same was continually inhabited and cultivated by the claimant, or those under whom he claims, for more than ten consecutive years next preceding. Confirmed.

No. 45.—MADAME HOTIN, widow of Benjamin Hotin, claims a tract of land, situate on the west side of the river Mississippi, in the county of German Coast, containing four arpents in front, and forty arpents in depth, and bounded on the upper side by land of Jean Adam Romel, and on the lower by land of Antoine Hymel.

The husband of the claimant having been regularly put in possession of this land by the proper surveyor, in the year 1776, and the land having been continually inhabited and cultivated until on and after the 20th December, 1803: Confirmed.

No. 46.—MADAME BECNEL claims a tract of land, situate on the river Mississippi, (west side,) in the county of German Coast, containing twelve arpents and twenty-three feet in front, and eighty arpents in depth, and bounded on the upper side by land of Nicholas and Jacques Haydel, and on the lower by land of George Haydel.

This claimant having continually inhabited and cultivated the first depth of forty arpents of the land now claimed for more than ten consecutive years prior to the 20th December, 1803, the Board confirm her claim to that extent, and reject it as to the second depth of forty arpents.

No. 47.—MATTHIAS CAMBER claims a tract of land, situate on the east side of the river Mississippi, in the county of German Coast, containing four arpents in front, and forty arpents in depth, and bounded on the upper side by land of Louis Folse, and on the lower by land of Jacques Seiche.

It appears that the land now claimed was inhabited and cultivated on the 20th December, 1803, and that the same was continually inhabited and cultivated by the claimant, or those under whom he claims, for more than ten consecutive years next preceding. Confirmed.

No. 48.—GEORGE LOUPE claims a tract of land, situate on the west side of the river Mississippi, in the county of German Coast, containing three arpents in front, and forty in depth, and bounded on the upper side by land of Madame Hotin, and on the lower by land of Charles Rhom.

It appears that the claimant did actually inhabit and cultivate the land now claimed on the 20th December, 1803, and that the same was continually inhabited and cultivated by him, or those under whom he claims, for more than ten consecutive years next preceding. Confirmed.

No. 49.—JEAN DESNOYERS claims a tract of land, situate on the west side of the river Mississippi, in the county of German Coast, containing eight arpents in front, and forty in depth, and bounded on the upper side by land of François Echtely, and on the lower by land of the parish church of St. Jean Baptiste.

It appears that the claimant did actually inhabit and cultivate the land now claimed on the 20th December, 1803, and for more than ten consecutive next preceding. Confirmed.

No. 50.—JEAN WEBER claims a tract of land, situate on the west side of the river Mississippi, in the county of German Coast, containing five arpents thirteen toises and five feet in front, and forty arpents in depth, and bounded on the upper side by land of George Weber, and on the lower by land of François Weber.

It appears that the claimant did actually inhabit and cultivate the land now claimed on the 20th December, 1803, and that the same was continually inhabited and cultivated by him, or those under whom he claims, for more than ten consecutive years next preceding. Confirmed.

No. 51.—MADAME DESLONDE, widow of George Deslonde, claims a tract of land, situate on the east side of the river Mississippi, in the county of German Coast, containing ten arpents in front, and forty arpents in depth, and bounded on the upper side by land of Michel Jacob, and on the lower by land of Matthias Camber.

It appears that the claimant did actually inhabit and cultivate the land now claimed on the 20th December, 1803, and that the same was continually inhabited and cultivated by her, or those under whom she claims, for more than ten consecutive years next preceding. Confirmed.

No. 52.—JACQUES FALGOUT claims a tract of land, situate on the west side of the river Mississippi, in the county of German Coast, containing three arpents and one toise in front, and eighty arpents in depth, and bounded on the upper side by land of Baptiste Camu, and on the lower by land of Charles Rixner.

The claimant having possessed the first depth of forty arpents of the land claimed for more than ten consecutive years prior to the 20th December, 1803; and having obtained from the Governor a regular warrant of survey, in the year 1786, for the second depth of forty arpents, the claim is hereby confirmed.

No. 53.—CHALES RIXNER claims a tract of land, situate on the west side of the river Mississippi, in the county of German Coast, containing three arpents and one toise in front, and eighty arpents in depth, and bounded on the upper side by land of Charles Falgout, and on the lower by land of Mr. Troxler.

It appears that the first depth of forty arpents of this land has been continually inhabited and cultivated for more than ten consecutive years next preceding the 20th December, 1803; and that Charles Falgout, under whose title the claimant holds, obtained a regular warrant of survey from Governor Miro, in the year 1786, for the second depth of forty arpents. Confirmed.

No. 54.—PIERRE RODRIGUES claims a tract of land, situate on the east side of the river Mississippi, in the county of German Coast, containing three arpents in front, and forty arpents in depth, and bounded on the upper side by land of ———, and on the lower by land of ———.

It appears that the claimant did actually inhabit and cultivate the land now claimed on the 20th December, 1803, and that the same was continually inhabited and cultivated by him, or those under whom he claims, for more than ten consecutive years next preceding. Confirmed.

No. 55.—NOEL DESLATTES claims a tract of land, situate on the east side of the river Mississippi, in the county of German Coast, containing three and a half arpents in front, and forty arpents in depth.

The land now claimed was surveyed in the year 1776 for Robert Lavingue, under whose title the claimant holds by virtue of successive sales; and it appearing that the land has been continually inhabited and cultivated for more than ten consecutive years prior to the 20th December, 1803: Confirmed.

No. 56.—ANTOINE DUPUY claims a tract of land, situate on the east side of the river Mississippi, in the county of German Coast, containing two arpents in front, and forty in depth, and bounded on the upper side by land of Jean Baptiste Foisel, and on the lower by land of Joseph Cuvillier.

It appears that the land now claimed was inhabited and cultivated on the 20th December, 1803, and that the same was continually inhabited and cultivated by those under whom the claimant holds for more than ten consecutive years next preceding. Confirmed.

No. 57.—GEORGE HAYDEL claims a tract of land, situate on the west side of the river Mississippi, in the county of German Coast, containing ten arpents in front, and eighty arpents in depth.

The first depth of forty arpents of this tract of land having been continually possessed by the claimant, or those under whom he claims, for more than ten consecutive years prior to the 20th December, 1803; and having obtained a regular order of survey for the second depth of forty arpents, in the year 1781, the claim is hereby confirmed.

No. 58.—MATTHIAS ROUSSEL claims a tract of land, situate on the west side of the river Mississippi, in the county of German Coast, containing eleven arpents in front, and forty arpents in depth, and bounded on the upper side by land of Jean J. Haydel.

It appears that the land now claimed was inhabited and cultivated on the 20th December, 1803, and that the same was continually inhabited and cultivated by the claimant, or those under whom he claims, for more than ten consecutive years next preceding. Confirmed.

No. 59.—MADAME DESLONDES, widow of Jacques Deslondes, claims a tract of land, situate on the east side of the river Mississippi, in the county of German Coast, containing four arpents in front, and forty arpents in depth, and bounded on the upper side by land of Mr. Andry, and on the lower by land of Madame George Deslondes.

It appears that the claimant did actually inhabit and cultivate the land now claimed on the 20th December, 1803, and for more than ten consecutive years next preceding. Confirmed.

No. 60.—NICHOLAS HAYDEL claims a tract of land, situate on the west side of the river Mississippi, in the county of German Coast, containing six arpents and three toises in front, and forty arpents in depth, and bounded on the upper side by land of Antoine Albert, and on the lower by land of Matthias Haydel.

The claimant having been put in possession of the land claimed before the year 1776, by the proper surveyor, and he having continually occupied and possessed the same since that period. Confirmed

No. 61.—MADAME MONTZ, widow of Antoine Montz, claims a tract of land, situate on the east side of the river Mississippi, in the county of German Coast, containing four arpents seventeen toises and three feet in front, and forty arpents in depth, and bounded on the upper side by land of Mr. Lasseigne, and on the lower by land of Christophe Achstigre.

It appears that the husband of the claimant was put in possession of this land in the year 1732, by the proper surveyor, and that it has been continually inhabited and cultivated ever since. Confirmed.

No. 62.—FRANCOIS WEBER claims a tract of land, situate on the west side of the river Mississippi, in the county of German Coast, containing three arpents four toises and four feet in front, and forty arpents in depth, and bounded on the upper side by land of Jean Weber, and on the lower by land of Jean Baptiste Labatut.

It appears that the claimant did actually inhabit and cultivate the land now claimed on the 20th December, 1803, and for more than ten consecutive years next preceding. Confirmed.

No. 63.—PIERRE ROUSSEL claims a tract of land, situate on the west side of the river Mississippi, in the county of German Coast, containing four arpents in front, and forty in depth, and bounded on the upper side by land of Noel Deslattes, and on the lower by land of the widow Roussel.

It appears that the claimant did actually inhabit and cultivate the land now claimed on the 20th December, 1803, and that the same was continually inhabited and cultivated by him, or those under whom he claims, for more than ten consecutive years next preceding. Confirmed.

No. 64.—CHARLES DARENSBOURG claims a tract of land, situate on the west side of the river Mississippi, in the county of German Coast, containing two arpents in front, and forty in depth, and bounded on the upper side by land of David Hymel, and on the lower by land of Louis Lagrange.

It appears that the land now claimed was inhabited and cultivated on the 20th December, 1803, and that the same was continually inhabited and cultivated by those under whom the claimant holds for more than ten consecutive years next preceding. Confirmed.

No. 65.—MATHIEU HOTTAR claims a tract of land, situate on the west side of the river Mississippi, in the county of German Coast, containing eight arpents and ten toises in front, and eighty arpents in depth, and bounded on the upper side by land of Noel Perret, and on the lower by land of Jean Boyer.

The claimant having continually possessed the first depth of the land claimed for more than ten consecutive years prior to the 20th December, 1803, the Board confirm his title to that extent. The balance, being claimed by virtue of a decree of the Intendant in 1801, the Board do not consider themselves authorized to confirm, and do therefore reject it.

No. 66.—ADAM WEBER claims a tract of land, situate on the west side of the river Mississippi, in the county of German Coast, containing six arpents and fourteen toises in front, and forty arpents in depth, and bounded on the upper side by land of Christophe Hymel, and on the lower by land of Antoine Weber.

It appears that the land now claimed was inhabited and cultivated on the 20th December, 1803, and that the same was continually inhabited and cultivated by those under whom the claimant holds for more than ten consecutive years next preceding. Confirmed.

No. 67.—ANTOINE WEBER claims a tract of land, situate on the west side of the river Mississippi, in the county of German Coast, containing four arpents and four feet in front, and forty arpents in depth, and bounded on the upper side by land of Mr. Lefebre, and on the lower by land of Antoine Borne.

It appears that the claimant did actually inhabit and cultivate the land now claimed on the 20th December.

1803, and that the same was continually inhabited and cultivated by him, or those under whom he claims, for more than ten consecutive years next preceding. Confirmed.

No. 68.—JACQUES TROXLER claims a tract of land, situate on the west side of the river Mississippi, in the county of German Coast, containing thirteen arpents in front, and forty arpents in depth, and bounded on the upper side by land of George Christophe, and on the lower by land of André Hymel.

It appears that the claimant did actually inhabit and cultivate the land now claimed on the 20th December, 1803, and that the same was continually inhabited and cultivated by him, or those under whom he claims, for more than ten consecutive years next preceding. Confirmed.

No. 69.—FREDERICK TOUPS claims a tract of land, being a second depth, and situate immediately behind a tract claimed by Madame Champagne, fronting on the river Mississippi, on the west side, in the county of German Coast, containing six arpents in front, and forty arpents in depth, and which said second depth now claimed contains the same quantity in front as that of Madame Champagne, and forty arpents in depth.

Pablo Toups, the ancestor of the present claimant, and from whom he derives title, having been put in possession of this second depth of forty arpents, by order of the Governor of the province, in the year 1779. Confirmed.

No. 70.—FRANCOIS TREPAGNIER claims a tract of land, situate on the east side of the river Mississippi, in the county of German Coast, containing twelve arpents in front, and forty in depth.

The claimant was put in possession of the land claimed, in the year 1779, by the Surveyor General of the province, by order of the Governor, and has continued to possess the same ever since that period. Confirmed.

No. 71.—ANTOINE BORNE claims a tract of land, situate on the west side of the river Mississippi, in the county of German Coast, containing four arpents in front, and forty arpents in depth, and bounded on the upper side by land of Jean Baptiste Rodrigue, and on the lower by land of Antoine Deslatte.

The claimant having purchased this land at a judicial sale made of it in the year 1788, and having continued in possession of the same ever since that period. Confirmed.

No. 72.—JOSEPH DELHOMME claims a tract of land, situate on the east side of the river Mississippi, in the county of German Coast, containing six arpents in front, and forty in depth, and bounded on the upper side by land of Mr. Dusieau, and on the lower by land of Mr. Trepagnier.

It appears that the claimant did actually inhabit and cultivate the land now claimed on the 20th December, 1803, and for more than ten consecutive years next preceding. Confirmed.

No. 73.—MADAME TREPAGNIER claims a tract of land, situate on the east side of the river Mississippi, in the county of German Coast, containing fifteen arpents and three toises in front, and forty arpents depth to nine arpents and three toises of said front, and a depth extending to the lake to the remaining six front arpents; and bounded on the upper side by land of Mr. Duez, and on the lower by land of François L'Hommer.

This tract of land having been occupied and possessed by those under whom the claimant holds for more than ten consecutive years prior to the 20th December, 1803, the Board confirm the title to the extent of the ordinary depth of forty arpents, and reject the claim to the second depth to six of the front arpents.

No. 75.—NICOLAS PICOU claims a tract of land, situate on the east side of the river Mississippi, in the county of German Coast, containing fourteen arpents in front, and forty arpents in depth, and bounded on the upper side by land of Antoine D. Degruis, and on the lower by land of Joseph V. Degruis.

It appears that the land claimed was surveyed for the present claimant by the proper officer, in the year 1787, and that he did, prior to that time, and ever since that period, possess the same. Confirmed.

No. 76.—GEORGE WEBER claims a tract of land, situate on the west side of the river Mississippi, in the county of German Coast, containing five arpents thirteen toises and five feet in front, and forty arpents in depth, and bounded on the upper side by land of the parish church of the parish of St. John the Baptist, and on the lower by land of Jean Weber.

It appears that the claimant did actually inhabit and cultivate the land now claimed on the 20th December, 1803, and for more than ten consecutive years next preceding. Confirmed.

No. 77.—ANTOINE BORNE claims a tract of land, situate on the west side of the river Mississippi, in the county of German Coast, containing nine arpents and a half in front, and forty arpents in depth.

It appears that this tract of land has been possessed and occupied either by the present claimant, or those under whom he claims, for more than ten consecutive years next preceding the 20th December, 1803. Confirmed.

No. 78.—GEORGE ROUSSEL claims a tract of land, situate on the west side of the river Mississippi, in the county of German Coast, containing four arpents and nineteen toises in front, and forty arpents in depth.

It appears that the land now claimed was inhabited and cultivated on the 20th December, 1803, and that the same was continually inhabited and cultivated by the claimant, or those under whom he claims, for more than ten consecutive years next preceding. Confirmed.

No. 79.—MATTHIAS ORY claims a tract of land, situate on the east side of the river Mississippi, in the county of German Coast, containing six arpents and a half in front, of which he claims to one arpent and a half the depth of eighty arpents, and to the remaining front arpents the ordinary depth of forty arpents.

It appearing that the land now claimed has been continually inhabited and cultivated for more than ten consecutive years prior to the 20th December, 1803, the Board confirm the title to the first depth of forty arpents, and reject the claim to a second depth of forty arpents to the one and a half arpent front.

No. 80.—MADAME RODRIGUE claims a tract of land, situate on the west side of the river Mississippi, in the county of German Coast, containing nine arpents in front, and forty arpents in depth.

It appears that the claimant did actually inhabit and cultivate the land now claimed on the 20th December, 1803, and that the same was continually inhabited and cultivated by her, or those under whom she claims, for more than ten consecutive years next preceding. Confirmed.

No. 81.—PIERRE BOSSIER claims a tract of land, situate on the west side of the river Mississippi, in the county of German Coast, containing six arpents seven toises and three feet in front, and forty arpents in depth, and bounded on the upper side by land of Madame Lagrange, and on the lower by land of George Bossier.

It appears that the claimant did actually inhabit and cultivate the land now claimed on the 20th December, 1803, and for more than ten consecutive years next preceding. Confirmed.

No. 82.—MADAME LAGRANGE, widow of Jean Baptiste Lagrange, claims a tract of land, situate on the west side of the river Mississippi, in the county of German Coast, containing four arpents in front, and forty arpents in depth, and bounded on the upper side by land of Jean Baptiste Barré, and on the lower by land of Pierre Bossier.

It appears that the claimant did actually inhabit and cultivate the land now claimed on the 20th December, 1803, and that the same was continually inhabited and cultivated by her, or those under whom she claims, for more than ten consecutive years next preceding. Confirmed.

No. 83.—BAUBERY TREPAGNIER claims a tract of land, situate on the east side of the river Mississippi, in the county of German Coast, containing four arpents in front, and forty arpents in depth, and bounded on the upper side by land of François Trepagnier, Senior.

It appears that the land now claimed was inhabited and cultivated on the 20th December, 1803, and that the same was continually inhabited and cultivated by those under whom the claimant holds for more than ten consecutive years next preceding. Confirmed.

No. 84.—FRANÇOIS TREPAGNIER, Jun. claims a tract of land, situate on the east side of the river Mississippi in the county of German Coast, containing four arpents in front, and forty in depth, and bounded on the upper side by land of Baubery Trepagnier, and on the lower by land of Pierre Pain, a free mulatto.

It appears that the land now claimed was inhabited and cultivated on the 20th December, 1803, and that the same was continually inhabited and cultivated by those under whom the claimant holds for more than ten consecutive years next preceding. Confirmed.

No. 85.—CHEVALIER DARENSBOURG claims a tract of land, situate on the west side of the river Mississippi, in the county of German Coast, containing nine arpents in front, and eighty arpents in depth.

It appears that the claimant did actually inhabit and cultivate the first forty arpents depth of this land for more than ten consecutive years next preceding the 20th December, 1803, and that he obtained a regular warrant of survey for the second forty arpents in depth in the year 1786. Confirmed.

No. 86.—LOUIS HABINE claims a tract of land, situate on the west side of the river Mississippi, in the county of German Coast, containing twenty-eight arpents in front, and eighty in depth, and bounded on the upper side by land of Pedro Baudoin, and on the lower by land of Madame Antoine St. Jago.

It appearing that the land now claimed was inhabited and cultivated on the 20th December, 1803, and for more than ten consecutive years prior, the Board confirm the title to the extent of the first depth of forty arpents, and reject the claim to the second depth of forty arpents.

No. 88.—JEAN FRANÇOIS PISEROS claims a tract of land, situate on the east side of the river Mississippi, in the county of German Coast, containing fifteen arpents one toise two feet and four inches in front, and a depth extending back to the lake, and bounded on the upper side by land of Louis M. C. De Trepy, and on the lower by land of Louis Augustin Menillon.

In the year 1773 Estevan Boré obtained a regular warrant of survey from Governor Unzaga for the first depth of forty arpents of this land; and for the second depth, being an extension back to the lake, he obtained a complete grant, in the year 1779, from Governor Galvez; the present claimant holds under the titles of said Boré. Confirmed.

No. 89.—GEORGE WENFRENDER claims a tract of land, situate on the east side of the river Mississippi, in the county of German Coast, containing eight arpents in front, and forty arpents in depth, and bounded on the upper side by land of Jacques Lagroire, and on the lower by land of Maurice O'Connor.

The claimant having purchased six arpents front of this land at a judicial sale made on the 2d of October, 1791, and the balance, being two arpents front, likewise at a judicial sale made in the year 1797; and the land having been occupied and possessed by him ever since that period. Confirmed.

No. 90.—ANTOINE ORY claims a tract of land, situate on the east side of the river Mississippi, in the county of German Coast, containing six arpents in front, and forty in depth, and bounded on the upper side by land of Gabriel Clautier, and on the lower by land of ——.

The claimant having purchased this land at two judicial sales, and those through whom he claims having occupied and possessed it for more than ten consecutive years prior to the 20th December, 1803. Confirmed.

No. 91.—ADAM VICUER claims a tract of land situate on the east side of the river Mississippi, in the county of German Coast, containing four arpents front, and eighty in depth, and bounded on the upper side by land of Balthazar Vicuer, and on the lower by land of Michel Carautin.

The claimant having occupied and possessed this tract of land for more than ten consecutive years prior to the 20th of December, 1803, the Board confirm his title to the extent of the first forty arpents depth, and reject the claim to the second depth of forty arpents.

No. 92.—Madame MICHEL CONRAD LIPS claims a tract of land, situate on the east side of the river Mississippi, in the county of German Coast, containing three arpents in front, and forty in depth, and bounded on the upper side by land of François Dupont, and on the lower by land of Jacques Conrad Lips.

It appears that the claimant did actually inhabit and cultivate the land now claimed on the 20th December, 1803, and that the same was continually inhabited and cultivated by her, or those under whom she claims, for more than ten consecutive years next preceding. Confirmed.

No. 93.—MICHEL LENNAN claims a tract of land situate on the west side of the river Mississippi, in the county of German Coast, containing five arpents and seventeen toises in front, and forty arpents in depth, bounded on the upper side by land of Pierre Mermillon, and on the lower by land of Jean Pierre Folse.

It appears that the land now claimed was inhabited and cultivated on the 20th December, 1803, and that the same was continually inhabited and cultivated by those under whom the claimant holds for more than ten consecutive years next preceding. Confirmed.

No. 94.—ANDRE CONRAD LIPS claims a tract of land, situate on the east side of the river Mississippi, in the county of German Coast, containing six arpents and six toises in front, and forty arpents in depth, and bounded on the upper side by land of Michel Jacob, and on the lower by land of Jean Helte.

It appears that the land now claimed was inhabited and cultivated on the 20th December, 1803, and that the same was continually inhabited and cultivated by those under whom the claimant holds for more than ten consecutive years next preceding. Confirmed.

No. 95.—JEAN HELTE claims a tract of land, situate on the east side of the river Mississippi, in the county of German Coast, containing three arpents and fourteen toises in front, and forty arpents in depth, and bounded on the upper side by land of Andre Conrad Lips, and on the lower by land of Jean Normand.

It appears that the claimant did actually inhabit and cultivate the land now claimed on the 20th December, 1803, and for more than ten consecutive years next preceding. Confirmed.

No. 96.—JACQUES CONRAD LIPS claims a tract of land, situate on the east side of the river Mississippi, in the county of German Coast, containing three arpents front, and eighty arpents in depth, and bounded on the upper side by land of Madame Michel Lips, and on the lower by land of Jean Bte. Picou.

It appears that the first depth of forty arpents of the land now claimed was inhabited and cultivated for more than ten consecutive years prior to the 20th December, 1803; and that Ponce Lasseigne, under whose title the claimant holds, obtained a grant for the second depth of forty arpents in the year 1789. Confirmed.

No. 97.—JEAN HELTE claims a tract of land, situate on the east side of the river Mississippi, in the county of German Coast, containing four arpents and two toises in front, and forty arpents in depth, and bounded on the upper side by land of Lorenzo Normand, and on the lower by land of Estevan, a free negro.

It appears that the land now claimed was inhabited and cultivated on the 20th December, 1803, and that the same was continually inhabited and cultivated by the claimant, or those under whom he claims, for more than ten consecutive years next preceding. Confirmed.

No. 98.—ANTOINE VICUER claims a tract of land, situate on the east side of the river Mississippi, in the county of German Coast, containing ten arpents in front, and forty in depth, and bounded on the upper side by land of François Dupont.

It appears that the claimant did actually inhabit and cultivate the land now claimed on the 20th December, 1803, and for more than ten consecutive years next preceding. Confirmed.

No. 99.—FRANÇOIS DUPONT claims a tract of land, situate on the east side of the river Mississippi, in the county of German Coast, containing two arpents in front, and forty in depth, and bounded on the upper side by land of Antoine Vicuer, and on the lower by land of Madame Michel Conrad Lips.

It appears that the claimant did actually inhabit and cultivate the land now claimed on the 20th December, 1803, and that the same was continually inhabited and cultivated by him, or those under whom he claims, for more than ten consecutive years next preceding. Confirmed.

No. 100.—ANTOINE FOLSE claims a tract of land, situate on the Lac des Allemands, in the county of German Coast, containing seven thousand five hundred superficial arpents, and bounded on the east and north by the aforesaid lake, on the south by the bayous Bœuf and Cabaha Nosse, and on the west by vacant land and the bayous Tigre, Chevreuil, le Haha, and Heron.

It appearing to the satisfaction of the Board that the claimant did, on and after the 1st day of October, 1800, inhabit and cultivate a part of said land, and continue thereon until on and after the 20th December, 1803, the Board confirm his title to six hundred and forty acres, to be laid off upon a base of sixteeen acres front, (including his improvement in the centre,) with the depth of forty acres, and reject his claim as to the balance.

No. 101.—MANUEL ANDRY claims a tract of land, situate on the east side of the river Mississippi, in the county of German Coast, containing thirteen arpents eighteen toises and two feet in front, and eighty arpents in depth, opening twenty-two degrees fifty-one minutes thirty seconds, and bounded on the upper side by land of the widow of Antoine Mantz, and on the lower by land of the widow of Jacques Delonde.

It appearing that the land now claimed was inhabited and cultivated on the 20th December, 1803, and for more than ten consecutive years prior, the Board confirm the claim to the extent of the first depth of forty arpents, and reject it as to the second depth of forty arpents.

No. 102.—JEAN BAPTISTE PICOU claims a tract of land, situate on the east side of the river Mississippi, in the county of German Coast, containing two arpents in front, and forty arpents in depth, and bounded on the upper side by land of Jacques Conrad Lips, and on the lower by land of Charles Robeau.

It appears that the claimant did actually inhabit and cultivate the land now claimed on the 20th December, 1803, and for more than ten consecutive years next preceding. Confirmed.

No. 103.—CHAUVIN and BOISCLAIR DELERY claim two tracts of land, situate on the west side of the river Mississippi, in the county of German Coast; one of said tracts containing five arpents and twenty toises in front, and forty arpents in depth, and bounded on the upper side by land of Antoine Dorvin, and on the lower by land of Edmond Fortier; and the other tract containing five arpents twenty toises and five feet in front, and forty arpents in depth, and bounded above and below by land of Antoine Dorvin.

It appears that the aforesaid tracts of land were inhabited and cultivated on the 20th December, 1803, and that they were continually inhabited and cultivated by those under whom the claimants hold for more than ten consecutive years next preceding. Confirmed.

No. 104.—EDMOND FORTIER claims a tract of land, situate on the west side of the river Mississippi, in the county of German Coast, containing thirteen arpents twenty-seven toises and three feet in front, and forty arpents in depth, and bounded on the upper side by land of Chauvin and Boisclair Delery, and on the lower by land of Madame Rixner.

It appears that the land now claimed was inhabited and cultivated on the 20th December, 1803, and that the same was continually inhabited and cultivated by those under whom the claimant holds for more than ten consecutive years next preceding. Confirmed.

No. 30.—PIERRE BOSSIER claims a tract of land, situate on the west side of the river Mississippi, in the county of German Coast, containing eighteen arpents in front, and forty arpents in depth, and bounded on the upper side by land of ———, and on the lower by land of ———.

It appearing that the land now claimed was inhabited and cultivated on the 20th December, 1803, and for more than ten consecutive years prior thereto, the Board confirm the claim to the extent of such depth as does not exceed forty arpents. Confirmed.

No. 87.—BERNARD BERNOUDY claims a tract of land, situate on the east side of the river Mississippi, in the county of German Coast, containing twenty-three arpents in front, and a depth extending back to the lake, and bounded on the upper side by land of ———, and on the lower by land of ———.

It appearing that the land now claimed was inhabited and cultivated on the 20th December, 1803, and for more than ten consecutive years prior, the Board confirm the claim to the extent of the first depth of forty arpents, and reject it as to the balance.

No. 74.—THE CHILDREN OF PAUL TOUPS claim a tract of land, situate in the county of Acadia, at the place called *les Coteaux de France*, at about the distance of three and a half leagues from the western bank of the Mississippi, containing eighteen arpents in front, and a depth of two leagues and a half. Paul Toups, the father of the claimants, obtained from the Baron de Carondelet a regular warrant of survey for this land in the year 1796, for the purpose of establishing a vacherie; and the conditions of the warrant of survey having been complied with on his part: Confirmed.

         P. GRYMES, *R. E. D. Orl. Ter.*
         JOSHUA LEWIS,
         THOMAS B. ROBERTSON.

————

Rejected claims from the books of William Wikoff, Jun., Deputy Register of the county of Pointe Coupée, and part of the county of Iberville.

No. 6.—DIEGO ARNDEZ claims a tract of land, situate on the west side of the river Mississippi, in the county of Iberville, containing ten arpents in front, and forty in depth, and bounded on the upper side by vacant land, and on the lower by land of Mr. Villier.

This claim is founded upon a petition (*requéte*) to the Governor of the province, dated the 29th of January, 1799, with the certificate of the commandant of the district, stating that the land was vacant, and might be granted without prejudice, &c. It does not appear that the Governor ever acted upon the petition. In the year 1802, the Intendant General of the province directed the commandant to make some inquiries ascertaining the nature of the claimant's pretensions to a grant; but it does not appear that the Intendant ever made any final order or decree on the petition. It appearing, also, in evidence, that the claimant did not occupy or inhabit the land on or prior to the 20th of December, 1803, they are of opinion that he is not entitled to the land under any law, usage, or custom of the Spanish Government, or under any act of Congress; and do therefore reject his claim.

No. 9.—GREGOIRE MELANSON claims a second depth or concession of forty arpents, lying immediately back of a first depth, situate on the west side of the river Mississippi, in the county of Iberville, and bounded on the upper side by land of Joseph Ignatio Landry, and on the lower by land of Simon Melanson.

This claim to a second depth is founded solely upon a petition (*requéte*) to the Intendant General of the province, dated the 29th of July, 1802, accompanied with the commandant's certificate that the land was vacant, and might be granted without injury, &c. Had the Intendant even a right at that period to grant the land, it does not appear that he ever acted upon the petition, or that it was ever presented to him. We are therefore of opinion that this claim to a second concession ought not to be confirmed under any law, custom, or usage of the Spanish Government; and do reject it.

No. 8.—OLIVIER ARNANDEZ claims a second depth or concession of forty arpents, lying immediately back of a first depth of four arpents front, situate on the west side of the river Mississippi, in the county of Iberville, and bounded on the upper side by land of Joseph Hebert, and on the lower by land of Thomas Hebert.

This claim to a second concession is founded upon a petition (*requéte*) to the Intendant General of the province, dated the 29th of June, 1802, together with the commandant's certificate that the land was vacant, and might be granted without prejudice, &c. Had the Intendant even a right to grant the land at that period, he has never acted upon the petition, nor does it appear that it was ever presented to him. We are of opinion that this claim to a second concession ought not to be confirmed under any law, usage, or custom of the Spanish Government; and do therefore reject it.

No. 10.—MATHURIN LANDRY claims a second depth or concession of forty arpents, lying immediately back of a first depth of five arpents and one hundred and thirty-four feet front, and situate on the west side of the river Mississippi, in the county of Iberville, and bounded on the upper side by land of Jean Baptiste Leblanc, and on the lower by land of Joseph Ignatio Landry.

The pretensions to this second depth are in all respects similar to those in the two preceding claims, being founded on a petition, dated the 29th of July,

1802, to the Intendant General, accompanied by the commandant's certificate; which petition does not appear to have been acted upon or seen by the Intendant. We are therefore of opinion that this claim to a second depth ought not to be confirmed under any law, custom, or usage of the Spanish Government; and do therefore reject it.

No. 20.—BARTHOLOMEW HAMILTON claims a second depth of forty arpents, lying immediately back of a first depth already confirmed to him in No. 20 among the confirmed claims.

The claimant shows no other evidence of title to this second depth than having occupied the front and first depth, and having occasionally supplied himself with timber from this second depth. According to the laws, customs, and usages of the Spanish Government, no front proprietor could, by any act of his own, acquire a right to lands further back than the ordinary depth of forty arpents; and although the Spanish Government has invariably refused to grant the second depth to any other than the front proprietor, yet nothing short of a grant or warrant of survey from the Governor could confer a title or right to the land; we do therefore reject the claim.

No. 23.—JOSEPH MOLLERE claims a tract of land, situate on the west side of the river Mississippi, in the county of Iberville, containing eight hundred superficial arpents, and bounded on the upper side by vacant lands, and on the lower by land of Estevan Watts.

The claimant, on the 26th of November, 1798, petitioned Governor Gayoso for this land; and the Governor, on the 14th of February, 1799, issued an order of survey, directing the Surveyor General of the province to put the claimant in possession of the land. The land was surveyed in 1800, but it appears that the claimant did not inhabit or cultivate the land on 1st day of October, 1800, as required by the act of Congress, nor has he since that time; nor does it appear that he ever complied with the requisite conditions of the order of survey, to wit, making the road and levée on the land. We are therefore of opinion that his claim ought to be rejected.

No. 25.—LOUIS MOLLERE claims a tract of land, situate on the west side of the river Mississippi, in the county of Iberville, containing six hundred superficial arpents, and bounded on the upper side by land of Estevan Watts, and on the lower by vacant land.

The claimant, on the 1st of January, 1799, petitioned Governor Gayoso for this land; and the Governor, in the same month and year, issued an order directing the Governor of Baton Rouge to cause the surveyor of the district to survey the land petitioned for, in order that proper titles should be made to the same. The land was, in consequence, surveyed in 1800; but it does not appear that other titles were ever made by the Spanish Government, and it does appear that the land has never been inhabited or cultivated. We are therefore of opinion that the claim ought to be rejected.

No. 31.—FRANCIS MARIONNEAUX claims a second depth or concession of forty arpents, lying immediately back of a first depth of seven arpents and fourteen feet in front, situate on the west side of the river Mississippi, in the county of Iberville, and bounded on the upper side by land of Magloire Dupuis, and on the lower by land of Mr. Leonard.

This claim is founded solely upon a petition, (requête,) in the year 1801, to the Intendant General of the province, accompanied with a certificate of the commandant, stating the land to be vacant, and might be granted without injury, &c. It does not appear that the Intendant ever acted upon the petition, even if he had a right to grant the land at that period. We are of opinion that this claim to a second depth ought not to be confirmed under any law, usage, or custom of the Spanish Government; and do therefore reject it.

No. 34.—BELONY HEBERT claims a second depth or concession of forty arpents, lying immediately back of a first depth of four arpents and twenty-one toises front, and situate on the west side of the river Mississippi, in the county of Iberville, and bounded on the upper side by land of Daniel Benoit, and on the lower by land of Alexis Hebert.

This claim to a second depth is founded upon pretensions in every respect similar to the preceding; the claimant having produced only a petition, with the Commandant's certificate to the Intendant General of the province in the year 1802; which petition was never acted upon by the Intendant General. We are of opin-

ion that this claim to a second concession ought not to be confirmed under any law, usage, or custom of the Spanish Government; and do therefore reject it.

No. 35.—JEAN CHARLES JUILLIER, a guardian of Joseph Trahan and Marie S. Trahan, infant children of Jean Marie Trahan, deceased, claims a tract of land, situate on the west side of the river Mississippi, in the county of Iberville, containing six arpents in front, and forty in depth, and bounded on the upper side by land claimed by Francis J. Juillier, and on the other by land of ———.

It appears, in support of this claim, that Jean Marie Trahan was put in possession of this tract of land, in the year 1787, by the commandant of the district, and that he resided but a short time upon it, when he abandoned it, by reason of the inundation of the river. There appears, also, in support of the claim, the affidavit of two inhabitants of the district, stating that said Trahan made a levée on the land, and that it has always been considered by the inhabitants of the district as his property; but there being no other title than a short possession with the permission of the proper Spanish officer, the land having been abandoned for a great length of time, and possession of it never resumed until long since the change of Government, we are of opinion that this claim ought to be rejected.

No. 36.—JEAN CHARLES JUILLIER claims a tract of land, situate on the west side of the river Mississippi, in the county of Iberville, containing six arpents front, and forty in depth, and bounded on one side by land claimed by the heirs of Jean Marie Trahan, deceased, and on the other by land claimed by Francis J. Juillier.

It appears, in support of this claim, that the claimant took possession of this land some time about the year 1786, by permission of the Spanish commandant; that he remained upon it but a short time, when he was forced to abandon it, by reason of the inundation of the river. There is also an affidavit stating that he made a levée on the land, and that the same has been always considered by the inhabitants of the district as his property. But for the reasons assigned in the preceding claim, which equally apply to the present, we are of opinion that this claim ought to be rejected.

No. 37.—FRANÇOIS ISIDORE JUILLIER claims a tract of land, situate on the west side of the river Mississippi, in the county of Iberville, containing six arpents in front, and forty in depth, and bounded on the upper side by land claimed by Baptiste Legendre, and on the lower by land of Jean Charles Juillier.

It appears, in support of this claim, that the claimant was put in possession of this land in the year 1787, by the commandant of the district; that he remained upon it but a short time, when he was forced to abandon it, by reason of the inundation of the river. There are also affidavits stating that he made a levée on the land, and that it has always been considered by the inhabitants of the district as his property. But for the reasons assigned in claim No. 35, which equally apply to the present, we are of opinion that the claim ought to be rejected.

No. 46.—ETIENNE FOREST claims a tract of land, situate on the west side of the river Mississippi, in the county of Iberville, containing two hundred and thirty-four and thirty-two hundredths superficial acres, and adjoining on one side land claimed by Enoch Budwell.

This claim is founded solely upon a settlement made, in the year 1805, upon vacant land, which is the only pretension the claimant has to a title. We do therefore reject the claim.

No. 48.—MICHEL MAHIER claims a tract of land, situate on the west side of the river Mississippi, in the county of Iberville, containing twenty arpents in front, and forty in depth, and bounded on each side by vacant land.

The claimant shows a petition (requête) to the Governor for this land, dated 1794, and a certificate of the commandant stating that the land is vacant, and may be granted without injury, &c. It does not appear that his petition was ever acted upon or seen by the Governor. He also claims under a settlement right; but, it appearing that the land was not inhabited or cultivated on the 20th December, 1803, or before, either by the claimant, or any one for him, we are of opinion that his claim ought to be rejected.

No. 51.—ELENOR TRANTHAM, widow of Martin Trantham, claims a tract of land, situate on the west side of the river Mississippi, in the county of Pointe Coupée, containing six hundred and forty superficial acres, and bounded on each side by vacant lands.

This claim is founded on a settlement made by Martin Trantham, the claimant's husband, by permission of the commandant of the district, which permission was given in consequence of a direction in writing from Governor Salcedo, in the year 1802, to the commandant, to permit said Trantham to settle on any vacant land in his district. It appears, from affidavits produced by the claimant, that Martin Trantham, her husband, did, in the year 1802, clear and cultivate a small part of the tract now claimed; but it does not appear that the claimant or her husband did actually inhabit and cultivate the land on the 20th December, 1803; on the contrary, it appears, from part of the evidence produced in support of the claim, that they did not live on the land, but cultivated a small part of it. We are therefore of opinion, the requisitions of the act of Congress not having been complied with, that the claim ought to be rejected.

No. 52.—WILLIAM STARKS claims a tract of land, situate on the west side of the river Mississippi, in the county of Iberville, containing six arpents in front, and forty in depth, and bounded on one side by land of William Cunningham, and on the other by vacant land.

This claim is founded upon a petition (requéte) to the Governor for this land, in the year 1795, with the certificate of the commandant stating the land to be vacant, and that it might be granted without injury, &c. It does not appear that the Governor ever acted upon or saw the petition. There are also produced affidavits, stating that Alexis Hebert, under whose title the present claimant holds, was put in possession of this land by the commandant, in the year 1795. But it appearing that the land was never inhabited or cultivated until after the 20th December, 1803, we are of opinion that the claim ought to be rejected.

No. 58.—JOSEPH JAFFRION claims a tract of land, situate on the west side of the river Mississippi, in the county of Pointe Coupée, containing ten arpents in front, and forty arpents in depth, and bounded on the upper side by land claimed by Pierre Landreno, and on the lower by land of the claimant.

The claimant, in the year 1777, petitioned Governor Galvez for this land; in 1778, the Governor issued an order to the commandant of the district, directing him to put the claimant in possession of the land. But it appears that he did not remain on the land long before he was forced to abandon it, by reason of the inundation of the river, and settled himself on other lands; and that he has never resumed possession of it until since the change of Government. We are therefore of opinion that his claim ought to be rejected.

No. 63.—FRANCIS HACKETT claims a tract of land, situate on the west side of the river Mississippi, in the county of Iberville, containing twelve arpents in front, and forty in depth, and bounded on one side by land claimed by Joseph Sharp, and on the other by land claimed by ——

The claimant produces, in support of this claim, the affidavits of different persons, stating that Joseph Sharp, from whom the claimant purchased this land, was put in possession of it by the commandant of the district about the year 1781; that he had made a levée on the land, and that, for about three years prior to that time, (the 25th of December, 1806,) he had had a person actually residing on it: but, it appearing in evidence that the land was never inhabited or cultivated either by the aforesaid Sharp, or any one for him, until after the 20th December, 1803, we are therefore of opinion that this claim ought to be rejected.

No. 66.—THOMAS CRAPPER claims a tract of land, being part of a second depth, situate about seventy arpents back from the river Mississippi, in the county of Iberville, and containing two hundred superficial acres, and bounded on one side by land of Auguste Richard, and on the other by land of Pierre Breau.

The claimant purchased this part of a second depth, in the year 1805, from Felix Athanas Darden, but he has produced no manner of evidence whatever to show that said Darden had a title to the land. It appearing that the land was never inhabited or cultivated until since the 20th December, 1803, we are of opinion that his claim ought to be rejected.

No. 94.—PIERRE ALLAIN, Jun. claims a second depth of forty arpents, lying immediately back of a first depth belonging to Pierre Allain, Sen., and situate on the river Mississippi, in the county of Iberville; and the aforesaid second depth containing five hundred and ninety-four and forty-two hundredths superficial acres.

In the year 1787 the claimant petitioned Governor Miro to grant him this tract of land, which is situated immediately at the end of a tract of land forty arpents deep, belonging to the claimant's father, and to be bounded by the lines of his father's land, and continued to the extent of a second depth of forty arpents. The Governor refused to grant him the land, because the second depth ought to be granted to the front proprietor only; and there being no other evidence of title, we are of opinion that the claim ought to be rejected.

No. 100.—JOSE LEGENDRE claims a tract of land, situate on the west side of the river Mississippi, in the county of Iberville, containing six arpents in front, and forty in depth, and bounded on one side by land of the widow Batista Legendre, and on the other by land of Mr. Hebert.

The claimant produces, in support of this claim, the affidavit of two inhabitants of the district, stating that, about the year 1787, the claimant was put in possession of this land by the Spanish commandant; that he made a levée and other improvements on it, and resided on it for a few years, when he was forced to abandon it by reason of the inundation of the river; and that the land has always been considered by the inhabitants of the district as his property; but he claims no other title than a short time of possession, with the permission of the proper Spanish officer. The land having been abandoned for a great length of time, and possession never resumed until long since the change of Government, we are of opinion that his claim ought to be rejected.

No. 108.—SIMON MELANSON claims a second concession or depth of forty arpents, lying immediately back of a first depth of four and a half arpents front, situate on the west side of the river Mississippi, in the county of Iberville, and bounded on the upper side by land of Gregoire Melanson, and on the lower by land of Joseph Hebert.

The claimant, being owner of the first depth of forty arpents, and desirous of obtaining an additional concession, for the purpose of being supplied with timber, petitioned the Intendant General of the province, in the year 1802, to grant him a second depth for that purpose; which petition was accompanied with a certificate of the commandant, stating the land to be vacant, &c. It does not appear that the petition has been in any manner acted upon by the Intendant; we are therefore of opinion that this claim to a second depth ought to be rejected.

No. 109.—CHARLES HEBERT claims a tract of land, situate on the right bank of the bayou Placquemines, in the county of Iberville, containing ten arpents in front, and forty in depth, and bounded on the upper side by land of Joseph Leblanc, and on the lower by vacant land.

In the year 1801 the claimant petitioned the Intendant General of the province for this land, for the purpose of establishing his children; and his petition was accompanied with the certificate of the commandant, stating that the land was vacant, having been abandoned about sixteen years before. In the year 1802 there were some directions given by the Intendant to the commandant to make inquiry as to the pretensions of the claimant to a grant; but it does not appear that he ever made any final decree. And it appearing that the land was not inhabited or cultivated until since the 20th December, 1803, we are of opinion that his claim ought to be rejected.

No. 112.—MICHEL LAMBREMONT claims a second concession or depth of forty arpents, lying immediately back of a first depth of five arpents and nineteen toises front, situate on the west side of the river Mississippi, in the county of Iberville, and bounded on the upper side by land of Joseph Aubry Dupuis, and on the lower by land of Jean Dupuis.

The claimant, being owner of the first depth of forty arpents, and desirous of obtaining an additional concession, for the purpose of being supplied with timber, petitioned the Intendant General, on the 22d of September, 1799, to grant him a second depth for that purpose; which petition was accompanied with the certificate of the commandant, stating it to be vacant, &c. It does not appear that the petition has in any manner been acted upon or seen by the Intendant; we are therefore of opinion that this claim to a second concession ought to be rejected.

No. 116.—THE WIDOW OF LOUIS LEGENDRE claims a tract of land, situate on the west side of the river Mississippi, in the county of Iberville, containing six arpents in front, and forty in depth, and bounded on the upper side by land claimed by the heirs of Jean Marie Trahan, and on the lower by land claimed by Daniel Benoit.

The claimant produces, in support of this claim, the affidavit of two inhabitants of the district, stating that Louis Legendre, the deceased husband of the claimant, was put in possession of this land about the year 1787, by the commandment of the district; that he made improvements and a levée on the land, and resided on it some years, when he was forced to abandon it by reason of the inundation of the river; and that it has always been considered by the inhabitants of the district as his property. But the land having been abandoned for so great a length of time, and possession never resumed until since the change of Government; and it having been customary, and almost invariably the case under the Spanish Government, to obtain other lands in lieu of those abandoned; we are of opinion that this claim ought to be rejected.

No. 120.—FRANCIS MAVEUX claims a tract of land, situate on the west side of the river Mississippi, in the county of Pointe Coupée, containing two arpents in front, and forty in depth, and bounded on one side by land of Simon Lacour, and on the other by land of Jacques Larche.

The claimant produces, in support of this claim, the affidavit of two inhabitants of the district, stating it to be within their knowledge that the claimant purchased the land about twenty-six or twenty-seven years ago, at a sale of the estate of Madame Pierre Jaffrion, deceased, and that he had quietly possessed the same ever since, until that date, (the 27th December, 1806.) But there being incontrovertible evidence that the original proprietor of the land was forced to abandon it, by reason of the inundation of the river, between twenty-five and thirty years ago, and that possession had never been resumed until some time since the change of Government, we are therefore of opinion that the claim ought to be rejected.

No. 123.—PIERRE L'EGLISE claims a tract of land, situate on the west side of the river Mississippi, in the county of Pointe Coupée, containing sixteen arpents in front, and forty in depth, and bounded on one side by land of François Moreau, and on the other by land of J. B. Rabelais.

The claimant purchased this land, in the year 1806, from the heirs of Jean Pierre Darquilon, and produces, in support of his claim, the affidavit of two of the inhabitants of the district, stating that it was within their knowledge that Jean Pierre Darquilon was proprietor of, and did inhabit and cultivate this land upwards of twenty-five years ago, and that it had always been considered as his property ever since that period, until the time of making the affidavit, (on the 28th December, 1806.) But there being incontrovertible evidence that the land was abandoned, by reason of the inundation of the river, upwards of twenty-five years ago, and that possession had never since been resumed until after the change of Government, we are of opinion that the claim ought to be rejected.

No. 124.—PIERRE L'EGLISE claims a tract of land, situate on the west side of the river Mississippi, in the county of Pointe Coupée, containing six arpents in front, and forty in depth, and bounded on each side by land claimed by Belony Chately.

The claimant produces, in support of his claim, the affidavit of two inhabitants of the district, stating that it was within their knowledge that Baptiste Lemoine, from whom the claimant purchased the land in the year 1806, was proprietor of, and did inhabit and cultivate the same upwards of twenty-five years before that date, (the 28th December, 1806,) and that it had always been considered as his property. But there being positive evidence of the abandonment of it for upwards of twenty-five years, we are, for the reasons assigned in the preceding claim, which equally apply to the present, of opinion that this claim ought to be rejected.

No. 125.—PIERRE L'EGLISE claims a tract of land, situate on the west side of the river Mississippi, in the county of Pointe Coupée, containing eight arpents in front, and forty in depth, and bounded on the one side by land claimed by Mr. Moreau, and on the other by land claimed by Louis Gremillon.

The claimant produces, in support of this claim, the affidavit of two inhabitants of the district, stating that it is within their knowledge that Joseph Dufriend, from whom the claimant purchased this land in the year 1806, was proprietor of, and did inhabit and cultivate the same upwards of twenty-five years before that date, (the 28th December, 1806,) and that it had always since been considered as his property. But there being incontrovertible evidence of the abandonment of it upwards of twenty-five years ago, we are, for the reasons assigned in claim No. 123 of the same claimant, and which equally apply to the present, of opinion that his claim to this land ought to be rejected.

No. 142.—MARTIN TUNOIR claims a tract of land, situate on the west side of the river Mississippi, in the county of Pointe Coupée, containing eight arpents in front, and forty arpents in depth, and bounded on the upper side by land of ———, and on the lower by land of Jean Baptiste Tunoir.

The claimant pretends title to this land by virtue of a deed made to him by the inhabitants of Pointe Coupée, dated the 8th of October, 1806; the inhabitants claimed and sold it, as belonging to them in common, for having made the levée, at the upper part of Pointe Coupée, by which they pretend that the land was reclaimed. This being altogether an assumed title on the part of the inhabitants, the Board reject the claim in toto.

No. 151.—JEAN BAPTISTE TUNOIR claims a tract of land, situate on the west side of the river Mississippi, in the county of Pointe Coupée, containing five arpents in front, and forty in depth, and bounded on the upper side by land claimed by Hypolite Baron, and on the lower by land claimed by P. Bacon.

The claimant states that he purchased this land from Marguerite Simon, in the year 1802, but he produces no manner of evidence in support of the claim. And it appearing in evidence to the Board that the land has, for a great length of time, been abandoned, and possession never resumed until after the change of Government, we are of opinion that the claim ought to be rejected.

No. 154.—JOSEPH ENNET claims a tract of land, situate on the west side of the river Mississippi, in the county of Pointe Coupée, containing eighty arpents in front, and forty in depth, and bounded on each side by vacant lands.

This claim is founded upon a sale made by Louis Sauvage, an Indian, to the claimant of this land, in the year 1806. The Indian is, in the instrument of sale, stated to be the grandson of a chief who had a grant of the land from the Spanish Government; and as an evidence of which are produced one or two certificates, not sworn to, certifying that it was within the knowledge of the person who gave the certificates that the said chief had a grant for the land from the Spanish Government. These are the only pretensions that the claimant has to a title; and there being no such grant on record, we do therefore reject his claim.

No. 161.—ZENO LACOUR claims a tract of land, situate on the west side of the river Mississippi, in the county of Pointe Coupée, containing seven arpents in front, and forty arpents in depth, and bounded on one side by land claimed by Mr. Lemoine, and on the other by land claimed by Pierre Mouran.

The claimant purchased this land, in the year 1806, from Joseph Jaffrion, who purchased it from Messrs. Dufreme and Lemoine; and he produces no evidence whatever of title in the original proprietors. But it is in evidence before the Board that the land has been abandoned for a great length of time, and possession never resumed until since the change of Government. We are therefore of opinion that his claim ought to be rejected.

No. 173.—MADELAINE and AGNES CLAUSE each claim a tract of land, situate on the west side of the river Mississippi, in the county of Iberville; both of which tracts contain ten arpents in front, and forty in depth, and adjoining each other, and bounded on the upper side by land of ———, and on the lower by land of ———.

The claimants produce, in support of their claims, an order from Governor Galvez, in the year 1778, to the commandant, directing him to put François Clause, the father of the claimants, in possession of ten arpents in front, and forty in depth, which he had petitioned for; they also produce the affidavits of different persons, stating that about twenty-three or twenty-four years before that time, (1806,) they had seen said Clause on the land, which he had inhabited and cultivated for many years previously. But it appearing in evidence to the Board that the land has for a great number of years been abandoned, and never claimed again until within a few years past, since the change of Government, we are of opinion that the claim ought to be rejected.

No. 186.—CHARLES DUFOUR, Jun, claims a tract of land, situate on the west side of the river Mississippi, in the county of Pointe Coupée, containing six arpents in front, and forty in depth, and bounded on one side by land claimed by Joseph Decuir, and on the other by land of Baptiste Lemoine.

The claimant produces, in support of this claim, the affidavits of two of the inhabitants of the district, stating that Auguste Jumeau, from whom the claimant purchased the land in 1806, was the proprietor of the same about twenty-five years before that time, (1806) and that he did inhabit and cultivate the land for a long time. But it being in evidence to the Board that the land has been abandoned for more than twenty-five years, by reason of the inundation of the river, and that it has never been claimed again until some time after the 20th December, 1803, we are of opinion that the claim ought to be rejected.

No. 187.—EBENEZER COOLY claims a tract of land, situate on the west side of the river Mississippi, in the county of Pointe Coupée, containing twenty arpents in front, ten on each side of the bayou Atanache, and forty in depth, bounded on the upper side by land claimed by the claimant, and on the lower by vacant lands.

It appears that one Joseph Bourgeat made a settlement on this tract of land upwards of forty years ago, and resided on it some years; one witness, a kinsman of the claimant, says ten or twelve consecutive years. This part of the river was settled by a number of families, of which Bourgeat's was one, about the same time; and a few years afterwards they abandoned it, by reason of a great inundation from the river, and settled elsewhere. Neither Bourgeat nor any of his family has ever resumed possession of the land, or exercised any act of ownership over it. The claimant purchased this land of Bourgeat's widow, in the year 1806. We consider that Bourgeat forfeited all claim to this land, after having left it and established himself elsewhere, having no other title than a naked possession; and it is probable that neither Bourgeat, nor his heirs, nor any person claiming under him, would have pretended any claim to this land, had not its value been so much enhanced by the change of Government. We have no doubt that, according to the usages of the Spanish Government, the Governor would not have hesitated to grant this land to any other individual, with a full knowledge of Bourgeat's claim, after he had left it and settled elsewhere. We are of opinion that the claim is unwarranted by any law, usage, or custom of the Spanish Government, or any law of the United States; and do accordingly reject it.

No. 194.—JOHN DELOY claims a tract of land, situate on the west side of the river Mississippi, in the county of Iberville, containing ten arpents in front, and forty in depth, and bounded on the upper side by land of ——, and on the lower by land of ——.

The claimant produces, in support of this claim, the petition (requête) of François Clause for this land, dated the 23d of January, 1771, and an order from Governor Unzaga, in the same year, directing the commandant of the district to put him in possession of ten arpents front, and two in depth. This appears to be part of the land claimed in No. 175, by the daughters of said Clause, which we have already rejected; and the same evidence appearing in this claim, to wit, abandonment for a great number of years, and not being claimed again until after the 20th December, 1803, we are of opinion that this claim ought to be rejected.

No. 201.—Madame JEAN BAPTISTE LACOUR claims a tract of land, situate on the west side of the river Mississippi, in the county of Iberville, containing six hundred superficial arpents, and bounded on the upper side by land of ——, and on the lower by land of——.

The claimant states, in her notice, that her claim to this land is founded on a grant from the Spanish Government; but of this she produces no evidence, nor of any other kind of title. And it appears in evidence to the Board, that, if ever the land was settled, it has been for a great length of time abandoned, and never claimed again, nor possession resumed, until after the 20th December, 1803. We are therefore of opinion that her claim ought to be rejected.

No. 209. ALEXIS CLOTIER claims a tract of land, situate in the county of Pointe Coupée, containing four arpents in front, and forty in depth, and bounded on the upper side by land of ——, and on the lower by land of ——.

The claimant produces an order of Governor Galvez, in the year 1777, to the commandant of the district, directing him to put Antoine Provost in possession of three arpents front, and forty in depth, which he had petitioned for; but he does not show in what manner the land has been transferred to him. It appearing in evidence that the land was abandoned by the original proprietor a great number of years past, by reason of the inundation of the river, and never again claimed until since the change of Government, we are of opinion that the claim ought to be rejected.

No. 212.—FRANÇOIS CHESSE claims a tract of land, situate on the west side of the river Mississippi, in the county of Pointe Coupée, containing four arpents in front, and forty arpents in depth, and bounded on the upper side by land of ——, and on the lower by land of ——.

The claimant purchased this land in the year 1806, from Francis and Augustin Allain, who purchased it, in the year 1777, from Augustin Roy; but he produces no manner of evidence of title in those under whom he claims. It is in evidence to the Board that the land has been abandoned for upwards of twenty-five years, by reason of the inundation of the river, and never claimed again until since the 20th December, 1803; we are therefore of opinion that the claim ought to be rejected.

No. 219.—Madame ANTOINE PROVOST, alias LATOUR, claims a tract of land, situate in the county of Pointe Coupée, containing three arpents and one perch in front, and forty arpents in depth, and bounded on the upper side by land of ——, and on the lower by land of ——.

The claimant states in her notice that Antoine Provost, alias Latour, obtained for this land an order of survey, from Governor Galvez, in the year 1777. This appears to be the same land claimed in No. 209, by Alexis Clotier, which we have already rejected; and it appearing to the satisfaction of the Board that the land has been for a great number of years past abandoned, by reason of the inundation of the river, and never claimed, or possession resumed, until since the 20th of December, 1803, we are of opinion that this claim ought to be rejected.

No. 225.—AUGUSTIN BOURGEAT claims a tract of land, situate in the county of Pointe Coupée, containing twenty-four arpents in front, and forty in depth, and bounded on the upper side by land of ——, and on the lower by land of ——.

The claimant states, in his notice, that he purchased this land from Madame Bourgeat, and that the same was inhabited and cultivated by Joseph Bourgeat, her husband, upwards of twenty-five years ago; but he produces no manner of evidence of title in those under whom he claims. It appearing to the satisfaction of the Board that, if ever the land was settled, it has been abandoned for more than twenty-five years, and possession never resumed until since the change of Government, we are of opinion that the claim ought to be rejected.

No. 227.—PHILIP BIDON claims a tract of land, situate on the west side of the river Mississippi, in the county of Iberville, containing forty arpents in front, and forty in depth, and bounded on the upper side by Fausse river.

It appears that this land was sold, in the year 1774, by Pierre Perrot to Joseph Hebert, the uncle of the claimant, and from whom he claims it; but in what manner he does not show, nor does he produce any evidence whatever of a title in either Perrot or Hebert. And it appearing in evidence to the Board that, if the land was formerly settled it was abandoned for a great length of time past, and possession never resumed until after the 20th December, 1803, we are of opinion that this claim ought to be rejected.

No. 257.—CHARLOTTE LARCHE, wife of J. P. Manchaussé, claims a tract of land, situate on the west side of the river Mississippi, in the county of Pointe Coupée, containing twenty arpents in front, and forty in depth, and bounded on the one side by land of Julian Poydras, and on the other by the bayou Charlotte.

The claimant produces, in support of her claim, the affidavits of two inhabitants of the district, stating it to be within their knowledge that, about twenty-five or thirty years before, Charles Larche and his wife, the parents of the claimant, lived on this land, and that the same has always since been considered as their property. But it appearing that the land was abandoned for a great length of time, and possession never resumed until after the change of Government, we are of opinion that the claim ought to be rejected.

No. 272.—PIERRE RIVET claims a second concession or depth of forty arpents, lying immediately back of a first depth, situate on the west side of the river Mississippi, in the county of Iberville.

This claim to a second depth is founded solely upon a petition (*requéte*) to the Intendant General of the province, in the year 1802, accompanied with the commandant's certificate that the land was vacant, &c. It does not appear that the petition was ever in any manner acted upon or seen by the Intendant. We are of opinion that this claim to a second depth ought not to be confirmed under any law, custom, or usage of the Spanish Government; and do therefore reject it.

No. 286.—BERNARD DAUTERIVE claims a tract of lan l, situate on the west side of the river Mississippi, in the county of Iberville, containing six arpents in front, and forty in depth, and bounded on the upper side by land of Gregoire Melanson, and on the lower by land of Thomas Hebert.

The claimant shows no other evidence of title to this land than a sale to him from John McHough and William Webb, in the year 1799. But it being fully proven that this land has been abandoned for a great length of time, and has never been inhabited or cultivated since, until after the 20th December, 1803, either by the claimant, or any one for him, or any one under whom he holds, we are of opinion that this claim ought to be rejected.

No. 287.—ALEXANDER PLANCHE claims a tract of land, situate on the west side of the river Mississippi, in the county of Pointe Coupée, containing twelve arpents in front, and forty in depth, and bounded on the upper side by land claimed by Charles Dufour, Jun., and on the lower by land claimed by Julian Poydras.

It appears that this land was, at a judicial sale of the same made in the year 1771, sold to one Simon Lancour, and by his heirs, in the year 1806, conveyed to the present claimant. It appears, also, that Lacour abandoned the land for more than twenty-five years, by reason of a great inundation from the river, and settled elsewhere, and that it has never been inhabited or cultivated since, until after the 20th December, 1803. We have no doubt that, according to the usages of the Spanish Government, the Governor would not have hesitated to grant this land to any other individual, with a full knowledge of Lacour's claim, after he had left it and settled elsewhere. We are of opinion that the claim is unwarranted by any law, usage, or custom of the Spanish Government, or any law of the United States; and do accordingly reject it.

No. 278.—PIERRE PAILLAUX claims a tract of land, situate on the west side of the river Mississippi, in the county of Iberville, containing six arpents in front, and forty arpents in depth, and bounded on one side by land of Joes Legendre, and on the other by land of Isidore Juillier.

It appears that Baptiste Legendre, whose widow the present claimant married, and now claims in her right, was put in possession of this land about the year 1787, by the commandant of the district; that he resided a short time upon it, when he abandoned it, by reason of the inundation of the river, and settled elsewhere; and the land has never been inhabited or cultivated since that period, until after the 20th December, 1803, either by Legendre, or those that claim under him. We are of opinion, for reasons before assigned in claims similarly situated, that this claim is unwarranted by any law, usage, or custom of the Spanish Government, or any law of the United States; and do therefore reject it.

No. 311.—IOHN MYERS claims a tract of land, situate on the bayou known by the name of the bayou Jacques, in the county of Iberville, containing ten arpents in front, and forty in depth, and bounded on the upper side by land of Antoine Lanclos, Sen., and on the lower by land of Jean Bte. Villars, a free negro.

The claimant states that Felix Brand purchased this tract of land, in the year 1802, of the Chetimachas tribe of Indians, who at that time occupied under the authority of the Spanish Government; that this purchase was made by the consent and authority of the Intendant; and that the claimant has since purchased the right of Felix Brand to the land. There is no evidence, either written or verbal, to show that the Intendant even authorized such sale, had he even the power to do so; and the Indians, under the Spanish Government, were not permitted to sell the lands they occupied without the act of Government concurring in the sale, and granting the land to the purchaser. We are therefore of opinion that the claim ought to be rejected.

No. 312.—ANTOINE GUILLEAU claims a tract of land, situate on the left bank of the bayou Placquemines, in the county of Iberville, containing ten arpents in front, and forty in depth, and bounded on the upper side by land of Pierre Gruner, and on the lower by land belonging to the Chetimachas tribe of Indians.

The claimant produces, in support of his claim, an order of survey, made by the Baron de Carondelet, in the year 1797, in favor of Joseph Bertonier, and states that he purchased the land of Bertonier; but it appearing in evidence to the Board that the land was not inhabited and cultivated on the 1st day of October, 1800, as required by the act of Congress, in cases of incomplete titles, nor until after the 20th day of December, 1803, we do therefore reject the claim.

No. 314.—ALEXANDRE LANDRY claims a second concession or depth of forty arpents, lying immediately back of a first depth, which we have already confirmed to him in No. 314 among the confirmed claims.

This claim to a second depth is founded solely upon a petition (*requéte*) to the Intendant General of the province in the year 1789, with the commandant's certificate that the land was vacant, and might be granted without injury, &c. Had the Intendant even a right at that period to grant the land, he has never acted upon the petition, nor does it appear that it has ever been presented to him. We are of opinion that this claim to a second concession ought not to be confirmed under any law, custom, or usage of the Spanish Government ; and do therefore reject it.

No. 318.—JAMES MATHER, Jr. claims a second depth of forty arpents, lying immediately back of a first depth, which we have already confirmed to him in No. 318 among the confirmed claims.

The claimant has no other foundation for his title to the second depth than having occupied the front and first depth, and having occasionally supplied himself with timber from the second depth. According to the laws, usages, and customs of the Spanish Government, no front proprietor, by any act of his own, could acquire a right to lands further back than the ordinary depth of forty arpents ; and although the Spanish Government has invariably refused to grant the second depth to any other than the front proprietor, yet nothing short of a grant or order of survey from the Governor could confer a title or right to the land. We do therefore reject the claim.

No. 320.—JEAN BTE. VILLARS, a free negro, claims a tract of land, situate on the bayou Jacques, in the county of Iberville, containing five arpents in front, and forty in depth, and bounded on the upper side by land of John Mayers, and on the lower by land of Jean Troxelles.

The claimant purchased this land in the year 1805 from Dominique Bourgeois, who purchased it, together with a large tract, from the Chetimachas tribe of Indians, in 1804. The Indians, under the Spanish Government, were not permitted to sell the lands they occupied, without the act of Government concurring in the sale, and granting the land to the purchaser. We consider that, since the cession of the territory to the United States, the Indians had no right to sell this land without the authority and concurrence of Government; and are therefore of opinion that this claim ought to be rejected.

No. 321.—JEAN TROXELLES claims a tract of land, situate on the bayou Jacques, in the county of Iberville, containing five arpents in front, and forty in depth, and bounded on the upper side by land of Jean Bte. Villars, and on the lower by land of Antoine Lanclos.

This is part of the tract of land mentioned in the preceding claim to have been purchased in the year 1804, by Dominique Bourgeois, from the Chetimachas tribe of Indians. We are of opinion that the Indians had no right to sell this land without the authority and concurrence of the Government of the United States, for the reasons we have assigned in the preceding claim, No. 320; and that this claim ought to be rejected.

No. 325.—ANTOINE LANCLOS, Sen. claims a tract of land, situate on the bayou Jacques, in the county of

Iberville, containing four arpents in front, and forty in depth, and bounded on the upper side by land of Jean Troxelles, and on the lower by land of Francis Nero.

The claimant purchased this land in the year 1805 from Dominique Bourgeois, who purchased it, together with a larger tract, in 1804, from the Chetimachas tribe of Indians. We are of opinion, for the reasons assigned in claim No. 320, which is part of the same land purchased by Bourgeois, that the Indians had no right to sell this land without the authority and concurrence of the Government of the United States, and that this claim ought to be rejected.

No. 338.—JOACHIM ESCALINE claims a second depth of forty arpents, lying immediately back of a first depth, which we have already confirmed to him in No. 338 among the confirmed claims.

The claimant has no other foundation for his title to this second depth than having occupied the front and first depth, and having occasionally supplied himself with timber from the second depth. According to the laws, usages, and customs of the Spanish Government, no front proprietor could, by any act of his own, acquire a right to lands further back than the ordinary depth of forty arpents; and although the Spanish Government has invariably refused to grant the second depth to any other than the front proprietor, yet nothing short of a grant or warrant of survey from the Governor could confer a title or right to the land. We do therefore reject the claim.

No. 345.—JACQUES DE VILLIERS claims a tract of land, situate on the east side of the river Mississippi, in the county of Iberville, containing forty-seven arpents in front, and such depth as forms a superficies of eight hundred and fifty-four arpents, and bounded on the upper side by land of the claimant, and on the lower by land of Urbain Gagné.

This claim is founded solely upon a petition (requéte) to the Governor of the province, in the year 1797, with the certificate of the commandant of the district stating the land to be vacant, and that it might be granted without injury, &c. It does not appear that the petition has in any manner been acted upon, or ever seen by the Governor ; and as it appears that the land has never been inhabited or cultivated until after the 20th of December, 1803, we are of opinion that the claim ought not to be confirmed under any law, usage, or custom of the Spanish Government, or any act of Congress; and do therefore reject it.

No. 350.—JOSEPH ORILLON claims a tract of land, situate on the right bank of the bayou Placquemines, in the county of Iberville, containing twenty arpents in front, and forty in depth, and bounded on the upper side by land of Alexander Darden, and on the lower by vacant land.

This claim is founded solely upon a petition (requéte) to the Intendant General, in the year 1799, with the commandant's certificate stating that the land was vacant, and might be granted without injury, &c. It does not appear that the petition was ever in any manner acted upon or seen by the Intendant; and it appearing that the land was never inhabited or cultivated until after the 20th December, 1803, we are of opinion that the claim ought to be rejected.

No. 357.—SALVADOR PAMIAS claims a tract of land, situate on the west side of the river Mississippi, in the county of Pointe Coupée, containing eight arpents in front, and forty in depth, and bounded on the upper side by land claimed by Charlotte Larche, and on the lower by land claimed by François Moran.

The claimant purchased this land in the year 1808, from the agent of Jean Baptiste Desmaret; but he produces no evidence whatever in support of Desmaret's title; and it appearing in evidence that the former proprietor of the land abandoned it for upwards of twenty-five years, by reason of the inundation of the river, and settled elsewhere, and that it has never been inhabited or cultivated until since the 20th December, 1803, either by Desmaret, or any one for him, or by the present claimant, we are of opinion that the claim is unwarranted by any law, usage, or custom of the Spanish Government, or any law of the United States; and do accordingly reject it.

No. 360.—ISIDORE LEBAURE claims a second concession or depth of forty arpents, lying immediately back of a first depth, situate on the river Mississippi, in the county of Iberville.

The claimant states that he petitioned the Governor of Baton Rouge for this second depth, in the year 1799, and that he directed the commandant to put the claimant in possession of the land until the approbation of the Intendant General should be obtained; that the papers were sent to the Intendant for approbation, and were by some means lost; but of this he produces no evidence: and it appearing that the proceedings were never sanctioned by the Intendant, we are of opinion that his claim ought to be rejected.

No. 363.—JAMES SMITH YARBOROUGH claims a tract of land, situate in the county of Iberville, containing four hundred and forty-five superficial acres, and adjoining on one side the land of Jordan and James Yarborough.

The claimant produces no manner of evidence whatever in support of this claim; and, although not claimed as a second concession, it appears to be immediately back of a tract claimed by him, and fronting on the bayou Manchack. It appears also that the land has never been inhabited or cultivated until since the 20th December, 1803. We are of opinion that the claim ought to be rejected.

No. 367.—DOMINIQUE ACOSTA claims a tract of land, situate on the bayou Jacques, in the county of Iberville, containing two hundred and four superficial acres, and bounded on the upper side by land of Jean Troxelles, and on the lower by land of Mr. Robichaux.

The claimant purchased this land in the year 1807, from the Chetimachas tribe of Indians. The Indians, under the Spanish Government, were not permitted to sell the lands they occupied without the act of Government concurring in the sale, and granting the land to the purchaser. We consider that, since the cession of the territory to the United States, they had no right to sell this land without the authority and concurrence of Government; and we are therefore of opinion that the claim ought to be rejected.

No. 368.—JEAN LOUIS CHAMPAIN, ANTHONY MARCHON, AND MADAME FRANÇOIS, as chiefs of the Chetimachas tribe of Indians, claim a tract of land, situate on the bayou Placquemines, in the county of Iberville, and containing one thousand and twenty-three and nineteen hundredths superficial acres.

This tract of land has been for a long time settled by a number of families of the Chetimachas tribe of Indians, by permission of the Spanish Government. The present claimants are the chiefs of these families. Long since the change of Government, some speculators have prevailed on these families to part with their title to this land; and finding that the Indians could not convey a title in fee simple without the consent and concurrence of Government, they have taken a lease of it for ninety-nine years. Since the making of this lease, the Indians have quit the possession of this land, and settled on other land in its neighborhood belonging to the public; and, although this claim is filed in the name of the chiefs of these families, it is no act of theirs, and is intended only for the benefit of the lessees. We are therefore of opinion that the claim ought to be rejected.

No. 369.—JEAN TROXELLES claims a tract of land, situate on the bayou Jacques, in the county of Iberville, containing one hundred and eighty-six and sixty-six hundredths superficial acres, and bounded on the upper side by land claimed by Francis Nero, and on the lower by land belonging to the Chetimachas tribe of Indians.

The claimant purchased this land in the year 1807, from the Chetimachas tribe of Indians. The Indians, under the Spanish Government, were not permitted to sell the lands they occupied without the act of Government concurring in the sale, and granting the land to the purchaser. We consider that, since the cession of the territory to the United States, they had no right to sell this land without the authority and concurrence of Government; and are therefore of opinion that the claim ought to be rejected.

No. 370.—ATHANAS DARDEN claims a tract of land, situate on the bayou Placquemines, in the county of Iberville, containing two hundred and three superficial acres, and bounded on one side by land belonging to the Chetimachas tribe of Indians.

The claimant purchased this land in the year 1807, from the Chetimachas tribe of Indians; and the claim being in every way similar to the preceding, No. 369, we are of opinion that it ought to be rejected.

No. 372.—ANNA BERRY claims a tract of land, situate on the west side of the river Mississippi, in the county of Pointe Coupée, containing six hundred and forty superficial acres.

The claimant pretends title to this land in right of a settlement made prior to the 20th December, 1803, by one John White, the former husband of the claimant; but she produces no evidence of permission from the proper Spanish officer, nor any to prove that the land was actually inhabited and cultivated prior to the 20th December, 1803; and there being evidence that the land was not inhabited or cultivated until after that period, we are of opinion that the claim ought to be rejected.

No. 375.—JEAN FRANÇOIS CHIBOIS claims a tract of land, situate on the bayou known by the name of Grand Bayou, in the county of Pointe Coupée, containing two thousand superficial arpents, and adjoining on one side to lands claimed by Love Alexandre Rebout.

The only pretension which the claimant has to a title to this land is a *requête*, or petition, which he states to have been made to the Spanish Government, in the year 1797, with the certificate of the commandant stating that the land was vacant, and might be granted without injury, &c.; but of this he produces no evidence, written or verbal, nor does he even state that the petition was ever presented to the Governor: and it appearing that the land has never been inhabited or cultivated to this day, either by the claimant or any one for him, we are of opinion that the claim is unwarranted by any law, usage, or custom of the Spanish Government, or any law of Congress; and do therefore reject it.

No. 376.—LOVE ALEXANDRE REBOUT claims a tract of land, situate on the bayou known by the name of the Grand Bayou, in the county of Pointe Coupée, containing one thousand superficial arpents, and adjoining on one side land claimed by Jean François Chibois.

This claim is in every respect founded on the same pretensions as the preceding, No. 375, claimed by Jean François Chibois; we do therefore reject it.

No. 377.—ZENO BOURGEAT claims a tract of land, situate on the west side of the river Mississippi, in the county of Pointe Coupée, containing three arpents and one perch in front, and eighty arpents in depth, and bounded on the upper side by land claimed by François Mayeux, and on the lower by land claimed by Alexis Clotier.

The claimant purchased this land from Pierre Latour, who is stated to have purchased it formerly from one Larche, who is said to have obtained a grant from the Spanish Government for the second depth, and that the evidence of the grant has been lost; but of this there is no proof whatever; and there is positive evidence that the first settler of the land abandoned it for more than twenty-five years, by reason of the inundation of the river, and settled elsewhere, and that the land has never been inhabited or cultivated since that period, until after the 20th December, 1803, either by the claimant, or by those under whom he holds: we are therefore of opinion that the claim ought to be rejected.

No. 378.—JEAN BAPTISTE MAJOR claims a tract of land, situate on the west side of the river Mississippi, in the county of Pointe Coupée, containing six arpents in front, and forty arpents in depth, and bounded on the upper side by land claimed by Belony Chately, and on the lower by vacant land.

The claimant purchased this land in the year 1808, from Labarthe Delisle, who is stated to have purchased it from the agent of Marie Louise Courtesy, the original proprietor. It appears in evidence, that the first settler of this land abandoned it for more than twenty-five years, by reason of the inundation of the river, and settled elsewhere, and that the land has never been inhabited or cultivated since that period, until after the 20th December, 1803, either by the first settler, or any person claiming under her. We are therefore of opinion that the claim ought to be rejected.

No. 53.—JULIAN POYDRAS claims a tract of land, situate on the river Mississippi, in the county of Pointe Coupée, containing twelve arpents in front, and forty in depth, and bounded on one side by land claimed by Charles Larche, and on the other by land claimed by Mr. Duplussine.

The claimant purchased this land in the year 1775, from Paul Moro, who does not appear to have had more than a possession by the permission of the proper officer. Some time after the present claimant purchased this land, he was compelled to leave it, by reason of the in-

undation of the river: he afterwards, it appears, placed a tenant on the land prior to the 20th December, 1803. We consider that his having been off the land for so many years (more than twenty-five) was a strong proof of his having abandoned it; and of his last settlement, prior to the 20th of December, 1803, he cannot avail himself, as a donation, under the act of Congress, because he has received grants of other lands from the Spanish Government. We are therefore of opinion that his claim ought to be rejected.

P. GRYMES, *R. E. D. Orl. Ter.*
JOSHUA LEWIS,
THOS. B. ROBERTSON.

Rejected claims from the register of A. Trouard, Deputy Register for the county of German Coast.

No. 6.—MADAME MILLET, widow of Jean Millet, claims a second depth of twenty-one arpents, lying immediately back of a first depth, which we have already confirmed to her in No. 6 among the confirmed claims.

This second depth of twenty-one arpents was sold, together with the front and first depth, to the husband of the claimant, in the year 1782, by Jean Mayer; but the claimant shows no other evidence of title to this part of the land in Mayer than his having occupied the front and first depth, and having occasionally supplied himself with timber from this second depth. According to the laws, customs, and usages of the Spanish Government, no front proprietor, by any act of his own, could acquire a right to land further back than the ordinary depth of forty arpents; and although the Spanish Government has invariably refused to grant the land to any other than the front proprietor, yet nothing short of a grant or warrant of survey from the Governor could confer a title or right to the land. We are therefore of opinion that the claim ought to be rejected.

No. 23.—ALEXANDRE LABRANCHE claims a second depth, extending back to the lake, and lying immediately behind a front or first depth of forty arpents, which we have already confirmed to him in No. 23 among the confirmed claims.

This second depth, extending back to the lake, appears to have been sold to the claimant, together with the front and first depth; but there is produced no evidence of title to it in those under whom he holds. According to the laws, customs, and usages of the Spanish Government, no front proprietor could, by any act of his own, acquire a right to lands further back than the ordinary depth of forty arpents; and although that Government has invariably refused to grant the second depth to any other than the front proprietor, yet nothing short of a grant or warrant of survey from the Governor could confer a title or right to the land. We are therefore of opinion that the claim ought to be rejected.

No. 35.—ACHILLE TROUARD claims a second depth of forty arpents, lying immediately back of a first depth of twelve arpents front, part of a larger front, which we have already confirmed to him in No. 35 among the confirmed claims.

The claimant has no other foundation for his title to this second depth than having occupied the front and first depth, and having occasionally supplied himself with timber from this second depth. According to the laws, usages, and customs of the Spanish Government, no front proprietor, by any act of his own, could acquire a right to lands further back than the ordinary depth of forty arpents; and although the Spanish Government has invariably refused to grant the second depth to any other than the front proprietor, yet nothing short of a grant or warrant of survey from the Governor could confer a title or right to the land. We are therefore of opinion that this claim to a second depth ought to be rejected.

No. 46.—MADAME BECUEL claims a second depth of forty arpents, lying immediately back of a front and first depth, which we have already confirmed to her in No. 46 among the confirmed claims.

The claimant has no other foundation for her claim to this second depth than having occupied the front and first depth, and having occasionally supplied herself with timber from this second depth. We are of opinion, for reasons assigned in the preceding claim, No. 35, and other claims similarly situated, that the claim to this second depth ought to be rejected.

No. 73.—MADAME TREPAGNIER claims a second depth, extending back to the lake, and lying immediately back of a front or first depth of six and a quarter arpents front, part of a larger front, which we have already confirmed to her in No. 73 among the confirmed claims.

The claimant purchased this second depth, together with fifteen arpents front, in the year 1806, from Antoine Foucher; but she shows no title in Foucher to the second depth. We are of opinion, for the reasons assigned in the claim No. 23, which equally apply to the present, that the claim to a second depth ought to be rejected.

No. 65.—MADAME HOTTAR claims a second concession of forty arpents in depth, and lying immediately back of a front or first depth, which we have already confirmed to her in No. 65 among the confirmed claims.

The claimant's title to this second concession is founded upon a decree of the Intendant General of the province, in favor of the claimant, in the year 1801. Unless the Government of the United States consider that the Intendant had a right to grant the land subsequent to the 1st day of October, 1800, we are of opinion that this claim ought to be rejected.

No. 79.—MATTHIAS ORY claims a second depth of forty arpents, lying immediately back of the first depth of one arpent and a half front, part of a larger front, which we have already confirmed to him in No. 79 among the confirmed claims.

The claimant purchased this second depth, together with the front and first depth, in the year 1791, from Jean Treguer; but he shows no evidence of title in Treguer to the second depth. We are of opinion that this claim to a second depth ought to be rejected.

No. 87.—BERNARD BERNOUDY claims a second depth, extending back to the lake, and lying immediately behind a front or first depth of forty arpents, which we have already confirmed to him in No. 87 among the confirmed claims.

The claimant produces no evidence in support of his claim to the second depth; we are therefore of opinion, for reasons assigned in claims similarly situated, that this claim ought to be rejected.

No. 91.—ADAM VICUER claims a second depth of forty arpents, lying immediately back of a first depth, which we have already confirmed to him in No. 91 among the confirmed claims.

The claimant has no other foundation for his title to this second depth than having occupied the front and first depth, and having occasionally supplied himself with timber from the second depth. According to the laws, customs, and usages of the Spanish Government, no front proprietor, by any act of his own, could acquire a right to land further back than the ordinary depth of forty arpents; and although that Government has invariably refused to grant the land to any other than the front proprietor, yet nothing short of a grant or order of survey could confer a title or right to the land. We are therefore of opinion that the claim ought to be rejected.

No. 100.—ANTOINE FOLSE claims a tract of land, situate on the Lac des Allemands, in the county of German Coast, containing seven thousand five hundred superficial arpents.

It appears that the claimant made an establishment on this land prior to the year 1800, and that he has inhabited and cultivated it since that period, until after the 20th December, 1803. He does not pretend that he ever obtained a title from the Spanish Government which would give him a right to the quantity of land here claimed. We are of opinion that, according to the act of Congress, he is entitled to the quantity of six hundred and forty acres, which we have already confirmed to him; and do therefore reject the balance of his claim.

No. 101.—MANUEL ANDRY claims a second depth of forty arpents, lying immediately back of a first depth of forty arpents, which we have already confirmed to him in No. 101 among the confirmed claims.

The claimant has no other foundation for his title to this second depth than having occupied the front and first depth, and having occasionally supplied himself with timber from the second depth. According to the laws, usages, and customs of the Spanish Government, no front proprietor could, by any act of his own, acquire a right to lands further back than the ordinary depth of forty arpents; and although the Spanish Government has invariably refused to grant the land to any other than the front proprietor, yet nothing short of a grant or order

of survey from the Governor could confer a title or right to the land. We are therefore of opinion that this claim ought to be rejected.

P. GRYMES, R. E. D. Orl. Ter.
JOSHUA LEWIS,
THOMAS B. ROBERTSON.

Decisions of the Board of Commissioners for the eastern district of the Territory of Orleans of land claims registered in the books of Bela Hubbard, Deputy Register for the county of La Fourche.

No. 1.—JEAN BAPTISTE LANDRY AND ALEXANDRE LANDRY claim a tract of land, situate on the right bank of the bayou La Fourche, in the county of La Fourche, containing six arpents and twelve toises in front, and forty arpents in depth, and bounded on the upper side by land of Alin Bourg, and on the lower by land of Madame Bourg.

This land was surveyed in the year 1779, in favor of Joseph Guedry, who obtained a complete grant for the same, in the year 1792, from the Baron de Carondelet; under which grant the present claimants hold, by virtue of successive regular transfers. Confirmed.

No. 2.—PIERRE PLE. claims a tract of land, situate on the left bank of the bayou La Fourche, in the county of La Fourche, containing six arpents and seventeen toises in front, and forty arpents in depth, and bounded on the upper side by land of Simon Landry, and on the lower by land of Amable Landry.

This land was surveyed in the year 1790 for Juan Pedro Landry, under whose title the claimant holds, by virtue of successive sales. The land having been inhabited and cultivated ever since the above period, until on and after the 20th of December, 1803. Confirmed.

No. 3.—ETIENNE GUITROS claims a tract of land, situate on the bayou La Fourche, in the county of La Fourche, containing on each side of the bayou a front of forty arpents, and depth of four arpents, and bounded on the upper side by land of Joseph Cherami, and on the lower by land of Valentin Saulet.

It appears that the claimant obtained a regular warrant of survey for this land from the Spanish Government, in the year 1794, and that the same has been continually inhabited and cultivated ever since that period. Confirmed.

No. 4.—JEAN PIERRE GUEDRY claims a tract of land, situate on the right bank of the bayou La Fourche, in the county of La Fourche, containing five arpents in front, and forty in depth, and bounded on the upper side by the land of Oliviero Guedry, and on the lower by land of Louis Estiven.

It appears that this land was inhabited and cultivated on the 20th December, 1803, and that the same was continually inhabited and cultivated by those under whom the claimant holds for more than ten consecutive years next preceding. Confirmed.

No. 5.—PIERRE DASPIC ST. AMAND claims a tract of land, situate on the left bank of the bayou La Fourche, in the county of La Fourche, containing eleven arpents and twelve toises in front, and forty arpents in depth, and bounded on the upper side by land of Joseph Savoi, and on the lower by land of Louis Achez.

It appears that the land now claimed was inhabited and cultivated on the 20th December, 1803, and that the same was continually inhabited and cultivated by those under whom the claimant holds for more than ten consecutive years next preceding. Confirmed.

No. 6.—AUGUSTE VERRET claims a tract of land, situate on the left bank of the bayou La Fourche, in the county of La Fourche, containing three hundred and forty-seven superficial arpents, and bounded on the upper side by land of Alexis Tollet, and on the lower by land of Nicholas Verret.

This land was surveyed in the year 1792, in favor of the claimant, who obtained a complete grant for the same from the Spanish Government in the year 1796. Confirmed.

No. 7.—PEDRO BLANCHARD claims a tract of land, situate on the right bank of the bayou La Fourche, in the county of La Fourche, containing four arpents and twenty toises in front, and forty arpents in depth, and bounded on the upper side by land of Louis Blanchard, and on the lower by land of Lorenzo Blanchard.

This land was surveyed for the claimant, by order of Governor Miro, in the year 1790; and having been inhabited and cultivated ever since, until on and after the 20th of December, 1803: Confirmed.

No. 8.—ANTONIO MOULARD claims a tract of land, situate on the left bank of the bayou La Fourche, in the county of La Fourche, containing six arpents and seventeen toises in front, and forty arpents in depth, and bounded on the upper side by land of Pedro Gotrau, and on the lower by land of Carlos Bourg.

This land was surveyed in the year 1790, for the claimant, by order of Governor Miro; and having continued to be inhabited and cultivated ever since, until on and after the 20th December, 1803: Confirmed.

No. 9.—JOSEPH COMEAU claims a tract of land, situate on the right bank of the bayou La Fourche, in the county of La Fourche, containing five arpents and twenty-six toises in front, and forty arpents in depth, and bounded on the upper side by land of Amand Landry, and on the lower by land of Paul Landry.

This land was surveyed for the claimant, in the year 1792, by order of the Spanish Government; and having continued to be inhabited and cultivated ever since that period, until on and after the 20th December, 1803: Confirmed.

No. 10.—NICHOLAS VERRET claims a tract of land, situate on the left bank of the bayou La Fourche, in the county of La Fourche, containing twelve arpents and a half in front, and forty arpents in depth, and bounded on the upper side by land of Auguste Verret, and on the lower by land of Santiago Verret.

This land was surveyed for the claimant, by an order of the Spanish Government, in the year 1790; and having been continually inhabited and cultivated ever since that period, until on and after the 20th December, 1803: Confirmed.

No. 11.—JEAN DAIGLE claims a tract of land, situate on the left bank of the bayou La Fourche, in the county of La Fourche, containing six arpents twenty-seven toises and five feet in front, and forty arpents in depth, and bounded on the upper side by land of Joseph Aucoin, and on the lower by land of Jean Richard.

The land was surveyed for the claimant, by virtue of an order from the Spanish Government, in the year 1790; and having been continually inhabited and cultivated ever since that period, until on and after the 20th December, 1803: Confirmed.

No. 12.—FABIEN GUILLOT claims a tract of land, situate on the right bank of the bayou La Fourche, in the county of La Fourche, containing one hundred and ninety-seven superficial arpents, and bounded on the upper side by land of Joseph Hebert, and on the lower by land of Francisco Blanchard.

This land was regularly granted in the year 1791, by Governor Miro, to Maria Dugas, representing the succession of her deceased husband, Prosper Geroir. The present claimant purchased of the aforesaid Maria Dugas. Confirmed.

No. 13.—PIERRE BOURG claims a tract of land, situate on the left bank of the bayou La Fourche, in the county of La Fourche, containing five arpents in front, and forty arpents in depth, the lines opening three degrees, and bounded on the upper side by land of Mathurin Ossitet, and on the lower by land of Charles Forest.

This land was surveyed for Jean Charles Ossitet, by virtue of an order of Governor Miro, in the year 1790. The present claimant purchased from said Ossitet; and the land having been inhabited and cultivated ever since the above period, until on and after the 20th December, 1803: Confirmed.

No. 14.—JEAN BAPTISTE BERGERON claims a tract of land, situate on the right bank of the bayou La Fourche, in the county of La Fourche, containing thirteen arpents in front, and forty arpents in depth, and opening thirteen degrees, and bounded on the upper side by land of Baptiste Bourgeois, and on the lower by land of Mathurin Leblanc.

It appearing to the satisfaction of the Board that this land was settled, by permission of the proper Spanish officer, prior to the 20th day of December, 1803, and that the same was actually inhabited and cultivated on that day: Confirmed.

No. 15.—VALENTINE SAULET claims a tract of land, situate on the bayou La Fourche, in the county of La Fourche, containing on each side of the bayou a front of one hundred and twenty arpents, and a depth of four arpents, and bounded on one side by land of Guitros, and on the other by land of Jean Buafinal, a free man of color.

This claim is founded upon two different orders of survey: the one obtained by the claimant from the Spanish Government, in the year 1790; and the other obtained by Alexander Daspit St. Amand (under whose title the claimant holds by purchase,) in the year 1793; and it appearing that the land has been inhabited and cultivated ever since the respective dates of the aforesaid orders of survey. Confirmed.

No. 16.—MARIE BLANCHARD, widow of Mathurin Trahan, claims a tract of land, situate on the right bank of the bayou La Fourche, in the county of La Fourche, containing four arpents and three-quarters in front, and forty in depth, and bounded on the upper side by land of Madame Joseph Moise, and on the lower by land of Laurent Blanchard.

This is part of a tract of nine arpents and three-quarters front, on the ordinary depth, surveyed in favor of Mathurin Trahant, deceased, (the husband of the claimant,) by order of Governor Miro, in the year 1790. The land having been inhabited and cultivated ever since that period, until on and after the 20th December, 1803. Confirmed.

No. 17.—LAURENT BLANCHARD claims a tract of land, situate on the right bank of the bayou La Fourche, in the county of La Fourche, containing five arpents in front, and forty in depth, and bounded on the upper side by land of Marie Blanchard, and on the lower by land of Francis Trillons.

This is part of the tract of land mentioned in the preceding, No. 16, surveyed in the year 1790, for Mathurin Trahant, deceased, and by his widow, Marie Blanchard, conveyed to the present claimant; and having been inhabited and cultivated ever since the above period, until on and after the 20th December, 1803. Confirmed.

No. 18.—ELIAS BLANCHARD claims a tract of land, situate on the right bank of the bayou La Fourche, in the county of La Fourche, containing three arpents and ten toises in front, and forty arpents in depth, and bounded on the upper side by land of Francisco Giroir, and on the lower by land of Madame Ambroise Dugas.

This is part of a tract of land of six arpents and twenty toises in front, and forty arpents in depth, surveyed in favor of Francisco Blanchard, by order of Governor Miro, in the year 1790. The present claimant holds under the title of the said Francisco Blanchard; and the land having been inhabited and cultivated ever since the before-mentioned period, until on and after the 20th December, 1803. Confirmed.

No. 19.—FRANCISCO GIROIR claims a tract of land, situate on the right bank of the bayou La Fourche, in the county of La Fourche, containing three arpents and ten toises in front, and forty arpents in depth, and bounded on the upper side by land of Prosper Giroir, and on lower by land of Elias Blanchard.

This is part of the tract of six arpents and twenty toises front, on the usual depth, surveyed for Francisco Blanchard, as mentioned in the preceding claim. The present claimant holds under the title of said Blanchard, by virtue of intermediate sales; and the land having been inhabited and cultivated ever since the year 1790, until on and after the 20th December, 1803. Confirmed.

No. 20.—EUSTACHE DAILE, widow of Charles Daigle, deceased, claims a tract of land, situate on the right bank of the bayou La Fourche, in the county of La Fourche, containing five arpents and twenty-eight toises in front, thirty-one and a half arpents in depth, and bounded on the upper side by land of Isaac Hebert, and on the lower by land of Fabien Aucoin.

This land was surveyed for Charles Daigle, the deceased husband of the claimant, by an order of Governor Miro, in the year 1790; and it having been inhabited and cultivated ever since that date, until on and after the 20th December, 1803. Confirmed.

No. 21.—VINCENT DAILE claims a tract of land, situate on the left bank of the bayou La Fourche, in the county of La Fourche, containing three arpents in front, and forty in depth, and bounded on one side by land of F. B. Corvaisier.

This is part of a tract of land of five arpents front, surveyed for Jean Bte. Ossitet, by virtue of an order of Governor Miro, in the year 1790. The present claimant holds under the title of said Ossitet, by various intermediate sales; and the land having been inhabited and cultivated ever since that period, until on and after the 20th December, 1803. Confirmed.

No. 22.—F. B. CORVAISIER claims a tract of land, situate on the left bank of the bayou La Fourche, in the county of La Fourche, containing two arpents in front, and forty in depth, and bounded on one side by land of Vincent Dales.

This is part of a tract of land of five arpents front, on the ordinary depth, surveyed for Jean Baptiste Ossitet, in the year 1790, as mentioned in the preceding claim. The present claimant holds under the title of said Ossitet, by virtue of divers intermediate sales; and the land having been inhabited and cultivated ever since the above period, until on and after the 20th December, 1803. Confirmed.

No. 23.—F. B. CORVAISIER claims a tract of land, situate on the left bank of the bayou La Fourche, in the county of La Fourche, containing three arpents and twenty toises in front, and forty arpents in depth, and opening five degrees, and bounded on the upper side by land of Jean Baptiste Ossitet, and on the lower by land of Jean Charles Ossitet.

This land was surveyed in favor of Mathurin Joseph Ossitet, by order of Governor Miro, in the year 1790. The claimant purchased of said Ossitet; and the land having been inhabited and cultivated ever since the above period, until on and after the 20th December, 1803, Confirmed.

No. 24.—FELIX BOURG claims a tract of land, situate on the left side of the bayou La Fourche, in the county of La Fourche, containing four arpents in front, and forty in depth, and bounded on the upper side by land of Jean Gotreau, and on the lower by land of Jerome Guerin.

It appears that the claimant did actually inhabit and cultivate the land now claimed on the 20th of December, 1803, and that the same was continually inhabited and cultivated by him, or those under whom he claims, for more than ten consecutive years next preceding. Confirmed.

No. 25.—MARGUERITE BOUDREAU, widow of Jean Baptiste Boudreau, claims a tract of land, situate on the right bank of the bayou La Fourche, in the county of La Fourche, containing five arpents in front, and forty in depth, and bounded on the upper side by land of Gregoire Landry, and on the lower by land of C. F. Girod.

It appears that the land now claimed was inhabited and cultivated on the 20th December, 1803, and that the same was continually inhabited and cultivated by the claimant, or those under whom she claims, for more than ten consecutive years next preceding. Confirmed.

No. 26.—FRANCOIS HEBERT claims a tract of land, situate on the left bank of the bayou La Fourche, in the county of La Fourche, containing one hundred and two and nine-twelfths superficial acres, and bounded on the upper side by land of Charles Bark, and on the lower by land of Peter Hebert.

It appears that the land now claimed was inhabited and cultivated on the 20th December, 1803, and that the same was continually inhabited and cultivated by the claimant, or those under whom he claims, for more than ten consecutive years next preceding. Confirmed.

No. 27.—PIERRE HEBERT claims a tract of land, situate on the right bank of the bayou La Fourche, in the county of La Fourche, containing six arpents in front, and forty in depth, and bounded on the upper side by land of Vincent Daineny, and on the lower by land of the claimant.

This land was surveyed for Simon Dugas, by order of Governor Miro, in the year 1790. The present claimant holds under the title of said Dugas; and the land having been inhabited and cultivated ever since the afore-mentioned period, until on and after the 20th December, 1803. Confirmed.

No. 28.—PIERRE SEVILLE claims a tract of land, situate on the left bank of the bayou La Fourche, in the county of La Fourche, containing one hundred and eighty-two and nine hundreths superficial acres, and

bounded on the upper side by land of Noel Victor Boudreau, and on the lower by land of Jean Baptiste Boudreau.

It appears that the land now claimed was inhabited and cultivated on the 20th December, 1803, and that the same was continually inhabited and cultivated by those under whom the claimant holds for more than ten consecutive years next preceding. Confirmed.

No. 29.—VICTOR COULON and PIERRE AUBERT claim a tract of land, situate on the left bank of the bayou La Fourche, in the county of La Fourche, containing eleven arpents in front, and forty in depth, and bounded on the upper side by land of Gregoire Benoit, and on the lower by land of Julien Crochet.

It appears that the land now claimed was inhabited and cultivated on the 20th December, 1803, and that the same was continually inhabited and cultivated by the claimants, or those under whom they claim, for more than ten consecutive years next preceding. Confirmed.

No. 30.—CLAUDE F. GIROD claims a tract of land, situate on the left bank of the bayou La Fourche, in the county of La Fourche, containing two arpents twenty-seven toises and four feet in front, and forty arpents in depth, and bounded on the upper side by land of Francisco Boudreau, and on the lower by land of Pedro Monté.

This land was surveyed by order of Governor Miro, in the year 1790, in favor of Francisco Gautreau, from whom the claimant purchased; and it having been inhabited and cultivated ever since that period, until on and after the 20th December, 1803. Confirmed.

No. 31.—CLAUDE F. GIROD claims a tract of land, situate on the left bank of the bayou La Fourche, in the county of La Fourche, containing twenty-six and a half arpents in front, and forty arpents in depth, and bounded on the upper side by land of Germin Bergeron, and on the lower by land of Mr. Landremon.

This land was surveyed by order of Governor Miro, in the year 1790; twenty arpents front in favor of Joacinthe Bernard, and the remaining six and a half arpents front in favor of Joseph Leblanc; under which titles the present claimant holds; and the land having been inhabited and cultivated ever since the above period, until on and after the 20th December 1803. Confirmed.

No. 32.—CLAUDE F. GIROD claims a tract of land, situate on the right bank of the bayou La Fourche, in the county of La Fourche, containing seven hundred and ninety-nine superficial acres and nineteen hundreths of an acre, and bounded on the upper side by land of Marguerite Boudreau, and on the lower by land of Philip Joel Bow.

It appears that the land now claimed was inhabited and cultivated on the 20th December, 1803, and that the same was continually inhabited and cultivated by the claimant, or those under whom he claims, for more than ten consecutive years next preceding. Confirmed.

No. 34.—THOMAS DE VILLANUEVA claims a tract of land, situate on the right bank of the bayou La Fourche, in the county of La Fourche, containing nine arpents in front, and forty arpents in depth, and bounded on the upper side by land of Etienne Guitrod, and on the lower by land of Jacques Lamotte.

It appears that the land now claimed was inhabited and cultivated on the 20th December, 1803, and that the same was continually inhabited and cultivated by those under whom the claimant holds for more than ten consecutive years next preceding. Confirmed.

No. 36.—VINCENT DUMENY claims a tract of land, situate on the right bank of the bayou La Fourche, in the county of La Fourche, containing six and a half arpents in front, and forty arpents in depth, and bounded on the upper side by land of Estevan Dupuy, and on the lower by land of Simon Dugas.

This land was surveyed in the year 1790, in favor of the claimant, by order of Governor Miro; and it having been inhabited and cultivated ever since that period, until on and after the 20th December, 1803. Confirmed.

No. 37.—JOSEPH DAIGLE claims a tract of land, situate on the right bank of the bayou La Fourche, in the county of La Fourche, containing one hundred and thirty superficial arpents, and bounded on the upper side by land of Santivez Crochet, and on the lower by land of Jean Pierre Hebert.

This land was surveyed in the year 1790, in favor of the claimant, by order of Governor Miro; and it having been inhabited and cultivated ever since that period, until on and after the 20th December, 1803. Confirmed.

No. 38.—ETIENNE DUPUIS claims a tract of land, situate on the right bank of the bayou La Fourche, in the county of La Fourche, containing six arpents and twenty toises in front, and forty arpents in depth, and bounded on the upper side by land of Joseph Dupuis, and on the lower by land of Vincent Dumeny.
This land was surveyed in the year 1790, in favor of the claimant, by order of Governor Miro; and it having been inhabited and cultivated ever since that time, until on and after the 20th December, 1803. Confirmed.

No. 39.—JOSEPH AUCOIN claims a tract of land, situate on the left bank of the bayou La Fourche, in the county of La Fourche, containing six arpents and twenty-six toises in front, and forty arpents in depth, and opening twenty-five degrees, and bounded on the upper side by land of —— Church, and on the lower by land of Jean Daigle.
This land was surveyed in the year 1790, in favor of the claimant, by order of Governor Miro; and it having been inhabited and cultivated ever since that period, until on and after the 20th December, 1803. Confirmed.

No. 40.—JOSEPH DUPUIS claims a tract of land, situate on the right bank of the bayou La Fourche, in the county of La Fourche, containing six arpents and nine toises in front, and forty arpents in depth, and bounded on the upper side by land of Fabien Aucoin, and on the lower by land of Estevan Dupuis.
This land was surveyed in the year 1790, in favor of the claimant, by order of Governor Miro; and it having been inhabited and cultivated ever since that period, until on and after the 20th December, 1803. Confirmed.

No. 42.—JEAN RICHARD claims a tract of land, situate on the left bank of the bayou La Fourche, in the county of La Fourche, containing seven arpents and three toises in front, and forty arpents in depth, and opening twenty-five degrees, and bounded on the upper side by land of Jean Daigle, and on the lower by land of Jean Baptiste Giroir.
This land was surveyed for the father of the claimant, (from whom he inherited it,) in the year 1790, by order of Governor Miro; and it having been inhabited and cultivated ever since that period, until on and after the 20th December, 1803. Confirmed.

No. 43.—JEAN PIERRE HEBERT claims a tract of land, situate on the right bank of the bayou La Fourche, in the county of La Fourche, containing six arpents and nineteen toises in front and forty arpents in depth, and bounded on the upper side by land of Joseph Daigle, and on the lower by land of Isaac Hebert.
This land was surveyed in the year 1790, in favor of the claimant, by order of Governor Miro; and it having been inhabited and cultivated ever since that period, until on and after the 20th December, 1803. Confirmed.

No. 44.—JEAN GREGOIRE BLANCHARD claims a tract of land, situate on the right bank of the bayou La Fourche, in the county of La Fourche, containing three hundred and fifty superficial arpents, and bounded on the upper side by land of Pierre Landry, and on the lower by land of Jean Chetedeau.
This land was surveyed in the year 1790, in favor of the claimant, who obtained a complete grant for the same in the same year, from the then Governor of the province, Don Manuel Gayoso de Lemos. Confirmed.

No. 45.—PIERRE AUCOIN claims a tract of land, situate on the right bank of the bayou La Fourche, in the county of La Fourche, containing seven arpents and thirteen toises in front, and forty arpents in depth, and bounded on the upper side by land of Ambroise Garidel, and on the lower by land of Louis Aucoin.
This land was surveyed in favor of the claimant, by order of Governor Miro, in the year 1790: and it having been inhabited and cultivated ever since that date, until on and after the 20th December, 1803. Confirmed.

No. 46.—JEAN PIERRE BOURG claims a tract of land, situate on the right bank of the bayou La Fourche, in the county of La Fourche, containing six arpents and twenty toises in front, and forty arpents in depth, and bounded on the upper side by land of François Trilloux, and on the lower by land of Pierre Goutreau.
This land was surveyed in favor of the claimant, by order of Governor Miro, in the year 1790; and it having

been inhabited and cultivated ever since that period, until on and after the 20th December, 1803. Confirmed.

No. 47.—LOUIS AUCOIN claims a tract of land, situate on the right bank of the bayou La Fourche, in the county of La Fourche, containing six arpents and one toise in front, and forty arpents in depth, and opening one degree, and bounded on the upper side by land of Pedro Aucoin, and on the lower by land of Ellis Blanchard.
This land was surveyed in the year 1790, in favor of the claimant, by order of Governor Miro; and it having been inhabited and cultivated ever since that period, until on and after the 20th December, 1803. Confirmed.

No. 48.—CHARLES P. P. RICHARD claims a tract of land, situate on the left bank of the bayou La Fourche, in the county of La Fourche, containing three and a half arpents in front, and forty arpents in depth, and bounded on the upper side by land of Jean Baptiste Giroir, and on the lower by land of Jean Raphael Landry.
This land was surveyed for the claimant, by order of Governor Miro, in the year 1790; and it having been inhabited and cultivated ever since that period, until on and after the 20th December, 1803. Confirmed.

No. 49.—MADAME BOUDREAU, widow of Benjamin Boudreau, claims a tract of land, situate on the left bank of the bayou La Fourche, in the county of La Fourche, containing four arpents and four toises in front, and forty arpents in depth, and bounded on the upper side by land of Charles Boudreau, and on the lower by land of Armand Fremin.
This land was surveyed, by order of Governor Miro, in the year 1790, part of it in favor of Charles Boudreau, who conveyed to Benjamin Boudreau; and the balance in favor of Benjamin Boudreau, the late husband of the claimant. The land having been inhabited and cultivated ever since that period, until on and after the 20th December, 1803. Confirmed.

No. 50.—PIERRE HEBERT claims a tract of land, situate on the left bank of the bayou La Fourche, in the county of La Fourche, containing six arpents and twenty-two toises in front, and forty arpents in depth, and bounded on the upper side by land of François Hebert, and on the lower by land of François Thibodeaux.
It appears that the land now claimed was inhabited and cultivated on the 20th December, 1803, and that the same was continually inhabited and cultivated by the claimant, or those under whom he claims, for more than ten consecutive years next preceding. Confirmed.

No. 51.—JEAN BAPTISTE GIROIR claims a tract of land, situate on the left bank of the bayou La Fourche, in the county of La Fourche, containing seven arpents and twenty toises in front, and forty arpents in depth, and bounded on the upper side by land of Jean Richard, and on the lower by land of Pierre Richard.
It appears that the claimant did actually inhabit and cultivate the land now claimed on the 20th December, 1803, and for more than ten consecutive years prior thereto. Confirmed.

No. 52.—GEROME GUERIN claims a tract of land, situate on the left bank of the bayou La Fourche, in the county of La Fourche, containing seven arpents and ten toises in front, and forty arpents in depth, and bounded on the upper side by land of Maria Mariana Charles, and on the lower by land of Pedro Bertelot.
It appearing to the satisfaction of the Board that this land was settled, by permission of the proper Spanish officer, prior to the 20th December, 1803, and that the same was actually inhabited and cultivated on that day: Confirmed.

No. 53.—VINCENT HERNANDEZ claims a tract of land, situate on the left bank of the bayou La Fourche, in the county of La Fourche, containing nine and a half arpents in front, and forty arpents in depth, and bounded on the upper side by land of Francis Martinez, and on the lower by land of Manuel Hernandez.
This land was surveyed in the year 1790, in favor of the claimant, by order of Governor Miro; and it having been inhabited and cultivated ever since that period, until on and after the 20th December, 1803: Confirmed.

No. 54.—JOSEPH LANDRY claims a tract of land, situate on the left bank of the bayou La Fourche, in the county of La Fourche, containing five arpents and five toises in front, and forty arpents in depth, and bounded on the upper side by land of Jean Raphael Landry, and on the lower by land of Fabien Guillot.

This land was surveyed in the year 1793, in favor of the claimant, by order of Governor Miro; and it having been inhabited and cultivated ever since that period, until on and after the 20th December, 1803: Confirmed.

No. 55.—PIERRE GOTRO claims a tract of land, situate on the right bank of the bayou La Fourche, in the county of La Fourche, containing six arpents in front, and forty arpents in depth, and bounded on the upper side by land of Jean Pierre Bourg, and on the lower by land of Marin Gotro.

This land was surveyed in the year 1790, in favor of the claimant, by order of Governor Miro; and it having been inhabited and cultivated ever since that period, until on and after the 20th December, 1803: Confirmed.

No. 56.—CHARLES BOUDREAU claims a tract of land, situate on the left bank of the bayou La Fourche, in the county of La Fourche, containing five arpents in front, and forty arpents in depth, and bounded on the upper side by land of François Arcenaux, and on the lower by land of Benjamin Boudreau.

It appearing to the satisfaction of the Board that this land was settled, by permission of the proper Spanish officer, prior to the 20th day of December, 1803, and that the same was actually inhabited and cultivated on that day: Confirmed.

No. 57.—JEAN BAPTISTE DAIGLE claims a tract of land, situate on the right bank of the bayou La Fourche, in the county of La Fourche, containing four arpents and seven toises in front, and forty arpents in depth, and bounded on the upper side by land of Pierre Leblanc, and on the lower by land of Simon Simoneau.

This land was surveyed in the year 1790, in favor of the claimant, by order of Governor Miro; and it having been inhabited and cultivated ever since that period, until on and after the 20th December, 1803: Confirmed.

No. 58.—PIERRE BERTELOTTE claims a tract of land, situate on the left bank of the bayou La Fourche, in the county of La Fourche, containing five arpents and three toises in front, and forty arpents in depth, and bounded on the upper side by land of Gerome Guerin, and on the lower by land of François Arcenaux.

It appearing to the satisfaction of the Board that this land was settled, by permission of the proper Spanish officer, prior to the 20th day of December, 1803, and that the same was actually inhabited and cultivated on that day: Confirmed.

No. 59.—FABIEN GUILLOT claims a tract of land, situate on the right bank of the bayou La Fourche, in the county of La Fourche, containing four arpents and seventeen toises in front, and forty arpents in depth, and bounded on the upper side by land of Domingo Esteves, and on the lower by land of Juan Carlos Landry.

This land was, in the year 1790, by order of Governor Miro, surveyed in favor of Francisco Landry, under whose title the claimant holds by purchase; and the same having been inhabited and cultivated ever since the above period, until on and after the 20th December, 1803: Confirmed.

No. 60.—FRANÇOIS AISEME claims a tract of land, situate on the left bank of the bayou La Fourche, in the county of La Fourche, containing two and a half arpents in front, and forty arpents in depth, and bounded on the upper side by land of Pedro Bertelot, and on the lower by land of Carlos Boudreau.

This land was surveyed in the year 1800, in favor of the claimant, by virtue of a decree of the Intendant General of the province, in the year 1799; and it having been inhabited and cultivated ever since the last mentioned period, until on and after the 20th December, 1803: Confirmed.

No. 61.—JOSEPH SIMONEAU claims a tract of land, situate on the right bank of the bayou La Fourche, in the county of La Fourche, containing six arpents in front, and forty arpents in depth, and bounded on the upper side by land of Madame Simoneau, and on the lower by land of Joseph Landry.

This land was surveyed by Don Carlos Trudeau, Surveyor General, in the year 1779, in favor of Benjamin Leblanc, from whom the present claimant purchased; and the same having been inhabited and cultivated ever since that period, until on and after the 20th December, 1803: Confirmed.

No. 62.—PIERRE JOSEPH LANDRY claims a tract of land, situate on the right bank of the bayou La Fourche in the county of La Fourche, containing six arpents in front, and forty arpents in depth, and bounded on the upper side by land of Benjamin Leblanc, and on the lower by vacant land.

This land was surveyed by Don Carlos Trudeau, in the year 1780, in favor of the claimant; and it having been inhabited and cultivated ever since that period, until on and after the 20th December, 1803: Confirmed.

No. 63.—SIMON LANDRY claims a tract of land, situate on the left bank of the bayou La Fourche, in the county of La Fourche, containing three arpents and twenty-four toises in front, and forty arpents in depth, and bounded on the upper side by land of François Thibodeaux, and on the lower by land of Jean Pierre Landry.

This land is part of a tract which was surveyed, by order of Governor Miro, in the year 1790, in favor of Prospère Landry, deceased, from whom the claimant (his son) inherited; and it having been inhabited and cultivated ever since the above period, until on and after the 20th December, 1803: Confirmed.

No. 64.—FRANÇOIS THIBODEAUX claims a tract of land, situate on the left bank of the bayou La Fourche, in the county of La Fourche, containing three arpents in front, and forty arpents in depth, and bounded on the upper side by land of Charles Forest, and on the lower by land of Simon Landry.

This is part of a tract of land of six arpents and twenty-four toises in front, on the depth of forty arpents, surveyed by order of Governor Miro, in the year 1790, in favor of Prospère Landry, deceased, from whom Simon Landry, his son, inherited it, and who conveyed it to the present claimant; and the land having been inhabited and cultivated ever since the afore-mentioned period, until on and after the 20th December, 1803: Confirmed.

No. 65.—ESTEVAN HERNANDEZ claims a tract of land, situate on the right bank of the bayou La Fourche, in the county of La Fourche, containing six arpents and twelve toises in front, and forty arpents in depth, and bounded on the upper side by land of Jean Charles Landry, and on the lower by land of Jean Liqueur.

The claimant was put in possession of this land in the year 1793, by the Surveyor General, in conformity to an order of the Spanish Government; and it having been inhabited and cultivated ever since that period, until on and after the 20th December, 1803: Confirmed.

No. 66.—STEPHEN DAIGLE claims a tract of land, situate on the left bank of the bayou La Fourche, in the county of La Fourche, containing three arpents and thirteen and a half toises in front, and forty arpents in depth.

This is part of a tract of six arpents twenty-seven toises and five feet in front, with the ordinary depth of forty arpents, surveyed for Jean Daigle, as mentioned in claim No. 11, and conveyed by said Daigle to the present claimant. Confirmed.

No. 67.—CARLOS FOREST claims a tract of land, situate on the left bank of the bayou La Fourche, in the county of La Fourche, containing seven arpents and a half in front, and forty arpents in depth, and bounded on the upper side by land of Jean Charles Ossitet, and on the lower by land of Simon Landry.

This land was surveyed in the year 1790, in favor of the claimant, by order of Governor Miro; and it having been inhabited and cultivated ever since that period, until on and after the 20th December, 1803: Confirmed.

No. 68.—CLAUDE FRS. GIROD claims a tract of land, situate on the left bank of the bayou La Fourche, in the county of La Fourche, containing three arpents and seven toises in front, and forty arpents in depth, and bounded on the upper side by land of Pierre Hebert, and on the lower by land of Jean Baptiste Gros.

This land was surveyed in the year 1800, in favor of François Thibodeaux, by virtue of a decree of the Intendant General, made in 1799. The present claimant holds by conveyance from the aforesaid Thibodeaux; and the land having been inhabited and cultivated ever since that period, until on and after the 20th December, 1803: Confirmed.

No. 69.—FRANÇOIS BOURG claims a tract of land, situate on the left bank of the bayou La Fourche, in the county of La Fourche, containing three arpents and twenty-two toises in front, and forty arpents in depth, and bounded on the upper side by land of Nicholas Bertrand, and on the lower by land of Olivier Trahant.

This land was surveyed in the year 1790, in favor of Orette Brasseur, by order of Governor Miro. The present claimant holds under the title of said Brasseur, by virtue of successive transfers; and the land having been inhabited and cultivated ever since the above-mentioned period, until on and after the 20th December, 1803. Confirmed.

No. 70.—JOSEPH HEBERT claims a tract of land, situate on the right bank of the bayou La Fourche, in the county of La Fourche, containing three arpents nine toises and one foot in front, and twenty-three arpents twenty-eight toises and three feet in depth, and bounded on the upper side by land of Simon Dugas, and on the lower by land of the claimant.

This land was surveyed in the year 1791, by order of Governor Miro, in favor of Pierre Hebert, from whom the present claimant purchased, and the same having been inhabited and cultivated ever since the above period, until on and after the 20th December, 1803. Confirmed.

No. 71.—JOSEPH HEBERT claims a tract of land, situate on the right bank of the bayou La Fourche, in the county of La Fourche, containing three arpents nine toises and one foot in front, and twenty-six arpents and three-fifths of an arpent in depth, and bounded on the upper side by land of the claimant, and on the lower by land of Prospère Giroir.

This land was surveyed in the year 1791, in favor of the claimant, by order of Governor Miro; and it having been inhabited and cultivated ever since that period, until on and after the 20th December, 1803. Confirmed.

No. 72.—FRANÇOIS LANDRY claims a tract of land, situate on the right bank of the bayou La Fourche, in the county of La Fourche, containing six arpents seven toises and three feet in front, and forty arpents in depth, and bounded on the upper side by land of Pedro Leblanc, and on the lower by land of Neil McDonel.

This land was surveyed in the year 1780, by Don Carlos Trudeau, in favor of the claimant; and it having been inhabited and cultivated ever since that period, until on and after the 20th December, 1803. Confirmed.

No. 73.—PIERRE BOURG claims a tract of land, situate on the left side of the bayou La Fourche, in the county of La Fourche, containing three arpents twenty-two toises and three feet in front, and forty arpents in depth, and bounded on the upper side by land of Orette Brasseur, and on the lower by land of Evan Jones.

This land was surveyed in the year 1790, by order of Governor Miro, in favor of Maria Brasseur and Olivier Trahant, who conveyed it to the present claimant; and it having been inhabited and cultivated ever since that period, until on and after the 20th December, 1803. Confirmed.

No. 74.—MADAME BOURG, widow of Fabien Bourg, claims a tract of land, situate on the right bank of the bayou La Fourche, in the county of La Fourche, containing six arpents and twelve toises in front, and forty arpents in depth, and bounded on the upper side by land of Jean Baptiste Bourg, and on the lower by land of Ambroise Dugas.

This land was surveyed in the year 1790, in favor of Fabien Bourg, (the late husband of the claimant,) by order of Governor Miro; and it having been inhabited and cultivated ever since that period, until on and after the 20th December, 1803. Confirmed.

No. 75.—PIERRE BOURG claims a tract of land, situate on the right bank of the bayou La Fourche, in the county of La Fourche, containing six arpents and twenty toises in front, and forty arpents in depth, and bounded on the upper side by land of Joseph Guedry, and on the lower by land of Santyvez Crochet.

This land was surveyed in the year 1790, by order of Governor Miro, in favor of Maria Naquin, who conveyed it to the present claimant; and it having been inhabited and cultivated ever since that period, until on and after the 20th December, 1803. Confirmed.

No. 76.—JOSEPH NICHOLAS HEBERT claims a tract of land, situate on the left bank of the bayou La Fourche, in the county of La Fourche, containing five arpents and one toise in front, and forty arpents in depth, and bounded on the upper side by land of Santi-

ago Bavillon,' and on the lower by land of Pedro Bertran.

This land was surveyed in the year 1790, in favor of the claimant, by order of Governor Miro; and it having been inhabited and cultivated ever since that period, until on and after the 20th December, 1803. Confirmed.

No. 77.—JUAN MONZON claims a tract of land, situate on the left bank of the bayou La Fourche, in the county of La Fourche, containing seven arpents in front, and forty arpents in depth, and bounded on the upper side by land of Vincente Fernandez, and on the lower by land of Lorenzo Acosta.

This land was surveyed in the year 1800, in favor of the claimant, by virtue of a decree of the Intendant General made in the year 1799; and the same having been inhabited and cultivated ever since the last mentioned period. Confirmed.

No. 78.—ANSELME BELLISLE claims a tract of land, situate on the right bank of the bayou La Fourche, in the county of La Fourche, containing six arpents in front, and forty arpents in depth, and bounded on the upper side by land of Anselme Blanchard, and on the lower by land of Joseph Melanson.

This land was surveyed in the year 1780, by Don Carlos Trudeau, in favor of the claimant; and it having been inhabited and cultivated ever since that period, until on and after the 20th December, 1803. Confirmed.

No. 79.—JUAN VIVES claims a tract of land, situate on the left bank of the bayou La Fourche, in the county of La Fourche, containing thirteen arpents in front, and forty arpents in depth, and bounded on the upper side by land of Lorenzo Acosta, and on the lower by land of Antonio Martinez.

This land was surveyed in the year 1790, in favor of the claimant, who obtained a complete grant for the same from the Intendant General of the province in the year 1801; and the same having been inhabited and cultivated ever since the year 1790, until on and after the 20th December, 1803. Confirmed.

No. 80.—MADAME DAIGLE, widow of Jean Baptiste Daigle, claims a tract of land, situate on the right bank of the bayou La Fourche, in the county of La Fourche, containing five and a half arpents in front, and forty arpents in depth, and bounded on the upper side by land of Jean Charles Boudreau, and on the lower by land of Jean Boudreau.

This land was surveyed in the year 1790, in favor of Jean Baptiste Daigle, (the late husband of the claimant,) by order of Governor Miro; and it having been inhabited and cultivated ever since that period, until on and after the 20th December, 1803. Confirmed.

No. 81.—ISAAC LANDRY claims a tract of land, situate on the left bank of the bayou La Fourche, in the county of La Fourche, containing two arpents twenty-seven toises and four feet in front, and forty arpents in depth, and bounded on the upper side by land of Joseph Gotreau, and on the lower by land of François Gotreau.

This land was surveyed in the year 1794, by an order of Governor Miro issued in 1790, in favor of François Boudreau, who conveyed it to the present claimant; and the same having been inhabited and cultivated ever since that last period, until on and after the 20th December, 1803. Confirmed.

No. 82.—JEAN BAPTISTE BOURG claims a tract of land, situate on the right bank of the bayou La Fourche, in the county of La Fourche, containing four arpents and twenty-one toises in front, and forty arpents in depth, and bounded on the upper side by land of Pierre Bourg, and on the lower by land of Fabien Bourg.

This land was surveyed for the claimant in the year 1790, by order of Governor Miro; and it having been inhabited and cultivated ever since that period, until on and after the 20th December, 1803. Confirmed.

No. 83.—JOAQUIN BLANCHARD claims a tract of land, situate on the right bank of the bayou La Fourche, in the county of La Fourche, containing five arpents and a half in front, and forty arpents in depth, and bounded on the upper side by land of Jean Doucron, and on the lower by land of Soulia Blanchard.

This land was surveyed for the claimant in the year 1790, by order of Governor Miro; and it having been inhabited and cultivated ever since that period, until on and after the 20th December, 1803. Confirmed.

No. 84.—SOULIA BLANCHARD claims a tract of land, situate on the right bank of the bayou La Fourche, in the county of La Fourche, containing five arpents and twenty toises in front, and forty arpents in depth, opening one degree, and bounded on the upper side by land of Joaquin Blanchard, and on the lower by land of Charles Blanchard.

This land was surveyed in the year 1790, in favor of the claimant, by order of Governor Miro, and it having been inhabited and cultivated ever since that period, until on and after the 20th December, 1803. Confirmed.

No. 85.—MADAME AUCOIN, widow of Charles Aucoin, claims a tract of land, situate on the right bank of the bayou La Fourche, in the county of La Fourche, containing six arpents in front, and forty arpents in depth, and bounded on the upper side by land of Anselme Bellisle, and on the lower by land of Pierre Leblanc.

This land was surveyed in the year 1780, in favor of Joseph Melançon, and by him conveyed to the present claimant; and it having been inhabited and cultivated ever since the above period, until on and after the 20th December, 1803. Confirmed.

No. 86.—PEDRO MARIA THERIOT claims a tract of land, situate on the right bank of the bayou La Fourche, in the county of La Fourche, containing four arpents and five toises in front, and forty arpents in depth, and bounded on the upper side by land of Juan Boudreau, and on the lower by land of Santiago Doucron.

This land was surveyed in the year 1790, in favor of the claimant, by order of Governor Miro; and it having been inhabited and cultivated ever since that period, until on and after the 20th December, 1803. Confirmed.

No. 87.—JOACHIN PORCHE claims a tract of land, situate on the right bank of the bayou La Fourche, in the county of La Fourche, containing five arpents and six toises in front, and forty arpents in depth, and bounded on the upper side by land of Lorenzo Blanchard, and on the lower by land of Baptiste Bourg.

This land was surveyed by order of Governor Miro, in the year 1790, in favor of Pierre Bourg, who conveyed it to the present claimant; and it having been inhabited and cultivated ever since the above-mentioned period, until on and after the 20th December, 1803. Confirmed.

No. 88.—JOACHIN PORCHE claims a tract of land, situate on the right bank of the bayou La Fourche, in the county of La Fourche, containing six arpents in front, and forty arpents in depth, and bounded on the upper side by land of Pierre Blanchard, and on the lower by land of Pierre Bourg.

This land was surveyed, by order of Governor Miro, in the year 1790, in favor of Lorenzo Blanchard, who conveyed it to the claimant; and it having been inhabited and cultivated ever since the above period, until on and after the 20th December, 1803. Confirmed.

No. 89.—JOACHIN PORCHE claims a tract of land, situate on the right bank of the bayou La Fourche, in the county of La Fourche, containing nine arpents in front, and forty arpents in depth, and bounded on the upper side by land of Louis Aucoin, and on the lower by land of Pierre Blanchard.

This land was surveyed, by order of Governor Miro, in the year 1790, in favor of the widow of Louis Blanchard, deceased, under whose title the present claimant holds by virtue of successive transfers; and the same having been inhabited and cultivated ever since the aforementioned period until on and after the 20th December, 1803. Confirmed.

No. 90.—ANTOINE VIVES claims a tract of land, situate on the right bank of the bayou La Fourche, in the county of La Fourche, containing two arpents twenty-seven toises and three feet in front, and forty arpents in depth, opening seventeen degrees, and bounded on the upper side by land of Jean Chetido, and on the lower by land of Alin Bourg.

This land was surveyed, by order of Governor Miro, in the year 1790, in favor of Pierre Landry, under whose title the claimant holds by virtue of successive intermediate transfers; and the same having been inhabited and cultivated ever since the above-mentioned period, until on and after the 20th December, 1803. Confirmed.

No. 91.—MADAME DUGA, widow of Hypolite Duga, claims a tract of land, situate on the right bank of the

bayou La Fourche, in the county of La Fourche, containing five arpents and two toises in front, and forty arpents in depth, and bounded on the upper side by land of Joseph Boudreau, and on the lower by land of Jean Baptiste Daigle.

This land was surveyed, by order of Governor Miro, in the year 1790, in favor of Jean Charles Boudreau, under whose title the present claimant holds by virtue of successive transfers; and the same having been inhabited and cultivated ever since the above period, until on and after the 20th December, 1803. Confirmed.

No. 92.—AUGUSTIN DOMINGUER claims a tract of land, situate on the left bank of the bayou La Fourche, in the county of La Fourche, containing eleven arpents and twenty-three toises in front, and forty arpents in depth, and bounded on the upper side by land of Joseph Dias, and on the lower by land of Louis de Leon.

This land was surveyed in the year 1790, in favor of the claimant, by order of Governor Miro; and it having been inhabited and cultivated ever since that period, until on and after the 20th December, 1803. Confirmed.

No. 93.—AUGUSTIN DOMINGUER claims a tract of land, situate on the left bank of the bayou La Fourche, in the county of La Fourche, containing three arpents sixteen toises and three feet in front, and thirty arpents in depth, and bounded on the upper side by land of the claimant, and on the lower by land of Santiago Verret.

This land was surveyed, by order of Governor Miro, in the year 1790, in favor of Louis de Leon, under whose title the claimant holds; and it having been inhabited and cultivated ever since the above period, until on and after the 20th December, 1803. Confirmed.

No. 94.—AUGUSTIN DOMINGUER claims a tract of land, situate on the left bank of the bayou La Fourche, in the county of La Fourche, containing three arpents and fifty-five feet in front, and such depth, not exceeding forty arpents, as may appear on the plat of survey, and bounded on the upper side by land of the claimant, and on the lower by land of Lorenzo Fillamen.

This land was surveyed, by order of Governor Miro, in the year 1790, in favor of Santiago Verret, under whose title the present claimant holds in virtue of successive intermediate sales; and the same having been inhabited and cultivated ever since that period, until on and after the 20th December, 1803. Confirmed.

No. 95.—JOSEPH VINCENT, alias LANDRY, claims a tract of land, situate on the right bank of the bayou La Fourche, in the county of La Fourche, containing four and a half arpents in front, and forty arpents in depth, and bounded on the upper side by land of Carlos Blanchard, and on the lower by land vacant.

This land was surveyed, in the year 1793, (by an order of Governor Miro in 1790,) in favor of Pedro Monter, under whose title the present claimant holds by virtue of successive transfers; and the same having been inhabited and cultivated ever since the above-mentioned period, until on and after the 20th December, 1803. Confirmed.

No. 96.—PIERRE CENZIANI claims a tract of land, situate on the left bank of the bayou La Fourche, in the county of La Fourche, containing four arpents and twelve toises in front, and forty arpents in depth, and bounded on the upper side by land of Joseph Grange, and on the lower by land of Joseph Gautreau.

This land was surveyed, by order of Governor Miro, in the year 1790, in favor of Juan Landry, who conveyed it to the present claimant; and the same having been inhabited and cultivated ever since the above-mentioned period, until on and after the 20th December, 1803. Confirmed.

No. 97.—ARMAND FREMIN claims a tract of land, situate on the left bank of the bayou La Fourche, in the county of La Fourche, containing five arpents twenty-six toises and three feet in front, and forty arpents in depth, and bounded on the upper side by land of Benjamin Boudreau, and on the lower by land of Pedro Henry.

It appears that the claimant did actually inhabit and cultivate the land now claimed on the 20th December, 1803, and for more than ten consecutive years prior thereto. Confirmed.

No. 98.—CARLOS B. BLANCHARD claims a tract of land, situate on the right bank of the bayou La Fourche, in the county of La Fourche, containing five arpents and twenty toises in front, and forty arpents in depth, and bounded on the upper side by land of Julia Blanchard, and on the lower by land of Pedro Monter.

This land was surveyed, in the year 1790, in favor of the claimant, by order of Governor Miro; and it having been inhabited and cultivated ever since that period, until on and after the 20th December, 1803. Confirmed.

No. 99.—BELONY BLANCHARD claims a tract of land, situate on the left bank of the bayou La Fourche, in the county of La Fourche, containing five arpents and twenty-six toises in front, and forty arpents in depth, and bounded on the upper side by land of Olivier Aucoin, and on the lower by land of Alexis Sotch.

This land was surveyed in the year 1790, in favor of the claimant, by order of Governor Miro; and it having been inhabited and cultivated ever since that time, until on and after the 20th December, 1803. Confirmed.

No. 100.—JEAN LICAIRE, alias LAVIOLET, claims a tract of land, situate on the right bank of the bayou La Fourche, in the county of La Fourche, containing five arpents and twenty seven toises in front, and forty arpents in depth, and bounded on the upper side by land of Estevan Hernandez, and on the lower by land of Armand Landry.

This land was surveyed in favor of the claimant, by an order of Governor Miro, in the year 1790; and it having been inhabited and cultivated ever since that time, until on and after the 20th December, 1803. Confirmed.

No. 101.—ALIN BOURG claims a tract of land, situate on the right bank of the bayou La Fourche, in the county of La Fourche, containing six arpents and thirteen toises in front, and forty arpents in depth, and bounded on the upper side by land of Pierre Landry, and on the lower by land of Joseph Guedry.

This land was surveyed by order of Governor Miro, in the year 1790, in favor of the claimant; and it having been inhabited and cultivated ever since that time, until on and after the 20th December, 1803. Confirmed.

No. 102.—ISAAC HEBERT claims a tract of land, situate on the right bank of the bayou La Fourche, in the county of La Fourche, containing one hundred and forty superficial arpents, and bounded on the upper side by land of Jean Pierre Hebert, and on the lower by land of Charles Daigle.

This land was surveyed in the year 1790, in favor of the claimant, by order of Governor Miro; and it having been inhabited and cultivated ever since that period, until on and after the 20th December, 1803. Confirmed.

No. 103.—ARMAND LANDRY, CADET DEPRE, and HENRY LANDRY claim a tract of land, situate on the right bank of the bayou La Fourche, in the county of La Fourche, containing five arpents and twenty toises in front, and forty arpents in depth, and bounded on the upper side by land of Jean Liquer, and on the lower by land of Joseph Coumo.

It appears that the land now claimed was actually inhabited and cultivated on the 20th December, 1803, and that the same was continually inhabited and cultivated by the claimants, or those under whom they claim, for more than ten consecutive years next preceding. Confirmed.

No. 104.—ALAIN LANDRY claims a tract of land, situate on the right bank of the bayou La Fourche, in the county of La Fourche, containing five arpents sixteen toises and three feet in front, and forty arpents in depth, and bounded on the upper side by land of Manuel Ordona, and on the lower by land of François Landry.

This land was surveyed, by order of Governor Miro, in the year 1790, in favor of Domingue Esteve, under whose title the present claimant holds by virtue of divers intermediate sales; and the same having been inhabited and cultivated ever since the period above mentioned, until on and after the 20th December, 1803. Confirmed.

No. 105.—HILAIRE BREAU claims a tract of land, situate on the right bank of the bayou La Fourche, in the county of La Fourche, containing two arpents in front, and forty arpents in depth, and bounded on the upper side by land of Paul Breau, and on the lower by land of Pierre Landry.

This is part of a tract of land of four arpents front, on the ordinary depth of forty, surveyed, in the year 1792, in favor of Paul Landry, by order of Governor Miro. The present claimant holds under the title of said Landry by virtue of successive transfers; and the land having been inhabited and cultivated ever since the aforesaid period, until on and after the 20th December, 1803. Confirmed.

No. 106.—PAUL BREAU claims a tract of land, situate on the right bank of the bayou La Fourche, in the county of La Fourche, containing two arpents in front, and forty arpents in depth, and bounded on the upper side by land of Joseph Coumeau, and on the lower by land of Hilaire Breau.

This is the remaining part of the tract of land mentioned in the preceding claim as surveyed for Paul Landry in the year 1792. The present claimant holds under the title of said Landry, by virtue of successive transfers; and the land having been inhabited and cultivated ever since the above mentioned period. Confirmed.

No. 108.—BAPTISTE LANDRY and JOACHIN ZERINGUE claim a tract of land, situate on the right bank of the bayou La Fourche, in the county of La Fourche, containing five arpents in front, and forty arpents in depth, and bounded on the upper side by land of Simon Simoneau, and on the lower by land of Manuel Ordona.

This land was surveyed by order of Governor Miro, in the year 1790, in favor of Joseph Gomez, under whose title the claimants hold by virtue of successive intermediate transfers; and the land having been inhabited and cultivated ever since the above period, until on and after the 20th December, 1803. Confirmed.

No. 109.—ALEXIS TOLET claims a tract of land, situate on the left bank of the bayou La Fourche, in the county of La Fourche, containing eleven arpents in front, and forty arpents in depth, and bounded on the upper side by land of Jean Baptiste Forest, and on the lower by land of Pierre Daspic.

This land was surveyed for the claimant, in the year 1800, by virtue of a decree of the Intendant General of the province in the year 1799; and the same having been inhabited and cultivated ever since the last mentioned period, until on and after the 20th December, 1803. Confirmed.

No. 110.—JOSEPH PHILIP HENRY claims a tract of land, situate on the right bank of the bayou La Fourche, in the county of La Fourche, containing three arpents in front, and forty arpents in depth, and bounded on the upper side by land of François Boudreau, and on the lower by land of Nicolas Metras.

It appears that the claimant did actually inhabit and cultivate the land now claimed on the 20th December, 1803, and that the same was continually inhabited and cultivated by him, or those under whom he claims, for more than ten consecutive years next preceding. Confirmed.

No. 111.—NICOLAS METRAS claims a tract of land, situate on the right bank of the bayou La Fourche, in the county of La Fourche, containing three arpents in front, and forty arpents in depth, and bounded on the upper side by land of Joseph Philip Henry, and on the lower by land of Bartholomew Henry.

It appears that the claimant did actually inhabit and cultivate the land now claimed on the 20th December, 1803, and that the same was continually inhabited and cultivated by him, or those under whom he claims, for more than ten consecutive years next preceding. Confirmed.

No. 112.—JEAN CHARLES LANDRY claims a tract of land, situate on the right bank of the bayou La Fourche, in the county of La Fourche, containing five arpents and five toises in front, and forty arpents in depth, and bounded on the upper side by land of Francisco Landry, and on the lower by land of Estevan Hernandez.

This land was surveyed in the year 1790, in favor of the claimant, by order of Governor Miro; and it having been inhabited and cultivated ever since that period, until on and after the 20th December, 1803. Confirmed.

No. 114.—JEAN DUGAS claims a tract of land, situate on the left bank of the bayou La Fourche, in the county of La Fourche, containing seven arpents in front, and forty arpents in depth, and bounded on the upper side by land of Jean Martez Terriot, and on the lower by land of Antonio Lepine.

It appears that the land now claimed was inhabited and cultivated on the 20th December, 1803, and that the

same was continually inhabited and cultivated by the claimant, or those under whom he holds, for more than ten consecutive years next preceding. Confirmed.

No. 115.—JOSEPH SIMONS claims a tract of land, situate on the bayou La Fourche, in the county of La Fourche, containing twenty-one superficial acres and fifty-six hundredths, and bounded on one side by land of Jean Daigle, and on the other by land of Simon Simoneau.

It appears that the land now claimed was inhabited and cultivated on the 20th December, 1803, and that the same was continually inhabited and cultivated by the claimant, or those under whom he holds, for more than ten consecutive years next preceding. Confirmed.

No. 116.—JOSEPH MICHEL claims a tract of land, situate on the left bank of the bayou La Fourche, in the county of La Fourche, containing one hundred and twelve superficial acres, and seventy-eight hundredths of an acre, and bounded on the upper side by land of Peter Guillot, and on the lower by land of Simon Blanc.

It appears that the land now claimed was inhabited and cultivated on the 20th December, 1803, and that the same was continually inhabited and cultivated by the claimant, or those under whom he claims, for more than ten consecutive years next preceding. Confirmed.

No. 117.—GREGORY LANDRY claims a tract of land, situate on the right bank of the bayou La Fourche, in the county of La Fourche, containing four hundred and fifteen and fifty-nine hundredths superficial acres, and bounded on the upper side by land of Marguerite Boudreau, and on the lower by land of Joseph Landry.

It appears that the land now claimed was inhabited and cultivated on the 20th December, 1803, and that the same was continually inhabited and cultivated by the claimant, or those under whom he claims, for more than ten consecutive years next preceding. Confirmed.

No. 118.—RAPHAEL LANDRY claims a tract of land, situate on the left bank of the bayou La Fourche, in the county of La Fourche, containing eleven hundred and eighty-two and ninety-two hundredths superficial acres, and bounded on the upper side by land of Edward Daigle, and on the lower by land of ———.

It appears that the land now claimed was inhabited and cultivated on the 20th December, 1803, and that the same was continually inhabited and cultivated by those under whom the claimant holds for more than ten consecutive years next preceding. Confirmed.

No. 120.—JOSEPH DUGAS claims a tract of land, situate on the left bank of the bayou La Fourche, in the county of La Fourche, containing two hundred and forty-three and sixteen hundredths superficial acres, and bounded on the upper side by land of Oliver Peters, and on the lower by land of Francis Dugas.

It appears that the claimant did actually inhabit and cultivate the land now claimed on the 20th December, 1803, and for more than ten consecutive years prior thereto. Confirmed.

No. 121.—ARMAND LANDRY claims a tract of land, situate on the right bank of the bayou La Fourche, in the county of La Fourche, containing four arpents in front, and forty in depth, and bounded on the upper side by land of Pierre Landry, and on the lower by land of Jean Gregoire Landry.

Jean Louis Landry was put in possession of this land by the Surveyor General of the province in the year 1792, in conformity to an order of the Spanish Government. The present claimant holds under the said Landry by purchase; and the land having been inhabited and cultivated ever since the above-mentioned period, until on and after the 20th December, 1803. Confirmed.

No. 122.—SIMON SIMONEAU claims a tract of land, situate on the right bank of the bayou La Fourche, in the county of La Fourche, containing five arpents and fourteen toises in front, and forty arpents in depth, and bounded on the upper side by land of Jean Baptiste Daigle, and on the lower by land of Joseph Gomez.

This land was surveyed, in the year 1790, in favor of the claimant by order of Governor Miro; and it having been inhabited and cultivated ever since that period, until on and after the 20th December, 1803. Confirmed.

No. 123.—PIERRE LANDRY claims a tract of land, situate on the right bank of the bayou La Fourche, in the county of La Fourche, containing seven arpents and four toises in front, and forty arpents in depth, opening fifteen degrees, and bounded on the upper side by land of Paul Landry, and on the lower by land of Jean Louis Landry.

This land was surveyed in the year 1792, in favor of the claimant, by an order of Governor Miro; and the land having been inhabited and cultivated ever since that period, until on and after the 20th December, 1803. Confirmed.

No. 124.—FRANÇOIS FRILLONS claims a tract of land, situate on the right bank of the bayou La Fourche, in the county of La Fourche, containing ten arpents one toise and two feet in front, and forty arpents in depth, and bounded on the upper side by land of Mathurin Truhant, and on the lower by land of Jean Pierre Bourg.

This land was surveyed in the year 1790, in favor of the claimant, by order of Governor Miro; and it having been inhabited and cultivated ever since that period, until on and after the 20th December, 1803. Confirmed.

No. 125.—MATHURIN AYEUX claims a tract of land, situate on the left bank of the bayou La Fourche, in the county of La Fourche, containing six arpents twenty-one toises and four feet in front, and forty arpents in depth, and bounded on the upper side by land of Estevan Boudreau, and on the lower by land of Isaac Ducros.

This land was surveyed in the year 1800, in favor of the claimant, by virtue of a decree of the Intendant General made in the year 1799; and the same having been inhabited and cultivated ever since the last mentioned period, until on and after the 20th December, 1803. Confirmed.

No. 126.—JACQUES DOUCRON claims a tract of land, situate on the right bank of the bayou La Fourche, containing seven and a half arpents in front, and forty arpents in depth, and bounded on the upper side by land of Pierre Marie Theriot, and on the lower by land of Joseph Breau.

This land was surveyed in the year 1790, in favor of the claimant, by order of Governor Miro; and having been inhabited and cultivated ever since that period, until on and after the 20th December, 1803. Confirmed.

No. 127.—JEAN FRANÇOIS MAZIERE claims a tract of land, situate on the left bank of the bayou La Fourche, in the county of La Fourche, containing six arpents in front, and forty in depth, and bounded on the upper side by land of Graviel Hebert, and on the lower by land of François Godet.

This land was surveyed in the year 1790, in favor of the claimant, by order of Governor Miro; and having been inhabited and cultivated ever since that period, until on and after the 20th December, 1803. Confirmed.

No. 128.—FRANÇOIS TRILLONS, Jun. claims a tract of land, situate on the left bank of the bayou La Fourche, in the county of La Fourche, containing one hundred and thirty-five superficial arpents, and bounded on the upper side by land of Pierre Lebaure, and on the lower by land of Antoine Monlar.

This land was surveyed, by order of Governor Miro, in the year 1790, in favor of Pedro Goutreau, who conveyed to the present claimant; and it having been inhabited and cultivated ever since the above-mentioned period, until on and after the 20th December, 1803. Confirmed.

No. 129.—JEAN BAPTISTE PETRE claims a tract of land, situate on the left bank of the bayou La Fourche, in the county of La Fourche, containing three arpents and seventeen toises in front, and forty arpents in depth, and bounded on the upper side by land of Joseph Petre, and on the lower by land of Joseph Theriot.

This is part of a tract of land of seven arpents and four toises in front, and forty arpents in depth, surveyed by an order of Governor Miro, in the year 1790, in favor of Tranquille Petre, who conveyed to the present claimant; and the land having been inhabited and cultivated ever since the above-mentioned period, until on and after the 20th December, 1803. Confirmed.

No. 130.—JOSEPH PETRE claims a tract of land, situate on the left bank of the bayou La Fourche, in the county of La Fourche, containing three arpents and seventeen toises in front, and forty arpents in depth, and bounded on the upper side by land of Pedro Monter, and on the lower by land of Jean Baptiste Petre.

This is the balance of the tract of land surveyed by order of Governor Miro, in the year 1790, (as mentioned in the preceding claim,) in favor of Tranquille Petre, who conveyed it to the present claimant; and the land having been inhabited and cultivated ever since the above period, until on and after the 20th December, 1803. Confirmed.

No. 131.—ANTONIO DOMINGUER claims a tract of land, situate on the left bank of the bayou La Fourche, in the county of La Fourche, containing five arpents and twenty-six toises in front, and such depth, not exceeding forty arpents, as may be found upon the plat of survey, and bounded on the upper side by land of Antonio Truillo, and on the lower by land of Joseph Dias.

This land was surveyed in the year 1790, by order of Governor Miro, in favor of Juan Roderiguen Mena, who conveyed to the present claimant; and the land having been inhabited and cultivated ever since the period above mentioned; until on and after the 20th December, 1803. Confirmed.

No. 132.—USEBE ARSENEAU claims a tract of land, situate on the right bank of the bayou La Fourche, in the county of La Fourche, containing one hundred and thirty-three and one-third superficial arpents, and bounded on the upper side by land of Jean Baptiste d'Aigle, and on the lower by Pierre Marie Theriot.

This land was surveyed, in conformity to an order of Governor Miro, in the year 1790, in favor of Juan Boudreau, under whose title the present claimant holds by virtue of successive intermediate transfers; and the land having been inhabited and cultivated ever since the above period, until on and after the 20th December, 1803. Confirmed.

No. 133.—BLAS ACOSTA claims a tract of land, situate on the left bank of the bayou La Fourche, in the county of La Fourche, containing three arpents and two and a half feet in front, and forty arpents in depth, and bounded on the upper side by land of the claimant, and on the lower by land of François Plazencia.

It appears that the land now claimed was inhabited and cultivated on the 20th December, 1803, and that the same was continually inhabited and cultivated by those under whom the claimant holds for more than ten consecutive years next preceding. Confirmed.

No. 134.—MANUEL HERNANDEZ claims a tract of land, situate on the left bank of the bayou La Fourche, in the county of La Fourche, containing two arpents and twenty-eight toises in front, and forty arpents in depth, and bounded on the upper side by land of Vincent Hernandez, and on the lower by land of Antoine Truillo.

This land was surveyed in the year 1790, in favor of the claimant, by order of Governor Miro; and having been inhabited and cultivated ever since that period, until on and after the 20th December, 1803. Confirmed.

No. 135.—MADAME MAYEUX ANDRE claims a tract of land, situate on the left bank of the bayou La Fourche, in the county of La Fourche, containing five hundred superficial arpents, and bounded on the upper side by land of Santiago Verret, and on the lower by land of —— Bertran.

This land was surveyed in the year 1791, in favor of Marius Bringier, who obtained a complete grant for the same in the same year, from Don Estevan Miro, then Governor; under which grant the present claimant holds by a conveyance from the aforesaid Bringier. Confirmed.

No. 136.—MADAME MAYEUX ANDRE claims a tract of land, situate on the left bank of the bayou La Fourche, in the county of La Fourche, containing nine and a half arpents in front, and forty arpents in depth, and bounded on the upper side by land of Nicolas Verret, and on the lower by land of the claimant.

This land was surveyed in the year 1791, in favor of Santiago Verret, who obtained a complete grant for the same, in the same year, from Don Estevan Miro, then Governor; under which grant the present claimant holds in virtue of a conveyance from said Verret. Confirmed.

No. 137.—JEAN GUILFOS claims a tract of land, situate on the left bank of the bayou La Fourche, in the county of La Fourche, containing six arpents and one toise in front, and forty arpents in depth, and bounded on the upper side by land of Balthazar Plazencia, and on the lower by land of Pablo Navarro.

It appears that the claimant did actually inhabit and cultivate the land now claimed on the 20th December, 1803, and for more than ten consecutive years prior thereto. Confirmed.

No. 138.—CARLOS BOURG claims a tract of land, situate on the left bank of the bayou La Fourche, in the county of La Fourche, containing three arpents five toises and four feet in front; and forty arpents in depth, and bounded on the upper side by land of Pierre Henry, and on the lower by land of François Hebert.

This land was surveyed in favor of the claimant, by virtue of a decree of the Intendant General, in the year 1799; and the land having been inhabited and cultivated ever since that period, until on and after the 20th December, 1803. Confirmed.

No. 139.—FRANCISCO PLACENTIA claims a tract of land, situate on the left bank of the bayou La Fourche, in the county of La Fourche, containing three arpents and two and a half feet in front, and forty arpents in depth, and bounded on the upper side by land of Juan Aleman, and on the lower by land of Balthazar Placentia.

It appears that the claimant did actually inhabit and cultivate the land now claimed on the 20th December, 1803, and that the same was continually inhabited and cultivated by him, or those under whom he claims, for more than ten consecutive years next preceding. Confirmed.

No. 140.—FABIEN AUCOIN claims a tract of land, situate on the right bank of the bayou La Fourche, in the county of La Fourche, containing one hundred superficial arpents, and bounded on the upper side by land of Charles Daigle, and on the lower by land of Joseph Dupuis.

It appears that the claimant did actually inhabit and cultivate the land now claimed on the 20th December, 1803, and that the same was continually inhabited and cultivated by him, or those under whom he claims, for more than ten consecutive years next preceding. Confirmed.

No. 141.—PIERRE HENRY claims a tract of land, situate on the left bank of the bayou La Fourche, in the county of La Fourche, containing three arpents five toises and four feet in front, and forty arpents in depth, and bounded on the upper side by land of Armand Fremin, and on the lower by land of Carlos Bourg.

This land was surveyed in favor of the claimant, by virtue of a decree of the Intendant General, in the year 1799 ; and having been inhabited and cultivated ever since, until on and after the 20th December, 1803. Confirmed.

No. 142.—LOUIS GOLLE claims a tract of land, situate on the left bank of the bayou La Fourche, in the county of La Fourche, containing three arpents in front, and forty arpents in depth, and bounded on the upper side by land of Mathurin Ayeux, and on the lower by land of Estevan Boudreau.

This land was surveyed, by virtue of a decree of the Intendant General, issued in the year 1799, in favor of Isaac Ducron, under whose title, by different conveyances, the present claimant holds ; and the land having been inhabited and cultivated ever since the aforementioned period, until on and after the 20th December, 1803. Confirmed.

No. 143.—ESTEVAN BOUDREAU claims a tract of land, situate on the left bank of the bayou La Fourche, in the county of La Fourche, containing seven arpents fourteen toises and three feet in front, and forty arpents in depth, and bounded on the upper side by land of Jean Mayet, and on the lower by land of Mathuin Ayeux.

This land was surveyed in favor of the claimant, by virtue of a decree of the Intendant General, in the year 1799 ; and having been inhabited and cultivated ever since that time, until on and after the 20th December, 1803. Confirmed.

No. 144.—JOSEPH ROBICHO claims a tract of land, situate on the left bank of the bayou La Fourche, in the county of La Fourche, containing one hundred and fifty and twenty-nine hundredths superficial acres, and bounded on the upper side by land of Pierre Dugat, and on the lower by land of Pierre Naquin.

It appears that the claimant did actually inhabit and cultivate the land now claimed on the 20th December, 1803, and for more than ten consecutive years prior thereto. Confirmed.

No. 145.—HENRY RENTHROP claims a tract of land, situate on the right bank of the bayou La Fourche, in the county of La Fourche, containing twelve arpents in front, and forty arpents in depth, and bounded on the upper side by land of the claimant, and on the lower by land of Michel Bourgeois, Jun.

It appears that the land now claimed was inhabited and cultivated on the 20th December, 1803, and that the same was continually inhabited and cultivated by those under whom the claimant holds for more than ten consecutive years next preceding. Confirmed.

No. 146.—HENRY RENTHROP claims a tract of land, situate on the left bank of the bayou La Fourche, in the county of La Fourche, containing one hundred and eighty-seven and ninety-two hundredths superficial acres, and bounded on the upper side by land of C. F. Girod, and on the lower by land of Pierre Guillot.

It appears that the claimant did actually inhabit and cultivate the land now claimed on the 20th December, 1803, and that the same was continually inhabited and cultivated by the claimant, or those under whom he holds, for more than ten consecutive years next preceding. Confirmed.

No. 147.—IVES BOUDREAU claims a tract of land, situate on the left bank of the bayou La Fourche, in the county of La Fourche, containing three arpents in front, and forty arpents in depth, and bounded on the upper side by land of Jean Mayet, and on the lower by land of Estevan Boudreau.

This is part of a tract of land, confirmed in the name of Estevan Boudreau, (see claim No. 143,) who conveyed the quantity here claimed to his son, the present claimant. Confirmed.

No. 148.—BELONY BERTRAND claims a tract of land, situate on the left bank of the bayou La Fourche, in the county of La Fourche, containing five arpents and twenty-six toises in front, and forty arpents in depth, and bounded on the upper side by land of Joseph Nicolas Hebert, and on the lower by land of the claimant.

This land was surveyed in the year 1790, by order of Governor Miro, in favor of Pedro Bertrand, under whose title the claimant holds in virtue of successive transfers; and the land having been inhabited and cultivated ever since the above-mentioned period, until on and after the 20th December, 1803. Confirmed.

No. 149.—GEORGE MATHEU claims a tract of land, situate on the left bank of the bayou La Fourche, in the county of La Fourche, containing three arpents in front, and forty arpents in depth, and bounded on the upper side by land of Antoine Barras, and on the lower by land of Dominick Bergeron.

This is part of a tract of land of six arpents in front, and forty in depth, surveyed in the year 1790, by order of Governor Miro, in favor of Jean Nicolas Bertrand, deceased, under whose title the claimant holds by virtue of a conveyance from the widow of said Bertrand; and the land having been inhabited and cultivated ever since the above-mentioned period, until on and after the 20th December, 1803. Confirmed.

No. 150.—JOSEPH BOUDREAU claims a tract of land, situate on the right bank of the bayou La Fourche, in the county of La Fourche, containing five arpents and two toises in front, and forty arpents in depth, and bounded on the upper side by land of Ambrosio Dugas, and on the lower by land of Juan Carlos Boudreau.

This land was surveyed in the year 1790, in favor of the claimant, by order of Governor Miro; and having been inhabited and cultivated ever since that period, until on and after the 20th December, 1803. Confirmed.

No. 151.—AMABLE LANDRY claims a tract of land, situate on the left bank of the bayou La Fourche, in the county of La Fourche, containing six arpents and twenty-seven toises in front, and forty arpents in depth, and bounded on the upper side by land of Jean Pierre Landry, and on the lower by land of Joseph Guerin.

This land was surveyed in the year 1790, in favor of the claimant, by order of Governor Miro; and it having been inhabited and cultivated ever since that period, until on and after the 20th December, 1803. Confirmed.

No. 152.—MARIN GOUTREAU claims a tract of land, situate on the right bank of the bayou La Fourche, in the county of La Fourche, containing eight arpents in front, and forty arpents in depth, and bounded on the upper side by land of Pierre Goutreau, and on the lower by land of Jean Olivier Hebert.

This land was surveyed in the year 1790, in favor of the claimant, by order of Governor Miro; and it having been inhabited and cultivated ever since that time, until on and after the 20th December, 1803. Confirmed.

No. 153.—ANTONIO RODRIGUEZ claims a tract of land, situate on the left bank of the bayou La Fourche, in the county of La Fourche, containing three arpents in front, and forty in depth, and bounded on the upper side by land of Isabel Sanchez, and on the lower by land of Lorenzo Acosta.

It appears that the claimant did actually inhabit and cultivate the land now claimed on the 20th December, 1803, and for more than ten consecutive years next preceding. Confirmed.

No. 154.—ETIENNE BOUDREAU claims a tract of land, situate on the left bank of the bayou La Fourche, in the county of La Fourche, containing four arpents twenty-seven toises and five feet in front, and forty arpents in depth, and bounded on the upper side by land of Isaac Ducros, and on the lower by land of Blas Boudreau.

This land was surveyed in favor of the claimant, by virtue of a decree of the Intendant General, in the year 1799, and it having been inhabited and cultivated ever since that period, until on and after the 20th December, 1803. Confirmed.

No. 155.—ETIENNE BOUDREAU claims a tract of land, situate on the left bank of the bayou La Fourche, in the county of La Fourche, containing six arpents and twenty-one toises in front, and forty arpents in depth, and bounded on the upper side by land of Blas Boudreau, and on the lower by land of Pablo Boudreau.

This land was surveyed, by virtue of a decree of the Intendant General, in the year 1799, in favor of Joseph Boudreau, who conveyed to the present claimant; and the land having been inhabited and cultivated ever since that period, until on and after the 20th December, 1803. Confirmed.

No. 156.—MARIE HEBERT, widow of Joseph Moise, claims a tract of land, situate on the right bank of the bayou La Fourche, in the county of La Fourche, containing six arpents and thirteen toises in front, and forty arpents in depth, and bounded on the upper side by land of Isabel Dugas, and on the lower by land of Mathurin Trahant.

This land was surveyed in the year 1790, in favor of the claimant, by virtue of an order of Governor Miro; and having been inhabited and cultivated ever since that time, until on and after the 20th December, 1803. Confirmed.

No. 157.—BLAISE BOUDREAU claims a tract of land, situate on the left bank of the bayou La Fourche, in the county of La Fourche, containing five arpents twelve toises and four feet in front, and forty arpents in depth, and bounded on the upper side by land of Estevan Boudreau, and on the lower by land of Joseph Boudreau.

This land was surveyed in favor of the claimant, by virtue of a decree of the Intendant General, in the year 1799; and it having been inhabited and cultivated ever since that time, until on and after the 20th December, 1803. Confirmed.

No. 158.—GERMIN BERGERON claims a tract of land, situate on the left bank of the bayou La Fourche, in the county of La Fourche, containing two and a half arpents in front, and forty in depth.

This is part of a tract of ten arpents front, on the depth of forty, surveyed in the year 1790, by order of Governor Miro, in favor of Germin Bergeron, deceased, from whom his son, the present claimant, inherited the part now claimed; and the land having been inhabited and cultivated ever since the date of the survey, until on and after the 20th December, 1803. Confirmed.

No. 158.—AUGUSTE BERGERON claims a tract of land, situate on the left bank of the bayou La Fourche, in the county of La Fourche, containing two and a half arpents in front, and forty in depth.

This is part of the tract of ten arpents front, surveyed in 1790, in favor of Germin Bergeron, deceased, (as mentioned in the preceding claim,) and from whom the present claimant, his son, inherited the part now claimed; and the land having been inhabited and cultivated ever since the date of the survey, until on and after the 20th December, 1803. Confirmed.

No. 159.—BENOIT GOUTREAU claims a tract of land, situate on the left bank of the bayou La Fourche, in the county of La Fourche, containing five arpents in front, and forty in depth.

This is the balance of the tract of ten arpents front, (mentioned in the two preceding claims,) and surveyed in 1790, in favor of Germin Bergeron, deceased, at whose death the part now claimed was conveyed to the present claimant; and the land having been inhabited and cultivated ever since the date of the survey, until on and after the 20th December, 1803. Confirmed.

No. 160.—ALLEN and DONALDSON claim a tract of land, situate on the right bank of the bayou La Fourche, in the county of La Fourche, containing three and a half arpents in front, and forty in depth, and bounded on the upper side by land of Marin Goutreau, and on the lower by land of Firmin Aucoin.

This is part of a tract of land of six arpents and twenty-eight toises in front, on the usual depth of forty arpents, surveyed in the year 1791, by order of Governor Miro, in favor of Jean Olivier Hebert, under whose title the claimants hold by virtue of successive transfers; and the land having been inhabited and cultivated ever since the above-mentioned period, until on and after the 20th December, 1803. Confirmed.

No. 161.—MANUEL BARRIO claims a tract of land, situate on the left bank of the bayou La Fourche, in the county of La Fourche, containing one hundred and twenty-five superficial arpents, and bounded on the upper side by land of Louis Tolleret, and on the lower by land of Pierre Goutrean.

This land was surveyed in favor of Pierre Lebaure, by virtue of an order of Governor Miro, in the year 1790. The present claimant holds under the title of said Lebaure; and the land having been inhabited and cultivated ever since the year above mentioned, until on and after the 20th December, 1803. Confirmed.

No. 162.—JEAN MAYET claims a tract of land, situate on the left bank of the bayou La Fourche, in the county of La Fourche, containing seven arpents fourteen toises and three feet in front, and forty arpents in depth, and bounded on the upper side by land of Joes Rousseau, and on the lower by land of Estevan Boudreau.

This land was surveyed in favor of the claimant, by virtue of a decree of the Intendant General, in the year 1799; and having been inhabited and cultivated ever since that time, until on and after the 20th December, 1803. Confirmed.

No. 163.—JOSEPH BREAU claims a tract of land, situate on the right bank of the bayou La Fourche, in the county of La Fourche, containing seven arpents and twenty-seven toises in front, and forty arpents in depth, and bounded on the upper side by land of Simon Mazerole, and on the lower by land of Santiago Ducron.

This land was surveyed in the year 1790, in favor of the claimant, by order of Governor Miro; and having been inhabited and cultivated ever since that period, until on and after the 20th December, 1803. Confirmed.

No. 164.—BERNARD RIVIERE claims a tract of land, situate on the left bank of the bayou La Fourche, in the county of La Fourche, containing four arpents and one toise in front, and forty arpents in depth, and bounded on the upper side by land of Pedro Donzel, and on the lower by land of Juan Mendoza.

It appears that the claimant did actually inhabit and cultivate the land now claimed on the 20th December, 1803, and for more than ten consecutive years next prior thereto. Confirmed.

No. 165.—IVES CROCHET claims a tract of land, situate on the right bank of the bayou La Fourche, in the county of La Fourche, containing six arpents and nine toises in front, and forty arpents in depth, and bounded on the upper side by land of the widow Bourg, and on the lower by land of Joseph Daigle.

This land was surveyed in the year 1790, in favor of the claimant, by order of Governor Miro; and having been inhabited and cultivated ever since that period, until on and after the 20th December, 1803. Confirmed.

No. 166.—ANTOINE MARTINEZ claims a tract of land, situate on the left bank of the bayou La Fourche, in the county of La Fourche, containing two hundred and thirty-nine and two-ninths superficial arpents, and bounded on the upper side by land of Juan Vives, and on the lower by land of Francisco Martinez.

This land was surveyed in favor of the claimant, by an order of Governor Miro issued in the year 1790; and

having been inhabited and cultivated ever since that time, until on and after the 20th December, 1803. Confirmed.

No. 167.—FRANÇOIS SEVIN claims a tract of land, situate on the left bank of the bayou La Fourche, in the county of La Fourche, containing ten arpents and three toises in front, and forty arpents in depth, and bounded on the upper side by land of Juan Plazencia, and on the lower by land of Dominique Estevez.

This land was surveyed in favor of the claimant, by virtue of a decree of the Intendant General, in the year 1799; and the land having been inhabited and cultivated ever since that period, until on and after the 20th December, 1803. Confirmed.

No. 168.—ANTONIO TRUILLO claims a tract of land, situate on the left bank of the bayou La Fourche, in the county of La Fourche, containing eight arpents and two toises in front, and forty arpents in depth, and bounded on the upper side by land of Manuel Hernandez, and on the lower by land of Juan Rodriguez Minas.

This land was surveyed in the year 1790, in favor of the claimant, by order of Governor Miro; and having been inhabited and cultivated ever since that period, until on and after the 20th December, 1803. Confirmed.

No. 170.—PABLO LEBLANC claims a tract of land, situate on the right bank of the bayou La Fourche, in the county of La Fourche, containing four arpents and twelve toises in front, and forty arpents in depth, and bounded on the upper side by land of Pablo Boudreau, and on the lower by land of Edward Daigle.

This land was surveyed in favor of the claimant, by virtue of a decree of the Intendant General, in the year 1799; and the land having been inhabited and cultivated ever since that time, until on and after the 20th December, 1803. Confirmed.

No. 171.—FRANÇOIS GAUDET claims a tract of land, situate on the left bank of the bayou La Fourche, in the county of La Fourche, containing seven arpents and twenty-eight toises in front, and forty arpents in depth, and bounded on the upper side by land of Jean François Maziere, and on the lower by land of Louis Gaudet.

This land was surveyed in favor of the claimant, by virtue of a decree of the Intendant General, made in the year 1799; and the land having been inhabited and cultivated ever since that time, until on and after the 20th December, 1803. Confirmed.

No. 172.—LOUIS TOILLERET claims a tract of land, situate on the left bank of the bayou La Fourche, in the county of La Fourche, containing two hundred and forty superficial arpents, and bounded on the upper side by land of Santiago Verret, and on the lower by land of Pedro Lebaure.

This land was surveyed in favor of the claimant, by virtue of an order of Governor Miro, in the year 1790; and having been inhabited and cultivated ever since that period, until on and after the 20th December, 1803. Confirmed.

No. 173.—CLAUDE F. GIROD claims a tract of land, situate on the left bank of the bayou La Fourche, in the county of La Fourche, containing six arpents and five toises in front, and forty arpents in depth, and bounded on the upper side by land of Jean Mendez, and on the lower by land of Charles Reiner.

It appears that the land now claimed was inhabited and cultivated on the 20th December, 1803, and that the same was continually inhabited and cultivated by those under whom the claimant holds for more than ten consecutive years next preceding. Confirmed.

No. 174.—MAURICE SIMONEAU claims a tract of land, situate on the right bank of the bayou La Fourche, in the county of La Fourche, containing six arpents in front, and forty arpents in depth, and bounded on the upper side by land of François Landry, and on the lower by land of Benjamin Leblanc.

This land was surveyed, in the year 1780, in favor of Neil McDonald, under whose title the present claimant holds by virtue of successive transfers; and the land having been inhabited and cultivated ever since the above mentioned period, until on and after the 20th December, 1803. Confirmed.

No. 175.—JOSEPH GRANGE claims a tract of land, situate on the left bank of the bayou La Fourche, in the county of La Fourche, containing six arpents and six toises in front, and forty arpents in depth, and bounded on the upper side by land of Antonio B. Bertrand, and on the lower by land of Juan Landry.

This land was surveyed in the year 1790, in favor of the claimant, by order of Governor Miro; and having been inhabited and cultivated ever since that period, until on and after the 20th December, 1803. Confirmed.

No. 176.—RAPHAEL LANDRY claims a tract of land, situate on the left bank of the bayou La Fourche, in the county of La Fourche, containing two hundred superficial arpents, and bounded on the upper side by land of Carlos Pedro, and on the lower by land of Joseph Landry.

This land was surveyed in favor of the claimant, by order of Governor Miro, in the year 1790; and having been inhabited and cultivated ever since that period, until on and after the 20th December, 1803. Confirmed.

No. 177.—CARLOS BOURG claims a tract of land, situate on the left bank of the bayou La Fourche, in the county of La Fourche, containing six arpents and eighteen toises in front, and forty arpents in depth, and bounded on the upper side by land of Antonio Monlar, and on the lower by land of the church.

This land was surveyed in the year 1790, in favor of the claimant, by order of Governor Miro; and having been inhabited and cultivated ever since that period, until on and after the 20th December, 1803. Confirmed.

No. 178.—AMBROISE DUGA claims a tract of land, situate on the right bank of the bayou La Fourche, in the county of La Fourche, containing seven arpents front, and forty arpents in depth, and bounded on the upper side by land of Fabien Bourg, and on the lower by land of Joseph Boudreau.

This land was surveyed in favor of the claimant, by virtue of an order of Governor Miro, issued in the year 1790; and it having been inhabited and cultivated ever since that time, until on and after the 20th December, 1803. Confirmed.

No. 179.—MADAME CHEDOTO, widow of Jean Chedoto, claims a tract of land, situate on the right bank of the bayou La Fourche, in the county of La Fourche, containing three arpents in front, and forty in depth, and bounded on the upper side by land of Jean Gregoire Blanchard, and on the lower by land of Pierre Landry, Jun.

This land was surveyed in the year 1790, in favor of the claimant's husband, by order of Governor Miro; and having been inhabited and cultivated ever since that period, until on and after the 20th December, 1803. Confirmed.

No. 180.—LORENZO DE ACOSTA claims a tract of land, situate on the left bank of the bayou La Fourche, in the county of La Fourche, containing three arpents and three toises in front, and forty arpents in depth, and bounded on the upper side by land of Antonio Rodriguez, and on the lower by land of Juan Vives.

It appears that the claimant did actually inhabit and cultivate the land now claimed on the 20th December, 1803, and for more than ten consecutive years next preceding. Confirmed.

No. 181.—JEAN DORION claims a tract of land, situate on the right bank of the bayou La Fourche, in the county of La Fourche, containing five arpents and twenty-six toises in front, and forty arpents in depth, and bounded on the upper side by land of Lucette Breau, and on the lower by land of Joaquin Blanchard.

This land was surveyed in the year 1790, in favor of the claimant, by order of Governor Miro; and having been inhabited and cultivated ever since that period, until on and after the 20th December, 1803. Confirmed.

No. 182.—CHARLES BLANCHARD claims a tract of land, situate on the left bank of the bayou La Fourche, in the county of La Fourche, containing six arpents and twenty-three toises in front, and forty arpents in depth, and bounded on the upper side by land of Tranquille Petre, and on the lower by land of Germin Bergeron.

This land was surveyed in the year 1790, by order of Governor Miro, in favor of Joseph Theriot, who conveyed to the present claimant; and it having been inhabited and cultivated ever since the above-mentioned period, until on and after the 20th December, 1803. Confirmed.

No. 183.—PEDRO MONTE claims a tract of land, situate on the left bank of the bayou La Fourche, in the county of La Fourche, containing six arpents and four toises in front, and forty arpents in depth, and bounded on the upper side by land of François Goutreau, and on the lower by land of Tranquille Petre.

This land was surveyed in the year 1790, in favor of the claimant, by order of Governor Miro; and having been inhabited and cultivated ever since that time, until on and after the 20th December, 1803. Confirmed.

No. 184.—ISABEL DOUGAS claims a tract of land, situate on the left bank of the bayou La Fourche, in the county of La Fourche, containing six arpents and three toises in front, and forty arpents in depth, and bounded on the upper side by land of François Blanchard, and on the lower by land of Madame Moise.

This land was surveyed in the year 1790, in favor of the claimant, by order of Governor Miro; and having been inhabited and cultivated ever since that period, until on and after the 20th December, 1803. Confirmed.

No. 185.—JOSEPH DIAS claims a tract of land, situate on the left bank of the bayou La Fourche, in the county of La Fourche, containing eleven arpents and twenty-seven toises in front, and forty arpents in depth, and bounded on the upper side by land of Juan Rodriguez Miras, and on the lower by land of —— Augustin.

This land was surveyed in favor of the claimant, by an order of Governor Miro issued in the year 1790; and it having been inhabited and cultivated ever since that period, until on and after the 20th December, 1803. Confirmed.

No. 186.—LAURETTE BREAU claims a tract of land, situate on the right bank of the bayou La Fourche, in the county of La Fourche, containing six arpents and twenty-three toises in front, and forty arpents in depth, and bounded on the upper side by land of Carlos Goutreau, and on the lower by land of Juan Dueson.

This land was surveyed in the year 1790, in favor of the claimant, by order of Governor Miro; and having been inhabited and cultivated ever since that period, until on and after the 20th December, 1803. Confirmed.

No. 187.—JUAN CARLOS GOUTREAU claims a tract of land, situate on the left bank of the bayou La Fourche, in the county of La Fourche, containing six arpents and eighteen toises in front, and forty arpents in depth, and bounded on the upper side by land of Fabien Guillot, and on the lower by land of Olivier Aucoin.

This land was surveyed in the year 1790, in favor of the claimant, by order of Governor Miro; and having been inhabited and cultivated ever since that period, until on and after the 20th December, 1803. Confirmed.

No. 188.—DIEGO GONZALES claims a tract of land, situate on the left bank of the bayou La Fourche, in the county of La Fourche, containing one hundred and nineteen superficial arpents, and bounded on the upper side by land of François Martin, and on the lower by land of Antoine Alleman.

This land was surveyed, by virtue of an order of Governor Miro issued in the year 1790, in favor of Vicente Mora, who conveyed to the present claimant; and the land having been inhabited and cultivated ever since the above-mentioned period, until on and after the 20th December, 1803. Confirmed.

No. 189.—OLIVIER AUCOIN claims a tract of land, situate on the left bank of the bayou La Fourche, in the county of La Fourche, containing two hundred and twenty superficial arpents, and bounded on the upper side by land of Juan Carlos Goutreau, and on the lower by land of Belony Blanchard.

This land was surveyed in favor of the claimant, by virtue of an order of Governor Miro issued in the year 1790; and it having been inhabited and cultivated ever since that period, until on and after the 20th December, 1803. Confirmed.

No. 190.—MATHURIN DONNE claims a tract of land situate on the left bank of the bayou La Fourche, in the county of La Fourche, containing two hundred and thirteen and twenty-four hundredths superficial acres; and bounded on the upper side by land of Charles Guillot, and on the lower by land of Domingo Stepho.

It appears that the claimant did actually inhabit and cultivate the land now claimed on the 20th December, 1803, and for more than ten consecutive years next preceding. Confirmed.

No. 191.—PIERRE DUGA claims a tract of land, situate on the left bank of the bayou La Fourche, in the county of La Fourche, containing two hundred and twenty-seven and four hundredths superficial acres, and bounded on the upper side by land of Jean Boudreau, and on the lower by land of Joseph Robichaux.
It appears that the claimant did actually inhabit and cultivate the land now claimed on the 20th December, 1803, and for more than ten consecutive years prior thereto. Confirmed.

No. 192.—CHARLES GUILLOT claims a tract of land, situate on the left bank of the bayou La Fourche, in the county of La Fourche, containing two hundred and thirty-four and sixty-six hundredths superficial acres, and bounded on the upper side by land of Olivier Peters, and on the lower by land of Mathurin Donné.
It appears that the claimant did actually inhabit and cultivate the land now claimed on the 20th December, 1803, and for more than ten consecutive years prior thereto. Confirmed.

No. 193.—GREGOIRE BENOIT claims a tract of land, situate on the left bank of the bayou La Fourche, in the county of La Fourche, containing eighty-nine and fifty-five hundredths superficial acres, and bounded on the upper side by land of Louis Augeron, and on the lower by land of Jean Marie Benoit.
It appears that the claimant did actually inhabit and cultivate the land now claimed on the 20th December, 1803, and for more than ten consecutive years next preceding. Confirmed.

No. 194.—LOUIS EXNICIOUS claims a tract of land, situate on the left bank of the bayou La Fourche, in the county of La Fourche, containing four arpents in front, and forty arpents in depth, and bounded on the upper side by land of Blaise Boudreau, and on the lower by land of Paul Leblanc.
It appears that the land now claimed was inhabited and cultivated on the 20th of December, 1803, and that the same was continually inhabited and cultivated by those under whom the claimant holds for more than ten consecutive years next preceding. Confirmed.

No. 195.—JEAN BAPTISTE HEBERT claims a tract of land, situate on the right bank of the bayou La Fourche, in the county of La Fourche, containing one hundred and sixteen and seventy-three hundredths superficial acres, and bounded on the upper side by land of Jean Constant Boudreau, and on the lower by land of ——.
It appears that the claimant did actually inhabit and cultivate the land now claimed on the 20th December, 1803, and for more than ten consecutive years prior thereto. Confirmed.

No. 196.—ALEXIS AUCOIN claims a tract of land, situate on the right bank of the bayou La Fourche, in the county of La Fourche, containing one hundred and seventy-four and seventy-four hundredths superficial acres, and bounded on the upper side by land of Fabien Aucoin, and on the lower by land of ——.
It appears that the land now claimed was inhabited and cultivated on the 20th December, 1803, and that the same was continually inhabited and cultivated by the claimant, or those under whom he claims, for more than ten consecutive years next preceding. Confirmed.

No. 197.—LOUIS DUE claims a tract of land, situate on the left bank of the bayou La Fourche, in the county of La Fourche, containing one hundred and six and seventy-eight hundredths superficial acres, and bounded on the upper side by land of Jean Baptiste Phillippeaux, and on the lower by land of Pierre Richard.
It appears that the land now claimed was inhabited and cultivated on the 20th December, 1803, and that the same was continually inhabited and cultivated by the claimant, or those under whom he claims, for more than ten consecutive years next preceding. Confirmed.

No. 198.—PIERRE GUILLOTTE claims a tract of land, situate on the left bank of the bayou La Fourche, in the county of La Fourche, containing one hundred and eighty-six and ten hundredths superficial acres, and bounded on the upper side by land of Henry Renthrop, and on the lower by land of Joseph Mitchell.
It appears that the land now claimed was inhabited and cultivated on the 20th December, 1803, and that the same was continually inhabited and cultivated by the claimant, or those under whom he holds, for more than ten consecutive years next preceding. Confirmed.

No. 199.—JEAN BAPTISTE BOUDREAU claims a tract of land, situate on the right bank of the bayou La Fourche, in the county of La Fourche, containing fifty-eight and seventy-five hundredths superficial arpents, and bounded on the upper side by land of Ann Angelique Terriot, and on the lower by land of ——.
It appears that the land now claimed was inhabited and cultivated on the 20th December, 1803, and that the same was continually inhabited and cultivated by the claimant, or those under whom he claims, for more than ten consecutive years next preceding. Confirmed.

No. 200.—REYNAUD and PEYTAVIN claim a tract of land, situate on the left bank of the bayou La Fourche, in the county of La Fourche, containing five arpents in front, and forty arpents in depth, and bounded on the upper side by land of Marguerite Crochet, and on the lower by land of François Leblanc.
It appears that the land now claimed was inhabited and cultivated on the 20th December, 1803, and that the same was continually inhabited and cultivated by those under whom the claimants hold for more than ten consecutive years next preceding. Confirmed.

No. 201.—JEAN GUEDRY claims a tract of land, situate on the left bank of the bayou La Fourche, in the county of La Fourche, containing one hundred and two and thirty-nine hundredths superficial acres, and bounded on the upper side by land of Jean M. Leblanc, and on the lower by land of François Leblanc.
It appears that the land now claimed was inhabited and cultivated on the 20th December, 1803, and that the same was continually inhabited and cultivated by the claimant, or those under whom he claims, for more than ten consecutive years next preceding. Confirmed.

No. 202.—JEAN BAPTISTE HEBERT claims a tract of land, situate on the left bank of the bayou La Fourche, in the county of La Fourche, containing one hundred and forty-two and forty-nine hundredths superficial acres, and bounded on the upper side by land of Peter Nanchan, and on the lower by land of Alexis Hebert.
It appears that the land now claimed was inhabited and cultivated on the 20th December, 1803, and that the same was continually inhabited and cultivated by the claimant, or those under whom he claims, for more than ten consecutive years next preceding. Confirmed.

No. 203.—ANN ANGELIQUE TERRIOT claims a tract of land, situate on the right bank of the bayou La Fourche, in the county of La Fourche, containing one hundred and fourteen and thirty-eight hundredths superficial acres, and bounded on the upper side by land of Joseph Goatreau, and on the lower by land of ——.
It appears that the land now claimed was inhabited and cultivated on the 20th December, 1803, and that the same was continually inhabited and cultivated by the claimant, or those under whom she claims, for more than ten consecutive years next preceding. Confirmed.

No. 204.—JEAN BAPTISTE DELORME claims a tract of land, situate on the right bank of the bayou La Fourche, in the county of La Fourche, containing one hundred and eleven and sixty-eight hundredths superficial acres, and bounded on the upper side by land of Philip Jolibois, and on the lower by land of Joseph Bourg.
It appears that the claimant did actually inhabit and cultivate the land now claimed on the 20th December, 1803, and that the same was continually inhabited and cultivated by the claimant, or those under whom he claims, for more than ten consecutive years next preceding. Confirmed.

No. 205.—NICHOLAS PHOPTE claims a tract of land, situate on the left bank of the bayou La Fourche, in the county of La Fourche, containing sixty-five and thirty-one hundredths superficial acres, and bounded on the upper side by land of Jean Baptiste Grough, and on the lower by land of Jean Olivier.
It appears that the land now claimed was inhabited and cultivated on the 20th December, 1803, and that the same was continually inhabited and cultivated by the claimant, or those under whom he claims, for more than ten consecutive years next preceding. Confirmed.

No. 206.—PHILIP JOLIBOIS claims a tract of land, situate on the right bank of the bayou La Fourche, in the county of La Fourche, containing two hundred and eighty-three and seven hundredths superficial acres, and bounded on one side by land of C. F. Girod, and on the other by land of Jean Baptiste Delorme.

It appears that the claimant did actually inhabit and cultivate the land now claimed on the 20th December, 1803, and that the same was continually inhabited and cultivated by him, or those under whom he claims, for more than ten consecutive years next preceding. Confirmed.

No. 207.—PIERRE NAQUIN claims a tract of land, situate on the left bank of the bayou La Fourche, in the county of La Fourche, containing one hundred and four and forty-three hundredths superficial acres, and bounded on the upper side by land of Joseph Robichaux, and on the lower by land of Jean Hebert.

It appears that the land now claimed was inhabited and cultivated on the 20th December, 1803, and that the same was continually inhabited and cultivated by the claimant, or those under whom he claims, for more than ten consecutive years next preceding. Confirmed.

No. 208.—LOUIS OGERON claims a tract of land, situate on the left bank of the bayou La Fourche, in the county of La Fourche, containing ninety-five and thirty-four hundredths superficial acres, and bounded on the upper side by land of Marguerite Peters, and on the lower by land of Gregoire Benoit.

It appears that the claimant did actually inhabit and cultivate the land now claimed on the 20th December, 1803, and that the same was continually inhabited and cultivated by him, or those under whom he claims, for more than ten consecutive years next preceding. Confirmed.

No. 209.—MATHURIN AUCOIN claims a tract of land, situate on the right bank of the bayou La Fourche, in the county of La Fourche, containing one hundred and twenty-nine and fifty-two hundredths superficial acres, and bounded on the upper side by land of François Louret, and on the lower by land of Etienne Davois.

It appears that the claimant did actually inhabit and cultivate the land now claimed on the 20th December, 1803, and that the same was continually inhabited and cultivated by him, or those under whom he claims, for more than ten consecutive years next preceding. Confirmed.

No. 210.—HYACINTHE AUCOIN claims a tract of land, situate on the right bank of the bayou La Fourche, in the county of La Fourche, containing ninety and twenty-four hundredths superficial acres, and bounded on the upper side by land of William Aucoin, and on the lower by land of ———.

It appears that the land now claimed was inhabited and cultivated on the 20th December, 1803, and that the same was continually inhabited and cultivated by the claimant, or those under whom he holds, for more than ten consecutive years next preceding. Confirmed.

No. 211.—JEAN M. LEBLANC claims a tract of land, situate on the left bank of the bayou La Fourche, in the county of La Fourche, containing three arpents in front, and forty arpents in depth, and bounded on the upper side by land of Jean Guedry, and on the lower by land of Abar Billangier.

It appears that the land now claimed was inhabited and cultivated on the 20th December, 1803, and that the same was continually inhabited and cultivated by the claimant, or those under whom he holds, for more than ten consecutive years next preceding. Confirmed.

No. 212.—JOSEPH DAIGLE claims a tract of land, situate on the right bank of the bayou La Fourche, in the county of La Fourche, containing fifty-four and twenty-nine hundredths superficial acres, and bounded on the upper side by land of Joseph Tonelia, and on the lower by land of Anselme Bellisle.

It appears that the claimant did actually inhabit and cultivate the land now claimed on the 20th December, 1803, and for more than ten consecutive years next preceding. Confirmed.

No. 213.—JULIEN CROCHET claims a tract of land, situate on the left bank of the bayou La Fourche, in the county of La Fourche, containing one hundred and nine and eighty-five hundredths superficial acres, and bounded on the upper side by lands of Victor Coulon and Peter Aubart, and on the lower by land of Marguerite Crochet.

It appears that the claimant did actually inhabit and cultivate the land now claimed on the 20th December, 1803, and for more than ten consecutive years next preceding. Confirmed.

No. 214.—MATHURIN HEBERT claims a tract of land, situate on the right bank of the bayou La Fourche, in the county of La Fourche, containing one hundred and forty-six and ninety-two hundredths superficial acres, and bounded on the upper side by land of Jean Baptiste Hebert, and on the lower by land of ———.

It appears that the claimant did actually inhabit and cultivate the land now claimed on the 20th December, 1803, and for more than ten consecutive years next preceding. Confirmed.

No. 215.—JOCO ROUSSEAU claims a tract of land, situate on the left bank of the bayou La Fourche, in the county of La Fourche, containing two hundred and two and eighty-three hundredths superficial acres, and bounded on the upper side by land of Jean Olivier, and on the lower by land of Jean Maillet.

It appears that the claimant did actually inhabit and cultivate the land now claimed on the 20th December, 1803, and for more than ten consecutive years prior thereto. Confirmed.

No. 216.—SIMON LEBLANC claims a tract of land, situate on the left bank of the bayou La Fourche, in the county of La Fourche, containing eighty-two and twenty-eight hundredths superficial acres, and bounded on the upper side by land of Joseph Mitchel, and on the lower by land of Jean Goutreau.

It appears that the claimant did actually inhabit and cultivate the land now claimed on the 20th December, 1803, and that the same was continually inhabited and cultivated for more than ten consecutive years prior thereto. Confirmed.

No. 217.—FRANÇOIS LELORET claims a tract of land, situate on the right bank of the bayou La Fourche, in the county of La Fourche, containing one hundred and thirty and seventy-five hundredths superficial acres, and bounded on the upper side by land of Charles Richard, and on the lower by land of Mathurin Aucoin.

It appears that the claimant did actually inhabit and cultivate the land now claimed on the 20th December, 1803, and that the same was continually inhabited and cultivated by him, or those under whom he holds, for more than ten consecutive years next preceding. Confirmed.

No. 218.—BASIL and JEAN BAPTISTE PREJEAN claim a tract of land, situate on the left bank of the bayou La Fourche, in the county of La Fourche, containing one hundred and sixty-seven and forty-one hundredths superficial acres, and bounded on the upper side by land of Edward Daigle, and on the lower by land of Jean Boudreau.

It appears that the land now claimed was inhabited and cultivated on the 20th December, 1803, and that the same was continually inhabited and cultivated by the claimants, or those under whom they claim, for more than ten consecutive years next preceding. Confirmed.

No. 219.—The WIDOW AND CHILDREN OF JEAN HEBERT, deceased, claim a tract of land, situate on the left bank of the bayou La Fourche, in the county of La Fourche, containing one hundred and sixty-five and sixty-seven hundredths superficial acres, and bounded on the upper side by land of Alexis Hebert, and on the lower by land of Francis Dugas.

It appears that the land now claimed was inhabited and cultivated on the 20th December, 1803, and for more than ten consecutive years next preceding. Confirmed.

No. 220.—AMBROISE HEBERT claims a tract of land, situate on the left bank of the bayou La Fourche, in the county of La Fourche, containing one hundred and fifty-six and forty-one hundredths superficial acres, and bounded on the upper side by land of Jean Baptiste Boudreau, and on the lower by land of Simon Guillot.

It appears that the claimant did actually inhabit and cultivate the land now claimed on the 20th December, 1803, and for more than ten consecutive years prior thereto. Confirmed.

No. 221.—JEAN BAPTISTE GROUGH claims a tract of land, situate on the left bank of the bayou La Fourche, in the county of La Fourche, containing sixty-nine and five hundredths superficial acres, and bounded on the upper side by land of C. F. Girod, and on the lower by land of Nicholas Phopte.

It appears that the claimant did actually inhabit and cultivate the land now claimed on the 20th December, 1803, and that the same was continually inhabited and cultivated by him, or those under whom he claims, for more than ten consecutive years next preceding. Confirmed.

No. 222.—JOHN CLERMONT claims a tract of land, situate on the left bank of the bayou La Fourche, in the county of La Fourche, containing one hundred and twenty-three and eighteen hundredths superficial acres, and bounded on the upper side by land of Domingo Stepho, and on the lower by land of Noel Victor Boudreau.
It appears that the claimant did actually inhabit and cultivate the land now claimed on the 20th December, 1803, and that the same was continually inhabited and cultivated by him, or those under whom he claims, for more than ten consecutive years next preceding. Confirmed.

No. 223.—JOSEPH TONNELIA claims a tract of land, situate on the right bank of the bayou La Fourche, in the county of La Fourche, containing eighty-nine and ninety-six hundredths superficial acres, and bounded on the upper side by land of Andrew Green, and on the lower by land of Joseph Daigle.
It appears that the claimant did actually inhabit and cultivate the land now claimed on the 20th December, 1803, and that the same was continually inhabited and cultivated for more than ten consecutive years prior thereto. Confirmed.

No. 224.—STEPHEN POROR claims a tract of land, situate on the left bank of the bayou La Fourche, in the county of La Fourche, containing two hundred and thirty-three and ninety-two hundredths superficial acres, and bounded on the upper side by land of Pierre Paul Boudreau, and on the lower by land of ———.
It appears that the claimant did actually inhabit and cultivate the land now claimed on the 20th December, 1803, and for more than ten consecutive years prior thereto. Confirmed.

No. 225.—BARTHELEMI HENRY claims a tract of land, situate on the right bank of the bayou La Fourche, in the county of La Fourche, containing one hundred and ninety-five and seventy hundredths superficial acres, and bounded on the upper side by land of Nicholas Metras, and on the lower by land of Louis Richard.
It appears that the claimant did actually inhabit and cultivate the land now claimed on the 20th December, 1803, and that the same was continually inhabited and cultivated by him, or those under whom he claims, for more than ten consecutive years next preceding. Confirmed.

No. 226.—MARGARET CROSHIE claims a tract of land, situate on the left bank of the bayou La Fourche, in the county of La Fourche, containing one hundred and twenty-six and forty-four hundredths superficial acres, and bounded on the upper side by land of Julian Croshie, and on the lower by land of Reynard and Peytavin.
It appears that the claimant did actually inhabit and cultivate the land now claimed on the 20th December, 1803, and for more than ten consecutive years prior thereto. Confirmed.

No. 227.—JEAN BAPTISTE THIBODEAUX claims a tract of land, situate on the left bank of the bayou La Fourche, in the county of La Fourche, containing two hundred and seven and three hundredths superficial acres, and bounded on the upper side by land of Martin Petre, and on the lower by land of Claude Leblanc.
It appears that the land now claimed was inhabited and cultivated on the 20th December, 1803, and that the same was continually inhabited and cultivated by the claimant, or those under whom he claims, for more than ten consecutive years next preceding. Confirmed.

No. 228.—LOUIS ROBICHAU claims a tract of land, situate on the left bank of the bayou La Fourche, in the county of La Fourche, containing two hundred and seventy-nine and eighty-eight hundredths superficial acres, and bounded on the upper side by land of Stephen Pirerear, and on the lower by land of Joseph Bozier.
It appears that the land now claimed was inhabited and cultivated on the 20th December, 1803, and that the same was continually inhabited and cultivated by the claimant, or those under whom he claims, for more than ten consecutive years next preceding. Confirmed.

No. 229.—GUILLAUME AUCOIN claims a tract of land, situate on the right bank of the bayou La Fourche, in the county of La Fourche, containing one hundred and sixty-four and thirty-eight hundredths superficial acres, and bounded on the upper side by land of Joseph Bark, and on the lower by land of Hyacinthe Aucoin.
It appears that the land now claimed was inhabited and cultivated by the claimant, or those under whom he holds, for more than ten consecutive years next preceding. Confirmed.

No. 230.—JEAN OLIVIER claims a tract of land, situate on the left bank of the bayou La Fourche, in the county La Fourche, containing sixty-five and thirty-one hundredths superficial acres, and bounded on the upper side by land of Nicholas Phopte, and on the lower by land of Joes Rousseau.
It appears that the land now claimed was inhabited and cultivated by the claimant, or those under whom he claims, on the 20th December, 1803, and for more than ten consecutive years next preceding. Confirmed.

No. 231.—JOSEPH HEBERT claims a tract of land, situate on the right bank of the bayou La Fourche, in the county of La Fourche, containing one hundred and sixty-nine and thirty-five hundredths superficial acres, and bounded on the upper side by land of Mathurin Hebert, and on the lower by land of François Boudreau.
It appears that the land now claimed was inhabited and cultivated on the 20th December, 1803, by the claimant, and for more than ten consecutive years next preceding. Confirmed.

No. 232.—JEAN GOUTREAU claims a tract of land, situate on the left bank of the bayou La Fourche, in the county of La Fourche, containing eighty-nine and seventy-one hundredths superficial acres, and bounded on the upper side by land of Simon Leblanc, and on the lower by land of Felix Bourg.
It appears that the land now claimed was inhabited and cultivated on the 20th December, 1803, and that the same was continually inhabited and cultivated by the claimant, or those under whom he claims, for more than ten consecutive years next preceding. Confirmed.

No. 233.—JEAN CONSTANT claims a tract of land, situate on the right bank of the bayou La Fourche, in the county of La Fourche, containing one hundred and twenty-three and thirty-four hundredths superficial acres, and bounded on the upper side by land of Jean Bte. Boudreau, and on the lower by land of Jean Bte. Hebert.
It appears that the claimant did actually inhabit and cultivate the land now claimed on the 20th December, 1803, and that the same was continually inhabited and cultivated by him, or those under whom he claims, for more than ten consecutive years next preceding. Confirmed.

No. 234.—ANDREW GREEN claims a tract of land, situate on the right bank of the bayou La Fourche, in the county of La Fourche, containing one hundred and twenty and sixteen hundredths superficial acres, and bounded on the upper side by land of Antonio Albarado, and on the lower by land of Joseph Tonnelia.
It appears that the land now claimed was inhabited and cultivated on the 20th December, 1803, and that the same was continually inhabited and cultivated by those under whom the claimant holds for more than ten consecutive years prior. Confirmed.

No. 235.—CLAUDE F. GIROD claims a tract of land, situate on the left bank of the bayou La Fourche, in the county of La Fourche, containing one hundred and eighty-seven and forty-seven hundredths superficial acres, and bounded on the upper side by land of Louis Godet, and on the lower by land of Bte. Bourgeois.
It appears that the land now claimed was inhabited and cultivated on the 20th of December, 1803, and that the same was continually inhabited and cultivated by those under whom the claimant holds for more than ten consecutive years next preceding. Confirmed.

No. 236. ALEXIS HEBERT claims a tract of land, situate on the left bank of the bayou La Fourche, in the county of La Fourche, containing ninety-eight and fifty-six hundredths superficial acres, and bounded on the upper side by land of the heirs of Jean Hebert, deceased, and on the lower by land of Jean Bte. Hebert.
It appears that the land now claimed was inhabited and cultivated on the 20th December, 1803, and that the

same was continually inhabited and cultivated by those under whom the claimant holds for more than ten consecutive years next preceding. Confirmed.

No. 237.—NOEL VICTOR BOUDREAU claims a tract of land, situate on the left bank of the bayou La Fourche, in the county of La Fourche, containing ninety-one and ninety-six hundredths superficial acres, and bounded on the upper side by land of Jean Ilier Clermont, and on the lower by land of Peter Seville.

It appears that the land now claimed was inhabited and cultivated on the 20th December, 1803, and that the same was continually inhabited and cultivated by the claimant, or those under whom he claims, for more than ten consecutive years next preceding. Confirmed.

No. 238.—PIERRE RICHOUE claims a tract of land, situate on the left bank of the bayou La Fourche, in the county of La Fourche, containing one hundred and five and thirty-five hundredths superficial acres, and bounded on the upper side by land of Louis Duc, and on the lower by land of François Benoit.

It appears that the land now claimed was inhabited and cultivated on the 20th December, 1803, and that the same was continually inhabited and cultivated by those under whom the claimant holds for more than ten consecutive years next preceding. Confirmed.

No. 239.—JOSEPH MOURRAN claims a tract of land, situate on the right bank of the bayou La Fourche, in the county of La Fourche, containing six hundred and thirty-seven and eighty-five hundredths superficial acres, and bounded on the upper side by land of François Malbrough, and on the lower by land of William Hammond.

It appearing that the land now claimed was inhabited and cultivated on the 20th December, 1803, and for more than ten consecutive years prior, the Board confirm the claim to so much land as may be contained within the depth of forty arpents.

No. 240. PAUL BOUDREAU claims a tract of land, situate on the left bank of the bayou La Fourche, in the county of La Fourche, containing three hundred and seventy-eight and fifty-eight hundredths superficial acres, and bounded on the upper side by land of Andrew Timpley, and on the lower by land of A. Landry.

It appears that the claimant did actually inhabit and cultivate the land now claimed on the 20th December, 1803, and for more than ten consecutive years next preceding. Confirmed.

No. 241.—PAUL BOUDREAU claims a tract of land, situate on the right bank of the bayou La Fourche, in the county of La Fourche, containing one hundred and sixty-four and sixty-nine hundredths superficial acres, and bounded on the upper side by land of Joseph Foret, and on the lower by land of Louis Foret.

It appears that the land now claimed was inhabited and cultivated on the 20th December, 1803, and for more than ten consecutive years next preceding, by those under whom the present claimant holds. Confirmed.

No. 242.—CLAUDE F. GYROD claims a tract of land, situate on the left bank of the bayou La Fourche, in the county of La Fourche, containing twenty-seven arpents in front, and forty in depth, and bounded on the upper side by land of François Chauvin, and on the lower by land of Louis Bourgeois.

The claimant purchased this land in the year 1804, of Domingo Esteves, in whose favor it was surveyed, in the year 1790, by order of Governor Miro, and who continued to inhabit and cultivate the land from the date of the survey, until the time of the sale aforesaid. Confirmed.

No. 243.—PAUL and JOSEPH FORET claim a tract of land, situate on the right bank of the bayou La Fourche, in the county of La Fourche, containing one hundred and eleven and ten hundredths superficial acres, and bounded on the upper side by land of Joseph Boudreau, and on the lower by land of ——.

It appears that the land now claimed was inhabited and cultivated on the 20th December, 1803, and that the same was continually inhabited and cultivated by the claimants, or those under whom they claim, for more than ten consecutive years next preceding. Confirmed.

No. 244.—JOSEPH FORET claims a tract of land, situate on the right bank of the bayou La Fourche, in the county of La Fourche, containing two hundred and fifty-nine and ninety-one hundredths superficial acres, and bounded on the upper side by land of Constant Pierre, and on the lower by land of ——.

It appears that the claimant did actually inhabit and cultivate the land now claimed on the 20th December, 1803, and for more than ten consecutive years prior thereto. Confirmed.

No. 245.—LOUIS BOURDAIE claims a tract of land, situate on the left bank of the bayou La Fourche, in the county of La Fourche, containing three arpents in front, and forty in depth, and bounded on the upper side by land of Andrew Sanchez, and on the lower by land of Juan Monson.

This land was surveyed in the year 1790, by order of Governor Miro, in favor of Vincente Fernandez, who conveyed to the present claimant; and it having been inhabited and cultivated ever since the above-mentioned period, until on and after the 20th December, 1803. Confirmed.

No. 246.—DOMINGO CEVALLOS claims a tract of land, situate on the right bank of the bayou La Fourche, in the county of La Fourche, containing five arpents in front, and the side lines closing to a point within the depth of forty arpents, and bounded on the upper side by land of Vicente Rodriguez Mora, and on the lower by land of Maria Rodriguez Mora.

This land was surveyed in favor of the claimant, by order of Governor Miro, in the year 1790; and having been inhabited and cultivated ever since that time, until on and after the 20th December, 1803. Confirmed.

No. 247.—MARIA RODRIGUEZ claims a tract of land, situate on the right bank of the bayou La Fourche, in the county of La Fourche, containing one arpent in front, and forty arpents in depth, and bounded on the upper side by land of Domingo Cevallos, and on the lower by land of Gasper Falcon.

This land was surveyed by order of Governor Miro, in the year 1790, in favor of Domingo Cevallos, who conveyed to the present claimant; and it having been inhabited and cultivated ever since that period, until on and after the 20th December, 1803. Confirmed.

No. 248.—MARTIAL LE BŒUF claims a tract of land, situate on the left bank of the bayou La Fourche, in the county of La Fourche, containing three hundred and thirty and six hundredths superficial acres, and bounded on the upper side by land of Adam Matern, and on the lower by land of Solomon Verret.

It appears that the land now claimed was inhabited and cultivated on the 20th December, 1803, and that the same was continually inhabited and cultivated by the claimant, or those under whom he claims, for more than ten consecutive years next preceding. Confirmed.

No. 249.—SOLOMON VERRET claims a tract of land, situate on the left bank of the bayou La Fourche, in the county of La Fourche, containing one hundred and thirty-three and six hundredths superficial acres, and bounded on the upper side by land of Martial Le Bœuf, and on the lower by land of Edward Verret.

It appears that the land now claimed was inhabited and cultivated on the 20th December, 1803, and that the same was continually inhabited and cultivated by the claimant, or by those under whom he claims, for more than ten consecutive years next preceding. Confirmed.

No. 250.—EDWARD VERRET claims a tract of land, situate on the left bank of the bayou La Fourche, in the county of La Fourche, containing three hundred and sixty-one and thirty-three hundredths superficial acres, and bounded on the upper side by land of Solomon Verret, and on the lower by land of Duvergé Verret.

It appears that the land now claimed was inhabited and cultivated on the 20th December, 1803, and that the same was continually inhabited and cultivated by the claimant, or those under whom he claims, for more than ten consecutive years next preceding. Confirmed.

No. 251.—DUVERGE VERRET claims a tract of land, situate on the left bank of the bayou La Fourche, in the county of La Fourche, containing two hundred and fifty-one and twenty-eight hundredths superficial acres, and bounded on the upper side by land of Edward Verret, and on the lower by land of Basil Ricard.

It appears that the land now claimed was inhabited and cultivated on the 20th December, 1803, and that the same was continually inhabited and cultivated by the claimant, or those under whom he claims, for more than ten consecutive years next preceding. Confirmed.

No. 255.—JOSEPH HONORE BREAU claims a tract of land, situate on the right bank of the bayou La Fourche, in the county of La Fourche, containing two hundred and twenty-six and sixty hundredths superficial acres, and bounded on the upper side by land of Jean Baptiste Trahant, and on the lower by land of Jean Leblanc.

It appears that the claimant did actually inhabit and cultivate the land now claimed on the 20th December, 1803, and for more than ten consecutive years prior thereto. Confirmed.

No. 256.—CHARLES RICHARD claims a tract of land, situate on the right bank of the bayou La Fourche, in the county of La Fourche, containing two hundred and sixty-eight and ninety-four hundredths superficial acres, and bounded on the upper side by land of Alexis Aucoin, and on the lower by land of François Leloret.

It appears that the claimant did actually inhabit and cultivate the land now claimed on the 20th December, 1803, and for more than ten consecutive years prior thereto. Confirmed.

No. 257.—NICHOLAS LIRET claims a tract of land, situate on the right bank of the bayou La Fourche, in the county of La Fourche, containing one hundred and twenty-eight and forty-two hundredths superficial acres, and bounded on the upper side by land of Madame Liret, and on the lower by land of Joseph Hebert.

It appears that the claimant did actually inhabit and cultivate the land now claimed on the 20th December, 1803, and that the same was continually inhabited and cultivated by him, or those under whom he claims, for more than ten consecutive years next preceding. Confirmed.

No. 258.—JOSEPH MALBROUGH claims a tract of land, situate on the right bank of the bayou La Fourche, in the county of La Fourche, containing six arpents in front, and seventy arpents in depth, and bounded on the upper side by land of William Hammond, and on the lower by land of ——.

It appears that the land now claimed was inhabited and cultivated on the 20th December, 1803, and for more than ten consecutive years prior, the Board confirm the title to the extent of forty arpents in depth, and reject the claim as to the balance of thirty arpents depth.

No. 259.—CHARLES BOURG claims a tract of land, situate on the left bank of the bayou La Fourche, in the county of La Fourche, containing seventy-nine and twenty-four hundredths superficial acres, and bounded on one side by land of François Hebert, and on the other by land of Pierre Henry.

It appears that the land now claimed was actually inhabited and cultivated by the claimant on the 20th December, 1803, and for more than ten consecutive years prior thereto. Confirmed.

No. 260.—JEAN DELAUNE claims a tract of land, situate on the right bank of the bayou La Fourche, in the county of La Fourche, containing two hundred and fourteen thirty-six hundredths superficial acres, and bounded on the upper side by land of Joseph Felix Boudreau, and on the lower by land of Pierre Goutreau.

It appears that the claimant did actually inhabit and cultivate the land now claimed on the 20th December, 1803, and that the same was continually inhabited and cultivated by him, or those under whom he claims, for more than ten consecutive years next preceding. Confirmed.

No. 261.—JOSEPH LANDRY claims a tract of land, situate on the right bank of the bayou La Fourche, in the county of La Fourche, containing one hundred and ninety-four and forty-nine hundredths superficial acres, and bounded on the upper side by land of Jean Baptiste Robichaux, and on the lower by land of Jean Baptiste Bourgeois.

It appears that the land now claimed was inhabited and cultivated on the 20th December, 1803, and that the same was continually inhabited and cultivated by those under whom the claimant holds for more than ten consecutive years next preceding. Confirmed.

No. 262.—ALEXIS LEJEUNE claims a tract of land, situate on the right bank of the bayou La Fourche, in the county of La Fourche, containing one hundred and twenty-five and one hundredth superficial acres, and bounded on the upper side by land of Jean Lejeune, and on the lower by land of ——.

It appears that the land now claimed was inhabited and cultivated on the 20th December, 1803, and that the same was continually inhabited and cultivated by the claimant, or those under whom he claims, for more than ten consecutive years next preceding. Confirmed.

No. 263.—ALEXIS LEJEUNE claims a tract of land, situate on the left bank of the bayou La Fourche, in the county of La Fourche, containing two hundred and six and one hundredth superficial acres, and bounded on the upper side by land of Joseph Hebert, and on the lower by land of François Dubois.

It appears that the land now claimed was inhabited and cultivated on the 20th December, 1803, and that the same was continually inhabited and cultivated by the claimant, or those under whom he claims, for more than ten consecutive years next preceding. Confirmed.

No. 264.—JOSEPH LEJEUNE claims a tract of land, situate on the right bank of the bayou La Fourche, in the county of La Fourche, containing two hundred and thirty-seven and sixty-two hundredths superficial acres, and bounded on the upper side by land of Alexis Lejeune, and on the lower by land of ——.

It appears that the claimant did actually inhabit and cultivate the land now claimed on the 20th December, 1803, and for more than ten consecutive years prior thereto. Confirmed.

No. 265.—PIERRE MENOUSE claims a tract of land, situate on the right bank of the bayou La Fourche, in the county of La Fourche, containing one hundred and forty-one and twenty-five hundredths superficial acres, and bounded on the upper side by land of Joseph Lejeune, and on the lower by land of ——.

It appears that the land now claimed was inhabited and cultivated on the 20th December, 1803, and that the same was continually inhabited and cultivated by the claimant, or those under whom he claims, for more than ten consecutive years next preceding. Confirmed.

No. 266.—LOUIS DANTIN claims a tract of land, situate on the right bank of the bayou La Fourche, in the county of La Fourche, containing five hundred and eighty and seventy-one hundredths superficial acres, and bounded on the upper side by land of Louis Pinelle, and on the lower by land of Joseph Hebert.

It appears that the land now claimed was inhabited and cultivated on the 20th December, 1803, and that the same was continually inhabited and cultivated by the claimant, or those under whom he claims, for more than ten consecutive years next preceding. Confirmed.

No. 267.—JOSEPH CHIASSON claims a tract of land, situate on the left bank of the bayou La Fourche, in the county of La Fourche, containing eighty-nine and thirty-six hundredths superficial acres, and bounded on the upper side by land of Pierre Chiasson, and on the lower by land of François Doucette.

It appears that the land now claimed was inhabited and cultivated on the 20th December, 1803, and that the same was continually inhabited and cultivated by the claimant, or those under whom he claims, for more than ten consecutive years next preceding. Confirmed.

No. 268.—FRANÇOIS TOURNIER claims a tract of land, situate on the right bank of the bayou La Fourche, in the county of La Fourche, containing two hundred and sixty-four and twenty-nine hundredths superficial acres, and bounded on the upper side by land of François Savoie, and on the lower by land of Paul M. Boudreau.

It appears that the land now claimed was inhabited and cultivated on the 20th December, 1803, and that the same was continually inhabited and cultivated by the claimant, or those under whom he claims, for more than ten consecutive years next preceding. Confirmed.

No. 269.—MICHEL AUCOIN and JOSEPH BOURG claim a tract of land, situate on the right bank of the bayou La Fourche, in the county of La Fourche, containing six and a half arpents in front, and forty arpents in depth, and bounded on the upper side by land of Simon Mazerole, and on the lower by land of Lucette Breau.

This land was surveyed in the year 1790, in favor of Carlos Goutreau, by order of Governor Miro, who at the same time put him in possession, by the surveyor; and it has continued to be inhabited and cultivated ever since the time of making the survey. The present claimants hold it by regular deeds. Confirmed.

No. 270.—Jacques Barrillo claims a tract of land, situate on the left bank of the bayou La Fourche, in the county of La Fourche, containing six arpents and thirteen toises in front, and forty arpents in depth, and bounded on the upper side by land of Madame Barillo, and on the lower by land of Joseph Nicolas Hebert.

This land was surveyed in the year 1790, in favor of the claimant, by order of Governor Miro; and it having been inhabited and cultivated ever since that period, until on and after the 20th December, 1803. Confirmed.

No. 271.—Jacques Barrillo claims a tract of land, situate on the left bank of the bayou La Fourche, in the county of La Fourche, containing six arpents (wanting four toises) in front, and forty arpents in depth, and bounded on the upper side by land of Pedro Bertrand, and on the lower by land of Joseph Grangé.

This land was surveyed in the year 1790, by order of Governor Miro, in favor of Ambrosio Belonie Bertrand, under whose title the present claimant holds in virtue of several intermediate conveyances; and the land having been inhabited and cultivated ever since the aforesaid period, until on and after the 20th December, 1803. Confirmed.

No. 274.—J. F. Bourg claims a tract of land, situate on the right bank of the bayou La Fourche, in the county of La Fourche, containing eighty-four and fifteen hundredths superficial acres, and bounded on the upper side by land of Urbin Echetté, and on the lower by land of Jean Baptiste Leonard.

It appears that the land now claimed was inhabited and cultivated on the 20th December, 1803, and that the same was continually inhabited and cultivated for more than ten consecutive years prior thereto. Confirmed.

No. 275.—Bartholomew Henry claims a tract of land, situate on the right bank of the bayou La Fourche, in the county of La Fourche, containing one hundred and one and fifteen hundredths superficial acres, and bounded on the upper side by land of Joseph Naquin, and on the lower by land of Nicolas Albert.

It appears that the land now claimed was inhabited and cultivated on the 20th December, 1803, and that the same was continually inhabited and cultivated by the claimant, or those under whom he claims, for more than ten consecutive years next preceding. Confirmed.

No. 276.—Augustin Domingues claims a tract of land, situate on the left bank of the bayou La Fourche, in the county of La Fourche, containing nine hundred and twenty-four and seventy-one hundredths superficial acres, and bounded on the upper side by land of Alexis Jollet, and on the lower by land of Antoine Bessé.

It appears that the land now claimed was inhabited and cultivated on the 20th December, 1803, and that the same was continually inhabited and cultivated by those under whom the claimant holds for more than ten consecutive years next preceding. Confirmed.

No. 278.—Jean Baptiste Leonard claims a tract of land, situate on the right bank of the bayou La Fourche, in the county of La Fourche, containing seventy-nine and seventy-seven hundredths superficial acres, and bounded on the upper side by land of Joseph Bourg, and on the lower by land of Joseph Bye.

It appears that the land now claimed was inhabited and cultivated on the 20th December, 1803, and that the same was continually inhabited and cultivated by those under whom the claimant holds for more than ten consecutive years next preceding. Confirmed.

No. 281.—Jean C. Terriot claims a tract of land, situate on the left bank of the bayou La Fourche, in the county of La Fourche, containing two hundred and twenty-one and sixteen hundredths superficial acres, and bounded on the upper side by land of Basil Richard, and on the lower by land of Jean Dugat.

It appears that the claimant did actually inhabit and cultivate the land now claimed on the 20th December, 1803, and that the same was continually inhabited and cultivated by him, or those under whom he claims, for more than ten consecutive years next preceding. Confirmed.

No. 283.—François Bandeloche claims a tract of land, situate on the right bank of the bayou La Fourche,

in the county of La Fourche, containing one hundred and fifty-nine and sixty-two hundredths superficial acres, and bounded on the upper side by land of André Candolles, and on the lower by land of Jean Baptiste Leonard.

It appears that the claimant did actually inhabit and cultivate the land now claimed on the 20th December, 1803, and for more than ten consecutive years prior thereto. Confirmed.

No. 286.—Pierre Amarin claims a tract of land, situate on the right bank of the bayou La Fourche, in the county of La Fourche, containing two hundred and three and eighty-five hundredths superficial acres, and bounded on the upper side by land of Charles Bolot, and on the lower by land of Joseph Naquin.

It appears that the claimant did actually inhabit and cultivate the land now claimed on the 20th December, 1803, and for more than ten consecutive years prior thereto. Confirmed.

No. 287.—Jean Guillotte claims a tract of land, situate on the right bank of the bayou La Fourche, in the county of La Fourche, containing six hundred and eight and seventeen hundredths superficial acres, and bounded on the upper side by land of Jean Roger, and on the lower by land of Jean Lejeune.

It appearing that the land now claimed was inhabited and cultivated on the 20th December, 1803, and for more than ten consecutive years prior, the Board confirm the claim to such quantity of land as may be contained within the first forty arpents in depth, and reject it as to the balance.

No. 290.—Jean M. Trahant claims a tract of land, situate on the left bank of the bayou La Fourche, in the county of La Fourche, containing ninety-six and a half acres, and bounded on the upper side by land of François Dubois, and on the lower by land of Pierre Chiasson.

It appears that the land now claimed was inhabited and cultivated on the 20th December, 1803, and that the same was continually inhabited and cultivated by the claimant, or those under whom he claims, for more than ten consecutive years next preceding. Confirmed.

No. 291.—Gregoire Aucoin claims a tract of land, situate on the left bank of the bayou La Fourche, in the county of La Fourche, containing three arpents in front, and forty arpents in depth, and bounded on the upper side by land of Jean Landry, and on the lower by land of François Boudreau.

This land was surveyed in the year 1790, by order of Governor Miro, in favor of Joseph Goutreau, under whose title the claimant holds by virtue of divers intermediate transfers; and the land having been inhabited and cultivated ever since the above-mentioned period, until on and after the 20th December, 1803. Confirmed.

No. 295.—Andre Hebert claims a tract of land, situate on the left bank of the bayou La Fourche, in the county of La Fourche, containing one hundred and six and eighty hundredths superficial acres, and bounded on the upper side by land of François Benoit, and on the lower by land of Jean Boudreau.

It appears that the land now claimed was inhabited and cultivated on the 20th December, 1803, and that the same was continually inhabited and cultivated by those under whom the claimant holds for more than ten consecutive years next preceding. Confirmed.

No. 296.—Joseph Bye claims a tract of land, situate on the right bank of the bayou La Fourche, in the county of La Fourche, containing seventy-six and six hundredths superficial acres, and bounded on the upper side by land of Jean Baptiste Leonard, and on the lower by land of the widow Vincent.

It appears that the land now claimed was inhabited and cultivated on the 20th December, 1803, and that the same was continually inhabited and cultivated by the claimant, or those under whom he claims, for more than ten consecutive years next preceding. Confirmed.

No. 297.—Celeste Lamotte claims a tract of land, situate on the right bank of the bayou La Fourche, in the county of La Fourche, containing one hundred and ninety-three and ninety-three hundredths superficial acres, and bounded on the upper side by land of Joseph Molaison, and on the lower by land of ——.

It appears that the land now claimed was inhabited and cultivated on the 20th December, 1803, and that the

same was continually inhabited and cultivated by those under whom the claimant holds for more than ten consecutive years next preceding. Confirmed.

No. 298.—URSULE VINCENT claims a tract of land, situate on the right bank of the bayou La Fourche, in the county of La Fourche, containing eighty-four and eighty-six hundredths superficial acres, and bounded on the upper side by land of Joseph Bye, and on the lower by land of Louis Pinelle.
It appears that the claimant did actually inhabit and cultivate the land now claimed on the 20th December, 1803, and for more than ten consecutive years prior thereto. Confirmed.

No. 300.—LOUIS PINELLE claims a tract of land, situate on the right bank of the bayou La Fourche, in the county of La Fourche, containing one hundred and seventy and seventeen hundredths superficial acres, and bounded on the upper side by land of the widow Vincent, and on the lower by land of Louis Dantin.
It appears that the claimant did actually inhabit and cultivate the land now claimed on the 20th December, 1803, and for more than ten consecutive years prior thereto. Confirmed.

No. 301.—BAZIL RICARD claims a tract of land, situate on the left bank of the bayou La Fourche, in the county of La Fourche, containing one hundred and eleven hundredths superficial acres, and bounded on the upper side by land of Duvergé Verret, and on the lower by land of Jean C. Terriot.
It appears that the land now claimed was inhabited and cultivated on the 20th December, 1803, and that the same was continually inhabited and cultivated by those under whom the present claimant holds for more than ten consecutive years next preceding. Confirmed.

No. 303.—JACQUES THIBAUDEAUX claims a tract of land, situate on the right bank of the bayou La Fourche, in the county of La Fourche, containing one hundred and sixty-five and fifty-two hundredths superficial acres, and bounded on the upper side by land of Jean Robichaux, and on the lower by land of François Lassin.
It appears that the land now claimed was inhabited and cultivated on the 20th December, 1803, and that the same was continually inhabited and cultivated by the claimant, or those under whom he claims, for more than ten consecutive years next preceding. Confirmed.

No. 304.—GEORGE FOLGANT claims a tract of land, situate on the left bank of the bayou La Fourche, in the county of La Fourche, containing one hundred and forty-six and ninety-three hundredths superficial acres, and bounded on the upper side by land of Jean Charles Bourgeois, and on the lower by land of Jean Baptiste Phillippeaux.
It appearing that the land now claimed was inhabited and cultivated on the 20th December, 1803, and for more than ten consecutive years next preceding, the Board confirm so much land as may be contained within the ordinary depth of forty arpents.

No. 305.—JEAN MARIE BENOIT claims a tract of land, situate on the left bank of the bayou La Fourche, in the county of La Fourche, containing ninety-four and twenty-eight hundredths superficial acres, and bounded on the upper side by land of Pierre Sylvie, and on the lower by land of Jean Baptiste Boudreau.
It appears that the land now claimed was inhabited and cultivated on the 20th December, 1803, and that the same was continually inhabited and cultivated by the claimant, or those under whom he claims, for more than ten consecutive years next preceding. Confirmed.

No. 306.—PIERRE BOURGEOIS claims a tract of land, situate on the left bank of the bayou of La Fourche, in the county of La Fourche, containing one hundred and one and forty-one hundredths superficial acres, and bounded on the upper side by land of Antoine L'Epine, and on the lower by land of ——.
It appears that the claimant did actually inhabit and cultivate the land now claimed on the 20th December, 1803, and that the same was continually inhabited and cultivated by him, or those under whom he claims, for more than ten consecutive years next preceding. Confirmed.

No. 307.—JEAN BAPTISTE PHILLIPPEAUX claims a tract of land, situate on the left bank of the bayou of La Fourche, in the county of La Fourche, containing one

hundred and twelve and eighty-one hundredths superficial acres, and bounded on the upper side by land of Pierre Goutreau, and on the lower by land of Louis Déré.
It appears that the claimant did actually inhabit and cultivate the land now claimed on the 20th December, 1803, and for more than ten consecutive years prior thereto. Confirmed.

No. 308.—JEAN BAPTISTE TRAHAN claims a tract of land, situate on the right bank of the bayou of La Fourche, in the county of La Fourche, containing two hundred and ten and nineteen hundredths superficial acres, and bounded on the upper side by land of William Arseman, and on the lower by land of Homoré Breaux.
It appears that the land now claimed was inhabited and cultivated by the present claimant on the 20th December, 1803, and for more than ten consecutive years prior thereto. Confirmed.

No. 310.—FRANÇOIS DUBOIS claims a tract of land, situate on the right bank of the bayou of La Fourche, in the county of La Fourche, containing one hundred and thirteen and seven hundredths superficial acres, and bounded on the upper side by land of Alexis Lejeune, and on the lower by land of Jean M. Trahan.
It appears that the land now claimed was inhabited and cultivated on the 20th December, 1803, and that the same was continually inhabited and cultivated by the claimant, or those under whom he claims, for more than ten consecutive years next preceding. Confirmed.

No. 311.—ANDRE TEMPLY claims a tract of land, situate on the left bank of the bayou of La Fourche, in the county of La Fourche, containing two hundred and nine and sixty-two hundredths superficial acres, and bounded on the upper side by land of François Rogers, and on the lower by land of ——.
It appears that the claimant did actually inhabit and cultivate the land now claimed on the 20th December, 1803, and for more than ten consecutive years prior thereto. Confirmed.

No. 312.—JOSEPH NAQUIN claims a tract of land, situate on the right bank of the bayou of La Fourche, in the county of La Fourche, containing two hundred and seventy five and nineteen hundredths superficial acres, and bounded on the upper side by land of Pierre A. Duzat, and on the lower by land of Barthelemy Henry.
It appears that the land now claimed was inhabited and cultivated on the 20th December, 1803, and that the same was continually inhabited and cultivated by the claimant, or those under whom he claims, for more than ten consecutive years next preceding. Confirmed.

No. 317.—JEAN TYSON claims a tract of land, situate on the right bank of the bayou of La Fourche, in the county of La Fourche, containing two hundred and nine and sixty hundredths superficial acres, and bounded on the upper side by land of the parish, and on the lower by land of Rutan Cassa.
It appears that the land now claimed was inhabited and cultivated on the 20th December, 1803, and that the same was continually inhabited and cultivated by those under whom the claimant holds for more than ten consecutive years next preceding. Confirmed.

No. 318.—JACQUES TERRIOT claims a tract of land, situate on the left bank of the bayou of La Fourche, in the county of La Fourche, containing two hundred and four and forty-six hundredths superficial acres, and bounded on the upper side by land of Amable Landry, and on the lower by land of ——.
It appears that the land now claimed was actually inhabited and cultivated by the claimant on the 20th December, 1803, and for more than ten consecutive years prior thereto. Confirmed.

No. 319.—LOUIS HALLE claims a tract of land, situate on the right bank of the bayou of La Fourche, in the county of La Forche, containing one hundred and four and twenty-four hundredths superficial acres, and bounded on the upper side by land of Jean Leblanc, and on the lower by land of Theodore Bourg.
It appears that the land now claimed was inhabited and cultivated on the 20th December, 1803, and that the same was continually inhabited and cultivated by those under whom the present claimant holds for more than ten consecutive years next preceding. Confirmed.

No. 320.—CLAUDE F. GIROD claims a tract of land, situate on the right bank of the bayou of La Fourche, in the county of La Fourche, containing nine hundred and two and forty-six hundredths superficial acres, and bounded on the upper side by land of A. Hebert, and on the lower by land of Michel Mourran.

It appears that the land now claimed was inhabited and cultivated on the 20th December, 1803, and that the same was continually inhabited and cultivated by those under whom the claimant holds for more than ten consecutive years next preceding. Confirmed.

No. 326.—LAURENT PICHOFF AND HEIRS OF JOSEPH PICHOFF, deceased, claim a tract of land, situate on the right bank of the bayou of La Fourche, in the county of La Fourche, containing one hundred and six and ninety-two hundredths superficial acres, and bounded on the upper side by land of ——, and on the lower by land of ·——.

It appears that the land now claimed was inhabited and cultivated on the 20th December, 1803, and that the same was continually inhabited and cultivated by those under whom the claimants hold for more than ten consecutive years next preceding. Confirmed.

No. 330.—PIERRE PAUL AUCOIN claims a tract of land, situate on the right bank of the bayou of La Fourche, in the county of La Fourche, containing seven and a half arpents in front, and forty arpents in depth, and bounded on the upper side by land of Joseph Breme, and on the lower by land of Carlos Goutreau.

This land was surveyed in the year 1790, in favor of Simon Mazerole, by order of Governor Miro. The present claimant holds under the title of said Mazerole, by virtue of successive transfers; and the land having been inhabited and cultivated ever since the aforesaid period, until on and after the 20th December, 1803. Confirmed.

No. 332.—LUTHER SPENCER claims a tract of land, situate on the left bank of the bayou La Fourche, in the county of La Fourche, containing four arpents twenty toises and five feet in front, and forty arpents in depth, and bounded on the upper side by land of Joseph Roger, and on the lower by land of André Templet.

This land was surveyed by virtue of a decree of the Intendant General, made in the year 1799, in favor of Francisco Roger, who conveyed it to the present claimant; and it having been inhabited and cultivated ever since the above period. Confirmed.

No. 333.—GEORGE FOLGANT claims a tract of land, situate on the left bank of the bayou La Fourche, in the county of La Fourche, containing four arpents and twenty toises in front, and forty arpents in depth, and bounded on the upper side by land of Louis Robichaux, and on the lower by land of Francisco Roger.

This land was surveyed by virtue of a decree of the Intendant General, in the year 1799, in favor of Joseph Roger, who conveyed it to the present claimant; and it having been inhabited and cultivated ever since that period, until on and after the 20th December, 1803. Confirmed.

No. 334.—JACQUES ROUSSEAU claims a tract of land, situate on the left bank of the bayou of La Fourche, in the county of La Fourche, containing eight arpents in front, and forty in depth, and bounded on the upper side by land of Pedro Allemand, and on the lower by land of François Delemand.

It appears that the land now claimed was inhabited and cultivated on the 20th December, 1803, and that the same was continually inhabited and cultivated by those under whom the claimant holds for more than ten consecutive years next preceding. Confirmed.

No. 345.—CHARLES BELOT claims a tract of land, situate on the right bank of the bayou of La Fourche, in the county of La Fourche, containing one hundred and sixty-six and forty hundredths superficial acres, and bounded on the upper side by land of Louis Richard, and on the lower by land of Pierre Amazin Dugas.

It appears that the land now claimed was inhabited and cultivated on the 20th December, 1803, and that the same was continually inhabited and cultivated by those under whom the claimant holds for more than ten consecutive years next preceding. Confirmed.

No. 349.—MARIE ROSALIE claims a tract of land, situate on the left bank of the bayou of La Fourche, in the county of La Fourche, containing three hundred and twenty-six and seventy-eight hundredths superficial acres, and bounded on the upper side by land of Antoine Bessé, and on the lower by land of Jacques Lamotte.

It appears that the claimant did actually inhabit and cultivate the land now claimed on the 20th December, 1803, and for more than ten consecutive years prior thereto. Confirmed.

No. 350.—JACQUES LAMOTTE claims a tract of land, situate on the left bank of the bayou of La Fourche, in the county of La Fourche, containing nine hundred and twenty and sixteen hundredths superficial acres, and bounded on the upper side by land of Marie Rosalie, and on the lower by land of Alexandre St. Amand.

This is part of a tract of land of seventy arpents in front on each side of the bayou, for which the claimant obtained an order of survey from Governor Miro, in the year 1790; and it appearing that the land has been inhabited and cultivated ever since that period, until on and after the 20th December, 1803. Confirmed.

No. 351.—JACQUES LAMOTTE claims a tract of land, situate on the right bank of the bayou La Fourche, in the county of La Fourche, containing nineteen hundred and twelve and sixty-five hundredths superficial acres, and bounded on the upper side by land of Thomas Villanueva, and on the lower by land of Claude F. Girod.

This is part of a tract of land of seventy arpents front on both sides of the bayou, for which the claimant obtained an order of survey from Governor Miro, in the year 1790; and it appearing that the land has been inhabited and cultivated ever since that period, until on and after the 20th December, 1803. Confirmed.

No. 352.—SIMON GUILLOTTE claims a tract of land, situate on the left bank of the bayou of La Fourche, in the county of La Fourche, containing one hundred and eighty-five and seventy-seven hundredths superficial acres, and bounded on the one side by land of Marguerite Peters, and on the other by land of Ambroise Maturin Hebert.

It appears that the claimant did actually inhabit and cultivate the land now claimed on the 20th December, 1803, and for more than ten consecutive years prior thereto. Confirmed.

No. 357.—OLIVIER GUEDRY and JOSEPH SARVIE claim a tract of land, situate on the left bank of the bayou of La Fourche, in the county of La Fourche, containing seventeen hundred and nine and ninety-two hundredths superficial acres, and bounded on the upper side by land of Jean Dugas, and on the lower by vacant land.

It appears that the land now claimed was inhabited and cultivated on the 20th December, 1803, and that the same was continually inhabited and cultivated by the claimants, or those under whom they claim, for more than ten consecutive years next preceding. Confirmed.

No. 358.—JEAN MARIE GAUTREAU claims a tract of land, situate on the right bank of the bayou La Fourche, in the county of La Fourche, containing one hundred and twenty-one and ninety-five hundredths superficial acres, and bounded on the upper side by land of Alexis Lenon, and on the lower by land of ——.

It appears that the land now claimed was inhabited and cultivated on the 20th December, 1803, and that the same was continually inhabited and cultivated by the claimant, or those under whom he claims, for more than ten consecutive years next preceding. Confirmed.

No. 359.—PIERRE GOUTREAU claims a tract of land, situate on the right bank of the bayou of La Fourche, in the county of La Fourche, containing one hundred and twenty and thirteen hundredths superficial acres, and bounded on the upper side by land of Jean Marie Goutreau, and on the lower by land of ——.

It appears that the land now claimed was inhabited and cultivated on the 20th December, 1803, and that the same was continually inhabited and cultivated by the claimant, or those under whom he claims, for more than ten consecutive years next preceding. Confirmed.

No. 363.—FRANÇOIS DUGAS claims a tract of land, situate on the left bank of the bayou La Fourche, in the county of La Fourche, containing one hundred and eighty superficial acres, and bounded on the upper side by land of the widow Hebert, and on the lower by land of Joseph Dugas.

It appears that the claimant did actually inhabit and cultivate the land now claimed on the 20th December,

1803, and for more than ten consecutive years prior thereto. Confirmed.

No. 364.—Martin Pike claims a tract of land, situate on the left bank of the bayou of La Fourche, in the county of La Fourche, containing one hundred and forty-two and fifty hundredths superficial acres, and bounded on the upper side by land of Jean Boudreau, and on the lower by land of Jean Thibaudeux.

It appears that the land now claimed was inhabited and cultivated on the 20th December, 1803, and that the same was continually inhabited and cultivated by the claimant, or those under whom he claims, for more than ten consecutive years next preceding. Confirmed.

No. 365.—Madame Jean Liret claims a tract of land, situate on the right bank of the bayou of La Fourche, in the county of La Fourche, containing one hundred and sixty-five and forty-two hundredths superficial acres, and bounded on the upper side by land of Hugh Gaston Johnson, and on the lower by land of Nicolas Liret.

It appears that the claimant did actually inhabit and cultivate the land now claimed on the 20th December, 1803, and for more than ten consecutive years next prior thereto. Confirmed.

No. 366.—Etienne Boudreau claims a tract of land, situate on the left bank of the bayou of La Fourche, in the county of La Fourche, containing five hundred and twenty-eight and seven hundredths superficial acres, and bounded on the upper side by land of Jean Baptiste Ducier, and on the lower by land of Pierre Goutreau.

It appears that the land now claimed was inhabited and cultivated on the 20th December, 1803, and that the same was continually inhabited and cultivated by the claimant, or those under whom he claims, for more than ten consecutive years next preceding. Confirmed.

No. 367.—Jean Etienne Boudreau claims a tract of land, situate on the right bank of the bayou La Fourche, in the county of La Fourche, containing three hundred and fifty-one and sixty-one hundredths superficial acres, and bounded on the upper side by land of François Gache, and on the lower by land of Joseph Daigle.

It appears that the land now claimed was inhabited and cultivated on the 20th December, 1803, and that the same was continually inhabited and cultivated by those under whom the claimant holds for more than ten consecutive years next preceding. Confirmed.

No. 372.—Jean Baptiste Ducet claims a tract of land, situate on the left bank of the bayou La Fourche, in the county of La Fourche, containing three hundred and seventy-eight and fifty-nine hundredths superficial acres, and bounded on the upper side by land of François Ducet, and on the lower by land of Etienne Boudreau.

It appears that the claimant did actually inhabit and cultivate the land now claimed on the 20th December, 1803, and for more than ten consecutive years prior thereto. Confirmed.

No. 373.—The Heirs of Louis Gaude, deceased, claim a tract of land, situate on the left bank of the bayou La Fourche, in the county of La Fourche, containing one hundred and ninety-eight and fifty-six hundredths superficial acres, and bounded on the upper side by land of François Gaude, and on the lower by land of C. F. Girod.

It appears that the land now claimed was inhabited and cultivated on the 20th December, 1803, and that it was continually inhabited and cultivated for more than ten consecutive years prior thereto. Confirmed.

No. 374.—Antoine Hernandez claims a tract of land, situate on the right bank of the bayou La Fourche, in the county of La Fourche, containing one hundred and sixty-six and seventy-seven hundredths superficial acres, and bounded on the upper side by land of Mathurin Daigle, and on the lower by land of Louis Angeron.

It appears that the claimant did actually inhabit and cultivate the land now claimed on the 20th December, 1803, and for more than ten consecutive years prior thereto. Confirmed.

No. 375.—Joseph Michel claims a tract of land, situate on the left bank of the bayou La Fourche, in the county of La Fourche, containing one hundred and twelve and seventy-eight hundredths superficial acres, and bounded on the upper side by land of Pierre Guillot, and on the lower by land of Simon Leblanc.

It appears that the land now claimed was actually inhabited and cultivated by the claimant on the 20th December, 1803, and for more than ten consecutive years prior thereto. Confirmed.

No. 376.—Achille Foret claims a tract of land, situate on the right bank of the bayou La Fourche, in the county of La Fourche, containing two hundred and fifty-two and ninety-four hundredths superficial acres, and bounded on the upper side by land of Joseph Sarvie, and on the lower by land of Olivier Gadre.

It appears that the land now claimed was inhabited and cultivated on the 20th December, 1803, and that the same was continually inhabited and cultivated by the claimant, or those under whom he claims, for more than ten consecutive years next preceding. Confirmed.

No. 377.—Pierre Paul Bourgeois claims a tract of land, situate on the left bank of the bayou La Fourche, in the county of La Fourche, containing two hundred and one and forty-nine hundredths superficial acres, and bounded on the upper side by land of Joseph Belony Babin, and on the lower by land of Stephen Piroc.

It appears that the land now claimed was inhabited and cultivated on the 20th December, 1803, and that the same was continually inhabited and cultivated by the claimant or those under whom he claims, for more than ten consecutive years next preceding. Confirmed.

No. 378.—Jean Baptiste Bourgeois claims a tract of land, situate on the left bank of the bayou La Fourche, in the county of La Fourche, containing two hundred and one and seventy-eight hundredths superficial acres, and bounded on the upper side by land of Belony Babin, and on the lower by land of ——.

It appears that the land now claimed was inhabited and cultivated on the 20th December, 1803, and that the same was continually inhabited and cultivated by the claimant, or those under whom he claims, for more than ten consecutive years next preceding. Confirmed.

No. 379.—Jean Baptiste Foret claims a tract of land, situate on the left bank of the bayou La Fourche, in the county of La Fourche, containing four hundred and two and fifteen hundredths superficial acres, and bounded on the upper side by land of Joseph Bourgeois, and on the lower by land of Alexis Jollet.

It appears that the claimant did actually inhabit and cultivate the land now claimed on the 20th December, 1803, and for more than ten consecutive years prior thereto. Confirmed.

No. 380.—George Toops claims a tract of land, situate on the left bank of the bayou La Fourche, in the county of La Fourche, containing eighty-seven and fifty-five hundredths superficial acres, and bounded on the upper side by land of Dominic Broussard, and on the lower by land of ——.

It appears that the land now claimed was inhabited and cultivated on the 20th December, 1803, and that the same was continually inhabited and cultivated by the claimant, or those under whom he claims, for more than ten consecutive years next preceding. Confirmed.

No. 381.—Anselme Landry claims a tract of land, situate on the left bank of the bayou La Fourche, in the county of La Fourche, containing two hundred and seventy-nine and seventy-eight hundredths superficial acres, and bounded on the upper side by land of Paul Boudreau, and on the lower by land of ——.

It appears that the claimant did actually inhabit and cultivate the land now claimed on the 20th December, 1803, and for more than ten consecutive years prior thereto. Confirmed.

No. 382.—Hypolite Leblanc claims a tract of land, situate on the right bank of the bayou La Fourche, in the county of La Fourche, containing three hundred and ninety and ninety hundredths superficial acres, and bounded on the upper side by land of Mathurin Leblanc, and on the lower by land of Joseph Sarvie.

It appears that the land now claimed was inhabited and cultivated on the 20th December, 1803, and that the same was continually inhabited and cultivated by the claimant, or those under whom he claims, for more than ten consecutive years next preceding. Confirmed.

No. 383.—HENRY S. THIBODAUX claims a tract of land, situate on the right bank of the bayou La Fourche, in the county of La Fourche, containing two hundred and seventeen and forty hundredths superficial acres, and bounded on the upper side by land of Mr. Trillons, and on the lower by land of Alexis Jollet.

It appears that the land now claimed was actually inhabited and cultivated by the claimant on the 20th December, 1803, and for more than ten consecutive years prior thereto. Confirmed.

No. 384.—JEAN BAPTISTE ROBICHO claims a tract of land, situate on the right bank of the bayou La Fourche, in the county of La Fourche, containing one hundred and fifty-eight and twenty-seven hundredths superficial acres, and bounded on the upper side by land of E. Millet, and on the lower by land of Fernandez Estaves.

It appears that the land now claimed was inhabited and cultivated on the 20th December, 1803, and that the same was continually inhabited and cultivated by the claimant, or those under whom he claims, for more than ten consecutive years next preceding. Confirmed.

No. 385.—JOSEPH THIBODAUX claims a tract of land, situate on the right bank of the bayou La Fourche, in the county of La Fourche, containing one hundred and six and seventy-one hundredths superficial acres, and bounded on the upper side by land of Nicolas Albert, and on the lower by land of Jean Anesin.

It appears that the land now claimed was inhabited and cultivated on the 20th December, 1803, and that the same was continually inhabited and cultivated by the claimant, or those under whom he claims, for more than ten consecutive years next preceding. Confirmed.

No. 386.—JEAN AUCOIN claims a tract of land, situate on the right bank of the bayou La Fourche, in the county of La Fourche, containing one hundred superficial acres and fifty-four hundredths, and bounded on the upper side by land of Joseph Thibodaux, and on the lower by land of Guillaume Arseman.

It appears that the land now claimed was inhabited and cultivated on the 20th December, 1803, and that the same was continually inhabited and cultivated by the claimant, or those under whom he claims, for more than ten consecutive years next preceding. Confirmed.

No. 387.—FRANCOIS AUCOIN claims a tract of land, situate on the right bank of the bayou La Fourche, in the county of La Fourche, containing ninety and thirty-one hundredths superficial acres, and bounded on the upper side by land of Joacinthe Aucoin, and on the lower by land of ———.

It appears that the claimant did actually inhabit and cultivate the land now claimed on the 20th December, 1803, and for more than ten consecutive years next preceding. Confirmed.

No. 388.—NICOLAS ALBERT claims a tract of land, situate on the right bank of the bayou La Fourche, in the county of La Fourche, containing one hundred and two and ninety-one hundredths superficial acres, and bounded on the upper side by land of Bartholomew Henry, and on the lower by land of Joseph Thibodaux.

It appears that the land now claimed was inhabited and cultivated on the 20th December, 1803, and that the same was continually inhabited and cultivated by the claimant, or those under whom he claims, for more than ten consecutive years next preceding. Confirmed.

No. 389.—JEAN LOUIS HEBERT claims a tract of land, situate on the left bank of the bayou La Fourche, in the county of La Fourche, containing two hundred and two and fifty-one hundredths superficial acres, and bounded on the upper side by land of Guillaume Hebert, and on the lower by land of François de la Maziere.

It appears that the claimant did actually inhabit and cultivate the land now claimed on the 20th December, 1803, and for more than ten consecutive years prior thereto. Confirmed.

No. 390.—ETIENNE DAVOIS claims a tract of land, situate on the right bank of the bayou La Fourche, in the county of La Fourche, containing one hundred and thirty-two and seventy-one hundredths superficial acres, and bounded on the upper side by land of Mathurin Aucoin, and on the lower by land of ———.

It appears that the claimant did actually inhabit and cultivate the land now claimed on the 20th December, 1803, and for more than ten consecutive years prior thereto. Confirmed.

No. 391.—PIERRE LEBLANC claims a tract of land, situate on the right bank of the bayou La Fourche, in the county of La Fourche, containing one hundred and forty-nine and twenty-six hundredths superficial acres, and bounded on the upper side by land of the middle parish of La Fourche, and on the lower by land of Jean Robicho.

It appears that the land now claimed was inhabited and cultivated on the 20th December, 1803, and that the same was continually inhabited and cultivated by the claimant, or those under whom he claims, for more than ten consecutive years next preceding. Confirmed.

No. 392.—GUILLAUME HEBERT claims a tract of land, situate on the left bank of the bayou La Fourche, in the county of La Fourche, containing one hundred and seventy-four and thirty-five hundredths superficial acres, and bounded on the upper side by land of Basil Richard, and on the lower by land of ———.

It appears that the claimant did actually inhabit and cultivate the land now claimed on the 20th December, 1803, and for more than ten consecutive years prior thereto. Confirmed.

No. 393.—Madame MARIE BABIN claims a tract of land, situate on the right bank of the bayou La Fourche, in the county of La Fourche, containing two hundred and forty-three and ninety-seven hundredths superficial acres, and bounded on the upper side by land of the church, and on the lower by land of Mr. Millet.

It appears that the land now claimed was inhabited and cultivated on the 20th December, 1803, and that the same was continually inhabited and cultivated by the claimant, or those under whom she claims, for more than ten consecutive years next preceding. Confirmed.

No. 397.—LOUIS GABRIEL RICHARD claims a tract of land, situate on the right bank of the bayou La Fourche, in the county of La Fourche, containing one hundred and twenty-three and thirty-eight hundredths superficial acres, and bounded on the upper side by land of Bartholomew Henry, and on the lower by land of Charles Bolot.

It appears that the land now claimed was inhabited and cultivated on the 20th December, 1803, and that the same was continually inhabited and cultivated by the claimant, or those under whom he claims, for more than ten consecutive years next preceding. Confirmed.

No. 398.—MATHURIN LEBLANC claims a tract of land, situate on the right bank of the bayou La Fourche, in the county of La Fourche, containing nine hundred and twenty-one and thirty-three hundredths superficial acres, and bounded on the upper side by land of Michel Mourran, and on the lower by land of Hypolite Leblanc.

It appears that the claimant did actually inhabit and cultivate the land now claimed on the 20th December, 1803, and for more than ten consecutive years prior thereto. Confirmed.

No. 400.—PIERRE VINCENT LERRONS claims a tract of land, situate on the right bank of the bayou La Fourche, in the county of La Fourche, containing sixty-two and fifty-nine hundredths superficial acres, and bounded on the upper side by land of Pierre Menons, and on the lower by land of ———.

It appears that the land now claimed was inhabited and cultivated on the 20th December, 1803, and that the same was continually inhabited and cultivated for more than ten consecutive years next preceding. Confirmed.

No. 402.—ARMAND FREMAN claims a tract of land, situate on the left bank of the bayou La Fourche, in the county of La Fourche, containing one hundred and sixty-three and ninety-eight hundredths superficial acres, and bounded on the upper side by land of the heirs of Benjamin Henry Boudreau, and on the lower by land of Peter Henry.

It appears that the claimant did actually inhabit and cultivate the land now claimed on the 20th December, 1803, and for more than ten consecutive years prior thereto. Confirmed.

No. 403.—JEAN ROBICHO claims a tract of land, situate on the right bank of the bayou La Fourche, in the county of La Fourche, containing one hundred and six and thirty-three hundredths superficial acres, and bounded on the upper side by land of Pierre Leblanc, and on the lower by land of Jacques Dubois.

It appears that the land now claimed was inhabited and cultivated on the 20th December, 1803, and that the

same was continually inhabited and cultivated by the claimant, or those under whom he claims, for more than ten consecutive years next preceding. Confirmed.

No. 404.—JOSEPH MOLAISON claims a tract of land, situate on the right bank of the bayou La Fourche, in the county of La Fourche, containing two hundred and thirty-five and fifty eight hundredths superficial acres, and bounded on the upper side by land of François Crochet, and on the lower by land of ———.
It appears that the claimant did actually inhabit and cultivate the land now claimed on the 20th December, 1803, and that the same was continually inhabited and cultivated for more than ten consecutive years prior thereto. Confirmed.

No. 405.—BASIL RICHARD claims a tract of land, situate on the left bank of the bayou La Fourche, in the county of La Fourche, containing three hundred and twenty-nine and seventy-nine hundredths superficial acres, and bounded on the upper side by land of Godé Leblanc, and on the lower by land of ———.
It appears that the claimant did actually inhabit and cultivate the land now claimed on the 20th December, 1803, and for more than ten consecutive years prior thereto. Confirmed.

No. 406.—JOSEPH BELONY BABIN claims a tract of land, situate on the left bank of the bayou La Fourche, in the county of La Fourche, containing one hundred and thirty-nine superficial acres, and bounded on the upper side by land of Baptiste Bourgeois, and on the lower by land of Peter Paul Bourgeois.
It appears that the claimant did actually inhabit and cultivate the land now claimed on the 20th December, 1803, and that the same was continually inhabited and cultivated for more than ten consecutive years prior thereto. Confirmed.

No. 407.—FERNANDE ESTEVE claims a tract of land, situate on the right bank of the bayou La Fourche, in the county of La Fourche, containing one hundred and twenty-two and seventy-one hundredths superficial acres, and bounded on the upper side by land of J. B. Robicho, and on the lower by land of Mathurin Daigle.
It appears that the claimant did actually inhabit and cultivate the land now claimed on the 20th of December, 1803, and for more than ten consecutive years prior thereto. Confirmed.

No. 408.—CLAUDE LEBLANC claims a tract of land, situate on the left bank of the bayou of La Fourche, in the county of La Fourche, containing two hundred and forty-one and sixty hundredths superficial acres, and bounded on the upper side by land of Jean Thibodeaux, and on the lower by land of Basil Richard.
It appears that the claimant did actually inhabit and cultivate the land now claimed on the 20th December, 1803, and for more than ten consecutive years prior thereto. Confirmed.

No. 409.—ANTOINE BESSE claims a tract of land, situate on the left bank of the bayou of La Fourche, in the county of La Fourche, containing two hundred and one and thirty-three hundredths superficial acres, and bounded on the upper side by land of Augustin Domingue, and on the lower by land of Jacques Lamotte.
It appears that the claimant did actually inhabit and cultivate the land now claimed on the 20th December, 1803, and for more than ten consecutive years prior thereto. Confirmed.

No. 410.—JEAN BAPTISTE MAZIERE claims a tract of land, situate on the left bank of the bayou of La Fourche, in the county of La Fourche, containing four hundred and nineteen and eighty-three hundredths superficial acres, and bounded on the upper side by land of Tranquille Arseman, and on the lower by land of ———.
It appears that the claimant did actually inhabit and cultivate the land now claimed on the 20th December, 1803, and for more than ten consecutive years prior thereto. Confirmed.

No. 411.—JOSEPH BOUDREAU claims a tract of land, situate on the right bank of the bayou of La Fourche, in the county of La Fourche, containing one hundred and forty-eight and eighty-seven hundredths superficial acres, and bounded on the upper side by land of Paul Boudreau, and on the lower by land of ———.
It appears that the land now claimed was inhabited and cultivated on the 20th December, 1803, and that the

same was continually inhabited and cultivated by the claimant, or those under whom he claims, for more than ten consecutive years next preceding. Confirmed.

No. 412.—MICHEL BOURGEOIS claims a tract of land, situate on the right bank of the bayou of La Fourche, in the county of La Fourche, containing two hundred and seventeen and thirty-four hundredths superficial acres, and bounded on the upper side by land of Henry Renthrop, and on the lower by land of Pierre Discord.
It appears that the land now claimed was inhabited and cultivated on the 20th December, 1803, and that the same was continually inhabited and cultivated for more than ten consecutive years next preceding. Confirmed.

No. 414.—JACQUES DUBOIS claims a tract of land, situate on the right bank of the bayou of La Fourche, in the county of La Fourche, containing one hundred and seventeen and eighty-seven hundredths superficial acres, and bounded on the upper side by land of Francis Aucoin, and on the lower by land of Mr. Boudreau.
It appears that the land now claimed was inhabited and cultivated on the 20th December, 1803, and that the same was continually inhabited and cultivated by the claimant, or those under whom he claims, for more than ten consecutive years next preceding. Confirmed.

No. 415.—MARGARET PETERS claims a tract of land, situate on the left bank of the bayou of La Fourche, in the county of La Fourche, containing eighty-four and forty-two hundredths superficial acres, and bounded on the upper side by land of Simon Guillot, and on the lower by land of Louis Ogeron.
It appears that the land now claimed was inhabited and cultivated on the 20th December, 1803, and that the same was continually inhabited and cultivated by the claimant, or those under whom she claims, for more than ten consecutive years next preceding. Confirmed.

No. 416.—MICHEL MORRAN claims a tract of land, situate on the right bank of the bayou of La Fourche, in the county of La Fourche, containing three hundred and seventy-seven and sixty-four hundredths superficial acres, and bounded on the upper side by land of Jean Pierre Janvier, and on the lower by land of Caylan Casas.
It appears that the land now claimed was inhabited and cultivated on the 20th December, 1803, and that the same was continually inhabited and cultivated by the claimant, or those under whom he claims, for more than ten consecutive years next preceding. Confirmed.

No. 417.—MICHEL MORRAN claims a tract of land, situate on the right bank of the bayou of La Fourche, in the county of La Fourche, containing three hundred and twenty-three and twenty-nine hundredths superficial acres, and bounded on the upper side by land of Pierre Defirmes, and on the lower by land of ———.
It appears that the land now claimed was inhabited and cultivated by the claimant, or those under whom he claims, for more than ten consecutive years prior to the 20th December, 1803. Confirmed.

No. 418.—MICHEL MORRAN claims a tract of land, situate on the right bank of the bayou of La Fourche, in the county of La Fourche, containing one hundred and twenty-five and fifty-five hundredths superficial acres, and bounded on the upper side by land of Baptiste Bergeron, and on the lower by land of Mathurin Leblanc.
It appears that the land now claimed was inhabited and cultivated on the 20th December, 1803, and that the same was continually inhabited and cultivated by the claimant, or those under whom he claims, for more than ten consecutive years next preceding. Confirmed.

No. 419.—FABIEN AUCOIN claims a tract of land, situate on the right bank of the bayou of La Fourche, in the county of La Fourche, containing one hundred and twenty-six and seventy hundredths superficial acres, and bounded on the upper side by land of Charles Bellegerent, and on the lower by land of ———.
It appears that the claimant did actually inhabit and cultivate the land now claimed on the 20th December, 1803, and for more than ten consecutive years prior thereto. Confirmed.

No. 423.—FRANCOIS SAVOYE claims a tract of land, situate on the right bank of the bayou of La Fourche, in the county of La Fourche, containing one hundred and forty-two superficial acres and twelve hundredths, and bounded on the upper side by land of Augustin Dominguer, and on the lower by land of Francois Fournier.

It appears that the land now claimed was inhabited and cultivated on the 20th December, 1803, and for more than ten consecutive years prior thereto. Confirmed.

No. 424.—FRANCOIS BOUDREAU claims a tract of land, situate on the right bank of the bayou of La Fourche, in the county of La Fourche, containing one hundred superficial acres and nineteen hundredths, and bounded on the upper side by land of Joseph Hebert, and on the lower by land of Philip Henry.

It appears that the claimant did actually inhabit and cultivate the land now claimed on the 20th December, 1803, and for more than ten consecutive years prior thereto. Confirmed.

No. 426.—GUILLAUME ARCEMAN claims a tract of land, situate on the right bank of the bayou of La Fourche, in the county of La Fourche, containing two hundred and twenty-nine and fifty-one hundredths superficial acres, and bounded on the upper side by land of Jean Aucoin, and on the lower by land of Jean Bte. Trahan.

It appears that the land now claimed was inhabited and cultivated on the 20th December, 1803, and that the same was continually inhabited and cultivated by the claimant, or those under whom he claims, for more than ten consecutive years next preceding. Confirmed.

No. 428.—MATHURIN DAIGLE claims a tract of land, situate on the right bank of the bayou of La Fourche, in the county of La Fourche, containing one hundred and forty-six and forty-three hundredths superficial acres, and bounded on the upper side by land of Jean Navarro, and on the lower by land of ———.

It appears that the land now claimed was inhabited and cultivated on the 20th December, 1803, and that the same was continually inhabited and cultivated by the claimant, or those under whom he claims, for more than ten consecutive years next preceding. Confirmed.

No. 429.—BAPTISTE BOURGEOIS claims a tract of land, situate on the right bank of the bayou of La Fourche, in the county of La Fourche, containing five hundred and forty-six and twenty hundredths superficial acres, and bounded on the upper side by land of ———, and on the lower by land of Baptiste Bergeron.

It appears that the land now claimed was inhabited and cultivated on the 20th December, 1803, and that the same was continually inhabited and cultivated by the claimant, or those under whom he claims, for more than ten consecutive years next preceding. Confirmed.

No. 430.—JEAN BAPTISTE BOUDREAU claims a tract of land, situate on the left bank of the bayou of La Fourche, in the county of La Fourche, containing one hundred and eleven and thirty-nine hundredths superficial acres, and bounded on the upper side by land of Peter Seville, and on the lower by land of Mathurin Hebert.

It appears that the land now claimed was inhabited and cultivated on the 20th December, 1803, and that the same was continually inhabited and cultivated by the claimant, or those under whom he claims, for more than ten consecutive years next preceding. Confirmed.

No. 431.—FRANCOIS BLANC claims a tract of land, situate on the left bank of the bayou of La Fourche, in the county of La Fourche, containing seventy-one and thirteen hundredths superficial acres, and bounded on the upper side by land of Reynaud and Peytavin, and on the lower by land of Jean Gadre.

It appears that the land now claimed was inhabited and cultivated on the 20th December, 1803, and that the same was continually inhabited and cultivated by the claimant, or those under whom he claims, for more than ten consecutive years next preceding. Confirmed.

No. 432.—JOSEPH GOUTREAU claims a tract of land, situate on the right bank of the bayou of La Fourche, in the county of La Fourche, containing one hundred and ninety-three and seventy-one hundredths superficial acres, and bounded on the upper side by land of Pierre Olivier Goutreau, and on the lower by land of ———.

It appears that the land now claimed was inhabited and cultivated on the 20th December, 1803, and that the same was continually inhabited and cultivated by the claimant, or those under whom he claims, for more than ten consecutive years next preceding. Confirmed.

No. 434.—JOSEPH LEBLANC claims a tract of land, situate on the right bank of the bayou of La Fourche, in

the county of La Fourche, containing two hundred and four and twenty-one hundredths superficial acres, and bounded on the upper side by land of Mathurin d'Aigle, and on the lower by land of Auguste Babin.

It appears that the land now claimed was inhabited and cultivated on the 20th December, 1803, and that the same was continually inhabited and cultivated by the claimant, or those under whom he claims, for more than ten consecutive years next preceding. Confirmed.

No. 435.—Jean Leblanc claims a tract of land, situate on the right bank of the bayou of La Fourche, in the county of La Fourche, containing one hundred and four and seventy-nine hundredths superficial acres, and bounded on the upper side by land of Joseph Honoré Breau, and on the lower by land of Louis Hallé.

It appears that the land now claimed was inhabited and cultivated on the 20th December, 1803, and for more than ten consecutive years next preceding. Confirmed.

No. 436.—VICENTE HERNANDEZ claims a tract of land, situate on the left bank of the bayou of La Fourche, in the county of La Fourche, containing one hundred and sixty-eight and eighty-seven hundredths superficial acres, and bounded on the upper side by land of Paul Leblanc, and on the lower by land of Baptiste and Basil Prejons.

It appears that the land now claimed was inhabited and cultivated on the 20th December, 1803, and that the same was continually inhabited and cultivated by the claimant, or those under whom he claims, for more than ten consecutive years next preceding. Confirmed.

No. 437.—JEAN BAPTISTE BELTERON claims a tract of land, situate on the right bank of the bayou of La Fourche, in the county of La Fourche, containing one hundred and thirteen and thirty-eight hundredths superficial arpents, and bounded on the upper side by land of Joseph Hebert, and on the lower by land of Marguerite Brodé.

It appears that the land now claimed was inhabited and cultivated on the 20th December, 1803, and that the same was continually inhabited and cultivated by the claimant, or those under whom he claims, for more than ten consecutive years next preceding. Confirmed.

No. 438.—JOSEPH HEBERT claims a tract of land, situate on the right bank of the bayou of La Fourche, in the county of La Fourche, containing one hundred and twenty-three and forty-five hundredths superficial acres, and bounded on the upper side by land of Louis Dantin, and on the lower by land of Jean Baptiste Belteron.

It appears that the claimant did actually inhabit and cultivate the land now claimed on the 20th December, 1803, and for more than ten consecutive years prior thereto. Confirmed.

No. 439.—JEAN BAPTISTE PHILLIPPEAUX claims a tract of land, situate on the left bank of the bayou of La Fourche, in the county of La Fourche, containing one hundred and sixty-five and sixty-four hundredths superficial acres, and bounded on the upper side by land of Etienne Boudreau, and on the lower by land of Louis Dué.

It appearing that the land now claimed was inhabited and cultivated on the 20th December, 1803, and for more than ten consecutive years prior thereto, the Board confirm the claim to such quantity of land as may be contained within the ordinary depth of forty arpents.

No. 440.—CONSTANT PITRE claims a tract of land, situate on the right bank of the bayou of La Fourche, in the county of La Fourche, containing one hundred and seventy-six and seventy-six hundredths superficial acres, and bounded on the upper side by land of Jean Boudreau, and on the lower by land of ———.

It appears that the land now claimed was inhabited and cultivated on the 20th December, 1803, and that the same was continually inhabited and cultivated by the claimant, or those under whom he claims, for more than ten consecutive years next preceding. Confirmed.

No. 442.—FRANÇOIS BENOIT claims a tract of land, situate on the left bank of the bayou of La Fourche, in the county of La Fourche, containing one hundred and twenty-one and sixty-one hundredths superficial acres, and bounded on the upper side by land of Pierre Riché, and on the lower by land of André Hebert.

It appears that the land now claimed was inhabited and cultivated on the 20th December, 1803, and that the

No. 443.—THEODORE BOURG, Jun. claims a tract of land, situate on the right bank of the bayou of La Fourche, in the county of La Fourche, containing one hundred and eighty-seven and fifty-seven hundredths superficial acres, and bounded on the upper side by land of Lambert Billardin, and on the lower by land of André Leblanc.

It appears that the land now claimed was inhabited and cultivated on the 20th December, 1803, and that the same was continually inhabited and cultivated by the claimant, or those under whom he claims, for more than ten consecutive years next preceding. Confirmed.

No. 446.—ANDRE LEBLANC claims a tract of land, situate on the right bank of the bayou of La Fourche, in the county of La Fourche, containing one hundred and twenty-three and seventy-nine hundredths superficial acres, and bounded on the upper side by land of Theodore Bourg, and on the lower by land of Hypolite Leblanc.

It appears that the land now claimed was inhabited and cultivated on the 20th December, 1803, and that the same was continually inhabited and cultivated by the claimant, or those under whom he claims, for more than ten consecutive years next preceding. Confirmed.

No. 447.—GUILLAUME HAMMOND claims a tract of land, situate on the right bank of the bayou of La Fourche, in the county of La Fourche, containing one hundred and twenty-five and eighty hundredths superficial acres, and bounded on the upper side by land of William Henry, and on the lower by land of Joseph Marlbro.

It appears that the claimant did actually inhabit and cultivate the land now claimed on the 20th December, 1803, and for more than ten consecutive years prior thereto. Confirmed.

No. 449.—MICHEL BOURGEOIS claims a tract of land, situate on the left bank of the bayou of La Fourche, in the county of La Fourche, containing one hundred and forty-three and eighty-three hundredths superficial acres, and bounded on the upper side by land of Louis Bourgeois, and on the lower by land of Joseph Bourgeois.

It appears that the land now claimed was inhabited and cultivated on the 20th December, 1803, and that the same was continually inhabited and cultivated by the claimant, or those under whom he claims, for more than ten consecutive years next preceding. Confirmed.

No. 450.—BERNARDO DE DERA claims a tract of land, situate on the left bank of the bayou of La Fourche, in the county of La Fourche, containing six arpents and seven toises in front, and forty arpents in depth, and bounded on the upper side by land of ———, and on the lower by land of Jean Baptiste d'Aigle.

This land was surveyed in the year 1790, by order of Governor Miro, in favor of Pedro Leblanc, under whose title the present claimant holds by virtue of intermediate transfers; and the land having been inhabited and cultivated ever since the above mentioned period, until on and after the 20th December, 1803. Confirmed.

No. 455.—MICHEL MORRAN claims a tract of land, situate on the right bank of the bayou of La Fourche, in the county of La Fourche, containing one hundred and sixty-four and two hundredths superficial acres, and bounded on the upper side by land of C. F. Girod, and on the lower by land of Henry Renthrop.

It appears that the land now claimed was inhabited and cultivated on the 20th December, 1803, and that the same was continually inhabited and cultivated by the claimant, or those under whom he claims, for more than ten consecutive years next preceding. Confirmed.

No. 457.—VINCENT MORA claims a tract of land, situate on the left bank of the bayou of La Fourche, in the county of La Fourche, containing six arpents and one toise in front, and forty arpents in depth, and bounded on the upper side by land of Juan Guelhé, and on the lower by land of Pedro Donzel.

This land was surveyed by the Surveyor General, in the year 1800, in favor of Pablo Navarro, under whose title the present claimant holds. The land having been inhabited and cultivated on, and for ten consecutive years prior to, the 20th December, 1803. Confirmed.

No. 461.—WALKER GILBERT claims a tract of land, situate on the right bank of the bayou of La Fourche, in the county of La Fourche, containing two hundred and twenty and eight hundredths superficial acres, and bounded on the upper side by land of Jean Guillot, and on the lower by land of Alexis Lejeune.

It appears that the land now claimed was inhabited and cultivated on the 20th December, 1803, and that the same was continually inhabited and cultivated by those under whom the claimant holds for more than ten consecutive years next preceding. Confirmed.

No. 463.—GUILLAUME BOURG claims a tract of land, situate on the left bank of the bayou of La Fourche, in the county of La Fourche, containing one hundred and twenty-three superficial acres, and bounded on the upper side by land of Pierre Bourg, and on the lower by land of Jean Baptiste Aucoin.

It appears that the land now claimed was inhabited and cultivated on the 20th December, 1803, and that the same was continually inhabited and cultivated by the claimant, or those under whom he claims, for more than ten consecutive years next preceding. Confirmed.

No. 464.—JEAN BAPTISTE AUCOIN claims a tract of land, situate on the left bank of the bayou of La Fourche, in the county of La Fourche, containing one hundred and sixty-four superficial acres, and bounded on the upper side by land of Guillaume Bourg, and on the lower by land of Vincent Dales.

It appears that the land now claimed was inhabited and cultivated on the 20th December, 1803, and that the same was continually inhabited and cultivated by those under whom the claimant holds for more than ten consecutive years next preceding. Confirmed.

No. 470.—CHARLES BERGERON claims a tract of land, situate on the right bank of the bayou of La Fourche, in the county of La Fourche, containing one hundred and eighty-five and ninety-five hundredths superficial acres, and bounded on the upper side by land of Augustin Babin, and on the lower by land of ———.

It appears that the land now claimed was inhabited and cultivated on the 20th December, 1803, and that the same was continually inhabited and cultivated for more than ten consecutive years next preceding, by the claimant, or those under whom he claims. Confirmed.

No. 472.—LORENZO ACOSTA claims a tract of land, situate on the left bank of the bayou of La Fourche, in the county of La Fourche, containing one hundred and sixty-four superficial acres, and bounded on the upper side by land of Antoine Sanchez, and on the lower by land of Antoine Rodriguez.

It appears that the land now claimed was inhabited and cultivated on the 20th December, 1803, and that the same was continually inhabited and cultivated by those under whom the claimant holds for more than ten consecutive years next preceding. Confirmed.

No. 477.—ALEXIS JOLLET claims a tract of land, situate on the right bank of the bayou of La Fourche, in the county of La Fourche, containing two hundred and thirty-two and seventy-eight hundredths superficial acres, and bounded on the upper side by land of H. S. Thibodeaux, and on the lower by land of Etienne Guitrod.

It appears that the land now claimed was inhabited and cultivated on the 20th December, 1803, and that the same was continually inhabited and cultivated by the claimant, or those under whom he claims, for more than ten consecutive years next preceding. Confirmed.

No. 478.—ALEXIS JOLLET claims a tract of land, situate on the left bank of the bayou La Fourche, in the county of La Fourche, containing three hundred and sixteen and sixty-six hundredths superficial acres, and bounded on the upper side by land of C. F. Girod, and on the lower by land of Augustin Domingue.

It appears that the land now claimed was inhabited and cultivated on the 20th December, 1803, and that the same was continually inhabited and cultivated by the claimant, or those under whom he claims, for more than ten consecutive years next preceding. Confirmed.

No. 479.—ALEXIS JOLLET claims a tract of land, situate on the left bank of the bayou La Fourche, in the county of La Fourche, containing two hundred and sixty-nine and twenty-one hundredths superficial acres, and bounded on the upper side by land of C. F. Girod, and on the lower by land of C. F. Girod.

It appears that the land now claimed was inhabited and cultivated on the 20th December, 1803, and that the same was continually inhabited and cultivated by the claimant, or those under whom he claims, for more than ten consecutive years next preceding. Confirmed.

No. 481.—Joseph Bourgeois claims a tract of land, situate on the left bank of the bayou La Fourche, in the county of La Fourche, containing one hundred and ninety-nine and eighty-two hundredths superficial acres, and bounded on the upper side by land of Michel Bourgeois, and on the lower by land of Jean Bte. Foret.

It appears that the land now claimed was inhabited and cultivated on the 20th December, 1803, and that the same was continually inhabited and cultivated by the claimant, or those under whom he claims, for more than ten consecutive years next preceding. Confirmed.

No. 482.—Louis Bourgeois claims a tract of land, situate on the left bank of the bayou La Fourche, in the county of La Fourche, containing three hundred and forty and forty-six hundredths superficial acres, and bounded on the upper side by land of C. F. Girod, and on the lower by land of Michel Bourgeois.

The claimant obtained a regular warrant of survey for this land, from the Baron de Carondelet, in the year 1787; since which time the land has been continually inhabited and cultivated. Confirmed.

No. 498.—Francis Marlbro claims a tract of land, situate on the right bank of the bayou La Fourche, in the county of La Fourche, containing one hundred and fifteen and thirty-four hundredths superficial acres, and bounded on the upper side by land of Etienne Davois, and on the lower by land of _____.

It appears that the land now claimed was inhabited and cultivated on the 20th December, 1803, and that the same was continually inhabited and cultivated by the claimant, or those under whom he claims, for more than ten consecutive years next preceding. Confirmed.

No. 501.—Joseph Lopez claims a tract of land, situate on the left bank of the bayou La Fourche, in the county of La Fourche, containing two arpents and seven-eighths of an arpent in front, and forty arpents in depth, and bounded on the upper side by land of Sebastian Suarez, and on the lower by land of Miguel Falcon.

It appears that the land now claimed was inhabited and cultivated on the 20th December, 1803, and that the same was continually inhabited and cultivated by the claimant, or those under whom he claims, for more than ten consecutive years next preceding. Confirmed.

No. 502.—Vincent Daillais claims a tract of land, situate on the right bank of the bayou La Fourche, in the county of La Fourche, containing one hundred and forty-six and eighty-five hundredths superficial acres, and bounded on the upper side by land of Mr. Labarthe, and on the lower by land of T. Villaneuva.

It appears that the land now claimed was inhabited and cultivated on the 20th December, 1803, and that the same was continually inhabited and cultivated by the claimant, or those under whom he claims, for more than ten consecutive years next preceding. Confirmed.

No. 506.—Miguel Falcon claims a tract of land, situate on the left bank of the bayou La Fourche, in the county of La Fourche, containing three arpents in front, and the side lines closing to a point at the depth of twenty-five arpents, and bounded on the upper side by land of Joseph Lopez, and on the lower by land of Jean Rodriguez.

It appears that the land now claimed was inhabited and cultivated on the 20th December, 1803, and that the same was continually inhabited and cultivated by the claimant, or those under whom he claims, for more than ten consecutive years next preceding. Confirmed.

No. 508.—Augustin Babin claims a tract of land, situate on the right bank of the bayou La Fourche, in the county of La Fourche, containing one hundred and twenty-eight and twenty-two hundredths superficial acres, and bounded on the upper side by land of Joseph Leblanc, and on the lower by land of _____.

It appearing that the land now claimed was inhabited and cultivated on the 20th December, 1803, and for more than ten consecutive years prior, the Board confirm the claim to so much land as is contained within the ordinary depth of forty arpents.

No. 512.—Sebastien Suarez claims a tract of land, situate on the left bank of the bayou La Fourche, in the county of La Fourche, containing three arpents in front, and the side lines closing to a point at the depth of twenty-seven arpents, and bounded on the upper side by land of Joseph Rodriguez, and on the lower by land of Joseph Lopez.

It appears that the land now claimed was inhabited and cultivated on the 20th December, 1803, and that the same was continually inhabited and cultivated by the claimant, or those under whom he claims, for more than ten consecutive years next preceding. Confirmed.

No. 514.—Theodore Bourg, Sen. claims a tract of land, situate on the right bank of the bayou La Fourche, in the county of La Fourche, containing two hundred and sixteen and six hundredths superficial acres, and bounded on the upper side by land of Louis Hallé, and on the lower by land of Lambert Billardin.

It appears that the claimant did actually inhabit and cultivate the land now claimed on the 20th December, 1803, and for more than ten consecutive years prior thereto. Confirmed.

No. 515.—Pierre Olivier Goutreau claims a tract of land, situate on the right bank of the bayou La Fourche, in the county of La Fourche, containing one hundred and fifty-five and ninety-five hundredths superficial acres, and bounded on the upper side by land of Jean Delaume, and on the lower by land of Joseph Goutreau.

It appears that the land now claimed was inhabited and cultivated on the 20th December, 1803, and that the same was continually inhabited and cultivated by those under whom the claimant holds for more than ten consecutive years next preceding. Confirmed.

No. 35.—Thomas de Villanueva claims a tract of land, situate on the right bank of the bayou La Fourche, in the county of La Fourche, containing three hundred and seventy-seven and thirty-seven hundredths superficial acres, and bounded on the upper side by land of Vincent Daillais, and on the lower by Pierre Mercier.

It appearing to the satisfaction of the Board that the land now claimed was settled previous to the 1st of October, 1800, and that the same was continually inhabited and cultivated by those under whom the present claimant holds, until on and after the 20th of December, 1803. Confirmed.

No. 113.—Jean Duga claims a tract of land, situate in the county of La Fourche, on the left side of the bayou of La Fourche, containing one thousand seven hundred and thirty-seven and sixty-seven hundredths superficial acres, and bounded on the upper side by land of Raphael Landry, and on the lower by land of Louis Le Baubé.

It appearing to the satisfaction of the Board that the land now claimed was settled prior to the 1st of October, 1800, and that it was continually inhabited and cultivated by those under whom the claimant holds, until on and after the 20th December, 1803, the Board confirm the claim to the extent of six hundred and forty superficial arpents, and reject it as to the balance.

No. 119.—Joseph Cherami claims a tract of land, situate in the county of La Fourche, and containing sixty-six arpents in front on one bank of the bayou La Fourche, and seventy-three arpents in front on the other bank, with the ordinary depth of forty arpents, and bounded on the upper side by land of Estevan Guitro, and on the lower by lands of Pedro Daspic and Jean Bt. Morel.

This land was resurveyed in the year 1796, in favor of the claimant, by the Surveyor General of the province; and the claimant having continued to inhabit and cultivate the same ever since the aforesaid period, until on and after the 20th of December, 1803. Confirmed.

No. 169.—Stephen Guitrod claims a tract of land, situate in the county of La Fourche, on the left bank of the bayou La Fourche, containing thirty-five arpents in front, by forty in depth, and bounded on the upper side by land of Pedro Daspic, and on the lower by land of Santiago Lamotte.

This land was surveyed in favor of Pedro Bourgeois, on the 30th of April, 1800, by the Surveyor General of the province, in virtue of a decree of the Intendant, dated the 25th April, 1799. Said Bourgeois conveyed the land to the present claimant; and the same having been inhabited and cultivated on the 1st day of October, 1800, and since. Confirmed.

No. 252.—EDWARD DAIGLE claims a tract of land, situate on the left bank of the bayou La Fourche, in the county of La Fourche, containing one thousand three hundred and sixty-six and sixty-five hundredths superficial acres, and bounded on one side by land of Raphael Landry, and on the other by land of —— Duga.

It appearing to the satisfaction of the Board that this land was settled prior to the 1st October, 1800, and that the same was continually inhabited and cultivated until on and after the 20th of December, 1803, they confirm the claim to the quantity of six hundred and forty arpents, so as to include the improvements in the centre, and reject it as to the balance now claimed.

No. 253.—MARGARET BRODE claims a tract of land, situate in the county of La Fourche, on the right bank of the bayou of the same name, containing one hundred and eighty-two and eighty hundredths superficial acres, and bounded on one side by land of Joseph Hebert.

It appearing that the land now claimed was settled by the claimant prior to the 1st of October, 1800, and that she has continued to inhabit and cultivate the same until on and after the 20th December, 1803. Confirmed.

No. 288.—PIERRE CHIASSON claims a tract of land, situate on the bayou La Fourche, in the county of La Fourche, containing ninety-eight and eleven hundredths superficial acres, and bounded on one side by land of Jean Marie Trahan, and on the other by land of Joseph Chiasson.

It appearing that the claimant settled this land prior to the 1st of October, 1800, and that he continued to inhabit and cultivate the same until on and after the 20th of December, 1803. Confirmed.

No. 289.—JEAN BAPTISTE DOUCETTE claims a tract of land, situate on the left bank of the bayou of La Fourche, in the county of La Fourche, containing three hundred and seventy-eight and twenty-three hundredths superficial acres, and bounded on one side by land of François Doucette, and on the lower by land of Etienne Boudreau.

It appearing that the land now claimed was settled prior to the 1st of October, 1800, and that the same was continually inhabited and cultivated by those under whom the claimant holds, until on and after the 20th December, 1803. Confirmed.

No. 344.—CELESTE LAMATE claims a tract of land, situate on the left bank of the bayou La Fourche, in the county of La Fourche, (the quantity not expressed in the survey,) and bounded on the upper side by land of Jacques Verret, and on the lower by land of Valentin Saulet.

It appearing that this land was settled prior to the 1st of October, 1800, and that the same was continually inhabited and cultivated by those under whom the claimant holds until on and after the 20th December, 1803, the Board confirm the claim to the quantity of six hundred and forty acres, so as to include the improvements in the centre.

No. 353.—PIERRE DASPIT ST. AMAND claims a tract of land, situate in the county of La Fourche, on the right bank of the bayou La Fourche, containing one thousand and twenty-six and sixty-five hundredths superficial acres, and bounded on the upper side by land of Farny Verret, and on the lower by land of Joseph Cherami.

It appearing that the claimant settled this land previous to the 1st of October, 1800, and that he continued to inhabit and cultivate the same until on and after the 20th December, 1803, the Board confirm the claim to the quantity of six hundred and forty acres, so as to include the improvements in the centre, and reject it as to the balance claimed.

No. 354.—ALEXANDRE ST. AMAND claims a tract of land, situate in the county of La Fourche, on the left bank of the bayou La Fourche, containing three hundred and seventy-one and eighty-one hundredths superficial acres, and bounded on the upper side by land of Jacques Lamotte, and on the lower by land of Janot Voisin.

It appearing that the land now claimed was settled prior to the 1st of October, 1800, and that the same was continually inhabited and cultivated by those under whom the claimant holds, until on and after the 20th December, 1803. Confirmed.

No. 355.—ALEXANDRE ST. AMAND claims a tract of land, situate in the county of La Fourche, on the right bank of the bayou La Fourche, containing four hundred and seventy-nine and twenty-eight hundredths superficial acres, and bounded on the one side by land of Jacques Lamotte, and on the other by land of C. F. Girod.

It appearing that the land now claimed was settled prior to the 1st of October, 1800, and that the same was continually inhabited and cultivated by those under whom the claimant holds, until on and after the 20th December, 1803. Confirmed.

No. 356.—JACQUES LAMOTTE claims a tract of land, situate on the left bank of the bayou La Fourche, in the county of La Fourche, containing three hundred and fifty-nine and eight hundredths superficial acres, and bounded on the upper side by land of Jean Baptiste Phillippeaux, and on the lower by land of Adam Materne.

It appearing that this land was settled prior to the 1st of October, 1800, and that the same was continually inhabited and cultivated by those under whom the present claimant holds, until on and after the 20th December, 1803. Confirmed.

No. 361.—PIERRE GADRE claims a tract of land, situate on the right bank of the bayou La Fourche, in the county of La Fourche, containing seventy-seven and seventy-eight hundredths superficial acres, and bounded on the upper side by land of François Sapin, and on the lower by land of John Maronge.

It appearing that this land was settled prior to the 1st of October, 1800, and that it was continually inhabited and cultivated by those under whom the present claimant holds, until on and after the 20th December, 1803. Confirmed.

No. 362.—JEAN BAPTISTE ROBICHO claims a tract of land, situate on the right bank of the bayou La Fourche, in the county of La Fourche, containing four hundred and thirteen and fifty-one hundredths superficial acres, and bounded on the upper side by land of Michel Morran, and on the lower by land of Joseph Landry.

It appearing that the land now claimed was actually settled prior to the 1st of October, 1800, and that it was continually inhabited and cultivated until on and after the 20th December, 1803, by those under whom the present claimant holds. Confirmed.

No. 394.—ANTOINE BOUTARY claims a tract of land, situate in the county of La Fourche, on the right bank of the bayou La Fourche, containing three hundred and seventy-six and forty-one hundredths superficial acres, and bounded on one side by land of Marguerite Brodé.

It appearing that the land now claimed was settled prior to the 1st of October, 1800, and that the same was continually inhabited and cultivated by those under whom the claimant holds, until on and after the 20th December, 1803. Confirmed.

No. 395.—MARIE ANTOINE MILLIEU claims a tract of land, situate on the right bank of the bayou La Fourche, in the county of La Fourche, containing sixty-seven and fifty-one hundredths superficial acres, and bounded on one side by land of Louis Ogeron, and on the other by land of Augustin Domingue, Jun.

It appearing that the land now claimed was settled prior to the 1st of October, 1800, and that the same was continually inhabited and cultivated by those under whom the claimant holds, until on and after the 20th December, 1803. Confirmed.

No. 396.—JOSEPH FELIX BOUDREAU claims a tract of land, situate on the right bank of the bayou La Fourche, in the county of La Fourche, containing two hundred and four and seventy-nine hundredths superficial acres, and bounded on one side by land of Jacques Dubois, and on the other by land of John Deslomes.

It appearing that the claimant settled this land prior to the 1st of October, 1800, and that he continued to inhabit and cultivate the same until on and after 20th December, 1803. Confirmed.

No. 399.—JEAN C. BROUSSARD claims a tract of land, situate on the left bank of the bayou La Fourche, in the county of La Fourche, containing ninety-five and sixty-five hundredths superficial acres, and bounded on the upper side by land of George Toops.

It appearing that the claimant did actually settle this land prior to the 1st of October, 1800, and that he continued to inhabit and cultivate the same until on and after the 20th December, 1803. Confirmed.

No. 401.—ALEXIS LEVRON claims a tract of land, situate in the county of La Forche, on the right bank of the bayou La Fourche, containing one hundred and sixty-two and twenty-three hundredths superficial acres, and bounded on one side by land of Pierre Vincent Levron.

It appearing that the claimant did actually settle this land prior to the 1st of October, 1800, and that the same was continually inhabited and cultivated by him until on and after the 20th December, 1803. Confirmed.

No. 413.—PIERRE HACHE claims a tract of land, situate on the right bank of the bayou La Fourche, in the county of La Fourche, containing three hundred and eighty-one and forty-four hundredths superficial acres, and bounded on one side by land of Antoine Boutary.

It appearing that the land now claimed was settled prior to the 1st of October, 1800, and that the same was continually inhabited and cultivated by the claimant, or those under whom he claims, until on and after the 20th December, 1803. Confirmed.

No. 420.—DOMINIC BROUSSARD claims a tract of land, situate on the left bank of the bayou La Fourche, in the county of La Fourche, containing one hundred and fifty-six and seventy-one hundredths superficial acres, and bounded on one side by land of George Toops.

It appearing that the land now claimed was settled prior to the 1st of October, 1800, and that the same was continually inhabited and cultivated by those under whom the claimant holds, until on and after the 20th December, 1803. Confirmed.

No. 421.—PIERRE HUZET claims a tract of land, situate on the left bank of the bayou La Fourche, in the county of La Fourche, containing one hundred and fifty-six and fifty-four hundredths superficial acres, and bounded on one side by land of Pierre Haché.

It appearing that the land now claimed was settled prior to the 1st of October, 1800, and that the same was continually inhabited and cultivated by those under whom the claimant holds, until on and after the 20th December, 1803. Confirmed.

No. 422.—JEAN GUILLOTTE claims a tract of land, situate on the left bank of the bayou La Fourche, in the county of La Fourche, containing two hundred and fifty-three and ninety hundredths superficial acres, and bounded on the upper side by land of the heirs of Oliver Petre, and on the lower by land of Charles Guillotte.

It appearing that the land now claimed was settled prior to the 1st of October, 1800, and that the same was continually inhabited and cultivated by those under whom the present claimant holds, until on and after the 20th of December, 1803. Confirmed.

No. 425.—FRANÇOIS SAPIN claims a tract of land, situate in the county of La Fourche, on the left bank of the bayou La Fourche, containing eighty-five and thirty-four hundredths superficial acres, and bounded on one side by land of Jacques Thibodeaux, and on the lower by land of Pierre Gadre.

It appearing that the land now claimed was settled prior to the 1st day of October, 1800, and that the same was continually inhabited and cultivated by those under whom the claimant holds, until on and after the 20th December, 1803. Confirmed.

No. 427.—JOSEPH ARABY claims a tract of land, situate in the county of La Fourche, on the left bank of the bayou of La Fourche, containing three hundred and eighty and eighty-two hundredths superficial acres, and bounded on the upper side by land of Henry Brown, and on the lower by land of Jean Deplaisance.

It appearing that the claimant did actually settle this land prior to the 1st of October, 1800, and that he continued to inhabit and cultivate the same until on and after the 20th December, 1803. Confirmed.

No. 433.—JEAN M. NAVARRE claims a tract of land, situate on the right bank of the bayou La Fourche, in the county of La Fourche, containing one hundred and fourteen and forty-eight hundredths superficial acres.

It appearing that the land now claimed was settled prior to the 1st of October, 1800, and that the same was continually inhabited and cultivated by those under whom the claimant holds, until on and after the 20th December, 1803. Confirmed.

No. 441.—ALEXANDRE MILLET claims a tract of land, situate on the right bank of the bayou La Fourche, in the county of La Fourche, containing one hundred and ninety-seven and ninety-four hundredths superficial acres, and bounded on the upper side by land of the

widow Babin, and on the lower by land of Jean Baptiste Robichaux.

It appearing that the land now claimed was settled prior to the 1st of October, 1800, and that the same was continually inhabited and cultivated by those under whom the present claimant holds, until on and after the 20th December, 1803. Confirmed.

No. 444.—JEAN MORANGE claims a tract of land, situate in the county of La Fourche, on the right bank of the bayou La Fourche, containing one hundred and eighty-five and six hundredths superficial acres, and bounded on the upper side by land of Pierre Guedry, and on the lower by land of André Candolle.

It appearing that the land now claimed was settled prior to the 1st of October, 1800, and that the same was continually inhabited and cultivated by those under whom the present claimant holds, until on and after the 20th December, 1803. Confirmed.

No. 445.—JOSEPH CHERAMI claims a tract of land, situate in the county of La Fourche, on the right bank of the bayou La Fourche, containing nine hundred and sixty superficial acres, and bounded on the upper side by land of Joseph Daigle, and on the lower by vacant land.

It appearing that the land now claimed was settled prior to the 1st of October, 1800, and that the same was continually inhabited and cultivated by those under whom the claimant holds, until on and after the 20th December, 1803, the Board confirm the claim to the quantity of six hundred and forty acres, but reject it as to the balance.

No. 448.—JOSEPH CHERAMI claims a tract of land, situate on the right bank of the bayou La Fourche, in the county of La Fourche, containing one thousand two hundred and ten superficial acres, and bounded on the upper side by land of Daspit St. Amand, and on the lower by land of Madame Françoise Gotro.

It appearing that the land now claimed was settled prior to the 1st of October, 1800, and that the same was continually inhabited and cultivated by the claimant, or those under whom he claims, until on and after the 20th December, 1803, the Board confirm the claim to the quantity of six hundred and forty acres, and reject it as to the balance.

No. 454.—JEAN LABATT claims a tract of land, situate on the right bank of the bayou La Fourche, in the county of La Fourche, containing three hundred and thirty-four and forty-two hundredths superficial acres, and bounded on the upper side by land of Antoine Basse, and on the lower by land of Vincent Dallas.

It appearing that the land now claimed was settled prior to the 1st of October, 1800, and that the same was continually inhabited and cultivated by the claimant, or those under whom he claims, until on and after the 20th December, 1803. Confirmed.

No. 455.—ANDRE CANDOLLE claims a tract of land, situate on the right bank of the bayou La Fourche, in the county of La Fourche, containing one hundred and sixty-seven and twenty-six hundredths superficial acres, and bounded on the upper side by land of Jean Morange, and on the lower by land of François Beaudeloche.

It appearing that the land now claimed was actually settled prior to the 1st of October, 1800, and that the same was continually inhabited and cultivated by those under whom the claimant holds, until on and after the 20th December, 1803. Confirmed.

No. 465.—LOUIS OGERON claims a tract of land, situate on the right bank of the bayou La Fourche, in the county of La Fourche, containing one hundred and eighty-nine and ninety-two hundredths superficial acres, and bounded on the upper side by land of Hugh Gaston Johnson, and on the lower by land of Antoine Basse.

It appearing that the land now claimed was inhabited and cultivated prior to the 1st of October, 1800, and continually, by the claimant, or those under whom he claims, until on and after the 20th December, 1803. Confirmed.

No. 466.—HUGH GASTON JOHNSON claims a tract of land, situate on the right bank of the bayou La Fourche, in the county of La Fourche, containing seventy-one and eight hundredths superficial acres, and bounded on the upper side by land of Joseph Marlbrough, and on the lower by land of Madame Liret.

It appearing that the land now claimed was settled prior to the 1st of October, 1800, and that the same was continually inhabited and cultivated by the claimant, or those under whom he claims, until on and after the 20th December, 1803. Confirmed.

No. 468.—ANTOINE DIAS claims a tract of land, situate on the left bank of the bayou La Fourche, in the county of La Fourche, containing three hundred and ninety-nine and thirty-nine hundredths superficial acres, and bounded on the upper side by land of Alexis Jollet, and on the lower by land of Thomas Burns.
It appearing that the land now claimed was settled prior to the 1st of October, 1800, and that the same was continually inhabited and cultivated by those under whom the present claimant holds, until on and after the 20th December, 1803. Confirmed.

No. 471.—FAROY VERRET claims a tract of land, situate in the county of La Fourche, on the right bank of the bayou La Fourche, containing three hundred and thirty-one and seventy-four hundredths superficial acres, and bounded on the upper side by land of Pierre Mercier, and on the lower by land of Pierre Daspit.
It appearing that the land now claimed was settled prior to the 1st of October, 1800, and that the same was continually inhabited and cultivated by those under whom the claimant holds, until on and after the 20th December, 1803. Confirmed.

No. 473.—JANOT VOIZIN claims a tract of land, situate on the left bank of the bayou La Fourche, in the county of La Fourche, containing seven hundred and fifty-five and sixty-six hundredths superficial acres, and bounded on one side by land of Alexandre St. Amand, and on the other by land of François Shaust.
It appearing that the claimant did actually settle this land prior to the 1st of October, 1800, and that he continued to inhabit and cultivate the same until on and after the 20th December, 1803, the Board confirm the claim to the quantity of six hundred and forty acres, and reject it as to the balance.

No. 474.—JANOT VOIZIN claims a tract of land, situate on the bayou La Fourche, in the county of La Fourche, containing four hundred and eight and thirty-eight hundredths superficial acres, and bounded on one side by land of C. F. Girod, and on the other by land of Valentin Saulet.
It appearing that the land now claimed was settled prior to the 1st of October, 1800, and that the same was continually inhabited and cultivated by those under whom the claimant holds, until on and after the 20th December, 1803. Confirmed.

No. 475.—BELA HUBBARD, as agent for the parishioners of the middle parish, claims, as church land, a tract of land, situate in said parish, and in the county of La Fourche, on the right bank of the bayou La Fourche, containing ninety-two and seventy-seven hundredths superficial acres, and bounded on one side by land of Joseph Hebert, and on the other by land of Pierre Leblanc.
It appearing that the aforesaid land has been used by the parishioners, as church land, for upwards of twenty years, the Board do hereby confirm the claim.

No. 476.—BELA HUBBARD, as agent for the parishioners of the interior parish, claims, as church land, a tract of land, situate in said parish, and in the county of La Fourche, on the right bank of the bayou La Fourche, containing one hundred and ninety-seven and eighty-eight hundredths superficial acres, and bounded on the upper side by land of John Tyson, and on the lower by land of the widow Babin.
It appearing that the aforesaid land has been used and possessed by the parishioners, as church land, for upwards of fifteen years, the Board do hereby confirm the claim.

No. 480.—THOMAS BURNS claims a tract of land, situate on the left bank of the bayou La Fourche, in the county of La Fourche, containing four hundred and nine and twenty-three hundredths superficial acres, and bounded on the upper side by land of Antoine Dias, and on the lower by land of Alexis Jollet.
It appearing that the land now claimed was actually settled prior to the 1st of October, 1800, and that the same was continually inhabited and cultivated until on and after the 20th December, 1803, by the claimant, or those under whom he claims Confirmed.

No. 485.—JEAN DEPLAISANCE claims a tract of land, situate on the left bank of the bayou La Fourche, in the county of La Fourche, containing four hundred and twenty-one and thirty-six hundredths superficial acres, and bounded on the upper side by land of Joseph Araby, and on the lower by land of François Suver.
It appearing that the claimant did actually settle this land prior to the 1st of October, 1800, and that he continued to inhabit and cultivate the same until on and after the 20th December, 1803. Confirmed.

No. 486.—JOSEPH DAIGLE claims a tract of land, situate on the right bank of the bayou La Fourche, in the county of La Fourche, containing seven hundred and three and eighty-five hundredths superficial acres, and bounded on the upper side by land of Etienne Boudreau, and on the lower by land of Joseph Cherami.
It appearing that the claimant did actually settle this land prior to the 1st of October, 1800, and that he continued to inhabit and cultivate the same until on and after the 20th December, 1803, the Board confirm his claim to the quantity of six hundred and forty acres, and reject it as to the balance.

No. 495.—FRANÇOIS SUARES claims a tract of land, situate on the left bank of the bayou La Fourche, in the county of La Fourche, containing fourteen chains and fifty-five links in front, and the ordinary depth of forty arpents, and bounded on the upper side by land of ———, and on the lower by land of Michel Marven.
It appearing that the land now claimed was settled prior to the 1st of October, 1800, and that the same was continually inhabited and cultivated by the claimant, or those under whom he claims, until on and after the 20th December, 1803. Confirmed.

No. 503.—FRANÇOIS GACHET claims a tract of land, situate on the left bank of the bayou La Fourche, in the county of La Fourche, containing five hundred and ninety-seven and eighty-four hundredths superficial acres, and bounded on the upper side by land of Joseph Cherami, and on the lower by land of Etienne Boudreau.
It appearing that the land now claimed was actually settled prior to the 1st of October, 1800, and continued to be inhabited and cultivated by those under whom the claimant holds until on and after the 20th December, 1803. Confirmed.

No. 504.—JOSEPH SAVOYE claims a tract of land, situate on the right bank of the bayou La Fourche, in the county of La Fourche, containing one hundred and fifteen and twenty-one hundredths superficial acres, and bounded on the upper side by land of Hypolite Leblanc, and on the lower by land of Achille Forest.
It appearing that the claimant did actually settle this land prior to the 1st of October, 1800, and that he continued to inhabit and cultivate the same until on and after the 20th December, 1803. Confirmed.

No. 505.—ANTOINE BOSSE claims a tract of land, situate in the county of La Fourche, on the right bank of the bayou La Fourche, containing one hundred and forty-nine and sixty-four hundredths superficial acres, and bounded on the upper side by land of Louis Ogeron, and on the lower by land of Jean Labarthe.
It appearing that the claimant did actually settle this land prior to the 1st of October, 1800, and that he continued to inhabit and cultivate the same until on and after the 20th December, 1803. Confirmed.

No. 507.—FRANÇOIS FRILLON claims a tract of land, situate in the county of La Fourche, on the right bank of the bayou La Fourche, containing three hundred and six and seventy-one hundredths superficial acres, and bounded on the upper side by land of Pierre Discord, and on the lower by land of Henry S. Thibodeaux.
It appearing that the land now claimed was settled prior to the 1st of October, 1800, and that the same was continually inhabited and cultivated by those under whom the claimant holds, until on and after the 20th December, 1803. Confirmed.

No. 509.—PIERRE MERCIER claims a tract of land, situate on the right bank of the bayou La Fourche, in the county of La Fourche, containing two hundred and eighty-five and ninety hundredths superficial acres, and bounded on the upper side by land of Thomas de Villanueva, and on the lower by land of Farcy Verret.
It appearing that the land now claimed was settled prior to the 1st of October, 1800, and that the same con-

46

tinued to be inhabited and cultivated by those under whom the present claimant holds, until on and after the 20th December, 1803. Confirmed.

No. 510.—CLAUDE FRANÇOIS GIROD claims a tract of land, situate on the left bank of the bayou La Fourche, in the county of La Fourche, containing two hundred and eighty-five and ninety hundredths superficial acres, and bounded on the upper side by land of Alexis Jollet, and on the lower by land of said Jollet.

It appearing that the land now claimed was settled prior to the 1st of October, 1800, and that the same was continually inhabited and cultivated by those under whom the claimant holds, until on and after the 20th December, 1803. Confirmed.

No. 511.—CLAUDE FRANÇOIS GIROD claims a tract of land, situate on the right bank of the bayou La Fourche, in the county of La Fourche, containing three hundred and fifty-two and ten hundredths superficial acres, and bounded on the upper side by land of Alexandre St. Amand, and on the lower by land of Janot Voizin.

It appearing that the land now claimed was settled prior to the 1st of October, 1800, and that the same was continually inhabited and cultivated by those under whom the claimant holds, until on and after the 20th December, 1803. Confirmed.

No. 513.—LOUIS OGERON claims a tract of land, situate on the right bank of the bayou La Fourche, in the county of La Fourche, containing one hundred and sixty-three and nineteen hundredths superficial acres, and bounded on the upper side by land of A. Hernandez, and on the lower by land of Antoine Hernandez.

It appearing that the land now claimed was settled prior to the 1st of October, 1800, and that the same was continually inhabited and cultivated by those under whom the claimant holds, until on and after the 20th December, 1803. Confirmed.

No. 313.—JOSEPH M. BOUDREAU claims a tract of land, situate on each side of the bayou Darbonne, in the county of La Fourche, containing seven hundred and eleven and twenty-six hundredths superficial acres.

It appearing that the claimant did actually settle this land, with the permission of the proper Spanish officer, prior to the 20th of December, 1803, and that he did inhabit and cultivate the land on that day, the Board confirm the claim to the quantity of six hundred and forty acres, and reject it as to the balance.

No. 314.—CHARLES BILLOT claims a tract of land, situate on both sides of the bayou Darbonne, in the county of La Fourche, containing two hundred and fifteen and four hundredths superficial acres, and adjoining on one side to land of Charles Naquin.

It appearing that the claimant did actually settle this land, with the permission of the proper Spanish officer, prior to the 20th day of December, 1803, and that he did inhabit and cultivate the same on that day. Confirmed.

No. 315.—PIERRE BOUSQUE claims a tract of land, situate on both sides of the bayou Darbonne, in the county of La Fourche, containing one hundred and eighty-five and thirty-four hundredths superficial acres, and adjoining on one side to land of Charles Billot.

It appearing that the claimant did actually settle this land prior to the 20th December, 1803, by the permission of the proper Spanish officer, and that he did inhabit and cultivate the same on that day. Confirmed.

No. 339.—LOUIS SAUVAGE claims a tract of land, situate on both sides of the bayou Darbonne, in the county of La Fourche, containing eighty and forty-eight hundredths superficial acres, and adjoining on one side to land of Pierre Bourg.

It appearing that the claimant did actually settle this land, with the permission of the proper Spanish officer, prior to the 20th of December, 1803, and that he did inhabit and cultivate the same on that day. Confirmed.

No. 340.—CHARLES NANQUIN claims a tract of land, situate on both sides of the bayou Darbonne, in the county of La Fourche, containing one hundred and forty-five and thirty hundredths superficial acres, and adjoining on one side to land of Pierre Dugas.

It appearing that the claimant did actually settle this land, with the permission of the proper Spanish officer, prior to the 20th day of December, 1803, and that he did inhabit and cultivate the same on that day. Confirmed.

No. 341.—JEAN NANQUIN claims a tract of land, situate on both sides of the bayou Darbonne, in the county of La Fourche, containing four hundred and eighty-four superficial acres.

It appears that the claimant petitioned the Baron de Carondelet for this land in the year 1795, and that the Baron directed the Surveyor General to inform himself relative to the land being vacant, &c., and that the Surveyor General reported favorably to the claimant. The claimant never received any other title from the Spanish Government; but he having actually settled the land prior to the 1st of October, 1800, and continued to inhabit and cultivate the same until on and after the 20th December, 1803. Confirmed.

No. 342.—JEAN DUPRES claims a tract of land, situate on both sides of the bayou Darbonne, in the county of La Fourche, containing four hundred and thirty-six and ninety-six hundredths superficial acres, and adjoining on one side to land of Joseph M. Boudreau.

This claim, as to title, is in every respect similarly situated to that of Jean Nanquin, No. 341, preceding. Confirmed.

No. 343.—JEAN BAPTISTE THEODORE HENRY claims a tract of land, situate on both sides of the bayou Darbonne, in the county of La Fourche, containing seven hundred and seventy-six and thirty-two hundredths superficial acres.

It appearing that the claimant did actually settle this land, with the permission of the proper Spanish officer, prior to the 20th of December, 1803, and that he did inhabit and cultivate the same on that day, the Board confirm the claim to the quantity of six hundred and forty acres, and reject it as to the balance.

No. 368.—JOSEPH BILLOT claims a tract of land, situate on both sides of the bayou Darbonne, in the county of La Fourche, containing one hundred and fifty-nine and twelve hundredths superficial acres, and adjoining on one side to land of Marie Acies.

It appears that Jean Billot obtained from Governor Miro a regular warrant of survey for this land, in the year 1788, and that the land was inhabited and cultivated on the 1st day of October, 1800; and further, that said Jean Billot conveyed the land to the present claimant. Confirmed.

No. 369.—JEAN BILLOT, Jun. claims a tract of land, situate on both sides of the bayou Darbonne, in the county of La Fourche, containing one hundred and sixty eight and thirty-six hundredths superficial acres, and adjoining on one side to land of Joseph La Force.

It appears that Jean Chap obtained from Governor Miro a regular warrant of survey for this land, in the year 1787, and that the same was inhabited and cultivated on the 1st day of October, 1800, and further, that the said Chap conveyed it to the present claimant. Confirmed.

No. 370.—MARIE NERISSE claims a tract of land, situate on both sides of the bayou Darbonne, in the county of La Fourche, containing three hundred and twenty-one and seventy-four hundredths superficial acres.

It appears that the claimant obtained for this land a regular warrant of survey from Governor Miro, in the year 1788, and that the same was inhabited and cultivated by her on the 1st day of October, 1800. Confirmed.

No. 371.—JEAN BILLOT, Sen. claims a tract of land, situate on both sides of the bayou Darbonne, in the county of La Fourche, containing three hundred and forty-two and eighty-five hundredths superficial acres.

It appears that the claimant obtained from Governor Miro a regular warrant of survey for this land, in the year 1787, and that he did inhabit and cultivate the same on the 1st day of October, 1800. Confirmed.

No. 453.—JOSEPH MOLLERE claims a tract of land, situate on both sides of the bayou Darbonne, in the county of La Fourche, containing eight hundred superficial arpents, and bounded on the upper side by land of Thomas de Villanueva, and on the lower by vacant land.

This land was surveyed for the claimant, by the Surveyor General of the province, in 1802, conformably to a decree of the Intendant General, dated the 25th April, 1799; and it having been inhabited and cultivated ever since the last mentioned period, until on and after the 20th December, 1803. Confirmed.

No. 484.—JEAN BILLOT claims a tract of land, situate on both sides of the bayou Darbonne, in the county of La Fourche, containing one hundred and sixty-seven and fifteen hundredths superficial acres, and adjoining on one side to land of Louis Sauvage.

It appearing that Joseph La Force, under whom the present claimant holds, settled this land, with the permission of the proper Spanish officer, prior to the 20th day of December, 1803, and that he actually inhabited and cultivated the same on that day. Confirmed.

No. 496.—CHARLES BERGERON claims a tract of land, situate on both sides of the bayou Darbonne, in the county of La Fourche, containing one thousand three hundred and thirty-four and fifty-eight hundredths superficial acres, and adjoining on one side to land of Thomas de Villanueva.

It appearing that the claimant did actually settle this land, with the permission of the proper Spanish officer, prior to the 20th December, 1803, and that he inhabited and cultivated the same on that day, the Board confirm the claim to the quantity of six hundred and forty acres, and reject it as to the balance.

No. 497.—WILLIAM HAMMOND claims a tract of land, situate on both sides of the bayou Darbonne, in the county of La Fourche, containing one hundred and fifty five and fifty-nine hundredths superficial acres.

It appearing that the claimant settled this land, with the permission of the proper Spanish officer, prior to the 20th of December, 1803, and that he inhabited and cultivated the same on that day. Confirmed.

No. 499.—FRANÇOIS MARLBROUGH claims a tract of land, situate on both sides of the bayou Darbonne, in the county of La Fourche, containing two hundred and forty and forty-four hundredths superficial acres, and adjoining on one side to land of Joseph Marlbrough, and on the other to land of Thomas de Villanueva.

It appearing that the claimant did actually settle this land, with the permission of the proper Spanish officer, prior to the 20th December, 1803, and that he inhabited and cultivated the same on that day. Confirmed.

No. 500.—JOSEPH MARLBROUGH claims a tract of land, situate on both sides of the bayou Darbonne, in the county of La Fourche, containing four hundred and seventeen and fifteen hundredths superficial acres, and adjoining on one side to land of Charles Bergeron, and on the other to land of François Marlbrough.

It appearing that the claimant settled this land, with the permission of the proper Spanish officer, prior to the 20th December, 1803, and that he actually inhabited and cultivated the same on that day. Confirmed.

No. 33.—THOMAS DE VILLANUEVA claims a tract of land, situate in the county of La Fourche, on the right bank of the canal leading from bayou La Fourche, to lake Verret, containing five hundred and sixty and fifty-five hundredths superficial acres, and bounded above by land said to belong to Antoine Leblanc, and below by land claimed by Laurien Laviolet.

It appears that one John Fitzpatrick settled this land, by permission of the proper Spanish officer, prior to the 20th day of December, 1803, and that he did actually inhabit and cultivate the same on that day. It appears, also, that, at the decease of said Fitzpatrick, the land was sold by the commandant of the district, at public sale, on the 19th day of May, 1805, to Alexander Milles, who afterwards conveyed it to the present claimant. Confirmed.

No. 279.—GREGOIRE AUCOIN claims a tract of land, situate on the bayou Bœuf, in the county of La Fourche, containing four hundred and forty-six and sixty-two hundredths superficial acres, and adjoining on one side to land of François Aucoin.

It appears that the land was actually settled, by permission of the proper Spanish officer, prior to the 20th of December, 1803, and that the same was inhabited and cultivated on that day. Confirmed.

No. 285.—JEAN BAPTISTE FALTEMENT claims a tract of land, situate in the county of La Fourche, on the right bank of the canal leading from the bayou La Fourche to lake Verret, containing two hundred and ninety-three and fifty three hundredths superficial acres.

It appearing that the claimant did actually settle this land, with the permission of the proper Spanish officer, prior to the 20th December, 1803, and that he inhabited and cultivated the same on that day. Confirmed.

No. 292.—HYPOLITE DAGBERT claims a tract of land, situate in the county of La Fourche, on the left bank of the canal leading from the bayou La Fourche to lake Verret, containing six hundred and sixty and seventy-three hundredths superficial acres, and adjoining on one side to land of François Guitreau, and on another to land of Jean Pierre Landry.

It appearing that the claimant settled this land, with the permission of the proper Spanish officer, prior to the 20th December, 1803, and that he did actually inhabit and cultivate the same on that day, the Board confirm the claim to the quantity of six hundred and forty acres, and reject the balance.

No. 316.—JOSEPH BOUDREAU claims a tract of land, situate in the county of La Fourche, on the right bank of the canal leading from the bayou La Fourche to lake Verret, containing one hundred and fifty-eight superficial acres, and bounded on the upper side by land of Jean B. Faltement, and on the lower by land of Pierre Moriaux.

It appearing that this land was settled, with the permission of the proper Spanish officer, prior to the 20th of December, 1803, and that the same was actually inhabited and cultivated by those under whom the present claimant holds, on that day. Confirmed.

No. 325.—MATHURIN OSSITET claims a tract of land, situate in the county of La Fourche, on the right bank of the canal leading from bayou La Fourche to lake Verret, containing one hundred and sixty superficial acres, and bounded on the upper side by land of Joseph Boudreau, and on the lower by land of the claimant.

It appearing that the land now claimed was settled, with the permission of the proper Spanish officer, prior to the 20th of December, 1803, and that the same was actually inhabited and cultivated by those under whom the present claimant holds. Confirmed.

No. 327.—THOMAS DE VILLANUEVA claims a tract of land, situate in the county of La Fourche, on the left bank of the canal leading from bayou La Fourche to lake Verret, containing one hundred and forty-three and twelve hundredths superficial acres, and bounded on the upper side by land of Jean Baptiste Roger, and on the lower by land of Louis Sync.

It appearing that this land was settled, with the permission of the proper Spanish officer, prior to the 20th of December, 1803, and that the same was actually inhabited and cultivated on that day by those under whom the claimant holds. Confirmed.

No. 329.—THOMAS DE VILLANUEVA claims a tract of land, situate on the left bank of the canal leading from the bayou La Fourche to lake Verret, and in the county of La Fourche, containing two hundred and six and thirty-one hundredths superficial acres, and bounded on the upper side by land claimed by Julian Ossitet, and on the lower by land claimed by Louis Bringier.

It appearing that this land was settled, with the permission of the proper Spanish officer, prior to the 20th December, 1803, and that the same was actually inhabited and cultivated, by those under whom the present claimant holds, on that day. Confirmed.

No. 335.—CHRISTOPHE BRYANT claims a tract of land, situate in the county of La Fourche, on the lake Verret, on each side of the canal leading from the bayou La Fourche, containing six hundred and twenty-seven superficial acres.

It appearing that the claimant actually settled this land, with the permission of the proper Spanish officer, prior to the 20th day of December, 1803, and that he inhabited and cultivated the same on that day, the Board confirm his claim to be laid off with a front of sixteen acres on lake Verret, so as to include the mouth of the aforesaid canal in its centre, and a depth of forty acres, removing back in the direction of the canal.

No. 346.—SAMUEL RUSSEL RICE claims a tract of land, situate in the county of La Fourche, on the bayou Bœuf, containing six hundred and fifty-three and thirty-six hundredths superficial acres, and adjoining on one side land of Samuel Rice.

It appearing that the land now claimed was settled, with the permission of the proper Spanish officer, prior to the 20th day of December, 1803, and that the same was inhabited and cultivated on that day by those under whom the present claimant holds, the Board confirm the claim to the quantity of six hundred and forty acres, and reject the balance.

No. 347.—SAMUEL RUSSEL RICE claims a tract of land, situate on the bayou Bœuf, in the county of La Fourche, containing six hundred and fifty-five and eighty hundredths superficial acres.

It appearing that the land now claimed was settled, by the permission of the proper Spanish officer, prior to the 20th December, 1803, and that the same was actually inhabited and cultivated on that day by those under whom the present claimant holds, the Board confirm the claim to the quantity of six hundred and forty acres, and reject the balance.

No. 348.—SAMUEL RICE, Sen. claims a tract of land, situate in the county of La Fourche, on the bayou Bœuf, at the place usually called Coupen Island, containing six hundred and ninety-four hundredths superficial acres.

It appearing that this land was actually settled, by the permission of the proper Spanish officer, prior to the 20th of December, 1803, and that the same was inhabited and cultivated on that day by those under whom the claimant holds. Confirmed.

No. 460.—THOMAS ALLEN claims a tract of land, situate in the county of La Fourche, on the canal leading from the bayou La Fourche to lake Verret, and containing two hundred and ten superficial acres.

Gilbert Leblanc obtained a regular order of survey from the Baron de Carondelet, in the year 1787, for this land; the said Leblanc conveyed it to the present claimant; and the land having been inhabited and cultivated on the 1st of October, 1800. Confirmed.

No. 280.—JEAN BAPTISTE HENRY claims a tract of land, situate in the county of La Fourche, on the bayou Bœuf, containing one hundred and eighty-six and sixty-eight hundredths superficial acres, and adjoining on one side to land of Jean Baptiste Jaunier.

It appearing that the land now claimed was actually settled, with the permission of the proper Spanish officer, prior to the 20th of December, 1803, and that the same was inhabited and cultivated on that day. Confirmed.

P. GRYMES, R. E. D. Orl. Ter.
JOSHUA LEWIS,
THOMAS B. ROBERTSON.

Rejected claims from the books of Bela Hubbard, Deputy Register for the county of La Fourche.

No. 113.—JEAN DUGAT claims a tract of land, situate in the county of La Fourche, on the left bank of the bayou La Fourche, containing one thousand seven hundred and thirty-seven and sixty-seven hundredths superficial acres; six hundred and forty of which have been confirmed to him in No. 113 among the confirmed claims.

This land is claimed in virtue of a settlement made prior to the 1st of October, 1800, and cultivation on the 20th of December, 1803. We have already confirmed the claim to the quantity of six hundred and forty acres, and do therefore reject the balance claimed.

No. 252.—EDOUARD DAIGLE claims a tract of land, situate on the left bank of the bayou La Fourche, in the county of La Fourche, containing one thousand three hundred and sixty-six and sixty-five hundredths superficial acres; six hundred and forty of which have been confirmed to him already in No. 252 among the confirmed claims.

This land is claimed by virtue of a settlement made, with the permission of the proper Spanish officer, prior to the 1st of October, 1800, and cultivation on the 20th of December, 1803. We have already confirmed the claim to the quantity of six hundred and forty acres, as authorized by the act of Congress, and do therefore reject the balance.

No. 258.—JOSEPH MARLBROUGH claims a second depth of thirty arpents, lying immediately behind a front of six arpents and a depth of forty, situate on the right bank of the bayou La Fourche, in the county of La Fourche, and which we have confirmed to the claimant among the confirmed claims.

The claimant pretends no other title to this second depth than his being proprietor of the front and first depth, we therefore reject his claim.

No. 287.—JEAN GUILLOTTE claims a second depth of land, lying back of a front and first depth, situate on the right bank of the bayou La Fourche, in the county of

La Fourche, and which we have confirmed to him in No. 287 among the confirmed claims.

The claimant pretends no other title to this second depth of land than the absurd one of its having been granted to him by one of the American deputy surveyors. We do therefore reject the claim as being entirely a feigned one.

No. 353.—PIERRE DASPIT ST. AMAND claims a tract of land, situate in the county of La Fourche, on the right bank of the bayou La Fourche, containing one thousand and twenty-six and sixty-five hundredths superficial acres; six hundred and forty of which we have confirmed to him in No. 353 among the confirmed claims.

This land is claimed in virtue of a settlement prior to the 1st of October, 1800, and cultivation on the 20th December, 1803. We have already confirmed the claim to the extent of six hundred and forty acres, and do therefore reject the balance.

No. 445.—JOSEPH CHERAMI claims a tract of land, situate on the right bank of the bayou La Fourche, in the county of La Fourche, containing nine hundred and sixty superficial acres; six hundred and forty of which we have confirmed to him in No. 445 among the confirmed claims.

This claim is founded upon a settlement, by permission of the proper Spanish officer, prior to the 1st of October, 1800, and cultivation on the 20th of December, 1803. We have already confirmed the claim to the quantity of six hundred and forty acres, and do therefore reject the balance.

No. 448.—JOSEPH CHERAMI claims a tract of land, situate on the right bank of the bayou La Fourche, in the county of La Fourche, containing one thousand two hundred and ten superficial acres; six hundred and forty of which have been confirmed to him in No. 448 among the confirmed claims.

This claim is founded on a settlement, with the permission of the proper Spanish officer, prior to the 1st of October, 1800, and cultivation on the 20th of December, 1803. We have already confirmed this claim to the extent of six hundred and forty acres, and therefore reject it as to the balance.

No. 473.—JANOT VOIZIN claims a tract of land, situate on the left bank of the bayou La Fourche, in the county of La Fourche, containing seven hundred and fifty-five and sixty-six hundredths superficial acres; six hundred and forty of which have been confirmed in No. 473 among the confirmed claims.

This claim is founded upon a settlement made, with the permission of the proper Spanish officer, prior to the 1st of October, 1800, and cultivation on the 20th of December, 1803. We have already confirmed this claim to the extent of six hundred and forty acres, and therefore reject the balance.

No. 486.—JOSEPH DAIGLE claims a tract of land, situate on the right bank of the bayou La Fourche, in the county of La Fourche, containing seven hundred and three and eighty-five hundredths superficial acres; six hundred and forty of which we have already confirmed to him in No. 486 among the confirmed claims.

This claim is founded upon a settlement made, with the permission of the proper Spanish officer, prior to the 1st of October, 1800, and cultivation on the 20th of December, 1803. We have already confirmed the claim to the extent of six hundred and forty acres, and therefore reject it as to the balance.

No. 313.—JOSEPH M. BOUDREAU claims a tract of land, situate in the county of La Fourche, on both sides of the bayou Darbonne, and containing seven hundred and eleven and twenty-six hundredths superficial acres; six hundred and forty of which we have confirmed in No. 313 among the confirmed claims.

This claim is founded upon settlement, with the permission of the proper Spanish officer, prior to the 20th of December, 1803, and cultivation on that day. We have already confirmed the claim to the extent authorized by the act of Congress, and therefore reject the balance.

No. 338.—JEAN BAPTISTE VARDIN, for himself and his brothers, claims a tract of land, situate on each side of the bayou Darbonne, in the county of La Fourche, containing six hundred and twenty-six and thirty-six hundredths superficial acres.

The claimants state that they settled on this land about the year 1792 or 1793, and they show sufficient proof to substantiate the fact; but it also appears satisfactorily to the Board, that they left the land, and settled elsewhere, previous to the 1st of October, 1800, and have never resumed possession of it since. We are therefore of opinion the claim ought to be rejected.

No. 343.—JEAN BAPTISTE THEODORE HENRY claims a tract of land, situate in the county of La Fourche, on both sides of the bayou Darbonne, containing seven hundred and seventy-six and thirty-six hundredths superficial acres; six hundred and forty of which have been confirmed in No. 343 among the confirmed claims.

This claim is founded upon a settlement made, by the permission of the proper Spanish officer, prior to the 20th December, 1803, and cultivation on that day. We have already confirmed the claim to the quantity of six hundred and forty acres, and therefore reject the balance.

No. 469.—MICHEL DEVAL claims a tract of land, situate in the county of La Fourche, on both sides of the bayou Darbonne, containing four hundred and six and twenty-four hundredths superficial acres.

The claimant pretends title to this land from his having gone on it in the year 1802, marked trees, and cleared a road; to which facts he produces one or two affidavits; but the land having never been inhabited and cultivated until after the 20th December, 1803, we therefore reject the claim.

No. 496.—CHARLES BERGERON claims a tract of land, situate in the county of La Fourche, on both sides of the bayou Darbonne, containing one thousand three hundred and thirty-four and fifty-eight hundredths superficial acres; six hundred and forty of which we have confirmed to him in No. 496, among the confirmed claims.

This claim is founded upon a settlement made, with the permission of the proper Spanish officer, prior to the 20th of December, 1803, and cultivation on that day. We have confirmed the claim to the extent of six hundred and forty acres, and therefore reject the balance.

No. 254.—ALEXANDRE LANDRY claims a second depth of land, situate in the county of La Fourche, and lying back of a front and first depth of the claimant, and containing five hundred and eighty-four and seventy hundredths superficial acres.

The claimant produces in support of this second depth, the certificate of the commandant of the district, who states that he permitted the claimant, in the year 1802, to take possession of this land. The land appears not to have been inhabited and cultivated; and we are of opinion that, according to the usages and customs of the Spanish Government, the claim ought to be rejected.

No. 272.—JOHN HENRY claims a tract of land, situate in the county of La Fourche, on the bayou Bœuf, containing six hundred and fifty-six and forty-five hundredths superficial acres.

The claimant states that he went on this land, with the permission of the proper Spanish officer, some time in the month of July, 1803; but we have satisfactory evidence that the land was never settled until after the 20th of December, 1803, and do therefore reject the claim.

No. 273.—FRANÇOIS AUCOIN claims a tract of land, situate in the county of La Fourche, on the bayou Bœuf, containing one hundred and sixty and sixty-seven hundredths superficial acres.

The claimant states that he settled this land some time in the month of July, 1803, with the permission of the proper Spanish officer; but it appearing satisfactorily in evidence to the Board that the land was not inhabited and cultivated until after the 20th December,1803, they therefore reject the claim.

No. 282.—BENOIT GOUTREAU claims a tract of land, situate in the county of La Fourche, on the bayou Bœuf, containing six hundred and sixteen and thirty hundredths superficial acres, and adjoining on one side land of Jean Baptiste Henry.

The claimant states that this land was settled, with the permission of the proper Spanish officer, some time in the month of July, 1803; but it appearing, from the best testimony the Board have been able to procure, that the land was not inhabited and cultivated until after the 20th December, 1803, they therefore reject the claim.

No. 284.—ANTHONY REED claims a tract of land, situate in the county of La Fourche, on lake Verret, at the mouth of the canal leading from bayou La Fourche, containing four hundred and forty-five and eighteen hundredths superficial acres.

The claimant sets up a title to this land as having been settled, with the permission of the proper Spanish officer, in the year 1801, by one Stout. It appears from the evidence produced by the claimant, that said Stout was on the land in the year 1801 or 1802; but it appears also that he left it some time prior to the 20th December, 1803. We do therefore reject the claim.

No. 293.—JEAN PIERRE LANDRY claims a tract of land, situate in the county of La Fourche, on the left bank of the canal leading from the bayou La Fourche to lake Verret, containing four hundred and seventy-eight superficial acres.

The claimant states that he settled this land, with the permission of the proper Spanish officer, prior to the 20th December, 1803, and that he inhabited and cultivated the same on that day; but it appearing in satisfactory evidence to the Board that the land was not inhabited and cultivated until after the 20th December, 1803, the Board do therefore reject the claim.

No. 291.—MICHEL DEVAL claims a tract of land, situate on the bayou Bœuf, in the county of La Fourche, containing one hundred and eighty-one and ninety-two hundredths superficial acres, and adjoining land of Jean Saunier.

The claimant states that he settled this land, with the permission of the proper Spanish officer, prior to the 20th of December, 1803, and cultivated and inhabited the same on that day; but it appearing in evidence to the Board that the land was not inhabited and cultivated until after the 20th December, 1803, they therefore reject the claim.

No. 299.—RAPHAEL LANDRY claims a tract of land, situate in the county of La Fourche, on the canal leading from the bayou La Fourche to lake Verret, containing three hundred and twenty-six and a half superficial acres, and adjoining on one side land claimed by James Orvens, and on the other by land claimed Jean Pierre Landry.

The claimant states that the land now claimed was settled by him, with the permission of the proper Spanish officer, prior to the 20th December, 1803, and that the same was inhabited and cultivated by him on that day; but it appearing, from satisfactory testimony, that the land was not settled until after the 20th December, 1803, the Board do therefore reject the claim.

No. 302.—JEAN BROCUMON claims a tract of land, situate in the county of La Fourche, on the bayou Bœuf, containing one hundred and seventy-six and ninety-six hundredths superficial acres, and adjoining on one side land claimed by Michel Deval.

The claimant states that he settled this land, with the permission of the proper Spanish officer, prior to the 20th December, 1803, and that he did inhabit and cultivate the land on that day; but it appearing, from the most satisfactory evidence, that the land was not settled until after the 20th December, 1803, the Board therefore reject the claim.

No. 309.—JAMES OWENS claims a tract of land, situate in the county of La Fourche, on both sides of the canal leading from the bayou La Fourche, to lake Verret, containing six hundred and forty superficial acres.

The claimant states that the land now claimed was settled by him, with the permission of the proper Spanish officer, prior to the 20th of December, 1803, and that he did actually inhabit and cultivate the same on that day; but it appearing, from satisfactory evidence, to the Board, that the land was not settled until after the 20th December, 1803, they therefore reject the claim.

No. 321.—JEAN BAPTISTE ROGER claims a tract of land, situate in the county of La Fourche, on the left bank of the canal leading from bayou La Fourche to lake Verret, containing one hundred and forty-two superficial acres, and bounded on the upper side by land of Thomas de Villanueva, and on the lower by land claimed by Julian Osselet.

The claimant states that this land was settled, by permission of the proper Spanish officer, prior to the 20th December, 1803, and that it was inhabited and cultivated on that day; but it appearing to the Board, from the most satisfactory testimony, that the land was never settled until after the 20th of December, 1803, they therefore reject the claim.

No. 322.—JEAN BAPTISTE PRELLE claims a tract of land, situate in the county of La Fourche, on the right bank of the canal leading to lake Verret, containing one hundred and ninety superficial acres, and bounded on one side by land claimed by Mathurin Osselet, and on the other by land claimed by Julian Osselet.

The claimant states that he settled this land, with the permission of the proper Spanish officer, prior to the 20th December, 1803, and that he inhabited and cultivated the same on that day; but it appearing to the Board, from satisfactory testimony, that the land was not settled until after the 20th December, 1803, they therefore reject the claim.

No. 323.—LOUIS BRINGIER claims a tract of land, situate on the left bank of the canal leading to lake Verret, in the county of La Fourche, containing two hundred and fifty superficial acres, and bounded on the upper side by land claimed by Louis Syng, and on the lower by land claimed by François Goutreau.

The claimant states that the land now claimed was settled, with the permission of the proper Spanish officer, prior to the 20th day of December, 1803, and inhabited and cultivated on that day; but it appearing, from the most satisfactory evidence, that the land was not settled until after the 20th December, 1803, the Board reject the claim.

No. 324.—MATHURIN OSSELET claims a tract of land, situate in the county of La Fourche, on the right bank of the canal leading to lake Verret, containing six hundred and fifty superficial acres, and adjoining on one side land of Pierre Moraux.

The claimant states that he settled this land, with the permission of the proper Spanish officer, prior to the 20th December, 1803, and inhabited and cultivated it on that day; but it appearing to the Board, from satisfactory evidence, that the land was not settled until after the 20th December, 1803, they therefore reject the claim.

No. 328.—FRANÇOIS GOUTREAU claims a tract of land, situate in the county of La Fourche, on the left bank of the canal leading to lake Verret, containing two hundred and sixty-four superficial acres, and bounded on the upper side by land claimed by Louis Bringier, and on the lower by land claimed by Hypolite Dagbert.

The claimant states that he settled this land, by permission of the proper Spanish officer, prior to the 20th of December, 1803, and inhabited and cultivated it on that day; but it appearing to the Board, from satisfactory testimony, that the land was not settled until after the 20th of December, 1803, they therefore reject the claim.

No. 331.—CLAUDE F. GIROD claims an island, situate in the county of La Fourche, about four leagues west of the entrance of the bayou La Fourche into the sea, and separated from the high land by swamp.

The claimant shows no manner of evidence in support of his title to this land, or tract of land, and we do therefore reject the claim.

No. 336.—CORNELIUS BALDWIN claims a tract of land, situate in the county of La Fourche, on the canal leading from the bayou La Fourche to lake Verret, and containing six hundred and forty-six and thirty-six hundredths superficial acres.

The claimant states that this land was settled, with the permission of the proper Spanish officer, prior to the 20th December, 1803, and inhabited and cultivated on that day; but of this he produces no evidence. We therefore reject the claim.

No. 337.—JACOB HENRY claims a tract of land, situate in the county of La Fourche, on the bayou Bœuf, containing one hundred and fifty-four and fifty-nine hundredths superficial acres, and adjoining on one side land claimed by Alexandre Daniel, and on the other by land of William Knight.

The claimant states that he settled this land some time in the month of May, 1803, and that he inhabited and cultivated the same on the 20th of December, 1803. He does not pretend to have settled by permission of the proper Spanish officer; and it appearing, from satisfactory evidence, to the Board, that the land was not actually settled until after the 20th of December, 1803, they reject the claim.

No. 360.—LOUIS BRINGIER claims a tract of land, situate in the county of La Fourche, on the left bank of the canal leading to lake Verret, containing two hundred and fifty-seven and eighty hundredths superficial acres, and adjoining on one side land claimed by Louis Syng, and on another land claimed by J. Goutreau.

The claimant states that the land was settled, by permission of the proper Spanish officer, prior to the 20th of December, 1803, and inhabited and cultivated on that day. But it appearing to the Board, from the most satisfactory testimony, that the land was not settled until the 20th of December, 1803, they reject the claim.

No. 451.—BERNARDO DE DERO claims a tract of land, situate in the county of La Fourche, on the bayou St. Bernard, or Grand Bayou, containing twelve hundred and eighty-six superficial acres, and bounded on each side by vacant lands.

The claimant founds his title to this land upon a petition to the commandant of the district in 1802, which petition was granted by the commandant to the extent that he was authorized. But the claimant produces no evidence whatever of an actual settlement of the land; and, from the best information we have been able to obtain, if the land has ever been settled to this day, it was not until after the 20th of December, 1803. We do therefore reject the claim.

No. 452.—JAMES OWENS claims a tract of land, situate in the county of La Fourche, on both sides of the canal leading to lake Verret, containing three hundred and forty-five superficial acres, and adjoining on one side land claimed by Raphael Landry, and on another land claimed by Julian Osselet.

The claimant produces, in support of his claim to this land, the permission of the commandant of the district, in the year 1802, to one James Simpson to settle any vacant land; and he produces also an affidavit, stating said Simpson to have inhabited and cultivated the land in the month of March, 1803; but it appearing, from satisfactory testimony, that the land was not inhabited and cultivated on the 20th of December, 1803, the Board therefore reject the claim.

No. 459.—FRANÇOIS FRILLON claims a tract of land, situate in the county of La Fourche, on both sides of the canal leading to lake Verret, containing two hundred and ninety-four and sixteen hundredths superficial acres.

The claimant states that he settled this land, with the permission of the proper Spanish officer, prior to the 20th of December, 1803, and that he inhabited and cultivated the same on that day; but it appearing to the Board, from the most satisfactory evidence, that the land was not actually settled until after the 20th of December, 1803, they therefore reject the claim.

No. 462.—WILLIAM KNIGHT claims a tract of land, situate in the county of La Fourche, on the bayou Bœuf, containing six hundred and forty-six and eighty-six hundredths superficial acres, and adjoining on one side land of John Henry.

The claimant states that this land was settled, with the permission of the proper Spanish officer, prior to the 20th of December, 1803, and that the same was actually inhabited and cultivated on that day; but it appearing, from the most satisfactory evidence, that this land was not settled until after the 20th December, 1803, the Board therefore reject the claim.

No. 467.—PIERRE LECONTE claims a tract of land, situate in the county of La Fourche, on the bayou Bœuf, containing one hundred and thirty-nine and forty-six hundredths superficial acres, and adjoining land claimed by Etienne Peniçon.

The claimant does not pretend to have settled the land prior to the 20th December, 1803; and we conceive the claim to be entirely a feigned one, and do accordingly reject it.

No. 483.—GREGOIRE AUCOIN and BENOIT GOUTREAU claim a tract of land, situate in the county of La Fourche, on the bayon Bœuf, containing one hundred and sixty-nine and seventy-six hundredths superficial acres, and adjoining on one side land claimed by Felix Boudreau.

The claimants state that they settled this land, with the permission of the proper Spanish officer, prior to the 20th of December, 1803, and that they actually inhabited and cultivated the same on that day; but it appearing to the Board, from satisfactory evidence, that the land was not settled until after the 20th December, 1803, they reject the claim.

No. 487.—CHARLOTTE HALL claims a tract of land, situate in the county of La Fourche, on the bayou Bœuf, containing one hundred and fifty-nine and thirty-three hundredths superficial acres, and adjoining on one side land claimed by William Knight.

The claimant does not even pretend that she settled this land prior to the 20th of December, 1803. We consider the claim to be entirely a feigned one, and therefore reject it.

No. 488.—ALEXANDRE DANIEL claims a tract of land, situate in the county of La Fourche, on the bayou Bœuf, containing one hundred and fifty-nine and sixty hundredths superficial acres, and adjoining on one side land claimed by John Henry, and on the other land claimed by Jacob Henry.

The claimant does not even pretend that this land was settled prior to the 20th December, 1803. We consider the claim to be entirely a feigned one, and do accordingly reject it.

No. 489.—JEAN M. LAGRANGE claims a tract of land, situate in the county of La Fourche, on the bayou Bœuf, containing one hundred and sixty and sixty-three hundredths superficial acres, and adjoining on one side land claimed by Jean Olivier, and on the other land claimed by Bte. Jaunier.

The claimant does not even pretend to have settled this land prior to the 20th December, 1803. We consider the claim to be a feigned one, and do accordingly reject it.

No. 490.—JEAN OLIVIER claims a tract of land, situate in the county of La Fourche, on the bayou Bœuf, containing one hundred and sixty and thirty-nine hundredths superficial acres, and adjoining on one side land claimed by Jean M. Lagrange.

The claimant does not even pretend to have settled this land prior to the 20th of December, 1803. We con-

sider the claim to be entirely a feigned one, and do accordingly reject it.

No. 491.—JEAN BAPTISTE JANNE claims a tract of land, situate in the county of La Fourche, on the bayou Bœuf, containing one hundred and sixty and sixty-three hundredths superficial acres, and adjoining on one side land claimed by Felix Boudreau, and on the other land claimed by Jean M. Lagrange.

The claimant pretends not to have settled this land prior to the 20th of December, 1803. We consider the claim to be entirely a feigned one, and do accordingly reject it.

No. 492.—ETIENNE PENIÇON claims a tract of land, situate in the county of La Fourche, on the bayou Bœuf, containing one hundred and thirty-nine and forty-four hundredths superficial acres, and adjoining on one side land claimed by Jean Baptiste Lagrange.

The claimant does not even pretend to have settled this land prior to the 20th December, 1803. We consider the claim a feigned one, and therefore reject it.

No. 493.—ETIENNE PENIÇON claims a tract of land, situate in the county of La Fourche, on the bayou Bœuf, containing sixty-nine and seventy-five hundredths superficial acres, and adjoining on one side land of Jean Baptiste Henry.

This claim is in every respect similar to the preceding one, claimed by the same; and we therefore reject it.

No. 494.—FELIX BOUDREAU claims a tract of land, situate in the county of La Fourche, on the bayou Bœuf, containing one hundred and sixty and sixty-three hundredths superficial acres, and adjoining on one side land claimed by Jean Baptiste Jeanne.

The claimant does not even pretend to have settled this land prior to the 20th December, 1803. We consider the claim to be entirely a feigned one, and do therefore reject it.

P. GRYMES, *R. E. D. Orl. Ter.*
JOSHUA LEWIS,
THOS. B. ROBERTSON.

12th CONGRESS. **No. 194.** 1st SESSION.

REVISION OF THE LAWS FOR THE SALE OF PUBLIC LANDS.

COMMUNICATED TO THE SENATE FEBRUARY 19, 1812.

Mr. WORTHINGTON made the following report:

The committee appointed to inquire if any, and what, further provisions or alterations are necessary in the laws of the United States for the sale of public lands, submit to the consideration of the Senate a bill, with a report, stating the reasons of the proposed alterations.

The alterations and amendments the bill contemplates in the present system are the following, viz:

1st. To sell the public lands in half-quarter sections.
2d. To reduce the price in future sales.
3d. To discontinue the credit now allowed by law: and
4th. To extend the time of payment to purchasers who have not completed their instalments.

The committee are aware that alterations, in a system like that under consideration, ought to be adopted with great caution, especially when its operations would seem to have been successful, (as, indeed, they have been to a certain extent,) and would most probably continue so to be within narrow limits. On examination, however, it will be found that this system, now in the course of experiment, has not been, so far as its practical operations have been ascertained, without strong objections and evils, both as it regards the public and individuals; and that a continuation of it, spread over a very extended tract of country, may, and it is believed will, produce effects very injurious to the public interests. The committee consider it their duty to present to the Senate a general view of the subject, and, for that purpose, have obtained from the Secretary of the Treasury the information contained in his letter, statements, &c., all of which accompany this report, and show the total amount of land sold by the United States; the amount sold and

remaining unsold in each land district; the amount of lands to which the Indian title is extinguished and unextinguished; the whole amount of lands claimed by the United States east of the river Mississippi; and the annual amount of sales and receipts of moneys in each land district since the establishment of land offices, &c.

The first alteration proposed is, to offer the public lands for sale in half-quarter sections. All experience has proved, that as the size of the tracts offered for sale have been from time to time lessened, the sales have increased. By the act of May 18, 1796, the public lands were offered for sale, one half in sections of 5,120 acres, the other half in quarter townships, or tracts of 5,120 acres. The sales, under this act, for four years, amounted to 121,540 acres. The act of May 10, 1800, directed that the lands west of the Muskingum river, before offered for sale in quarter townships, should be divided into half sections, and those east of the same river into sections, and so offered for sale. The sales under this act for an equal term (four years) amounted to 919,603 acres. The act of the 26th of March, 1804, provides, that all the public lands of the United States shall be offered for sale in half-quarter sections, or tracts of 160 acres. The sales under this act, for the next four years after its passage, amounted to 1,750,308 acres. The committee do not mean to suggest that the subdivision of the public lands from time to time has been the sole cause of the increased sales; but they can have no hesitation in believing that these subdivisions of the tracts, having suited them to the ability of a greater number of purchasers, have been the principal cause of the increase of the sales under each succeeding act.

The subdivision of the public lands in the manner proposed does not alter the general system adopted for